European Peace Movements and the Future of the Western Alliance

European Peace Movements and the Future of the Western Alliance

Edited by

Walter Laqueur and Robert Hunter

Published in Association with the
Center for Strategic and International Studies,
Georgetown University, Washington, D.C.

Transaction Books
New Brunswick (U.S.A.) and Oxford (U.K.)

Published by Transaction Books.

Copyright ©1985 by the Center for Strategic & International Studies, Georgetown University, Washington, D.C. 20006.

Library of Congress Catalog Number: 84-24423

ISBN: 0-88738-035-2 (cloth)

Printed in the United States of America

Library of Congress Cataloging in Publication Data
Main entry under title:

European peace movements and the future of the Western Alliance.

   1. Peace—Societies, etc.   2. Antinuclear movement—European.
3. North Atlantic Treaty Organization.   4. Europe—Foreign relations
—United States.   5. United States—Foreign relations—Europe.
I. Laqueur, Walter, 1921–   .   II. Hunter, Robert Edwards, 1940.
JX1952.E97   1985   327.1′72   84–24423
ISBN 0-88738-035-2

CONTENTS

ACKNOWLEDGMENTS

The editors gratefully acknowledge the following publications for permission to use previously published material:

Irving Kristol, "Uncertain Future—NATO after 35 Years," originally published as "What's Wrong with NATO?" in *New York Times Magazine,* 25 September 1983.

Henry Kissinger, "A Plan to Reshape NATO," *Time,* 5 March 1984, pp. 20-24.

Theodore Draper, "The Western Misalliance," based in part on an article published in *Washington Quarterly,* Winter 1981.

ABBREVIATIONS

ABM	Antiballistic Missile
AFSC	American Friends Service Committee
ARD	German Television
ARP	Anti-Revolutionary Party
ASF	In the Name of Atonement/Peace Services
ATOM	Astronomical Telescope Orientation Mount (NASA)
BDKJ	Federation of German Catholic Youth
BRPF	Bertrand Russell Peace Foundation
CALC	Clergy and Laity Concerned
CDA	Christian Democratic Appeal (Dutch)
CDA-VVD	Liberal Party
CDFP	Campaign for a Democratic Foreign Policy
CDS	Christian Democratic Party (Dutch)
CDU	Christian Democratic Union
CERES	Left-wing Socialist Party (French)
CFDT	French Labor Union
CHU	Christian Historical Union (Dutch)
CND	Campaign for Nuclear Disarmament Peace Movement
CNFMP	Coalition for a New Foreign and Military Policy
CNFP	Ad Hoc Coalition for New Foreign Policy
CODENE	Committee for the Denuclearization of Europe
CPN	Communist Party—Netherlands
CPSU	Communist Party—Soviet Union
CPUSA	Communist Party—United States of America
CSCE	Conference on Security and Cooperation in Europe
CSF	Coalition to Stop Funding the War
CSIS	Center for Strategic and International Studies

CSSR	Czechoslovak Socialist Republic
CSU	Christian Socialist Union
D'66	Democratics '66
DAC	Direct Action Committee (British)
DDR	Deutsche Democratische Republik
DGB	Trade union umbrella organization (German)
DKP	German Communist Party
EC	European Community
EEC	European Economic Community
EKD	Evangelical Churches of Germany, Council of
END	European Nuclear Disarmament
EVP	Evangelical People's Party
FAR	Force d'Action Rapide
FAS	Federation of American Scientists
FBS	Forward Based Systems
FDP	Free Democratic Party
FOR	Fellowship for Reconciliation
FRG	Federal Republic of Germany
GDR	German Democratic Republic
GLCMs	Guided Missile Countermeasures
GNP	Gross National Product
HADES	Missile
ICBM	Intercontinental Ballistic Missile
ICDP	International Confederation for Disarmament and Peace
IKV	Dutch Interchurch Peace Council
INF	Intermediate Nuclear Forces
KGB	Soviet Secret Police
KOR	Committee for Defense of the Workers
KVP	Catholic People's Party (Dutch)
LCNP	Lawyer's Committee on Nuclear Policy
LOVO	Dutch peace organization
LRTNF	Long-Range Theater Nuclear Forces

MBFR	Mutual and Balanced Force Reductions
MFS	Mobilization for Survival
MX	Missile Experimental
NATO	North Atlantic Treaty Organization
NCASF	National Council American-Soviet Friendship
NCC	National Council of Churches
NTA	No to Nuclear Weapons
NWFC	Nuclear Weapons Freeze Campaign, Inc.
OCV	Consultation Center for Peace (Belgium)
PCF	French Communist Party
PS	Socialist Party
PSP	Party of Political Radicals
PSU	Unified Socialist Party
PVdA	Labor Party (Dutch)
RPR	Gaullists
SACEUR	Supreme Allied Commander—Europe
SALT	Strategic Arms Limitation Talks
SAM	Strategic Airborne Missile
SANA	Scientists Against Nuclear Arms
SANE	National Committee for a Sane Nuclear Policy (SANE alone used as an organization name)
SDP	German Social Democratic Party
SLBM	Submarine Launched Ballistic Missile
SPD	Social Democratic Party
SSBN	Missile launching nuclear Submarines
START	Strategic Arms Reduction Talks
TACT	Tories Against Cruise and Trident
TNF	Tactical Nuclear Forces
TUC	Technology Utilization Center
UCS	Union of Concerned Scientists
UDF	Union Defense Force (British)
USPC	United States Peace Council
USSR	Union of Soviet Socialist Republics
VAKA	Flemish Action Committee Against Atomic Weapons

VELKD	United Evangelical-Lutheran Churches of Germany
VVD	Liberals (Dutch)
WDC	World Disarmament Campaign
WILPF	Women's International League for Peace and Freedom
WPC	World Peace Council
WRL	War Resisters League
WSP	Women Strike for Peace
ZdDK	Central Committee of German Catholics

1

INTRODUCTION

Walter Laqueur and Robert Hunter

This book concerns the future of the Western alliance and the development of the peace movement in Europe and—to an extent—in the United States. These two topics are frequently discussed as though they were one. They are not, of course, although the relationship between them is obvious. On the one hand, it is virtually certain that the future of NATO would have become an item very high on the international agenda even if the North Atlantic Council had not taken the so-called double-track decision in 1979 on intermediate-range nuclear forces. Peace movements, on the other hand, were active in Western Europe and the United States back in the 1950s, long before recent nuclear debate in the alliance.

It is not surprising that nations from time to time examine the *raison d'être* of an alliance. There are no eternal alliances. They come into being in specific historical conditions, last a few years or decades in fulfilling the specific political or military purposes for which they were created, and then modify themselves, fade away, or fall apart as circumstances change. NATO came into being more than three decades ago in response to a specific threat and as a result of Western Europe's inability to defend itself without U.S. help. Whether there was, in fact, danger of a Soviet military invasion in 1949-50 is a question that can neither be proved nor disproved, because, from the Soviet point of view, such an attack might not have been necessary to establish its hegemony in Europe. However weak the Soviet Union was in the postwar period, Western Europe was even weaker, and neither nature nor politics suffers a vacuum gladly. Defensive alliances are created as much to resist political pressure as to deter military attack, as NATO's early history attests. It can hardly be questioned that, but for U.S. help, Western Europe would have been in a poor position to resist such pressure from the Soviet Union. What kind of Western Europe would have emerged but for NATO?

It is improbable that Britain, France, and Western Germany would have become so-called people's democracies such as Poland or Czechoslovakia. Their economies and social structure would probably have developed on lines not very different from what we see today; their sovereignty as far as domestic affairs are concerned would perhaps not have been greatly affected. At the same time, however, the Soviet Union would have expected to deal with West European leaders who would, broadly speaking, have been in sympathy with the aims of Soviet foreign policy and would have shown the respect due to the most powerful country in Europe. Moscow would have expected close economic cooperation with Western Europe, and it would have been resentful if West Europeans had meddled in world affairs rather than minding their own business. In short, while not insisting on slavish support for every Soviet initiative, Soviet leaders would have expected proper regard for their interests. They would probably not have considered such a state of affairs as permanent but as a transitional phase toward internal changes in Western Europe and a more clearly defined client status. But the interim phase might have lasted for many decades; it is doubtful whether Soviet leaders had any clear idea about the more distant future.

Both in Western Europe and in the United States, there was opposition to NATO from the very beginning. Opponents included not only the Communists but also the German Social Democrats (until the late 1950s), the Gaullists, sections of the British Labour party and the Italian socialists, and, of course, U.S. isolationists. At the time, the most fervent Atlanticists could be found in the smaller European countries such as Holland and Belgium. In most European countries there was opposition not only from the Left but also from the Right: in West Germany 40 percent or more of the population fairly consistently expressed its preference for neutrality over an alliance.

But such neutrality seemed beyond reach, and during the late 1950s and early 1960s the alliance became more popular both in the United States and in Western Europe, with the sole exception of France. This fact did not preclude differences of opinion, however, sometimes far-reaching—as is no doubt inevitable in any voluntary coalition. The erosion of the allied consensus began in the late 1960s and had more than one reason; for example, Western Europe had been rebuilt from the ravages of war but its economic strength was not matched by either political unity or political and military power. Quite frequently, West European countries dissented from U.S. policies, but they were usually unable to juxtapose agreed-upon strategies of their own and, in any case, lacked the power to back them up.

With detente came a change in appraisals of the Soviet threat that had been the prime motive for the creation of the alliance. Differences in substance between Western Europe and the United States were usually not that profound, but there was one basic difference in approach: only the United States was a global power with worldwide interests and commitments. By contrast, Western Europe had no such commitments nor did it want them. Hence the willingness on the part of the European allies to accept detente even if it were restricted to Europe. The United States took a different view, and this was bound to lead to growing conflict. Last, there were the well-known differences of opinion among various European countries with regard to nuclear strategies, between them and the United States and also within each country. Thus, sooner or later, a reexamination of the purpose of the alliance was bound to take place in any case. The resurgence of a strong peace movement in recent years simply provided additional impetus.

THE EUROPEAN PEACE MOVEMENT

In analyzing various peace movements in the West, it is important to make a critical distinction. Being for arms control—even, in the United States, for a mutual and verifiable freeze of strategic nuclear weapons—is not the same as being for the West's unilateral abstention from nuclear competition. Every candidate for the presidency in 1984, in both political parties, has portrayed himself as a champion of arms control.

As opposed to U.S. emphasis on strategic nuclear weapons, the European movements are more directly germane to security in Europe and to the future of the alliance. They are in general more far-reaching in their prescriptions, and some of them are more potent in their political effects. It is also perhaps ironic that pressure for the so-called no first use of nuclear weapons in NATO doctrine began in the United States among individuals with prior responsibilities for national security, and has not so far resonated in Western Europe to the same degree.

While there are differences within the European peace movement, central themes can be summarized as follows: The use of nuclear weapons will lead to the destruction not only of civilization and of most (or all) of humanity but also very likely of earth itself ("exterminationism"). As long as these weapons exist, there is the danger that they will be used; indeed, in history all new weapons have been used sooner or later. Hence there is a need to freeze, to reduce, and ultimately to abolish nuclear weapons—bilaterally if possible, unilaterally if necessary. In the longer run, Europe will survive only if the present military blocs are dissolved.

As for deterrence and the balance of power, some unilateral disarmers maintain that neither ever existed, while others claim that during the last five years NATO (meaning the United States) has acquired a first-strike capacity. They deny the claim of Western governments that the deployment of Pershing II and cruise missiles was essential in view of the buildup of Soviet SS-20s on the one hand and of great Soviet conventional strength on the other. According to this view, the conventional strength of the superpowers in Europe is more or less equal. In fact, therefore, the Soviet threat is largely mythical, is generated by pathological fear of a nonexistent enemy, or is deliberately fanned by the military-industrial complex.

These unilateral disarmers also argue that the deployment of the Euromissiles gives NATO a decisive advantage; they are highly vulnerable and therefore useless for second-strike purposes. Generally speaking, the logic runs, the purpose of NATO's strategy of flexible response is to carry out atomic warfare in Europe while saving the United States. Thus the stationing of nuclear weapons in Europe may be in the U.S. interest but endangers Europe's survival. Western Europe has more to fear from the United States than from any other quarter because NATO strategy relies upon first use of nuclear weapons. For Western Europe to survive, therefore, a nuclear-free zone has to be established from Poland to Portugal, to be followed by the retreat of all foreign troops from European territory and by the Europeanization (and neutralization) of Europe.

In general political debate within the alliance, however, there is no dispute about the consequences of a nuclear war; the real debate is, or at least should be, about how to prevent it. Yet Western strategy since the 1950s has implied a critical weakness because of NATO's concentration on the role of nuclear weapons to the detriment of conventional defense. Even today, it is unlikely that the Soviet Union has any significant nuclear advantage over the West. But since it has matched the West in the nuclear field, it has acquired a major advantage in view of its superior conventional strength. In these circumstances, "deterrence" was bound to become more problematical: Nuclear weapons may indeed deter a nuclear attack, but the same is not necessarily true of conventional war. At the same time, the danger of accidental war is minimal but it cannot be dismissed altogether. Last, there is the danger, nay, the near-certainty, of nuclear proliferation that will make the world an even more dangerous place.

On these facts there is broad agreement in the West. But within the peace movement there is widespread belief that it is more aware than others are of the dangers facing humankind and that it has a greater feeling of responsibility for posterity. Others—including, according to an extreme view, even individuals committed to less-uncompromising arms control—may be so blinded by fanatical, ideological hate that they do not realize that their strategies are bound to lead to a cosmic disaster. Historically, feelings of this kind have not been uncommon in humankind, especially among religious and political sectarians. To give but one example: the belief that God had chosen the small neutral countries to make peace between the aggressive big powers was widespread among the Protestant churches of Scandinavia and Benelux in the early phase of World War II.

But is it fair to generalize about the European peace movement? It is, after all, a coaliton of disparate groups, including highly motivated and well-informed men and women as well as others whose opposition is limited to missiles stationed this side of the inner-German border. The peace movement deserves to be taken seriously despite its inability to provide satisfactory answers to such basic questions as how to disinvent nuclear energy. After all, even the destruction of all nuclear devices would be no more than a temporary palliative. The more radical disarmers have correctly insisted on more far-reaching solutions, such as the establishment of a world state: As long as nation-states exist, there will be conflicts among them. Indeed, if the dilemma were the choice between being "red" or dead, the answer would be obvious because the destruction of humankind would end history, whereas there is always a chance that a Communist regime might at some future stage mellow or wither away (in which case the nuclear threat would resurface!). As Mr. Lafontaine and others in Germany have argued, life in Hungary and even in Poland is preferable to not living at all. But the dilemma is false: there is every reason to assume that even a Communist world would be constituted of nation-states and, as the recent past has shown, the conflicts between them are as intense as those between other countries. Nuclear weapons might still be used by a minority in a civil war, by nuclear terrorists, or through some other means. In short, whatever the merits of unilateral disarmament, the removal of the danger of nuclear war is not among them.

Most nuclear disarmers maintain that the less nations depend on nuclear weapons, the less the risk of nuclear war. With some qualifications, this is correct; and some observers—disarmers and their opponents alike—have accordingly suggested that the West should make greater efforts to strengthen conventional defenses. But conventional defense is expensive; with the improvement of arms technologies, it also happens to be increasingly deadly; and there has been long-standing argument in Western Europe that increased attention to conventional defenses makes some war more likely, by decreasing the chances that it would escalate to nuclear combat.

In these conditions, the attachment of many nuclear disarmers to conventional defense has been largely platonic. One can always think of reasons that conventional defense should *not* be strengthened. The economic situation at home is bad, the Soviets are weak and incompetent, or (by contrast) the Soviets are strong and may react violently. From these arguments, it is only one step to the eccentricities of "social" or "civilian" defense. This concept refers to passive resistance à la Gandhi or active resistance as offered by Solidarity. Such strategies may or may not be of some efficacy in the case, say, of a Swedish invasion of Norway (where civilian defense is practiced to some degree); they are unlikely to work in most other conditions. The tactics of the brave Soldier Schweik have not been effective in Czechoslovakia of late (there has been a deplorable decline in the sense of humor all around).

A PEACE MOVEMENT IN THE EAST?

Last, members of Western peace movements frequently invoke the existence of a peace movement in the Communist bloc. It is perfectly true that thinking people in East European countries are afraid of nuclear war, even though local governments and media shield them from excessive exposure to the nuclear facts of life and death. A few East Europeans have even demonstrated their dissent. But the idea that this movement is bound to grow by leaps and bounds until it is a major if unwelcome factor in Communist policies, corresponding to the peace movement in the West, belongs to the realm of fantasy. A few dozen courageous men and women in Moscow and East Germany have tried to generate greater public awareness of these dangers. A few Green delegations from West Germany have proceeded to Moscow and East Berlin and unfurled their slogans for two minutes. In 1983, *Neues Deutschland*, the East German daily, even printed a couple of letters questioning Soviet intentions to deploy nuclear weapons in the DDR. But there still is no Eastern peace movement; only a few individuals in prison or under threat of arrest or—as in the case of some East Germans—expelled to the West. There is no symmetry between West and East, and it is disingenuous even to pretend that there will be such symmetry in the foreseeable future.

Soviet support for the West European peace movement is natural. In fact, the "fight for peace" has replaced the "international class struggle" as the main Communist objective and slogan in Soviet strategy. But the importance of Soviet help for and Communist penetration of West European peace movements should not be exaggerated. Some money has been passed, organizational and public relations know-how has been provided, but such help does not usually amount to political control. Nor is the peace movement an unmixed blessing from the Soviet point of view: there is always the danger that some "unstable elements" in the peace movements will draw attention to the Soviet nuclear buildup or even equate the two superpowers concerning the threat to world peace. For the West European peace movement, open Soviet support is something of an embarrassment for reasons that need hardly be spelled out in detail.

THE ROLE OF THE CHURCHES

More significant is the prominent part played in the peace movement by influential sections of the churches. The Protestant churches of Northern Europe have been among the most active warners against a nuclear holocaust. Indeed, apocalyptic traditions have deep roots in European history, and on more than one occasion fear has been exploited for educational purposes. The apocalyptic fears can be traced back to the old Nordic sagas on the twilight of the gods and the destruction of the globe by a great fire. But it was above all Martin Luther who was firmly convinced that the world was soon coming to an end. To be sure, by the 1960s the apocalyptic element had virtually disappeared from Protestant theology, but it has recently had a theological and political revival not unconnected with the rise of the peace movement. The commitment of sections of the Catholic Church to the peace movement—stronger in the United States than in Europe—has yet other sources that cannot be discussed in this framework in any detail.

In Europe, the events of the 1930s and 1940s certainly had a delayed shock effect. The stand of the churches *vis-à-vis* the fascist dictators had not been above reproach, and there has been an ardent desire not to repeat the mistakes of the past but rather to resist the forces of evil from the beginning. This factor has led the churches into political discussions—a perfectly legitimate enterprise and one that has contributed to public debate on nuclear issues, but one for which they had no special competence or political authority.

CHANGE IN THE ALLIANCE

How can one explain the accelerated erosion of the consensus on European defense in recent years? Various reasons have been adduced: oppressive rhetoric and relative lack of consultation on Washington's part at least through 1983, the aversion of Social Democratic leaders to Republican, antisocialist administrations in the White House, a growth of cultural anti-Americanism in Europe, and other factors. But although these factors may have contributed to the process, they cannot explain the extent of the drift, for if U.S. rhetoric has been excessive on more than one occasion, U.S. deeds have on the whole been cautious. If there has in recent years been insufficient consultation by the United States with its allies, it is also true that Reagan's predecessor was criticized for lack of leadership. The neoconservative policies of Republicanism may be disliked by Social Democrats in Europe, but it would be a mistake to overrate the importance of domestic issues in international affairs: De Gaulle quarreled almost constantly with Washington, and he certainly was no Marxist. The fact that China, Yugoslavia, and Romania have Communist governments has not prevented the maintenance of fairly good relations. The issue at stake is partly ideological aversion to communism; but above all, it is opposition to expansionism.

The drift is also one consequence of a change of guard in Western Europe and, to a certain extent, also in the United States. For the new generation of leaders, the 1930s, World War II, and the outbreak of the Cold War are no more than distant recollections. The lessons painfully learned by their parents are no longer self-evident. There is a tendency to take peace and national sovereignty for granted and to depreciate the threats to them. At the same time, the generation of "Europe Firsters" in the United States is also gradually disappearing from the political scene. As seen from Washington, Western Europe is still very important, but the feeling of a special relationship and automatic commitment is weakening.

Apart from the question of generations, there are differences of substance. There is greater fear in some NATO countries and in many cases greater willingness to consider political concessions to the Soviet Union. Unfortunately, very few concrete results have been achieved in recent East-West arms control talks, hardly more under Carter (when the domestic constituency for SALT II fell apart) than under Reagan. This is not to denigrate the value of pursuing arms control but quite the reverse; it is, rather, to indicate that for much of the recent past arms control has not helped to bridge the gap across the Atlantic.

Furthermore, U.S. attention to Western Europe has been seen to shift for substantive reasons: especially new challenges to Western interests in the Persian Gulf—a development that has also intensified U.S. sensitivity to the West Europeans' not bearing their share of the burden, even where their interests are more directly at stake. Regarding the Soviet strategic buildup, Western leaders have been faced, broadly speaking, with the alternatives of either ignoring it or of counterbalancing and matching it. According to one school of thought in Western Europe, there has been no need to match the Soviet buildup because it constitutes no major new threat to the West. By contrast, in the United States and also among the major West European governments, there has been firm belief that unilateral concessions will not make Europe more secure.

Making these differences of viewpoint more intense have been developments outside the realms of strategy and alliance politics on East-West matters. Most important has been a continuing sense of European economic malaise, largely engendered by the end of the period of almost unrestrained economic growth. This malaise has sapped energies and optimism about the success of the European Community and, with it, a sense of purpose for Western Europe. The onset of systemic difficulties in Western economies has also created a higher degree of economic competition and strain across the Atlantic. In turn, these developments have inevitably increased the difficulties of resolving broader defense and East-West issues, both directly—as with pressures against increasing conventional defense and squabbling over trade with the East—and in a general erosion of common purpose.

ALLIANCE ALTERNATIVES

Given these differences of mood and opinion, different proposals for the future of the alliance were bound to emerge. Most West Europeans and Americans still support the continuation of the alliance as a matter of principle. But unless there is also a meeting of minds on specific strategies, such general agreement might not be of sufficient consequence. There is even some danger that the alliance could become less relevant with regard to the crises likely to arise in the late 1980s and 1990s. Even now, countries nominally still members of NATO, led by Greece, have ceased to cooperate in certain respects. Elsewhere, main opposition parties make attacks against NATO. A change in government in these countries would at least raise questions about whether the number of reluctant allies would be extended, and it would possibly have more negative consequences.

This state of affairs has put the United States at a psychological disadvantage, with U.S. statesmen and generals beseeching, cajoling, or threatening reluctant Europeans to do more for Western Europe's defense, as though the United States could or should be more European than the Europeans themselves. Such an approach strengthens the belief among some West Europeans that the conflict is essentially between the two superpowers, with Europe in the role of the innocent bystander, becoming involved in a brawl that is really none of its concern.

Such U.S. behavior may thus in time prove to be politically counterproductive. If doubts increase in some circles in Europe about the character of the conflict and the possibility (or the desirability) of defending Western Europe, U.S. leaders may not be able to work effectively with established governments to dispense sufficient infusions of political will. These are problems that Europeans have to thrash out among themselves, something more easily said than done. If all (or most) of Western Europe would either enthusiastically support or emphatically reject NATO, a decision by the United States would be less difficult—though in the latter case certainly deeply troubling. But at present there is a division in West European opinion, with a majority favoring NATO but substantial minorities opposing it. These complications make the choices available to U.S. leaders exceedingly vexatious.

A case can still be made for continuing the alliance in its present form. The direction of the mood in Western Europe may reverse itself in the near future, or the Soviets may change in a way that makes the need for an alliance either more or less obvious. In short, time will be gained, and it will become easier to find a common denominator for new strategies that will make the alliance more widely acceptable than at present. But there is also the danger that the erosion of the consensus will continue and that sticking to old concepts and commitments will make finding a new understanding more difficult. In the meantime, U.S. overeagerness could strengthen the belief among some Europeans that the United States needs Western Europe more than vice versa, which in turn would increase anger and frustration in the United States because of a view of the "one-sided" character of the alliance.

Among those in Western Europe who advocate abolishing the alliance, few would rejoice if such actually came to pass. They know in their hearts that Western Europe has remained free and (relatively) prosperous only because of the existence of a balance of power. Even Swedish Socialists know that, but for the existence of NATO, Sweden would be a very different country today. As all opinion polls have shown, an overwhelming majority of West Europeans favor the continued existence of NATO in one form or another, as long as the Warsaw Pact is not effectively abolished. This group includes the majority of the British Labour party and German Social Democrats and probably also not a few West European Communists, especially in Italy and Spain. But the kind of alliance that many of these critics envisage would hardly be in a position to defend Europe. There would be doubts about what useful purpose U.S. participation in such an organization would serve.

There is a third scenario, namely, a gradual U.S. disengagement from NATO as it is now constituted and the search for new forms of defense cooperation. This seems to be favored by a small but growing number of Americans, including many who see U.S. interests refocusing on the Pacific or the Western Hemisphere. While, of course, it is not now nor likely soon to be official U.S. policy, growing pressure in this direction should be expected in the next few years if the current drift continues. This view on the part of some Americans is based in part on their analysis that Western Europe is strong enough in manpower and resources to defend itself against outside threats but that the political, economic, and perhaps above all psychological effort needed will never be made unless the United States compels West Europe to make a decision. There would be major difficulties involved in the establishment of a European defense community, but in this scenario these would have to be left to European leaders, to be resolved in consultation with Washington if that was desired. Such a disengagement could be envisaged in stages over a prolonged period, and it might perhaps result in a new agreement between the United States and a European defense community as distinct from the present mechanism.

It would be idle to deny that any U.S. disengagement would involve considerable and perhaps fatal risks. Cynics may argue that if (as many West Europeans profess to believe) widely held U.S. fears of Soviet intentions are wrong or exaggerated, Western Europe would have little reason for concern even if the nuclear umbrella should be withdrawn. By contrast—following this logic—if that portion of U.S. opinion that emphasizes Soviet challenge has been right, a few years of exposure to the harsh winds blowing from the East would be of considerable educational value for Europe. Political experience and insight cannot be bequeathed; it must be relearned by each successive generation. Yet world affairs is not a laboratory with no penalties for wrong experiments; Western Europe might be galvanized into action, but it is equally possible that it might be paralyzed and, once having entered the Soviet sphere of influence, would find the road back to sovereignty and independence barred.

To be sure, this last dire scenario need not come to pass. There are common security interests between Western Europe and the United States that still argue persuasively for the continuation of the alliance. But to make it work effectively in the future will require an exercise of collective national will that has been all too absent in recent years. Some *modus vivendi* on visions of the Soviet threat and the best means for dealing with it has to emerge from the growing differences of opinion that have been increasingly evident. The economies of the Western world need a fresh resolve to cooperate rather than compete to the point of mutual loss. Thorny security issues—conventional, strategic, and arms control—need to be sorted out time and time again in an uncertain international environment. New agreements need to be reached concerning the definition of threats to allied interests beyond the NATO area, along with greater West European willingness to share the burdens involved. Last, a younger generation of West Europeans and Americans need to relearn old lessons—and accept almost on trust the folly of experimenting with basic security interests.

The alternative need not be a final collapse of the alliance. But it is bound to lead to a common disillusionment with old compacts and bargains and to the erosion of the political and psychological basis for taking national decisions in a larger-than-national interest. In these circumstances, it is not certain whether the democratic nations of Western Europe would still be masters of their own destinies to the same degree that they are today.

There are, in brief, no obvious solutions to the problems facing the United States and Europe today: All possible courses of action entail grave burdens and risks. But so does abstention from action. The contributions to this volume, written from different vantage points, all address themselves to this crucial debate, which will preoccupy the United States and Western Europe for years to come.

The editors wish to thank the Fritz Thyssen Foundation for its generous support of this project. They also wish to thank the Center for Strategic and International Studies of Georgetown University, under whose auspices this project was conducted, and Ms. Sophia Miskiewicz for her invaluable assistance.

2

THE PEACE MOVEMENTS, EUROPEAN NEUTRALISM, AND THE FUTURE OF THE ATLANTIC ALLIANCE

William G. Hyland

The great irony of the last decade is that as Soviet military power has grown the alliance created to thwart it has weakened. Of course, an anti-Soviet alliance ought to weaken only at times of great Soviet adversity. The reason for the current paradox is simply that the alliance has lost confidence: there is little agreement on objectives and growing confusion over strategy and capabilities. A vicious circle is being created: if the United States tries to assert its interests, it encounters European doubts and criticism; Washington then retreats into a sullen resentment; Europe is dismayed, redoubles its criticism, and the pattern repeats itself. The end is not in sight. It could prove to be a mid-life crisis that will eventually be overcome. This is unlikely. It could lead to a slow, agonizing demise of the Atlantic partnership. This is possible, but not probable. It could, most probably, lead to a transformation in the political relations within the West and between East and West on the European continent.

THE CRISIS OF CONFIDENCE

U.S. critics of NATO are fond of reminding the present generation that NATO's founding fathers in the United States were very dubious about the alliance. Supposedly they saw only a temporary U.S. rescue mission, to hold the line until Europe revived and could counter the Soviet Union without much outside assistance. This is now presented as a justification for ending U.S. involvement on the continent. After all, it is argued, why should the present leaders be more pro-NATO than the founders? If Acheson intended to bring the troops home as soon as possible, why not now, thirty-five years later?

This is, of course, the worst sort of historical revisionism in the service of current political polemics. True, the founding fathers in the United States had to sell a skeptical Congress on a new alliance; they did this in part by stressing the old isolationist virtues: no entangling alliances, at least no long-term entanglements. But surely Truman and Acheson, also the fathers of the Marshall plan and the Truman doctrine, knew that a long-term engagement was the real contract. The United States would be in Europe for a lengthy period, if only because the military threat would not dissipate. Indeed, it is worth remembering that in 1949, when the United States had a monopoly on nuclear weapons, it was generally believed that the West was even then too weak for a general settlement with the USSR. And this view persisted. The founding fathers did not really anticipate a change in the balance with the USSR until the late 1950s.

By then, the late 1950s, the military threat loomed even larger. Under the impact of the missile-gap crisis, the West came to believe that it might be confronting a permanent change in the balance of strategic power and—foreshadowing the 1980s—this led to a strong antinuclear movement in Germany. But an underlying strain of confidence ran through the 1950s and 1960s, especially after the Cuban crisis. Even though the inexorable growth of Soviet striking power was shifting the balance toward a strategic stalemate, most of the Western nations, including the United States, continued to believe that the USSR was deterred from a frontal attack and forced to probe around the edges of the alliance. To be sure, there were voices of doubt raised, but no serious challenge to NATO strategy was mounted during the critical years. Nor, it must be added, was any serious program put forward for a European settlement. Western confidence, for example, was enunciated by a latter-day critic, Denis Healy, who expounded the prevailing view in 1968:

> NATO could not forgo reliance on nuclear escalation in case of large-scale attack without an order of increase in European military budgets which in present circumstances is beyond the realm of practical possibility. Moreover, it is far from clear that NATO would be acting wisely in seeking to achieve security in Europe through the building of a Maginot Line of conventional forces . . . there is the

unanswered question: Why change a strategy which has worked and shows every sign of continuing to work very well?[1]

At the very moment of this statement, two factors were in fact combining to alter the history of the alliance and sow the seeds of the current crisis: (1) the French defection from the alliance in all but name, and (2) the turn toward detente, especially German detente. Both events were consistent with a reading of the state of East-West relations. De Gaulle foresaw that in an era of nuclear stalemate the U.S. nuclear guarantee would diminish. Europe would have to compensate by greater reliance on its own forces. At the same time, German leaders saw that in an era of strategic stalemate there might be a chance for a political rapprochement. De Gaulle saw the dangers of a protracted stalemate, while Brandt saw the opportunities of a protracted balance.

In retrospect the French withdrawal from the NATO's unified commands was a devastating blow, though no NATO member wished to recognize it as such. It was rationalized as brought on by the peculiarities of the French or of the general. His critique of the nuclear equation was largely dismissed. Curiously, it was in the United States where he was taken more seriously, though only in certain quarters. In the Nixon-Kissinger period, de Gaulle and the Gaullist view were accorded a serious hearing, perhaps even too much so. By 1969, U.S. doubts over the stability of nuclear balance were forming much along the lines of de Gaulle's own apprehensions. But for the United States there was no easy answer. A massive conventional buildup was too costly and too alarming for the alliance, especially during a war crisis in Indochina. A crash strategic effort might have been approved under Nixon, but the congressional revolt against Vietnam deeply eroded support for any military response to a rising growth in Soviet power.

What happened was not a military response but nearly the reverse. Detente in Europe was embraced as the alternative to a new military strategy, while in the United States arms control loomed as a substitute for a defense buildup. This was most dramatically evident in the narrow, national debate over the antiballistic missile system in 1969-71, which constantly skirted the strategic alternative of building up the option of a defense of the United States rather than relying on an indefinite offensive standoff. The negotiating option seemed infinitely preferable. It is easily forgotten, in an era of "star wars," that the ABM was approved by only one vote in the Senate in 1969. Twenty years earlier the West could have negotiated from enormous strength.

Twenty years later it no longer could do so. It was the Europeans who invented the detente of the 1970s and speculated endlessly about its benefits. Even the skeptical French encouraged the idea, though in the slightly perverse form of a new Europe entity stretching from the Atlantic to the Urals (excluding the United States, of course).

The invasion of Czechoslovakia in August 1968 was scarcely a ripple on this placid European outlook. The alliance punished the USSR by a freeze of diplomatic contacts; the only practical effect of which was that it had to be lifted on the twentieth anniversary of NATO, in April 1969, to allow the new U.S. administration to approach the Soviets on strategic arms talks, which were urged by all the European allies. The real focus of the new eagerness was Germany. Well before Willy Brandt launched his own version of *Ostpolitik,* German policy was shifting in an eastward direction. One observer, Theo Sommer, wrote in 1968: "At last we can say that the Bonn Government is pursuing a sincere, decisive, and clear-sighted policy of detente with Eastern Europe." [2]

What Brandt did was to shift the focus from Eastern Europe, where Bonn had hoped to slide into detente through the back door, to the frontal approach of dealing directly with Moscow itself. And, of course, he succeeded. By the mid 1970s European detente was flourishing and dramatized by Brandt's humane act of penance in Auschwitz. All of Europe was prepared to fall into the ranks of detente. Even the United States, despite doubts since confirmed by both Nixon and Kissinger in their memoirs, had to pursue a parallel line in Europe, if only to redeem the Berlin issue, and thereby guarantee the completion of Brandt's initial approach. This is not to say that the United States did not have its own interests in detente. A high point for Europe followed in 1975, when all the European leaders plus the United States president and Canadian prime minister gathered in Helsinki to ratify the new European settlement, thus finally ending World War II with a synthetic peace treaty. The problem was that the military dimensions of the new European order had not been settled. This left a void that could be partially filled only by a new Western consensus on strategy and further East-West accommodation.

It is the Western failure to fill this void that has produced a major crisis in which the very rationale for the North Atlantic alliance is challenged. After Helsinki, detente diverted the alliance from the task of reexamining nuclear strategy in the era of superpower parity. Strategy seemed almost irrelevant in an era of SALT agreements and security conferences. The failure to press a European military settlement with Moscow in conjunction with the political settlement, however, meant that the USSR had a relatively free hand in Europe. This became painfully evident to European governments in 1977. The Soviets began building a new European missile force, the infamous SS-20s, and the SALT negotiations turned toward limiting the very U.S. systems that might counter the Soviet buildup. The result was a mild European revolt, which took the form of a now-famous speech by Helmut Schmidt in which he seemed to call for a new Euro-strategic balance to complement the intercontinental balance. The net result was to raise the question of the nuclear defense of Western Europe, or as it is known in the jargon, the credibility of "extended deterrence." Even this serious intervention from Europe might have been accommodated had it not been for the political fiasco growing out of the decision to employ the neutron bomb in Germany. This crisis was to have a major impact on the emerging nuclear debate in both Germany and the United States.

Before examining that episode, it is worth reviewing the broad U.S. effort to deal with the new era of parity and detente. The U.S. authorities, much more than the Europeans, foresaw the consequences of a new balance of power. While Nixon was still in office, a serious effort was initiated to reexamine the concept of deterrence and to devise alternatives to a policy of massive nuclear strikes on civilian targets. As a by-product of this general review of nuclear policy, the nuclear link to Europe also had to be reexamined, but to a lesser extent. Presumably, the restoration of strategic credibility would resolve the European problem. The initial result was the "Schlesinger doctrine" of flexible options: the United States would have the alternative of using nuclear weapons in a number of discrete ways, and would no longer be bound to an inexorable escalation to a general nuclear war. While intellectually and strategically sound, the political impact of this debate was to shift the focus of attention from deterrence to "war-fighting." This would have a devastating long-term consequence. As long as the vague notion of deterrence was the predominant strategy, the debate, in effect, was closed. Clearly deterrence was mandatory. But when deterrence became blurred and blended with war-fighting, there was bound to be political backlash. The message seemed to be that the United States and its allies were more concerned with how to fight a nuclear war than how to prevent it. All subtleties were washed out by a new political outcry, stimulated by the furor over the neutron bomb.

The neutron crisis was a self-inflicted wound. No government on either side of the Atlantic wanted to provoke a genuine debate about nuclear weapons. So Washington shifted the decision to Europe (in effect to Bonn), but the Europeans were unaccustomed to taking nuclear responsibility, which had always rested with Washington (which was also convenient in allowing Europe to escape any political blame). The result is well known. There was an outcry in Germany against the immorality of designing and deploying weapons to kill people but not buildings or equipment. What the neutron controversy did was to provide an entering wedge for the Greens to pry open the question of Western strategy, which had been the almost exclusive preserve of the governments and experts. At the same time, the outcome persuaded the U.S. government not to repeat the process when confronted by the next issue: the stationing of new U.S. missiles in Europe. The Carter administration was determined to reach agreement within the alliance, even at the cost of accepting a badly flawed solution. The decision was to deploy a strange mixture of new land-based missiles, and a collision became inevitable. The antinuclear movement was looking for a new issue, and the alliance inadvertently provided the catalyst in the decision of December 1979 (to install 572 new U.S. medium-range missiles in Europe). Had the U.S. government realized the political consequences, perhaps it would have insisted on its preference for less-visible and less-vulnerable weapons stationed at sea rather than allowing the weapons desired for deterrence to undermine the very concept.

In the years that followed the fateful decision of December 1979, strategy abdicated in favor of politics, and politics in turn gave way to public relations. The debate shifted from the threat emanating from Soviet missiles to the threat that would be created by U.S. missiles. To ensure political support for the recipient governments, the alliance was forced to adopt the inane position of offering to give up entirely the very weapons that were intended to reestablish the frayed links between European defense and the U.S. nuclear guarantee, (i.e., the "zero option"). It reached the point that prominent and influential Europeans finally raised the explosive question of whether the insistence on deploying U.S. nuclear weapons was not, in fact, undermining the alliance by failing to provide "reassurance."

Not only were U.S. weapons attacked on political grounds but the firmer terrain of deterrence underwent considerable erosion. Prominent Americans raised questions about the validity of the U.S. nuclear guarantee: they did so with the best of motives—to spark a new debate over strategy at a time of the political crisis over the new missiles. But the effect was to place in doubt the fundamental rationale: that U.S. nuclear power would dissuade any Soviet adventure in Europe. Now, it seemed, the Americans themselves did not believe in the strategy so long espoused—the strategy of flexible response. It was inevitable that once the sanctuary of strategy had been breached, the next step would be to advocate its dismantling—hence, the proposals by prominent Americans that would abandon the strategy itself. It could have been no real surprise that several advocated dropping the idea of first use of nuclear weapons by the alliance. Again, their motives were pure: to stimulate an increased conventional defense of Europe. But again, the net result was an assault on the vital center—the traditional wisdom of NATO defense. So, the alliance found itself internally weakened by its traditional supporters at the very moment of attack from the far Left that focused on the denuclearization of Europe. What had begun as a strategic response to the Soviet Union had degenerated into a test of loyalty of the alliance. NATO and the United States could not even negotiate effectively for fear of encouraging the antinuclear forces by any hint of irresolution. A major opportunity for a settlement in 1982—the "walk-in-the-woods"—was sacrificed in the name of managing a faltering alliance. A sad commentary on the state of the alliance, to say nothing of the sorry state of U.S. foreign policy.

BLURRING THE SUPERPOWER IMAGE

The nuclear crisis enhanced a second process already under way in the 1970s. This was the increasing tendency in Europe to equate the two superpowers, to blur the distinction between the United States and the USSR. The process has taken different forms. On an intellectual level, there has been the continuation and intensification of revisionism, in which the cold war has been rewritten as a mutual and reciprocal affair, staged by two malefactors, that consequently had become self-perpetuating, as E.P. Thompson wrote:

> It is in the very nature of the Cold War show that there must be two adversaries: and each move by one must be matched by the other. This is the inner dynamic of the Cold War.

Almost the same sentiment is reflected in the attitudes of the Green movement in Germany. Indeed, the language is so close as to suggest a mutually self-reinforcing movement. Rudolf Bahro argues that,

> what accounts for the danger of East-West competition is not Soviet repression or expansion, but a mutual "self perpetuating battle for hegemony between the elite ruling circles of both powers." [3]

From blurring the Soviet and U.S. image, it was a short step to proposing a European policy of neutrality between the two superpowers. This, of course, was an old theme and not the official position of any European government, but it infected the debate over missiles by introducing a "third way." While the two superpowers were being drawn into a global contest, Europe, East and West, was moving in another direction, toward closer cooperation and parallel views; this was at least one thesis. Thus, during the Afghanistan crisis, clearly brought on by the Soviet invasion, both halves of Europe reacted to try to limit the crisis and to preserve detente in Europe. The United States, it was argued, acted to aggravate and escalate the confrontation. The Iranian crisis served to stimulate a further evolutionary turn. The idea was that if Europe was to escape from the superpowers' embrace, it had to encourage them to abandon their respective European empires. The aim, of course, was neutralization through denuclearization. In its extreme argument the position was that West Europe should split from the United States as an inducement to the USSR to allow its East European satellites to free themselves.

The elimination of U.S. nuclear weapons thus became the precondition to establishing a new European order. It followed, of course, that the NATO decision of 1979 had to be resisted and reversed. Hence, proposals for postponing, freezing, and so on became the rallying point for the opposition in Germany and the Low Countries, as well as in Britain. One by–product was to encourage a nuclear freeze movement in the United States; it too reflected a blurring of the image. All nuclear weapons suddenly became equal; the weapons themselves were the root of the danger, not the policies that lay behind them. There was essentially no difference between the two sides. This view was stimulated by doomsday predictions by scientists, and pseudoscientists. A relatively moderate antinuclear group in the United States produced a book on the Soviet Union that discussed the attitude of the USSR toward "stability," and cynically concluded: "As you can see, 'stability' like beauty is very much in the eye of the beholder. Nonetheless, you can expect each side to continue to speak of destabilizing moves by the other that could 'spiral' into a new arms race, increase the risk of war and so forth." [4]

This mind-set was not confined to the "arms race" or opposition groups. It spread to vital areas of the alliance—how to conduct policy in dealing with the Soviet threat. In the aftermath of the Polish imposition of martial law in December 1981, the differences at the official level began to reflect the erosion at the unofficial, antinuclear peace movement level. The Europeans chose to treat the Polish crisis as an internal affair of the Communist bloc to be evaluated by its consequences for the settled European order rather than as a new and heartening phase in the East-West struggle. In both the United States and Western Europe the ghost of Yalta was suddenly invoked. Supposedly, the Polish problem and the Soviet predominance in East Europe had been settled by the two superpowers in their meeting in the Crimea; it would be the height of hypocrisy to repudiate the fundamental bargain in the 1980s, at the very time when some pan-European rapprochement seemed likely. This attitude, in turn, infuriated Americans, especially conservatives, who retaliated by threatening to denounce Yalta altogether. This was a contretemps compared to the battle over economic sanctions and the Soviet gas pipeline. But it was symbolic of the erosion of solidarity within NATO on a vital issue.

The blurring of the U.S. image spread beyond European problems. There has always been a latent suspicion in Europe that the United States is not qualified to conduct a truly global policy. This suspicion was deepened by the fiasco of Vietnam, when the United States threatened to become an obstacle to European detente because of its obsession with the global contest. Strangely, Europeans were nevertheless not content to accept a "regional" role. They complained bitterly when Kissinger assigned them this limited mission in his famous "Year of Europe" speech in April 1973. Yet, when they did exert an influence outside Europe, it was invariably in the guise of a third party rather than as a partner of the United States. During the 1973 oil crisis, European pandering to insulate Europe from Arab wrath was nearly obscene. The Europeans nonetheless reappeared in this guise in the aftermath of Camp David. During 1980, the French courted the Arabs shamelessly, trying to strike a bargain over oil in return for recognition of the Palestine Liberation Organization. It reached a point that even the mild-mannered Cyrus Vance complained that the French had "gotten in the way." But the Europeans insisted on pursuing their own policies, which culminated in the declaration of Venice in 1980, which recognized the "legitimate rights" of the Palestinians. As it turned out, it was irrelevant; Europe has no real leverage, and all parties recognized it. But it confirmed what was already apparent—the distancing of Europe from the United States.

The latest episode, again of blurring the two images, occurred after the U.S. invasion of Grenada. It was greeted in Europe not only by new anti-United States demonstrations—this was to be expected—but by a revival of the notion that there was no difference between the

Soviet invasion of Afghanistan and the U.S. invasion of Grenada. Even the redoubtable Margaret Thatcher joined in by transforming a limited U.S. action into a universal principle of interventionism, a sort of Reagan Doctrine. The reaction of others was far sharper, of course. Not a single European ally supported the United States in the United Nations. Clearly, a low point for the alliance was reached. It led to the predictable U.S. reaction, which was to revive the question of the value of the alliance. This was not a transitory phenomenon, born out of pique. It reflected a simmering anti-Europeanism, a trend not well understood in Europe. There is, in fact, a growing disenchantment with Europe in the United States, especially among the strongest anticommunists; this is not purely anti-Europeanism. Indeed, some in the United States argue that Europe ought to want to be more autonomous, even to the point of advocating U.S. assistance in creating a European nuclear force.

The overall impact of the growing European split with the United States has been to encourage a reexamination of the fundamentals of postwar U.S. foreign policy. It is a strongly held view within the strongly anticommunist circles that the old internationalism of the postwar period has exhausted itself. The "liberal" concept of foreign policy, involving a broad activist role for the United States ended in 1980. The old elite that largely agreed with the predominant view of the European elites lost its influence. The Reagan election marked a watershed as one particularly astute critic wrote: "We are in the process of witnessing a basic sea change in American foreign policy, although it may take some years before it emerges in a recognizable form . . . . The United States is becoming a much more nationalistic country . . . . The new national mood in the United States could wreck the Atlantic alliance."[5]

THE IMPACT OF REAGAN

The new tensions between the United States and Europe were not produced by Ronald Reagan or his administration. It is clear that the split began much earlier, perhaps as early as 1973, at the time of the failure of the "Year of Europe," the U.S. nuclear alert, and the oil crisis that followed the Yom Kippur war. True, there was a period when the differences evident in that crucial year seemed dormant. But they erupted again, and all too easily, during the conflict and confusion over the neutron bomb in 1978, and then became deadly serious during the Afghan and Iranian crisis. U.S. disgust with Europe is plain in the memoirs of Zbigniew Brzezinski (*Power and*

Principle, 1983). By the time of the U.S. election campaign, the distance between Europe and the United States had grown to serious proportions. Reagan's campaign stance, especially his attack on the SALT II treaty, was indeed worrisome to Europe, but disenchantment with Carter was also widespread. Thus, in Europe Reagan seemed a welcome change. Moreover, the Europeans, like the Soviets, seemed to believe that the Reagan administration would simply become another version of the Nixon administration. The appointment of Alexander Haig to the cabinet undoubtedly reinforced this view.

The view was, of course, quite wrong. Reagan brought to Washington a strong ideology and an unyielding commitment to defense, but no concept of an operational foreign policy. Within the first year this was reflected in deadly infighting within the administration over the primacy of ideology over pragmatic policies. But the Europeans were more or less convinced that on the level of reality the administration was open to influence and persuasion. They were alarmed, nonetheless, by language that evoked the cold war. The overall impact was that Europe was further polarized by the Reagan administration: the Greens on the one hand; the Atlanticists on the other. The deepening division in Europe created a vicious circle. As the struggle within the administration intensified, European reactions provided ammunition for the debate between the U.S. factions. The ideologues argued that the United States had to go it alone; the pragmatists argued that allied support was essential, especially in conducting the confrontation policies that the ideologues seemed to want.

What had begun as a general debate, gradually came to focus on the issue of arms control negotiations, and in particular, the negotiations over intermediate-range forces in Europe. By the summer of 1981 two years had passed since the NATO decision to install 572 new U.S. missiles to counter the Soviet buildup of SS-20 missiles. Under prodding from Helmut Schmidt the Soviets had agreed to negotiate, but little had come from the first round because by the winter of 1980 Carter had been defeated. Reagan came to office with no plan of action, neither a negotiating scenario nor a political strategy. If there was any clear tendency, it was to treat the issue as a test of alliance fortitude rather than as an issue for East-West accommodation. Nevertheless, it appears that Haig, sensing the European discontent, pressed for opening the INF negotiations while agreeing to hold off the START talks, as a sop to the far Right ensconced in the Pentagon. But this compromise did not settle the issue of what to negotiate, and the struggle within the administration collided with concerns of the European countries about pressure from their peace movements.

Rather than negotiating for a genuine compromise, which might have seduced the Soviets at the onset of a new administration, the U.S. position was to adopt the radical "zero option," proposed in November 1981. This had as its aim to placate European opinion, but it ensured that the negotiations would be immediately deadlocked. No serious analysts believed that the Soviets would tear down their entire missile establishment. So the net effect was disastrous: the antinuclear groups in Europe were not appeased but incensed; they went even further in demanding the complete denuclearization of Europe, and, of course, they rallied to the nuclear freeze. Similarly, in the United States the freeze movement gained ground because the Reagan approach to arms control was sluggish and, in their view, suspect.

Within six months the official position was collapsing. The public relations gains were short-lived and marginal. The attempt to reorient the U.S. position in the spring of 1982 coincided with the outbreak of the most bitter conflict within the alliance since Suez: the dispute over the gas pipeline and sanctions against the USSR for the Polish imposition of martial law. This dispute brought out the latent animosities on both sides. The Americans found it inexplicable that the Europeans would grant the Soviets such huge concessions at a time of East-West crisis. But the Europeans found it equally inexplicable that the Americans would grant the Soviets the invaluable concession of relieving their ghastly agricultural crisis. The stalemate was broken only by the advent of George Shultz, who liquidated the crisis by retreating in ignominy from the untenable position he inherited.

THE THIRD WAY

It is important to note that this particular incident of the Atlantic conflict had little to do with the pacifist movement. Indeed, on both sides of the Atlantic there was a brooding silence over Poland among the antinuclear groups. Yet, the crisis in Warsaw strengthened these groups because it strengthened the European view that the United States was unilateralist, and if this trend was allowed to persist unchecked, it would spread to the entire field of nuclear weaponry. The movement for denuclearization was thus reinforced. And correspondingly, as this movement was strengthened particularly in Great Britain and Germany, the unilateralist sentiment in U.S. policy was strengthened as a reaction.

The stalemate deepened. It was finally relieved if not broken by domestic developments in Europe. The German Social Democratic party, shifting ever leftward, was defeated at the polls in March 1983. And the British Labour party, which was undergoing an even more radical shift, was also defeated. This removed the last obstacle to the first U.S. missile deployments in December 1983. But the price was high. Whereas there had been a consensus in Great Britain and Germany in 1979, with the opposition parties supporting the governments' decisions, in 1983 the consensus collapsed. Not only were two of Europe's largest and most influential parties in opposition but they decided to break completely with the NATO decision that they had helped to shape. Indeed, the formal repudiation of that NATO decision by the German Social Democrats in November 1983 was probably a turning point in postwar history. The former chancellor, Willy Brandt, put it quite clearly when he said that the two superpowers were "too strong for the good of the world." It was in this light that his colleague Hans Joachim Vogel put forward what has to be considered as a strategic alternative for Germany: not neutralism as commonly but mistakenly feared but a sort of new German nationalism that takes the form of reducing the power and position of both superpowers in order to magnify the power of Germany. Indeed, Vogel, in explaining a "comprehensive" strategy of denuclearization of Europe, called for increasing the "importance of Europe, especially within the Alliance." A brand of German Gaullism was emerging at the close of 1983, not in the government but in the ranks of the opposition. But it is important to note that the new government of Christian Democrats had not abandoned *Ostpolitik*. Indeed, at the height of the missile crisis, both German states seemed concerned with insulating their relationship from the confrontation between their superpower patrons.

THE NEW ERA

It is clear that the era of European security dominated by the superpowers is waning. Mutual deterrence resting on the fear of nuclear conflict has less and less public support, and far from engendering political confidence, has become the source of growing fears. The United States has endeavored to cope with the coming of nuclear parity but has been only partly successful. On a technical level the United States has gone far to redress the imbalances in intercontinental striking power. Indeed, the advent of an entire family of more modern strategic weapons—the B-1, the Trident submarine and missile system, and eventually the MX—promises to create a new balance that will be more favorable to the United States, no matter what the near-term Soviet response. Moreover, the United States has made strides in such exotic but essential correlated fields as nuclear targeting, and command and control. Finally, with considerably less success, the United States has tried to devise a new strategic doctrine—called by the Carter administration "countervailing strategy"—based on the simple but effective concept of denying "victory" to the Soviets under any conceivable circumstances. The Reagan administration, unfortunately, muddied the picture by introducing some tangential thoughts, such as the grisly idea of prolonged nuclear war. As a result of such aberrations, plus some incredibly insensitive rhetoric, the status of strategic doctrine is nearly chaotic, even though the material balance continues to shift toward the United States (a similar uncertainty over doctrine seems to have taken place in the USSR).

The grave uncertainties about strategic deterrence have aggravated the uncertainties about the defense of Europe (as already noted). This was the core issue in the debate and contest over the deployment of new U.S. Pershing IIs and cruise missiles. But even though the first, crucial phase ended in U.S. success and a resounding Soviet defeat, the basic issue was not resolved until the winter of 1983–84. The United States may make progress in restoring a measure of regional deterrence, but the question of what Michael Howard has called "reassurance," the second function of the U.S. nuclear guarantee, remains open. On the whole, Europe has not been reassured. This is a political rather than military task, and it is to this issue that U.S. policy must turn its attention, lest the erosion of support for the United States gain such a momentum that both sides of the Atlantic will be forced into another agonizing reappraisal.

What this means for U.S. policy is that a new concept of European security must be developed. It must include both a credible defense policy, and the general outlines of an acceptable accommodation with the USSR in Europe.

To begin, the United States and the allies need to address forthrightly the question of the nuclear component of European defense. The popular aversion to nuclear matters will continue, and may even become stronger in Europe. The cliché has become that the only answer is the strengthening of defense with nonnuclear means. This solution embraces the moderate Left and the moderate Right, and includes many prominent U.S. political leaders. It has become a near obsession, and it is always put forward as an antidote to the strategists' addiction to nuclear weapons. The burden of these various proposals and advocacies is that nuclear strength cannot substitute for conventional forces and weapons. But the obverse—that conventional forces can substitute for the deterrent function of nuclear weapons—is not automatically valid. NATO's dilemma will not disappear: Soviet conventional forces are likely to remain stronger than NATO's in the only truly critical area, Central Europe. Geography in this area favors the Soviet Union and its ability to bring massive forces to bear in a relatively short time. But alliance politics rules out the most effective positive defense: an elastic defense to contain Soviet attacks. Forward defense is the price the alliance pays to retain Germany. The result, of course, is that Germany remains vulnerable to a Soviet blitzkrieg. Even a limited thrust would leave Germany largely behind Soviet front lines. Such a catastrophe naturally has to be deterred. But deterrence cannot rest solely on NATO's conventional forces. The USSR will never be entirely persuaded that it cannot break through conventional defenses. And there can be no certainty that the Soviet Union would not use nuclear weapons tactically to achieve a breakthrough. Where would such a contingency leave the West?

Clearly, the United States and its allies need to develop a nuclear posture in Europe that is credible to the USSR and reassuring to Europe itself—no easy task. A starting point is the deployment of the new family of Pershing II and cruise missiles. How they will be used, and when, is far from clear. Tactical prudence dictates ambiguity but politics demands clarity. This deployment must be accompanied by a continuing and genuine effort to find a compromise with the USSR. Such a compromise may not be possible. Yet the U.S. effort remains a test of U.S. good faith in Europe. Washington cannot, of course, placate the far Left and the more determined antinuclearists, e.g., the Greens in West Germany. But it can satisfy the moderate Center, which is under a constant assault from the Left in nearly every European country. U.S. negotiating efforts thus far have failed to win significant support, and the Soviet Union is bent on exploiting this situation. At some point it is probable that the Soviets, having failed to reverse the deployments, will make a new offer to freeze the U.S. deployment at a little more than a token level. This will be the moment of truth for Europe, for which it is woefully prepared.

The second problem in sorting out the nuclear equation is to define the status of French and British nuclear forces. The British and French systems present two problems: one tactical, the other strategic. The tactical problem is how to relate these systems to various arms control negotiations. This is not an insurmountable problem. It will probably be worked out eventually in some variant of the START talks. More important is the strategic problem of relating these systems to the defense of Europe and to the U.S. nuclear forces. This is rarely discussed, out of sensitivity to alliance politics. Nevertheless, the theory on which both the British and French systems rest is increasingly doubtful. In the final analysis, both countries gamble that the Soviets will be persuaded by the sheer irrationality of their strategy: the threat to annihilate a few Soviet cities even though the consequences could be the destruction of Great Britain and France; theoretically, no gain in Europe would be worth this risk; these systems are relatively invulnerable at sea, which adds to their deterrent value; no Soviet first strike could be truly effective.

This may have been valid in the 1960s, but today it raises serious questions. What would be worth the risk of confronting Moscow? A Soviet attack on Germany? This would pose the gravest threat to the security of France, a lesser threat to England. But de Gaulle's eternal question now arises: Would France risk Paris to save Bonn? If not, would the British then resort to the nuclear threat to deter the Soviets from occupying the Channel forts? Both Britain and France evade the issue by claiming that their nuclear forces are not tied directly to NATO but are weapons of last resort. They are national forces in the broad sense. In this very narrow construction of a last desperate threat, these forces may indeed be credible. France would fight for France. But this does not deal with a Russian conventional attack, limited in scope but nevertheless disastrous for Central Europe. Moreover, the expansion of these forces makes no particular strategic sense, though possibly justified on technical grounds of modernization. And if the ABM treaty breaks down, and both superpowers proceed with a new "star wars" defense, British and French forces could become meaningless.

The appearance in Europe of U.S. Pershing missiles also challenges the role of British and French forces. The Pershings' short flight time will make the Soviets far more conscious of the European theater. A preemptive strike on the Pershings could include a strike on British cruise missiles bases. What would be the British response? Indeed, what would be the U.S. response? All of this boils down to a proposition that Britain and France may no longer enjoy the luxury of independent nuclear systems that bear no relationship to U.S. deterrent forces. Some strategic coordination is required, if a viable defense posture is to be restored. It would facilitate both defense and arms control. And perhaps most important, it might dilute the growing attack in Great Britain against foreign bases and the British nuclear forces themselves. The demand for a "dual" key over U.S. cruise missiles that arose in late 1983 was a harbinger of increasing pressure in Great Britain to exert control over Great Britain's own destiny. Failure to make significant progress in rationalizing the British and French forces might encourage the other allies to oppose Britain and France in their nuclear roles, especially if they appeared to be the obstacle to effective arms control.

Finally, the United States must recognize the sentiment in favor of a European nuclear entity, which is beginning to come into vogue as an alternative to dependence on the United States. For the United States, settling the role of Britain and France is vital, lest it merge with a demand for the withdrawal of U.S. nuclear weapons, on the grounds that a European force would somehow be "safer." Why the Soviets would regard a European deterrent as effective remains a mystery in this fanciful dream of European independence. But even if it could be created, why would the United States maintain over 200,000 troops facing the Red Army without any nuclear cover? A European nuclear force is no answer to NATO's anguish.

In any case, questions of nuclear strategy need to be seen in a larger context, if only because denuclearization is becoming the centerpiece of an alternative view of European security. This is the main proposal that bridges the more extreme views of, say, E.P. Thompson, and the moderate views of the British Left (in the SDP and Liberal Alliance) and the German Social Democrats. It appeals to U.S. liberals as well. As outlined by the German SPD, the road to European security runs through the following litany: renunciation of the first use of nuclear weapons, a nonaggression pact between NATO and the Warsaw Pact, and a battlefield zone free of nuclear weapons. All of this proceeds under the theme of security "partnership" with the East. It is not avowedly anti-American, but that is the objective tendency of the proposals. It is closely akin to Thompson's search for the "circumstances" in which both superpowers would "loosen the military grip which settled upon Europe in 1945." Thompson sees two alternatives: the destruction of European civilization or the reunification of European political culture, (when it was in fact unified is an interesting historical question). His program is also to seek "limited nuclear free zones," along with measures of conventional disarmament and the withdrawal of both Soviet and NATO forces from both Germanys. This is virtually the return of the classical disengagement of the 1950s: the creation of a large gray zone in Europe, free of U.S. tutelage and protection, only four hundred miles from Soviet divisions in Byelorussia. It is a dangerous pipe dream, but alluring to a frightened Europe.

These alternatives raised a serious question of what the Western alliance envisions. There is obviously a growing impatience and opposition to the eternal verities of European security, i.e. the gradual rapprochement of East and West based on Western strength. NATO needs a new definition of security that will endure. It should not, and cannot, give in to pressures of the street, but in the long run it cannot settle for the status quo. Europe is restless, and this includes Germany. U.S. influence is declining. Tensions with the Soviet Union have the effect of worsening the position of the United States in Europe. The paradox is that the U.S. defense of Europe, though objectively more critical than ever before, is becoming part of the problem rather than the solution. The ultimate European answer, of course, is neutralism. For the United States this is an immense threat, no matter how distant. It threatens to wipe out all that has been achieved since 1945, to change the balance of power, and, in the end, to force another war. To thwart this contingency—which is still only a nightmare—the United States needs to reexamine its policy in concert with its European friends. The alliance needs a new, common strategy. More than five years have been lost since the neutron fiasco of 1978. Time is beginning to run out.

NOTES

1. *Orbis* [13] (Spring 1969): 51.
2. Theo Sommer, "Bonn's New Ost-politik," *International Affairs* 1 (1968).
3. *The Greens of West Germany,* Special Report (Institute for Foreign Policy Analysis, August 1983), p. 69.
4. *Ground Zero, What about the Russians—and Nuclear War?* (Pocket Books), p. 173.
5. Irving Kristol, "What's Wrong with NATO?" *New York Times Magazine,* 25 September 1983, p. 62.

3

UNCERTAIN FUTURE—NATO AFTER 35 YEARS

Irving Kristol

According to a recent report by the International Institute for Strategic Studies, the London-based research center, NATO is in trouble. Western Europe and the United States, the study points out, appear to have different attitudes and policies toward the Middle East, Central America, and Poland, different perceptions of the Soviet threat, different conceptions of the proper economic relations between the West and the Russians; and there seems to be a belief in Europe that the Reagan administration is somewhat too casual about the possibilities of nuclear war.

Such commentary is true as far as it goes, but it does not go far enough. The cracks keep appearing in this antiquated, bureaucratic alliance that has been in existence now for more than three decades. We keep papering over the cracks, but they resurface faster than we can repair them. It is becoming ever clearer that the Atlantic alliance, as we have understood it and been comfortable with it for so many years, is gradually emptying itself of all meaning. In fact, the public disillusionment on both sides of the Atlantic with Europe's security arrangements—especially the excessive reliance on nuclear weapons —is such that a radical reconstruction may be the only way to keep NATO from disintegrating entirely.

I think we can look back and see that three faults have appeared in the Atlantic alliance, and they are truly basic.

The first has to do with the so-called nuclear umbrella—the U.S. nuclear umbrella—over Europe. About four years ago, at a NATO conference in Brussels, I read a paper called "Does NATO Exist?" to a small seminar. My answer was in the negative, based on my belief that the nuclear umbrella no longer offered real shelter. The talk was not well received, but the NATO aides did not take it too seriously.

The following day, however, Henry Kissinger gave a speech to the conference—a public speech with representatives of all the media of Europe present—and strongly implied that the U.S. nuclear umbrella no longer existed. At which point all hell broke loose.

Every European chancellery immediately got onto the State Department and demanded to know, "Does this signify a change in American policy?" And the State Department got onto Kissinger and said, "My God, what have you done?" And Kissinger then issued a "clarification," saying he had been completely misunderstood, that of course the nuclear umbrella was still there, in place, and the Europeans could have absolute confidence in the determination of the United States to use intercontinental nuclear weapons in the defense of Europe.

Kissinger had evidently forgotten that he really did not have freedom of speech. When you are Henry Kissinger you cannot say what you mean because everyone assumes that you speak either for the State Department or for some sovereign power or, in his case, for yourself as a sovereign power. But there is no question as to what he meant, just as there is no question as to where the truth lies.

It should be obvious to everyone that, once the Soviet Union achieved nuclear parity with the United States, the whole notion of the nuclear umbrella became much less credible. It is one thing for the United States to say, and for Europeans to believe, that we shall send ICBMs to destroy the Soviet Union if it presumes to attack Western Europe—all this at a time when the Soviets cannot respond in kind. It is quite another thing for the president of the United States to declare that "because the Russians have dared to attack Western Europe, I will press the red button, even if it means that my country will be destroyed in a nuclear exchange with Moscow."

Will any president actually do that? I have discussed this matter with friends (and former friends) in the Pentagon and the State Department. Their reaction is: "You must not write those things, you must not say those things—the Russians will hear you. So long as they believe the president will press the red button, that is all that counts." When I persist in asking, "But will the president press that red button?" they say, "Well, it is not certain that he won't."

That is the official view—it is not certain that he won't. In my view, it is as certain as anything can be in the political universe that he won't. It strikes me as absurd to think that a president is going to risk the destruction of the United States by inaugurating a nuclear holocaust because Soviet tanks have moved into West Germany and our conventional forces on the Continent have failed to stop them.

Today the nuclear umbrella is 99 percent bluff. Mutual assured destruction, the threat upon which the umbrella over Europe relies, really no longer exists as a believable strategy. One can imagine the United States responding to a Soviet attack on its homeland with, in effect, a suicidal gesture, saying, "All right, you are going to obliterate us, we will obliterate you, just for the satisfaction of it." But it is unimaginable, really, that the United States is going to engage in a mutual holocaust with the Soviet Union to protect Western Europe.

How is it possible, then, that so many European leaders are willing to join the Pentagon and the State Department in pretending that the umbrella exists? Part of this pretense is wishful thinking. There is a fantasy that has been popular in Europe for many years now that the next European war will consist of Soviet missiles and U.S. missiles flying over Europe and obliterating the two superpowers while leaving Europe untouched. A seductive fantasy, from the European point of view.

But the main reason that the idea of the nuclear umbrella has any credibility among Europeans is the presence over there of something like 200,000 U.S. troops and their dependents. Europe does not need 200,000 U.S. soldiers to fight a conventional war; it has plenty of soldiers of its own and the military significance of the U.S. soldiers is marginal. In the European mind, they are there as hostages to make certain that if the Soviet Union does overrun Western Europe in a conventional war, the president will be under severe pressure, seeing a U.S. army decimated, to press that red button.

Which is one reason those troops are not going to remain in Europe for very long. This situation can be accurately perceived in the United States as well as in Europe, and members of Congress can now be heard wondering aloud whether it truly makes sense to have those hostages over there. I have little doubt that, in the years ahead, this concern will become more acute. There is no active public opinion in favor of keeping those troops in Europe, only public passivity before a long–standing commitment. Nor is there any active congressional opinion in favor of it if the only function of those troops is to act as sacrificial hostages. Sooner or later such passive acceptance of an inherited military strategy will drain away into nothingness.

The second fault in the Atlantic alliance as now constituted is a reliance on the doctrine of graduated deterrence. Under this doctrine, we provide conventional forces in Western Europe to help the Europeans cope with a conventional Soviet attack; our combined forces are not large enough to defeat a Soviet attack, but they are strong enough to give the Soviets some pause. If they do not pause, then we will shoot tactical atomic weapons at them—and that should give them pause. If they then fire back tactical atomic weapons at us, we will let loose the intermediate-range nuclear missiles now scheduled to be placed in Europe, wreaking havoc on crucial Soviet military installations all the way to Moscow. And if the Soviets reply by destroying Western Europe with their SS-20s, already in place—well, then the elected leaders of the United States, Britain, and France press their red buttons and give us mutual assured destruction.

This whole idea of graduated deterrence was inaugurated in the late 1950s and early 1960s as a way of saving Europe the trouble of permanent, large-scale military mobilizations and of providing a much cheaper defense than would large standing armies with conventional weaponry. Somehow, the possibility that the Soviets would quickly achieve parity or better in tactical nuclear weapons and intermediate-range weapons was never seriously explored. They have done so, of course.

The upshot is that the strategy of graduated deterrence now scares Western Europe more than it does the USSR. That, I think, helps explain the strength of the antinuclear movement in Western Europe—a movement that is absurd in its dreams of a nonnuclear world but perfectly understandable in its human origins, for it is truly insane for Western Europe to begin any nuclear exchange that could well end in its annihilation. Moreover, a great many Europeans suspect that, once Europe is destroyed in a limited nuclear exchange and the United States faces mutual assured destruction, U.S. leaders will sit down with Soviet leaders and negotiate. And who can say with confidence that such a scenario is unlikely?

When one raises this issue with NATO officials, they say: "Well, we really don't expect to have a nuclear exchange in Germany at the level of tactical nuclear weapons or even intermediate-range nuclear weapons; that is not the point of the strategy. The point is to deter the Russians." Yes, of course—but there is no such thing as a surefire deterrent. What if, after all, the Soviets are not deterred? Is NATO bluffing about its tactical nuclear weapons? The answer one gets is: "But they don't know whether or not we are bluffing and the truth is that we don't know whether or not we are bluffing." Is this a sensible military policy, to engage in bluffing the enemy and bluffing yourself at the same time? It creates a significant uncertainty for the Soviet Union, to be sure, but also for the democratic polities of Western Europe—and it is becoming clear that the totalitarian Soviet Union can endure such uncertainties with greater fortitude.

Moreover, we can rely on the Soviets, who are very astute in their strategic thinking, to probe the bluff. It is most unlikely that Soviet tanks are going to start rolling en masse through West Germany. There is no reason to think the Soviets want, literally, to occupy Western Europe as distinct from "Finlandizing" it. They have enough problems with their East European satellites. Besides, they have more interesting alternatives. They might, for instance, consider a new Berlin blockade—using SAM missiles to prevent an airlift. What would NATO do in the face of such an action? Would it really send its tanks rolling through East Germany or would it choose to negotiate West Berlin away? To ask this question is to answer it.

Or let us assume that one day the Soviets say they have been provoked (they are very easily provoked) in northern Norway—someone has done something nasty to some submarine—and they then proceed to occupy the northern littoral of Norway. Not many Norwegians live there but it is an area of considerable strategic importance. Now, as it happens, Norway is a member of NATO. So what do we do if the Soviets occupy the northern strip, an area that is indefensible against their conventional forces? Do we start sending troops to fight a war —perhaps, eventually, a nuclear war—on Norwegian soil? How will the Norwegians react to that idea? Or do we use NATO forces against a Soviet target closer at hand, say, East Germany?

The fact is we have no credible plan to cope with any such probes, not in Berlin, not in Norway, not in Turkey. Yet if such probes prove successful, the demoralization of Western Europe would proceed apace.

In truth, there really is only one viable military strategy for Western Europe. That is to build up NATO's conventional war against the Soviet Union, while at the same time possessing a second-strike tactical and strategic nuclear capability strong enough to inhibit the Soviets from initiating nuclear warfare. We must stop frightening the citizenry of Western Europe to death, which is what we are doing with our overemphasis on nuclear warfare and nuclear weapons. We need conventional forces of sufficient size and strength to inflict military defeat upon an aggressor.

And, obviously, since even a conventional conflict on NATO territory could be devastating to the area, NATO planning should be such that any conventional war should be fought not in Western Europe but in Eastern Europe. Nations that are serious about defending themselves do not hunker down behind a Maginot line, which is what NATO is doing.

The kind of buildup of conventional forces required for such a viable strategy would be very expensive and would require a significant mobilization of Western Europe's resources. The question is: Does the will to make these sacrifices for European security exist among the peoples and governments of Western Europe? When one discusses this issue with informed European observers, one is quickly assured that it does not exist, that it is unrealistic to think that the British government or the West German government or the Danish government will spend more money on military hardware and troops and inevitably slow down their spending on the various programs lumped together under the rubric of social welfare. No government can do it, these observers insist, and no government has the will even to try to do it. But the people who say this do not fully realize the import of what they are saying. What they are saying is, in effect: "Look, we can't have larger armies. We can't cut our social expenditures. The political will for that just does not exist. But when it comes to using nuclear weapons and risking nuclear annihilation, you can count on us."

That is hardly a plausible assurance. A nation unwilling to curb its social expenditures to build up its conventional military forces will not take upon itself the burden of igniting a nuclear war on its own territory. It will figure out ways and reasons for not doing so. If the will for conventional warfare is lacking, the will for nuclear warfare is lacking, *a fortiori*—and the whole NATO doctrine of graduated deterrence makes no sense whatsoever.

What the Europeans really hope is that any confrontation with the USSR will escalate quickly into a Soviet-U.S. nuclear confrontation, so that those "graduated" stages, during which they may be annihilated, will be passed over. In effect, the governments of Western Europe are asking the United States to run the risk of a nuclear holocaust so that they do not have to cut their social-welfare budgets. This is not a very attractive proposition from the point of view of the U.S. national interest. The U.S. national interest—and in the longer term, I think, the European national interest as well—is to try to see to it that any conflict that might emerge in Europe will remain at the conventional level rather than move quickly to the nuclear level. Of course, if the Soviets initiate a nuclear attack, we would presumably respond in kind. But short of that prospect, it seems clear that the willingness to use strong conventional forces in conventional ways on enemy territory must be revived in Europe. Otherwise NATO is void of meaning.

As NATO is now constituted, European suspicion of U.S. intentions is so active as to subvert the will to resist Soviet pressure. The question constantly being posed is: "Who is using whom?" More and more Europeans are convinced that the United States would prefer to see a nuclear war confined to Western Europe, and that the U.S. commitment to "go the last mile" in nuclear warfare is suspect. This is a reasonable suspicion, based on a sensible reading of the U.S. national interest. And it is an ineradicable suspicion, given the present structure and strategy of NATO.

The third fault in the Atlantic alliance involves differences in attitudes and policies toward the Soviet Union. It is often said that these differences flow from varying perceptions and theories as to what the Soviet system is like, whence it has come, whither it is going. I think this is a half-truth. The other half is that the differences flow from the different conceptions the United States and Western Europe have of their own roles in the world.

The United States is, and its people wish it to be, a world power. In fact, the people wish it to be *the* world power—which may not be entirely possible. But no president of the United States is going around saying that the United States must be No. 2. Presidents still say the United States must be No. 1, even though they understand that being No. 1 is not so easy anymore, and that it is not even clear exactly what being No. 1 means. In any case, the people do have the sense of themselves as a world power, which means they have some sense of themselves as shaping a world order and world civilization that will be congruent, however imperfectly, with U.S. interests and U.S. ideas.

Western Europe, in contrast, has entered what can fairly be described as a regional-isolationist phase, with a policy toward the Soviet Union based on the assumption of permanent military inferiority, a policy that one might call, at the risk of giving offense, "therapeutic appeasement." The rationale for this policy is that "time is on our side"—that the Soviet Union is a young country, that the Communist socioeconomic system has its troubles, and that as the Soviets "mature" they are bound to become more civil in their foreign policy. Therefore, many Europeans say, we should help them mature, help them build a more productive economic infrastructure through trade and investment, negotiate with them ceaselessly even if it is, temporarily, unproductive.

The rationale for U.S. policy is much less sophisticated, though not necessarily less valid. It is that the Soviet Union is an immoral, brutal, expansionist power and has been so under successive leaderships, and that so long as it is a *Soviet* Union—that is, a Communist regime —it will continue to be so.

Nothing better exemplifies the clash between the two perspectives than the sham arms-control negotiations that we are now involved in with the Soviet Union. I use that word *sham* advisedly. The Reagan administration never wanted to enter these negotiations, because in the past the Soviets always used such occasions to gain a military advantage. The United States was dragged into the current negotiations by the leaders of the West European governments, who said they had to demonstrate to their people that their intentions were honorably peaceful before any intermediate-range nuclear missiles could be installed to balance the Soviets' SS-20s. Is it not a little odd that these democratically elected governments of Western Europe should have to prove to their people that they are not "warmongers," and that the best way to accomplish this is to engage in arms-control negotiations that will be at best pointless and at worst the prelude to a treaty that further increases Soviet military superiority in Europe?

In short, the governments of the Western alliance have been for some time now engaged in miseducating and misleading their own public opinion on the possibilities of arms control, encouraging all sorts of wishful thinking about Soviet intentions. So wishful is this thinking, and so successful have our own governments been in deluding us, that in all of the controversy over the SS-20s, Pershings, and cruise missiles, no one seems to have asked the question: "Why did the Soviets in the mid-1970s begin to put those SS-20s in place?" They did not have to, if it was merely military security they were concerned about. They already had a preponderance of power in Europe, a preponderance of nuclear as well as conventional power. So why did the Soviet leaders decide to do what they must have known would be exceedingly provocative, namely, install those new, very powerful, very accurate missiles? The only possible explanation is that the Soviets are not satisfied with having a clear edge in the balance of power in Europe; they want an overwhelming preponderance of power over Western Europe. They want Western Euope to be radically inferior militarily—radically vulnerable—to the Soviet Union. One can further assume that if they wish to achieve such overwhelming superiority they intend to do something with it, like intimidating the nations of Western Europe to pursue policies, economic and political, that are skewed toward the interests of the Soviet Union.

The question of Soviet intentions has not been addressed by the Europeans because it raises the troublesome question of Soviet ideology. Unlike the Europeans, most Americans do see themselves as engaged in an ideological war with the Soviet Union, one that will determine the nature of the future world order. Will it be an order that, in some sense, continues the liberal, democratic, capitalist traditions of the West, or will it be some version of Soviet communism, Chinese communism or some other kind of communism yet to be invented? That this is the fundamental issue the Soviet government and the American people (if not always the U.S. government) understand clearly enough.

It is fascinating to listen to Western Europeans who complain that the trouble with Americans is that they think they are in an ideological war with the Soviet Union—even though the Soviets say plainly, over and over again, that they are in an ideological war with us. Finding it inconvenient to face up to the reality of that ideological war, Europeans refuse to take Soviet ideological statements seriously. But that the statements are seriously meant is evidenced by the way those within the Soviet orbit are treated when they fail to take them seriously.

President Reagan is accused of igniting the cold war all over again. But, in reality, the cold war has never ended, not since the conclusion of World War II. Our State Department, our presidents, all the leaders of Western Europe have talked about detente, but there is no detente and there never has been. And most Americans, despite their miseducation at the hands of the media, the State Department, and successive administrations, have never succumbed to this mirage. Indeed, to the extent that President Reagan speaks as if the cold war were a reality, he is merely bringing U.S. rhetoric into line with U.S. opinion, as well as with world realities.

In fact, I think we are in the process of witnessing a basic change in American foreign policy, although it may take some years before it emerges in a recognizable form. The era of liberal internationalism, extending from World War II until 1980, has pretty much petered out. The old liberal establishment that ran U.S. foreign policy and that basically agreed with the European view of the world has lost, to a large degree, its credibility, its authority, and its political influence. We do not hear people talking about "winning the hearts and minds" of Europeans or Africans or Asians anymore; that phrase has vanished from the American vocabulary. The United States is becoming a much more nationalistic country, a country much more concerned about its national interest and more willing to act unilaterally if necessary to pursue its national interest.

This is the real predicament that NATO now faces. The new national mood in the United States could wreck the Atlantic alliance unless certain basic changes are made—though it is the reconstruction of the Western alliance that most Americans would certainly prefer. After all, the nations of Western Europe are democracies; they share our political values, we want them as allies, and we want them to want us as an ally. To achieve a firm alliance, however, papering over the cracks will not work. What we need to do is to reconstruct NATO before it falls apart.

If we have learned anything from the NATO experience of the past thirty years, it is the rediscovery of an old truth: dependency corrupts and absolute dependency corrupts absolutely. To the degree that Europe has been dependent upon the United States, the European will has been corrupted and European political vitality has diminished. A reconstructed NATO could reverse that process. But it would have to be an all-European NATO, with the United States an ally but not a member.

An all-European NATO, with its own nuclear weapons and its own military strategy, would not have to worry about whether it was serving U.S. interests, not its own, in pursuing this or that policy. If it wanted intermediate-range nuclear missiles, we would provide them, but only on request. If it wanted them at sea, instead of on land, it could put them at sea. The only way the nations of Western Euope are going to regain the self-confidence that they should have—and the will to engage in international affairs in a resolute way—is if there is a European NATO with a large degree of military independence from the United States. An independent NATO, with its own nuclear deterrent, responsible for the defense of Western Europe, willing to make the sacrifices to fight (with U.S. help, if necessary) and win a conventional war with the Soviet Union should such a war break out, that is the NATO of the future, if NATO is to survive at all.

Such a European alliance might regain its self-respect and a feeling of control over its own national destinies, and, above all, it might recapture the spirit of nationalism that is indispensable to any successful foreign policy. A country cannot in this century have a successful foreign policy that does not encompass the nationalist impulse. One of the problems with the involvement of the United States in NATO is that it dilutes that nationalist impulse. Nationalism in Western Europe is up for grabs, and unless it is seized by political parties that believe in our values and traditions, it could be seized by people with less palatable aspirations.

A new Atlantic alliance between the United States and an all-European NATO would be possible and desirable, with Europeans as willing partners of the United States under terms to be freely negotiated. But if this is to come about, we must subject the NATO that now exists, a very sick NATO, to shock treatment. Nothing less will suffice.

4

A PLAN TO RESHAPE NATO

Henry Kissinger

Lebanon and the Soviet succession have preoccupied us in recent weeks [March 1984], but the Atlantic alliance must remain the pivot of U.S. policy. On its unity depends the security of free peoples. From its cohesion will flow whatever hopes the Soviet succession offers for a new dialogue. Unfortunately, just as storms recur in nature, crises recur in the Atlantic alliance. Nearly every administration for a generation has been involved in them. However, the present controversies in NATO are both unprecedented and unsettling.

In West Germany, Scandinavia, the Low Countries, and even in Britain (though to a lesser extent), "peace" movements have been pulling governments in the general direction of their policies, even though those governments disagree with their premises. In addition, the main opposition parties in West Germany and Great Britain—which, in the nature of democratic politics, can be expected to get into office eventually—are advocating policies that amount to unilateral nuclear disarmament for their countries. Because these groups hold sway over key segments of public opinion, too many European leaders—even conservative ones—have yielded to the temptation to demonstrate their peaceful intentions the easy way, by pretending to be reining in a bellicose and insensitive United States through their ministrations. As a result, among those who shape public attitudes—and thereby set what become the limits of the politically possible—there is less intellectual or philosophical agreement than in any previous period.

This creates an exceedingly dangerous situation. An alliance cannot live by arms alone. To endure it requires some basic agreement on political aims that justify and give direction to the common defense. If military arrangements provide its only bond, it will sooner or later stagnate. It will surely prove unable to take advantage of diplomatic opportunities for an easing of tensions. That is the central issue before the Atlantic alliance today. It requires a remedy that is fundamental, even radical—in the literal sense of going to the root. Four problems in particular are gnawing at the alliance:

Lack of an agreed, credible strategy. The gap between NATO's formal strategy and what the public will support has widened dangerously. The so-called flexible response devised in the 1960s remains NATO's official doctrine. It contemplates a defense of Europe that begins with conventional weapons and then goes up the ladder of nuclear escalation—until it reaches whatever level is necessary to halt Soviet aggression. In today's circumstances this doctrine has a fatal weakness: neither existing nor projected NATO conventional ground forces are adequate to repel a major Soviet conventional attack. Therefore, the doctrine would require a nuclear response at an early stage. Yet strategic nuclear parity deprives the threat of strategic nuclear war of much of its credibility; mutual suicide cannot be made to appear as a rational option. And no alternative nuclear strategy has been developed. Partly for this reason, public opinion, essentially unopposed by most NATO governments, is moving powerfully against *any* reliance on nuclear weapons—even tactical ones.

The alliance is thereby trapped in a precarious combination of (a) inadequate conventional forces, leading to (b) reliance on nuclear weapons in (c) a strategic environment that makes the threat of their use, and therefore their deterrent value, less and less credible, and (d) a public climate of growing nuclear pacifism that undermines what credibility remains. Lack of a coherent defense policy leaves the alliance, possessing a huge stockpile of enormously destructive weapons, disarming itself psychologically.

Intermediate-range weapons and arms control. The arrival of the new U.S. intermediate-range weapons in Europe late last year was properly hailed as a major success, for if public demonstrations and Soviet pressure had succeeded in blocking that deployment, the Soviet Union would in effect have achieved a veto over NATO's military dispositions. But unless the alliance clarifies the purpose of these missiles, the accomplishment is likely to be transitory because the basic European attitude toward the missiles is that of a host toward a now unwanted guest whose invitation to dinner it would be too awkward to withdraw. Some prominent Europeans purport to see in the missiles' presence a hidden U.S. design to confine a nuclear war to Europe. Others treat them as one of those peculiar U.S. aberrations that periodically upset the alliance's equilibrium. Too few recognize, and even fewer are willing to admit, that in fact the missiles link the strategic nuclear defense of Europe and the United States. Weapons capable of reaching Soviet territory stake the American homeland to the defense of Europe; they do not enable the United States to remain immune.

European ambivalence makes it excruciatingly difficult to define "progress" toward arms control while the nearly desperate eagerness with which progress is pursued makes its attainment less likely. The Soviets have refused even to discuss any proposal balancing U.S. intermediate-range missiles in Europe against the Soviet arsenal at a lower level. They insist on total withdrawal of the missiles while retaining a large number of their own. The goal of leaving Europe vulnerable to Soviet nuclear blackmail is obvious. Yet significant segments of European opinion persist in blaming the United States for the deadlock. In Europe and in the United States, this attitude must in time erode the public support needed not only for missile deployment but also for coherent arms control.

East-West relations. Behind the sharp differences over defense strategy and arms control lies a parallel dispute over the alliance's posture toward the Soviet Union. Too many Europeans accept the caricature of a United States run by trigger-happy cowboys whose belligerence has provoked Soviet intransigence. Many Americans, on the other hand, consider such European notions naive and believe that together with the pacifist and neutralist demonstrations, they reflect a trend toward appeasement that encourages Soviet intransigence.

Relations with the Third World. Most European leaders believe that they have a special opportunity to establish preferential relationships with Third World countries. In the flash points of the Middle East, Africa, and Central America, they see U.S. approaches as hopelessly tainted by an obsession with Soviet ambitions; some hope to win favor in the Third World by an ostentatious dissociation from the United States. More than a few Americans view such behavior as a free ride paid for by U.S. sacrifices or as a positive incitement to Third World radicalism.

These differences could be healthy if they led to compatible and constructive policies for the 1980s and 1990s. So far this has not happened. Mutual recriminations have created opportunities for Soviet political warfare even during this period of stagnation in the Kremlin leadership. The Politburo is obviously convinced that the West has become so paralyzed concerning nuclear weapons that there is no urgency about nuclear arms control; the Soviets can simply wait for a while to harvest the fruits of Western anxieties. By contrast, there may be concern in Moscow that NATO will move to close the gap in conventional forces; hence the willingness to resume the talks, moribund for ten years, about limiting conventional arms. Does this reflect a genuine interest in arms control, or is it a means to thwart the desperately needed Western conventional buildup by creating the same conditions by which public opinion was mobilized on the missile question? And what is one to make of the almost deferential pleas by all major NATO countries for the resumption of a dialogue that the Soviets have interrupted? Or of the upgrading of all major European delegations except the French to the Andropov funeral, compared with the Brezhnev rites fifteen months ago—especially when Andropov's rule was marked by the flagrant attempt to influence the German election, the walkout from arms control talks, and the shooting down of the Korean airliner, not to speak of Andropov's fifteen-year stewardship of the KGB?

Will the Soviets see Western pleas for dialogue as a demonstration of goodwill, or will they learn from the compulsion to demonstrate good intentions after months of harassment that intransigence pays because the West has weak nerves? Will we fail to relax tensions because the Soviets conclude that atmospherics can substitute for dealing with the real causes dividing the world? Europe is not moderating the United States, and the United States is not stiffening Europe's spine, as the folklore on each side would have it. More likely, each is in danger of paralyzing and demoralizing the other. Western disunity is perhaps the principal obstacle to progress in East-West negotiations.

This state of affairs has deeper causes than particular policies on either side. The present NATO structure is simply not working, either in defining the threat or in finding methods to meet it.

Existing arrangements are unbalanced. When one country dominates the alliance on all major issues—when that one country chooses weapons and decides deployments, conducts the arms-control negotiations, sets the tone for East-West diplomacy, and creates the framework for relations with the Third World—little incentive remains for a serious joint effort to redefine the requirements of security or to coordinate foreign policies. Such joint efforts entail sacrifices and carry political costs. Leaders are not likely to make the sacrifice or pay the cost unless they feel responsible for the results.

An imbalance such as the one now existing cannot be corrected by "consultation," however meticulous. In the long run, consultation works only when those being consulted have a capacity for independent action. Then each side takes the other seriously; then each side knows that the other's consent has to be won. Otherwise consultation becomes "briefing." Agreement reflects not conviction but acquiescence for want of an alternative.

The present imbalance is not new. It has existed ever since World War II. But military dependence on another nation has a cumulative impact. When dependence no longer results from wartime destruction but from a policy choice, made under conditions of relative prosperity, it can breed guilt, self-hatred, and a compulsion to display *independence* of the United States wherever doing so is safe, especially with regard to some Third World issues and certain aspects of East-West relations.

The problem has become even more acute because the generation of leaders that built NATO has virtually disappeared. Those who governed Europe during the early postwar years were still psychologically of the era when Europe bestrode the world. Global thinking came naturally. European leaders assumed responsibility for their own security policies and gave it up only reluctantly because of special circumstances. But nearly forty years have passed since the end of World War II. The new leaders were reared in an era when the United States was preeminent; they find it politically convenient to delegate Europe's military defense to us. Too many seek to position themselves somewhere between the superpowers—the first step toward psychological neutralism. Thus Europe's schizophrenia: a fear that the United States might not be prepared to risk its own population on a nuclear defense of Europe, coupled with the anxiety that the United States might drag Europe into an unwanted conflict by clumsy handling of Third World issues or East-West relations.

The rush to condemn our actions in Grenada by so many of our European allies is a case in point. What could have been in the minds of their leaders? Even making allowance—especially in the case of Britain—for totally inadequate consultation, they could hardly have wanted us to fail. That would surely have affected our willingness to run risks in defense of other areas, ultimately including even Europe. Rather, they must have assumed that their actions were irrelevant and costless: that we would not be deterred, that we would exact no penalty, and that therefore it was safe to use the incident to score points with "progressives" at home and with Third World radicals abroad.

The change in the nature of European leadership has been paralleled in the United States. Our new elites do not reject NATO any more than do their European counterparts. But for them, too, the alliance is more a practical than an emotional necessity, more a military arrangement than a set of common political purposes.

On both sides of the Atlantic, we find ourselves threatened by the dominance of domestic politics over global political strategy. In Europe this leads in too many countries to a faintly disguised neutralism. In the United States it accelerates our already strong tendency toward unilateralism and isolationism.

U.S. leaders have too often adjusted foreign policies to political pressures, bureaucratic infighting, or changing intellectual fashions. The history of the U.S. attitude toward intermediate-range missiles in Europe is an example. These were proposed to the Europeans in 1957-58, installed in Britain, Italy, and Turkey by 1960, and withdrawn in 1963. They reappeared later in 1963 as part of a NATO multilateral force, and were abandoned once again by 1965. They were put before NATO for the third time in 1978 and accepted once again in 1979. Not surprisingly, Europeans organizing to stop the current deployment are encouraged by the knowledge that previous U.S. decisions have not proved immutable.

Similarly, our allies have had to adjust from passionate U.S. advocacy of SALT II to its rejection, and then to the fact that we have chosen to observe a treaty we refuse to ratify; from a strategic doctrine of massive retaliation to one of flexible response; from a policy of detente to one of confrontation and back to conciliation, not to speak of the gyrations in our Middle East policy—all in addition to the reassessments that occur whenever a new administration comes into office. Each change of course leaves victims among European leaders who have staked their domestic positions on policies that the U.S. later abandons. Each lurch encourages a kind of neutralism, as Europeans seek to avoid being made hostage to sudden swings in U.S. policy.

A continuation of existing trends is bound to lead to the demoralization of the Western alliance. An explicit act of statesmanship is needed to give new meaning to Western unity and a new vitality to NATO. In my view such an effort must have three components: (a) more significant role for Europe within NATO, (b) a reform of the NATO organization, and (c) a reassessment of current NATO deployment.

A NEW ROLE FOR EUROPE

During the entire post-World War II period it has been an axiom of U.S. policy that for all the temporary irritation it might cause us, a strong, united Europe was an essential component of the Atlantic partnership. We have applied that principle with dedication and imagination, insofar as it depended on U.S. actions, in all areas except security. With respect to defense, the United States has been indifferent at best—at least since the failure of the European Defense Community—to any sort of Europeanization. Many in this country seemed to fear that a militarily unified Europe might give less emphasis to transatlantic relations or might botch its defense effort and thus weaken the common security. The opposite is almost certainly the case.

In the economic field, integration was bound to lead to transatlantic competition, even to some discrimination. What defines a common market, after all, is that its external barriers are higher than its internal ones. In the field of defense, by contrast, increased European responsibility and unity would promote closer cooperation with the United States. A Europe analyzing its security needs in a responsible manner would be bound to find association with the United States essential. Greater unity in defense would also help to overcome the logistical nightmare caused by the attempt of every European nation to stretch already inadequate defense efforts across the whole panoply of weapons. For example, there are at least five kinds of battle tanks within NATO, different types of artillery, and different standards for calculating the rate of consuming ammunition. In a major conflict it would be nearly impossible to keep this hodgepodge of forces supplied.

Thus the paradox: the vitality of the Atlantic alliance requires Europe to develop greater identity and coherence in the field of defense. I am not talking about traditional "burden sharing," paying more for the existing effort. I have in mind something more structural: a more rational balance of responsibilities. The present allocation of responsibilities fails to bring the allies to reflect naturally about either security or political objectives. Everyone has been afraid to take the initiative in changing the present arrangement, lest doing so unravel the whole enterprise. But since drift will surely lead to unraveling—if more imperceptibly—statesmanship impels a new approach.

STRUCTURAL REFORM

Structural reform cannot substitute for a sense of purpose and clear doctrine. But if pursued with care and sensitivity, it can help catalyze the development of shared political purposes. These common objectives require that European judgments on security, East-West diplomacy, and other matters emerge from Europe's own analysis. Mere acquiescence in U.S. decisions, briefings, and pressures provides a facade of unity; shared purposes require a deeper sense of participation. Specifically:

1. By 1990 Europe should assume the major responsibility for conventional ground defense. This is well within the capability of a group of countries with nearly one and one-half times the population and twice the GNP of the Soviet Union. The Soviets, moreover, have to divide their forces on at least two fronts.
2. This requires that planning for Europe's defense become a more explicitly European task. Heretofore, the Supreme Allied Commander Europe (SACEUR) has been an American. In the new arrangement a European officer should take that traditionally American place, probably with a U.S. deputy. Such a change is also likely to give a new perspective to allied strategic planning. The United States has generally achieved its military successes by the weight of the equipment that our vast industrial potential has made available. This has tended to tempt our military leaders to equate strategy with logistics. European nations have rarely enjoyed such a material margin; rather, they have had to rely on superior leadership, training, initiative, and tactics—precisely what NATO needs in an age of nuclear parity and renewed emphasis on conventional defense.
3. Since the beginning of NATO, the secretary-general, who is responsible for running the alliance's political machinery, has been a European. In the new structure, with its greater emphasis on political coordination, it would make more sense for this official to be an American—whenever the new secretary-general, Lord Carrington, decides to retire. Meantime, no Western leader is better qualified for guiding NATO's transition than the wise and thoughtful Carrington.
4. Europe should take over those arms-control negotiations that deal with weapons stationed on European soil. The INF negotiations with the Soviets (for intermediate-range missiles) and MBFR negotiations (on conventional forces) have heretofore been conducted by U.S. delegations. Both of these negotiations should be "Europeanized" as quickly as possible, with a European chairperson, a U.S. deputy, and a mixed, though predominantly European, delegation.

The structure that I am proposing would enable Europeans to confront—on their own initiative and in their own context—issues that have been evaded for at least two decades: the precise definition of an adequate conventional defense; the nature of the so-called nuclear threshold, that is, the point where there is no choice except conventional defeat or nuclear escalation; and the relationship between strategy and arms control. Because nuclear weapons would presumably be used only if conventional defense failed, Europe would be responsible for setting the nuclear threshold by its own efforts; it could relieve its nuclear anxieties by the simple expedient of augmenting its conventional defenses.

By the same token, European leadership in the MBFR and INF negotiations would place final responsibility for both conventional-force levels and intermediate-range missile deployment in Europe with the leaders whose countries will have to bear the brunt—for good or ill—of the outcome of these negotiations. This is especially important with respect to the U.S. intermediate-range missiles in Europe. That deployment makes sense only if the allies genuinely believe that the prospect of a nuclear blow from Europe on Soviet territory will help deter a Soviet conventional attack or nuclear blackmail. If our principal allies do not share this conviction, the psychological basis for the deployment will evaporate.

European chairmanship of the INF talks would oblige Europe's leaders to face the issue head-on; their domestic critics would no longer be able to argue (as they do now) that U.S. intransigence is the principal obstacle to arms control.

As for the United States, it would of course participate in these deliberations—in a less dominant position—through its continued membership in the integrated command, its responsibility for nuclear defense, and its ground, naval, and air forces in Europe.

REDEPLOYMENT

The issue of redeploying U.S. forces touches raw European nerves like no other. The slightest hint of altering present arrangements jangles sensibilities; it evokes fears of U.S. withdrawal and prospects of European neutralism. But if present trends continue, it is certain to become a central issue in the alliance relationship. Before dealing with it in the context of a program of NATO reform, a few facts must be noted:

1. The present NATO deployment of five U.S. divisions and supporting air and naval forces evolved in the 1950s, when NATO's doctrine was massive retaliation—to react to aggression with an immediate and overwhelming nuclear blow against Soviet territory. Massive retaliation paradoxically required that the total forces on the Continent be kept below the level required for conventional defense. NATO did not wish to tempt Soviet conventional aggression by doing anything to suggest that a Western response would

be limited to nonnuclear means. Hence the U.S. conventional deployment in Europe reflected political, not military, criteria: it was intended to give us no choice about nuclear retaliation and to leave the Soviets no doubt that this would be the consequence of even a conventional war. European conventional forces represented a similar political decision: they too were conceived as a trip wire for our nuclear riposte. From the birth of NATO a full conventional defense has been part neither of its strategy nor of its efforts.

2. This situation became anomalous when the growth of Soviet strategic forces deprived general nuclear war of much of its credibility. Yet NATO deployment has been essentially unaffected by the change. NATO has improved its conventional defenses but has not closed the gap in such forces. As the current NATO commander made clear recently, even counting the five U.S. divisions that have remained in Europe, the alliance is still unprepared to withstand a major Soviet ground attack for more than a few days. European ambivalence continues thirty five years after NATO's creation. Our allies remain unwilling to develop forces strong enough to provide an alternative to nuclear weapons—and yet much of their public opinion shies away from even thinking about nuclear deterrence.

3. Were we to start all over again, we would therefore hardly repeat the decision of the 1950s in today's circumstances. Let us assume a group of wise men and women from both sides of the Atlantic came together to plan a global strategy unconstrained by the past. Assume further that it started from the premise that ultimately the defense of the West is indivisible and that Europe should be viewed under the aspect of the defense of the West in Europe—as a thoughtful French observer, François de Rose, put it. Such a group would almost surely conclude that the sensible division of responsibilities would be for Europe, with economic resources and manpower exceeding those of the Soviet Union, to concentrate on the conventional defense of the Continent. To maintain the global balance of power—by definition as essential for Europe as for the United States—the United States would emphasize highly mobile conventional forces capable of backing up Europe and contributing to the defense of, for example, the Middle East, Asia, or the Western Hemisphere.

Such a division of responsibilities would also enable our military establishment to shift some of its intellectual energies and scientific research from a hypothetical esoteric war in an area where we have major allies to the defense of regions where conflict is much more likely. In such regions our allies are less prone to see their interests immediately engaged, and the countries being threatened are in a worse position to assist in the defense effort.

Even if we were to start all over again, an irrefutable case would exist for maintaining considerable U.S. ground forces in Europe. This would be essential to keep our allies from feeling abandoned and to eliminate any Soviet misunderstanding that the defense of Europe no longer reflects a vital U.S. interest. In a new division of responsibilities we should also preserve and preferably strengthen existing U.S. land-based air power on the Continent. And we should continue our responsibility for both strategic and tactical nuclear defense, assuming that we and the Europeans could agree on a strategy for the latter. U.S. intermediate-range missiles should remain in Europe to "couple" the nuclear defenses of both sides of the Atlantic so long as European leaders desired them. No change in naval deployments would be involved.

Why, then, is such a division of responsibilities not realized? The principal obstacle is psychological. For all their criticisms of U.S. policy, Europeans dread a return to isolationism in the United States. Americans fear that any tinkering with deployment would drive Europe into explicit neutralism. And some in the Pentagon would rather maintain our troops in Europe in a less than rational deployment than return a portion to the United States where they are more exposed to congressional budget cutters.

In my view, persisting in a deployment that is losing its rationale accelerates these attitudes. Pacifism and neutralism are on the march in Europe even under the present setup; isolationism in the United States is not so vocal but is being powerfully encouraged by endless allied disputes. An alliance that cannot agree on its political premises cannot sustain itself by clinging to military arrangements decided a generation ago in totally different circumstances. With current trends, the issue of the rationale for the NATO deployment will become unavoidable. If it arises not as an integral component in a comprehensive design but as a single question of whether to continue stationing U.S. troops in Europe, unilateral changes will be arbitrarily imposed by the potentially most destructive means—the U.S. budgetary process. Then indeed we might see in the United States a psychological wrench away from Europe, and in Europe a panicky resentment against the United States. A change in deployment without a positive political and strategic purpose, withdrawal for its own sake, might shock our allies into neutralism; it could mislead our adversary and tempt aggression.

There is an urgent need for serious and rapid reexamination of NATO doctrine, deployment, and policies, conducted by men and women known for their dedication to Western unity. The group—to be formed immediately after our elections—must begin with one of the most divisive issues before the alliance: an agreement on the nature and scope of the threat. The group must avoid the tendency of previous such efforts, which set unrealistic goals and thereby magnified the problem. A deadline for completion should be set—certainly no longer than two years.

Theoretically, such a study could lead to one of three outcomes: (1) The group could come to the same conclusions about the optimum division of responsibilities in an agreed global strategy outlined above. Given the disagreements about the nature of the interests involved in regions outside Europe and the domestic priorities of most European countries, such a conclusion, however rational, is extremely improbable. (2) The group could agree that the strategic interests of the West require a full conventional defense, but that for practical and psychological reasons, Europe can undertake the required effort only if the present U.S. ground deployment in Europe is maintained intact. (3) The group could decide that the realities of European domestic politics preclude more than the current gradualistic, marginal improvement of defense efforts.

I hope very much that Europe would choose the second option. If Europe should agree to build a full conventional defense and were prepared to express that commitment in unambiguous yearly obligations to increase its forces, the United States should accept the judgment that its present ground forces in Europe are an indispensable component. Such a decision might in fact invigorate the conventional arms-reduction talks and in time lead to stability at a lower level. But if Europe should opt for a perpetuation of the present ambivalence or for only a token improvement, then the United States will owe it to the overall requirements of global defense to draw certain conclusions. If Europe by its own decision condemns itself to permanent conventional inferiority, we will have no choice but to opt for a deployment of U.S. forces in Europe that makes strategic and political sense. If nuclear weapons remain the ultimate deterrent to even conventional attack, a gradual withdrawal of a substantial portion, perhaps up to half, of our present ground forces would be a logical result. To provide time for necessary adjustments, that withdrawal could be extended over five years. To ease the transition further, we could, if Europe agreed, keep the excess ground forces in Europe for a time afterward in a new status analogous to that of the French forces, prepared for use in Europe but also available for use in emergencies outside it. Any withdrawal would make sense only if the redeployed forces were added to our strategic reserve; if they were disbanded, the effect would be to weaken the overall defense.

The proposed redeployment would leave intact air and naval forces, as well as intermediate-range missiles, so long as Europe wants them. A useful by-product of the process would be a systematic reevaluation of the existing inventory of very short range tactical nuclear weapons, a legacy of three decades of *ad hoc* decisions; these weapons now represent at one and the same time an increment to deterrence and the greatest danger of unintended nuclear war because, being deployed so far forward, they are unusually subject to the exigencies of battle.

In this scheme, withdrawal would be not an end in itself—as it will if frustrations on both sides of the Atlantic go much further—but one component of an adaptation to new circumstance extending over some eight years that rededicates the United States to the alliance for the indefinite future.

Psychology is immensely important in international relations, especially when policies turn not only on cold, professional assessments of the national interest by trained political leaders but on public opinion. I would like to believe that restructuring the alliance to give Europeans greater responsibility for their own defense, while important U.S. forces remain in Europe, will be seen not as an abandonment but as an embrace of Europe. It is a means of enlisting Europeans as full partners in the process of decision on which their safety as well as ours depends. For a son of Europe reared on the existing NATO orthodoxy, the very idea of even a partial redeployment is painful—all the more so after Lebanon. But we will not be fulfilling our obligations to the West if we fail to put forward an initiative to forestall the crisis that will otherwise confront us in much worse circumstances.

POLITICAL OBJECTIVES

By themselves, neither organizational nor doctrinal adaptations can remedy the political incoherence rending NATO. This article has emphasized security issues. However, a few general observations on the alliance's political problems are necessary.

1. Those leaders on either side of the Atlantic who value the alliance, with all its failings, as the ultimate guardian of Western freedom must seek urgently to end political disputes over East-West relations and North-South policy, especially Western conduct in the flash points of conflict in the Third World. The tendency to

grandstand before domestic audiences, the growing self-righteousness, will in time make a mockery of the key assumption of the Atlantic alliance: we share a common approach to security. Defense requires, after all, *some* agreed political purpose in the name of which it is conducted. The Atlantic alliance must urgently develop a grand strategy for East-West problems and Third World relations applicable for the rest of this century. Otherwise, it will tempt constant pressures and crises.

2. The United States cannot lead the alliance or even contribute to its cohesion if we do not restore bipartisanship to our foreign policy. Ever since the Vietnam war, we have disquieted our friends and confused, where we have not emboldened, our adversaries by periodic wide swings on essential elements of our policies. But the national interest does not change every four or eight years. At some point the national interest must be accepted by our public as clearly recognizable and constant. Otherwise, we shall become a source of dangerous instability, still relevant for our power but irrelevant for our ideas. A presidential election year is probably not an ideal time to forge a bipartisan consensus. But whoever wins the presidential election faces no more important and urgent challenge than to restore the element of bipartisanship to our foreign policy.

3. European governments must meet head-on the disturbing trends toward pacifism and neutralism in their countries. These movements are led by people of conviction; they cannot be defused by accommodation. They can be resisted only with a compelling vision of a new future. If European governments continue to humor those who profess to see the danger to the peace in a bellicose United States, not an intransigent Soviet Union, they will find themselves making concession after concession and will become hostages of their critics.

The current condition of the alliance cries out for a rethinking of its structure, its doctrine, and its unifying purposes. The creativity and courage with which we approach this challenge will determine whether the alliance enters a new and dynamic period or gradually withers.

I have outlined proposals to reinvigorate allied cohesion by defining clear responsibilities for each side of the Atlantic, to be implemented over a period of years. On that basis European leaders could defend cooperation with the United States as something they sought as a matter of their own conviction and in their own national interest

U.S. leaders would have a rational, understandable policy to defend and would benefit from dealing with a more equal partner. A new era of allied creativity and U.S. dedication could give inspiration to the generation that has come to maturity since World War II and since the postwar crises that infused NATO's founders with their sense of common purpose.

We must not let our future pass by default to the neutralists, pacifists, and neoisolationists who systematically seek to undermine all joint efforts. The nations bordering the North Atlantic need above all faith in themselves and the will to resist the siren calls of those who use fear and panic as instruments of policy or domestic debate. In the end we must fulfill our trust: to preserve and strengthen a North Atlantic alliance that represents the hope of human dignity and decency in our world.

5

THE WESTERN MISALLIANCE

Theodore Draper

The crisis of the Western alliance is an old story. What is new is the nature of the crisis. The crisis in the past was mainly about the reliability of the commitment of the United States to come to the aid of Western Europe. The crisis in the present is about the reliability of Western Europe to aid the United States whenever its far-flung interests or prestige are endangered. This reversal of roles has been gradually approaching, and none of the main factors that have entered into it is actually new. What is new is the crystallization of these factors by events that have forced divergent interests and policies to come out into the open. What is also new is the popular consciousness of a changed relationship among the allies, so that it has become the raw material on which journalists steadily feed. A succession of "new eras" has been regularly proclaimed since World War II; this one may well be the first that unquestionably deserves the name.

One symptom of the present crisis was the question peremptorily raised at the head of a column by James Reston, the senior political commentator of the *New York Times*, on 14 November 1979. The telltale question was: "Where Are the Allies?" Reston was referring to the lack of action on the part of allies of the United States for the release of the hostages in Iran. President Carter, wrote Reston, "cannot deal with this diplomatic and religious tangle alone." He needed, Reston went on, a diplomatic boycott of Iran by the allies and, if that failed, an economic boycott too.

The question was raised again five months later on 10 April 1980,

56

this time officially. In a major address, President Carter declared that it was "vital that the burden of sacrifice be shared among our allies and among other nations." He was referring to the burden of U.S. retaliatory measures against Iran and the Soviet Union. He claimed not to know as yet what the answer to the question was. "I cannot tell," he said, "what those allies and other friends of ours might actually do."

Almost six weeks later, on 21 May 1980, a leading editorial in the *New York Times* sought to answer Reston's original question. The United States, it charged, "is being routinely defied by its major allies." The defiance was demonstrated by the failure of Western Europe and Japan to impose effective sanctions against Iran, by the encouragement of a Palestinian state on the West Bank of the Jordan, and other such departures from U.S. policy. If this trend continued, the editorial predicted ominously, the result was going to be the erosion of the basic military alliance between Western Europe and the United States, the purpose of which was "to combine European, Japanese and American economic power for the defense of democratic values."

Four months later, in September 1980, an article in the *New Yorker* again revealed some of the popular confusion attending the alliance. It explained that the North Atlantic Treaty relationship, which had started out as a "simple U.S. military guarantee to Europe"—and a qualified military association of the North Atlantic nations, was "soon expanded" into "an extremely ambitious political framework." The article counseled that what the United States and Western Europe needed was "not closer alliance, restored alliance, or improved alliance, but less alliance" without the "political ambitions that have become attached to it." The underlying assumption of the article seemed to be that the alliance had long ago become a political instrument and that its outmoded politicization had made it in important respects an "anachronism." [1]

By the end of 1983, the question "Where Are the Allies?" had become even more acrimonious and anguished. Commentators in the *New York Times* reflected the mutual recriminations that resulted from the Lebanese crisis and the Grenadan intervention. On 11 November of that year, a column by Flora Lewis was headed "Europe's Queasy Feeling." She reported that "a sense that Washington lacks appropriate restraint and risks irresponsible impulses is spreading." In return, "American officials tend to brush aside allies' qualms, retorting that Europeans make a vocation of complaining about the U.S. role."

The most extreme U.S. counterattack came on 13 November from William Safire in a column headed "NATO After Grenada." He represented those who were fed up with "this chorus of denunciation from our European allies," and asked, What does it "teach us about the Western alliance?" It taught, according to him, that "our NATO partners are interested exclusively in having the United States defend Europe and are resentful of any action the U.S. takes elsewhere to protect its own security." The NATO alliance was now a "one-way street" that the United States should no longer travel. It was time to think of removing U.S. troops from Europe and forcing Europe to defend itself independently without "the rental of our troops."

Americans were thus constantly reminded of their seemingly unaccountable and inexcusable disappointment in "our allies." Almost imperceptibly, a sea change had come over the place of the United States in the world. When the alliance was formed, the United States did not need European allies; they needed the United States. There was nothing in the alliance that was supposed to work automatically, even in the event of a military attack on one or more of its parties. The alliance had nothing to do with combining "European, Japanese and American economic power for the defense of democratic values." It had never developed a political framework, ambitious or otherwise; on the contrary, all efforts to give it such a framework had failed. If such myths can find their way into leading editorials and articles, one can imagine how far illusions and misconceptions about the "alliance" have gone in less well informed quarters.

Thirty-one years have passed since the alliance was formed, and even people whose business it presumably is to know such things have but a dim and mistaken notion of what the alliance was and is all about. Thirty-one years is a long time for an alliance to last; this one goes so far back that a new generation can hardly be expected to recall the circumstances that brought it about and that gave it its particular purpose.

Before we ask, "Where Are the Allies?" and why are they not sharing the "burden of sacrifice," it seems necessary to recall what the alliance was supposed to do. The terms *allies* and *alliance* are being used so loosely that they have come to mean little more than friends and friendships, the implications of which are decided arbitrarily by whoever happens to use the words. The Kennedy administration's "Alliance for Progress" represented an even looser use of the term; it was no real alliance and resulted in little, if any, progress. President Kennedy anticipated the editorial in the *New York Times* that made the North Atlantic Treaty Organization (NATO) alliance something it had never been and was not intended to be. In 1961, in one of his more fanciful flourishes, he declared that NATO was "remarkable among the alliances of history in its combination of political, military, economic, and even psychological components."[2] It was nothing of the sort, except for the military component, and Kennedy did nothing to make it so. As a result, the idea of an alliance has been so corrupted that it is well on its way to becoming completely useless. There are diplomatic terms for looser connections: *entente, consultation pact, nonaggression pact, community of interest,* and the like. An alliance is something else.

For an alliance to be invoked, it is necessary to know in advance just what definite, formal commitments were made, who made them, and in what circumstances.[3] Alliances that are not clearly defined have little chance of being successfully invoked—not that clear definitions guarantee success. The alliance that is now being invoked in the United States is clearly of the traditional kind, and it is widely assumed that the United States has a right to count on its allies, as if they had agreed on some clear and specific mutual obligations or had arrived at some general undertaking to come to one another's assistance whatever the place or issue. It may come as a surprise to some that the United States has no alliance with Western Europe or Japan that could conceivably apply to any of the most recent trouble spots: Angola, Ethiopia, Iran, Afghanistan, Pakistan, the Iran-Iraq war, or the Middle East. No ally has defaulted in these areas because no commitment was ever made to act in concert in any of them. In fact, they were deliberately left out of the treaty on which the alliance is based.

That alliance is based on the North Atlantic Treaty of 4 April 1949, better known as NATO, though the North Atlantic Treaty Organization was formed the following year as the military structure. The treaty is the only diplomatic instrument that has any bearing on our rights and our allies' obligations. It is still in force because, unlike most such agreements, it was intended to last indefinitely unless one or more of the signatories chose to denounce it after a period of twenty years. It was originally entered into by the United States and ten other countries—Canada, Denmark, France, Iceland, Italy, Luxembourg, the Netherlands, Norway, Portugal, and Great Britain. Before charges of European default get to be too deafening, it is well to recall just what the European countries entered into.

NATO was designed for one purpose and one purpose only: security. It was not concerned with "the defense of democratic values"; if it had been, Portugal, which was then ruled by the Salazar dictatorship, could not have been one of the members. The heart of the treaty was the commitment in Article 5 that "an armed attack against one or more of them in Europe or North America shall be considered an attack against them all." No provision was made for automatic implementation.

Article 4 merely provided for "consultation" whenever one of the parties decided that it faced a threat to its "territorial integrity, political independence or security." Secretary of State Dean Acheson, the chief U.S. architect of the treaty, repeatedly assured congressional committees that the United States would decide in its own good time whether, when, and how to do anything in support of the treaty. He knew that Congress would never have ratified it if it had provided for anything less equivocal.

When the treaty went into effect, as Acheson admitted in secret testimony that was not made public until 1974, by which time it attracted little attention, the United States did not have the military force to defend Europe against a major attack. "There is nothing to meet it at all," he told a senatorial committee at the end of 1950. It would take eighteen months to have "something," two years for "something more," and four years for "something really substantial." [4] The outbreak of the Korean war that year began the remilitarization of NATO. At its inception, then, NATO was made up of a defenseless Europe and an unprepared United States. It began life as little more than "a mere political commitment," as Acheson put it in retrospect. [5] The original idea was to encourage Europe to defend itself by giving it an assurance that the United States would immediately be drawn into any new European war. The theory was that Europe could succeed in defending itself if it were united; it needed the U.S. assurance to gain time and confidence for unification to proceed. It is difficult, decades later, to recapture the faith and hope that were put in a truly united Europe; without that faith and hope NATO might never have won the support of the Americans, who were among the most devout converts to the cause of European unity.

The alliance was deliberately limited in scope. One limitation was geographical. Article 6 restricted it to Europe and North America but, peculiarly, went on to mention Algeria and islands in the North Atlantic "north of the Tropic of Cancer." The French were so worried that the reference to Europe might be narrowly interpreted that they insisted on explicitly including Algeria, though it was then an official part of France. The Tropic of Cancer was dragged in to establish a definite southern boundary. As a harassed Acheson explained in further secret testimony, Alaska was in but the Panama Canal Zone was out. The Canary Islands were problematic, but Crete was definitely out. A U.S. or French battleship attacked by a Soviet submarine in the Indian Ocean was not protected by the treaty. Syria was offered as an example of a Middle Eastern state that was definitely excluded. [6] Later, when Turkey and Greece were admitted to NATO in 1952, the North Atlantic area was defined as extending from the eastern frontier of Turkey to the Bering Straits. [7] In effect, any crisis outside this area did not come within the terms of this alliance, the very name of which was made obsolete by the admission of Turkey and Greece.

The alliance was also limited in function. The Canadians at first wanted it to include cultural, economic, and social cooperation. Acheson found that the senators would have none of it. [8] As a result, Article 2 was watered down to promote "stability and well-being" and to encourage "economic collaboration," without any indication that anything had to be done about them. In practice, NATO has consistently ignored these vague sentiments. [9] Efforts to use them to enlarge the scope of NATO, especially one by German Chancellor Konrad Adenauer in 1956-57, have consistently failed. In 1957, a report by the NATO Committee of Three, known as "The Three Wise Men," made up of Lester Pearson of Canada, Halvard Lange of Norway, and Gaetano Martino of Italy, advocated a much greater degree of political cooperation by enhancing the role of the NATO Council. Nothing came of it. [10]

The United States may have reason to expect the support of Western Europe for its policies in the Iranian and Afghanistan crises, but not on the basis of this alliance. Indeed, it is even questionable whether the North Atlantic Treaty represented an alliance in any true sense of the term. We habitually refer to "allies of the United States," and the use of the term in this connection may be unavoidable, but it conceals as much as it reveals.

On the surface, Europe promised to defend the United States if attacked, and the United States promised to defend Europe if attacked. But that was not the reality. No one expected Europe to be capable of defending the United States; the problem was always to ensure the defense of Europe by the United States. To this extent, the alliance was hopelessly one-sided. The Americans, to be sure, did not enter into it for purely philanthropic reasons. They acted on the assumption that European independence and recovery were essential to U.S. security and well-being; that another war in Europe was sure to drag the United States in anyway; and that the best way to prevent such a war from breaking out was to make sure that everyone knew the United States would be in it from the outset. Nevertheless, the alliance was strictly Europe-centered; the interest of the United States in Europe was fundamentally to keep Europe from being taken over or dominated by the Soviet Union and thus putting its enormous economic, technical, and other resources at the disposal of the Soviet Union. NATO was realistically intended to prevent Europe from being used against the United States, not to ensure Europe's aid to the United States. In effect, the European members of NATO are allies in their own self-defense; they are allies in no other sense.

The question arises whether such a one-sided arrangement was ever a true alliance. "The distribution of benefits within an alliance," states a classic text by the late Professor Hans J. Morgenthau, "should ideally be one of complete mutuality; here the services performed by the parties for each other are commensurate with the benefits received." The ideal is seldom attained, of course, but the principle of mutuality is still essential in alliances. If "one party receives the lion's share of benefits while the other bears the main bulk of burdens," Morgenthau continues, "such an alliance is indistinguishable from a treaty of guarantee." [11] A decade and a half after the North Atlantic Treaty was signed, Henry Kissinger thought that it amounted to just that: "a unilateral American guarantee." [12] He was not the only one, and this view persists to this day, at least with respect to the strategic element of NATO's defenses. The alliance was certainly a unilateral U.S. guarantee at its inception, and there is no reason to believe that it has ever changed in essence. The European end of the alliance was long accustomed to think of the alliance unilaterally, not without U.S. encouragement, with the result that coming to the aid of the United States was hardly something that Europeans ever contemplated.

The transition of the North Atlantic Treaty from a mainly political and diplomatic structure to a predominantly military system was originally demanded by the Europeans, who were not satisfied with a mere declaration of intent. Ironically, the French regime of the day, headed by Prime Minister Henri Queuille and Foreign Minister Robert Schuman, was most exigent on this score. Europe was too cold, hungry, fragile, and fearful to trust in a mere piece of paper; it wanted substantial evidence that the Americans would live up to their word and not come in, as Queuille put it, to "liberate a corpse." The Americans, especially the armed forces, were soon glad to oblige, and their own General Dwight D. Eisenhower was appointed NATO's first supreme commander. The French at different times have been the most extreme exponents of two contradictory European tendencies: to give the Americans military responsibility for

NATO, and to accuse them for that very reason of exercising "American hegemony." [13]

NATO has been a peculiar alliance—we will agree to use the term—for a peculiar military reason that Walter Millis, the military historian, once ascribed to a peculiar dilemma: NATO's planners could not decide "what kind of war they were preparing to fight." [14] This dilemma is as baffling as ever. For the past three decades, it has been expressed by a succession of catchwords and slogans, such as "massive retaliation," "flexible response," "deterrence," and "stability." There is as yet no escape from them, even if the terminology is sometimes changed to escape boredom or feign originality. We need not refight the doctrinal battles that have raged over them, but the past, present, and future dilemma of the alliance is so deeply enmeshed in them that it is necessary to look back to see how the present impasse came about. Our interest is not so much in the military problem as in its bearing on the alliance.

At the outset, the kind of war NATO's planners were preparing themselves to fight could not be a war with conventional weapons because the Soviets' preponderance in conventional warfare was so great that there would have been no point in fighting the Soviets at all. If atomic weapons were usable, however, conventional arms seemed to be superfluous or at best good enough for a holding operation until a decision could be made to employ nuclear weapons. By the 1950s, U.S. military doctrine, somewhat reluctantly adopted by NATO, gave up fighting a conventional war altogether and switched over to the idea of nuclear war or nothing—the now notorious doctrine of "massive retaliation." This position implied that Europe was not going to be defended at all on the ground, or at least was not going to participate in its own defense. The implications of massive retaliation were so disagreeable that then Secretary of State John Foster Dulles, its main public proponent, had to back away from it almost as soon as he had propounded it. [15] By the end of the 1950s, the dilemma was excruciatingly acute: the next war could not be a conventional war and it could not be a nuclear war. What then could it be?

It was opportunely discovered, or at least believed, that the seemingly hopeless choice between conventional and nuclear warfare had an escape hatch. The way out was "deterrence." It apparently offered a solution to the dilemma that conventional warfare was unprofitable and nuclear warfare was unthinkable. The ultimate weapon, it now appeared, was not intended to fight a war; it was intended to deter one. No one then knew—or now knows—how to defend Europe without destroying Europe. No one then knew—or now knows—how to fight a nuclear war without destroying the nuclear powers. But if the purpose was to deter, not to fight, the problem could be evaded, though not solved. Deterrence for this reason played such a large part in the military-political thinking of the past era, down to the present. So far as the alliance was concerned, however, the doctrine of deterrence hinged on U.S. nuclear superiority and hence unhinged any mutuality inherent in the alliance. This more than anything else gave rise to the view that the alliance was really a unilateral U.S. guarantee.

But nuclear deterrence unhinged the alliance in a still more disturbing way. The difficulty with deterrence was that it was soon seen to be mutual. If U.S. atomic or nuclear forces could deter the Soviets, Soviet atomic or nuclear forces could deter the United States. But deter the two nations from what? From a nuclear war or any kind of war? From wars between themselves or wars waged by other means and in other places? These questions hung in the air unresolved. In January 1955, the National Security Council foresaw for the first time the mere possibility of "a condition of mutual deterrence." By 1958, military circles were familiar with the joint themes of "nuclear parity" and "mutual deterrence." [16] But what effect parity and deterrence would have on the alliance was much less clear and much less clearly confronted.

A new element was introduced in the second half of the 1950s. It was brought about by the development of intermediate nuclear weapons, placed in Europe but long enough in range to reach the Soviet Union. They were developed, built, and effectively controlled by the United States. These theater nuclear weapons or forward-based systems, as they were called, were intended to counteract the Soviets' advantage in conventional warfare without resorting to strategic or intercontinental nuclear weapons. The theater nuclear weapons, together with a NATO buildup of conventional forces, created the need for a new doctrinal move in the effort to escape from the straitjacket of all-out intercontinental nuclear war or nothing.

The new doctrine of "flexible response" posed a different kind of dilemma for the alliance, one no more reassuring than that of "massive retaliation." The new dispensation sought to combine conventional, theater and intercontinental nuclear weapons in an indeterminate mixture depending on unforeseen circumstances. To have given "flexible response" a chance, it would have been necessary to build up NATO's conventional forces to within range of Soviet strength in this category. No such effort was ever made. It could not be made without knowing just what kind of war NATO's planners were preparing to fight. If the war was to be a largely conventional war, it was bound to be fought mainly in Europe—a horror that the European allies were determined to avoid at all costs. The addition of theater nuclear weapons to conventional forces promised to make it an even more frightful European war; it could be assumed that the Soviets would seek to take them out at once; and it was hard to believe that a nuclear exchange would stop there. If the war turned into a full-fledged nuclear war, without the use of conventional or theater nuclear weapons, it would be fought over the heads of Europeans on Soviet and U.S. soil.

The kind of war, then, determined whose ox was going to be gored first or last. The allies could not help viewing these options from the viewpoint of national interest and survival. Europeans ultimately preferred to put their trust in the U.S. "nuclear umbrella" to avoid, at least theoretically, a conventional plus theatre nuclear war in Europe. The United States put more and more stock in the buildup of NATO's conventional arms. In the end, "flexible response" was apt to be more flexible in theory than in practice; it all depended on how long a conventional war could be fought in Europe and whether Europeans really wanted another and more ruinous conventional war fought in Europe at all.

The doctrine of deterrence was so agreeable because it seemed to avoid all of these dreadful options. If the buildup of conventional and nuclear arms was necessary primarily to deter rather than to fight a war, Europeans did not need to care whether it would be fought in Europe; and Americans, whether it would be fought over Europe. Deterrence, however, had two disagreeable aspects. One was that it might not work, in which case it was still necessary to plan for fighting some kind of war. The other was that it encouraged Europeans to put their real reliance on U.S. strategic nuclear weapons, the ultimate deterrent. The European reluctance to give up nuclear deterrence is another way of saying that Europe would like to be defended outside Europe if the deterrent should fail to deter.

By the 1960s a new escape hatch—stability—was discounted. It implied that it was a good thing for neither the United States nor the Soviet Union to possess a military advantage. If a stable military balance could be achieved, neither side would be tempted to take advantage of the other, on pain of unacceptably destructive retaliation. Stability theorists took the position that Soviet strategic parity with the United States actually benefited the United States by committing the Soviet Union to the mutual-assured-destruction doctrine. [17]

But what of the alliance? If a stable nuclear balance could be assured, the deterrence of nuclear war would become automatic. The stability theory is thus the deterrence doctrine writ large. For the alliance, the dilemma of mutual deterrence would be extended indefinitely, not removed. The European allies could count less than ever on the United States' using the "ultimate deterrent" to save them. Even if it were credible, which is highly doubtful, stabilization is no escape hatch or nuclear panacea. Stabilization, like parity, is a will-o'-the-wisp because it means, in reality, repeated stabilizations at increasingly higher levels. The only way to stabilize once and for all is to put an absolute and permanent end to technological and scientific development, a cure that might be worse than the disease, even if it were feasible.

One reason for bringing up all this is that "deterrence" and "flexible response" are still very much with us. They appear to be the poles of present-day military doctrine from which there is no escape. Whatever problems were posed by "massive retaliation" and "flexible response" for the alliance in the past are not likely to go away in the future.

The very nature of the alliance dictated that the issue of nuclear versus any other kind of war should be the heart of the matter. The issue is not as abstruse or esoteric as nuclear-arms experts like to make it. The grand lines of strategy have always been recognized as relatively simple and fundamental, however complicated the tactics or technology may be to carry them out. There is nothing mysterious or incomprehensible about what makes nuclear weapons different strategically from all previous innovations in weaponry. The difference lies in the level of destructiveness. The unimaginable horror of that level is what makes nuclear weapons unique. In all past history, new weapons, such as the machine gun and the tank, were used to wage wars, not to deter them. The doctrine of deterrence applied to nuclear weapons implies that they are so destructive that they cannot be used for any rational purpose based on any calculation of more gain than loss. Such a weapon is different in kind, not merely in degree. Yet the temptation to figure out some way to use nuclear arms in actual war never seems to go away.

By now, however, it is clear that nuclear arms can at best deter nuclear war only. They cannot deter any other kind of war. The struggle for power goes on, and is obviously going on, below the level of nuclear war. A position of dominance in world affairs may be established by a power or group of powers using force considerably short of the level of nuclear war; and a position of inferiority may be suffered without its going so far as self-destruction. Even as a last resort, suicide is not a rational or inevitable course. The idea that the struggle for power must escalate to nuclear war is a form of political blackmail put forward, especially in the United States, as a means of persuasion to give up the struggle for power altogether. Yet as long as the struggle for power persists, the danger of nuclear war cannot be ruled out.

The paradox of the alliance is that it was founded on the U.S. monopoly of atomic arms. Such weapons have also been its unbearable burden and dilemma. It is richly worth reconsidering what those old warriors, Charles de Gaulle and Konrad Adenauer, thought of the alliance.

De Gaulle's original program called for an alliance with the Soviet Union, not with the United States. In December 1944, before the end of World War II, de Gaulle had in mind, as he told Stalin in Moscow, a three-stage system. A Franco-Soviet alliance was to be the first stage, followed by Anglo-Soviet and Anglo-French alliances in the second stage. He included the United States in the third stage only within the general framework of the United Nations. De Gaulle's aim was then to form a bloc of European states to act as "the arbiter between the Soviet and Anglo-Saxon camps." [18] Inasmuch as de Gaulle regarded Britain as part of the Anglo-Saxon camp with the United States, his second stage of alliances with Britain lacked the verisimilitude of his first-stage alliance with the Soviet Union. An "arbiter" was hardly in a position to be an ally.

De Gaulle's opening move came to nothing. Stalin had no intention of dealing with de Gaulle as an equal or taking his advice. A ravaged, distraught Western Europe begged for U.S. aid and, with it, U.S. leadership. By the time de Gaulle had retired from office for the first time, in 1946, his program had collapsed for lack of support from any quarter, including his own people.

But de Gaulle's second try, after his return to power in 1958, was more fruitful. In a show of nonpartisanship, he denounced the "two hegemonies" of Soviet Russia and the United States. He came to regard NATO as no more than a U.S. appendage, demeaning to France. His goal was now a "European Europe," which partly included the USSR, according to his formula of a Europe "from the Atlantic to the Urals," and totally excluded the United States. His "European Europe" was to be led by France in contradistinction to the "Atlantic Europe" led by the United States. To fulfill this vision, de Gaulle no longer took the direct route of a Franco-Soviet alliance. He now set out for the same destination by an indirect route.

The road to Moscow went through the suburbs of detente, which began to take shape in the spring of 1965. In February 1966, de Gaulle announced the French intention to withdraw from the military organization of NATO but not from the North Atlantic Treaty itself, thus keeping a foot in the door. In June of that year, he visited the Soviet Union to make official the new Franco-Soviet detente. At that time, Soviet leader Leonid I. Brezhnev thought the time ripe to come forth with a proposal for a European security conference including the Soviet Union but excluding the United States. De Gaulle himself soon made clear that detente was only a first step, according to this formula "detente, entente, and cooperation." A Franco-Soviet detente was not a substitute for an alliance; it might, depending on circumstances, be the first stage of one. There is this in Gaullism, a tradition of playing the Soviet card against "American hegemony." It is only one strand of that tradition; that this strand has reappeared in a neo-Gaullist guise should not be so surprising or mystifying. Implicit in this schema of Gaullism were three limiting conditions. De Gaulle's willingness to take the risk of moving closer to the Soviet Union and further from the United States cannot be understood without them.

France, de Gaulle recognized, was no match for the Soviet Union. Before he engaged in the negotiations that led to the Franco-Soviet detente, de Gaulle undertook to arrive at a Franco-German understanding with Chancellor Adenauer. A Franco-German entente was the precondition for a Franco-Soviet detente. De Gaulle's German gambit was initially successful because it appealed to Adenauer's ardent sympathy for what was then known as European Union. The Adenauer-de Gaulle honeymoon did not last long but it set a precedent for another Franco-German honeymoon in the present circumstances.

The second Gaullist precondition rested on a determination of which of the two "hegemonies" was the weaker. It was a Gaullist principle to support the weaker of the two so as to create a balance of power between them within which a French-led Europe could operate most successfully. In de Gaulle's time, the Soviet Union was considered to be the weaker of the two, thus permitting France to lean over in its favor.

The third precondition of Gaullist policy assumed that the United States, in its own interest, was bound to come to the support or rescue of Western Europe in any serious crisis. For this reason, there was no need for Europe to pay for U.S. protection that it could get for nothing, or at least without the necessity of binding itself to the United States in a formal military organization. The presumption of

U.S. support, and the assumption that support had in the last analysis to rest on the threat of nuclear deterrence, made possible the military withdrawal of France from NATO without ostensible sacrifice of anything that was really essential to France in the NATO setup.

De Gaulle, however, became increasingly dubious about the third point. In a notable statement in November 1959, he raised the question whether the atomic "equilibrium" between the Soviet Union and the United States could last. "Who can say," he asked, "what will happen tomorrow?" He speculated that the two superpowers might "divide the world" between them or agree not to wage atomic war against each other. He even speculated that one day the Soviet Union might annihilate Western Europe, while the United States did the same thing to Central Europe. [19]

In another famous statement in 1963, de Gaulle went further. He acknowledged that France had to have allies, but immediately insisted on France's need to have "the free disposition of itself" because alliances have no "absolute virtues, whatever may be the sentiments on which they are based." In the atomic age France could be destroyed at any moment unless "the aggressor is deterred from the attempt by the certainty that he too will suffer frightful destruction." An alliance with the United States had once been justified as a means of preventing such an eventuality because the Americans had long been the only ones to possess nuclear arms. The United States could protect France when the former had a monopoly of those arms and the will to use them as soon as Europe was attacked. Deterrence worked so long as these two conditions were fulfilled. But conditions had changed as soon as the Soviets had come into possession of nuclear weapons powerful enough to threaten the United States with direct destruction on its own territory.

"In these conditions," de Gaulle summed up, "no one in the world, particularly no one in America, can say if, where, when, and to what extent American nuclear weapons would be employed to defend Europe." Yet de Gaulle was not willing to give up the employment of those weapons altogether, for in the very next sentence he turned around and allowed that "this does not at all prevent American nuclear weapons, which are the most powerful of all, from remaining the essential guarantee of world peace." How those weapons could guarantee world peace or even peace in Europe without the certainty that they would be used he did not explain. In other statements that same year, he took the same line of questioning the reliability of the U.S. nuclear deterrent without giving it up. [20]

In effect, de Gaulle reduced the Europe-United States alliance from a unilateral U.S. guarantee to a European insurance policy. The difference was that Europeans had put their trust in the guarantee as their first and only line of defense, not so much to beat back an attack as to prevent one; they now wanted to have other options, leaving the U.S. deterrent as a last line of defense if all else failed. His battle cry of "independence" gave France full freedom of action in every contingency except the ultimate one of nuclear attack; for that he reserved the right to call on the "alliance" with the United States for the extreme unction of nuclear deterrence. His juggling act was of the now-you-see-it-now-you-don't kind in which he manipulated three balls at once: one marked "Independence"; a second "Alliance"; and a third, "No Faith in the Alliance." It was a dazzling performance—so long as de Gaulle was speaking to a sympathetic French audience.

As the French experience showed, detente and the alliance have a most uneasy relationship. De Gaulle's policy with respect to the Soviet Union immediately, inevitably, and drastically changed the French position within the North Atlantic alliance. The French detente was not merely a step toward the Soviet Union; it was also a step away from the United States. It is of the nature of detente, whatever else it may do, that it changes the existing balance of forces. The United States could not get closer to Communist China without getting further from Communist Russia. Making friends with someone else's enemy or rival cannot fail to be disturbing and even threatening. Detente is a seemingly innocent word that implies the spread of goodwill and peaceful intentions where they did not exist before. In the real world, however, its influence is not so innocent. It does not easily do away with the underlying, long-term enmities and rivalries; rather, it indicates a shift, however great or little, in the lineup. De Gaulle's methods were open and brutal enough to make unmistakably clear that the lineup had changed. Whenever de Gaulle supported the United States, as during the Cuban missile crisis of 1962, he did so to prevent the balance of forces from moving too sharply in favor of the Soviet Union, not because he thought that the alliance required him to come to the assistance of the United States. Detente was for him—and for the Soviets—a weapon, not a token of affection or reward for good behavior.

For all his special pleading, de Gaulle cannot easily be dismissed. He saw some things more clearly than others of his time and dared to speak out about them with vision and eloquence. He was justified to mistrust nuclear deterrence as soon as it had become mutual deterrence. When he wondered aloud whether the United States would use strategic nuclear weapons in the defense of Europe if it were open to similar nuclear destruction, he knew what he was talking about. But Gaullism should not be confused with neutralism. The ideal Gaullist world would permit Europe under French leadership to act independently of the two superpowers, using whatever means necessary to achieve its ends as circumstances dictated. These means might include siding with the Soviet Union or the United States, siding with neither, going off on an independent tack against both, or taking refuge in neutralism—but none of these as a matter of principle. Since all these options would depend on how much power was available to carry them out, the less power Europe or France could actually muster, the more likely it would be to fall back on some form of Swedish-type neutralism or even Finnish-type accommodation. In practice, then, Gaullism may be far more neutralist than it is in theory. A successful Gaullism would take a strong line with both the Soviet Union and/or the United States, as de Gaulle was wont to do from time to time; a failed or illusory Gaullism would run the risk of progressive Swedenization or Finlandization as it came under more Soviet than American pressure.

De Gaulle's view of mutual deterrence was not original. Its implications had already occurred to responsible Americans. In 1956, the army's chief of staff, General Maxwell D. Taylor, had written an article, which he was not permitted to publish, in which he had held that, in the condition of mutual deterrence, "the only war worth preparing for is surprise, nuclear attack on the United States." [21] In 1958, the army, navy, and marine corps combined to advocate that "the United States and the USSR would be increasingly restrained from deliberately initiating a general nuclear war except where national survival was directly at stake." This position, which was at that time vetoed by the Air Force, held: "This fact had become so apparent that it was doubtful whether either the Soviets or our Allies believed that we would use our retaliatory power for anything other than to preserve our own existence." [22] In 1959, the same year that de Gaulle first brought up the subject, Dulles's successor as secretary of state, Christian A. Herter, testified at his confirmation hearing: "I can't conceive of the President of the United States involving us in an all-out nuclear war unless the facts showed clearly that we are in danger of devastation ourselves, or that actual moves have been made toward devastating ourselves." Herter also said: "I am sorry that the alliance does not relate to the whole world, but I do not think that is in the cards at the present time." [23] A different line was taken by spokesmen of the following Kennedy administration, especially by Secretary of

Defense Robert McNamara. In 1963 he assured Western Europe that its defense was as vital "to us as the defense of our own continent" and that the United States was prepared "to back up our commitments there with our strategic nuclear power no matter what degree of damage might result should the deterrent aspect of this policy fail." [24] But ten years later, David Packard, deputy secretary of defense from 1969 to 1971, was equally sure that "with the present nuclear balance the United States will not use its nuclear force against the Soviet Union short of a dire threat to the survival of the United States." [25]

Whom to believe? That was just the question de Gaulle had asked: "Who can say what will happen tomorrow?" No U.S. president had ever faced such a decision. There was no precedent for nuclear war. The only thing sure about what the United States would do in the event of an attack on Western Europe and on Western Europe alone was that no one could be sure.

What did all of this have to do with the alliance? The answer depended on one's point of view. For the Americans by and large, with the exception of such heretics as Hans Morgenthau and the early Henry Kissinger, the alliance was safe in U.S. hands. From the Gaullist standpoint, nuclear weapons, as General Pierre Gallois argued in 1963, made the alliance obsolete because no nation would jeopardize its survival for others. [26] It was as if the alliance could hold together only so long as it was not put to the acid test. NATO, in effect, had begun to resemble the Locarno Treaty of 1925, whereby Great Britain and Italy had guaranteed the Franco-German and Belgian-German borders. "The treaty of Locarno," wrote A.J.P. Taylor, "rested on the assumption that the promises given in it would never have to be made good—otherwise the British government would not have given them." [27]

Adenauer apparently began to worry about the alliance almost as soon as it was put together. As early as 1950, he thought it significant enough to record in his memoirs that he had asked an important American political figure whether the United States would use atomic weapons if Eastern forces invaded West Germany. The answer was: No. [28] The German chancellor became increasingly disturbed about the NATO alliance as a purely military structure. By 1956, he thought it necessary to change it into a more political instrument, by which he meant that a common foreign policy was necessary to make a common military policy effective. When he raised the issue with Secretary of State Dulles in 1956, the reply was nominally favorable to the idea but Dulles offered an objection that then and later precluded any serious effort to do anything about the matter: the United States, unlike Europe, had worldwide interests that other countries could not be permitted to constrain. [29]

In 1957, after the Soviet "Sputnik," Adenauer's conviction that something had to be done to transform the members of NATO into political "partners" deepened. In December of that year, he wrote a memorandum that still seems to have lost little of its force. He criticized the United States for neglecting NATO politically because he thought the United States wanted to have a free hand in Asia and the Near East. Like de Gaulle but earlier, he wondered whether a president of the United States could really be counted on to employ nuclear weapons for Europe now that Soviet Russia had missiles with nuclear heads that could directly attack the United States. The lesson for him was ominous: "As soon as the people of Western Europe become more strongly conscious of these facts, the inclination to capitulate to the Soviet Union will presumably become very strong." He concluded that the NATO alliance would continue to have purpose only if it developed into a "political alliance." [30]

What the United States, alarmed by the Iranian and Afghanistan crises, now wants from its allies is just such a common foreign policy, a "political alliance," as Adenauer had suggested, albeit one that follows the U.S. lead. The United States wants this kind of alliance to operate outside Western Europe. When Adenauer prematurely pointed in this direction, the United States held back; when the United States finally wanted to go in the same direction, Western Europe held back.

De Gaulle soon said publicly what Adenauer had written privately. The French had already had some chastening experiences with the Europe-fixation of the North Atlantic Treaty. As soon as they found themselves in serious trouble in Indochina, they wanted help outside Europe. In December 1952, the French cabinet adopted a resolution affirming that the French union "deserved" to receive support "without fail" from its Atlantic allies. [31] Two years later, the French government vainly appealed to the Eisenhower administration for air strikes to save its garrison at Dien Bien Phu. And in 1956, the Eisenhower administration not only failed to give help to the Suez operation of Great Britain and France but implicitly cooperated with the Soviet Union to frustrate it.

The United States, of course, thought that the French did not deserve support at Dien Bien Phu or Suez, but that was not the point for the embattled Europeans. The deeper issue was whether the United States should decide when and if the French or British deserved support, as in the future the French and Germans might decide when and if the United States deserved support. Two or more could play at that game, but the sides were then so unequal that the rules seemed to permit the United States to make all the decisions for the entire team. In any case, the United States refused to aid France and Britain outside the European area in their hours of need; and European memories tend to be much longer than American in these matters.

For this and other reasons, de Gaulle made at least two efforts to broaden the decision making of the alliance. In September 1958, he proposed the formation of a directorate of the United States, Great Britain, and France to shape the global policies of their alliance. His proposal was generally received as a self-serving bid to increase France's power and was never taken seriously. Eisenhower's reply to de Gaulle put him and France in their places in a way that must have deeply rankled. One reason given by Eisenhower was that the United States did not wish to give other allies the impression that "basic decisions affecting their own vital interests are being made without their participation"—as if the United States had not been making such decisions. The second reason had more serious implications for the future. Eisenhower also rejected de Gaulle's proposal on the ground that it was an effort "to amend the North Atlantic Treaty so as to extend its coverage beyond the areas presently covered." [32] The United States, in effect, was perfectly content with an alliance that formally left it with a free hand outside Europe without allied meddling—as if the day would never come when the United States might need allied support outside Europe.

Two years later, just before the Kennedy administration came in, de Gaulle tried again. On 25 September 1960, he made a more far-reaching proposal. He recalled that in 1949, when the North Atlantic Treaty was signed, the immediate question had been the security of Europe. For that reason, the alliance had been limited to Europe within "a very narrow zone of action." But much had changed in ten years. There were now possibilities of conflict and military operations outside Europe extending throughout the world, especially in Africa and the Middle East. Europe, and particularly France, had recovered economically and socially. An alliance narrowly limited to Europe was outmoded, and something more was needed. "We think," he said, "that, at least among the world powers of the West [by which he meant the United States, France, and Great Britain], something must be organized, as far as the Alliance is concerned, with regard to the political and occasionally strategic conduct of the Alliance outside Europe, particularly in the Middle East and Africa where these three powers are constantly involved." He made the very preservation of the alliance dependent on its expanded coverage. "If there is no agreement among the principal members of the Atlantic Alliance on matters other than Europe, how can the Alliance be indefinitely maintained in Europe? This must be remedied." [33]

President Kennedy apparently did not know what to make of de Gaulle's proposal. [34] After mulling the question over for almost two years, he appropriated the general idea for a speech on 4 July 1962, in which he offered U.S. readiness "for a Declaration of Interdependence" with a United Europe to form "a concrete Atlantic Partnership" that would also serve "as a nucleus for the eventual union of all free men." Kennedy was obviously taking no chances that anything would come of the idea by linking it to a United Europe and inflating it rhetorically to the bursting point. The following year, Kennedy also spoke of building an "Atlantic partnership—an entity of interdependent parts, sharing equally both burdens and decisions," though he did nothing to share burdens or decisions. [35]

Others played around with the idea. In 1965, Henry Kissinger was sufficiently inspired by the Gaullist critique to take the position that the Atlantic alliance needed "a common foreign policy" if it were to retain "any vitality." More concretely than others he proposed creating "a political body at the highest level for concerting the policies of the nations bordering the North Atlantic." He suggested making this body the executive committee of the NATO Council, with representatives of the United States, Britain, France, West Germany, Italy, and one rotating member representing the smaller NATO countries. The larger goal was "an Atlantic Commonwealth." [36]

The question, then, that arose back in the 1950s was: More than NATO—or less? It is the same question that haunts the alliance today.

The Atlantic alliance was reduced to less from the European side by an upsurge of neo-Gaullism of both French and German varieties. As in the past, France took the lead, but Germany has followed more closely behind than it had ever dared in the past.

The foreign policy of former President Giscard d'Estaing clearly took its inspiration from the legacy left by de Gaulle; the controlling concept in both cases was that of an "independent" French policy. In an interview on 23 May 1980, Giscard was asked to explain why the French ambassador in Moscow was the only Western diplomat to present himself at the reviewing stand of the 1 May demonstration, and why Giscard himself soon afterward met with Soviet leader Brezhnev in Poland following arrangements so secretive that they betrayed an uneasiness that France's "allies" might have interfered if they had known about the meeting too far in advance. With evident rancor, Giscard replied that France had the right "to have an independent policy without immediately being accused of breaking with Western solidarity." He pledged himself to continue to carry out "an independent policy, in natural solidarity with our partners in Europe and in the world." [37] Independence always came first with solidarity hitching lamely along.

For Giscard as for de Gaulle, "independence" was not enough. It had to be an independence that enabled France to fall back on Western solidarity if all else failed. Giscard's foreign minister, Jean François-Poncet, had the month before struck the same keynote of "an independent French foreign policy in its conception and in its practice." At the same time, however, he insisted that France was still faithful to the Atlantic alliance, though he denied that it was of the nature of "a protector and its protégés." He even spoke of the "solidarity which unites us with the United States" in the matter of the U.S. hostages in Iran, while again emphasizing that France alone could decide what measures, if any, to take. [38] In this balancing act between independence and solidarity, independence decides what form solidarity will take or whether there will be any solidarity at all.

De Gaulle also used to reject Atlantic union in favor of European union without going so far as to break all ties with the United States. Yet the break after the French military withdrawal from NATO in 1966 between de Gaulle's regime and the post-Adenauer government headed by Chancellor Ludwig Erhard was, in the Gaullist view, precipitated by the difference of outlook between France and Germany with respect to the United States. De Gaulle's foreign minister, Maurice Couve de Murville, scornfully recalled in his memoirs how the West German government was "flabbergasted and terrified" at the prospect of following "French dynamism, audacity, and independence," whenever the United States disapproved of French actions. [39]

The real break with the Adenauer tradition came at the end of 1966 with the so-called Grand Coalition headed by the Christian Democratic Chancellor Kurt Kiesinger and Social Democratic Foreign Minister Willy Brandt. They began the redirection of German policy that was consummated in the fall of 1969, when the Grand Coalition fell apart and Brandt took over as chancellor with the Free Democratic party as junior partner. The new leitmotiv was made up of equal parts of *Ostpolitik* and detente. They performed as the ideological accompaniment to the Soviet-German treaty in August 1970 and the Polish-German treaty the following November. On the occasion of the first, Brandt made a notable address from Moscow to his compatriots in which he clearly signified that the treaty had decreased the distance between West Germany and the Soviet Union and had increased the distance between West Germany and the United States. The new balancing act between East and West was explained by Brandt in these words: "Our national interest does not permit us to stand between the East and West. Our country needs cooperation and harmonization with the West and understanding with the East." Brandt defined this "understanding" as a form of partnership: "Russia is inextricably woven into the history of Europe, not only as an adversary and danger but also as a partner—historical, political, cultural and economic."[40] These carefully chosen words unmistakably represented a basic shift in West Germany's foreign policy and foreign relations.

In this way, a German variety of Gaullism or in the beginning a German appendage of Gaullism came into existence after de Gaulle himself had left the scene. Chancellor Helmut Schmidt inherited this German neo-Gaullism, which he carried out with somewhat more adroitness than his predecessor. When Schmidt was replaced by the Christian Democrat Helmut Kohl, German foreign policy changed little, if at all, just as French foreign policy did not change all that much when Francois Mitterand replaced Giscard d'Estaing.

De Gaulle himself, however, was a premature Gaullist. Europe did not have the economic, political, and military resources to back him up. France byitself was not weighty enough. As a result, de Gaulle tried to make up in acts of will and outbursts of oratory what France lacked in instruments of power. The resurgence of Gaullism without de Gaulle suggested that Gaullism was not merely the emanation of one man, that it had authentic roots in French and European conditions, and that, as an expression of independence from the United States, Gaullism could also take a German or other European form. Gaullism was the solvent that first began to dissolve the Atlantic alliance. Its deeper sources enabled it to outlive the commanding figure from whom it took is name.

What role was left for the United States? The answer used to be clear and simple: if the United States, as the saying goes, sneezed, its allies took out their handkerchiefs. But that day has passed. Whatever "United States leadership" means today, it does not mean what it once meant.

Official admissions of the change go back at least as far as President John F. Kennedy, though he can be quoted on both sides of the issue. In 1961, he told the American people to face the fact that "the

United States is neither omnipotent nor omniscient," and "there cannot be an American solution to every world problem." [41] Presumably, the United States had previously considered itself omnipotent and omniscient, with a solution to every world problem, and needed to be admonished that that era had come to an end. But this comedown did not mean that Kennedy was willing to give up assuming responsibility for freedom everywhere. In 1963, he called on his generation to recognize that it was—"by destiny rather than choice—the watchman on the walls of world freedom." [42]

It took another decade for a president of the United States to give up the status of "dominance" within the Western alliance. Nixon did so in terms that also reflected on U.S. behavior in the past when he acknowledged that "the United States had led without listening, talked to our allies instead of with them, and informed them of new departures instead of deciding with them." By early 1970, Nixon announced that the time had come to move "from dominance to partnership." [43] None of this newfound enthusiasm for partnership was original. Kennedy had already in the previous decade held out to the European allies such phrases as "partners in aid, trade, defense, diplomacy, and monetary affairs," "a partner with whom we could deal on a basis of full equality," "a full and equal partner," and "partners for peace." [44] Phrases they were, and phrases they remained, until Nixon picked them up again. Nixon's own offer of partnership was soon qualified. In early 1971 he saw fit to assure European allies and friends that "the United States will continue to play a role of leadership, commensurate with our position in the world." He then offered allies "more nearly equal partnership" based on "sharing the responsibilities of leadership." [45] These formulas were slippery enough to mean anything or nothing, mainly nothing. Something had clearly changed in the relations among the allies, but what and how much were not so clear.

The difficulty of moving from dominance to partnership is that "real partnership is possible only between equals." [46] Partnerships with senior and junior partners tend to give juniors the privilege of obeying the seniors. If the partnership is really between equals, it might last just as long as their interests were equal and the same—a condition not often encountered in the real world. Real partnership is not the only thing possible between equals; independence and antagonism are not only possible but probable. These contradictions and paradoxes of alliances would be easier to deal with if nations were single-minded in their aims and interests. In fact, nations pursue a variety of aims and interests not usually compatible with one another. Substituting partnership for dominance in the U.S. diplomatic vocabulary was more a matter of form than of substance.

Subsequently, the Nixon-Kissinger policy toward the alliance differed from that of the past, but not in the way it was advertised. Partnership continued to be just as far away as ever. Instead, the United States bore down less heavily on Europe because the United States ignored Europe. Embroiled in the Vietnam war, the Nixon administration had little time or mind for anything else. Nixon admitted as much in 1971 when he said that the tendency had for five to six years past been "for us to obscure our vision almost totally of the world because of Vietnam." [47] Kissinger told President Nguyen Van Thieu of South Vietnam in 1972 that the United States had for the past four years "mortgaged our whole foreign policy to the defense of one country." [48] The United States had no claim on Europe to take part in the Vietnam war because it was far outside the limits set by the North Atlantic Treaty, and Europe had no claim on U.S. attention because Vietnam was all-absorbing and all-consuming.

Another reason that the alliance changed very little during the Nixon-Kissinger years was the division of labor allotted to it in U.S. policy. It had long been an axiom of U.S. policy that the United States was the only power in the alliance able and willing to bear global responsibilities and that its European "partners" were supposed to mind their own business except where Europe itself was directly concerned. [49] The policy was restated by Kissinger in his "Year of Europe" speech in 1973: "The United States has global interests and responsibilities. Our European allies have regional interests." [50] Kissinger had played variations on this theme ever since 1965. [51] As U.S. foreign policy increasingly turned toward the "underdeveloped," "Third World" areas, Europe was left largely without a role to play outside itself. U.S. policymakers complained that Europe was regional-minded, introspective, and provincial to fit into U.S. policy. When de Gaulle had tried to break out of this European straitjacket, he had been treated as an interloper, a spoiler, or a dreamer. After several presidents had suffered from his bitter protests and unsolicited advice, President Johnson had decided simply to ignore him as the best way to deal with his irritating presence.

Still, the Nixon-Kissinger revision of U.S. policy did make some difference in U.S. policy in regard to the European allies. It told them that they could not expect the United States to carry the entire burden in their defense, that they had to expect less from the United States, which had to divert more of its hard-pressed resources elsewhere. It did not ask the Europeans to do more for the United States outside Europe, for that would have cut the ground from under the principle that the United States had global and Europe only regional interests and responsibilities. Such suggestions as were made about a wider role for Europe were so vague and general that no one took them seriously.

Kissinger himself acutely reflected the ambivalence of the United States toward its European allies. Until 1969, when his White House years began, he was one of the most sympathetic academic protagonists of Europe. He had advocated a change "from tutelage to equality," and his visionary "Atlantic commonwealth" went far beyond the terms of the Atlantic alliance. Once in office, however, Kissinger found the Europeans just as frustrating and exasperating as his predecessors had found them. The global-regional distinction that he made in his "Year of Europe" speech came too late to be received in Europe without resentment and defiance. It did not take long for the Europeans to annoy the United States by stretching out beyond their region to the Middle East and beyond, either by going their own way or by refusing to go along with the United States. Familiarity apparently bred contempt, because Kissinger's memoirs do not deal kindly with the European allies. Of NATO, he wrote that it was "an accidental array of forces in search of a mission." About the prospect of nuclear war, he makes this biting observation:

> They [the European allies] wanted to make the Soviet Union believe that any attack would unleash America's nuclear arsenal. If the bluff failed, however, they were not eager to have us implement the threat on their soil. Their secret hope, which they never dared to articulate, was that the defense of Europe would be conducted as an intercontinental nuclear exchange over their heads; to defend their own countries, America was invited to run the very risk of nuclear devastation from which they were shying away. [52]

The secret hope of the United States, Kissinger might have added, was that the defense of the United States would be conducted in or through Europe—or at least anywhere but in the United States. The two secret hopes did not make for secret confidence between the United States and its allies.

Kissinger's successor as assistant for national security affairs, Zbigniew Brzezinski, had a still different view of the place of the alliance in U.S. policy. Brzezinski had for years promoted a theory that sought to replace the Atlantic community with a "larger conception." It envisaged "a future cooperative community, involving eventually four major units, America and Russia as the peripheral participants, and West and East Europe as the two halves of the inner cores (in time perhaps becoming still more closely linked)." He maintained that this cooperative community "would promote a more constructive and politically appealing image of tomorrow than a troubled Western partnership." The Atlantic community could be but one component in this East-West-Soviet-U.S. "partnership," first put forward by him in 1965. [53]

Two years later, Brzezinski again envisaged the ultimate objective as "a world of cooperative communities," including this time Japan as well as the United States, Western Europe, Eastern Europe, and the Soviet Union. Communism, according to Brzezinski, was now "dead" in the sense that "it was no longer capable of mobilizing unified global support," though how it could be said to be "dead" if it was still able to mobilize something less than global support he did not explain. As for the "Atlantic concept," it would have to adapt itself "to the post-cold war era," which he assumed had come into its own. In this period, the Western alliance as such clearly had no significant or secure place in Brzezinski's scheme of things. [54]

By 1968, Brzezinski cut the ground from under the original, and still-accepted, *raison d'être* of the alliance: to protect its members against the real or potential threat of the Soviet Union. For the rest of the century, he announced, the United States was less likely to be concerned with "fighting communism." In quasiutopian fashion, he gave the United States the task of "helping to develop a common response with the rest of mankind to the implications of a truly new era." [55] This new era was Brzezinski's version of the by now familiar postindustrial society to which he gave a more pretentious title, the "technotronic age," a name that never caught on. In his book on the subject, he considered that the Atlantic world or concept was "now historically and geographically limited" and had to be replaced by "a broader, more ambitious, and more relevant approach." He wanted "a community of the developed nations" because it was "historically more relevant" than the Atlantic community. [56]

In 1973, the year that Brzezinski godfathered the Trilateral Commission, to which Jimmy Carter was an early recruit, his two basic premises again directed attention away from the Western alliance. The first held that "the primacy and centrality of American-Soviet conflicts has ended." The second replaced Europe with Asia as potentially the more dangerous to the international order. [57] If Brzezinski was right, the Western alliance was located in the wrong place, without a real opponent to be allied against. In any case, it is clear where President Carter derived the inspiration for the much-quoted statement at Notre Dame on 22 May 1977, that "we are now free of that inordinate fear of communism." Brzezinski had been trying to rid the United States of the inordinate fear of communism, especially as embodied in the Soviet Union, for at least a decade. If the Soviet invasion of Afghanistan in 1979 made Brzezinski as well as his chieftain suddenly and dazzling see the light out of the East in its true intensity, the revelation was so sudden and dazzling because it had reversed their whole system of belief about the Soviet Union and its candidature for the world's cooperative community. Those who have written about Brzezinski's inveterate anti-Soviet hawkishness seem never to have read what he had written, often and at length.

Thus, two successive assistants for national security affairs, the chief intellectual conceptualizers in two adminstrations, had found no real or important place for the alliance. Yet the worst crisis that can befall a nation is the one at home, and the crisis of the alliance was, historically, culturally, politically, and spiritually, a crisis at home. While the United States was neglecting Europe and Europe was pulling away from the United States, the common European-U.S. heritage was falling apart. The primacy and centrality of U.S.-Soviet conflicts are never so acute and critical as when they move into the European arena. Yet for the eight years of the Nixon-Kissinger-Ford regime and the first three years of the Carter-Brzezinski regime, Europe was the aggrieved stepchild of U.S. policy. Worst of all, theories such as Brzezinski's had long tried to persuade U.S. policymakers that the Soviet-U.S. conflict and the European connection were less important than they had long been and were long to be.

European allies who have criticized the makers of U.S. foreign policy for their ineptitude and instability have had more than enough reason to complain. From a longer perspective, however, the trouble goes much deeper; its roots cannot be found in individuals or individual decisions. More important than anything else are the structural changes that have taken place since the alliance was formed. These can be understood and heeded; they cannot be repealed, no matter who is in the White House or State Department.

One of the most far-reaching structural changes has been economic. At the end of World War II, the United States had a virtual monopoly of the world's productive capacity and monetary reserves. One estimate put Great Britain and France at no more than 6 to 7 percent of the "free world's power" in the 1950s and the United States at 70 percent. [58] In the ten-year period 1946-55, the U.S. trade surplus was so great that the current-account deficit of the world with the United States reached $38 billion, with almost the entire deficit occurring in 1946-49. [59] Looking back at 1946, a veteran U.S. foreign correspondent recalled in wonder: "The United States was not just a super-power; it was the monopower of the earth." [60] Exaggerations of this kind were common; only the United States emerged from the war immensely strengthened; the rest of the world, including the Soviet Union, appeared to be hopelessly devastated or at least mutilated.

The first danger signals came early enough to have given plenty of warning. Europe recovered with surprising speed, helped by the Marshall Plan, but too quickly and too fully to be attributed primarily to U.S. aid, no matter how large it may have been ($26 billion for 1946-55). German production, the hardest hit by the war, almost doubled between 1949 and 1955. Europe as a whole went from a $7 billion deficit on goods and services in 1947 to a small but telling surplus of almost $1 billion in 1952, and $2 billion in 1954. By 1955, Europe's exports of goods and services had risen to more than two and a half times the volume of 1947. The then six Common Market countries more than doubled their reserves between 1958 and 1967; U.S. reserves steadily declined from nearly $23 billion in 1949 to about $16 billion in 1957 to only $7 billion at the end of 1960. The "dollar crisis" was born. [61]

If the alarm bell first rang in any one year, it was in 1958. It was the year of the first U.S. postwar downturn. It was also the year the U.S. balance of payments went into a permanent state of deficit. Arthur F. Burns, the former longtime head of the Federal Reserve Bank, described what happened that year to bring on the alarm:

> During 1958, imports rose sharply, exports fell, and our stocks of gold were cut by two billion dollars. More ominous still, foreign financiers, who hitherto apeared to have unbounded faith in American finances, began to whisper serious doubts whether the integrity of the dollar could be counted on in the future. [62]

The shock effects were felt the following year. The Eisenhower administration, nearing its end, was sufficiently disturbed to send Under Secretary of the Treasury Douglas Dillon to Europe at the end of 1959 to ask the Europeans to reduce their protective tariffs against U.S. goods. As one unkind version preferred to put it, he went "tin cup in hand, to solicit contributions from the Europeans." [63] He asked politely, but the United States was still too proud and self-important to insist or twist arms. The urgency of the problem was hushed up by succeeding administrations in the interest of refraining from drawing back from the international commitments and commanding presence of the United States in the world. By 1963, ninety-five countries and territories were receiving some form of U.S. assistance. By 1969, the United States had 302 major and 2,000 secondary military bases abroad. Meanwhile, the trade balance had begun to shrink. By 1965, the first year of the massive intervention in Vietnam, the alarm bells should have been earsplitting. The war was ruinous to Vietnam, and to the U.S. political and social fabric, and economic system. President Johnson's Council of Economic Advisers recommended in January 1966 that the war should be paid for by increased taxation. [64] Afraid that it would make an unpopular war even more unpopular, Johnson took the easier way out by resorting to "deficit spending." In effect, Johnson financed the Vietnam war with massive inflation. This in turn encouraged a massive rise in imports into the United States and a massive drop in exports, which were progressively priced out of foreign markets. As the U.S. economic system weakened, U.S. multinational corporations invested more heavily abroad in what one economic historian called a "defensive investment" made "to forestall the relative decline of American economic and political power." [65] What was in part U.S. invasion of foreign economies was also a flight from the U.S. economy.

The result was a balance-of-payments crisis that finally could not be covered up or contained. The U.S. trade surplus began to decline sharply by 1967 and turned into a trade deficit by 1971. Productivity suffered, dropping in the decade 1960-70 to the lowest percentage of growth of any non-Communist country (United States, 2.8 percent; West Germany, 5.5 percent; Japan, 10.8 percent). The U.S. Treasury's gold stocks, symptomatic of the exploding balance-of-payments crisis, fell from $24 billion in 1949 to $18 billion by 1960, and to $11 billion by 1970. In 1971, the United States found itself with its first trade deficit in a century. The monetary ystem could stand no more pressure. On 15 August 1971, President Nixon ended the convertibility of the dollar into gold, bringing about the long-delayed devaluation of the dollar, which proceeded to fall by about 40 percent. The postwar era of the U.S. economy had officially come to an end—if there is such a thing as the end of an era.

The United States had been asking for the cooperation and forbearance of its European allies in the economic sphere ever since the end of the 1950s. Little had been forthcoming, partly because the Europeans had their own economic grievances against the United States. Foremost among them was the European financial burden caused by the enormous balance-of-payments deficit incurred by the United States. The position of the dollar as the European reserve currency had forced European countries to accumulate increasing hoards of dollars that were worth less and less as U.S. inflation rose higher and higher. Europe, in effect, was made to finance a part of the U.S. deficit. Europe complained of the dollar glut, and the United States complained of unfair European and Japanese trade practices. The abruptness with which the Nixon administration went off the gold standard in 1971 demonstrated that the United States had lost control of an international financial system based on the stability of the dollar and set up at Bretton Woods in 1944.

This structural change altered beyond recognition the economic relationship of the United States with its allies. In the initial phase, the United States could afford to run up large deficits in its balance of payments while large surpluses were built up in Western Europe. The United States encouraged the creation of a preference area in Western Europe that discriminated against U.S. goods. Japanese expansion was promoted even as Japan hindered U.S. companies from entering the Japanese market. In the later phase, the U.S. economy had hopelessly overextended itself. Its monetary system and key economic sectors could not compete even on equal terms. A decade after Nixon's devaluation, a former chairman of the Council of Economic Advisers was still convinced that "the United States carries on with an economic leadership out of proportion with its economic power." [66] He might have said the same about the political leadership.

Official recognition of the structural change in the U.S. economy was long put off and thus made worse when it came. But coming down was much harder than going up, and the United States still has not come fully to terms with the facts. The conflict inherent in this structural change is, however, not between the United States and the Soviet Union; it is between the United States and its allies. The Soviets have benefited from it without lifting a finger.

The second structural change is strategic. It is directly related to the Soviet-United States balance of power but rebounds against the relationship of the United States with its allies.

The original military problem had been characteristic of the period of decisive U.S. nuclear superiority. Despite this acknowledged superiority, the essential points had been made by former President Eisenhower: in 1953, that the new weapons had almost totally eliminated the former unique physical security of the United States; and, in 1955, that it was more important to have "enough" of the new weapons than to have "a lot more." [67] This line of thought, embellished by others, had later brought about the strategic doctrines of "mutual deterrence" and "mutual assured destruction," which implied that both the United States and the Soviet Union were equally endangered by the use of nuclear weapons. Yet the North Atlantic alliance had hinged on the ability and willingness of the United States to use nuclear weapons in defense of Western Europe if the ultimate need arose. The paradox of "mutual deterrence"—that it deterred the United States from deterring the Soviet Union—was recognized without being faced.

Nevertheless, so long as the United States was clearly and generally understood to enjoy decisive nuclear superiority, the paradox of an alliance resting on mutual deterrence was not psychologically or politically demoralizing. If deterrence was mutual, the emphasis could be put on the deterrence of the Soviet Union without enquiring too closely about how such deterrence would work if the United States was also deterred. The alliance struggled with its strategic conundrum, blew hot and cold, from massive retaliation to flexible response, and somehow seemed to survive.

The structural change came about with the recognition that the United States no longer enjoyed strategic superiority. Indeed, it is now debated whether the Soviet Union has gained strategic superiority. At best, the United States and the Soviet Union have sought to place themselves in a position of nuclear parity since the SALT agreement. The alliance was never meant to function on this basis. Yet it had been coming on for some time, even though it has only lately aroused acute anxiety, mainly in the United States.

The strategic changeover came in the 1960s. The Soviet fallback during the Cuban missile crisis of 1962 apparently determined the Soviet leadership never again to be caught in such an embarrassing position in a state of strategic inferiority. Though President Kennedy continued to emphasize U.S. strategic superiority, it is now said by one of his closest aides that he really agreed with Raymond Aron that the Soviets had achieved strategic parity as early as 1959-60, before the Cuban missile crisis, when they had begun to possess a significant number of intercontinental missiles. [68] In any event, the Soviet leadership was taking no chances and clearly intended by mid-decade to catch up and even surpass the United States. By late 1964 or early 1965 at the latest, it is believed, the Soviets set out on this course. At about the same time, U.S. policymakers decided that the Soviets would be unwilling to pay the price for nuclear parity. [69] As a result, the Johnson administration decided in 1966 to build no more nuclear weapons and to limit itself to the improvement of existing weapons. [70] Just then, the Soviets were building new nuclear weapons and improving all existing weapons furiously. [71]

During Henry Kissinger's tenure in the Nixon and Ford administration, the response of the United States to the change in the strategic balance was to aim at nuclear parity through the SALT negotiations. Kissinger—or one part of him—was then convinced that the
difficulty of conceiving "a national objective for general nuclear war"
on either side had made such a war most unlikely or at least much
less likely than conventional wars, defined as anything below the
threshold of nuclear war. [72] By 1976, toward the end of the Ford administration, Kissinger's State Department had made resistance to
attack in Western Europe by conventional forces "central to a realistic strategy." [73] The swing away from reliance on nuclear weapons
could hardly have gone further.

Out of office, however, Kissinger felt free to speak his mind. In
September 1979 at a conference in Brussels, he shocked an audience
of professional students of strategy with his brutal candor. He was
certain that in the 1980s

> the United States will no longer be in a strategic position to reduce a
> Soviet counter-blow against the United States to tolerable levels. In-
> deed, one can argue that the United States will not be in a position in
> which attacking the Soviet strategic forces makes any military sense,
> because it may represent a marginal expenditure of our own strategic
> striking force without helping greatly in ensuring the safety of our
> forces.

He then stunned his auditors with some advice and a confession.
He noted caustically that NATO had always wanted "additional reas-
surances of an undiminished American military commitment."
Whenever the commitment was given, NATO ministers could return
home "with a rationale for not increasing defense expenditures." If
his analysis was correct, he went on, the words in the U.S. commitment "cannot be true, and if my analysis is correct we must face the
fact that it is absurd to base the strategy of the West on the credibility
of the threat of mutual suicide."
Then came the confession:

> And therefore I would say, which I might not say in office, the Euro-
> pean allies should not keep asking us to multiply strategic assurances
> that we cannot possibly mean, or if we do mean, we should not want
> to execute because if we execute, we risk the destruction of civiliza-
> tion.

In other words, U.S. leaders, including Kissinger, had been accustomed to giving the Europeans in NATO assurances that the Americans could not possibly have meant and that the Europeans should

stop asking for because they merely forced the Americans to dissemble. [74]

Of all the Europeans, the Germans had the hardest time reconciling themselves to the twists and turns of U.S. policy. Detente had become almost an obsession in German governmental circles, whatever the party in power. In concrete terms, it had come to mean vastly increased trade with the Soviet Union and Eastern Europe, and closer relations with East Germany, with the ultimate goal of German reunification. To gain these benefits from detente, though, it was necessary to interpret it primarily in terms of German, or at most European, interest. Detente held out short-run gains that could be less promising in the long run. A strictly German-Soviet or European-Soviet detente holds the Soviets' European front quiet and stable while Soviet expansionism has a free hand elsewhere. Moreover, a German-Soviet detente may work at cross-purposes with German-U.S. relations when a Soviet-U.S. detente breaks down. These contradictory and dangerous aspects of detente present Germany with difficult choices that it did not have before when its options were far more limited. The German conceptualizers also have their work cut out for them if they are to make all pieces of German policy fit together.

Take the case of Theo Sommer, a noted German political commentator and copublisher of the important journal *Die Zeit,* of Hamburg, Chancellor Schmidt's unofficial organ. In an article invitingly entitled "Europe and the American Connection," he gave a fair account of what Europeans understand by detente:

> Most Europeans—with the possible exception of the British—have long believed that detente along the central front must be insulated against the effects of peripheral turbulence; that linkage was not only impractical but unwise. . . . Europe must not become an area of tension simply because there is tension elsewhere.

If Sommer had stopped there, he might have been ahead. But he knew or suspected that this isolationist or insulationist view of European detente might leave something to be desired by Americans. So on the very next page he offered a somewhat different version:

> A French-German axis of interest is emerging whose leaders are intent not on cancelling detente in Europe but extending it to the outlying areas, on continuing the dialogue with Moscow across the endangered European front while containing Russian transgression and aggression in Asia and Africa. [75]

Detente had now been given three functions: to insulate Europe from tension elsewhere; to be extended to outlying areas of peripheral turbulence; and to contain Russian aggression in faraway Asia and Africa. How could the Franco-German axis extend detente to outlying areas without getting itself drawn into the tension of those areas? And how could that lovely new detente and that horrible old containment—in Asia and Africa no less—be legally joined in political holy wedlock?

Or take the strange case of the neutron bomb. It was supposed to have the virtue of achieving its end without causing as much indiscriminate destruction as its predecessors. Inasmuch as the Europeans had always complained that they were not consulted about U.S. military innovations even when they were intended for Europe, the Carter administration decided to ask its European allies for their opinions. This maneuver proved most embarrassing. As Marion Grafin Donhoff, coeditor of *Die Zeit* and long an outstanding figure in German political life, explained: "The Europeans, however, wanted the bomb but did not want to say so publicly." As for Germany, Countess Donhoff reported: "But the Federal Republic wanted to be pushed into accepting it rather than openly come out in its favor." [76] President Carter decided that the bomb was causing more political trouble in Europe than it was worth, and its production was put off indefinitely.

None of the parties involved in the neutron bomb fiasco had reason to be proud of his performance. The Germans charged that President Carter double-crossed them by failing to live up to a private agreement to go ahead with the bomb if it could be stationed in Germany and one other European country. [77] Chancellor Schmidt thought that his agreement to station the bomb in Germany was already such a political risk for him that the Americans should have bailed him out by accepting final responsibility for the decision. President Carter went through his usual flip-flop with more than his usual clumsiness. The deeper lesson of the neutron bomb affair was, however, that the Europeans wanted more political influence without accepting responsibility for more power. When the Europeans want something but do not want to say so publicly, they want to benefit if all goes well and blame the United States if all does not. It is a game that has lost its charm for the United States, which has taken about all the blame it can absorb.

Another contretemps arose over theater nuclear weapons or forward-based systems. Former Chancellor Schmidt used the Alastair

Buchan Memorial Lecture of the International Institute for Strategic Studies in London in October 1977 to make himself the spokesman for European misgivings about the SALT negotiations. It was little appreciated in the United States how greatly SALT had troubled European officials and observers. The fundamental premise of the first SALT negotiations had limited them solely to Soviet and U.S. strategic weapons, defined as those that can reach the Soviet Union from the United States and the United States from the Soviet Union. This arrangement deliberately left out the medium-range or theater nuclear weapons that could reach Europe from the Soviet Union and the Soviet Union from Europe. The Europeans, as usual, wanted a combination of incompatibilities. They insisted that theater weapons should be excluded from SALT. At the same time, they worried that, if such weapons were excluded, the achievement of Soviet-U.S. parity as the aim of SALT would leave the Soviet Union with increasing superiority in theater nuclear as well as conventional forces. Though both sides had deployed theater weapons ever since the mid-1950s, the Soviet Union had seized the advantage by modernizing and augmenting its theater arsenal first. The presumed balance between Soviet-U.S. intercontinental strategic nuclear weapons and the assumed imbalance between the theater nuclear and conventional weapons of the two sides set the stage for Schmidt's lecture-sermon.

Schmidt bravely took on SALT. By codifying the nuclear strategic balance between the Soviet Union and the United States, he complained, SALT "neutralizes their strategic nuclear capabilities." By so doing, it magnifies "the significance of the disparities between East and West in nuclear tactical and conventional weapons" in Europe. The principle of parity was "sensible," but it should not be limited to Soviet-U.S. strategic intercontinental nuclear weapons. It "must" apply to all categories of weapons, that is, theater nuclear and conventional. If it did not, Schmidt charged, SALT would actually endanger Western Europe:

> But strategic arms limitations confined to the United States and the Soviet Union will inevitably impair the security of the West European members of the Alliance vis-à-vis Soviet military superiority in Europe if we do not succeed in removing the disparities of military power in Europe parallel to the SALT negotiations.

This was refreshingly tough talk, aimed primarily at the Americans, who were implicitly accused of impairing the security of their Western European allies by concentrating on strategic parity with the

Soviet Union. Schmidt volunteered that there were only two ways, in theory, to correct the imbalance. Either the Western alliance had to "undertake a massive buildup of forces and weapons systems," or both sides had to reduce their armed forces massively in all categories. Unfortunately, Schmidt observed with regret, the Soviet Union had shown no willingness "to accept the principle of parity for Europe, as she did for SALT." The inevitable conclusion seemed to be that the Western alliance had to build up its theater nuclear and conventional forces massively to equal those of the Soviet Union. Otherwise, SALT was implicitly equivalent to the imperilment and betrayal of the Western allies of the United States. [78]

The Americans as it turned out, were delighted with Schmidt's recommendation of a massive buildup of European theater nuclear weapons. In December 1979, at U.S. urging, NATO agreed to deploy 572 new medium-range missiles in Europe by approximately 1983. But this deployment was made contingent on negotiations with the Soviet Union to reduce the medium-range weapons on both sides. This so-called two-track policy gave the Soviets a foot in the door of Western decision making. The West had nothing to say about the Soviets' massive deployment of SS-20s and other weapons targeted on Europe, but now the Soviets were given an implicit intrusion in the ultimate deployment of the U.S. cruise missiles and Pershing IIs in Europe.

The Soviets soon launched a campaign of intimidation against those Europeans hardy enough to entertain the aim of parrying the Soviet advantage in intermediate nuclear weapons. If NATO went through with the planned theater-nuclear buildup, the Soviets threatened to take countermeasures of their own. Since the theater nuclear weapons were produced and controlled by the United States, not Europeans, the Soviets considered these weapons to be as much a part of the U.S. nuclear arsenal as the strategic intercontinental nuclear arms stationed in the United States or at sea. They had a point—the Soviet theater nuclear weapons could reach Europe but not the United States, whereas NATO's theater nuclear weapons could reach the Soviet Union.

The European allies had been offered a "dual-key" arrangement in 1979 when the decision to deploy the cruise missiles had been made; the system would have given ownership of the launchers to the host countries and the warheads to the United States, so that one could not be used without the other, implying joint control. This offer had been rejected. Partly to avoid responsibility for the weapons, partly to avoid the cost (estimated by the British government at $1,000 million), the European allies were quite content to take on themselves the entire obligation for both production and control. As a result, the full brunt of the virulent propaganda and mass opposition against the deployment of cruise missiles and Pershing IIs in Europe was borne by the United States.

When Schmidt's own Social Democratic party voted at a special party congress on 19 November 1983 against the deployment of the new intermediate missiles by the one-sided margin of 383 to 14, the United States was left with little more than half the German political representation in favor of the weapons. A more unfavorable political climate for installing them could hardly be imagined. The German predicament was so dis-eased because the German people were asked not whether they wanted more German missiles in Germany but whether they were willing to permit more U.S. missiles in Germany. The wrong question was sure to bring the wrong answer.

The main European apprehension about a buildup of theater nuclear as well as conventional arms is older and deeper. Such a buildup raises the specter of "decouplement." This term refers to the European fear that the United States might prefer to wage a war against the Soviet Union, if it ever came to that, from Europe rather than from the United States. To use Europe as its main forward base, the United States would find it necessary to build up the medium-range nuclear and conventional arms stationed in Europe. At present, NATO's plans call for resistance to attack in Europe for ninety days to provide a period of deliberation before any resort to the strategic nuclear forces stationed in the United States. [79] Any delay worries Europeans that they will be the first targets of Soviet attack, and more particularly that it will be necessary at the outset for the Soviet nuclear forces to take out the anti-Soviet theatre arms stationed in Europe. The stronger the forward-based systems in Europe become, the more incentive the Soviets have to knock them out at the earliest possible moment and the more reason the United States has to rely on them before resorting to presumably suicidal strategic nuclear warfare. The specter of decouplement is that of disjoining a future war in Europe from the U.S. nuclear deterrent, with which Europeans want to prevent an attack on Europe altogether rather than to hold the deterrent in reserve until it could deter nothing but a Soviet nuclear attack on the United States itself.

This confusion of aims and interests should be enough to show that the problem is objectively head-cracking; politicians, American or European, good or bad, clever or foolish, cannot be blamed for it. It is of a piece with the European dilemma, which has been described in these terms: "Europe wants a theatre nuclear posture that leaves the Soviet Union with absolutely no doubt that the weapons will be used in defense of NATO—and the NATO members with absolutely no worry that they will ever have to be." [80] The problem of nuclear war is, inherently, both how to wage it and how to avoid it.

All of these variations on the theme of nuclear war testify to the structural change that has taken place in the military relationship between the Soviet Union and the United States and between the United States and its European allies. A French commentator has, as usual, defined the problem most clearly without giving any practical advice about what can be done about it: "Things were clear and simple when the United States took us under their own umbrella of deterrence and any Soviet attack against Western Europe would bring about a strategic response based on American territory. We now know that time has passed." [81]

The third structural change has significantly altered the relationship between the United States and its European allies. It can, however, hardly fail to influence the relations between the Soviet Union and the United States as well as between the Soviet Union and Western Europe.

As we have already noted, such doubts or questions as there used to be about the U.S.-European relationship turned mainly on what the United States could or would do for Europe. What is new in the present situation is the growing doubt about what Europe can or should do for the United States. The changeover had been coming gradually, but it had reached an acute stage when the senior political commentator of the *New York Times* could ask, "Where Are the Allies?" as if they were supposed to be where we wanted them to be, and the president of the United States could publicly berate the allies for having failed to live up to their supposed obligations.

President Carter's litany of allied woes of 10 April 1980 may well be the classic U.S. statement of the contradictions tearing the alliance apart:

> Nations ask us for leadership. But at the same time, they demand their own independence of action.
>
> They ask us for aid. But they reject any interference.
>
> They ask for understanding. But they often decline to understand us in return.
>
> Some ask for protection, but are wary of the obligation of alliance.
>
> Others ask for firmness and certainty. But at the same time, they demand flexibility required by the pace of change and the subtlety of events.

The European response might go as follows:

• If the United States had provided more adequate leadership, we might have demanded less independence of action.
• The aid asked for from the United States in the realm of security, which is the only aid provided for in the treaty of alliance, has become more and more problematic. This aid in no way implied interference in European affairs in any other respect.
• Past U.S. policy itself restricted the obligation of alliance to European security.
• Firmness is not the same as certainty, and flexibility is not the same as unpredictability, vacillation, inconsistency, and even incoherence.

When allies talk to each other in these terms, there is more than misunderstanding at stake. They have begun to understand each other only too well. The contradictions and incompatibilities in their aims and interests have become too flagrant to hide or disguise. An alliance made in response to one set of conditions was coming apart in response to another.

Oddly, a leading member of President Carter's cabinet soon explained why the United States could not count on its allies to share the burden of defending Persian Gulf oil. "It's going to be very difficult to do that because the alliance, by its own terms, is confined to the territory of its members," said Secretary of Defense Harold Brown. "Moreover, except for the U.S., the forces are ill-suited for operation outside the region of the alliance." [82] The lesson seemed to be that, for purposes outside the region of the present alliance, the United States needed a different kind of alliance. For President Carter to ask for European cooperation so far afield as Iran and Afghanistan was sure to subject the alliance to intolerable strain. The alliance of 1949 was not suited to the crises of 1979-80 or 1983. As a result, the European responses were in almost every case grudging, ineffectual, or hostile. Just when it was more necessary than ever for the Western powers to act decisively, they had never appeared to be so far apart.

What lies ahead?

As for the United States, it is no longer governed by policy; it is ruled by necessity. Whatever its politicians say or promise, they have less and less control over events. The economic and military fat that used to give the United States a protective layer has all but disappeared. Global power must in any case derive from an adequate base of domestic economic power and depend on political acceptance of its cost.

As for the Europeans, their ideal world would be made up of three parts:

- Economic competition: unconditional and unlimited.
- Global politics: complete and unqualified independence.
- European defense: ultimate dependence on the United States.

There is nothing inherently wrong in these aims, singly or together. Every nation or group of nations has the right to pursue those policies that it considers to be in its interest. The United States has been doing just that throughout its history; its most philanthropic acts have been defended on the ground that they were also good business or in the national interest. The problem for Europe is not whether it ought to adopt this program but whether it can get away with it. How far can independence from the United States be stretched without breaking the ties that have bound them for almost four decades? How close are we to the point of no return?

In economic competition, that point has just about been reached. Europe is not responsible for the U.S. economic decline. The basic reason for that decline is structural: too many years of vast and easy profits; weakening of the competitive fiber; an almost deliberate abdication in the mass-consumption industries, which had been the glories of the economy; a decade or two of wrongheaded and short-sighted decisions by those who manage the economy. European nations and Japan cannot be blamed for taking advantage of their opportunities. But in a contest for economic survival, blame is beside the point.

By 1980, the U.S. business community could no longer hide from itself the acuteness of its crisis and the direction from which the main threats came. One of the leading U.S. business organs, *Business Week,* in its issue of 30 June 1980, demanded nothing less than "The Industrialization of America" for reasons that must have shaken many of its readers. Industry's loss of competitiveness over the past two decades had been "nothing short of an economic disaster." In 1960, the United States had over 25 percent of the manufacturing exports of industrial nations; it lost 16 percent of its share in the 1960s and 23 percent in the 1970s. Among the industries in crisis were: automobile, steel, rubber, textile, machinery, metal-working machinery, consumer electronics, apparel, and shoes. Where did all these losses go?

"America's major allies are now its chief competitors in global markets." What was the remedy? The prescription came suspiciously close to threatening a trade war. The partial U.S. economic recovery by 1983 eased but by no means eliminated the basic causes that had brought on this spasm of alarm.

Political independence and economic advantage are particularly hard to bear from allies supposedly dependent on U.S. military protection. The lifeblood of every power, and especially every great power, is economic, and that lifeblood has been draining away from the United States. It cannot, at any rate, sustain the kind of sovereign style to which Americans had become accustomed after World War II. It tells much about the seriousness of the economic decline that so many industries should now think of themselves as fighting for survival, not style. No economic war, with enemies or allies, could fail to have incalculable political consequences. These political consequences were dramatically demonstrated by the increasingly conspicuous isolation of the United States in the United Nations.

Western Europe's growing independence in global politics, outside the NATO area, is a question about which there is no right or wrong. There is no law, certainly no NATO law, that says that Western Europe should not be as independent as it pleases. There is no international morality that requires Europeans to obey the political dictates of the United States, to which they had deferred for so long. There is only the practical question of what such European independence is likely to do to its relations with the United States, assuming that Europe does not wish those relations to change too much or in ways that might damage Europe's other interests.

European independence almost always takes the form of independence from the United States. The trouble is that there is no shortage of other nations in the world that are habitually independent from and, indeed, hostile to the United States. Vote after vote in the United Nations in recent years testifies to that. When Europeans join the independence-from-the-United States bloc, they make it almost unanimous. In a world of conflicts, there is no such thing as *Ding-an-Sich* independence. Every independence from one side leans over toward independence in favor of another side, sometimes by strengthening one side, sometimes by weakening the other.

European independence is increasingly isolating the United States. How far that isolation has gone has been reflected in the United Nations between 1980 and 1983. One vote came on 29 July 1980, in the General Assembly on a resolution sponsored by Arab nations calling for the formation of a Palestinian state. In November 1979, six of the

West European allies had voted with the United States against a similar resolution. Only eight months later, all nine members of the European Common Market, almost the entire corps of nominal European allies, broke with the United States by collectively abstaining. The United States was left with only six other countries, including Israel, to vote against the resolution. The issue itself had not changed all that much in eight months; what had changed was the relationship between the United States and Western Europe.

Another vote came a month later, on 30 August 1980, in the Security Council on a resolution calling on all nations with embassies in Jerusalem to withdraw them. This time the vote was 14 to 0 with one abstention, that of the United States. The Western allies on the Security Council, including France and Great Britain, had chosen to isolate the United States even more demonstratively than in the previous vote in the General Assembly.

Three years later, the United States was ostentatiously isolated on a matter of direct concern. On 28 October 1983, the Security Council passed a resolution "deeply deploring" the U.S. military intervention in Grenada. The vote was 11 to 1, with the United States casting the lone negative vote and thus exercising its veto power. Two European allies, France and the Netherlands, voted for the resolution; Great Britain abstained. On 2 November of that year, a similar resolution was passed, without debate, by the UN Assembly. Only 10 votes out of 158 were cast against the resolution. Not a single member of NATO voted in favor of the U.S. position.

Despite the presumably similar political views of the Thatcher and Reagan administrations, and the reputation of Britain as the "staunchest ally" of the United States, the British reaction was the most startling and far-reaching. Never since the short-lived Gaullist experiment of the Heath government had a British regime endorsed a quasi-Gaullist independence of the United States. Foreign Secretary Sir Geoffrey Howe urged Britain's partners in the European Community to adopt a foreign policy independent of United States. Without actually naming the United States, he said that events in Grenada had served as a reminder that "there are times when Europe needs to be a voice independent even of its closest allies." He came out for exerting "a real influence over events" as "the Ten [rather] than as separate European nations."

The "moderate" Labourite spokesman on foreign affairs, Denis Healey, was even more explicit. Writing in the *New York Times* of 16 November 1983, he warned that "the strain on relations between America and Europe has never been greater. This strain must be relaxed or the alliance could fall apart." To relax the strain, he demanded that the United States should take actions in Lebanon, Central America, and Grenada that would bring it into line with European policies.

UN votes are rarely based on abstract rights and wrongs; they almost always represent national or regional interests. The United Nations hardly ever makes history, but it can register history that is made in the world outside. These votes were just such registrations. Never before had European states so strikingly demonstrated that, in anything except their own self-defense, they had a political alliance among themselves, not with the United States. If UN votes are mainly symbolic, this was the symbolism of the votes in 1980 and 1983.

The North Atlantic Treaty had not called for anything else, but neither had it foreseen any such eventuality. The founding fathers of the alliance had devoutly believed in European unity, recovery, and eventual independence. They had assumed that such a Europe would be able to defend itself and be better able to stand with the United States as a strong and loyal ally. What they did not anticipate was that after more than thirty years Europe would still not be able to defend itself but would use its increasing unity and recovery to make itself more independent of the United States, at the expense of U.S. influence and prestige throughout the world. European independence from the United States is only one side of the coin; the other side is U.S. independence from Europe. U.S. isolationism can make a comeback via U.S. isolation.

Yet U.S. isolationism is still the terror of Europe. It was abandoned so completely with World War II that even the disillusionment of the Vietnam war could not bring it back. It can, however, reappear in another guise, that of de facto isolation within a *de jure* alliance.

The most critical and painful aspect of the present reality is the problematic defense of Western Europe. It has already been noted that Western Europe was supposed to be protected by U.S. atomic power to compensate for the Soviet advantage in conventional arms and until Western Europe could defend itself. The population and resources of Western Europe were theoretically equal to the task. The missing link was believed to be the political and economic unity of Western Europe, the necessary condition for its ability to use its manpower and resources to the fullest.

The original balance of Soviet conventional power against U.S. atomic power was then unbalanced by the acquisition of nuclear arms by both the United States and the Soviet Union. As the hope for

European unity faded and as it was replaced by the reality of a West European trading bloc, each member bargaining in its own interest and combining against everyone else's interest, Europe's relationship to the United States changed drastically. Thus developed the paradox that Raymond Aron has characterized with his accustomed lucidity: "The United States appears as a rival and protector, a rival in the economic field, and a protector from the military standpoint." [83] This duality was fixed by the mid-1950s, and it might have brought about a mortal crisis for the alliance if the United States had not then felt so confident that it could afford the rivalry and so pleased that it could play the role of military protector.

The facts of life are now that the U.S. commitment can no longer rest on a treaty made in 1949 under quite different political and economic circumstances. The validity of the commitment was always based on the U.S. perception that it was a matter of unimpeachable national interest to keep Western Europe friendly to the United States or at least out of Soviet control and exploitation. This perception is still widely held in the United States, but no treaty can make it automatically operative. The question is how favorable or unfavorable the circumstances will be when it is put to the test.

Nuclear parity or superiority is no panacea because it is inherently unstable. Neither the United States nor the Soviet Union is ever likely to accept outright inferiority passively. The very search for parity or superiority implies a recognition of temporary inferiority or superiority that must be corrected by moving upward or downward. The quest for parity or superiority guarantees a nuclear seesaw, not a state of blissful nuclear equality. The mirage of parity is a standing invitation to escalation because no one can be sure what parity is or when it has been achieved. McGeorge Bundy has argued that parity has prevailed between the United States and the Soviet Union for the past twenty years and has proven itself to be an effective guarantee. [84] If he is right, the United States did not possess the superiority that it claimed to have had in all those years. Yet the figures emanating from Washington in most of those years were said to show clear superiority. It apparently did not matter very much.

Parity—whether anyone really knows what it means for two such different military systems as the Soviet or American, and how it could be maintained whatever it means—cannot be the answer because it is illusory. The key to the puzzle of nuclear peace or stalemate may well be President Eisenhower's dictum: enough is enough. The point is worth repeating in his own words: "There comes a time, possibly, when a lead is not significant in the defensive arrangements of a country. If you get enough of a particular type of weapon, I doubt that it is particularly important to have a lot more of it." Eisenhower at that time was thinking of what was enough to deprive the United States of its formerly unique physical security. The long-range bomber and "the destructive power of a single bomb" were then enough in his opinion to produce a fundamental structural change in U.S. defense. Curiously, President Carter made almost the same kind of observation a quarter of a century later about the destructive power of another weapon—but aimed at the Soviet Union. In his State of the Union Message in January 1979, he declared: "Just one of our relatively invulnerable Poseidon submarines, comprising less than 2 percent of our total nuclear force, carries enough warheads to destroy every large and medium-size city in the Soviet Union." That much power, multiplied fifty times, would seem to be enough of any particular weapon and make it doubtful that "it is particularly important to have a lot more of it."

The Eisenhower principle of "enough" may be defined in a general sense as whatever level of destructive power would make more such destructive power wasteful and unnecessary. Another test of "enough" would be the level of destruction necessary to deprive nuclear war of "a rational objective," as Kissinger put it in his less politically intoxicated days. Unless one assumes that the United States or the Soviet Union would have to have a rational objective to wage a mutually suicidal nuclear war, all calculation is vain, all bets are off. The concept of "enough" does not mean that the nuclear guard can be let down; one inviolate condition is that the ability to deliver must be ensured. But that is not the same as the competitive conditions of nominal parity. "Enough" needs no negotiations to establish alleged equalities of equivalences; it is not a numbers game; it is not determined by SALT-type bargaining. It has at least an upper limit determined by rationality rather than by competition. That limit may from time to time move up or down as technological requirements dictate; it would not change merely to keep pace numerically with the Soviet Union, which, in that case, would paradoxically possess the power to dictate U.S. requirements.

McGeorge Bundy was right about the effectiveness of parity over the past twenty years, but the parity he had in mind was not that of numbers of correlations of different kinds of weapons. By "underlying parity" he specified that he meant "mutual destructive power." That kind of destructive power can exist whether the numbers favor the United States, as they did in the Kennedy years, or the Soviet Union, if that should ever be the case, or neither side. Any numerical change that leaves untouched the capacity of each nuclear superpower to destroy the other cannot change the fundamental strategic balance between them; a numerical change may save them money; it will not save lives. SALT-type negotiations will never bring about stable parity acceptable to both sides; they will merely register the progress of an arms race and periodically change the essential question from "What's enough?" to "Who's ahead?"

Yet Europeans shudder at the prospect of the failure of the negotiations; they shudder at a parity that inexorably implies mutual destruction; they shudder that SALT leaves them out; they would shudder even more if they had to take part in the negotiations and make up their own minds about just what they wanted. As former Chancellor Schmidt once had the hardihood to suggest, SALT has been a divisive force in the alliance because parity between the United States and the Soviet Union leaves out Western Europe. The inclusion of Western Europe will not make the already formidable task of parity-mongering any easier.

What does the Soviet Union want of Western Europe? At this stage, the Soviet Union clearly does not seek to add Western Europe to its political and military empire. The Soviets have enough to cope with for quite a while. What the Soviet Union wants for the time being is to make Western Europe serve Soviet purposes in the struggle for power against the United States.

Western Europe can serve the Soviet Union in essentially two ways. One, by making its economic and technological resources available to the Soviet Union. Virtually anything that the Soviet Union cannot get from the United States it can get from Western Europe. Huge factories have been put up in the Soviet Union and Eastern Europe by Italian, German, French, and combined enterprises. The chief limit on this transfer of Western resources and technology seems to be the credits that Western countries are willing to hand out. There has been no such phenomenon since the early years of the Soviet regime. Western help was then needed for the Soviet regime to survive; it is now needed for the Soviet regime to gain ascendancy. The more the Western economies come to the rescue of Soviet nonmilitary production, the more the Soviets can pour into their military economy, which operates on a separate and higher level.

It pleases Western European leaders for the present to pretend that economic collaboration with the Soviet Union and economic rivalry with the United States do not have political consequences. They know better, of course, but the presence of illusion is necessary to insulate the military alliance with the United States from the economic association with the Soviet Union. The intimate relationship between politics and economics is such a commonplace in European thought, from which it spread to the rest of the world, that it would seem to be insulting to bring it to the attention of Europeans. Still, official European policy prefers to put economic relations with the Soviet Union and political relations with the United States into separate compartments.

The second way by which Western Europe can serve the Soviet Union is by being more docile and independent. Docility and independence do not usually go together but they are able to cohabit in this case. Docility is for the Soviet Union; independence for the United States, for there is a peculiar thing about European independence—it is invariably independence from the United States. The stronger the U.S. line toward the Soviet Union is, the more independent Europe becomes. European independence never seems to work the other way. If the United States takes a weak line with the Soviet Union, as it has done occasionally, Europe never seems to pull independently for a strong line.

Because Europe is not strong enough to stand midway between U.S. and Soviet power, holding off both equally, independence from the United States and abhorrence of a strong line with the Soviet Union makes for greater docility. Or if docility offends European sensibilities, let us say that more distant relations with the United States and closer relations with the Soviet Union are symbiotic.

The Soviet Union does not and need not demand in this phase of its expanding power that Western Europe should align itself with the Soviet bloc. Such a precondition for Soviet favor would be politically unrealistic, frightening too many antagonistic or fence-sitting Europeans into the anti-Soviet or even pro-United States camp. The next best thing, and almost as rewarding, is the encouragement of European independence, with the consequent further isolation of the United States. The removal of a U.S. ally is itself a gain for the Soviet Union by changing the balance of forces against the United States; the attachment of that ally to the Soviet Union may be left open and need not even be murmured about at this historical juncture. The Soviet Union has everything to gain and nothing to lose by playing the anti-United States rather than the pro-Soviet side of the street in Western Europe, though of course nothing prevents it from doing one or the other whenever the opportunity offers.

Detente can also take a negative form. At minimum, it requires that Western Europe should do nothing to disturb relations with the Soviet Union, though half-hearted and make-believe gestures may be tolerated. In practice, this negative detente takes the form of European criticism of, or even holy horror at, any U.S. policy that may disturb the Soviet Union. Detente thereby gives the Soviet Union an effective, if under-the-table, veto over European policy. Whenever Western Europe does or says anything that may ruffle Russian sensibilities, detente is immediately said to be threatened, and the specter of nuclear war—which detente is supposed to be holding off—is brought forward. The junction of detente and independence leads Europe into a one-way street that takes it further and further away from the United States.

The immediate reward to Europe for such a policy should not be underestimated. It provides the political underpinning for ever-growing trade with the Soviet Union and Eastern Europe. It enables Europe to deluge the Soviet bloc with credits with which to finance the trade, the same credits that can threaten the stability of the European financial system if they should be defaulted in case the trade breaks down. Local European Communist parties, especially of the unreconstructed variety, fine tune their domestic opposition to take account of European foreign policies of which the Soviet Union approves or at least does not strenuously disapprove. West Germany is most vulnerable to this political and economic blackmail. Soviet Russia has it in its power to determine the state of East and West German relations, which are played like an accordion. For West Europeans, the compensations for not unduly disturbing the Soviet Union are concrete, lucrative, and immediate; the compensation for maintaining a friendly alliance with the United States in the event of war is hypothetical, uncertain, and abhorrent to contemplate. It is all too understandable and even in the nature of things. The one thing not easily forgivable is the pretense that such a state of affairs does not exist, that it does not strengthen the Soviet Union, and that Soviet demands on Western Europe will not rise with the changing "balance of forces."

For years after World War II, the deafening anti-Americanism of European intellectuals seemed to be a luxury the United States could afford. Not that there was lacking more than enough in the United States to criticize. But this type of European anti-Americanism struck even a critical American as obsessive and repetitive to the point of psychopathology, especially when countries and systems deserving of far more strident criticism were let off with threadbare alibis and tattered apologies. There were notable European exceptions, but they were scorned, shunted off to a kind of intellectual ghetto, and sometimes more severely penalized. As much as intelletual pro-Americanism was in short supply in Europe, political parties and leaders were still loath to give up the U.S. connection. Even that has changed. "Unlike the fifties, and to some extent the sixties," a prominent German international-affairs expert reported in 1979, "there is today almost an absence of distinctly pro-American political parties in Western Europe" and "a positive stand on preferential cooperation with the United States is not currently seen to pay political dividends." Yet the same writer considers ties with the United States "the single most important element in the foreign relations of any Western European member-state." [85] How the two manifestations can continue to coexist remains a mystery.

A former British ambassador in Washington, Peter Jay, has been moved to warn against "this systematic European ambivalence, willing to wound but afraid to strike, tempted by the glamour of status and gestures but shy of the responsibilities and burdens of real power." Of the European attitude toward the United States he has written: "But it boosted and boosts European morale to spotlight American errors, to sour its failures, to exploit its market, to resent its overseas investments, to have a critic's ringside seat at its global tribulations, to mock its culture, to deride its leaders and to bewail the 'weakness' of its currency." [86]

Americans have been slow or reluctant to draw the full implications of Europe's increasingly demonstrative independence. It was formerly the policy of U.S. administrations to indulge Europe psychologically as if to make up for its physical weakness. This indulgence mixed with indifference encouraged further alienation by spreading the illusion that a price would never have to be paid for it. As always, the longer the illusion continued, the higher the price was sure to be.

Hans Morgenthau foresaw more than a decade ago that the Western alliance had three ways to go. It could maintain the status quo, which he considered "unviable"; it could go forward to "a much more intimate cooperation among members of the Alliance," which he viewed as unlikely; or it could go backwards toward "a narrower and more specific definition" of its scope. He believed that it was necessary to narrow the gap between "our comprehensive legal commitments and the limited sphere within which our interests and policies coincide with those of our allies." [87]

The alliance has certainly not remained the same. It has certainly not gone forward. It has gone backward, almost far enough to defy recognition. The gap between legal commitment and coincidence of interest has widened dangerously. But it has not been widened by common understanding or deliberate agreement. It has been widened by the force of events that have relentlessly undermined the original purpose of the alliance. Americans and Europeans have drifted from alliance to misalliance by staking out their own territories of independent action. A series of accomplished facts has reduced the credibility of the 1949 treaty to the vanishing point. It is typical of such unorchestrated changes that recriminations should fly in all directions. As matters stand, the only thing that Europe really wants of the alliance is that the United States should defend Europe, if necessary by nuclear arms; and the one thing the United States needs from the alliance is that Europe should support U.S. global policies, outside the area of the treaty on which the alliance rests. A house divided by such an alliance cannot stand.

It is easy enough to say that if the alliance cannot remain the same and should not go backward, it must go forward. When these things are easy to say they are said, without anything being done about them. In this case, nothing will be done without facing the reality that the alliance of 1949 cannot provide a basis for forward movement. It is fixed in its own time and circumstances, based on a different Europe, a different United States, and a different world. It was, even in its heyday, a unilateral military guarantee more than a true alliance. Its fatal flaw, as Adenauer and de Gaulle tried vainly to get across, was that it lacked an adequate political dimension. A unilateral military guarantee may have been enough in a period of seemingly unchallengeable U.S. nuclear superiority when Europe was obsessively interested in the threat of attack and was far from seeing itself as the main economic rival of the United States or as a protagonist of its very own independent global politics. Today, Europe prefers detente with the Soviet Union to U.S. nuclear protection to exorcise the threat of attack, and it sets no bounds on its economic rivalry and independent global politics, even if they are sure to cause embarrassment and anger in Washington.

The alliance is mortally ill because it cannot much longer pretend that a unilateral U.S. military guarantee or nuclear insurance policy is enough. It was long ago recognized that an alliance resting on a purely military foundation was dangerously fragile. In 1962, McGeorge Bundy, then speaking for the Kennedy administration, said: "The problem of defense in the nuclear age is as much psychological as military." [88] In 1963, Dean Acheson wrote: "In short, a successful military policy is possible when, and only when, it is one of at least three strands of the policies of the allied countries. The other two are the political and the economic." [89] And yet, in 1979, Professor

Michael Howard thought it necessary to protest against the tendency to ignore "the social dimension of strategy" and the "societal implications" for any defense of the West. [90] If the problem of defense is psychological, political, economic, and social, as well as military and technological, then the Western alliance must be psychological, political, economic, and social, as well as military and technological. It is much easier to count troops, tanks, and missiles than to assess the fortitude necessary to use them.

The obsolescence of the alliance does not mean that the Western powers and Japan cannot take common action in case of need. If they do so, however, it will be because they have been driven to it, not because the alliance has called for it. They will act together, if at all, on an *ad hoc,* intermittent, circumscribed, concrete basis. They will be guided by immediate self-interest, not by the ties and trust that make alliances work. Yet, if these occasions of common danger and common action should recur often enough, a new compact may well emerge. Alliances arise out of just such compelling experiences, not out of well-meaning but futile preachments. For the time being, however, we are most likely heading into a period when the new West European alignment will have to run its course, without or against the United States.

Meanwhile, a first step toward a new compact would be to face the present reality and see the old alliance in all its nakedness. If we are engaged in any kind of war, it is a war of attrition with many twists and turns, ups and downs. The decisive weapons in such a war are political, economic, social, and cultural, not the missiles of the apocalypse. A new Western front will be restored only when the isolation of the United States is seen as the greatest danger to Europe, and the estrangement from Europe is seen as the greatest danger to the United States. An isolated United States and an insulated Europe could threaten to bring about a condition of the greatest ultimate peril to both.

NOTES

1. William Pfaff, *New Yorker,* 1 September 1980, pp. 30-34.
2. *Public Papers of the Presidents of the United States: John F. Kennedy, 1961* (April 10), p. 255.
3. "The essence of a genuine alliance system is that both the commitments and aid to be expected are precisely defined." G.F. Hudson, in *Diplomatic Investigations,* ed. Herbert Butterfield and Martin Wight (London: George Allen & Unwin, 1966), p. 178.
   "An alliance adds precision, especially in the form of limitation, to an

existing community of interests and to the general policies and concrete measures serving them." Hans J. Morgenthau, *Politics Among Nations* (New York: Knopf, 1967), p. 176.

4. Senate Committee on Foreign Relations, *Reviews of the World Situation: 1949-1950: Hearings Held in Executive Session,* 81st Cong., 1st, 2d sessions, Historical Series, 1974, pp. 382-83.

5. Senate Subcommittee on National Security and International Operations, *Hearings: The Atlantic Alliance* 89th Cong., 2d sess., 27 April 1966, p. 10.

6. Senate Comittee on Foreign Relations, *The Vandenberg Resolutions and the North Atlantic Treaty: Hearings held in Executive Session,* 80th Cong., 2d sess., and 81st Cong., 1st sess., May-June 1948 and 2-6 June 1949, Historical Series, August 1973, pp. 143-44.

7. Secretary of State Dean Rusk, *Hearings: The Atlantic Alliance,* p. 231.

8. Dean Acheson, *Present at the Creation* (New York: Norton, 1969), p. 277.

9. Canadian Secretary of State for External Affairs Lester B. Pearson fought most strenuously to implement Article 2 and later admitted: "Article 2 remained virtually a dead letter for substantive action in economic matters. . . . The reality is that the spirit to implement the economic aspects of Article 2 was never there and that an economic basis for the realization of its larger political goal was never created." *Mike: The Memoirs of the Right Honourable Lester B. Pearson* (New York: Quadrangle/New York Times Co., 1973) p. 66.

10. Ibid., pp. 93-97.

11. Morgenthau, *Politics Among Nations,* p. 178.

12. Henry Kissinger, *The Troubled Partnership* (New York: McGraw-Hill, 1965), p. 108.

13. We are going to limit ourselves to the Western alliance and exclude Japan, though it is often referred to as if it were a Western ally in the East. In fact, Japan represents an even more extreme case of a unilateral U.S. military guarantee rather than a true alliance. The most recent formal treaty with Japan consists of little more than verbiage elaborating on what the first United States-Japanese Security Treaty of 1951 stated explicitly: to permit the maintenance of U.S. armed forces in Japan "so as to deter attack upon Japan." Most recently, Japanese Prime Minister Zenko Suzuki reiterated the traditional policy of "meeting small-scale, limited aggression with Japan's own defense capability and relying upon the deterrent strength of the U.S. under Japan-U.S. security arrangements to meet situations beyond our capabilities" *(New York Times,* 20 September 1980). Whatever mutuality and reciprocity may be lacking in the relationship between the NATO allies, these are virtually nonexistent in respect to Japan. The Japanese "alliance" is either a courtesy title or a convenient fiction.

14. Walter Millis, *Arms and Men* (New York: G.P. Putnam's Sons, 1956), p. 330.

15. It has been little noted that Dulles himself formulated what later became known as "flexible response": "To deter aggression, it is important

to have the flexibility and the facilities which make various responses available." *Foreign Affairs* (April 1954): 358.

16. Maxwell D. Taylor, *The Uncertain Trumpet* (New York: Harper & Bros., 1959), pp. 26-27, 58.
17. Jerome Kahan, *Security in the Nuclear Age* (Washington, D.C.: Brookings Institution, 1975), p. 272.
18. Charles de Gaulle, *Memoires de guerre* (Paris: Plon, 1959), 3: 62-70.
19. Charles de Gaulle, *Discours et messages* (Paris: Plon 1970), 3: 134.
20. Ibid., 4: 71-73 (14 January 1963); p. 96 (19 April 1963); p. 124 (19 April 1963).
21. Taylor, *The Uncertain Trumpet*, p. 44.
22. Ibid., p. 61.
23. Senate Commitee on Foreign Relations, *Hearing: Nomination of Christian A. Herter* 86th Cong., 1st sess., 21 April 1959, pp. 10, 44.
24. Cited by William W. Kaufmann, *The McNamara Strategy* (New York: Harper & Row, 1964), p. 165.
25. David Packard, in *The New Atlantic Challenge*, ed. Richard Mayne (London: Charles Knight & Co., 1975), p. 208.
26. Gallois's view was cited with reason by Kissinger in *The Troubled Partnership*, p. 13.
27. Alan J. Taylor, *English History, 1914-1945* (New York: Oxford University Press, 1965), p. 222.
28. Konrad Adenauer, *Erinnerungen*, vol. 1, *1945-1953* (Stuttgart: Deutsche Verlags-Anstalt, 1965), p. 351.
29. Ibid., vol. 3, *1955-1959*, pp. 159, 163, 166.
30. Ibid., pp. 320, 334-36.
31. André Fontaine, *L'alliance atlantique a l'heure de degél* (Paris: Calmann-Levy, 1959), p. 73.
32. *Hearings: The Atlantic Alliance*, pt. 7 (supp. 15 August 1966), pp. 230-31.
33. De Gaulle, *Discours et messages*, 3: 247-48.
34. Theodore Sorenson, *Kennedy* (New York: Harper & Row, 1965), p. 561. Arthur M. Schlesinger, Jr., devotes two sentences to Kennedy's statement, as if he could not take it seriously. *A Thousand Days* (New York: Houghton Mifflin, 1965), p. 856.
35. *Public Papers of the Presidents of the United States: John F. Kennedy, 1963* (25 June), p. 518.
36. Kissinger, *The Troubled Partnership*, pp. 246-48.
37. *Le Monde*, 25-26 May 1980.
38. Ibid., 18 April 1980.
39. Maurice Couve de Murville, *Une politique étrangère 1958-1969* (Paris: Plon, 1971), p. 273.
40. *Bundeskanzler Brandt Reden und Interviews* (Hamburg: Hoffmann & Campe, 1971), pp. 203-4.
41. *Public Papers of the Presidents of the United States: John F. Kennedy, 1961* (16 November), p. 726.
42. Ibid., *1963*, p. 894 (prepared but not delivered).
43. *U.S. Foreign Policy for the 1970s. A Report to the Congress* (18 February 1980), pp. 29, 31.
44. John F. Kennedy, *The Burden and the Glory* (New York: Harper & Row, 1964), pp. 16, 106, 111, 114.

45. *U.S. Foreign Policy for the 1970s: Building for Peace. A Report to the Congress* (25 February 1971), pp. 28, 44.
46. Kissinger, *The Troubled Partnership,* p. 236.
47. 6 July 1971 (in *Department of State Bulletin,* 26 July 1971): 93.
48. Henry Kissinger, *White House Years* (Boston: Little, Brown & Co., 1979), pp. 1, 386.
49. The axiom was stated by former Secretary of State Christian Herter in 1966: "I think we are the only nation today, if you want to exclude Russia and China, that feels global responsibilities. It is a question of the extent to which we can exercise our power wherever it might be required or be desirable in the world. Obviously we cannot do everything alone. We have to have partners. We have to retain them on the European scene. If possible, we ought to keep partners on the Asian scene." *Hearings: The Atlantic Alliance,* p. 119.
50. *Department of State Bulletin* (14 May 1973): 594.
51. In Kissinger, *The Troubled Partnership*; and "Central Issues of American Foreign Policy," *Agenda for the Nation* (Washington, D.C.: Brookings Institution, 1968).
52. Kissinger, *White House Years,* p. 83.
53. Zbigniew Brzezinski, *Alternative to Partition* (New York: McGraw-Hill, 1965), p. 175.
54. *Department of State Bulletin* (3 July 1967).
55. *Encounter* (January 1968): 25.
56. Zbigniew Brzezinski, *Between Two Ages* (New York: Viking Press, 1970), pp. 305-8.
57. Brzezinski, in *The New Atlantic Challenge,* ed. Richard Mayne (London: Charles Knight & Co., 1975), p. 315.
58. W.W. Rostow, *The Diffusion of Power* (New York: Macmillan, 1972), p. 214.
59. Robert Triffin, *Europe and the Money Muddle* (New Haven: Yale University Press, 1957), p. 9.
60. C.L. Sulzberger, *New York Times,* 21 December 1974.
61. This paragraph is largely based on Robert Triffin, *Europe and the Monetary Muddle;* idem, *Our International Monetary System* (New York: Random House, 1968); and Charles P. Kindleberger and Andrew Shonfield, eds., *North American and Western European Economic Policies* (New York: St. Martin's Press, 1971), p. 68.
62. Arthur F. Burns and Paul A. Samuelson, *Full Employment: Guideposts and Economic Stability* (Washington, D.C.: American Enterprise Institute for Public Policy Research, 1967), p. 8.
63. Raymond Vernon, *Foreign Policy* (Winter 1971-72): 56.
64. This aspect of the Vietnam war deserves far more study and publicity than it has received. It is mentioned by Arthur M. Okun, former chairman of the Council of Economic Advisers, in *The Political Economy of Prosperity* (Washington, D.C.: Brookings Institution, 1970), p. 70, and by James Tobin in *The New Economics One Decade Older* (Princeton: Princeton University Press, 1974), pp. 34-36. For some of the "dubious practices" used to doctor statistics to conceal the unfavorable results of Johnson's decision, see Milton Gilbert, *Quest for World Monetary Order* (New York: John Wiley & Sons, 1980), pp. 140-41.

65. Robert Gilpin, *U.S. Power and the Multinational Corporation* (New York: Basic Books, 1975), p. 163.
66. Paul W. McCracken, *Wall Street Journal,* 17 June 1980.
67. "We know that our former unique physical security has almost totally disappeared before the long-range bomber and the destructive power of a single bomb" (*Public Papers of the Presidents of the United States: Dwight D. Eisenhower, 1953,* p. 205). "There comes a time, possibly, when a lead [in hydrogen bombs] is not significant in the defensive arrangements of a country. If you get enough of a particular type of weapon, I doubt that it is particularly important to have a lot more of it" (ibid., *1955,* p. 47). To which may be added the view of former Secretary of Defense Robert S. McNamara: "You cannot make decisions simply by asking yourself whether something might be nice to have. You have to make a judgment on how much is enough" (20 April 1963).
68. McGeorge Bundy, "The Future of Strategic Deterrence," *Survival* (November-December 1977): 269. Bundy also observes: "We did assert that we had strategic superiority and we did assert that having it made a difference. What we did not say was that the principal use of this numerical superiority was in its value as reassurance to the American public and as a means of warding off demands for still larger forces" (p. 270).
69. Walter Slocombe, "The Political Implications of Strategic Parity," *Adelphi Papers,* no. 77, May 1971, p. 5.
70. Deputy Secretary of State Kenneth Rush, *Department of State Bulletin* (23 April 1973): 479.
71. The publicly announced Soviet military budget rose from 12.8 billion rubles in 1965 to 13.4 in 1966, to 14.5 in 1967, 16.7 in 1968, 17.7 in 1969, and 17.9 in 1970—an increase of 40 percent. The real resources, including secret and hidden allocations, devoted to the Soviet military amounted of course to much more. Thomas W. Wolfe, *Soviet Power and Europe, 1945-1970* (Baltimore: Johns Hopkins University Press, 1970), p. 429.
72. Senate Committee on Foreign Relations, *Hearings: Nomination of Henry A. Kissinger,* September 1973, pt. 1:101.
73. Department of State, *United States Foreign Policy: An Overview,* January 1976, p. 16.
74. "NATO: The Next Thirty Years," *Survival* (November-December 1979): 265-66.
75. *Foreign Affairs,* Special Issue: *America and the World* (1979): 634-35.
76. *Foreign Affairs* (Summer 1979): 1062-63.
77. Ibid., p. 1063.
78. The next of Schmidt's lectures appeared in *Survival* (January-February 1978): 2-10.
79. Kissinger, *White House Years,* p. 393.
80. Cited by Alton Frye from an unnamed commentator, *Survival* (May-June 1980): 102.
81. Maurice Duverger, *Le Monde,* 19 February 1980. Duverger went on to assert that if nuclear arms that can strike the USSR are stationed in Europe but controlled by the United States, they should count as part of the nuclear potential of the United States, which decides whether to

employ them. But, if no theatre nuclear arms are emplaced, only the French nuclear force is left. And the French force, unfortunately, is not strong enough to defend Europe. A reader might pardonably not know what to conclude.

82. *U.S. News and World Report,* 4 August 1980, p. 26.
83. *Hearings: The New Atlantic Challenge,* p. 37.
84. *Survival* (November-December 1979): 271.
85. Uwe Nerlich, "Western Europe's Relations with the United States," *Daedalus* (Winter 1979): 96, 99.
86. Peter Jay, "Europe's Ostrich and America's Eagle," *Economist* (8 March 1980): 25-26.
87. Hans J. Morgenthau, *A New Foreign Policy for the United States* (New York: Praeger, 1969), p. 7.
88. At a meeting of the Atlantic Treaty Association, Copenhagen, 27 September 1962.
89. *Foreign Affairs* (January 1963): 248.
90. Ibid. (Summer 1979): 975-86.

6

PACIFISM AND EAST-WEST RELATIONS

Pierre Hassner

To grasp such an international and intangible phenomenon as pacifism any help is welcome. Two formulas coming from French and German literature spring to mind. One is the title of a French novel, *L'Amour, c'est beaucoup plus que l'Amour.* The other is the famous call of Goethe's sorcerer's apprentice: *"Die Geister die ich rief, die werd' ich nicht mehr los. . . ."*

The first observation to make about the current wave of pacifism is that it represents both much less and much more than pacifism. Many followers of or sympathizers with the so-called peace movement are indignantly refusing the label of "pacifism." And it is quite true that pacifists in a classical radical sense opposing any use of violence and rallying under slogans such as *"ohne Waffen leben," "Frieden Schaffen ohne Waffen,"* "swords into ploughshares," or "better red than dead" are but a minority within a movement that includes many who oppose only nuclear weapons, or NATO strategy, or the deployment of Euromissiles in Europe, or who advocate partial solutions such as a nuclear freeze, a declaration of no first use of nuclear weapons, an exclusive reliance on defensive weapons, the creation of denuclearized zones, or a reduction of military expenditures. One may well accept the distinction proposed by Christopher Coker and Heinz Schulte between pacifism and strategy critique as the two sources of the West European peace movement.[1] But one must immediately add that the two streams are not separate but feed into each other through an inner dynamic that leads the same individuals or parties from one position to the other.

Above all, one must add that both pacifism and strategy critique draw much of their force and inspiration from other trends or attitudes that, in turn, they encourage or legitimize. Many in the United States or in France suspect that the real driving force behind German pacifism is nationalism or neutralism. Many in Europe see the U.S. nuclear freeze movement or the pastoral letter of the U.S. bishops as an expression of isolationism. Behind universalistic moral and theological arguments, it is easy to discover conscious or unconscious divergences of geopolitical interests or of generational attitudes. Is the search for security just a convenient code for the search for identity, or is the search for identity based on a feeling of insecurity?[2] The question is unanswerable in terms of causal origins or of priority. But the point is that pacifism affects the whole fabric of international relations and is affected by them. Whether as a consequence, a symptom or a cause, it can be understood only in the light of a much broader examination of the relation between objective structure and constraints and subjective perceptions, aspirations, and attitudes within the present international order.

Nor can this examination remain a purely static one. More than anything else, pacifism today is a social movement or, at least, one component of a complex and contradictory evolution. But nothing is more unpredictable than a social movement—its spread, its exhaustion, its long-run, diffuse consequences. It is here that our second quotation is relevant. Pacifism is less important in itself than by the way it is manipulated by existing national and international forces, by parties, churches, unions, or governments, and by the way it affects their continuing game. But those who try to manipulate or to control it may well find themselves in the situation of Goethe's sorcerer's apprentice. Several familiar dialectical developments may set in, with unknown, unexpected, or unpredictable results. For instance, in West German domestic politics, it remains an open question between the SPD and the Greens as to who is manipulating or coopting whom. It seems, at the time of this writing, that the SPD is having considerable success in defusing the Greens by adopting some of their themes but at the price of breaking the strategic and political consensus in the Federal Republic and perhaps in the long run within NATO.

In East-West relations it used to seem obvious (and to this writer still seems so in the long run) that the structural asymmetries

between the two alliances and the two types of regimes cause whatever similarities and contacts that may emerge between pacifist
movements in Western and Eastern Europe to be overshadowed by
the contrast in their influence upon the policies of their respective
governments. Yet, today, it appears that the main West European
countries involved (the FRG, Britain, and Italy) are proceeding to deploy U.S. missiles with less difficulty than was expected, while in the
Soviet bloc Rumania, but also Hungary and Bulgaria, seem to be resisting Soviet pressures to accept the deployments called for by Moscow. The two countries that do accept them—the GDR and the
CSSR—seem to acknowledge greater domestic resistance than expected and to fear the consequences of their own severe campaigns
about the dangers of war. On the surface, NATO seems more united
than expected, and the Warsaw Pact less so; Moscow may have cause
to wonder whether both its deployment of SS–20s and its encouragement of the Western peace movement have not boomeranged.

Personally, we shall not argue for the above. Rather, as with detente
or Eurocommunism, Moscow, while it may be disappointed by the
effect of such movements in the West and worried by their fallout in
the East, still has the better cards for limiting the damage in its own
empire and drawing whatever political and military advantages it can
(even if they are not as great as it would have liked) out of their
greater force in the West, or rather out of the lesser ability of Western
governments or structures to ignore or repress them. But this, of
course, is only a guess that may be true only for the middle run. The
crucial notion that we will try to develop is that of the unequal rate
of development of pacifism in different countries within the two alliances and between the two alliances themselves. Pacifism, more than
one would have thought, is present everywhere (except, to some extent and for the time being, in France), but its strength and its ability
to affect societies and governmental policies vary from case to case.
It is these variations that cause conflicts and imbalances between
allies and between the two camps. Whether the existing institutional
and strategic structures and constraints will once again show their
resiliency in the face of these new conflicts and imbalances, or
whether the latter will provoke a more accelerated erosion in the
West and more decisive explosions in the East than was the case for
other trends and movements that balance remains to be seen. [3]

We shall examine the problem essentially by looking at the impact
of the peace movements upon the relations between state and society
within the different countries, at the consequences of this impact
upon relations within the two alliances, and, ultimately, at the

balance sheet in terms of the balance and the relations between East and West. But first, to approach it, we shall briefly try to identify the structural problems of the relations between the two Europes and the two superpowers at the level of the overall balance of states and of societies, the types of new attitudes born in reaction to these problems (pacifism, neutralism, and nationalism), and the ways in which these attitudes are manifested at the various levels of social and political life (that of social moods, of political movements, and of party and governmental policies). And finally, we shall try to raise the question of the historical significance of the present crises in terms of the postwar history of recurrent strains, resilient structures, and repressed evolutions.

THE PROBLEM

In trying to analyze East-West relations from a European perspective, this writer has found it useful, over the years, to distinguish between three levels: that of the strategic system (dominated by the division of Europe and by its direct link to the intercontinental balance of the superpowers, present through their troops and their nuclear weapons); that of the political actions and reactions of states; and that of the evolution and revolution of societies. The first, dominated by the military balance, was the most stable; the second, the diplomatic level, was characterized by the (usually sterile) search of some smaller and middle power for flexibility; and the third, the social (i.e. ideological and cultural on the one hand, economic on the other) level, was characterized by long periods of subterranean evolution or erosion, punctuated by movements of explosion or revolution.

While so far the fate of the European continent more than that of any other has been dominated by the first level and still is, this dominance was almost absolute at the time of the first cold war up until the middle sixties. De Gaulle's policies of detente, German *Ostpolitik,* Kissinger's acrobatics, Rumania's exercise in semi-independent diplomacy, and Moscow's attempts at getting various Western powers to compete for special bilateral relationships with the Soviet Union indicated a certain revival of diplomacy in the late sixties and early seventies. But already during this period the Prague Spring, the youth revolt and the counterculture in the West, the fall of the right-wing dictatorships in Southern Europe, and the progress of the Left in Western Europe indicated the emergence of social movements that were encouraged by detente but produced new imbalances and new conflicts. Partly as a result, we have witnessed since 1973-74 and even more clearly since 1979-80 a return to the primacy of confrontation and to the preoccupation with military dangers, but this is accompanied by the persistence and the growth of social movements, partly directed against the new cold war or inspired by the new fear of nuclear war. They in turn express, encourage, or provoke new feelings of national or Continental identity or interests, and hence a revival of Gaullism in new places and in a new form. [4]

If this very sketchy framework and this even sketchier periodization have any validity, they should help us understand the rise and limits of peace movements and neutralism. The basic structure of East-West relations is still provided—in 1984 as well as in 1945—by the coincidence of strategy and ideology, of the two alliances led by the two nuclear superpowers and the two political regimes of liberal democracy and communism. The basic structure of Europe, as far as security is concerned, is still determined by the direct presence of these two superpowers and their nuclear weapons and in particular by their direct control over the two most crucial states of the Continent, namely the two German ones. But the new period of tension, coupled with the perception of a new and more dangerous round in the arms race, has revived and given unprecedented force to another dimension: the danger of war and the hostility to nuclear weapons. Whatever one may think of the truth of this perception or of the effect of the attitudes it inspires, certainly the problem of avoiding war and controlling—if not eliminating—nuclear weapons is a genuine one that transcends the East-West opposition.

However, if the problem is universal, situations and perceptions of vulnerability are different according to geographical location, or to possession or nonpossession of nuclear weapons. Hence the new awareness of the problem of nuclear war serves to reveal and to focus, to legitimize and to encourage, a new awareness of separate identities between the United States and Western Europe, between France and Germany, and even between Eastern Europe and the Soviet Union. By the same token, it tends to *relativize* the basic East-West opposition. It is being used to foster not only the notion that the real danger lies less in the Soviet Union than in nuclear weapons but also the notion that the two Germanys as the two most exposed potential victims, or the small and middle states of Europe as opposed to the two superpowers, or even the whole of Europe including the USSR, as Continental powers that have suffered from war on their soil as opposed to the irresponsible United States, have a common interest in peace.

Hence the problem of the political confrontation between the two systems, or seen from the West, of the containment of Soviet expansionism, becomes separated from and subordinated to the avoidance of war and the assertion of national and European interests. The East-West struggle, when it is not negated or attributed to U.S. economic imperialism or ideological Manichaeism, is seen as concerning only the superpowers engaged in a mad arms race, or in a global confrontation for hegemony in the Third World, whereas Europe—East and West—can find peace, independence, and reconciliation in disengagement. [5]

The three dimensions of the three problems—peace, freedom, and independence—or the avoidance of war, of conquest, and of alienation, lead to the three current movements of pacifism, neutralism, and nationalism. While the three problems may seem to point toward divergent priorities, the three movements appear to be psychologically and logically linked. However, in both cases, the relationships are more complicated and they vary according to definitions, to countries, and to periods.

The crisis of deterrence derives from a convergence of technological, military, and political developments. The coming of strategic parity, combined with the increase in Soviet local superiority, has challenged the balance of imbalances and the credibility of extended deterrence through the threat of escalation upon which the security of Western Europe had been based. The evolution of technology toward greater accuracy and hence greater vulnerability has encouraged the sudden perception that nuclear weapons, which had been tolerated since the last wave of antinuclear protest in the late fifties and early sixties, might actually be used to fight and not only to deter. The period of toleration had more or less coincided with that of detente. The deterioration of the latter, the breakdown of arms control and the renewed saliency of the East-West conflict, has, even more than technological developments, changed the light in which nuclear weapons and the arms race were perceived. The simultaneous deterioration of prosperity and full employment has contributed to the atmosphere of pessimism and to the divergence of interests, or at least of priorities, among alliance partners. The coming to power of the Reagan administration has sharpened these divergencies into conflicts of military (especially nuclear) and of political (especially East-West) strategies.

These conflicts are rooted in different experiences both of vulnerability to the threat of war and of gains and losses in the experience of detente. Perhaps even more fundamentally they are rooted in the generational problem. [6] On both sides of the Atlantic, the new generation not only has fewer shared memories and less awareness of common interests but is being "deinternationalized" by its search for roots, by the increased priority sometimes of national, sometimes of subnational, regional, ethnic, community, or individual concerns. Furthermore, to the extent it keeps an international outlook, this outlook is itself shifting in centrifugal directions: toward the West and the South in the United States, due to its demographic transformation and to the growth of Asian economic and Latin American political challenges, and toward the East in the Federal Republic due to its renewed Central European consciousness and to its human and economic links with the GDR.

While nothing is more dangerous than indulging in mechanical symmetries between East and West, enough of the same phenomena (at least concerning the rediscovery of historical national roots, and the increase of conflicting economic interests within the bloc and of the need for interdependence with the other half of Europe) are present to make their manipulation by the Soviet Union both tempting and dangerous for both sides. Much of course, depends upon the coherence or the contradictions within and between the pacifist, neutralist, and nationalist movements.

We have already mentioned the variety of meanings of the concept of pacifism and, more important, the variety of factions within the peace movements. If one divides them into three categories—the radical nonviolent and unilateral disarmers, the anti-NATO and antinuclear revisionists, and the arms controllers and "new conventionalists" [7]—it is our thesis that increasingly the more important stream will be the middle one. While the pacifists proper have provided much of the religious fervor behind the peace movement, particularly in Protestant countries including the GDR, and may continue to do so, and while the need for arms control and a decreased reliance on nuclear weapons is likely to be accepted by all meaningful political actors, including the hawkish Reagan administration and the traditionally nuclear French government, the real challenge—after deployments of the Euromissiles commence—is likely to come from that spectrum of critics and revisionists who question NATO's strategic doctrine or the very idea of nuclear deterrence and are engaged in a search for alternative strategies and security systems.

Something similar may occur for the two other trends of neutralism and nationalism. The notion of neutralism may have a maximum meaning, which itself ranges from legal neutrality to positive neutralism or nonalignment but at any rate excludes participation in an alliance. At the other extreme, many U.S. critics have tended to brand any European disagreement with U.S. policy or any notion of distinct European or national interests as neutralist. But in between there is an area that, while keeping within existing structures, notably that of the Atlantic alliance, tends to go from as geographically and functionally restricted a definition of these institutions as possible to an effective destruction of their substances, either by a moral stand of "equidistance" (or even a sentimental preference for the other side) or by the claim to total freedom of action. Again it is this middle trend that may make itself felt most powerfully in the coming debates over NATO strategy and nuclear-free zones and disengagement. The role of Greece is a present illustration and a possible warning.

Finally, nationalism. Many Germans react with indignation to the identification of their peace movement as an expression of nationalism. They tend to see in it an implicit suspicion of a return to Nazism or to Prussian *Machtpolitik,* and they see themselves on the contrary in the role of victims or of apostles of peace, love, and understanding. On the other hand, they freely acknowledge a renewed search for identity and an increased awareness of national interests and of the limitations on the sovereignty of the two German states.

Again, between the two extremes of nationalism proper (in the traditional aggressive or in an inverted missionary or moralistic sense), and the Bundesrepublik's behaving—or aspiring to behave—more like a normal nation-state, there is a wide intermediary area. It includes, first, the rediscovery of the values of *Heimat* and *Gesellschaft* by the apolitical romanticism of the Greens. Then, there is the emphasis upon the special character of German interests, their opposition to those of their nuclear neighbors or those of the United States, and their convergence with those of the other German state or of all small and middle European states. Finally, one finds the notion that within the existing structures, Germany has a special role consisting of promoting East-West reconciliation, and should for that purpose have an individual strategy that implies no longer being taken for granted by its allies. It is this middle ground that, especially through its adoption by the SPD, is likely to play an increasing role in the debates over NATO strategy, over the European Community and over East-West relations. In the German case the meaning of nationalism is made particularly obscure and open to question by the problem of the division: Are "German interests" to be defined as those of the Bundesrepublik? Of the German people? Of the two German states? Of an "all-German *kulturnation?*" Or of a past and possibly future German state?[8] But the scope and content of the new national feelings remain obscure in the case of other Europeans and Americans as well, because it can be expressed by assertiveness or by withdrawal, by the search for influence or for isolaton, by a new regionalism or a new globalism.

The crucial question is that of the relationship among these three trends within a given country, and from one country and one continent, one alliance to the other. In some cases, pacifism, neutralism, and nationalism tend to counteract or compensate one another; this is, for the time being, the case in France, where an early experience with a moderate dose of neutralism and nationalism seems to have acted as a vaccination against pacifism. For France, the aspiration to independence is satisfed by the possession of an independent nuclear deterrent and by an active diplomacy that, rather than aspiring to disengagement, combines contradictory or complementary engagements: with NATO against the Soviet Union in Europe, with Cuba and Nicaragua against the United States in Latin America. In Germany, on the other hand, and in some other traditionally faithful NATO allies (for example, the Netherlands), the trends toward pacifism, neutralism, and nationalism tend to go hand in hand because the fear of war tends to lead to revolt against the American protector and because, conversely the only conceivable form of nationalism is, for the time being at least, of the pacifist variety. As Egon Bahr has said concerning nuclear weapons, the only way a nonnuclear state can exercise its sovereignty is by refusing their presence on its territory. To this motivation, shared by all Atlanticist and nonnuclear states, is added in the German case the double fact that traditional nationalism has been discredited by Nazism, and that the most national (in whatever uncertain, confused, or diluted form) goal of the FRG has to do with links with East Germany and hence if not with East-West reconciliation, at least with the refusal of East-West confrontation.

What is more unpredictable are the reactions of countries to one another's evolutions. They may vary among parallelism, imitation, reaction, and prevention. The German example clearly serves as a model in some of the smaller Protestant countries, where the Protestant churches influence the Catholic churches. One of the clearest examples of mutual reinforcement is between the Protestant churches and, through them, the pacifist movements of the two German states. But elsewhere the effect is rather one of contrast or of preventive reaction. Clearly European pacifism and U.S. isolationism feed upon each other and produce a common result of reciprocal transatlantic acrimony. More unexpectedly, one of the main reasons for the weakness of the peace movement in France and for the new French emphasis on Western cohesion is the strength of the German peace movement and the fear of German neutralism. Conversely, to the extent that the fear seems exaggerated and that the structure of European security seems reconsolidated, French nationalist and neutralist (rather than pacifist) tendencies may well revive under the form of a new dialogue with Moscow, designed to balance a resurgent U.S. strength or a renewed Washington-Bonn axis.

I have spoken in the same breath of moods like the antinuclear one, of movements such as the Greens, the nuclear freeze, or the Campaign for Nuclear Disarmament, and of policies—those of established institutions like political parties, churches, or unions, and ultimately those of governments.[9] Yet this is of course the most crucial distinction of all. Generational moods may inspire policies but they do not make them; the mediation of political forces is essential. Through the past years we have witnessed this process of mediation and translation, with forces attempting to profit from the mood and governments attempting to placate or to preempt it. However, spectacular gaps have remained between silent majorities and active minorities, clearly visible in the mass media and the policies of legitimately elected governments. Again it is probably at the middle level, above all that of West European Social Democratic parties, the unions, and the churches, including the U.S. Catholic ones, that the effects are likely to be the most lasting. But in the remainder of this chapter, we shall be preoccupied essentially with their indirect effects upon the states and their policies toward one another.

A TALE OF TWO GAPS

Because the difference between totalitarian, authoritarian, and democratic governments has essentially to do with the difference in relations between state and society, it is not surprising that the story of the impact of peace movements upon East-West relations could be told essentially in terms of this difference. It is more striking that in West-West relations, too, the main question may well be whether difference between the two sides of the ocean or between two countries like the Federal Republic and France are caused, or, on the contrary, attenuated or compensated, by differences between each state and its own society.

For this writer, at least, "peace-watching" since 1979 has consisted above all in watching the interplay between the respective widening or narrowing of these two gaps: the intra-Western and the intranational. The dominant trend in practically every Western country has been a crisis of the welfare state and a cry for less state control. In the United States this went together with an aspiration for more leadership and a more energetic foreign policy; in Western Europe— especially in the Federal Republic and in the Nordic countries—the mood was more directed toward social, domestic priorities and more hostile to authority and to foreign assertiveness. The trend in foreign policy, confirmed by the election of Reagan and the reelection of Schmidt, was for the United States to question detente and for Europeans to confirm their attachment to it. In the more general area of social values, the "greening of America" was replaced by the favoring of authority, the work ethic, and technology, while the "greening" of Germany—the revolt against Prussian values as well as against technocracy, the assertion of individualism as well as the thirst for community and nature—was in full swing. This led me to the hypothesis that the two crucial countries of the Atlantic alliance, the United States and West Germany, were drifting apart in their fundamental attitudes, as the two fervent minorities that claimed to represent the moral majority of each were pushing toward right-wing moralistic fanaticism in one case and left-wing pacifistic fanaticism in the other. [10] In Catholic countries like France and Italy, more passivity and more acceptance of the requirements of reason of state were checking this evolution.

A year later, the explosion of the peace movement in the United States with Ground Zero week, the freeze movement, the stand of the Catholic bishops, and, on the other hand, the election of conservative governments in Great Britain and in the Federal Republic seem to have blurred this opposition, both between Americans and Europeans and between Protestants and Catholics. Government policies have appeared to follow this convergence; the Reagan administration has toned down its nuclear rhetoric, has made all the right declarations about the impossibility of winning a nuclear war. Even more important, it has resumed arms–control negotiations and, at least on intermediate nuclear forces, has made all the concessions requested by its West European, particularly German, allies. Conversely, the three major governments concerned, the FRG, Britain, and Italy, have agreed to deploy the U.S. missiles, with the vocal support of socialist France. They have actually started the deployment with less difficulty than expected, thereby giving the lie to the apocalyptic prophecies of the peace movements and the dire warnings of the Soviet Union.

Everything, then, seems quiet and harmonious, at least on the peace and East-West fronts. But this is where the other, and perhaps more fundamental gap, reappears: between state and society or, more precisely, between governments, articulate minorities, and popular (electoral or polled, silent or vocal) majorities. Here it may be instructive to reflect on a comparison that has been as striking during the same period as the European-United States one, namely that between France and the Federal Republic. In the seventies and early eighties, it has been possible to observe that the policies of the two governments on East-West relations have not been so different, nor are the attitudes of the two populations as revealed by the polls. If anything, both neutralism and the fear of war seemed more widespread in France than in Germany. But the intellectual atmosphere and the media were in complete contrast; they were dominated by pacifism and anti-Americanism in Germany, and by antitotalitarianism coupled with the acceptance of nuclear deterrence (as well as of civilian nuclear energy) in France. The troubling question was whether the discrepancy among the three levels within each of the two countries could be maintained indefinitely or if not, which one would prevail over the others. [11]

The provisional answer seems to be that the combination of mass movements expressed by demonstrations, and by the intellectuals and the media, has not changed the position of governments (at least on the basic immediate options) but that it has significantly affected popular attitudes. In the Federal Republic, while acceptance of the Atlantic alliance has remained very high, acceptance of the missiles has gone down from a narrow majority to a minority of 15 percent. More significant still, between 1982 and 1983 those who see the main answer to the problem of Western security in effective cooperation between Europe and the United States have declined from 53 percent to 34 percent; those who see it in the strengthened economic unity of Western Europe have gone from 35 percent to 21 percent; those who favor greater defense cooperation among Western European countries have gone from 28 percent to 17 percent; and those who see the answer in continued dialogue and contacts with the Soviet Union have increased from 33 percent to 42 percent. [12]

The influence of articulate minorities seems then to have been greater, so to speak, downward upon popular opinion than upward upon governments. But the notion should immediately be corrected by the obvious fact that these governments have been elected by these same populations, and that the latter do not seem to have reacted with a feeling of betrayal or with active rage to the fact that, in this case, their elected governments acted against their preferences. Of course, this is due to the fact, which emerges from polls as well as from elections, that economic considerations (as in Germany) and the personal authority of leaders or lack of authority of their opponents (as in Great Britain) play a greater role than foreign policy. There is, then, a gap between government and society on the peace issue, but a gap that is made tolerable by the relatively low saliency of the issue. It could become worrisome, however, if the confidence enjoyed by governments on other issues erodes, or if the issue of war and peace (or, especially in Germany of national unity and sovereignty) were to acquire greater saliency, or both. And this is all the more important and dangerous as the main opposition parties (Labour and the SPD in the two countries we mentioned) and some of the most important institutionalized forces (the DGB and the TUC, the Protestant churches, and the Church of England) are leaning in the pacifist direction, at least to the extent of questioning the principle of nuclear deterrence.

Does this situation extend to the United States or to France, as well, or does it contribute to reopening the transatlantic or the Franco-German gap? Here, the answer must be extremely tentative. International polls show that the U.S. public shares the same concern for the future of detente as its European—particularly German—counterparts. Indeed, the number of those who see continued dialogue and contracts with the Soviet Union as the main answer to the problem of security has increased more in the United States, from 25 percent in 1962 to 40 percent in 1983, than anywhere else. Primary concern with the threat of war increased from 25 percent to 28 percent in the FRG over this period; from 25 percent to 45 percent in the United States. Concern with nuclear weapons went from 18 percent to 37 percent in the United States (and, remarkably, from 18 percent to 26 percent in France), and only from 32 percent to 38 percent in Germany (where it even decreased, in October, from a maximum of 42 percent in March 1983). [13]

It seems, then, that anxiety over detente, over nuclear weapons, and over the handling of these issues by the Reagan administration is more or less comparable throughout the Western world. In the United States, the confidence expressed in Reagan's overall performance, including his handling of the economy, stands in sharp contrast with judgments on his policies regarding these peace issues: according to the Harris Poll, one American out of four thinks he is doing a good job in avoiding war; three out of four think the United States must take part of the blame for the grim state of U.S.-Soviet relations. [14]

If, on the other hand, one puts these answers in the broader context of foreign policy and of social attitudes, one sees the differences re-emerging. Concern with the Soviet buildup, which remained stable (but at a very high level) in Germany from 1982 to 1983 (55 percent), shot up from 27 percent to 52 percent in the United States and from 21 to 30 percent in France. It is to be noted, however, that concern with the U.S. military buildup follows more or less the same pattern: relative stability at a high level in the FRG (from 39 percent in 1982 to 41 percent in 1983); a comparatively sharp increase in the United States (from 11 percent to 25 percent); and almost as much in France (from 14 percent to 24 percent) and Great Britain (from 15 percent to 24 percent). But the pattern of worry on the extension of Soviet influence is markedly different; it shoots up from 22 percent to 37 percent in the United States; only slightly less so (from 19 percent to 27 percent) in France; and actually decreases in Britain (from 19 percent to 17 percent) and in the Federal Republic (from 28 percent to 25 percent). [15]

Needless to say, skepticism may be warranted on all these figures, and much remains unexplained even for those who take them seriously. To this observer, they seem to indicate that the common interest in peace and detente and worry over nuclear weapons and U.S. imprudence (in which the French are slowly tending to follow the other countries) is counterbalanced very significantly, in the United States and also if to a lesser extent in France, by a continuing desire for a policy of resistance to Soviet expansionism, while faith in detente is much more solid in Britain and in West Germany. The favorable response of the U.S. public to the invasion of Grenada, and the signs of a new patriotism and of a new popularity of things military in the United States have been shown to have some equivalent in Britain by the attitudes of the public and of the media to the Falklands war. But in the Federal Republic whatever tendencies in this direction may exist are submerged by the predominance of attachment to detente and hostility to nuclear weapons. The government's relief at the maintenance of good relations with the GDR in spite of the missile deployments and its constant and Pollyannish insistence on interpreting every Soviet statement as conciliatory reflect this mood, which aims above all at avoiding conflict, danger, and agonizing choices. This may be connected with the divergences in broader attitudes toward technology, toward the future, and toward life in general that could be discerned in 1981, particularly in the younger generations, and that seem to remain just as valid.

Of course, it is perfectly possible that the passive and pessimistic attitudes of the majority of Germans could be transformed by economic recovery and by a new belief in competition, which the Kohl government is trying to encourage, just as it is even more possible that the evangelical romanticism of the Left prevalent in the Green and peace movements may one day lead to an assertive and aggressive romanticism of the Right. Conversely, if dangers of confrontation with the Soviet Union and of nuclear escalation seem more serious than they were over Grenada, the antiwar impulse may prevail more spectacularly in the United States over the assertive or resisting mood than it does today. Still, one cannot avoid the impression that differences in geopolitical situations and interests, in social situations, and in cultural moods are sufficiently deep to make an assertive U.S. policy much more likely than a German one. While the attitude toward nuclear weapons shows a shared distrust of military government experts (which is not, or not yet, the case in France), episodes like the popular German reactions to the projected census or to cable television show a unique distrust of government and of technology. This has added to the more active and strident role of the environmentalists (which—for a time at least—amounted to a kind of veto power over civilian nuclear energy) and creates special constraints for German defense and foreign policy.

THE ATLANTIC ALLIANCE: AFTER THE STORM OR BEFORE THE FALL?

Writing in the winter of 1983, after the deployment of the first Pershing II and cruise missiles in Europe, one hesitates between two slogans, expressed by the titles in two leading European weeklies: "The Normalizing of Germany" (*The Economist,* 29 October) and "In the Waiting Room of History" (*Die Zeit,* 6 January 1984) In a sense, the alliance has weathered the storm; the vicious spiral that many expected on both sides of the Atlantic (refusal of the Europeans to deploy the very missiles they had asked for, serving as an alibi for U.S. troop withdrawals) has been avoided. European pacifists and U.S. isolationists are both on the defensive, and the Soviet Union, apparently at a loss for the next move, beyond withdrawal from arms control negotiations, is in no good position to help them.

On the other hand, without going so far as to call NATO's victory on the missiles issue a pyrrhic one, the fact remains that it is only a battle that has been won, not the war itself. The point is not merely that the deployments are supposed to be spread over a five-year period, with corresponding opportunities for trouble. Nor is the point that the pacifists' defeat may be compensated for by the victory's consisting in having won over, at least in part, the Social Democratic parties and hence having the prospect of victory if and when they come to power [16] (because the conventional wisdom holds that to do so, they would have to return to the center and disengage from the Greens or unilateralist embrace). The point, rather, is the coincidence of this breaking of the consensus between political parties and forces, the shifting in public opinion, and the coming into the open of new and even more, of old, repressed issues, all of which may converge, for the first time, and put into question the alliance itself.

An indication of this direction could be seen in the Congress of the SPD in Cologne in November 1983. It was remarkable in three respects. The most conspicuous was the overwhelming rejection of the deployments and the victory of Willy Brandt over Helmut Schmidt. Atlanticist Social Democrats point out, however, that the Congress also witnessed an attempt by the leadership to put a stop to the fight over the missiles by reaffirming its commitment to NATO and its acceptance of the decision as legitimate if mistaken, and by dissociating itself from the illegal actions of the radical peace movement and calling for a focus on other issues. But the most important respect may be the third one: among these new subjects a foremost one is NATO strategy—which may revive or reinforce all the divisive issues of the deployment issue in an even more explosive form. [17]

In a recent interview, one of the most significant exponents of the area of convergence between the left wing of the SPD and the moderate wing of the Greens, Jo Leinen, indicates NATO strategy and German sovereignty as the two emerging themes for mobilization and action. [18] One may formulate the same thought by distinguishing three issues in the coming Atlantic debate: nuclear versus conventional weapons; centralized integration versus national decentralization; and defense versus offense. All three lead from the military to the political, and from the West-West dimension to the East-West one.

The most obvious and general aspect is that the genie of the nuclear issue is out of the bottle, and that it will take more than the dying out of the deployment dispute to put it back. It may well be that the wave of anxiety and controversy will recede again, as it did after the early sixties; there may be no substitute for nuclear deterrence, but the only way to live with it may well be to unleash collective doubts and fears as well as an unfruitful search for alternatives once every generation. [19] It may also be that the issue is not as divisive for the Atlantic alliance as it looks. First, there is a convergence between the U.S. and the European peace movements on this issue. On both sides of the Atlantic, the radicals (more powerful in Europe than in the United States) are for the abolition of nuclear weapons; the moderate wing of the peace movement agrees on such U.S. proposals as the freeze or no first use, on European-American proposals such as that of the Palme Commission for a zone free of battlefield nuclear weapons, and, more generally, on the goal of a conventional defense. Indeed this goal is a prevalent trend in the military establishment (including General Rogers) and in the strategic establishment (including within the Reagan administration). Conventional weapons, especially the new sophisticated ones, appear as the panacea likely to make up for the lost nuclear superiority of the United States and to appease the peace movement. To the extent that this view meets with criticism, the fronts are not clearly drawn across the Atlantic. A minority of U.S. strategists, a majority of the NATO and European military establishment, and a quasi-unanimity within the French strategic and military establishment believe that a purely conventional balance is not possible and that if it were, it would be less stable than the present balance based on the threat of escalation, despite the latter's declining credibility.

It is remarkable that while many on the European Left suspect the United States of wanting to wage limited nuclear war in Europe, and point to the Euromissiles and to field manual 100-5 of the U.S. army, which foresees an integrated use of nuclear and chemical weapons on the second echelon of the Warsaw Pact forces,[20] most point, on the contrary, to the U.S. tendency to go in the direction of a maritime-plus conventional strategy and to abandon the idea of using the threat of nuclear response to a conventional attack. Of course, some, in the peace movement and elsewhere, do not hesitate to affirm in the same breath that the United States will never use nuclear weapons to defend Europe, and that theater nuclear weapons are dangerous because of their vulnerability and their precision, which make the first-strike weapon subject to the "use-them-or-lose-them" effect.[21] But precisely all this confusion on both sides may serve to preserve the ambiguity on which NATO doctrine and posture have been based from the beginning.

This is not the most plausible possibility, however. Both the changes in the balance of power and changes in public mood make it likely that once exposed, ambiguity, as a substitute for consensus, will be more and more difficult to sustain. If all U.S. nuclear weapons were withdrawn from Germany or Central Europe, or from all nonnuclear countries (as Egon Bahr suggests) it would probably be the end of NATO. But even if this were not the case, and even if the more likely scenario were the case—where only the number and role of nuclear weapons in Europe were reduced and only short-range battlefield nuclear weapons were eliminated—disagreements over nonfighting and deterrence doctrine, thresholds, the duration of local weapons, and the desirability of escalation would be revived and multiplied. The traditional solution, moreover, so well described by Catherine Kelleher under the name "retreat to the trip-wire," [22] would still be likely, but would look less and less satisfactory to strategists and less and less reassuring to the people at large. The peace movement would not have created the problem but it would have made the solution more difficult, if only because under its influence, nuclear problems tend to be discussed in broad daylight, rather than in the cozy seclusion of the nuclear planning group.

But the difficulty is compounded by the two other dimensions with which the peace movement has been associated: that of sovereignty and that of relations with the East. Already on nuclear matters, the specter that haunted the West during the fifties and sixties and that produced and wrecked such schemes as the European Defense Community or the Multilateral Force, German sovereignty, is again rearing its head in nuclear matters—not in the form of a national deterrent (although some isolated voices, outside Germany, are beginning to raise the issue) but in that of a double key or of a real participation, certainly in strategy and probably in control. [23] Whether this search for an independent role is expressed negatively (as in the Dutch trend toward disengaging from nuclear missions and getting into a "Nordic" posture) or positively (in a search for nondiscrimination and influence), the dilemmas of deterrence, credibility, and political acceptability are likely to grow, and the days of grumbling acceptance of each successive U.S. strategy may well be over.

One fact has not yet been fully realized: the rush to a conventional posture is not more likely to solve these problems than the retreat toward the trip wire because the same differences of attitude and the same dilemmas are now beginning to apply to the conventional field as well. The trend among Americans as well as among Germans may well be away from coalition warfare. The problems of sovereignty and nationalism may take the form of the search for global and theater mobility on the U.S. side; for national and local retrenchment on the European, particularly the German, side. The new strategic concepts developed by the United States for conventional warfare—whether Airland Battle 2000, developed by the army, or the notion of horizontal escalation—require more operational integration and centralization than before, and more political agreement on the global nature of the conflict and of the enemy. [24] On the other hand, the natural tendency of the Europeans is toward a more restricted definition of their interests; the natural tendency of the Germans is away from their special degree of integration in NATO, toward a posture more similar to that of the other allies.

But, above all, the dilemma that conventional strategy is beginning to raise even more sharply than nuclear strategy is that of the offensive and the defensive. For nuclear strategy, the dilemma may have a certain reality (in terms of planning or not for counterforce systems and, even more, if the issue of antimissile defense becomes central). But it is really more a matter of rhetoric and suspicions, for, all progress in accuracy and all increased talk about war-fighting notwithstanding, the restraints on any U.S. government against launching a first strike will remain enormous, as will be, on the other hand, the credibility deficit of an extended deterrence posture based on pure mutual assured destruction, even in the eyes of the Europeans most hostile to the quest for superiority. But in terms of conventional warfare the problem is real enough, for the prevailing U.S. trend, and indeed, for strategic logic as such, a conventional option has to be an offensive (or, if one prefers, a counteroffensive) one. [25] It cannot leave the benefit of initiative and surprise to the opponent, and it can even less forgo the option of extending the battlefield to its rear and of striking its second echelon forces. But for the Germans and to some extent the Europeans, the fear of war by preemption or misunderstanding (which would be much more likely with the new conventional weapons than with the old nuclear ones), the desire to be seen to be defensive, and that of sparing the territory of Eastern Europe (particularly East Germany), combine in pushing toward resistance to this trend. In the past this has led NATO to adopt a static defense, which in principle could neither retreat nor advance, and which the Federal Republic has called *Vorne Verteidigung* instead of *Vorwarts Verteidigung* to emphasize its defensive character. It is still too offensive for the peace movement, which is searching for alternative strategies that would be both purely conventional and purely defensive. [26] The most elaborate option is that developed by Horst Afheldt, with the sponsorship of C.F. von Weizsäcker (who, during the electoral campaign, was the security adviser of the SPD candidate Hans Joachim Vogel). Its concept, which goes by the name of "technoguerrilla," calls for a combination of precision-guided munitions (especially new antitank weapons) and for local defense; this would supposedly stop a Soviet conventional attack, while the retention of a minimum retaliatory U.S. nuclear force should deter the Soviets from resorting to nuclear weapons. [27]

This scheme is far from attracting unanimous support. Many in the peace movement find it too conservative, and want to sever all links with the United States or with nuclear weapons and rely purely on a nonviolent defense; [28] many in the SPD find it unrealistic and would, at least at the present time, be content with a posture closer to the present one but eliminating battlefield or theater nuclear weapons. The point is that in the peace movement as well as in the SPD, the search for alternative strategies is the order of the day, and this certainly means a search for alternatives to U.S. doctrines of mobility and counteroffensive, and possibly a search for alternatives to NATO.

The CDU-FDP government, caught between two fires, is likely to opt for the status quo, as it has already done by refuting the alternatives proposed by the peace movement and resisting those proposed by the U.S. Army. [29] Its position is strengthened by its firm and loyal stand on the deployment issues, but it is weakened by the inevitable demographic and economic constraints likely to affect the Bundeswehr. It may (as indeed some elements of the SPD and of the peace movement do) look for greater European cooperation to mitigate the dilemma but it still will be in no position to strengthen its forces significantly or to renounce the Atlantic connection or renounce detente, particularly with the GDR. In turn, this is likely to strengthen U.S. trends toward a maritime strategy and global unilateralism.

Hence, while NATO strategy is likely to be the focus of debate, the real stakes are likely to go beyond NATO and strategic matters proper; they concern the priority of the Atlantic connection within the framework of East-West relations, and the clash between U.S. views of global and multidimensional confrontation and European—particularly German views of Atlantic defense combined at the minimum with the pursuit of regional arms control and detente, and at a maximum with the search for overcoming the division of Europe.

EAST-WEST RELATIONS: A DELICATE BALANCE OF DISCONTENT?

We are reaching at last the true subject of this chapter. One thing the peace movement is not likely to advance is peace. One thing it is likely to encourage is division, within the countries of the Western alliance and between them. But the question that remains open is whether it is likely to affect the European balance and the division between East and West. The standard Western fear has been best expressed by President Mitterrand's formula: "The missiles are in the East and the pacifists are in the West." The pacifists are demonstrating at the wrong bases, but even if they were (as some of them belatedly but increasingly are) distributing their protest evenhandedly, they would affect the military programs of the West, not those of the East. Hence, even if they were not manipulated by Moscow they would risk tilting the balance in its favor. The answer of the peace movement is that there are, indeed, pacifists in the East, and that they are closely connected with many of them. Indeed, the main phenomenon according to the pacifists is that of a pan-European protest movement, ranging from Western disarmers to Eastern dissidents, against the main source both of oppression and the fear of war: Europe's occupation by the two superpowers. While most of the participants in such movements—for instance the CND and the Communist-led groups in the West, Solidarity in the East—disclaim or are hostile to the other movement, there is enough dialogue and even agreement among significant components (the two churches, the Berlin alternativists, and the protesters in the two Germanys, the London-based Campaign for European Nuclear Disarmament, and the Czechoslovak Charter 77) to legitimize the claim that these movements do constitute a link between the two Germanys and the two Europes that must cause some discomfort not only to the West but also to the Soviet rulers. This does not mean that they present a common, much less credible, "alternative to Yalta," and much less still a workable strategy toward such a goal. But their strong point is that a Western strategy based on NATO and on the containment of the Soviet military threat has nothing to offer East European aspirations to autonomy and communication with the West and to offer West European, particularly West German, desires for closer links with them and more generally for a new European order. If the European dilemma is that of security and change, it is not surprising that the Establishment and the majority of the population in the West should give priority to military security, but that many in Eastern Europe and in the new generation in the West, particularly in Germany, should converge in a willingness to run some risks for political change.

If a certain dialogue is becoming possible between certain portions of the peace movement in the West and of the human rights movement in the East, it is because peace and human rights, however valuable and valued by themselves, are also (and perhaps primarily) code words for the search for political alternatives.

Within the peace movement the trend in emphasis is clearly moving from the problem of the avoidance of war to that of the reassertion and the rapprochement of both German states and of both halves of Europe, from the Western framework to the pan-European one, or, in the language of the movement's critics, from pacifism to nationalism and neutralism.

The search for an alternative, nuclear-free defense is reviving, one after the other, all the schemes of the fifties and sixties for nuclear-free zones, for neutralizaation, and for disengagement. At that time, they were explicitly linked to the search for a solution of the German problem and for a European settlement. They are more and more so today. This is particularly the case in the Federal Republic, [30] where the link to the German problem through the idea of a demilitarization and neutralization of Germany as the only way to reunification (or at least of a special military status for the two German states leading to a special political one) has been given impetus by the collaboration of East German dissidents like R. Havemann and R. Bahro and Berlin "alternativists" like Peter Brandt. The Havemann letter to Brezhnev, published in October 1981, and signed by a number of East German and West German intellectuals, was a landmark in this respect. But on a European level, the initiative comes from the appeal of the Russell Foundation, in April 1980, for "a nuclear-free Europe from Poland to Portugal" and from the creation of the campaign for European nuclear disarmament led by E.P. Thompson, which increasingly distinguishes itself from the old "Campaign for Nuclear Disarmament" by its desire "to strike at the structures of the Cold War itself." The Dutch Inter-church Organization has expressed a similar all-European and antisuperpower orientation. [31]

At the level of political forces, the Federal Republic stands out much more among Western countries. The whole European Left is favorable toward detente, and the drive to anti-Americanism, neutralism, or unilateral disarmament is strong in the Socialist parties of Britain and the Netherlands. However they are not associated with a strong interest in Eastern Europe or an all-European vision. By contrast, France under Mitterand is pursuing the line of challenging the division symbolized, rightly or wrongly, by the Yalta agreement, of denouncing situations like the Polish one, and of calling for a future dissolution of the blocs. Meanwhile, however, it stresses the status quo and the need for an improved military balance and for closer Western—both Atlantic and European—ties, partly or precisely out of fear of West Germany sliding into neutralism.

In Germany, then, perhaps the most interesting position is that of the Berlin wing of the SPD (and, to some extent, of the CDU former Berlin mayor and future federal president, Richard von Weizsäcker). People like Egon Bahr and Günter Gaus clearly share the goals of the peace movement but find its tactics too open and impatient; [32] they prefer a long-range strategy starting from the status quo. Rather than calling for a united Germany, or for a dissolution of the blocs, they want, from within the two alliances, to carve out and consolidate a special position of the two Germanys and a special relation between them. [33] For this, the concern for security, nuclear weapons, and arms control is more and more clearly a means to an end, which is intra-German reconciliation. But they know that this is possible only in a certain European context of detente. This is why Egon Bahr, refusing Chancellor Kohl's alliance as belonging to the reason of state of the Bundesrepublik, puts forth, as an alternative, the notion that this reason of state consists of East-West reconciliation. [34]

Clearly the SPD, while for the time being wanting to sacrifice neither the alliance nor East-West reconciliation, is edging closer to the second than to the first. But the Kohl government and the CDU are themselves very far from taking an exclusive view of their own Western priority. They seem to have found the best or the least bad combination between Germany's various objectives and constraints. Having shown their pro-Western credentials and reassured their U.S. and French allies—not only by reaffirming the priority of the alliance and the refusal of a neutral or mediating role (hence Kohl's indefinitely reaffirmed formulation: "We are not wanderers between two worlds") but, above all, by sticking to the deployment decision despite the attacks of the peace movement and the risks to relations with the Soviet Union and the GDR—they feel free to pursue, toward both, the same *Ostpolitik* and *Deutschland-politik* based on the pursuit of human alleviations of the division, of arms control, and of detente, and on the instrument of economic trade and aid, illustrated in particular by the huge credit to the GDR in the summer of 1983. Even in this direction, they can point out that, although less afraid than their predecessors of speaking both of human rights and of German reunification (which Kohl did in Moscow in June 1983) they have not lost anything in bilateral relations, at least not with the GDR. Contrary to the threats and predictions about a new "ice age," intra-German relations are flourishing in spite of the change of government in Bonn and the missile deployments. Kohl and Honecker use the same language about a *Verantwortungsgemeinschaft* (community of responsibility), which has replaced the term *security-partnership* used by the Social Democrats, and about the need to minimize the damage created by the crisis of detente upon their mutual relations.

However, the Kohl government seems aware that this is, at least for the short run, all that it is engaged in: a holding pattern or damage-limiting operation. It knows that its strength in being able to work credibly along all three dimensions of the Atlantic partnership with the United States, of the Franco-German "alliance within the alliance" in the European direction, and of detente and economic cooperation with the East, particularly with the GDR, is based on the Federal Republic's weakness, which is its limited freedom of action. It knows that it can afford to abandon none of the three directions and that, by the same token, it can afford to pursue none of them to its ultimate logic. A balanced policy, dressed up in formulas such as the reference to the Harmel Report or to the Federal Republic's Western values and Central

European geographical situation, is the only reasonable one, and its pursuit can be seen as a success only from the point of view of German as well as European and Western interests. But this policy approach will always appear as frustratingly halfhearted to Germany's foreign partners and as frustratingly passive or paralyzed to those in the Federal Republic and elsewhere who look for decisive steps in the all-German and all-European directions.

Where, then, can these steps come from, in the eyes of the peace movement, and where can they lead? All are aware that the key is in Soviet hands, and hence all have to imagine a change in the behavior of Moscow and in the structure of the Soviet empire. But one can distinguish two types of scenarios and strategies, which are linked to two basic social visions that one may call reform from above and revolution from below.

For some (in particular those linked yesterday to the Gaullists and today to the left wing of the Social Democratic parties) the Soviet Union is basically defensive. What keeps it in Eastern Europe and above all in East Germany is the U.S. presence in Western Europe and in the Federal Republic, and, in particular the military threat of the missiles. If the West were to renounce them, or even to disarm unilaterally, or if Western Europe or the Federal Republic were to put an end to the U.S. presence, unilaterally or through negotiations with the Soviets, the latter would be happy to reciprocate by withdrawing from Eastern Europe, or by accepting German unity, or, in a more moderate version, by considerably relaxing its control. But for this it should not be made insecure by popular rebellions in the East or by help to these rebellions from the West.

For the other, more radical wing, the Soviet Union and the United States are equally tyrannical and driven by the logic of power and of "exterminism." It is only through the rebellion of the people, East and West, against the whole cold-war system that Europe can be liberated and reunited. The only way for the Western peace movement to avoid being manipulated by the Soviet Union is on the one hand to refuse the logic of compromise and negotiation, and on the other hand to adopt the cause of the Eastern dissidents as its own—thus giving birth to an all-European transbloc movement against the bipolar order. [35]

Rudolf Bahro seems to hold both views simultaneously. On the one hand he distinguishes between West and East and claims that the source of war danger ultimately still lies in capitalist imperialism, Soviet authoritarianism and militarism being essentially a reaction or a consequence; [36] on the other hand he believes that the protest movement—called peace movement in the West, dissident or human rights movement in the East—is but one movement that embraces the whole continent. Both its themes—ecology and peace—and the forces that favor its diffusion—the Protestant church and rock music—are common, and have in common their total independence from, and indifference toward, ideology and bipolarity. [37] To evaluate these claims it is necessary to consider, however briefly, the degree of reality of the peace movement in Eastern Europe and its relationship to the policies of East European governments and of the Soviet Union.

The distinction between popular moods, articulate minorities and government policies is even more important in the East than in the West, since the nature of the regimes forces a much clearer separation among the three levels. For the same reasons, the level of popular attitudes and perceptions is particularly difficult to ascertain. It is a fair guess, however, that with the exception of the revolt against Western culture, the moods of which the peace movement is an expression of in the West are much more widespread in the East. The fear of war, partly through the memories of World War II (particularly in the Soviet Union) partly through the backfiring of the regime's own propaganda (particularly in the GDR), [38] is much more genuine than in the West (with the possible exception of the Federal Republic). The renewed feeling of national identity, the search for historical and spiritual roots have been kept more alive than in the West by the resistance to the Communist regime (although we lack information as to the degree of separate East German, versus all-German, patriotism in the GDR, and as to the echo of the regimes' attempt to play upon these feelings by rehabilitating the whole of Prussian history). The spiritual feeling of the cultural unity of Europe is particularly strong in Central Europe, which feels itself as a part of the West kidnapped by the East. [39] There is no equivalent of neutralist feelings to the extent that the population is more likely than not to be pro-Western in Eastern Europe and to identify with Moscow as a world power threatened by its environment in the Soviet Union. But there certainly is, in East and Central Europe more than in the West, a diffuse rejection of the bipolar division symbolized by "Yalta."

Out of these various feelings, did a peace movement emerge in the East bearing any resemblance and relationship at all to the Western ones? The short answer is no, with one partial and specific exception (the GDR) and one partial and general qualification, namely, that the Soviet reaction to Western missile deployments may be creating one. [40]

The case of the GDR peace movement is unique for three interrelated reasons: the intra-German factor (with the role of the West German example, propagated by television, the human communications with the Greens and the Berlin alternativists, the national theme leading to plans for neutralization and reunification); the inner contradictions of the GDR regime on the military question, for it is both the most militarized and militaristic state in Eastern Europe and the only one that recognizes a social service for draft objectors); and the role of the Protestant church. The last is crucial in the two other respects themselves, because the Protestant church was decisive in the fight for a "social peace service" and in the criticism of the growing militarization and the education to hate of GDR youth, and because it maintains institutional links with the Evangelical church in the FRG. Although the GDR church goes even further than the latter in rejecting nuclear deterrence, the two churches have produced joint statements favoring the notion not only of a special responsibility for peace of the two German states leading to a special military status but also of a special responsibility for the safeguarding of the spiritual unity of the German nation. Both in the selection of the themes and, even more, through its role as a protector, a moderator, and a mediator, the Evangelical church in the GDR is playing a role not unlike that of the Catholic church in Poland. One may venture the thought that if Poland and (to an infinitely more modest degree) the GDR are the only two East European countries where social movements emerge in the open, it is because they are the only two countries where a fragmentary civil society has a recognized semi-independent existence, because the church gives it an institutional basis. At any rate, practically all collective demonstrations involving several hundred or even thousands of young people in Dresden in 1982 or in Jena in 1983, for example, are due to the efforts of young Christians. There exist, of course, other sources of dissent that have little to do with the peace issue, such as the Punk movement. Even among those who rally to the protective cover of the church, the motivations are not always self-evident: concern with peace and with religion may coexist with a political protest that adopts the presentation more likely to be tolerated. Concern with nuclear war, with intra-German reconciliation, and with intra-GDR reform are hard to disentangle; their respective weights are even harder to evaluate.

At the other extreme, in Poland, the situation is more clear. Solidarity was concerned neither with peace nor with ecology but with human and social rights; to the extent that they know it, the Polish people are suspicious of the Western peace movement because they suspect that it is manipulated by the Soviets and that it weakens the West. At the time of the Berlin peace meeting of May 1983, Western delegates of the END persuasion were rather disconcerted by a strong attack in the Polish clandestine press. [41] On the other hand, some groups associated with Solidarity, like the KOR and some Solidarity representatives in the West, have entered into a dialogue with the Western peace movement on the theme of the necessary link between peace and human rights.

This, indeed, is the prevalent attitude among East European independent peace groups. They try to use the existence of the peace movements in the West (and the fact that the Soviet and East European authorities have an interest in not discouraging and alienating them) to secure a forum abroad and protection at home for their own themes, which remain predominantly those of democracy and human rights.

Within this general framework, there are many different tactics partly dictated by the different national traditions and the different strengths of the respective groups in the various countries. In the Soviet Union and in Hungary, the independent peace groups try to distinguish themselves from the dissidents and to promote trust and dialogue between East and West without criticizing their own regime directly, while still emphasizing the need for democratization as a basis of detente. This has not, however, earned them any additional toleration from the authorities, certainly not in Moscow (where the leader of the groups, Batovrin, has been expelled after a period of internment in a psychiatric hospital, and Sakharov's dialogue with the U.S. arms-controller Sidney Drell [42] has been branded as treasonable), nor even in Budapest, where one group has had to announce its dissolution. [43]

Perhaps the most interesting case is Czechoslovakia. There, one finds no independent peace group as such, but does find the best illustration of the two basic attitudes of East European dissidents toward the Western peace movement. On the one hand, an historian writing under the pseudonym of V. Racek eloquently rebukes E.P. Thompson by stressing the opposition between freedom and totalitarianism and the primacy of the struggle against the latter as a condition of the struggle for peace. On the other hand, Charter 77 as such, through exponents like Hayek, Hejdanek, or Sabata, have engaged in a positive dialogue with E.P. Thompson and the Western peace movement. They declare their agreement both with its general goals, from nuclear disarmament to the overcoming of the division of Europe, and with its concrete proposals, such as the neutralization of Central Europe, but they emphasize the need to stress the organic connection between these goals and that of democratization; for them the internal peace of states, which can come only with the abandonment of repression, is the condition for international peace. [44] On this basis, they try unsuccessfully to engage in a dialogue with the official peace movements of the East (on the occasion of the Peace Congress in Prague, in June 1983) as well as with the unofficial ones in the West (in Berlin, May 1983).

What is even more interesting than the position taken by Charter 77, which can be interpreted as essentially tactical, is its relative success not in gaining toleration by the government but in embarrassing it, in revitalizing the movement and evoking a greater echo within the population than in the past. This is largely due to the phenomenon with which we started and with which we shall end, namely, the disquiet caused in the CSSR and the GDR by the announcement of the stationing of Soviet missiles in reaction against the NATO deployments. Obviously this does not change the realities of these countries' security, although the worry of the population may be justified by the perspective of an increase in the Soviet presence, in police control, and in the militarization of society. This, indeed, may be the only valid part in the argument of the Western peace movement against the deployments: they tend to harden the division of Europe and the repression of society in Eastern Europe even further.

But the surprising aspect lies in the population's discovery of aspects of Soviet military presence that it had ignored in its absorption of official propaganda about the danger of war associated with U.S. missiles, and in its turning the propaganda against the Soviet missiles. It lies even more in the embarrassed attitude of the respective governments, who seem, in the case of Czechoslovakia, to avoid being identified too closely with the counterdeployment decision and, in the GDR case, to go as far as taking the unprecedented step of publishing two dissenting letters emanating from Evangelical congregations in the party organ, *Neues Deutschland*. [45] As for Hungary, Bulgaria and Rumania, one does not know whether, as was intimated in particular by Rumania, they were invited to station new Soviet missiles and refused, or whether their turn might come later (perhaps once cruise missiles are deployed at Comiso), or whether the Soviet deployments concern only the northern tier with the exception of Poland, where Solidarity can be seen as being, objectively, the only peace movement that really succeeded in creating a situation that made such deployments unthinkable.

But clearly the Balkan countries are glad to have been spared thus far, which increases their enthusiasm for the Soviet-sponsored campaign for nuclear-free zones. The point, at any rate, is that two classes of East European satellites are created and that both the Soviet Union and the East European governments are faced with a new complexity of interests and tactics in dealing with their populations and with their neighbors. Clearly Honecker's alternations of repression and toleration of the peace movement (a campaign of arrests for instance, following a cordial reception of the Western Greens) have to do with the dual goal of encouraging the peace movement in the Federal Republic while curbing its contagious effects at home. Whether the relative toleration is inspired by the Soviets, as some dissidents like Pastor Eppelman [46] believe, or whether the warm relations with the FRG and the emphasis on Luther and national themes are signs of Honecker's margin of autonomy from a reluctant Soviet Union, as Klaus Bölling intimates, is very hard to decide. Similarly, in the South, the role of policy toward Yugoslavia and Greece in the treatment of Bulgaria and Rumania is a matter for speculation. [47]

Whether this new complexity may lead, as E. Kux thinks, to a destabilization of Eastern Europe that, in turn, would endanger European security, is much more doubtful still. The problem is linked to the permanent trade-off between the Soviets' control over Eastern Europe and their degree of influence over Western Europe. [48] It is expressed in their ambivalent relations with the Western peace movement, as shown by the stormy exchange of letters between Y. Jukow and the Russell Foundation over the control of the Berlin peace meeting. [49] Clearly the Soviets are dissatisfied with the raising of some uncomfortable issues, including the German one, and with the insufficient role of the Comunist parties in the Western peace movement. As an editorial in *Kommunist* puts it: "It is no secret that at first certain comrades were unable to grasp the nature of the antiwar movements . . . were not always able to overcome their prejudices against pacifist and ecological organizations, with their inconsistent and contradictory arguments, and did not perceive the members of these mass movements as their objective allies in the struggle for peace." [50] But it is also no secret that, as Gromyko pointed out in speaking of the peace movement in another editorial: "The question that must always be asked is 'Who stands to profit?' In politics it is not so important to know *who* is championing certain opinions. What is important is to know *who stands to profit* from these opinions". [51]

By this criterion, it is still likely that the balance sheet is not negative for the Soviet Union. Certainly, the peace movement and the Euromissile episode have given one more piece of evidence of the general dissatisfaction with the division of Europe and, in particular, with Soviet rule over its Eastern part. On the other hand, it has shown a similar unease with the idea of nuclear deterrence, which is the first obstacle in the way of Moscow's continental domination, and has sharpened the conflicts between the United States and Western Europe. For the time being, however, the prospects are that not pacifism nor neutralism nor nationalism, successful as they may be in exposing and deepening the gaps between the postwar bipolar system and the evolution of societies, will succeed in tearing the structure down. Nuclear deterrence and the division of Europe share the common fate of being less and less accepted but are not any likelier than before to be replaced by a credible substitute.

This is why it is so important to distinguish between immediate priorities and long-range perspectives. Europe has to live both with nuclear weapons and with the Soviet Union; but it can and must work at reducing excessive reliance on the former and excessive compliance with the latter. Those who decide to live as if the military danger and the division of Europe did not exist may well live in a world of dangerous illusion, all the more so because they are more likely to jeopardize the security of Western Europe than Soviet rule in Eastern Europe. Still, they do point to the historical perspective of an autonomous and reconciled Europe, and they do show that the iron constraints of the system do leave a margin of hope for the only genuine dialogue, that which starts from below.

NOTES

1. C. Coker and E. Schulte, "Strategiekritik und Pazifismus. Zwei Haupttendenzen in den Westeuropäischen Friedensbewegungen," *Europa-Archiv* 14 (25 July 1983): 413-20.
2. See, for the German case, the discussion between Alfred Grosser and Wilfrid von Bredow in the latter's "Friedensbewegung und Deutschlandpolitik," *Aussenpolitik und Zeitgeschichte* 46 (19 November 1983): 37.
3. See my "Recurrent Stresses, Resilient Structures", in R. Tucker and L. Wrigley, eds., *The Atlantic Alliance and Its Critics* (New York, 1982).
4. See the reference to Gaullism in P. Bender, *Das Ende des Ideologischen Zeitalters. Die Europäisierung Europas* (Berlin, 1981), pp. 166-67.
5. The most complete articulation of this view is Bender, *Das Ende des Ideologischen Zeitalters.*
6. See S. Szabo, ed., *The Successor Generation: International Perspectives of Postwar Europeans* (London, 1983).
7. The expression was coined by Josef Joffe, in "Stability and Its Discontents: Can Europe Live with Its Defense?" a paper prepared for the Chatham House Conference "The U.S. and Western Europe in the 1980s," 21-22 June 1983.
8. For all these distinctions, see my "Was geht in Deutschland vor? Wiederbelegung der deutschen Frag durch Alternativen und Friedensstaaten in Europa: Gibt es gemeinsame Interessen in der Internationalen Politik?" in *Die Identität der Deutschen,* ed. W. Weidenfeld (Bonn, 1983).
9. I have developed this distinction, inspired by James Q. Wilson's article: "Ronald Reagan and the Republican Revival," *Commentary* (October 1981), in my: "Arms Control and the Politics of Pacifism in Protestant Europe," in *The Western Panacea: Constraining Soviet Power through Negotiation,* ed. U. Nerlich, vol. 2 of *Soviet Power and Western Negotiating Politics* (Cambridge, Mass., 1983), pp. 117-53.
10. See my "The Shifting Foundation," *Foreign Policy,* Fall 1982.

11. See my "Pacifisme et terreur," in *Pacifisme et dissuasion,* ed. P. Lellouche (Paris, 1983).

12. Louis Harris Poll "Security and the Industrial Democracies," November 1983. The Atlantic Institute for International Affairs.

13. Ibid.

14. Harris Poll, as quoted by Alistair Cooke, *Letter from America,* The BBC, 1 January 1984.

15. The Atlantic Institute, Harris Poll.

16. This point is stressed forcefully by J. François-Poncet, "Certitudes et Incertitudes Allemandes," *Le Monde,* 10 November 1983.

17. Kurt becker, "Der Graben wird breiter," *Die Zeit,* 25 November 1983.

18. G. Hefty, "Die Diskussion wird sich um die NATO Drehen. Leinen zu Friedensbewegung und SPD," *Frankfurter Allgemeine Zeitung,* 30 November 1983.

19. This is the hypothesis of P. Lellouche, "Introduction," *Pacifisme et dissuasion,* ed P. Lellouche (Paris, 1983).

20. "NATO: Angriff als beste Verteidigung?" *Der Spiegel,* 21 November 1983. See also R. Halloran, "U.S. Military Ordered to Integrate Plans for Using Nuclear Arms," *International Herald Tribune,* 23 March 1983.

21. This has even been the case, recently, for Stanley Hoffmann. See the exchange in *Esprit,* February 1984.

22. Catherine Kelleher, "Thresholds and Theologies: The Need for Critical Reassessment," in CSIS, *Strategic Responses to Conflict in the 1980s,* ed. W. Taylor, S. Maaranen, and G. Gong (Los Angeles, 1983), pp. 352-57.

23. See K. Feldmeyer, "Atomare Mitbestimung im Bundnis," *Frankfurter Allgemeine Zeitung,* 17 October 1983.

24. See the contributions by C. Kelleher, A. Komer, and J. Record to the symposium mentioned in n. 21.

25. S. Amiel, "Deterrence by Conventional Forces," *Survival* (March-April 1978): 58-63.

26. See, among many others, the periodical *Uberleben-Zeitschrift für alternative Sicherheitspolitik,* particularly the special issue "Alternative Verteidigungskonzepte" 1, no. 3 November 1982.

27. H. Afheldt, *Verteidigung und Frieden* (Munich, 1976), and C.F. von Weizsäcker, *Wege aus der Gefahr* (1978).

28. See a good summary of the discussion by P. Lacroix, "Y a-t-il une alternative à l'actuelle doctrine de défense occidentale?" in *Eviter la guerre?* ed. P. Lacroix (Paris, 1983), pp. 283-300.

29. "Bonn Steht Fest zur NATO-Doktrin," *Süddeutsche Zeitung,* 25 October 1983, and "Wörner lehnt U.S. Gefechtskonzept ab," *Süddeutsche Zeitung,* 8 September 1983.

30. See two excellent reviews: one from a critical point of view von Bredow, "Friedensbewegung und Deutschlandpolitik"; the other from within the movement, U. Albrecht, *Deutsche Fragen—Europäische Antworten* (Berlin, 1983), pp. 97-121.

31. Interkirchliche Friedensrat (IKV), "Europa den Europäern," in *Deutsche Fragen—Europäische Antworten,* ed. V. Albrecht (Berlin, 1983), pp. 165-71.

32. See their contributions to *Deutsche Fragen—Europäische Antworten,* ed. V. Albrecht (Berlin, 1983), as well as Gaus's interview with Peter Brandt

and E. Kindler Bunte in *Ästhetik und Kommunication* 5 (1982), "Wie souverän ist die Bundesrepublik?"

33. See E. Bahr, *Was wird aus den Deutschen?* (Rowohlt, 1982); and G. Gaus, *Wo Deutschland lieqt. Eine Ortbestimmung* (Hamburg 1983).

34. See A. Fontaine, "Le pari de la bonne Allemagne," *Le Monde,* 18 November 1983.

35. See E.P. Thompson, *Beyond the Cold War* (London: Merlin Press, 1982); "We Must Strike Directly at the Structures of the Cold War Itself," *Guardian,* 21 February 1983.

36. R. Bahro, "The Russians Aren't Coming," in *Dynamics of European Nuclear Disarmament,* ed. A. Myrdal et al. (London, 1981) pp. 122-29.

37. "Ein Netz von erheblicher Spannungskraft," *Der Spiegel,* 13 December 1982.

38. For a brief description of this atmosphere of fear in the GDR, see R. Asmus, "Ten Days of Peace in the GDR," *FRE Research,* 14 November 1983. Apparently widespread rumors were leading many East Germans to expect the Soviets to start World War III on the day of the beginning of the Pershing II deployments in the FRG (oral communications).

39. See "Heart of Europe," a special issue of *Le Débat,* December 1983, especially the article by L. Kolakowski and M. Kundera, "L'Europe Centrale, un occident kidnappe."

40. For a good overview, see R. Asmus, "Is There a 'Peace Movement' in Eastern Europe?" *RFE Research,* 2 September 1983. For an elaboration concerning the GDR, see the same author's "Is There a Peace Movement in the GDR?" *Orbis* (Summer 1983): 301-43.

41. See *Taz* (Berlin), 16 May 1983.

42. *Foreign Affairs* (Summer 1983).

43. For information on these groups, see the special report of *END,* Moscow Independent Peace Group, and the New Hungarian Peace Group (1982), and the periodicals *END* (particularly no. 1, December 1982-January 1983), and *Alternative* (particularly the November-December 1983 issue).

44. See *Voices from Prague,* a special *END* report (London, 1983).

45. See R. Asmus, "Neues Deutschland. Points Dissenting Views on Arms Control," R.F.E. Report, 31 October 1983.

46. See Asmus, "Is There a Peace Movement in the GDR?"

47. K. Bölling, *Die Fernen Nachbarn* (Hamburg, 1983).

48. For two excellent reviews of the situation, see E. Kux "Moskaus Nach-Nachrüstung," *Neue Zürcher Zeitung,* 23 November 1983; and V. Meier, "Moskaus Schwierigkeiten bei der Verwirklichung der Gegenmassnahmen," *Frankfurter Allgemeine Zeitung,* 3 January 1984.

49. See my "Moscow and the Western Alliance," *Problems of Communism,* May-June 1981.

50. "Une polémique entre les Soviétiques et le Mouvement Pacifiste Occidental", *Le Monde,* 24 February 1983.

51. *Kommunist,* 12, 1983, quoted in RFE/RL, Sept 2, 1983.

7

THE NORDIC PEACE MOVEMENTS

Niels Jorgen Haagerup

The Nordic region is often considered a specific subsystem in international politics, at least as far as security matters are concerned. Hence it follows that the peace movements in the five Nordic countries may be discussed as a separate entity, apart from the European peace movements in general.

To view the Nordic countries as a distinct region is historically correct in that they have many common features and have close ties to one another, particularly in terms of culture and heritage. This is especially true of the three Scandinavian countries, Denmark, Norway, and Sweden. Today, however, the concept of a separate Nordic entity is changing. The interdependence between the Nordic area and the outside world has grown to a considerable extent, both in the economic and strategic spheres.

The rise of the peace movements in the Nordic countries should therefore be seen (at least in part) in the context of certain local factors, including significant changes in the military environment of the Scandinavian Peninsula (such as the Soviet naval buildup.) At the same time, the NATO double-track decision of 1979 has led in Denmark and Norway to protests similar in nature to those occurring in the Federal Republic of Germany, the Netherlands, and the United Kingdom.

In terms of mass support and organizational structure, the peace movements in the Nordic countries may not loom as large and as efficient as their counterparts in certain other West European countries. Nevertheless, they have a larger following than any previous movements of this nature. In political terms, their impact has been considerable, above all because the Social Democratic parties have to a large extent tried to identify themselves with the general objectives of the peace movements, if not always with their methods. With the Social Democratic parties dominant in the Nordic countries, the broad political consensus on security policy in the three Scandinavian countries is eroding, even if it does not go so far as to threaten Denmark's and Norway's membership in NATO, and the determination of Sweden to maintain a relatively strong national defense as the basis of its non-alignment policy. Still, cracks are appearing and the demands for a Nordic nuclear-free zone, one of the principal objectives of the Nordic peace movements, could conceivably weaken broad popular support for NATO if the Atlantic alliance is closely identified with U.S. nuclear policy.

Before looking at each of the Nordic countries, it seems appropriate to deal first with the area as a whole in an historical framework.

THE NORDIC COUNTRIES IN INTERNATIONAL POLITICS

Geographically, the Nordic countries are at the periphery of the European continent. For several centuries the main political and cultural developments in Europe only sporadically affected them.

Several kilometers south of the present Danish-German border the Eider-Stone was erected in 1671. The inscription on the side facing south ran: "Eidora Romani Terminus Emperii" (here ends the Roman Empire). On permanent exhibit in the Royal National Museum in Copenhagen, it is a reminder that the Nordic countries were never integrated into the Roman Empire. This fact had an important impact upon the separate development of the judicial system of the Nordic countries and probably on the development of social values as well. The closeness of the Scandinavian languages and a common historical heritage give credence to the nation of a separate Nordic identity.

Until late in the eighteenth century, Denmark and Sweden were frequently at war with each other. Genuine feelings of community throughout the Nordic region were not present until strong extraregional pressures began to create them in the latter half of the nineteenth century. By that time, the roles of the Nordic countries had been reduced to those of small countries, and the communal sense emerged in part as a consequence of the political and cultural defense erected against outside pressures. Among the major elements of this development were the creation of Germany as a major nation-state and the expanding power and influence of Russia (and later the Soviet Union.) Two world wars demonstrated the strategic significance of the Nordic area; in World War II Denmark and Norway were directly embroiled, as was Iceland.

It was not until after World War II that more systematic efforts were made to establish political and institutional structures to foster strong regional cooperation in various spheres. The first major attempt concerned defense. Shortly after the start of the cold war, Scandinavian defense negotiations were initiated by the Swedes and found widespread popular support in Denmark and Norway. Finland was excluded from participating because of its strong dependence on its Soviet neighbor. The negotiations failed due to Swedish insistence on strict nonalignment, which proved incompatible with the Norwegian demand for some link to the Western powers.

Attempts were made to bring about a Nordic customs union in the late 1950s, and a more ambitious try at creating a Nordic economic union was made ten years later, at a time when it was still uncertain whether the Common Market would be enlarged against General de Gaulle's persistent veto. Both initiatives were unavailing because in strategic and economic terms the dependence of the Nordic countries on the outside world had grown to such an extent that isolated Nordic solutions were no longer possible. Denmark, Norway, and Iceland have been members of NATO since 1949, and Denmark has been a member of the European Economic Community since 1973. The other Nordic countries have free-trade agreements with the EEC.

The Nordic Council was created as a substitute for the failed schemes for a Nordic defense union and a Nordic economic union. A rather loose framework for regional cooperation in political, social and cultural fields, the council is not a driving force for stronger integration but, rather, an instrument to promote and exploit the several features that bind the Nordic countries together. Regional community feelings remain strong and are frequently utilized consciously or not, as a defense against outside forces.

Even if the Nordic peace movements do not openly appeal to these Nordic community feelings very frequently, they obviously do try to exploit them with the aim of isolating the Nordic countries from European and East-West power politics. The campaign against nuclear weapons—there are none in the Nordic countries themselves—and the demand for a Nordic nuclear-free zone can be seen as a reflection of the traditional Nordic preference for being left outside the rivalries and tensions of other powers. The peace movements thereby keep alive a rather utopian view of politics, one that has always had stronger popular support in Scandinavia than in most other European countries.

THE NORDIC BALANCE

The concept of "the Nordic balance" was originated by Norwegian political scientists more than twenty years ago. It is now widely used, although the concept is more a descriptive term than an operational mechanism. It refers to the interdependence in strategic matters of Nordic countries (Iceland excepted), an interdependence that exists despite the different solutions chosen by each to provide security against the outside world.

When Norway and Denmark joined the Atlantic alliance in 1949 and Sweden decided to remain nonaligned, any idea of a common Scandinavian security policy was given up and is unlikely to be revived. Still, certain features of the security policies of the Nordic countries constitute a system of interdependence. Denmark and Norway chose early on to show considerable restraint in terms of accepting foreign bases or nuclear weapons (nuclear stockpiling) on their soil in peacetime. Finland has moved from total dependence on the Soviet Union to a somewhat more independent line of neutrality in world affairs, even if it continues to give its relationship with the Soviet Union absolute priority in all foreign policy matters. Sweden bases its nonalignment policy on a defense posture that even today remains rather impressive in view of the small size of the Swedish population.

It is generally assumed that changes in one part of this Nordic system could cause changes in other parts. The size of the Swedish defense effort and unilateral restraints by Denmark and Norway as to bases and nuclear weapons, for example, are thus seen to be tied to the relative independence of Finland's position vis-à-vis its large and generally suspicious Eastern neighbor.

In both a formal and real sense, Finnish-Soviet relations are dictated by the Treaty of Friendship, Co-operation and Mutual Assistance signed in 1948 and renewed at intervals. The Finns have themselves belied the popular term of "Finlandization" by their prudent and efficient policy toward the Soviet Union, which has allowed them to develop a more independent policy of neutrality. Surely, the dependence on the Soviet Union and the need to preserve good relations with it remain the cornerstone of Finnish foreign policy. Even so, Finland has managed throughout to maintain a Western style of democracy, and the transistion of Kekkonen to Koivisto marked a further step in the direction of a more independent Finnish posture in international relations.

One cannot state with any certainty that this development was made possible by the Danish and Norwegian stand against foreign military forces and nuclear weapons in the region, but it is at least commonly assumed that a drastic reversal of the Finnish position in the direction of more explicit Soviet control over Finnish affairs could have consequences for such Danish and Norwegian restraints and cause the Swedes to reconsider the terms of Swedish nonalignment policy. It should be added that for decades neither superpower appeared to be interested in interfering with developments in Finland, which has made the region a low-tension area. During the past few years, however, the situation has been eroding, and may now be coming to an end. Soviet military buildup on the Kola Peninsula, the growing significance of the Soviet naval and air bases in the North, and repeated evidence of Soviet submarine activity inside and outside Swedish waters in the Baltic indicate that the whole Nordic area is becoming more directly involved in the East-West and superpower conflict.

THE NORDIC PEACE MOVEMENTS

One can roughly divide the development of the peace movements in Scandinavia into three periods. Between the two world wars, the peace movements were small and sectarian. They consisted for the most part of devoted and sometimes fanatical pacifists who rejected all recourse to arms. Organized in clubs and small associations, they communicated more with one another than with the rest of the community by way of small magazines and occasional pamphlets.

Following World War II the peace movements began to take shape in the early and mid-1950s. Their main effort was directed against nuclear weapons. The Stockholm peace appeal and the movement "No to Nuclear Weapons" had a considerable following. Communist influence was too obvious to be denied and eventually compromised many of the followers at a time when the cold war was at its height.

The peace movement then lay dormant for many years, although several of its leaders were active in other and related fields, for instance the movement against the Vietnam war in the 1960s. When the peace movement developed into the mass movements of the late 1970s and the early 1980s, the survivors of the second stage joined the vanguard of a new generation. They were back on the barricades, reviving their old slogans, fighting the ever-increasing arsenal of nuclear weapons and other means of mass destruction; and campaigning actively against the insidious policies of the great powers, above all, the United States.

For the first time, the peace movements took on grass-roots characteristics. They were almost always sharply left-wing, if not openly or even covertly Communist-oriented. They were and are antiestablishment phenomena. They were related to, but not in all cases identical with, the ecological movements of the seventies. They were one class of several single-issue movements that grew up alongside and outside the political parties, which in many respects proved unable to channel these new waves of protest.

The movements cannot be said to have drawn their leaders from any one particular group, although the role of left-wing intellectuals such as university teachers, schoolteachers, and educators has been particularly influential. Certain priests and a few bishops have also contributed, but always in their role as individuals. Unlike the situation in some other European countries, the churches in Scandinavia play no real role in the peace agitation. This is due both to the existence of the Danish People's Church (state church), which includes the large majority of the Danes (Lutheran), and to the rather indifferent attitude most Danes have to religious affairs and to the churches.

One reason that the Social Democratic parties of Northern Europe have lent themselves so willingly to the general objectives of the peace movements is undoubtedly their anxiety not to be totally outflanked by these new movements. For parties that consider themselves to be progressive and left of center, it is imperative to be able to communicate (and if possible identify) with movements such as the peace movements. For revolutionary or semirevolutionary parties this represents no problem; their whole existence is based on an antiestablishment posture. For parties like the Scandinavian Social Democratic parties, the problem is more complex. Since the 1920s they have had a strong influence upon government policy and have more often that not been in government, either alone or in coalition with other political parties.

The Social Democratic parties are not equally important in all Nordic countries. The party-political structure of Iceland differs from that of the other Nordic countries. It has a Communist party, which at times ranks among the most important parties and is sometimes to be found holding a share of power in the country.

The Finnish party structure is also somewhat different from that of the other Nordic countries. For many years the Social Democrats were looked upon with the greatest suspicion by the Soviet Union, which largely accounted for the party's being unable to play a major role in Finnish politics. It is no coincidence that the longtime presidents Paasikivi and Kekkonen came from the Agrarian, later the Centre, party, which enjoyed a higher degree of Soviet favor. But this has changed. The president is a Social Democrat, and the Social Democrats constitute the largest party in the wide-ranging government coalition.

There are parallels among the three Scandinavian countries in regard to the Social Democratic party in each country. In Norway and Sweden it sometimes commands more than 50 percent of the electorate, and has been able to command an absolute majority in parliament. In Denmark the party is smaller, but thanks to the multiparty system, with at present ten parties represented in the Folketing, the Social Democratic party plays the same important role. It has even more leverage than its counterparts in Norway and Sweden. The Social Democratic party, the Socialist People's party, and the Left-Wing Socialists, constitute about 45 percent of the electorate. The long-established Radical Liberal party has strong pacifist traditions, and has been a faithful supporter of Social Democratic-led governments. The parties of the Left and the Radical Liberal party together normally command a majority in parliament.

When the Social Democrats identify with the peace movements, as has been the case in the early 1980s (at least so far as their fight against the new U.S. missiles for Western Europe is concerned), the conflict between government and opposition is sharpened. In Norway, the center-right government is holding a slight numerical edge over the Social Democratic opposition. In Denmark, the Social Democratic party forms part of the foreign policy majority supporting the center-right minority government, resulting in serious problems for the government when the Social Democrats ally themselves with parties to the left that favor anti-NATO and anti-EEC policies.

In fact, the Social Democrats were in government when the double-track decision was taken by NATO. This was the case in the Federal Republic of Germany, as well as in Denmark and Norway. It is therefore no coincidence that the Social Democratic parties of these countries—and a few others—have switched positions or, as they themselves prefer to call it, stiffened their attitudes toward nuclear weapons in general and the planned deployment of 572 medium-range missiles in Western Europe in particular. It is also a fact that the Social Democratic parties of Western Europe with the notable exception of the French and the Italian Socialist parties have cooperated closely, particularly on issues related to European and international security.

The so-called Scandilux cooperation among Social Democrats from Norway, Denmark, Holland, Belgium, and Luxembourg has had an important effect upon willingness on the part of these parties to be identified with the peace movements. The German Social Democratic party (SPD) and the British Labour party are taking part in the Scandilux meetings as observers. However, the influence of the SPD is incomparably stronger than that of the British Labour party, which years ago moved so far to the left and took such awkward positions with regard to defense, nuclear weapons, and the European Community that it became an embarrasment to most of the other Socialist and Democratic parties of Western Europe.

It is one of the most remarkable features of postwar German history that it is the German Social Democratic party that for several years has exercised great influence upon the attitudes of the Social Democratic parties of the smaller West European countries. This is due not only to the ties that have developed among the Socialists in these countries across the borders; the political stability achieved by the Federal Republic of Germany is widely recognized and respected throughout Europe, and the role of the SPD in this process is appreciated even by many non-Socialist parties.

One may recall that the SPD has traveled a long way from the very critical position toward the rearmament of Germany in the days of Kurt Schumacher to the more responsible position assumed by Erich Ollenhauer, Willy Brandt, and Helmut Schmidt. The fact that the Social Democrats managed to combine an active detente policy with a pro-NATO (first in coalition with the Christian Democrats and later in coalition with the much smaller FDP) policy made a strong impression on Social Democratic parties in other countries and contributed to cementing the support for the Western alliance. Since the SPD-FDP coalition broke up and the FDP switched sides to support a CDU/CSU government in Bonn, the German Social Democrats seem to be moving closer to their position of more than thirty years ago.

It is perhaps conceivable that the peace movements could have made considerable inroads in the other Social Democratic parties of the West European countries of Northern and Central Europe even without the change in the position of the SPD. As it is, the growing opposition to the deployment of nuclear missiles in Europe within the SPD rank and file and the party leadership has given respectability of a sort to similar or even more radical positions taken by other Social Democratic parties that are agitating against the deployment of the Pershing II and cruise missiles.

Because the Scandinavian countries do not have to deal with the deployment issue in their own countries, it is rather surprising that the Social Democratic parties in Scandinavia have aligned themselves with their sister parties in Germany, Holland, and Belgium against the deployment. The campaign against U.S. nuclear missiles is necessarily of a somewhat different nature for the former than for the latter, but their countries, as NATO members, are committed to the double-track decision and the infrastructure costs arising out of that decision. This is where the Norwegian Labour party and the Danish Social Democratic party have tried to put obstacles in the way of Norwegian and Danish coresponsibility for the final deployment, but their opposition to the necessary appropriations came rather late. The left-wing opposition to the Norwegian center-right government was a single vote short, and in Denmark the position of the anti-missile majority affected only that last envisaged slice from Denmark for the construction sites under the NATO infrastructure program, without seriously jeopardizing the program itself.

The Danish government has on several occasions in 1983 been embarrassed by the position of the antinuclear left-wing majority in the Folketing and its demand for an extraordinary meeting of the foreign and defense ministers of NATO to reconsider the deployment of the U.S. missiles. This discomfiture was caused by the peculiar circumstances in which the government has found itself: faced with a hostile majority in certain aspects of foreign and defense policy but not forced by that majority to resign. Thus it has remained in power, partly to offset the effects of opposition to the deployment of missiles in other NATO countries.

The alliance between the left wings in Denmark and Norway and the local peace movements should not be taken to mean that the identification between the two is total. It may indeed be argued that the Social Democrats in Denmark and the Labour party in Norway (the situation in nonaligned Sweden is, of course, somewhat different) remain faithful to membership in the Atlantic alliance. It is worth noting that, in terms of public opinion polls, support for continued Danish and Norwegian membership not only remains strong but is apparently stronger than ever. It seems evident that the public at large does not identify membership in NATO with acceptance of the deployment of nuclear missiles in Western Europe nor with the military posture and foreign policy views of the Reagan administration.

To maintain their credibility with the voters at large, it is important to Danish and Norwegian Socialists that support for NATO remains high even within their own ranks. The opposition to nuclear weapons and the sometimes vocal opposition to various aspects of the foreign policy of the Reagan administration can therefore be seen, in a somewhat paradoxical way, as an attempt to bolster that support by moving away from the more unpopular features of U.S. policy, including the planned deployment of missiles in Western Europe. The fact that the demand for such missiles originally came from Western Europe and that the deployment is based upon a unanimous decision by the NATO countries in 1979 is usually glossed over by referring to such "changed circumstances" as the nonratification of SALT II and the militant anticommunist stand of President Reagan. In addition, by backing the campaign against U.S. missiles and for the creation of a Nordic nuclear-free zone, the Danish and Norwegian Social Democrats are trying to draw attention away somehow from the more extreme demands of several peace movement leaders, such as for unarmed Danish neutrality between East and West.

Membership in NATO remains remarkably uncontroversial in both Denmark and Norway compared with the controversy still surrounding Denmark's membership in the EEC since 1973 and Norway's relationship with the European Community. Seen from the outside, the effect of the Scandinavian Social Democrats' working hand in hand with the peace movements in their countries might seem to be a weakening of the links between these countries and NATO, and certainly current NATO policy. Viewed from the inside, however, the effect may well be, at least for a while, to preserve the widespread favorable attitudes toward continued NATO membership while at the same time rejecting additional nuclear arms for NATO in Europe. This would represent a continuation of the position originally taken in the late 1950s by both countries not to allow nuclear weapons on their soil in peacetime.

Some, perhaps most, of the leaders of the peace movements would definitely like to see the links between their countries and NATO weaken, with the eventual goal a complete break. No doubt they realize that this is by no means a popular demand and they therefore concentrate on exploiting the current antinuclear mood by campaigning against the missiles and for the creation of a Nordic nuclear-free zone. They appear all the more successful to the public because of the Social Democrats' backing, and are apt—for the time being—to soft-pedal their anti-NATO and generally antidefense objectives.

The justification of some Scandinavian Social Democrats to identify with the peace movements is thus not only that they are grass-roots movements but also that they may indirectly contribute to maintaining the popular support for NATO within the parties' ranks. They point out that issues like the neutron bomb, nuclear missiles, and U.S. policy in Latin America tend to undermine that support. There is undeniably some truth in this, although it may well be argued that such tactical and subtle maneuvers are hardly conducive to furthering the public's understanding of vital foreign policy issues. The practical effect has certainly been that the broad consensus on foreign policy is being eroded in both Denmark and Norway.

Whereas the sentiment for continued NATO membership remains strong in both countries, there is no or little corresponding sympathy for the steps that must be taken by the alliance to adjust to the changing conditions of East-West relations and to offset the Soviet military buildup of both conventional and nuclear forces, including medium-range missiles.

This difficulty does not arise in Sweden, although the broad consensus on foreign policy and defense between the Social Democrats and the non-Socialist parties appears to be more fragile than before. Olof Palme, the Social Democratic prime minister, is not faced with any of the nuclear problems existing within the Western alliance. Still, his support for the peace movement stops short of supporting the demands for severe cuts in Swedish defense expenditures. On the other hand, he has publicly sided with the Greek Socialist government in demanding a six-month suspension of the deployment of NATO missiles in Western Europe, a move that is quite remarkable for a nonaligned country's head of government. But Palme is not only the prime minister; he is also chairman of his party and an internationally known leader eager to play a role on the world stage. He wants to be viewed as active in a peace campaign spearheaded by such prominent European Socialists as Willy Brandt, Bruno Kreisky —and Olof Palme.

THE NORDIC NUCLEAR-FREE ZONE

In Northern Europe, the most significant project against nuclear weapons is the twenty-year-old plan for a nuclear-free Scandinavia. Launched by Urho Kekkonen, at that time the president of Finland, it was given new life in Norway in 1980 within the Labour party and supported in Sweden by Palme, both when he was leader of the opposition and when he again became prime minister in 1982. In Helsinki on 1 June, 1983, Palme said: "The basic purpose of a Nordic nuclear-weapon-free zone is to improve the security of the Nordic states. We want to reduce the nuclear threat to the Nordic area. This could be achieved through a combination of undertakings on the part of the Nordic states not to allow nuclear weapons on their territories, either in wartime or in peacetime, and a number of undertakings on the part of the nuclear-weapon states. No threat of the use of nuclear weapons shall emanate from Nordic territory and, in return, the nuclear-weapon powers shall undertake not to use nuclear weapons against us or threaten to use them against us."

The declared aim of the Nordic peace movements is to achieve such a state of affairs. It would be difficult for Norway and Denmark to endorse this aim, given their membership in NATO, whose strategy has not ruled out a first use of nuclear weapons. Indeed, that option is a crucial part of the NATO deterrence strategy and applies to Norway and Denmark irrespective of the fact that these countries have refused to store nuclear weapons in peacetime. To renounce them in wartime would be tantamount to renouncing accepted NATO doctrine and strategy. The Norwegian Labor government appeared to be close to doing just that in 1981 but did not do so. At the same time, the Danish Social Democratic government voiced sympathy for a nuclear-free Scandinavia but did not endorse a particular plan.

When the Danish Social Democrats went into opposition in 1982, they had fewer qualms about Palme's idea. In late 1983 the Folketing adopted a resolution asking the government to work for the creation of a nuclear-free Scandinavia and did so without the approval of the government, with only the Socialists as the Social Democrats' allies. The prior statement by the Social Democratic leader, Anker Jorgensen, that Denmark should renounce nuclear weapons in both peace and war was, however, not explicitly endorsed.

The Social Democratic position, unlike that of the peace movements, is ambivalent. As do the Socialists in some other Western European countries, the party wants to suspend deployment of the U.S. medium-range missiles at least temporarily but has not rejected outright the NATO double-track decision of 1979. The party supports the idea of a nuclear-free Nordic area but has never committed Denmark to renouncing nuclear weapons in both peace and war, or stipulated detailed conditions for realizing such an idea.

It can be said that the peace movements have managed (1) to influence the policies of the Nordic Social Democratic parties; (2) to weaken the earlier broad political support in Denmark and Norway for current NATO strategy; and (3) to create greater confusion about the whole issue of nuclear weapons.

One day in late November 1983, the Danish Trade Union Council called for a five-minute work stoppage to demonstrate for peace and against the deployment of the 572 medium-range missiles in Western Europe. The trade unions are traditionally closely linked to the Social Democratic party. The brief demonstration was another indication that the antinuclear campaign of the peace movements has made deep inroads. The demonstration could also be seen as a Social Democratic gesture to preempt a Communist initiative in the same direction.

In party-political terms the Communist parties of Scandinavia (unlike those of Finland and Iceland) are numerically very weak. Those in Denmark and Norway cannot win even 2 percent of the votes and are therefore not represented in the parliaments. But in the grass-roots movements, the Communists play a much more significant role. This is especially true of the peace movements.

THE DANISH PEACE MOVEMENT

Pacifism has played an important political as well as ideological role in Danish politics. Having lost a significant part of its territory to the emerging Germany in 1864, Denmark was resigned to a policy of neutrality with a built-in bias favoring Germany due to its proximity and preponderant military power. Following World War I, antimilitary sentiments and the formation of a long-lasting Social Democratic-Radical Liberal government coalition encouraged the belief that Denmark could not rely on a national defense for its security.

In the wake of the humiliating surrender to Hitler's Germany in 1940 and the rise of a widespread resistance movement during the five years of occupation, the Danish outlook and position changed. Failing to form a Scandinavian defense union, Denmark and Norway in 1949 became founding members of the Atlantic alliance. The fundamental shift was as much a result of the trauma of the World War II experience as it was a clear appreciation of the Soviet threat and the need to meet it with a strong Western defense. After almost forty years of peace in Western Europe, support for NATO remains high and is even growing. However, the belief in the necessity for a strong defense and a deterrence strategy based upon the possible use of nuclear weapons may be waning, especially among the young and among the political parties of the Left.

But there are also signs that a positive attitude toward defense has taken root. The voluntary Home Guard of Denmark has grown remarkably, for example, especially during the last few years, now comprising nearly eighty thousand men and women. It would be misleading, therefore, to say that pacifist and neutralist sentiments are becoming predominant. More realistically, the postwar consensus on foreign and defense policies is gradually giving way to a polarization between two sharply opposing views, thereby making it possible for the peace movement to appeal to a wider part of the public than before.

The peace movement consists of a vast number of separate and independent organizations, each of which has specific sections of the population as its target. In the early 1980s, such groups as Women for

Peace, Teachers for Peace, Christians for Peace, Journalists for Peace, Workers for Peace, and so forth have sprung up. They join the few long-established peace organizations that have had limited influence and are generally viewed as sectarian. This great diversity combined with unity in demands gives the movement considerable strength and respectability, and makes it impossible to brand all members as Communists or Communist supporters. To work for peace has become almost synonymous with opposing the new NATO missiles, or at least "new missiles in the East and in the West," as it is often expressed. The local groups sponsor a vast range of activities—study groups, seminars, exhibitions, demonstrations—some of which are centrally inspired and organized.

On the national level only two organizations are of any real significance: Cooperation Committee for Peace and Security and No to Nuclear Weapons (NTA).

The Cooperation Committee was founded in 1973, shortly after a peace conference in Moscow in which about thirty Danes participated. Its first public activity was a campaign against the Danish purchase of the F-16 aircraft. The most rapid growth of the organization occurred during its campaign against the neutron bomb in 1978 when many local committees were founded. This development gained further momentum following the NATO double-track decision of 1979.

The central office of the Cooperation Committee is in Copenhagen, and its organizational structure is more hierarchical than is usual for grass-roots movements. According to the committee, it is a nonpolitical organization, aims to cut across party lines, and has representatives from the parties on its steering committees. The dominating faction of its leadership has strong leanings toward the Communist party, a fact that constitutes the committee's strength and its weakness. The strength comes from the high degree of activity and discipline characteristic of well-organized Communists, the weakness from its one-sided view of international politics and of the superpowers.

No to Nuclear Weapons—in its new form—was founded immediately after the NATO decision of December 1979. In November 1979 a small group of individuals had published an appeal to the public that drew much more public support than had been anticipated. In January 1980 the group arranged a peace seminar, the outcome of which was No to Nuclear Weapons. The backbone of the organization consists of many local groups and working committees, each specializing in specific tasks such as campaigning, communication, international relations, and editorial activities. Activities are directed from a central office in Copenhagen, and communication within the organization is maintained through a weekly newsletter. A periodical published about ten times a year addresses the public at large.

No to Nuclear Weapons has all the characteristics of a true grassroots organization: a loose, nonhierarchical structure, individual financial contributions, no formal membership, a rather inactive decision-making procedure, and last but not least, the burning enthusiasm of its members. Many acquired their first experiences with such activities by participation in protests against the Vietnam war in the late 1960s. Many are not Socialists, but their overall attitude toward security matters is radical in the American sense of the term. There is an apparent affinity between activists in No to Nuclear Weapons and such organizations as Greenpeace, for example.

Concerning attitudes toward international politics, there are apparent similarities between No to Nuclear Weapons and the British CND movement, although the Danish movement is less openly anticommunist. The organization tries very hard to uphold a nonaligned position in its criticism of both superpowers, and one of the points of action concerns relations to nonofficial peace movements in the Socialist countries.

The immediate goal of all components of the Danish peace movement is to prevent the deployment of NATO medium-range missiles in Western Europe. On this subject there is complete unity, which tends to direct the attention of the movement toward cooperative measures with German and Dutch organizations.

The current missile issue, however, cannot remain the focus forever. It is clear that in the not-too-distant future, the campaign for a Nordic nuclear-free zone will move to the center of the scene. Should the Danish peace movement succeed in acquiring as much broad popular support for the zone as has been the case regarding the missile deployment, difficulties could arise for maintaining official security policy in Denmark.

The above-mentioned resolution by the Folketing in November 1983 reinforced the antinuclear posture of Denmark—to the embarrassment of the center-right government of Poul Schlüter—and committed the government to "work actively" for a Nordic nuclear-free zone. The general elections called in Jauary 1984 came about, however, because of disagreements over the government's economic policy, not the security policy. The nuclear issues were frequently brought up during the brief campaign by the Social Democrats and, even more, by the extreme left-wing parties, who identify wholly with the peace movement but apparently without influencing the election results.

The coalition government—four center-right parties—strengthened its position and continued in office, but it did not obtain a majority. It may be in a better position to carry out its economic policy thanks to the support of the small Radical Liberal party, but that same party is likely to be on the side of the left-wing parties in their antinuclear and antimissile initiatives in the Folketing.

A confrontation over Denmark's continued NATO membership appears unlikely. Opinion polls indicate popular support for NATO is as strong as ever, and the peace movements seem to have had little if any impact upon it. But new initiatives by the antinuclear and antimissile majority in the Folketing could eventually erode the credibility of Denmark's NATO policy—paradoxically against the wishes of the majority of people and even of the MPs, but undoubtedly to the satisfaction of most leaders and organizers of the various peace groups.

THE SITUATION IN NORWAY

The similarities between the situation in Denmark and that in Norway arise mainly in the fact that both countries are NATO members. In geographical and strategic terms, the situations in the two countries are very different.

The growth of the Soviet navy, the activities of Soviet naval forces in the North Atlantic and the Norwegian Sea, and the military build-up in the Kola Peninsula have all contributed to making the northern parts of Scandinavia a highly significant strategic area. Fully aware of the implications of this development, both the previous Norwegian Labour government and the current conservative government (now a center-right government) have taken steps to ensure the maintenance of Norway's close connections with its Atlantic partners. Whereas Denmark is obviously closely connected to the Continent and therefore with Germany, Norway relies more on its Atlantic ties for its security.

As in Denmark, pacifism has run deep in parts of Norway. German aggression in 1940 and the subsequent war and occupation weakened the traditional pacifism of certain segments of the population, however, and Norway took the lead in 1949 in bringing about Norwegian and Danish membership in the Atlantic alliance.

Norway, like Denmark, has refused to accept the permanent stationing of allied forces and nuclear warheads on its soil in peacetime. Fundamental adherence to NATO remains unshaken, although certain neutralist tendencies have begun to emerge to the left of the Labour party (and even within the party) and in some other parties as well. Such developments do not constitute a serious threat to Norway's continued membership in NATO at this time, but they have encouraged the growth of the peace movement and support for a Nordic nuclear-free zone.

The Norwegian Labour government agreed in 1980 to the construction of facilities for the prestocking of heavy equipment for planned allied (mainly U.S.) reinforcements in times of war. A solid political majority was behind this decision, which nevertheless caused some discontent within the party. Because Norway also complied with the NATO decision to increase real defense expenditures by 3 percent annually, the broad consensus for Norwegian security based on NATO membership was somewhat strained, especially following the NATO double-track decision. This may, in part, explain the rise in Norway of the debate on the nuclear-free zone plan, something that until then had not had many proponents.

The Norwegian peace movement has gained support for its view that the prestocking agreement and the role of nuclear weapons in NATO's strategy tend to increase the risks for Norway in case of war. This view has been further reinforced by frequent criticism of the Reagan administration's foreign policies.

The new peace movement thus broadened the appeal of the former (and much more sectarian) Norwegian peace organization, which had as its targets the very existence of armed forces and their potential role within NATO strategy. The Norwegian Peace Committee is generally weaker and less influential than the corresponding Danish Cooperation Committee.

The peace movement has been reinforced by the important role played by a few influential intellectuals, such as Professor Johan Galtung, the founder and for many years the leader of the Peace Research Institute in Oslo. The security debate in Norway has been and remains lively, with an unusually large number of books being published on the subject, some of a very high standard.

As a mass movement, the Norwegian peace movement is unlikely to impact as strongly as corresponding movements in Germany and the Netherlands. However, the Labour party has to a large extent associated itself with the general objectives of the movement. This has had less dramatic effects than in Denmark, because the Norwegian government parties have a majority—if only a very small one—in the Storting. But although some kind of uneasy compromise may exist in Denmark between the government and the Social Democrats (unless the government is forced to resign), the situation in Norway is characterized by a permanent confrontation (between the Labour party and the present government) over a number of security issues. This could in turn affect the security policy of a later Labour government, as the broad consensus on foreign policy and security issues continues to be eroded.

THE ICELANDIC PEACE MOVEMENT

Iceland is as much "Nordic" as the four other Nordic countries—and in certain respects even more so. By virtue of its geographical location and its small population (less than 300,000 people), however, its position is very different from that of the other Nordic countries. Like Denmark and Norway, it is a founding member of NATO. It has no military forces of its own, and its strong economic dependence on fishing forces Icelanders to look at their foreign relations (including security policy) in terms of safeguarding the vital fishing industry. This has twice brought the country into a conflict of interest and an open clash, particularly with the United Kingdom. For a time during the so-called cod wars, Iceland's continued NATO membership appeared uncertain. Actually, the tense situation gave rise to an unusual demonstration in favor of participation in NATO among the population at large.

Although Iceland appears to be firmly tied to the Atlantic alliance, the U.S. base at Keflavik has been the target of certain groups, including peace activists. During several periods, above all in 1956 and 1971, opposition to the base was strong even among some of the political parties, nearly resulting in the abrogation of the Keflavik agreement. Protest against maintaining the base has since lost its momentum, due not so much to recognition of the strategic significance of the base (in view of the Soviet naval buildup) but to Iceland's preoccupation with its internal economic problems. The peace activists do not seem to have the same broad popular base that obtains elsewhere, and have even less support within the political parties. On the other hand, debate on foreign policy and security issues is rather limited for a number of reasons, and there is some sympathy among Icelanders at large for the view that the nation should try to keep out of superpower conflicts altogether. The fact that opposition to the Keflavik base has waned can probably be taken as a sign that the Icelanders realize there is little they can do to fulfill their wish to remain aloof from world affairs.

THE SITUATION IN SWEDEN AND FINLAND

A wide range of peace activists can be found in Sweden and Finland. If they appear to be less antiestablishment than those in

Denmark and Norway, it is mainly because NATO policy is not an internal source of dissenson, even if the nuclear policies of the Atlantic alliance are the object of some criticism from Finnish quarters. In general, however, Finland maintains a lower profile than Sweden in international relations, thereby offsetting its need to give absolute priority to friendly relations with the Soviet Union. A discrete Finnish silence in regard to the United States is the rule about matters on which Sweden may be particularly open and forceful in its criticism, such as the Vietnam war.

The peace movement strongly supports the idea of a Nordic nuclear-free zone, but because this policy is also favored by the governments concerned, there is no reason for conflict on the subject.

Insofar as the peace activists agitate against the Swedish military defense, they have found only a limited response among the public. It is generally recognized, and is rarely a point of contention among the political parties, that as a precondition of Sweden's nonaligned position in international affairs, it must maintain a reasonably strong military posture. Over the past few years, the discussion has tended to focus on the difficulties in maintaining an independent posture and a sufficiently strong one, above all in view of the Soviet naval buildup in the Baltic and elsewhere.

The activities of Soviet submarines in Swedish waters (including the much publicized episode in 1981 when a Soviet submarine ran aground just outside an important naval installation) have hardly enhanced arguments of the pacifists, who are advocating unilateral disarmament. The fact that the submarine carried nuclear arms, according to Swedish sources, made mockery of the plans for a Nordic nuclear-free zone, for there are no nuclear weapons in the Nordic area aside from the Soviet ones. Still, debate on the nuclear-free zone has been resumed and given new emphasis, above all by Palme, who is also known for the proposal (from the so-called Palme Commission) to establish a nuclear-free zone in Central Europe from which all battlefield nuclear weapons would be withdrawn.

There is simply no history of true pacifism in Finland. The peace campaigns are for the most part in full accordance with the official policy of the government, although groups both inside and outside the Social Democratic party are critical of the measures that have been taken to reinforce military defense. In the view of these groups, security policy should be implemented by political, military, means. However, unlike Denmark and Norway, Finland has no peace movement of any significance to challenge the basic security policy. Although "Finlandization" has become the more or less accepted term for a country's taking Soviet views and wishes into account in its conduct of foreign relations, the achievements of Finland's foreign policy are remarkable compared with those of other countries bordering on the Soviet Union.

CONCLUSIONS

The peace movements of the Nordic countries are too diversified, too different, too decentralized, and, especially in Denmark and Norway, too large to be under tight Communist leadership and domination. They are, in many respects, true grass-roots movements but the Communist influence is nevertheless considerable in terms of organization and political objectives.

The most important aspect of the peace movements, whether Communist-influenced or not, is the amount of respectability they have gained. In political terms, this is manifest in the willingness of the Social Democratic parties to identify themselves—not always fully—with the immediate objectives of the peace movements: opposition to the deployment of the 572 NATO missiles in Western Europe, and the establishment of a Nordic nuclear-free zone.

The state of East-West relations will remain the vital factor in gauging the degree of influence the peace movements have on the foreign and security policies of the Nordic countries, including the two NATO members, Denmark and Norway. The weakening or perhaps even the eventual dissolution of the alliance (or the Danish and Norwegian membership in it) may be the real target of the leading peace movement organizers, but unless additional, more serious isues jeopardize the future of the Atlantic alliance, this goal is likely to remain elusive. Nevertheless, in the current political climate, the Nordic peace movements have turned out to be important enough to cast serious doubts upon the continued consensus on foreign policy, which has been, until recently, a distinct feature of Scandinavian politics.

BIBLIOGRAPHY

Agrell, Vilhelm. *Om Kriget inte kommer.* Lund, 1981.
Alfsen, Erik. *A Nordic Nuclear-Free Zone.* END-papers, 5 (Spring 1983).
Apunen, Osmo. "Finland's Treaties on Security Policy." *Cooperation and Conflict* 15, no. 4 (1980).
Barth, Magne, ed. *Forhandslagring i Norge.* Oslo, 1980.
Bodin, Katarina. "The Nordic Countries and the Prospects for a Nuclear Weapon Free Zone." *Contemporary History,* no. 1386 (July 1981).
Moller, W. Christmas. Fredsbevaegelsen og Europas sikkerhed. *Dansk udenrigspolitisk Arbog* 1980.

Dansk sikkerhedspolitik og forslagene om Norden som kernevabenfri zone (with an English summary). Copenhagen, 1982.

Einhorn, Eric S. *National Security and Domestic Politics in Post-War Denmark.* Odense, 1975.

Espersen, Mogens. "Die dänische Verteidigungspolitik in der achtzieger Jahren." *Europa Archiv,* no. 10 (1980).

————. *Fredsbevaegelsen—folkelig bevaegelse eller sovjetisk redskab.* Copenhagen, 1983.

Grepstad, Jon. *The Peace Movements in the Nordic Counties.* END-papers, 4 (Winter 1983).

Gunnarson, Gunnar. "Icelandic Security Policy: Contexts and Trends." *Cooperation and Conflict* 17, no. 4 (1982).

Garden, Hugo. *Atomvaben-debatten.* Copenhagen, 1983.

Haagerup, Niels Jorgen. "Die europäische Sicherheitsdimension." *Europa Archiv,* no. 9 (1983).

Hakovirta, Herta. "Finland in the International Tension and Detente." In *Norden og den internationale spaending.* Copenhagen, 1982.

Heurlin, Bertel. "Danish Security Policy." *Cooperation and Conflict* 17, no. 4 (1982).

Heurlin, Bertel, ed. *Kernevabenpolitik i Norden.* Copenhagen, 1983.

Holst, Johan Jorgen, ed. *Five Roads to Nordic Security.* Oslo, 1973.

————. *Norwegian Security Policy for the 1980's.* NUPI-report no. 76. Oslo, 1982.

Jacobson, Max. *Finnlands Neutralitätspolitik zwischen Ost und West.* Wien, 1969.

Lindberg, Steve. "The Illusory Nordic Balance. Threat Scenarios in Nordic Security Planning." *Cooperation and Conflict* 16, no. 1 (1981).

Maud, George. "The Further Shores of Finlandization." *Cooperation and Conflict* 17, no. 1 (1982).

Militaerkritisk magasin Forsvar, nos. 2, 3, 4, 5, 8, 9, 10, 11.

Mottola, Kari, ed. *Nuclear Weapon and Northern Europe.* Helsinki, 1983.

Mouritzen, Hans. "Prediction on the Basis of Official Doctrine." *Cooperation and Conflict* 16, no. 1 (1981).

Noreen, Eric. "The Nordic Balance: A Security Concept in Theory and Practice." *Cooperation and Conflict* 18, no. 1 (1983).

Ofstad, Harald and Mariene Ohberg, eds. *Var rost en makt. Nordiske inlagg i fredsdebatten.* Sodertalje, 1982.

Petersen, Gert. "Das Alpha and Omega einer europäischen Friedensordnung." In *Deutsche Fragen—Europäische Antworten.* Edited by Ulrich Albrecht et al. Berlin, 1983.

————. *Om nodvendigheden af dansk fredspolitik.* Copenhagen, 1982.

Petersen, Nikolaj. "Danish Security Policy in the Seventies: Continuity or Change?" *Cooperation and Conflict,* no. 3/4 (1972).

——. "The Alliance Policies of the Smaller NATO Countries." In *NATO after Thirty Years*. Edited by Lawrence A. Kaplan and Robert N. Clawson. Wilmington, Del., 1981.

Security in the North: Report from a Seminar in Iceland (April 1982). Copenhagen, 1982.

Sjaastad, Anders C. "SALT II: Consequences for Europe and the Nordic Region." *Cooperation and Conflict* 15, no. 4 (1980).

Yearbook of Finnish Foreign Policy, 1982. Helsinki, 1983.

8

THE PRECARIOUS PEACE IN EUROPE: THE WEST IN SEARCH OF A POLITICAL STRATEGY

Uwe Nerlich

Europe has been without war for almost forty years. Few generations in the course of European history have been allotted a similar experience. In the dwindling numbers of those who were exposed to the violence unleashed in World War II, the memory of that catastrophe is fading. But discussion in the West today is determined no less by an increasingly common forgetting of how this peace that has since prevailed in Europe came to be, and of what has been the foundation for its precarious nature as much as for its beneficial permanence: a state of tension that succeeding generations are clearly finding increasingly difficult to endure. In the early eighties, that is after twenty years of attempted detente in relations with the Soviet Union, the Western public is becoming more aware than at any time since 1945 of the precarious nature of this peace.

DETERRENCE AND NEGOTIATIONS AS METHODS OF DEALING WITH THE SOVIET UNION

If the present peace in Europe is perceived as precarious, then one reason is surely that neither the deterrence policy nor the negotiating policy of the West, as they have been practiced in the past twenty years, can prevent a growing preponderance of Soviet military power in Europe. Current trends are pointing to a situation in which the progressive limitation of Western potential for action at both levels will change overall the dominant political structures in East-West relations. It remains for future Western policy to give deterrence as well as negotiating policy toward the Soviet Union an orientation that points the present development dynamic in Europe in another direction, or else to look forward to a totally changed situation as the consequence of current policy. The former will in any case amount to a strengthening of the U.S. role in Europe, the latter to a strengthening of the Soviet role. There is no third way.

At this point, however, there emerges not only the question of what margin still remains for Western deterrence and negotiating policy. The much more fundamental question arises—in fact squarely in the political arena at the beginning of the eighties—whether the past deterrence or negotiating policy toward the Soviet Union is not ultimately part of the problem rather than part of the solution, i.e. whether the methods of dealing with the Soviet Union have not decisively contributed to the precarious nature of the present peace in Europe.

Thus, many view this precariousness as grounded in the fact that deterrence is based on nuclear means for whose military use no policy could answer, or that negotiations with the Soviet Union take place under antagonistic conditions that preclude lasting agreements in the generally accepted interests of the West. Since the end of World War II, the one as well as the other criticism have been raised again and again. But beyond the question of the validity of the one or the other, deterrence *and* negotiations have been the two essential forms of dealing with the Soviet Union at every stage in this period; the Western community would neither have borne the burden of a full defense capability nor have sustained an antagonism without communication with the other side. The insulation of military power within society, a product of possessing nuclear weapons on a large scale and being able to dispense with far larger standing armies accords as much with the needs of Western democracies as does the search for consensus and compromise, which is embodied in negotiations even under antagonistic conditions. [1]

Yet the political acceptance of nuclear deterrence in the West—in the Soviet Union this presents no problem—was all the greater, the less the relation of forces was seen to require an actual employment. Thus, in the period of clear U.S. superiority in strategic weapons (and of an emerging French nuclear potential) in the first half of the sixties, the nuclear discretionary power could become truly the most important formative element in the political consolidation of the Western alliance. In similar fashion, negotiations with the Soviet Union permitted the broadest political consensus in the West *eo ipso* at a time when Moscow evidently saw incentives for real cooperation, that is, in the period 1971 to 1973. In the West these negotiations were assessed at that time as the genesis of new political structures in relations with the Soviet Union.

The Soviet Union has never failed to recognize the political dividends represented by strategic superiority and the potential of broad Western negotiating initiatives for the domestic and alliance policies of Western countries. Moreover, a strategic superiority of the West, even if it was designed simply to counterbalance the far greater capability for military action of the Soviet Union, had to lessen the political consequences of Soviet military power and aggravate any Soviet attempts to secure advantageous political tides against Western intervention. In precisely this way the Soviets regarded broad, consensus-based negotiating initiatives from the West as a constraint on Soviet potential for influence on the policy of Western countries, which called for shifting priorities and opportunities for playing off Western countries against one another; such initiatives also represented an aggravation of the Soviet attempt to shield Eastern Europe sufficiently from progressive political penetration by the West. The Soviet responses to these situations were simple. [2] In the one instance they accorded with the trust in military strength that is rooted in Russian tradition; in the other they met the need, peculiar to the regime, for depoliticization of all processes.

In the world after 1945, nuclear deterrence and negotiations between antagonists were thus for the West the lesser evil compared to the full buildup of military defense capability or an abandonment of diplomacy, and yet the conventionalizing of both would have been all the easier the more superfluous deterrence were to become [3] or the more negotiations were to result in a political order that did not call for surrendering Western values. Soviet policy has aggravated the one as well as the other, for the idea of leaving to their own dynamic critical political processes in the West that are accessible to it is alien to Soviet policy, but it would not have been able to do this so successfully without the political ambivalence that has characterized nuclear deterrence as well as negotiations with antagonists on the policy of the West in the past several decades.

THE AMBIVALENCE OF NUCLEAR DETERRENCE

The ambivalence of nuclear deterrence has had a political impact in three ways. First, in contrast to defense capability, which proves itself in conflict, nuclear deterrence requires a credibility that is supported by "important segments of public opinion," [4] while at the same time it is conditioned by an irresolvable value conflict, namely, that a moral order is to be secured by means that within this moral order itself admit of no ethical justification for their use. Second, nuclear deterrence was to offer a cheap substitute for traditional armed forces, though at no time could they be linked with the goal of maintaining a monopoly. Nuclear weapons thus had the function of "absolute" weapons vis-à-vis traditional forces or toward nonnuclear-weapons states. At the same time, however, nuclear deterrence was fundamentaly conditioned from the start by a nuclear arms rivalry that continually had to limit their effectiveness as "absolute" weapons, yet that evoked nuclear threats that, proportionate to their anticipated effectiveness, compelled a self-deterrence.

There are two consequences grounded in this ambivalence. First, nuclear deterrence—following the classical logic of *summa jus, summa injuria*—leads to a situation wherein nuclear rivals must not only reckon with the adversary's potential once a conflict has developed but, because nuclear weapons are operational with little preparation, find themselves under a constant threat, which gives rise to a common interest in avoiding a catastrophe. At the same time, however, nuclear deterrence provokes a mistrust that results from the realities of nuclear rivalry and that precludes the consensus that would be needed to sustain an agreeable reduction of this mutual danger. [5] From this situation there results—this is the second consequence—a constraint on communication with the nuclear competitor; this constraint demands tacit or even formal agreements, although the inherent difficulties of nuclear disarmament [6] increasingly disclose that diplomacy not only cannot keep pace with the nuclear rivalry but—what is more, because of the inseparable connection of nuclear deterrence with conventional imbalances—is running into increasingly narrow limits in disarmament of traditional forces in Europe. [7] A substantial reduction in the Western deterrence potential would necessitate a dismantling of the conventional superiority of the Soviet Union in Europe, which it is in fact designed to counterbalance, whereas the Soviet Union has at least counterbalanced precisely the nuclear superiority of the West so as to increase the political and, potentially, the military impact of the conventional disparity.

The third way in which the ambivalence of nuclear deterrence has an effect consists in the fact that nuclear deterrence—especially in view of the primary strategic and geographic distances between the two world powers—was designed to protect third powers, namely, in Western Europe, but as the nuclear rivalry progressed, the United States was more and more threatened itself, and so the deterrence protection of third powers has increasingly established a common interest with the Soviet Union that necessarily and repeatedly entered into a state of tension with protective functions and their political implications. At the same time, the nuclear rivalry opened up increasingly catastrophic prospects in the event of a breakdown of deterrence in Europe, which then in Western Europe met with a growing interest in agreement between the world powers or even in direct communication with the Soviet Union about the nuclear rivalry.

THREE POSSIBLE APPROACHES IN WESTERN SECURITY POLICY

Three fundamentally different lines of development open up for future security policy, namely, continuity, change through accommodation, and the attempt to restructure relations with the Soviet Union.

POLITICAL REALISM AS MANDATE: MERE CONTINUITY?

A simple continuity of the deterrence policy of the past decades will lead to a progressive decline in deterrence effect, for an inadequate implementation becomes all the more momentous the more persistently the Soviet Union seeks to deny NATO options through further, directed arms buildup. Similarly, the continuity of a negotiating policy that is essentially subordinated to the purposes of internal political crisis management will become less and less capable of keeping limitations of Soviet power on the agenda, much less achieving them, because the policy is under internal pressure for results and, in view of the steadily deteriorating balance of military forces, it will cease to have any disposable military bargaining quantity. Time and again in the seventies the Soviet Union has lauded as a politcal success the fact that its increasing military strength compels the West to negotiate. Should the divergence in the development of the military balance of power steadily grow wider in the eighties, then further negotiations will lose all perspective in the West, for any result would, because of the altered starting points of the two sides, only make the situation worse. But that too would then—as a consequence of the policy of the seventies—constitute a political success in Soviet eyes. Thus it is true of both methods of dealing with the Soviet Union that sheer continuity in the process will steadily weaken the state of Western security. In the case of a procedural linkage of the two methods, as is undertaken most explicitly thus far in the so-called NATO double-track decision, they will still reinforce each other's negative effects under such circumstances.

CHANGE THROUGH ACCOMMODATION

At present this continuity—and this is the second line—is jeopardized, primarily in Western Europe, where deterrence is regarded more and more as a threat and not as protection, and where negotiations as such are called for but in fact are viewed rather as a variant to unilateral self-denial. In such conceptions deterrence and diplomacy in dealing with the Soviet Union are replaced by sheer good conduct—on the expectation that accommodation will bring about beneficial changes internally as well as externally. Such a position is most prominently encountered in countries with more weakly defined political cultures, such as the Federal Republic, where the growing awareness of insufficient national identity coincides with the crisis of those international ties—and of the policies sustaining them—that over the past three decades have caused a strong national identity to be perceived as rather a disturbing relic. Such positions are also found most prominently in the younger generation, which has internalized the realities of Soviet policy in a period in which the suppression of freedom movements under the shadow of military power has been characterized initially as "accidental" (Michel Debré after the intervention in Czechoslovakia) and ultimately as "necessary" (former Chancellor Schmidt after the imposition of martial law in Poland) for the sake of maintaining world peace. [8]

These notions of change through accommodation are often imperturbably accompanied by the conviction that the previous policies of deterrence and negotiations have failed. Of course, they have not come together to form any new policy, but they have taken shape in a movement that can in any case refer to the obviously increasingly precarious character of the current peace in Europe and at the same time itself aggravates a continuity of past security policy or further precipitates negative consequences. In this general area there are also attempts to give such good conduct a political perspective. Not coincidentally, they link up with the European security plans proposed in the fifties in common with the United States, then in the sixties by de Gaulle at the expense of the United States, and aimed at a European security order. [9] Yet while there was in the grand designs of those early years not only the unquestioned protection from the United States but, as a conceivable possibility, a restructuring of political and military relations by way of a give and take, the current conceptions of a "Europeanization" of Europe rely solely on the notion that European good conduct ultimately accords with the self-interest of the United States and the Soviet Union in such a way that, to take up once again Kennan's formulation from the fifties, the "burden of bipolarity" is lifted from the European continent. [10]

What the relationship of the two global powers would look like following such a disengagement in Europe; what sort of structure

Europe could assume; why the Soviet Union should give up the sole attribute of a global power, its military strength or the political uses of that strength; or how it is that the United States, which is claimed to be dangerous as a guardian power under present circumstances, nevertheless should guarantee, out of self-interest, the political process of transition to a Europeanized Europe—all this is never even addressed within such conceptions. If this movement might be applauded for its again recalling European interests—in contrast to the narrowed perspectives of the last twenty years—interests that demand a different European order from that which is possible under the conditions of simple continuity in the relations with the Soviet Union in Europe, then Stanley Hoffmann's dictum on the constraints of the bipolar stalemate applies once again to these conceptions: "Dreams, then, are the victims of this system." [11]

It is precisely the growing internal weakness of the Soviet empire, from which the advocates of change through accommodation expect ever-greater areas of tolerance for political evolution, that will make it more difficult for any Soviet leadership in the foreseeable future to do without the preponderance of military means. Not only would this raise the power question in Moscow like no other process, it would also accelerate the imperial downfall that the Soviet leadership hopes to ward off precisely, as the most recent Polish experience shows once again, by means of the presence of overwhelming military forces. On the other hand, those advocates of change through accommodation who under present circumstances make the world-power role of the United States the fixed starting point of their criticism and who even tend to equate the United States with the Soviet Union nevertheless assume that the interests of the United States as a world power would shield Western Europe even under altered circumstances. Just such a view fails to recognize that the internal stength of the United States during the past decades, in which the United States has played the role of world power practically against its will, has derived again and again from forces that have pressed for precisely a limitation on this world-power role and that follow the U.S. impulse to avoid "European entanglements." It is primarily the will of Western Europe for cooperation with the United States that binds the United States in Europe and that thus upholds a defense of Western Europe by the United States. The question of what would be in the interests of the United States as a world power no more offers a key to future U.S. conduct than it is the key to the moral conduct to the European countries that advocate European change through accommodation to basing their own politics on anticipated world-power politics of the United States, which at the same time they never tire of stigmatizing. [12]

Thus one would have to say that a mere continuity in approach—in deterrence as in negotiating policy—will not be sufficient for maintaining a state of relative security, while a simple renunciation of both—good conduct instead of policy—will not change the current situation in the direction of "Europeanization" of Europe but, rather, will only accelerate the progressive deterioration that would be expected, just more slowly, if the past security policy were to continue. Just how precarious the current peace in Europe is thus substantially depends also on whether there is a third way for the future development of Europe. Such a way would be contained—rather than in continuity or renunciation—in a *fundamental change* of both the deterrence and the negotiating policy of the West.

DETERRENCE AND NEGOTIATIONS: POTENTIAL FOR A REORIENTATION?

An alteration of Western deterrence policy would have to proceed from four considerations. First, the Soviet Union, mainly over the past twenty years, and quite unlike the West, has built up its armed forces steadily and systematically, [13] and it has oriented this buildup always to military necessities, which then as such corresponded to political purposes as well. Because Soviet force planning has always given priority to conventional forces, [14] in the sense that nuclear weapons were designed to free these forces for their military effectiveness by means of effective counterdeterrence or actual neutralization of Western escalation capabilities, Soviet strategy has never been reduced to a deterrence strategy, which creates in fact far lesser military demands. Hence, the Soviet Union has not needed to make any distinction between war-fighting and deterrence requirements, but for that very reason the dilemma inherent in nuclear deterrence in the West has necessarily been heightened: The more the West's dependence on nuclear weapons increased under conditions of Soviet counterdeterrence, the more the political necessity of keeping deterrence requirements as vague as possible—for reasons of alliance consensus as well as political consent in the individual allied nations—came into conflict with the military necessity of being able to confront the Soviet Union at least with selective responses. Selective denial of Soviet military options capable of inhibiting Soviet decisions on the use of military force is thus equated in the political realm of the Western public with war-fighting capability; and the more selectivity, which then poses specific military demands too, proves to be the only possibility for Western deterrence capability, the more opinion in the West tries to sidestep the Soviet Union's increasing military capability for action by appealing to the political nature of deterrence, which is then presented in abstractions such as "equilibrium."

As long as the strategic potential of the United States—this is the second consideration—offered Western Europe a credible deterrence security, it was less necessary than under present conditions to base deterrence on strategic requirements. This applies especially to nuclear weapons in Western Europe, which by their ranges (more than 70 percent under 170 kilometers, 60 percent under 25 kilometers), yields, operational flexibility, and vulnerability were never established for purposes of flexible response as long as they were seen only as release mechanisms for the employment of strategic weapons. However, as specific deterrence functions would increasingly have to be considered for nuclear weapons in Western Europe too, all the more there is a repetition in Western Europe of the view propounded time and again by advocates of a minimal strategic deterrence in the United States since the beginning of the sixties: One relies—and not infrequently in the name of liberal morality—on the deterent effect of the apocalypse. This would then, however, serve to produce more and more simply self-deterrence, while measures for selectively denying Soviet options—which then in an emergency situation would result in a dramatic reduction of the effects, were deterrence nevertheless to fail—are characterized as destabilizing.

Instead of selectively exposing to military risk sensitive components of the offensive potential upon which the Soviet leadership would have to be able to rely in a conflict situation—e.g. its reinforcement potential—and in so doing reducing the collateral damages as far as possible by limiting the weapons effects, one raises to a principle of deterrence the notion that the Soviet leadership must be convinced that the West does not possess the means for a controlled and selective employment, as if this sort of limited response potential against a powerful offensive potential could appear as a provocation. Confidence in the irrationality of deterrence is thus accompanied by the fear that everything that makes a conflict more controllable and could deny the Soviet Union options also makes the conflict more probable.

This peculiar non sequitur has meanwhile had a long history, even though politically it has never gained as great an importance as in the present opposition to the modernization of the NATO TNF disposition in some of the countries of Western Europe. Here too anxiety is a poor counselor. The apocalyptic expectations designed to preserve the peace are seen endangered by the creation of selected response potentials, yet at the same time it is believed that with these potentials, designed to make the Soviets' use of military force more difficult, not only the conflict but also the occurrence of the apocalypse becomes more probable. Policy thus becomes a prisoner of the irrationality it first sought to employ only manipulatively.

But the military requirements of deterrence—this is the third consideration—not only are sacrificed to an absurd and even, by its own self-image, essentially irresponsible deterrence policy but are also subjected to all manner of political calculation. It is precisely the apparent arbitrariness of the requirements that result from pursuing deterrence only as a threat of irrational behavior that from the start misleads into abandoning any systematic conception as to which response potentials could constrain the use of Soviet military power and allowing other, i.e. political, considerations to predominate. Thus in the fifties primarily the cost factor was seen. As Dean Acheson later expressed it, Eisenhower's deterrence policy was determined above all by Treasury Secretary Humphrey. [15] In the early sixties, requirements of political control of nuclear weapons as a means to integrate the alliance were paramount. Finally, in the seventies, nuclear decisions increasingly became a function of internal political requirements, while in the conventional area easing the economic burden and symbolic foreign policy were decisive. In other words, nuclear deterrence was increasingly subjected first to express purposes of arms control policy, then to immediate internal political requirements of staying in power, while in the area of conventional defense, what was generally decisive were labor policy, export interests, protection of national industries, foreign policy considerations within the EC, institututional self-interest (for instance of the branches of armed forces), but, above all, budgetary deliberations.

If at present defense requirements are in many places subordinated politically to arms control, this is really nothing fundamentally new. Military requirements have been treated as such only in exceptional cases. However, there is a new element in that placing defense policy as such expressly and systematically, at the very least de facto, under the primacy of arms control is viewed as politically advantageous. Such a policy is grounded in the maintenance of a broad affirmation of the Atlantic alliance and in this sense is a legitimation of defense efforts, but the not surprising consequence is a progressive change of the alliance's function. Contrary to current interpretations, the alliance was still understood in the Harmel Report of 1967 primarily as a defense alliance; in the meantime, however, it appears, at least in many West European member states, rather, as the proper framework for the furtive transformation of East-West relations, in which framework then military requirements are presented only in abstract and suitably manipulable fashion as exigencies of equilibrium. For its part, this kind of policy has diminished even further the loss of political consent that a deterrence strategy must carry. As Stanley Hoffmann has put it, the more military power "is clouded by political calculations and restrictions, the less can the population understand, much less approve of, its use." [16]

This practice of Western deterrence policy is thus characterized by a far-reaching continuity in the validity of the strategy of flexible response and, at nearly all points, an inadequate implementation of this strategy. [17] Meanwhile, it has thus—this is the fourth consideration—fostered a development that has allowed the strategy of flexible response, which provided for a most limited and controllable possible employment of military means for countering acts of aggression, to degenerate de facto into a strategy of delayed massive retaliation. This in turn, in the sense of self-fulfilling prophecy, has given way to increasing vagueness of requirements in the face of the lack of credibility of a strategy of massive retaliation. This lack of credibility had already been amply manifested by the criticism of the strategy in the fifties but had, in logical fashion, contributed to the discrediting of the strategy of flexible response and thus in many ways to that of nuclear deterrence in general.

As long as Western policy does not simply accept the military predominance of the Soviet Union in Europe and rely on Soviet self-restraint, it is not a matter of alternatives to the strategy of flexible response but, rather, of its practical implementation. This is not simply a question of the availability of military means but, rather, primarily of the conceptions and procedures for such response modes as jeopardize, through selective action, the success of a Soviet offensive without unavoidable apocalypse, to the extent that this can turn the balance in Soviet decisions about war and peace. This restriction of rational Soviet decision possibilities for the political use of military power constitutes the purpose of deterrence.

POLITICAL DIMENSIONS OF EFFECTIVE DETERRENCE

The restriction of rational Soviet decision making is decisive for the direct effectiveness of the Western deterrence capability. However, it does have consequences—and this is even more important politically—for the political behavior of the states affected in peace and crisis situations. This behavior is largely determined by the assessment of virtual wars, to use Albert Wohlstetter's expression, that is, by the way the possible course and outcome of a diversity of conceivable conflicts are calculated by potential parties to conflict. [18] This is a critical determinant of the political utility of military power in peace and crisis situations. Accordingly, it also defines the probability of the occurrence of conflicts. Were the effectiveness of Western deterrence to decline in such a way that all the potential parties to conflict in the West, or at least those in Western Europe, come to the conclusion that all virtual wars will assume a catastrophic outcome, then this would mean that a defense of Western Europe by the United States is not possible, at least in the eyes of the West Europeans. In Soviet eyes this consequence would then represent a critical political success in the Soviet Union's policy toward the West, if the Soviet leadership appraises the risks of possible conflicts even higher still.

A strengthening of Western deterrence that diminishes the feeling of defenselessness in Western Europe thus has immediate consequences in peacetime and in times of crisis, consequences that will have a decisive influence on the structure of future political relations in Europe. This accords with the basic idea behind the strategy of flexible response: to respond to actual or virtual conflict situations in the most appropriate way possible, i.e. with the means for controlling a limited conflict and with possibilities for raising the stakes that could give the other side cause for desisting. The main alliance conflict is not simply a relatively improbable conflict situation, nor does preparing for it mean that one can then respond appropriately to all limited conflict situations. Deterrence requirements can thus be directed to very limited tasks; not taking them into account, however, would allow an originally limited conflict situation to escalate rapidly into an impending catastrophe.

From these considerations it follows that deterrence remains a political necessity, that the strategy of flexible response provides a conceptual framework for the perception of future strategic tasks, but that the past practice of deterrence policy requires a fundamental change. This practice must be geared primarily to the *military* requirements for controlling limited conflicts that endanger the viability of Western Europe as well as for selectively denying Soviet escalation possibilities. In contrast to Soviet practice, this would still not represent any comprehensive war-fighting capability, but it would perhaps strengthen the effectiveness of Western deterrence considerably. These military requirements can be derived not from abstract assumptions about equilibrium but, rather, from an evaluation of typical and potentially decisive limited virtual conflicts and the strategic options the Soviet Union has at its disposal in the given conflict.

In this perspective it is crucial that security policy be more than a function of domestic politics; domestic stability is considered a precondition. It helps not to overburden the system. However, it is also suggested that a perspective of eventual change in East-West relations is needed to prevent a steady erosion of the consensus on which security policies rest in the West. A mere continuation of established policies is considered unlikely to generate the support needed to stay in the competition. Prudent restoration of established policies, their more efficient implementation, and, to a degree, their decoupling from domestic politics are thus viewed as insufficient to maintain political stability. While return to centrism is welcomed, its endurance is not taken for granted. Moreover, previous policies have proved unable to prevent disarray precisely because their pursuit in a continuous process made them more susceptible to domestic manipulation. On the other hand, a mere restoration of established policies is regarded as indifferent toward profound changes in strategic and political circumstances as well as toward new opportunities that may open up, in particular within the Soviet orbit.

The imperative then in this perspective is a strategic approach in which policies are chosen on various levels with a degree of orchestration so as to approach the objective of eventual change via intermediate achievements. As Henry Kissinger has put it, the "moral imperative of our time [is] to keep open the prospect, however slim, of a fundamental change." [19] This, then, would require attempting to change Soviet leadership perceptions through *considered moves* of how successful Soviet policies of denial of Western options and of exploitation of Western weaknesses are. It would also require not simply the renewed continuity in the pursuit of policies but the restoration of political and strategic options for the West.

This approach is demanding as compared with recent practice. It is meant to deal more constructively with the Soviet Union, yet it is loaded with uncertainty. It assumes a change in the conduct of relations with the Soviet Union. It will not escape from the myriad of constraints that in the final analysis reflect the basic fact that "each generation is permitted only one effort of abstraction; it can attempt only one interpretation and a single experiment, for it is its one subject." [20] Even with Pierre Hassner's dictum in mind that "every period is by definition a time of transition," [21] the West is to be seen at a crucial juncture. The crucial issue is what political systems in the

West can bear, and what kinds of relations with the Soviet Union are needed to cope with Soviet power. In other words, Western security policy has to determine how much of an "abstraction" is affordable and needed, and to what extent this can be shaped by governmental policies toward the Soviet Union.

RELATING COMPETITION AND COOPERATION IN WESTERN POLITICAL STRATEGY

Political judgment on how competitive and cooperative policies toward the Soviet Union ought to be related can differ widely, and these divergencies are right in the center of political controversies between and within the United States and Western Europe. Under these circumstances a more refined conceptual framework for what constitutes a two-track approach needs to be developed or made more explicit than is embodied in documents like the Harmel Report, which tends to be an instrument of polemics or apologetics rather than a set of guiding principles for actual policies. [22]

It is noteworthy that the concept of a two-track approach was used originally to characterize the way in which high policy and trade policy were separated *within* the Atlantic alliance to keep the latter "suppressed" by regulatory mechanisms and thereby prevent it from intruding into high policy: "The establishment of rules governing international trade permitted trade issues to be discussed and resolved in their own realm without intruding into other areas of policy; it created what might be called a two-track system, with trade issues traveling along their own track, not interfering with traffic elsewhere." [23] In its original version it thus was a management approach to maximize advantages or at least increase efficiency on the two main levels of interaction within the Atlantic alliance: security policy and international economics. Using leverage on one level to induce favorable responses on the other was the exception to a rule that regarded the two-track system as a means for traffic regulation.

Undoubtedly, this management version of the double-track approach has often played a role in policies toward the Soviet Union to protect narrow interests that were confined to particular activities on a given level. The record of Western arms control policy provides abundant examples. Traffic regulation, however, can be, and sometimes is, seen to serve longer-term objectives that are not confined to one level of activity. What this means is that the mere continuity of one line of activity by which solutions are deliberately sought in a narrow framework that does not relate to other levels of activity can get associated with expectations of eventual outcomes in other areas that are desirable but cannot be addressed or at least are not seen to be susceptible to more direct approaches. In this management version of the double-track system, be it with or without associated long-term expectations, interference or mutual reinforcements between different action levels are assumed not to matter. Thus complementarity is not an applicable criterion in this case, however wrong actual judgments about the separability of the levels may turn out to be.

In retrospect, it has been obvious for years that the double-track system as a mere management device no longer works *within* the alliance. Trade issues time and again have become politicized in ways that affected security policy one way or another. This is another way of saying that the Atlantic alliance ceased at some point to function as a sufficiently homogeneous system in order to allow this kind of traffic regulation. However, if the double-track system does not work within the alliance it may seem futile to expect that it could function in East-West relations. Issues are bound to get politicized on all levels, no matter how strong the interest in dampening them may appear to be in the West. Moreover, conditions in East-West relations characteristically keep changing. The result is that interference between various levels of activities in East-West relations *is* a frequent occurrence, just as mutual reinforcement or increased leverage that can be applied to other levels is desirable in this kind of environment. Complementarity is thus a built-in requirement in multilevel Western approaches toward the Soviet Union. It is the political environment that makes it imperative.

What, then, are the essentials of the environment within which the West has to develop political strategies toward the Soviet Union? While Western political strategies are susceptible to modes of emphasis that vary along with domestic and other conditions, these are the fundamentals that have to be recognized or can be ignored only with penalties:

- *Political antagonism* between the Soviet Union and the West that is considered a basic condition for the maintenance of the Soviet system and that can be muted only along with internal changes of the Soviet power structure.
- *Division* of Europe and in particular Germany that exists under two conditions: the dividing line separates two different sociopolitical systems under conditions of continued political antagonism, and the division could prevail only under conditions of massive Soviet military presence in Eastern Europe. The result is an unprecedented

military confrontation in Europe and an unprecedented division of a state in terms of both competing sociopolitical systems and military confrontation.

* *Nuclear confrontation*, which, basic political and strategic asymmetries notwithstanding, has become an intrinsic element of East-West relations.

* *Some cooperation* that is necessitated and characterized by the unique conditions of nuclear confrontation and political antagonism in a divided Europe.

* A *Soviet long-term political strategy* that exists in the European context with these essentials: It is designed to change political structures gradually and to get accepted different structures of East-West relations in Europe that would imply different relations between Western Europe and the United States and inside Western Europe. It tries to channel the long-term process of change by employing two issues—extended deterrence and the division of Germany—to expand influence while shielding Eastern Europe to the extent possible. It is meant to maximize political advantages on all levels by confining the political competition to the military level and by inducing the West to subject the competition to an arms control regime that not only creates asymmetric restraints but is conducive to the structural change the Soviet Union is aiming at. However clumsy Soviet approaches often turn out to be—at times almost so as to become a Western last resort—they are orchestrating policies on various levels. In fact, this is comparatively easy not only because of Soviet decision patterns but because all policies are expected to serve a common set of objectives—with allowance for tactical variations or expected bonus effects. The distinction of competitive and cooperative policies does not make sense from a Soviet perspective because all policies are seen as competitive, but cooperation is seen as a way to induce structural change and expand influence, which requires Soviet commitments to cooperation where the Soviets cannot always hope to control outcomes, pending on how demanding Western cooperative policies are. There is thus little sense in describing Soviet approaches to the West in terms of the double-track paradigm. [24]

* *Strategic leverage* for the West that is modest in scope. The easiest road to move on has been that of exercising nuclear restraints or self-limitation and recognizing aspects of the political status quo, but in either respect the West has reached limits in the course of the last two decades. Still, U.S.-West European relations are the one area where Western concessions could invoke Soviet political responsiveness, yet this is precisely where Western governments have more reason than ever to abstain. Other than that, there are only two ways to exercise direct political influence. One is by providing

incentives, e.g. in the economic field; the other is by using the appropriate agents of change or stability as the case may be. Here the Polish situation has both reduced hopes and opened up alternative approaches.

- *Different roles* to be played within the Western alliance to protect national interests, to assume different responsibilities, and to maximize influence through appropriate division of labor.
- *A differential of global perspectives* within the West, with the United States facing the Soviet Union on a global scale, although the chances of both to influence outcomes in many areas may shrink, and facing countries like West Germany that want a degree of regional stability to be protected, although this cannot be separated from the global competition.
- *Domestic polarization* over how to deal with the Soviet Union in most Western countries, and often in ways that can importantly decide who gets access to power or stays in power.

These are elements inherent in the European situation that any political strategy has to reckon with somehow. Political strategy of the West can change any of them, but it has not created any nor could it do away with them. For example, cooperation is a European fact of life. What political strategy can or should consider is which purposes cooperation ought to serve in which way. Political strategy may be negligent of some aspects or try to get mileage out of changing the emphasis within this set of conditions. The less Western approaches are confined to muddling through, the more they will require strategic decisions.

The strategic issue, then, is which objectives the West ought to pursue through what kind of mix of competitive and cooperative policies and with what kind of interrelationships between the various levels of action. There is some mix of competitive and cooperative policies. Levels have to be related somehow. Most important, without political objectives as to how relations with the Soviet Union ought to be changed within some time perspective, no political strategy is feasible.

From the Soviet point of view all cooperative policies are regarded as competitive policies, and the choice of types of cooperation is determined in terms of competitive risks and advantages as the Soviets see them. [25] At the same time the Soviets' political strategy requires them to wage the political competition essentially by engaging the West in a military competition and then letting the West compete under an expanding arms control regime that without seriously constraining Soviet military power is widely viewed in the West as a vitally important part of East-West cooperation. In other words, the Soviet Union aims at reducing the competitiveness in East-West relations as perceived in the West to the lowest possible degree, reinforced by the "sanitized" political impact of growing military power on political behavior in the West.

As is the case for the Soviet Union, for the West, competition in East-West relations means both denial of disruptive options and inducement of political change. For the Soviet Union the competition is most promising if and when the West perceives it essentially as a military competition with cooperativeness spreading across the spectrum so as to blur Western perceptions of the nature of the competition. However, for the West it must mean the opposite: denial is the most immediate task simply because the Soviet Union is increasing military pressure on the West and the distribution of disruptive options is heavily and increasingly weighted in the Soviet Union's favor. This needs to be qualified in two ways.

First, Western military responses ought to be designed to minimize the political instrumentalities of growing Soviet military power, which stem not simply from intimidation and the potential for blackmail but from structural consequences within the West of a successful Soviet effort to deny NATO's strategy as the basis for military alliance cooperation. [26] At the same time they ought to deny the most possible uses of Soviet military power: the more the Soviet Union can hope to control escalation, the greater the Soviet capacity to limit war on Soviet terms and thus to consider war as a way to pursue political objectives that are by definition limited. The least likely thing the Soviet Union would invite is a Western military response in terms of a NATO-base case. Minimizing the growing Soviet military challenge in terms of both its political instrumentality and its potential role in limited war is the most immediate task before the alliance.

Second, defense policy and military strategy ought to be part and parcel of a long-term Western approach that reduces the role of military power in the evolution of political structures on the Continent and in other areas affected by the East-West competition. In other words, the approach should be seen, as it was by many in the fifties, as a holding operation, not an end in itself. Defense and nuclear deterrence are likely to remain perennial tasks simply because it transcends human imagination that forces of unprecedented size and power will simply disappear. But the nature of the competition in East-West relations will have to be shifted away from a narrow military competition. Successful military denial efforts are an essential prerequisite and arms control can be used as a means to bound the military competition, although the past record of Western arms-control policies offers little encouragement. In fact, arms control thus far has been part of the problem rather than the solution. It has made the task of military denial more difficult, yet has perpetuated the "fixation on external security" [27] that it was meant to mute, if not to discontinue. The way arms control has worked, it has served the ends of Soviet military and above all political strategy precisely because it made Western military responses even more difficult, while narrowing the competition further to the military level and reducing cooperation largely to arms negotiations. Once more Florence Nightingale comes to mind: "Whatever hospitals do, they should not spread the disease." Arms control thus should be supplementary also in practice [28] to defense efforts and to foreign policy toward the Soviet Union, as distinct from the dominant role arms control has increasingly played in both defense policy (e.g. the double-track decision) and foreign policy (emphasis on "military detente").

Military denial thus is the most indispensible part of Western competitive efforts, although with or without negotiated arms agreements an element of cooperation is part of it. To be successful, Western efforts that could interfere with chances to broaden the competition and induce political change may be needed. In fact, given the short-term nature of the military denial task and the long-term nature of political change, the former could be seen as foreclosing the chances for the latter. However, it is both in terms of regenerating political support and pursuing the competition across a much broader range that mitigating this kind of tension is of vital importance. The answer should not be to reduce denial efforts needed for the sake of vaguely specifiable long-term political effects but to define the denial effort as part of a long-term strategy of political change. This in turn may allow a better choice of military response options in the near term.

To meet Soviet political strategy and pursue Western long-term political interests, the important thing is to broaden the competition and to bring Western political and economic strength into play. This does not mean economic warfare or the mere propagation of Western values. The essential thing is to understand the political roles of cooperation in the enduring competition with the Soviet Union. From a Soviet point of view the ideal situation would be if Western willingness to cooperate would spread across the spectrum *and* lose its competitive character; this would provide maximum competitive advantages for Soviet cooperative policies. For the West it is essential to engage in a widening range of cooperation both perennially to rebuild public consensus and to create conditions for political change; it is equally important to understand that cooperation with the Soviet Union always has to be part of the competition. This must be so to deny the Soviets competitive advantages from cooperation and to design cooperative policies so as to fit long-term objectives of political change. This means that cooperation has to be genuine and increasingly substantive. But it must also be part of the West's political strategy of competition.

What this would suggest is that current disjunctions of competitive and cooperative policies hardly reflect Western political interest. Both require solutions that are responsive to the challenge or the opportunity as the case may be. But if Western political strategy is one of competing through denial *and* cooperation, Western policies that are pursued as part of this political strategy will always be mixed in character.

The broader the range of the competition, the more difficult it is to associate policies with different "tracks" or levels of activity. It may be worth recalling that the need for some kind of a double-track concept resulted from earlier developments that led to the indefinite postponements of political issues of East-West relations. This resulted in peripheral strategies that one hoped would gradually achieve what direct diplomacy no longer was expected to achieve. This began in 1956-57 and became an irreversible fact of international life when Kennedy firmly shifted to a peripheral policy. Arms control was to become one of the tools for peripheral policies, and it did not come as a surprise that what was regarded peripheral in the West with a view to a long-term process of change was soon discovered as a central issue area by the Soviet Union. The logic of this development then was bound to be that peripheral strategy eventually became the central strategy for the West as well. [29]

It is only in this context that something that was described later as the double-track approach became desirable and found its expression in the Harmel Report. The West was left with different kinds of long-term policies that could easily interfere with one another. To separate them and give each a purpose of its own, yet within a framework that made military security a precondition for political long-term solutions and political order the eventual rationale for a sustained military effort, made sense under the circumstances. However, the implicit disjunction of actual policies is as arbitrary as the subsequent disjunction of competitive and cooperative policies.

There are two requirements that a refined double-track concept should meet. It should assume a high degree of continuity or a marginal need for conceptual change with regard to major policies of denial and cooperation, and it should be defined in terms of a different disjunction of policies: the basic distinction should be between direct policies of denial and indirect policies of political change.

While policies of denial tend to be associated with a sense of urgency, they always have long-term implications. Conversely, policies of change depend on long-term processes that are hard to control, but desirable long-term outcomes can easily be foreclosed by inconsiderate instant actions. This was where many in the United States and in Western Europe differed most profoundly in 1982. The cleavages already tend to be forgotten, but underlying them is a basic difference in foreign policy orientation between the United States and West European countries: the United States not only carries the main burden of policies of denial, but is also basically committed to a static view of European affairs oriented toward the status quo, whereas European countries are more geared toward processes of change the more they are affected by the European partition. Typically, West Germany is least ambiguous in this respect, whereas its neighbors would want to square the circle, i.e. to overcome the partition, yet without loosening controls on West Germany.

Under these circumstances the major Western allies have to agree on a *modus vivendi* that could serve as a substitute for long-term objectives for how to restructure Europe. Without future efforts to strengthen NATO's defense, such strategies will be based on weak political foundations. Yet, with a more common notion of what the alliance does agree upon, processes in Eastern Europe and in other parts of the Soviet empire may in fact turn out to be reinforced by precisely this Western consensus. European peace continues to be precarious, but eventual Soviet political success could result only from Western failure to cope with the secular challenges Soviet military power and policies of expansion are posing.

NOTES

1. The first point is especially true of the United States, which has traditionally gotten by with small volunteer armies and which after 1945 would have found itself confronted with far greater tensions and demands of social control in the absence of nuclear deterrents and in the face of steadily growing military strength of the Soviet Union than was already the case under the actual conditions of the forces. Cf. Morris

Janowitz, *The Last Half-Century: Social Change and Politics in America* (Chicago, 1978), pp. 190ff., 205-17.

2. The Soviet striving for strategic parity, resulting in de facto superiority in times when the U.S. potential was essentially frozen (second half of the sixties) and when the United States was seeking to make relations with the Soviet Union more stable politically (early seventies), had to lead almost mechanically to the political crisis of nuclear deterrence in the West. In the same way, Soviet negotiating policy after 1973-74 was careful to avoid the impression of a consensus-building in East-West relations that Western countries could profit by, as it gave prominence to the routine continuity of the negotiations and denied the West as much as possible—except in the highly opportune case of the Federal Republic—opportunities for dramatic negotiating initiatives.

3. This has been expressed in the aperçu of I.I. Rabi that the nuclear weapons race will be eliminated "when people get bored with it" (quoted in Smith, *Doubletalk*, p. 36).

4. Cf. William W. Kaufmann's classic analysis of the credibility of nuclear deterrence in Kaufmann, ed., *Military Policy and National Security* (Princeton, 1956), p. 20.

5. This was a decisive factor on both sides right from the beginning of the nuclear rivalry. Cf. Barton J. Bernstein, "The Quest for Security: American Foreign Policy and International Control of Atomic Energy, 1942-1946," *Journal of American History,* 60 (March 1974): 1003-44; as well as David Holloway, *Entering the Nuclear Arms Race: The Soviet Decision to Build the Atomic Bomb, 1939-1945,* Wilson Center Working Papers, No. 9, (Washington, D.C., 1979).

6. A substantial reduction of nuclear weapons *can* increase instability. An agreement on radical reductions, which both sides view as designed to increase security, must therefore proceed basically from a common assessment of the differing strategic requirements, something that in previous dealings with the Soviet Union has not been within the realm of the possible.

7. Kennan recognized early on this structural consequence of nuclear deterrence and its inherent bipolarity as he still expressed the hope that if the burden of bipolarity were lifted from the European continent, then the political significance of armed force would also decline. George F. Kennan, *Russia, the Atom, and the West* (New York, 1957), pp. 88ff.

8. Former Chancellor Schmidt in an A.R.D. television interview from Guest-row in the GDR on 13 December, 1981.

9. Cf. Charles R. Planck, *Sicherheit in Europa. Die Vorschläge für Rüstungsbeschränkung und Abrüstung 1955-1965* (Munich, 1968), pp. 109ff., 156-219.

10. As a plea for such a policy of Europeanization, cf. Peter Bender, *Das Ende des Ideologischen Zeitalters. Die Europäisierung Europas* (Berlin, 1981), especially the final section ("Europa und die Zukunft: vier Stufen der Europäisierung"). Still, Bender seeks only to offer a "direction," not to submit a plan. Accordingly, it is of lesser consequence that certain issues remain open, that is, when current structures of European

security are to be given up and under what conditions the two world powers, the Soviet Union in particular, are to be expected to leave Europe essentially to itself. In this way, this remains romantic policy, policy without a discernible view of the future conditions, much less strategies that are to take European development in the desired direction of "Europeanization."

11. Stanley Hoffmann, *Gulliver's Troubles, or the Setting of American Foreign Policy* (New York, 1968), p. 55.

12. In this regard, however, the Latin-European Communist parties show a greater realism than is found in the left opposition of the SPD/FDP government in the Federal Republic. Cf., for instance, the statements by Santiago Carrillo in *Eurocommunism and the State* (Westport, Conn., 1978), pp. 108-9, 170-71.

13. In this period, what Albert Wohlstetter at the end of the fifties had formulated as a hardly realizable deterrence requirement for the West became a matter of course for the Soviet Union: deterrence as "a stable, steady-state peacetime operation." "Delicate Balance of Terror," *Foreign Affairs* 37 (January 1959): 219. The steadiness of the Soviet Union's military efforts is underscored by the constancy in the rates of growth of defense expenditures, although the amount of defense expenditures does not permit any direct conclusions about the force buildup.

14. The sole exceptions, which then proved to be politically costly, were the attempts by Malenkov in the mid-fifties and then above all by Khrushchev from the end of the fifties up to the 22nd Party Congress of the CPSU in 1962 to rely more heavily on nuclear deterrence (probably also under the impress of Eisenhower's "New Look" policy) and to reduce Soviet conventional forces substantially.

15. Dean Acheson, *Present at the Creation. My Years at the State Department* (New York, 1969), p. 934.

16. *Force in Modern Societies: Its Place in International Politics,* Adelphi Papers, No. 102, The I.I.S.S. (London, 1973), p. 6.

17. This strategy has been in effect in the United States since 1961–62, and in NATO since 1967. Because of its greater conventional demands, it was rejected at first by most West Europeans; later, in the main by France. Paradoxically, an adequate implementation of this strategy was impossible at first for lack of sufficient conventional forces, while the nuclear potential of the United States and NATO was increased more with a view to general nuclear responses, that is, comprehensive nuclear strikes, without selectivity requirements; then in the seventies substantial though insufficient improvements were undertaken in the conventional realm, but at the same time most attempts to develop more selectivity and flexibility for nuclear responses, without which a strengthening of conventional capabilities ultimately produces nothing, were discredited politically as steps toward a war-fighting capability. Cf. here also Uwe Nerlich, "Theatre Nuclear Forces in Europe: Is NATO Running out of Options?" in *NATO—The Next Thirty Years,* ed. Kenneth A. Myers (Boulder, Colo., 1980).

18. The concept is designed to express what is envisaged in more or less explicit power calculations of national policy as the outcome of possible conflicts. In this way it has been formed roughly analogous to the

concept of virtual motion, which in mechanics serves to make equilibrium problems solvable by treating dynamic problems as if they were static.

19. Henry A. Kissinger, *White House Years* (Boston, 1979), p. 1255.
20. Henry A. Kissinger, *A World Restored: The Politics of Conservatism in a Revolutionary Age,* Universal Library ed. (New York, 1964), p. 332.
21. Pierre Hassner, *Change and Security in Europe. Part I: The Background,* Adelphi Papers, no. 45, The I.I.S.S. (London, 1968), p. 1.
22. Double-track policies have been tried before, in particular in the early seventies, but they never met their own prime requirement: continuity of the process, i.e. the very thing suggested by the track metaphor. This relates to changed circumstances (as in the United States after Watergate) or to changing contents, as the fate of the so-called Harmel Report would suggest. While the report had called for a long-term effort toward political solution as the only condition that would obviate to a degree the need for military security, the NATO studies on which the report was based (in particular the so-called Schutz-Watson Report on political East-West relations) had established nonrecognition of the GDR as a basic precondition. It took only a few years until this condition had changed without ever reconsidering the principles on which the Harmel Report was founded. It thus shrunk to mean essentially that complementarity exists between whatever mix of cooperative and competitive policies a government would see fit.
23. Richard N. Cooper, "Trade Is Foreign Policy," *Foreign Policy* 9 (Winter 1972-73): 19.
24. As Kenneth Jowitt has pointed out, security and economic policies can serve the same Soviet structural objectives in a differentiated way. Faced with continuous choices between claims of hegemony and equality, economic policies at times are emphasized on the Soviet side to pursue structural objectives without raising issues of inequality (see Kenneth Jowitt, *Images of Detente and the Soviet Political Order* [Berkeley, 1977], p. 15). But again this is different from what is understood to be the double-track approach in a management sense. This is so in spite of the fact that for a long time the two-track system (which might have induced a similar approach on the Soviet side), did work within the Atlantic alliance. However, it was precisely the primacy of military cooperation within the previous Atlantic two-track system that reinforced Soviet interest in trying to confine the political competition essentially to the military level.
25. The implications of this for the prospects of mutual benefits vary according to how the nature of Soviet competitiveness and its limitations or universality is assessed in the West. On one extreme the Soviet economy is regarded essentially as a mobilization base and economic cooperation is thus in principle weighed as support for Soviet military objectives. On another extreme Soviet stakes in survival are considered in terms of a commonality of vital interest so as to expect essential self-restraints on Soviet military power a feasible objective of arms control, whatever competitive purposes both military power and arms control are meant to serve in the Soviet calculus.
26. See Phillip A. Karber's seminal study on the conventional arms competition in Europe in Uwe Nerlich, ed., *Soviet Power and Western*

Negotiating Policies, vol. 1: *The Soviet Asset: Military Power in the Competition over Europe* (Cambridge, Mass., 1983), chs. 1, 6.

27. Helmut Schmidt, *The Balance of Power* (London, 1971), p. 258.
28. Typically the double-track decision of December 1979 was based on a set of guiding principles the most important of which was that arms control should supplement defense, not substitute for it. Similarly, the now-famous Harmel Report was based in part on a study headed by Foy Kohler that explicitly stated that arms control should supplement policies of political change and not become a substitute for foreign policy, something that was openly reconfirmed in the Reykjavik Declaration of December 1968.
29. In a way the *modus vivendi* achieved in the early seventies can be regarded as a second indefinite postponement *(Ausklammerung)* of political issues with military and eventually economic detente as the predictable result, yet under circumstances where in each instance Western options were at a low point.

9

PACIFISM IN THE NETHERLANDS

Frans A.M. Alting von Geusau

In writing this chapter I have drawn from several studies, completed and/or published earlier:

- *"Die Niederlande und die Modernisierung der Kernwaffen," Europa Archiv* 37, no. 2 (January 1982).
- *Power Over Man and Peace among Nations.* To be published by the Ethics and Public Policy Center, Washington, D.C.
- *The Security of Western Europe. A Handbook.* To be published by Sherwood Press, London.

ABBREVIATIONS

CSCE   Conference on Security and Cooperation in Europe
CPSU   Communist Party of the Soviet Union
LRTNF   Long-Range Theater Nuclear Forces
NATO   North Atlantic Treaty Organization

On 19 August 1977, the Dutch Communist daily newspaper *De Waarheid*—Dutch for *Pravda*—launched an initiative for a broad popular campaign in the Netherlands against the planned introduction of "enhanced radiation reduced blast warheads" for U.S. NATO forces in Western Europe. Among the listed leaders of the campaign were representatives of a variety of parties, professions, and churches. It soon became clear that the Dutch Communist party had taken the initiative in the organization of the campaign, known as Stop the Neutron-Bomb.

The campaign was not a specifically Dutch affair. Three weeks earlier, on 30 July 1977, a Tass statement had called for a campaign against the neutron bomb. The World Peace Council, the most important international Communist-front organization, had already decided on an action-week against the weapon, 6-13 August. On 8 August twenty-eight Communist parties had issued a declaration calling upon all Social Democrats and Christians to take action against this "barbaric weapon."

The well-organized campaign in the Netherlands proved successful beyond expectation. Within months, with the help of hundreds of local action cells, over a million signatures were collected. In March 1978, the Dutch government informed the United States that a majority in parliament found production of the neutron weapons undesirable. The committee known as Stop the Neutron Bomb henceforth called itself the Cooperative Stop the Neutron Bomb/Stop the Nuclear Arms Race. The campaign against the neutron bomb thus marked the resurgence of pacifism and antinuclear protest in the Netherlands.

The Soviet-inspired campaign apparently fell on a fertile soil of rising fear of nuclear war, concern about deteriorating East-West relations, and growing irritation over the lack of progress in nuclear arms-control negotiations. For the Netherlands in particular, two other coinciding events may explain the sudden resurgence of pacifism and antinuclear protest. One was the launching by the Dutch Interchurch Peace Council (IKV) of its campaign "Help Rid the World of Nuclear Weapons, Starting with the Netherlands." The other was the formation, after a long governmental crisis, of a weak center-right coalition government of Christian Democrats (CDA) and Liberals (VVD), which constituted a small and unreliable majority in parliament. [1]

PACIFISM AND INTERNAL POLITICS

THE DUTCH INTERCHURCH PEACE COUNCIL

Concern over nuclear weapons is no new phenomenon for the Christian churches in the Netherlands. The synod of the main Protestant church had published its first pastoral letter on war and peace in 1952. In the early sixties, attention focused increasingly on the problem of nuclear weapons and the so-called nuclear arms race.

Unofficial reports on the issue were published by the other main churches; the report published in 1965 by the Dutch branch of the Catholic peace movement *Pax Christi* on peace in the atomic age also reflected the concern expressed worldwide by the Catholic church through the papal encyclical *Pacem in Terris* and the Second Vatican Council. It was, however, the synod of the main Protestant church that opened a new chapter in 1966, with its pastoral letter pronouncing "a radical no against nuclear weapons." Shortly thereafter, initiative was taken to form the Dutch Interchurch Peace Council, the IKV. In the following years the IKV became the ecumenical cooperative organization of nine denominations.[2] Under its own authority, the IKV was to:

- study problems of war and peace;
- stimulate awareness within the churches and inform on such problems;
- recommend appropriate actions to interested persons;
- conduct discussions with government and other policymakers; and
- assist church authorities in formulating their viewpoint.

For about ten years, IKV members focused on discussion and information among themselves and with the various churches.

The launching of the 1977 campaign "Help Rid the World of Nuclear Weapons, Starting with the Netherlands" marked an important change from discussion to agitation. According to the IKV's secretary-general (since 1974), the new campaign was to fulfill three conditions: (1) it was to have a specific aim; (2) it was to become a movement to mobilize the masses; and (3) it was to unsettle parliament and exert pressure for alternative security policies.

The specific aim was to terrify people by making them aware of the danger of nuclear war, showing them what "system" the country belonged to, where nuclear weapons were stored, and what new weapons were being produced. On this basis the masses were to be mobilized to protest against the development of deployment of specific nuclear weapons, first the neutron bomb and later the cruise missiles.[3] To unsettle parliament—particularly the center Christian Democrats with their strong links to the churches—the churches themselves were to be brought in. Strong pressure was exerted and continues to be exerted on official church bodies to give their moral blessing to the campaign slogan. For the same reason, it was considered necessary to present the slogan as the product of serious scientific research on alternative methods to control nuclear arms. The

IKV's essentially pacifist and unilateralist message was concealed in the alleged adoption of a proposal to work for reciprocal arms-control agreements by way of small unilateral steps. [4]

The adoption in 1977 of this new campaign strategy had important consequences for the nuclear debate in the Netherlands. The choice of a specific aim blurred the ideological distinctions between church-affiliated and Moscow-manipulated peace campaigns; furthermore, it facilitated cooperation between the IKV campaign and the Stop the Neutron Bomb activists. Whereas both campaigns sought to mobilize the masses, the successful formation of local cells in the Stop the Neutron Bomb campaign acted as a catalyst for the formation of local IKV action cells. In many instances, they would simply merge later.

The osmosis between the two campaigns strengthened the political impact of the unilateralist movement in parliament. Politically the IKV and the Stop the Neutron Bomb campaigns found their support primarily with the more extreme left-wing political opposition in parliament. [5] The IKV's approach, however, and its affiliation with the churches, did enable it to generate support beyond its political "constituency." It found such support within the opposition Labor party (PVdA) and with some parliamentarians of the Christian-Democrat party (CDS) who—for other reasons—were opposed to the governing coalition. Their combined votes could be sufficient in number to topple the coalition formed in December 1977. The peculiar Dutch political situation thus made the unsettling of parliament a real possibility, and gave the pacifists an influence that well surpassed the political support they enjoyed in the country.

THE INTERNAL POLITICAL PUZZLE IN THE NETHERLANDS

The excessive political influence of the Dutch nuclear pacifists since 1977 cannot be properly understood without a brief description of the internal political situation. Until 1967, the postwar Dutch political scene could be characterized as a multipillar system. The multiparty system in parliament was founded on a society made up of denominational or confessional groups held together by a strong feeling of social and religious identity and well-developed organizational ties. Common allegiance to the nation, the royal house, and democracy provided reasonable political stability. Postwar recovery had been largely due to the leaders of the moderate Labor party, the Center Catholic People's party, and, to a lesser extent, the Liberals and smaller confessional parties.

In 1967, the multipillar system began to erode precipitously through two related trends: (1) increasing political polarization, especially to the left in the Labor party; (2) rapid deconfessionalization inside the Center Catholic and Protestant parties. The Labor party tried to promote polarization through its efforts to split the deconfessionalizing center. The confessional parties[6] tried to contain the political consequences—dwindling electoral support—by merging their parties into the new Christian Democratic Appeal (CDA). The merger process proved to be a long and arduous one (from 1968 to 1980). During the 1972-73 government formation, the Labor party managed to divide the merging parties (KVP and ARP joined the coalition; the CHU stayed out) but failed to stop the merger process.

The left-center government from 1973-1977 made a specific effort to reorient Dutch policy, including foreign and security affairs. Its new "peace policy" in particular stressed the need for reducing the role of nuclear weapons in NATO's deterrence strategy, and for developing a more distinct (from the United States, that is) effort at arms control.

In 1977, renewed efforts to divide the merging Christian parties failed. The new center-right government was faced, however, with dissension within its own ranks (a situation existing in the present coalition since 1982). Continuation of the new "peace policy" of the previous cabinet and LRTNF modernization since 1978 were among the principal issues on which the CDA dissenters tended to align themselves with the Labor opposition. The coalition government from 1977 to 1981 thus faced a threefold internal political threat: the threat of the opposition to use the nuclear issue as a breaking point by finding enough support among the CDA dissenters to provoke a government crisis; the threat of the pacifists to generate sufficient support inside the CDA fraction for alternative security policies; and the threat of the CDA dissenters—who belonged overwhelmingly to one of the merging parties, the ARP—to prevent the completion of the merger.

Confronted with the choice between full support for NATO's 1979 double-track decision and survival of the coalition and the merger, the government gave priority to the latter. The choice has so far produced two rather unfortunate consequences. For one thing, it has required the government from 1979 to 1981 and again since 1982[7] to keep postponing the decision on the deployment of cruise missiles on Dutch territory. Second, it has prevented the government from properly influencing public opinion and challenging the message of the pacifists. The government thus gave the campaigners virtually free rein in their agitation against the NATO double-track decision, and against U.S. security policies in general. This in turn served to help rather than hinder Soviet efforts to divide the alliance.

The excessive political influence of the nuclear pacifists may thus be explained by the inability of the CDA to cope adequately with its dissenting minority, and by the weakness bordering on cowardice of the government. The two large demonstrations thus far against deployment of cruise missiles in the Netherlands—November 1981 and October 1983—did not indicate broad political support for nuclear pacifism in the country. Opinion polls conducted among the demonstrators show that an overwhelming majority among them would vote for the left-wing parties. Only 3.3 percent of the demonstrators would vote for the parties currently holding the majority in parliament.

PACIFISM AND INTERNAL POLITICS IN BELGIUM

In Belgium, both the return of pacifism and the internal political evolution differ markedly from those in the Netherlands.

Belgian pacifist agitation had resumed two years earlier—in 1975—with formation of the Consultation Center for Peace (OCV), an organization under direct control of the Belgian Communist party and with close links to the World Peace Council. The Flemish Action Committee Against Atomic Weapons (VAKA) was formed in 1979; a similar action committee for peace and development was formed in French-speaking Belgium.

Although a growing number of organizations have joined the network—among them the Belgian branch of Pax Christi—the Belgian Communist party appears to have maintained tight control over them, mainly through the OCV. Since 1981 the Belgian movements, following the example of the Dutch IKV, have tried to transform themselves into a mass movement with local action cells. Their impact on Belgian politics appears to be less than is the case in neighboring Netherlands. Apart from the more visible Communist control of the movement, at least two more fundamental reasons can be given for their lesser influence.

Belgium is a predominately Catholic country. For historical reasons, the Catholic church is much less inclined to intervene directly in political debates and has not been urged to speak out on nuclear weapons. Second, the focus of internal political conflict is much less related to foreign and security issues than has been the case for the Netherlands. Most of the political problems facing Belgium concern relations between the French and Flemish-speaking populations, and the intricate process of keeping the nation together in the transformation from a unitary to a federal state. Both of these factors have served to constrain the influence of pacifism on Belgian foreign policy.

PACIFISM AND INTERNATIONAL POLITICS

SMALL-POWER RESPONSES TO THE CHANGING INTERNATIONAL POLITICAL SITUATION

As the tragic East-West division of Europe took shape in the years following World War II, both the Netherlands and Belgium opted for full participation in the emerging system of Western cooperation. Belgian neutrality has twice—in 1914 and in 1940—been violated by Germany. The Dutch policy of aloofness from alliances had served the country well from 1839 to 1939, but in May 1940, the Netherlands, like Belgium had been invaded by Germany. The lessons from the two world wars appeared clear. Military considerations on the part of the strongest European power rather than neutrality had been decisive for the violation or nonviolation of their territorial integrity; their prewar neutrality had made them less defensible and less prepared to resist invasion and to face occupation.

As the cold war commenced in 1947–48, the two countries became staunch supporters of West European unification and Atlantic security cooperation. Reliance upon U.S. protection—the nuclear guarantee and the presence of U.S. troops in Western Germany—became the cornerstone of their external security policies. These policies were assured of broad political support from the democratic political parties at home. Relations with the United States were characterized by mutual confidence and essential agreement on the nature of the Soviet threat to their external security.

Participation in the multilateral system of Western cooperation also offered additional benefits to the two countries. The role they could play in Western and international politics went clearly beyond that to which small and/or neutral states had been accustomed. At least up until the mid-1960s alliance and unification served the two countries well in terms of security, influence, and welfare.

During the sixties and continuing into the seventies, significant changes in the international political situation seriously taxed the cohesion of the North Atlantic alliance. Faced with growing tension in European-American relations, erosion of transatlantic confidence, and stagnation in European unification efforts, Belgian and Dutch governments came under strong domestic pressure to reorient or at least readjust their foreign policies. Turbulence in the United States and the ill-fated U.S. involvement in the Vietnam war had eroded confidence in the United States as the leading power in the Atlantic alliance. In light of these serious problems, the governments of Western Europe embarked upon a search for a West European identity and role in international affairs, one that would distance them from the United States. East-West detente since the early sixties and particularly following the new German *Ostpolitik* of 1969 appeared to offer fresh opportunities for West European governments to improve bilateral East-West relations more independently.

In the climate of East-West detente, the evolution of nuclear weapons presented a myriad of increasingly serious political problems for the alliance. A first problem concerned the gradual disappearance of U.S. nuclear superiority over the Soviet Union. The effect was twofold: it undermined the credibility in Europe of the U.S. nuclear guarantee; and it raised the fear of nuclear war, for the alliance was now required to examine nuclear war-fighting scenarios so as to uphold the credibility of its new deterrence strategy of flexible response. Second, fear of nuclear war was enhanced by the danger of a further proliferation of nuclear weapons. Another concern expressed during the sixties in Western Europe was that of the insufficient control of European governments over allied nuclear strategy and the decision—if required—to use nuclear weapons. These issues divided the Americans and the Europeans, as well as the Europeans among themselves.

The issue of U.S.-Soviet nuclear arms-control negotiations presented yet a third problem for U.S.-European relations. As negotiations proceeded and results became increasingly difficult to attain, arms control grew into a highly sensitive political issue within the alliance and in domestic politics. Whenever results seemed imminent, West European governments would blame the United States for shortcomings in their arms-control policies.

The Belgian and Dutch responses to these intricate consequences of the changing international political situation have shown both some interesting similarities and differences. The governments of both countries saw the new situation as an opportunity to increase their roles in improving East-West relations and in promoting arms control. With respect to the latter, however, their policies were and are different: the Belgian government tended to focus more on increasing its role *within* the alliance; the Dutch emphasized expanding their role *outside* the alliance. Belgian Foreign Minister Tindemans took the initiative (which proved abortive) to relaunch political unification among the member states of the European Community.

The Dutch government sought to enhance its role in arms-control negotiations by operating more independently from its allies and by working in concert with like-minded smaller states outside the alliance. Shortly before the conclusion of the Final Act of the CSCE, the Dutch government issued the white paper "Disarmament and Security." It contained a strong plea for a more disarmament-oriented policy, "first and foremost by the repulsion of the role of nuclear weapons" within the totality of the "deterrence system." It rejected Dutch unilateral nuclear disarmament, but introduced restrictions that were at variance with current NATO strategy. Among them were an explicit rejection of suggestions to consider the introduction of so-called mininuclear weapons, and the proposed restriction of the role of nuclear weapons to one of deterring only a *nuclear* initiative of the adversary.

In its effort to outline a new policy, the white paper also reflected the hope that continuation of the detente would facilitate repulsion of t' role of nuclear weapons through East-West agreement. When that hope faded away with the rapid deterioration of East-West relations after Helsinki, the Dutch plea for repulsion began to lead a life of its own in Dutch politics. It has served as a slogan for the parliamentary opposition since 1977 against government policies. It was used by those who resisted the neutron bomb and U.S. efforts to restore the East-West military balance. The plea was also used to force the Dutch government in 1979 to postpone the decision on deployment of cruise missiles on Dutch territory. Today, it continues to be used within NATO as an argument for achieving a significant reduction of Dutch nuclear responsibility within the alliance, [8] and has thus strengthened the case of those who advocate unilateral nuclear disarmament.

Finally, the anti-United States bias in West European—especially Dutch—foreign policy has been enhanced by changes in the international economic situation. Since the mid-1960s, the United States and the European Community have experienced recurrent conflicts over trade and monetary policies. Since the first UN Development Decade and particularly following the energy crisis of the 1970s, European and U.S. development cooperation policies have taken divergent approaches. Dutch and other European assistance to Vietnam, Cuba, and Nicaragua, for example, underline the extent to which their responses to the changing international situation have differed from those of the United States.

THE CHANGING INTELLECTUAL CLIMATE

The resurgence of pacifism has certainly been facilitated by the political responses of the Netherlands and Belgium to the changing international situation. Pacifism and these political responses reflect a more serious problem, namely the breakdown of postwar democratic political consensus on essential Western security and foreign policies. The causes of this breakdown must be sought in the changing intellectual climate Western Europe has been experiencing since the 1960s. Evidence of the profound changes can be found in the rejection of political reality, in the substitution of abstract conceptions for concrete political phenomena, and in the European crisis of identity.

Pacifism in its various forms since the nineteenth century, between the two world wars, and as nuclear pacifism after World War II, has always been marked by a rejection of political if not human reality itself. Western pacifism [9] since World War I in particular can be characterized as an attitude rather than as a doctrine or a philosophy. As an attitude it combines unreasoning fear and flight from reality into a utopian vision. The human realities of conflict, iniquity, good, and evil in the world are rejected and replaced by the utopian vision of a humanity that strives and longs for peace. Only the political system in which they live or the political "elite" that rules their country prevent men and women from promoting trust among peoples and peace between nations. Pacifists, moreover, are driven more by a fear of war than by a concept of peace. They do not reject violence or the use of force as such, only violence in its more risky forms. Fear drives them to fighting the symptoms rather than the causes of warfare. It also drives them to an attitude of submissiveness toward the strongest and most dangerous power in the world. Ever since the horrors of World War I, Western pacifists have combined their resistance to the development of certain weapons involving their own country with submissiveness toward totalitarian states.

Pacifism since 1919 may thus be looked at as a permanent undercurrent in West European societies. It has intermittently acquired political relevance whenever any of the following conditions prevailed: (1) the need for a political decision on a major weapons-procurement or modernization program; (2) serious doubt about the values underlying democratic society and a crisis of confidence between governments and people; (3) awareness of the strength or superiority of the totalitarian adversary; and (4) the conduct of a "peace campaign" by the totalitarian adversary. The remarkable resurgence of pacifism since 1975 can be explained by the unique concurrence of the four conditions, in an intellectual climate that has made many people sensitive to the pacifist message.

Following the assassination of President Kennedy in 1963, the United States entered a period of domestic turbulence that centered on the civil rights problem and the war in Vietnam. Unrest and confrontation on U.S. college campuses also spread to the European universities. Initially, many European intellectuals joined their U.S. colleagues in attacking the involvement of the United States in the Vietnam war. After 1968 their ways parted. While U.S. intellectuals continued to challenge identifiable policies of their country, West European intellectuals increasingly became the victims of an ideologically biased criticism. Their criticism no longer aimed at specific policies but at the political system and democratic society at large. Their image of the United States changed from the trusted democratic liberator and ally to that of an untrustworthy and dangerous superpower (fostered by their perceptions of the Nixon administration and the Watergate crisis). This changing image coincided with Europe's own identity crisis. Europe's single forward-looking postwar political conception of federal unity was destroyed in the Gaullist-provoked crisis of the sixties, and nationalism returned to European politics. Until the first energy crisis in 1973, continuing economic progress still acted as a palliative for political disarray. When economic recession replaced prosperity, and interdependence became a factor of vulnerability instead of influence, political disarray provoked a serious European crisis of identity. It resulted in increasing domestic political polarization and a breakdown of confidence in the very democratic values by which Western Europe and the United States distinguished themselves from most of the outside world.

East-West detente during this era also transformed Western Europe's image of the Soviet Union. The reality of a Soviet totalitarian threat was reduced to an obsolescent Western perception. The image of the Soviet Union has evolved to one of a "satisfied" superpower; the behavior of the Kremlin was to be understood and condoned as a defensive response to historical experiences and continuing hostile encirclement.

Serious doubts about Western democratic values combined with the new perception of the Soviet Union tended to obfuscate the crucial distinction between democratic governnent and totaliarian repression in the minds of many intellectuals. Many even felt tempted by the "progressive" videology of Marxism-Leninism. The new intellectual "understanding" of totalitarianism along with the announcement by the Kremlin that detente had changed the "correlation of forces" in favor of "socialism" created a climate for submissiveness to Soviet military and political strength.

The need for an allied response to the Soviet military buildup shortly after the "greatest" achievement of detente, the Helsinki Final Act, could hardly have come at a worse moment. In a situation in which intellectuals and West European politicians had come to combine respect for Soviet power with contempt for U.S. policy and weakness, the climate was exceptionally favorable to a resurgence of pacifism. Because NATO as an organization of sovereign and democratic allies lacks sufficient unity to agree on a political response, it could not but focus on restoring military strength. In open societies, restoring military strength requires agreement on specific weapons-modernization decisions. During the late seventies, the Carter administration had already sought allied agreement at an early stage; the administration and NATO's 1979 double-track decision therefore became an obvious, easy, and long-lasting target for pacifist agitation.

The smaller allies were confronted with the need to assume coresponsibility for a major nuclear weapons modernization program at a time in which:

- confidence in the United States and the reliability of its nuclear guarantee had sunk to a low level;
- the perception of a Soviet threat had been replaced by fear of nuclear war; and
- the repulsion of the role of nuclear weapons and the promotion of arms control had become the overriding goals.

Several reasons may be given as to why the request to assume coresponsibility for nuclear weapons modernization met with resistance and resentment in Belgium and the Netherlands. For many years the smaller allied countries had taken the credibility of U.S. protection for granted. Reliance on the strategy of nuclear deterrence enabled the smaller states to maintain their defense expenditures at a low level. The perseverance of the Soviet threat in an era of detente gave rise to the perception that the Soviet threat had been overstated, rather than that NATO's deterrence had worked. In the prevailing intellectual climate of criticizing the United States and the West, being tempted by left-wing ideologies, and trying to understand the Soviet Union, new "scientific" approaches found easy acceptance.

Revisionist writings on the history of the cold war, behaviorism, and systems analysis competed in explaining the East-West conflict in a new way. The political reality of the Soviet totalitarian threat was reduced to an aberrant perception of security elites holding self-serving enemy images. The consistent Soviet military buildup was reduced to one side of an action-reaction pattern in a so-called arms race. Generalizations about military-industrial complexes replaced careful analysis about the political forces in the East-West conflict. A new tradition of "thinking" emerged in which abstractions about presumably similar military blocs, deterrence systems, or superpowers concealed the real differences between democratic states and totalitarian regimes. In this intellectual climate, the pacifists' call for withdrawal from responsibility found widespread response; it appealed especially to those who were critical of the United States and those who preferred the morally satisfying role of small countries keeping their distance from allied power politics.

CONFUSING REALIGNMENTS

On 8 August 1977, as mentioned above, twenty-eight Communist parties issued a declaration calling upon all Social Democrats and Christians for action against the U.S. neutron bomb. The fact that Social Democrats and Christians were singled out as useful partners for the Soviet peace campaign against NATO and the United States underscored a realignment of forces in Western Europe that had already been in progress for several years. By the late seventies, European Social Democrats and many Christian churches were no longer in the forefront of the battle against Soviet totalitarianism and communism, as in the postwar years. Peace, disarmament, and development had gradually emerged as their principal international political concerns.

For the sake of peace and disarmament, or in the name of detente, increasing contacts with Soviet and East European counterparts had been accepted and sought after ecumenism in the Christian churches gave an additional impetus to seeking contact with representatives of the Eastern and Russian Orthodox churches. The Soviet Communist party (CPSU) aptly began to exploit the desire for dialogue and the growing fear of nuclear war to serve its own ends in its recurrent peace campaigns against the West.

In 1958 the Christian Peace Conference—another international Communist-front organization—was set up in Prague, with the intent to generate Christian and theological support for Soviet "peace" policies. In 1959 the Central Committee of the CPSU addressed a special letter to the Sixth Postwar Congress of the Socialist International suggesting cooperation by "all detachments of the international workers movement" in the common task "to prevent a destructive new war and to rebuff the attempts at a reactionary offensive." [10] At the time, the letter was ignored. By 1981, however, Leonid Brezhnev could note that links had been established with several Western Social-Democratic parties and with the leadership of the Socialist International itself.

In 1961 the Russian and Eastern Orthodox churches joined the World Council of Churches. In the guise of ecumenism, representatives of these churches acting under CPSU instructions entered the network of cooperation among Christian churches.

In the name of peace, disarmament, and the prevention of nuclear war, West European Social Democrats moved away from the earlier consensus with other democratic parties and moved toward increased understanding and cooperation with the CPSU. The Belgian and Dutch Socialist parties were among those that responded earlier and favorably toward the CPSU offensive launched in 1971. Prominent Belgian Socialist leaders participated with the Belgian Communist party in the formation and activities of a new international Communist–front organization for detente, called the International Committee for European Security and Cooperation. [11] In November 1972, the Belgian Socialist party became the first to establish a formal cooperative relationship with the CPSU. The Dutch Labor party since 1972 has been strongly in favor of collaborating with the Communists (to educate and change them, as the official argument goes!). Links between the CPSU and the leadership of the Socialist International were forged in 1980. The net effect of these realignments has been that the Belgian and Dutch Socialist parties fully support the campaigns in their countries against the deployment of cruise missiles, while expressing great understanding for the policy and position of the Kremlin.

With respect to the Christian chuches, the realignment has been considerably more apparent in those churches that belong to the World Council of Churches than in the Roman Catholic church. As a consequence, the realignment in the Netherlands—with its strong ecumenical tradition—has been more apparent than in Belgium. Especially in the Netherlands, the pacifists found widespread support among Church leaders, who—given their ignorance about political reality—readily began to march behind pacifist slogans in the name of "peace on earth," the Sermon on the Mount, or fear of war.

PACIFISM AND THE PEACE MOVEMENTS

As we have seen, the 1977 Stop the Neutron Bomb campaign marked the resurgence of pacifism and antinuclear protest in the

Netherlands. Following the campaign's political success, pacifist movements directed their efforts against NATO's LRTNF modernization program as a step toward unilateral denuclearization of NATO forces in Western Europe. From the outset, two types of pacifist or so-called peace movements could be distinguished: Soviet-manipulated or useful pacifism, and virtuous pacifism.

The first—with its peace campaigns—was a product of the Soviet network of political warfare. The second was a product of genuine fear of nuclear war and impotence in regard to the ongoing arms competition. Though distinct in origin, the two strands of pacifism ominously grew into each other and soon reached a level of close cooperation, and jointly fostered popular and intellectual confusion.

USEFUL PACIFISM AND ITS IMPACT

Soviet-manipulated pacifism has appeared as a considerable political force inside the countries of Western Europe through the transmission belts of the Soviet network for political warfare. It is a form of pacifism that could be termed *useful pacifism* or the *pacifism of the deliberate lie.* The main purpose of the transmission belts is to integrate other Western pacifists, conscientious objectors, neutralists, members of religious communities, intellectuals, "peace-loving" progressive political forces, and others into Soviet political strategy. To this end, Communist control over the functioning of the transmission belts must be assured as far as possible. At the same time, this control must be concealed by attracting noncommunist collaborators to major conferences, by giving them posts on governing bodies, by creating broadly representative committees, and by seeking organized cooperation with other pacifist or peace movements. The principal transmission belts for the Soviet peace campaign are the international Communist-front organizations, in particular the World Peace Council, national Communist-front organizations, and the Russian Orthodox church. [12] As the maze of cooperative arrangements between these organizations and other West European pacifist movements has grown enormously in recent years, both sides have vigorously rejected the alleged existence of Soviet CPSU manipulation. Still, evidence is firm and overwhelming. Rejection of such evidence is not based on fact but on fiction; on the belief, namely, that the CPSU is conducting this campaign solely for the purpose of peacefully living side by side with the Western democracies, and dutifully complying with the agreements to protect basic human rights for its own population.

In October 1973, the World Peace Council and the Soviet Peace

Committee organized the World Congress of Peace Forces in Moscow. [13] During and after this conference, plans were worked out to create movements. In September 1980, the World Peace Council sponsored the World Parliament of Peoples for Peace in Sofia, attended by 2,260 delegates. It adopted the Program of Action 1981 unanimously; that is to say, with the concurrence of Western trade union leaders, Social Democrats, intellectuals, national liberation movement leaders (Arafat), and representatives of other peace movements, churches, youth, and women's organizations present. Among the points of the action program were:

- campaigns against the "new" U.S. "military doctrine" and the stationing of new U.S. nuclear weapons in Western Europe; also against the Camp David peace agreements between Egypt and Israel;
- campaigns of solidarity with Vietnam, Syria, Cuba, the PLO, and the Soviet puppet regime in Afghanistan. [14]

Between the two gatherings, action had been taken through the network effectively to promote campaigns inside West European countries against the neutron bomb and the NATO LRTNF decision. The clearest example to date is the coordinated Stop the Neutron Bomb campaign, launched officially on 30 July 1977 by Tass.

The Dutch Communist party achieved the most in its endeavors. The initiative and the campaign are good examples of the functioning of a national Communist-front organization: while the more than one hundred initiators included many well-known and noncommunist Dutch citizens, the organization was in the hands of trusted Communist party members. The campaign is a most instructive case of manipulated, useful pacifism. What was the basis for its success?

First, manipulation is successful only when it plays upon already existing grievances and unreasoning fear. Such fear can be exploited best if the debate is focused on specific (and necessarily gruesome) weapons, and waged according to the terms of actual war-fighting scenarios rather than of deterrence theory.

Second, genuinely concerned noncommunists who argue on moral bases are crucial assets for concealing manipulation. Invariably they are the ones who most vigorously denounce any evidence of being used.

Third, nothing succeeds like success. The campaign of the Dutch Interchurch Peach Council (IKV), Rid the World of Nuclear Weapons Starting with the Netherlands, which commenced in September 1977, first used the action model of the Stop the Neutron Bomb campaign.

Later the two campaigns merged into an inextricable cooperative network of local action groups, national campaign organizations, and international coordination efforts. These mergers became all the more apparent after the Stop the Neutron Bomb campaign transformed itself into the broader Stop the N-bomb/Stop the Arms Race campaign. Thenceforth, both campaigns focused first on preventing NATO's LRTNF modernization decision, and then on resisting the deployment of cruise missiles. Concern for the deployment of Soviet SS-20 missiles has been mutely expressed but never became a campaign issue.

Fourth, the exploitation of irrational popular fear as an instrument of extraparliamentary pressure against weak governments creates its own momentum. Whereas vocal minorities are useful tools for manipulated pacifism, they are easily presented as expressions of majority popular feeling by the other pacifists. Both therefore easily agree that more forceful methods of popular pressure are to be employed if the government decides to accept cruise missiles on Dutch soil. In February 1983, the Dutch deliberative body of peace organizations [15] (LOVO) agreed on a large-scale plan of action for 1983, including methods of civil disobedience if the government agreed to accept cruise missile deployment on Dutch territory. Civil disobedience as a method of political action thus easily grows into more forcible forms of undermining democratic societies.

Fifth, following the successful Stop the Neutron Bomb campaign the Dutch Communist party was urged to help internationalize the peace campaign. Two international forums were organized in Amsterdam during 1978; their organization was probably too rigidly controlled by the party and East European officials to have made any great impact. More effective international coordination, however, became a principal concern and activity of the combined Dutch peace movements thereafter.

Finally, the success of the Stop the Neutron Bomb campaign and consecutive developments have clearly shown that a flexible "popular-front" strategy within the maze of Western peace movements is the most promising one for productive and concealed manipulation. This formula has been adopted in the other West European countries as well.

The influence of Soviet-manipulated, useful pacifism on other pacifist movements is bound to remain a subject of controversy in Western Europe (though not in the CPSU, according to the enthusiastic reports in the Soviet media). Still, a number of clearly discernable facts can be established. The first fact is that pacifism in postwar Western Europe has known three waves of peace actions: in 1950, around 1960, and since 1977. Each of the three waves followed Soviet efforts to launch broad, pluralistic peace fronts. The first wave started with the Stockholm Appeal for a petition for peace but did not get very far. The second wave was marked by demonstrations against atomic weapons but failed to make a decisive impact. The third wave, as we saw, began in 1977. The building up of the Soviet "peace campaign" preceded each of the waves. Throughout the process, the Soviet network has expanded and become better organized. The timing of activities has invariably been set by the Soviet peace campaigns.

A second fact emerging during each of the campaigns has been the remarkable concurrence between the targets of the Soviet network and those of the other pacifists. Autonomous pacifist movements may have presented different or more far-reaching aims, but the common targets for action invariably have been NATO policies and NATO decisions. A comparison of the Program of Action 1983 of the World Peace Council with the action program of the autonomous peace movements in 1983 [16] reemphasizes the extent to which useful and autonomous pacifists concur in the timing of their agitation and the principal targets of their campaigns. In both cases, the second half of 1983 has been the decisive period for mass demonstrations. Both groups have adopted a nuclear freeze and the prevention of deployment by NATO of Pershing II and cruise missiles as their principal aims.

Yet a third fact is that no such campaigns have been conducted in any country of the Soviet bloc. For a brief period of time following the Polish crisis, the Dutch IKV spread the message that it was seeking cooperation with such independent East European movements as Solidarnosc, Charta '77, or Dialogue (in Hungary). It proved to be a false message. Communications from them—if forthcoming—were carefully edited to avoid indications that there might be any disagreement. For the sake of good contact with "official" Communist peace movements, such contacts have been deemphasized since the early fall of 1983.

VIRTUOUS PACIFISM

Virtuous pacifism, like useful pacifism, needs the existence of grievances or irrational fear to obtain popular support or have public impact. Virtuous pacifism in postwar Western Europe has been politically irrelevant outside the framework of Soviet peace campaigns.

Within that framework, virtuous pacifism is primarily interesting as an intellectual state of mind, and as a magnifier of the gospel of unilateral nuclear disarmament. Much better than the Communists, virtuous pacifists can generate social, political, and religious support for the idea that unilateral disarmament is the only path to peace. Only they can add the amount of honesty needed to convince the morally concerned.

Virtuous pacifism, as it appears today in the framework of the Soviet peace campaigns, is primarily nuclear pacifism. It is not based on any coherent political doctrine or theory but on a mixture of vague interpersonal morality and unreasoning fear. Its moral argument seems to be that states, like human beings, are inherently good. They can be made to act as "good" entities, thus enabling the adversary to do the same. Unilateral disarmament on the Western side will thus be followed by unilateral disarmament on the Soviet side. The reason that Western states have not yet adopted this course is because "the system" (security elites, the military-industrial complex, big industry, the deterrence system, and so forth) has prevented them from abiding by the popular will. Extraparliamentary popular campaigns are justified by the necessity to break through "the system" in order that the "good" majority may prevail. A highly interesting aspect of this moral argument is the moral indifference to (if not neglect of) the distinction between democratic societies and totalitarian regimes.

This moral indifference is related to another typical conviction of pacifism: that peace is the highest value, if not an absolute one, in relations between states. To preserve peace, the renunciation of the use of force becomes an absolute imperative, and unilateral disarmament becomes a morally necessary step, regardless of the consequences (e.g. better red than dead). Peace, however, is an undefined notion. It merely expresses a human desire and evokes positive associations. [17]

The elevation of peace to an absolute value and the renunciation of force to an absolute imperative reflect the moral position that nothing is more important than staying alive as a person or a group. The consequence of this moral position is that civic courage loses its character as a virtue, and that freedom, democracy, and human dignity lose their character as moral values. The moral argument of virtuous pacifism is thus linked to the exaggerated fear of the pacifists.

The pacifist renunciation of force is born of fear and the desire for tranquillity. Modern virtuous pacifists, however, do not renounce the use of force altogether but—as a result of their fear—only its more dangerous forms. They are disposed to employ less risky forms of violence. In essence virtuous pacifists do not protest against certain policies but against human reality itself. They deny the fact that Western states are confronted with the choice between preventing the use of force by force, or accepting their submission to totalitarian force. Such a denial, however, is concealed in the moral argumentation of the nuclear pacifists by dealing with the real world of international relations only in highly abstract terms. In discussing the concept of peace, for example, no differentiation is made between peace in the hearts of men and women, peace between human beings and God, peace between human beings, peace in relations between government and citizens, or peace in relations between sovereign states. Nor is differentiation made between states, whether a democratically governed ally such as the United States, or a totalitarian, antagonistic regime like the Soviet Union; both are simply referred to as superpowers, each with its own interests, ideologies, and enemies. Concealments of this nature lead to the neglect of such eminently ethical problems as the exercise of power over people, a government's legitimacy, its nature (repressive or democratic), and the obligation of protecting citizens from submission to regimes of terror.

Contemporary virtuous pacifism—as a product of a vague morality and unreasonable fear—has therefore assumed by necessity the form of nuclear pacifism. The principal aim of its campaign has been to spread fear by explicitly describing the horrors of nuclear war.

In the wake of this pacifism, religious leaders have been heard to declare that nuclear war is the greatest moral issue of our time. If it is to be avoided at all costs, nuclear weapons must be abolished, regardless of the consequences. The original moral argument that "good" behavior on one side generates equally good (disarming) behavior on the other side thus becomes an instrument for making unilateral disarmament more widely acceptable. Willingly or unwillingly, it serves to support Soviet campaigns for Western disarmament. If fear of nuclear war becomes the overriding consideration, submission to a totalitarian regime becomes a lesser evil, if an evil at all.

Nuclear pacifism in final analysis is not based on a philosophical conception or sound moral reasoning, but on a certain psychology or attitude. It expresses submissiveness to what is felt and feared to be superior power. It is for this very reason that virtuous pacifists easily cluster and cooperate with neutralists, ecologists, the useful pacifists, and other such groups. For the same reason, they viciously attack U.S. policies and NATO decisions, while going out of their way to comprehend or condone the Soviet military buildup, the invasion of

Afghanistan, or repression in Poland. They do not demonstrate against the LRTNF modernizations as such; they demonstrate for unilateral disarmament, but learned as campaign leaders that demonstrating against a specific weapon can generate more support. The fallacy of the moral argument is replaced by the power of the street. The evolution of the Catholic peace movement Pax Christi from a Catholic peace society into Pax Christi/IKV as a campaign organization of virtuous nuclear pacifists is an instructive example of this phenomenon. Pax Christi originated in France at the end of World War II as a bishops' initiative for German-French reconciliation. In the early fifties, it transformed itself into a Catholic peace movement for prayer, study, and action for peace in the service of the church. In the late sixties, it took the initiative in the Netherlands to create the Interchurch Peace Council (IKV). From 1967 to 1977 its character changed to a more autonomous organization advocating "progressive" views on such purely political issues as East-West detente, disarmament, development assistance, and the Middle East conflict. In 1977 it evolved to a campaign organization with the specific aim of mobilizing the masses as an instrument to force parliament in the direction of an alternative security policy, i.e. unilateral nuclear disarmament. Pax Christi/IKV kept its affiliation to the churches but in fact became a political pressure group, cooperating with the smaller political parties to the left of the Labor party. [18]

For the purposes of a successful campaign, the members of Pax Christi/IKV presented themselves not as nuclear pacifists but as advocates of a policy of unilateral initiatives designed to promote gradual mutual disarmament. To reassure skeptics, the proposed policy was presented as the fruit of scientific research and theory building. In fact it had been the fruit of one U.S. psychologist [19] who during the sixties had proposed another negotiating technique in the United States for dealing with the Soviet Union, which Pax Christi/IKV supported. The American based his proposed technique on the hypothesis that nations—the United States and the Soviet Union in particular—could cultivate mutual trust through unilateral disarmament initiatives and thus gradually move to broader agreement on the joint objective of a peaceful, just, and disarmed world. He underestimated the fact that tension and arms competition are symptoms rather than causes of conflict between states. His method, the politics of mutual example, had been attempted, the Soviet Union continued its military buildup, and by the late seventies the method no longer found much serious "scientific" support.

More important is that the method proposed a small step by the

United States that—in the absence of an adequate Soviet response—could be canceled. A small country like the Netherlands, having removed all nuclear weapons from its soil under popular pressure, obviously would not have proposed such a small step as the method suggests. It would have proposed a giant step toward unilateral disarmament, with no incentive for the Soviet Union—or possibility for a smaller Warsaw Pact state—to respond likewise. Pax Christi/IKV participation in the campaigns for unilateral disarmament since then warrant only one conclusion: resorting to the above method served only to win broader public and political support by concealing the real nuclear-pacifist motivation. It thus made Pax Christi/IKV a more attractive participant in the overall effort to fight the stationing of Pershing II and cruise missiles in Western Europe. Since 1980, the IKV and Stop the N-bomb/Stop the Arms Race campaigns are playing an increasingly prominent role as international coordinators of the pacifist campaigns in Western Europe. The large demonstrations such as those in Bonn, Paris, Rome, Brussels, London, and Amsterdam in the fall of 1981 and in 1983 against LRTNF modernization were initiated and coordinated by these groups.

Virtuous nuclear pacifism still distinguishes itself from useful pacifism in motivation and outlook. The aims of the virtuous pacifists do not always converge with those of the Soviet network. Virtuous pacifists neglect the major strategic problem facing the West, namely, Soviet conventional and nuclear offensive capacity in Central Europe. Useful pacifists are aware of this problem and see it as the principal Soviet asset in the effort to defeat the West without having to fight a war. Hence the useful pacifists advocate acceptance of slavery; virtuous pacifists advocate acceptance of impotence.

THE ALTERNATIVE POLITICAL SUBCULTURE OF PACIFISM

The combined network of so-called peace movements certainly at its core has evolved into what might be characterized as an alternative political subculture. In this subculture, activists of diverse background are held together by a climate of irrational fear, justifying their actions by irrational slogans. They are no longer affected by rational political argument, and reject discussion with acknowledged experts or their own governments. They no longer respond to facts, political realities, or historical experience. Their own "experts" manipulate data to serve the campaign slogans and shape opinion. They speak their own language and are insensitive to the political culture of democratic decision making and the rule of law in pluralistic democracies. Their alternative political subculture derives from an underlying current of rejection of Western society, its way of life, and its democratic values. As a consequence, the pacifists combine a psychological attitude of submissiveness to totalitarian superiority with a political attitude that rejects democratic weaknesses. They will thus employ their civil rights to demonstrate, to go to court, or to participate in politics as instruments to destroy the fabric of the very democratic societies that allow them to be heard and to exist as free persons.

In the last few years, the "autonomous peace movements" have increasingly sought international cooperation and common planning and strategy. The Dutch peace movements in particular have played a central role in international coordination. Among the six principal organizations of this kind, the International Peace Communication and Coordination Centre (created in 1981) is located at IKV headquarters in The Hague; Pax Christi has its international secretariat in Antwerp. The International Fellowship of Reconciliation is located in Alkmaar. The Women's International League for Peace and Freedom has offices in Amsterdam and Geneva. On the national Dutch level, the campaign against the deployment of cruise missiles has enabled the organizers to combine the agitation of groups as far apart as discontented middle-of-the-road Christian Democrats and Soviet-manipulated Communist-front organizations.

The demonstration of 29 October 1983, in The Hague was organized by the Committee Cruise-Missiles-No, set up in April 1983. Its membership consists of the IKV, Pax Christi, the cooperative campaign Stop the Neutron Bomb/Stop the Nuclear Arms Race, Women for Peace, Women Against Nuclear Weapons, Platform of Radical Peace Groups, Humanist Peace Council, Church and Peace, Federation of Trade Unions, Union of Conscripts, and the left-wing opposition political parties (Labor Party, D'66, PSP, PPR, EVP, CPN). The composition of the committee and of the demonstration itself shows both the societal danger and the political weakness of the alternative political subculture of pacifism in the Netherlands. The multipillar system that had given political stability to postwar Netherlands has apparently crumbled. It has been replaced by political polarization. Polarization, however, goes well beyond the issues of peace, security, and disarmament.

The peace movements have been able to associate persons and groups on a common denominator of dissatisfaction, but dissatisfaction on a great variety of issues. Among the participants were many adherents to the Labor party and the largest (but left-wing) trade union, as well as disgruntled churchleaders and cadre. This fact reflects a deepening split within parliament, inside the Labor party and the trade union itself, and within the Christian churches. As an overwhelmingly left-wing demonstration, it also points to a crisis of confidence between leaders and membership, and between church officials and believers. Inside this minority of the Dutch population, a majority favors harsher action and agitation if the government decides to proceed with deployment of cruise missiles.

REACTIONS TO THE PACIFIST MOVEMENTS

In recent years, pacifist agitation in the Netherlands (and to a lesser extent in Belgium) no longer goes unchallenged. Since 1980, a number of organizations have been formed that challenge the monopoly of the (pacifist) peace movements. These "alternative" peace movements support NATO's double-track decision and—if necessary—the deployment of cruise missiles on Dutch soil. They favor mutual and reciprocal disarmament through negotiations. The two most important organizations are the Interchurch Committee for Bilateral Disarmament (1980) and the Foundation for Peace Policy (1981); the latter is a coordinating framework for a variety of smaller, like-minded peace movements. Separate from them is the Legion of War Veterans (and its political foundations), which focuses on more direct attacks on the pacifists. It is probably too early to evaluate the organizations' impact on the political and public debate. As organizations, they obviously operate differently than does the pacifist network. Their emphasis is not on demonstration but on dialogue, not on agitation but on persuasion, not on the power of the street but on the strength of sound information and argument. As points of reference for a confused popular majority, they may help to restore some rationality and common sense to the security and peace debates.

RETROSPECT AND PROSPECTS

Pacifism as an undercurrent in the Western world dates from the early nineteenth century. It orginated in the United States and Britain, shortly after the Napoleonic wars. The first organization, the Netherlands Peace League, was formed only in 1871 (at the time of the German-French war). Pacifism was associated historically with certain nonconformist Protestant sects, and later it has been associated with socialism and anarchism as well. As we have seen, it has been a more permament undercurrent in Western society since 1919, acquiring political relevance intermittently and under certain conditions in the 1930s, and again in the 1950s and 1960s. It has always reflected an aversion to violence and an inclination—in difficult times—to delegate responsibility for the use of force to others. Although the Dutch have had some prominence in international pacifist movements since 1914, pacifism is neither specifically Dutch nor is it associated with neutrality or smaller powers in particular.

In a world in which democratic states are confronted with the danger of massive destruction by nuclear war and the danger of totalitarian repression and expansion, no clear solution is at hand to avoid both slavery and destruction. Western democracies do not live easily with such uncertainty in an age of mass media, instant news, and frequent crises.

The resurgence of pacifism since 1977 may have been a remarkable phenomenon, especially in the Netherlands. Its resurgence, however, reflects a profound crisis in the West rather than a specifically Dutch disease. It also reflects the achievement of a relentless, long-standing Soviet political warfare effort, unprecedented even in the history of our cruel twentieth century. The unique character of the resurgence makes it very difficult indeed to predict the prospects for pacifism and the peace movements in the Netherlands, Belgium, and Western Europe. I consider it highly unlikely that pacifism will simply fade away after deployment is completed, if only because a firm governmental decision cannot yet be ascertained. Popular support for pacifism will continue to diminish, but harsher actions by a dwindling manipulated minority are a realistic possibility.

Whether governments will be firmer in dealing with violence than with demonstrations and manipulations is anybody's guess. The impact of Dutch pacifism may be reduced if the other NATO allies go ahead with deployment, whatever the Dutch decide. I do not, however, exclude the danger that lasting harm has been done to the political cohesion and military strength of the North Atlantic alliance. If so, the unraveling will continue. Without a firm U.S. commitment to the defense of Western Europe, the security of our countries is no longer assured. Western Europe could then slowly slide into impotence against the Soviet Union, or become involved in the crises of the Soviet empire, which itself faces the explosive combination of internal decay with too much military and subversive power.

NOTES

1. Seventy-six out of 150 members.
2. The General Baptist church, the Lutheran church, the Evangelical Fraternity, the Dutch Calvinist churches, the Protestant church, the

Quakers, the "Old-Catholics," the Remonstrant Fraternity, the Roman Catholic church, and the Ecumenical Research Exchange.

3. According to the NATO double-track decision, forty-eight ground-launched cruise missiles are to be deployed in the Netherlands and in Belgium.

4. Discussed further below.

5. CPN: Communist party Netherlands
   D'66: Democratics '66
   PSP: Pacifist Socialist party
   EVP: Evangelical People's party
   PPR: Party of Political Radicals
   PVdA: Labor party (its left wing).

6. KVP: Catholic People's party
   ARP: Anti-Revolution party
   CHU: Christian Historical Union.

7. After the 1981 elections, a left-of-center government was formed (CDA, D'66, PvdA); it collapsed within a year and new elections were held in 1982, returning the CDA-VVD (Liberal party) Coalition to power with a majority of 81 out of 150.

8. On 12 December 1979 the Dutch ministers in the North Atlantic Council notified their allies that the Netherlands government was unable to decide on the deployment of GLCMs on its territory at this juncture; a decision was promised for December 1981 (postponed several times since). The minister of defense also expressed the belief "that any stationing of new weapon systems on The Netherlands territory should result in a reduction in the existing Netherlands nuclear tasks"; this latter issue is still under consideration.

9. Compare Karl Jaspers, *Die Atombombe und die Zukunft des Menschen* (Munchen, 1958).

10. See Arnold M. Silver, *The New Face of the Socialist International: The Institution Analysis* (Washington, D.C.: Heritage Foundation, October 1981).

11. Based in Brussels.

12. See further my *The Security of Western Europe. A Handbook* (forthcoming), ch. 3.

13. It was attended by over three thousand delegates and followed a consensus reached at the 1969 International Conference of Communist and Workers' Parties in Moscow to seek renewed association with popular movements in the West for the advancement of "socialism" and peace.

14. The program contained many more action points of the same persuasion. Obviously, the concurrence of so many Western delegates did not prove manipulation, only a happy coincidence of their concerns with those of the CPSU. The Soviet deployment of peace-loving SS-20 missiles or the invasion of Afghanistan are not among their unanimous concerns, of course.

15. A kind of supermerger of: IKV, Pax Christi (the Catholic peace movement), Stop the N-bomb/Stop the Arms-Race, Women for Peace, Women Against Nuclear Weapons, Humanists' Peace Council, and Platform of Radical Peace Groups. Each of these groups again has its

own ties with organizations belonging to the Soviet network. Similar mergers have taken place in other West European countries.

16. On the latter: *Disarmament Campaigns,* a monthly publication from the IKV in The Hague.

17. For this very reason, peace campaigns are the principal instrument of Soviet political warfare. Peace simply means Communist world control, according to Lenin and his successors.

18. Today, Pax Christi is strongest in the Netherlands (about twenty thousand members). It has about five thousand members in Belgium, according to *The Economist.*

19. Charles Osgood.

10

BRITAIN'S NUCLEAR DISARMERS

Martin Ceadel

The history of Britain's nuclear-disarmament movement divides neatly into four phases: from 1945 to 1957; and from 1965 to 1979 it scarcely existed; but from 1958 to 1964, and from 1980 to the time of writing, [1] it has been a major force in political life. This essay will outline the first three phases, then describe the post-1980 phase in more detail, and conclude by drawing implications for the future from a comparison between the original upsurge and the current resurgence.

Nuclear-disarmament movements, like antiwar movements in general, are hybrids. One component is the peace movement proper, consisting of those with a *principled* objection to nuclear weapons (and often to the underlying assumptions of all orthodox defense thinking). The other component is motivated by *prudential* considerations only: it comprises, for example, those who object to some or all nuclear weapons because they involve special risks to the areas in which they are stationed, because they are controlled by the United States, or because they divert resources from conventional defences.

Principled antiwar activity has historically been strong in Britain: not only has Britain's political culture, conditioned by liberalism and Protestantism, been conducive to peace movements, but so has its "semidetached" strategic position. (In wholly detached and therefore largely secure states, such as the United States before the development of the ICBM, antiwar feeling can most easily take the form of isolationism; in exposed states, such as France in 1940, it can take the form of defeatism. But in states enjoying moderate measures of security, haters of war must think of abolishing it, being unable simply to opt out of it, yet are generally able to promote ways of doing this without being branded cowards or traitors, as they would be in

218

vulnerable states.) The perspective that will here be adopted is that Britain's first antinuclear upsurge was mainly a principled protest against Britain's development of a hydrogen bomb, which largely explains why it outshone other such movements. Its second upsurge is part of a worldwide reaction to the arms race that has a strongly prudential element, however; and the fact that prudential arguments have traditionally had less impact in Britain helps to explain why it has in certain respects lagged behind its foreign counterparts.

THE FIRST PERIOD OF QUIESCENCE

What this perspective draws attention to is the remarkable absence, for more than a decade, of moralistic dissent from Britain's postwar foreign and defense policy, despite several features that would formerly have elicited strong condemnations from the peace movement and political opposition: peacetime conscription; acceptance of United States military bases, in some of which nuclear-capable bombers were stationed after July 1948, with minimal British controls over them; membership after April 1949 in NATO, involving an unprecedented degree of deference to an ally (the United States) and a novel commitment to forward defense in Europe; and the development by Britain of its own nuclear weapons, the deployment of which could be reconciled only with great difficulty, if at all, with traditional just-war thinking.

The lack of dissent can be explained in terms of secrecy, distrust of the United States, the cold war, and the state of the peace movement. The decision of January 1947 to develop a British atom bomb, initially a secret even from most members of the cabinet, seemed only prudent after the United States—which in the summer of 1940 had waited before offering the destroyers-for-bases deal of September to see whether Britain was going to collapse or not—had in 1946 reneged on what the British regarded as a promise to continue the wartime atomic collaboration. The same was true, in the early cold war when a severely damaged Europe felt itself at the mercy of Soviet expansionism, of the decision to sign the North Atlantic Treaty in April 1949. The peace movement was, moreover, itself at a low ebb: the pacifists had been discredited by Hitler, and liberal internationalists were frustrated by the deadlock at the new United Nations; only the federalists were optimistic, but they tended to regard the atomic bomb as but a symptom of deeper problems that structural reform alone could remedy and in many cases saw NATO as a step in the right direction, Communist aggression in the Korean War added to the peace movement's discomfiture, so that when in October 1952 the first British atomic bomb was tested, protest was virtually confined to a small group of Gandhian pacifists associated with the Peace Pledge Union and too obscure to be reported in the press.

Soon afterward, admittedly, a slight change in the climate of opinion occurred. Stalin's death and the ceasefire in Korea, both in 1953, produced the first partial thaw in the cold war. The fading of federalist hopes, and in particular the defeat of the proposed European Defence Community in 1954, forced the peace movement to focus on symptoms, such as nuclear weapons, instead of systemic change. And, in some quarters at least, the thermonuclear revolution, which saw the development of a hydrogen bomb a thousand times more powerful than its atomic predecessor, was viewed as a more truly qualitative change in warfare than had been the progression from the "conventional" fire-storm raids of World War II to the more efficient but quantitatively no more murderous destruction of Hiroshima and Nagasaki. The H-bomb had been first tested in November 1952 by the United States, with the Soviet Union (an atomic power since September 1949) following suit in August 1953; but, revealingly, it attracted little attention in Britain until the Americans began a new series of tests in March 1954. In a House of Commons debate on these tests, Prime Minister Winston Churchill asserted on 5 April 1954: "With all its horrors, the atomic bomb did not seem unmanageable as an instrument of war. . . . But the hydrogen bomb carries us into dimensions which had never confronted practical thought and have been confined to the realms of fantasy and imagination." And it was in 1954 that Bertrand Russell, formerly (as is notorious) a hawk over atomic weapons, warned in an influential radio broadcast that, though "the general public still thinks in terms of the destruction of cities," it was now clear that "a war with the hydrogen bomb is quite likely to put an end to the human race." [2] Russell did not yet abandon his belief in deterrence, however (denying as late as May 1957 that he was in favor of the abolition of nuclear weapons); and, indeed, the lesson most commonly drawn from this revolution in warfare was that Britain should acquire its own H-bomb, as the government had already decided to do, on the grounds that it was the first weapon powerful enough to enable a small country like Britain to pose a threat to one the size of the Soviet Union. The H-bomb was thus, in every sense, a great leveler.

A small antinuclear movement did emerge in 1954, to supplement the intermittent activities of the Gandhian pacifists, but it made little impact. After the 5 April 1954 Commons debate, the Labour party set up a Hydrogen Bomb National Campaign, which collected half a million signatures for a petition calling for multilateral nuclear disarmament and the strengthening of the United Nations but then faded away. Even the Bevanite Left of the party failed to take up the nuclear issue, seeming to find German rearmament a greater worry. In 1955 concern about the fallout's being detected by atmospheric tests led members of the Women's Cooperative Guild in Golders Green, north London, to set up a joint local committee for the abolition of nuclear bomb tests, but this attracted little publicity. Indeed it seemed in the autumn of 1956 that postwar Britain had submitted almost without demur to a foreign and defense policy several features of which would once have provoked bitter controversy.

THE FIRST RISE AND FALL OF THE CAMPAIGN
FOR NUCLEAR DISARMAMENT

In the space of little more than a year the situation was transformed and the Campaign for Nuclear Disarmament (CND) came into vigorous existence in January 1958.[3] This was the result of a fortuitous combination of six factors.

The first was the Suez invasion of November 1956 and its humiliating abortion in the face of U.S. economic pressure, which not merely revived the art of the political demonstration but provoked a bitter debate within Britain as to its world role, as a result of which a sizable minority concluded that Britain was too weak to be a major military power and should in future rely on its moral influence instead. The second factor, coinciding almost exactly, was the Soviet military repression of Hungary—both a further demonstration of the gulf between the power of ordinary states and that of the superpowers, and the cause of the departure from the Communist party of E.P. Thompson and others, who, in partnership with a number of young, university-educated Marxists such as Stuart Hall, formed the "New Left," later to be an influential minority component within CND.

The third factor was the publication in April 1957 of a defense white paper in which the new minister of defence, Duncan Sandys, finally made clear that British defense would in future be based largely on massive retaliation with the H-bomb. A British missile, Blue Streak, was to be built; conscription was to be ended and conventional capabilities reduced; and it was made explicit that there was "at present no means of providing adequate protection for the people of this country against the consequences of an attack by nuclear weapons." Spelling out in this way what had formerly been fudged had an undoubted public impact.

So did the fourth factor, Britain's first H-bomb test, at Christmas Island in May 1957, which contributed directly to the formation of two of CND's predecessors. Anticipation of this British test stimulated those concerned about fallout, and in February 1957 the north London joint local committee against nuclear bomb tests was metamorphosed, following a meeting at the National Peace Council, into the National Council for the Abolition of Nuclear Weapon Tests. And in April 1957 the Gandhian pacifists, who earlier in the decade had been mounting small-scale sit-down protests, set up the Emergency Committee for Direct Action Against Nuclear War (soon known as the Direct Action Committee or DAC for short). Originally formed to obstruct the British test by sailing a boat close to Christmas Island, DAC continued in existence despite the failure of that attempt to organize other antinuclear protests. DAC was in fact the original organizer of the first Aldermaston march at Easter 1958, although by then CND, with which it was cooperating uneasily, was gaining most of the publicity.

Moral outrage at a British test and increasing worry about radiation produced growing pressure among the Left during 1957 for a unilateral gesture by Britain. It was not surprising therefore that, when the Labour party met at Scarborough from 30 September to 4 October 1957 for its annual conference, many people hoped that it would give a lead, particularly as it had already called for a temporary suspension of British tests and also because Aneurin Bevan had been heard to claim that "tens of millions of people all over the world would once more lift up their eyes to Britain" if it renounced the bomb.[4] But, though wobbling almost to the last moment, Bevan remained true to his former position and spoke decisively against unilateral nuclear disarmament on the grounds that it would send the next British foreign secretary "naked into the conference chamber . . . to preach sermons." Labour's refusal to espouse unilateralism, thereby necessitating a separate campaigning body, was thus factor number five.

The sixth and last factor occurred on the day the Scarborough conference dispersed: the launching by the Soviet Union on 4 October 1957 of the first earth satellite, Sputnik-1, thereby demonstrating that the West was now within range of Soviet rocketry. In the United States alarm about a supposed "missile gap" led to a 1958 agreement with Britain to install (highly vulnerable) liquid-fueled Thor rockets in East Anglia, albeit under a dual-key control system. In Britain

Sputnik seems to have been the final catalyst for an influential *New Statesman* article by J.B. Priestley on 2 November, the favorable response to which prompted the editor, Kingsley Martin, to hold discussions with Canon John Collins of St Paul's Cathedral, historian A.J.P. Taylor, Labour politician Michael Foot, and others, which led in January 1958 to the winding up of the National Council for the Abolition of Nuclear Weapon Tests and its replacement by CND, of which Canon Collins was chairman and Bertrand Russell, rapidly moving toward unilateralism, president.

After a very brief hesitation designed (unsuccessfully) to accommodate the United Nations Association, CND in February 1958 declared itself unilateralist in the full sense: opposed to a British independent deterrent, to a British nuclear contribution to NATO or any other alliance, and to U.S. or any other foreign nuclear weapons on British soil. This message was disseminated by Easter marches (CND's most successful tactic, borrowed from DAC, as already noted), major public meetings, pamphlets, and leaflets—pressure-group methods reminiscent of past radical campaigns. Indeed, one of CND's best public speakers, A.J.P. Taylor, was self-consciously in the tradition of radical dissent from British foreign policy of which he had recently published a history.[5] CND's support encompassed a very broad range of political allegiances, but radicalism was its most characteristic ideology. (Unlike socialism or liberalism, radicalism does not seek structural changes in the economy or the system of states; it implies instead that peace is preserved when the popular will is allowed to prevail over vested interests and blinkered and self-serving rulers.)[6] CND's radical campaign survived the setback of a Conservative electoral victory in 1959 and reached its peak in 1960, in which year a Gallup poll in April found 33 percent support for giving up nuclear weapons entirely and a unilateralist motion was carried in September at the Labour party conference over the protests of leader Hugh Gaitskell.

That Gaitskell regained control of defense policy the following year was symptomatic of CND's loss of momentum after 1960, almost imperceptible at first but all too visible by 1964, which can be attributed to a combination of policy and organizational problems. Many of the most famous names who constituted CND's initially self-appointed executive committee were concerned mainly to protest against the British deterrent; their belief that its renunciation would have a dramatic impact on the rest of the world betrayed an egoism that led A.J.P. Taylor later to describe CND as a "last splutter of imperial pride."[7] But after France tested its first nuclear device in February

1960 (China following suit in October 1964), it was harder to believe that a moral gesture by Britain would of itself prevent nuclear proliferation. With the cancellation of the Blue Streak program in April 1960, moreover, it became clear that the "independent" deterrent would be dependent on a delivery system purchased from the United States. To both opponents and supporters alike, therefore, the British bomb did not seem as important as it had formerly.

CND's response was to make its policy more extreme. It came out against British membership in NATO in 1960—a step originally pressed for by its New Left element in the belief that the campaign had to be made aware of the political implications of its single-issue obsession with the morality of the British bomb but a step that also appealed to the isolationism that has commonly characterized British radicalism. The problem with this policy was that it left unclear what Britain's role outside NATO would be. The foreign policy of "positive neutralism" expounded by CND after 1961 (and including opposition to the EEC) lacked plausibility; and calling as it did for conventional disarmament while failing (with few and belated exceptions) to discuss alternative defense strategies, it presented no coherent nonnuclear defense policy either. Because, to preempt the charges of being parasitic upon the U.S. nuclear deterrent or of being pro-Soviet, CND also called for both superpowers to renounce their nuclear weapons unilaterally, it is not surprising that some of its most thoughtful supporters came to believe that it had espoused a policy that was too fundamentalist to have any chance of implementation. In particular the New Left, in the person of Stuart Hall, wished CND to have the flexibility to campaign against particularly disturbing nuclear policies (such as the MLF proposal), and caused controversy by pressing for a more gradualist approach. [8] Canon Collins had become dissatisfied with CND's little-Englandism: when the European Federation Against Nuclear Arms (launched by CND in January 1959) failed to make progress and the CND executive showed little enthusiasm for a new body, he went ahead on his own and in January 1964 formed an International Confederation for Disarmament and Peace (ICDP).

The espousal of more fundamentalist policy goals went ,hand in hand with the democratization of the movement—annual conferences were held from 1960, a national council was elected from April 1961, national membership was finally introduced in 1965—and the drifting away from it of many members of the original executive committee. It was also accompanied by the adoption of more extreme campaigning methods after 1960 by those including CND's president

Bertrand Russell who, falling increasingly under the influence of his abrasive American private secretary, Ralph Schoenman, a harbinger of late-1960s student radicalism, felt that to counter press hostility it was necessary to undertake civil disobedience as an attention-grabbing device. In September of that year, therefore, the Committee of 100 was set up to pursue on a mass scale the sit-down demonstrations ending in arrests and imprisonment that DAC had been mounting during 1958-59, somewhat to the CND leadership's embarrassment. What had radiated idealist Gandhian pacifism when practiced by DAC appeared as politically motivated defiance of the state in the hands of Schoenman and his associates. The Committee of 100 (which absorbed DAC in July 1961) was thus a mixed blessing for CND, which suffered the resignation of its president in a row between the two bodies:[9] CND attracted publicity for the nuclear-disarmament movement as a whole, but its confrontation with the police, and its unsustainable attempt to mount ever bigger demonstrations, caused it to be perceived by 1962 as disruptive and in decline. Even the Aldermaston marches changed in character. Younger and more militant marchers, including a prominent contingent of anarchists, were replacing the moderate and middle-aged worriers about fallout, partly because of two events on which it became CND orthodoxy to blame its loss of moderate support: the moratoriums on atmospheric testing that culminated in the partial test-ban treaty initialed in Moscow in July 1963; and the widespread belief that the Cuban missile crisis of October-November 1962 had shown nuclear deterrence to be working successfully.

By Easter 1964, when no Aldermaston march was held and Canon Collins felt unable to endure the chairmanship any longer, it was generally recognized that these policy and organizational difficulties had brought the campaign's first phase to an end. CND continued in existence (unlike the Committee of 100, which wound itself up in 1968), but its support dwindled rapidly. Many activists reverted to a more normal existence—marrying, and pursuing careers (in several cases in universities, which began to expand at this time)—giving rise to the theory that radical movements have a limited "natural" life expectancy. Others espoused new issues: the performance of Harold Wilson's 1964-70 Labour government (which, partly by means of its skillfully obfuscating the Atlantic Nuclear Force proposal, succeeded in distracting the Left's attention from its retention of nuclear weapons), the Vietnam war, student politics, Northern Ireland, ecology, and feminism. For a fifteen-year period nuclear weapons were not the subject of a parliamentary debate. It seemed that the British public had come to believe in the possibility of stable nuclear deterrence on the basis of mutual assured destruction.

Meanwhile, important and potentially destabilizing changes in nuclear policy were occurring. The doctrine of flexible response, officially ed by NATO in 1967, appeared to envisage an attempt at limited nuclear war in Europe. And the development of new weapons of an accuracy not required for mutual assured destruction seemed to jeopardize the stability formerly achieved. Yet the peace movement was too weak and distracted to draw the public's attention to these developments; and the start of the detente process and the SALT talks led most people to give the superpowers the benefit of the doubt. Only a return to cold war and the arms race, especially if domestic political conditions were also suitable, could guarantee a second phase of CND activity.

THE SECOND PHASE

CND reached its nadir in the early 1970s. By 1971, membership, at 2,047, had fallen low enough for the Communists (who had been supporting the campaign since 1960) to get one of their number, John Cox, elected as chairman. Thereafter there were increasing signs that the peace movement was, albeit slowly and from a low baseline, starting to revive. CND began to attract new recruits of high caliber: some, like Dan Smith and Mary Kaldor, brought with them an academic expertise about defense that the campaign had formerly lacked; and Mgr. Bruce Kent, who in 1977 replaced John Cox as chairman, brought the moral integrity of a Roman Catholic priest formerly active in the charity War on Want to an organization with an embarrassingly strong Communist (although not overtly pro-Soviet) minority.

In 1977 opinion polls throughout Western Europe began to show a steady increase, which was to peak in mid-1980, in public expectations of another war within ten years. [10] This may have been caused by mounting disillusionment with the results of SALT I and by the deteriorating prospects for SALT II. But a particular cause of disquiet in 1977 was the Carter administration's resumption in July of work on the "neutron bomb" (enhanced radiation weapon), a nuclear warhead perceived in Britain as being especially objectionable: like gas in World War I, it was seen as dirtier than a blast bomb, and its ability to irradiate tank crews without destroying the surrounding buildings made it the capitalist weapon par excellence in the eyes of the Left. Its abrupt cancellation by Carter in April 1978 merely reinforced two contradictory worries in Western Europe about U.S. defense policymaking. On the one hand, peace movements drew the moral that unnecessary weapons could be withdrawn in response to their protests (CND having in 1978 collected 162,000 signatures for a petition against the neutron bomb). [11] On the other hand, defense ministries concluded that they had been right to fear that the ending in the 1970s of the U.S. preponderance in strategic nuclear weapons made the United States a less dependable ally; it thus became important to avoid any NATO nuclear inferiority in the European theater (because deficiency in the theater balance of power could no longer be redressed by U.S. superiority in the global balance).

The widening divergence between public and official attitudes in Britain was symbolized by the events of spring 1978. From May to early July the first world disarmament meeting since that of 1932-33 was held in the form of a special session of the United Nations General Assembly in New York, with a second promised for four years later, by which time definite proposals were to have been formulated. But simultaneously NATO heads of government agreed to increase defense spending by 3 percent per annum in real terms, having already begun to investigate the possibility of modernizing their long-range theater nuclear forces (LRTNF) in Europe. [12] In July 1979, just after SALT II was signed, Carter approved detailed proposals for submission to the NATO Council in December; and a speech by Brezhnev in East Berlin on 6 October marked the start of a last-minute peace offensive designed to stop NATO from going ahead. It was the propaganda counteroffensive by NATO that prompted E.P. Thompson to revive his concern for the peace issue; [13] and in the same month the nonagenarian doyens of the British peace movement, Lords (Fenner) Brockway and (Philip) Noel-Baker, launched the World Disarmament Campaign in the hope that public opinion would force the governments of the world to take seriously the second United Nations special session on disarmament scheduled for 1982.

Other factors were helping to revive the peace movement at this time. The deepening economic recession stimulated the belief that scarce resources were being wasted on defense. This was probably less important, however, than the opposition to the civil use of nuclear energy, which had been growing throughout the 1970s; like atmospheric testing prior to 1963 it seemed to show that nuclear energy was dangerous even if military deterrence worked—an argument dramatized by the accident at Three Mile Island in March 1979. (It was on the first anniversary of this near-disaster that a new "eco-feminist network" was launched in the United States, Women and

Life on Earth; a British equivalent formed in September 1980 was to be instrumental in launching the celebrated Women's Peace Camp at Greenham Common.) [14] Another factor, to which Bruce Kent has attached importance, [15] was increased reporting of defense accidents and false alarms: in November 1979, in particular, an almost catastrophic accident at Lakenheath in 1956 was disclosed for the first time under the U.S. Freedom of Information Act; and a recent computer failure that placed United States defense forces on full alert for six minutes also attracted considerable attention. By late 1979, therefore, a revival of the peace movement, undetected by a book on CND that went to press as late as July of that year, had become visible. CND membership, for instance, though still only "a nominal 4,000," as Bruce Kent later put it, [16] had increased by 30 percent in the space of twelve months.

But it was not until the eleven-month period from December 1979 to November 1980 that full-scale peace activity was triggered by a combination of events reminiscent of thirteen years previously. This time seven factors could be identified.

The first factor was the NATO Council's dual-track decision of 12 December 1979 to approve LRTNF modernization unless new talks with the Soviet Union produced an agreement over the theater nuclear balance. The increased risk to Britain of a Soviet preemptive strike on the 160 ground-launched cruise missiles to be stationed on its soil under U.S. single-key control provoked a debate over the utility of existing civil defense capabilities to deal with even a limited nuclear attack of this kind. A letter from Professor Michael Howard in *The Times* on 30 January 1980, warning of the new situation, and the government's reluctant publication in March of an inept and formerly restricted official booklet, *Protect and Survive,* encouraged E.P. Thompson to write a highly publicized riposte, *Protest and Survive,* which appeared in April to mark the launching of a new group, the campaign for European Nuclear Disarmament (END).

END had grown out of discussion in February between Thompson and the Bertrand Russell Peace Foundation (BRPF), the body Russell had set up in September 1963 at Ralph Schoenman's prompting, following the decline of the Committee of 100, to carry on the stridently anti-American and ultraleftist peace campaigning of his last years. After 1966, when Schoenman devoted himself to a BRPF offshoot, the International War Crimes Tribunal (until dismissed by Russell in 1969), the BRPF's most influential figure was Ken Coates, a miner turned sociology lecturer; and in 1969 the foundation decamped from London to Nottingham, where it shared premises with Coates's newly established Institute of Workers' Control. (It was a sign of how far to the left some of its constituency parties had moved that in the 1983 general election Coates was the official Labour candidate in Nottingham South.) Like the New Left during CND's first phase, and Canon Collins's ICDP (which had proved ineffectual), Thompson and Coates disliked insular preoccupation with nuclear weapons in Britain to the detriment of practical campaigning to undermine alliance structures in Europe; END's goal was thus to make Europe a nuclear-free zone. This was endorsed at its launching at the House of Commons by sixty-eight MPs (including Tony Benn, Stuart Holland, and Neil Kinnock) and nearly two hundred other public figures. No individual members were to be enrolled, however, although an executive was appointed consisting of Thompson, Coates, Stuart Holland, Bruce Kent, Dan Smith, Mary Kaldor, and Peggy Duff (secretary of CND until 1967 and thereafter of the ICDP).

The second factor was the Soviet Union's military intervention in Afghanistan on 24 December 1979, which finally terminated the decade of detente and made certain that the United States Senate would not ratify the SALT I treaty signed in June. An unfettered arms race seemed inevitable, moreover: a prospect that scared many in Britain who did not favor one-sided disarmament by the West but felt nevertheless that a real effort to achieve multilateral disarmament was essential. Thus when on 12 April 1980 Lords Brockway and Noel-Baker held the first public meeting of their World Disarmament Campaign (WDC), they were gratified by the response: an audience of 2,600 in Central Hall, Westminster; Cardinal Basil Hume delivering the main address; and a cheque for £10,000 from the overseas-aid charity Oxfam in recognition of the WDC's insistence that money spent on armaments be diverted to help relieve Third World distress. In July 1980 the WDC was able to appoint as its secretary the former chief of staff of the UN peacekeeping force in Cyprus, Brigadier Michael Harbottle.

The third factor was the announcement on 17 June 1980 that the first batch of cruise missiles in Britain was to be based at Greenham Common, near Newbury, and that the second site was to be Molesworth in Cambridgeshire. This stimulated the local peace campaigns that have been so marked a feature of the 1980s peace movement: the Newbury Campaign Against Cruise Missiles (the leader of which, Mrs Joan Ruddock, was later elected chairperson of CND), Campaign ATOM in nearby Oxford, Cumbrians for Peace, Manchester Against the Missiles, and many others.

The fourth and fifth events both occurred in July 1980: the

announcement, after much speculation, that the British government was indeed to buy Trident from the United States to replace Polaris as its independent nuclear deterrent; and the issuing by Carter of Presidential Directive 59, which appeared to many as confirmation of their fears that U.S. nuclear planners were contemplating war-fighting rather than pure deterrence.

The sixth factor was the official return of the Labour party, at its October 1980 conference, to the unilateralist position it had adopted in 1960, 1972, and 1973. This change was attributable not merely to the growing ascendancy of the Left following the electoral defeat of 1979 and the worsening of the recession but also to an astonishing indiscretion by the new defense secretary, Francis Pym, who revealed that the outgoing Labour government had, contrary to its public statements and without even informing a majority of its own cabinet, approved the "Chevaline" project for improving Polaris warheads.

The Seventh and last factor was the election in November 1980 of Ronald Reagan, a president suited more to the deterrence of his country's enemies than to the reassurance of his country's allies.

In the space of eleven months these seven factors had produced in Britain a sharply increased perception that the arms race was out of control and, particularly on the Left, among women and among the young, a growing minority belief that NATO was at least as responsible for this as was the Soviet Union. (For whatever reason, the latter's deployment of SS-20s failed to catch the public imagination.) There was also a marked increase in public expressions of skepticism about the achievability of multilateral disarmament unless one state risked a "one-sided" initiative. "Multilateralism," as New Left veteran Professor Raymond Williams put it in the autumn of 1980, "is in fact a codeword for continued acquiescence in the policy of military alliances and the arms race." [17]

Nothing occurred to confound these judgments in the two and a half years after Reagan's election. No progress was made toward arms control. Reagan's initiatives in the European theater talks promised in the NATO Council's dual-track decision of 12 December 1979, such as the "zero option" of 18 November 1981 (abandoned early in 1983), did not appear constructive to his critics; and his assent to new strategic talks (START) in June 1982 was neutralized by his choice of hard-line negotiators and by his "star wars" speech of 23 March 1983. Margaret Thatcher's relishing of her "iron maiden" image, her government's announcement of 11 March 1982 that it would be buying the most advanced (D-5) version of Trident, and her resolute prosecution of the Falklands War all made her seem no less a "militarist" to the British peace movement. Only in 1983, as will be seen, were serious efforts made to present the government's case; and only in the middle of that year did the combination of factors assembled from December 1979 to November 1980 start at least partially to unravel.

The nuclear-disarmament movement that enjoyed unchecked growth in this period was organizationally more diverse than that of the years after 1958, when CND's monopoly had been challenged only by DAC and Committee of 100. As well as the (multilateralist) WDC, there were END and its local branches (for example in west Yorkshire), numerous local campaigns, peace camps, feminist groups, and a growing number of independent specialist bodies such as Scientists Against Nuclear Arms (SANA), which a CND vice-president, Professor Michael Pentz, set up in February 1981. Their relationship to the senior but long-dormant antinuclear organization, CND, which itself had a number of specialist sections (Labour, Christian, Green, etc.) as well as a youth group, was often unclear—a fact that did not trouble Bruce Kent, who in February 1980, with his church's consent took over as full-time general secretary, having relinquished the chairmanship to Lord Jenkins of Putney (former Labour MP Hugh Jenkins). As late as April 1980, the month the media first began to notice the revival of peace campaigning, it was still "not then clear that CND would be the major beneficiary and organiser" of that revival, as E.P. Thompson has acknowledged in partial explanation of that month's launching of the separate END campaign.[18] But, after 50,000 marched from Hyde Park to Trafalgar Square on 26 October 1980 (prompting *The Times* to acknowledge editorially "the second coming of CND"), CND was clearly once again the unofficial spearhead of antinuclear activity.

Under CND's leadership the nuclear-disarmament movement grew steadily. By the end of 1980 national CND membership had already reached 9,000, and the rate of growth was accelerating. In the course of 1981 national membership rose to 20,000, with an extra 200,000 estimated to belong to the burgeoning local peace groups; and during that year CND became increasingly aware of being part of a wider European campaign: when 150,000 people attended a Hyde Park rally on 24 October it was part of a weekend of demonstrations in which 25,000 turned out in Paris and 250,000 in Brussels. September 1981 also saw the quiet beginnings of the peace movement's best-publicized new tactic when a Women For Life on Earth group in South Wales marched to Greenham Common and decided to set up a permanent peace camp outside the gates. By November, when the articulate and photogenic Mrs. Ruddock soundly defeated John Cox in the contest to succeed Lord Jenkins as CND's chairperson, public support for unilateralism had reached 23 percent.

During 1982 national CND membership climbed to 50,000, and its major rally, in Hyde Park on 6 June, mobilized either 250,000 people (according to CND) or 125,000 (according to the police)—even the lower figure a remarkable achievement at the height of the Falklands War (which did not end until 14 June). In July the home secretary felt obliged to cancel the "Hard Rock" civil-defense exercise planned for the autumn owing to strong opposition from Labour-controlled local authorities; and by September support for unilateralism had reached 31 percent. In October a working party of the Church of England's Board of Social Responsibility, chaired by the bishop of Salisbury, produced a unilateralist report, *The Church and the Bomb.* And throughout the year the Greenham Common peace camp (declared women-only in February) [19] enjoyed the limelight because of its tenacity in face of eviction attempts (by October it was living under plastic sheets following the removal of its caravans), the willingness of its members to go to prison for acts of nonviolent civil disobedience, and its major demonstrations on 12 December, when 30,000 women formed a nine-mile chain round the perimeter fence of the base, which they covered with children's pictures and other decorations, and on the following day when 2,000 of them blockaded its entrance.

By 1983, a year that started with 44 Greenham campers climbing over the fence and performing a New Year's Day dance on the silos for an hour until arrested, the movement had become sufficiently important for attempts to be made—official, semiofficial, and independent—to denigrate it. In January Thatcher chose Michael Heseltine to be her new secretary of state for defence largely because of his public relations skills; and by March a special "defence secretariat 19" had been set up in his department to carry on the drive against unilateralism, or one-sided disarmament as the government increasingly preferred to call it. Its researches enabled Heseltine in April to exploit the CND national council's narrow vote in favor of sending two observers to a congress being organized in Prague by the (Soviet-controlled) World Peace Council by releasing details of the left-wing affiliations of CND's leading figures. Factual inaccuracies reduced the impact of this report, however, and what surprised informed observers was how few Communists (as distinct from Labour party members) could be identified: 3 out of 24 on the executive, and "more than a dozen" (as *The Times* put it) out of 107 members of the national council. [20] April 1983 saw a number of anti-CND initiatives: a junior minister, Dr. Gerard Vaughan, held back part of the grant to the Citizens' Advice Bureau, apparently from displeasure at the fact that Joan Ruddock was employed four days a week at the bureau in his Reading constituency, although he soon had to make an embarrassed "climb-down"; Bruce Kent was warned by Cardinal Hume of the danger of becoming too political (CND having inevitably become identified as strongly anticonservative, despite the existence of the small Tories Against Cruise and Trident [TACT] group); the semiofficial British Atlantic Committee set up a new public relations offshoot, Peace Through NATO; Tory journalist Lady Olga Maitland launched her counterpart to the Greenham women, a body called Women and Families for Defence; and the existence of an interlocking network of right-wing groups seeking to undermine CND, some which were alleged to be spreading lies (such as that CND was in receipt of Soviet funds or that Bruce Kent had once organized an IRA march), came to light when journalists investigated complaints by Kent against Conservative MP Winston Churchill. [21] (Earlier, on 23 March, a letter-bomb sent to CND headquarters had been safely disposed of.)

The effect of such anti-CND propaganda is hard to assess. The polls suggest that public support for unilateralism had already started to fall: from a 31 percent peak in September 1982, it was already down to 21 percent in January 1983, and to 19 percent by May (and to 16 percent by October). Opposition to cruise missiles did, however, drop from 61 percent to 54 percent between January and May 1983 (reaching 48 percent in October), as did opposition to Trident, albeit only from 56 percent to 54 percent (and to 50 percent in October). [22]

But opinion polls have long shown a surprisingly inexact correspondence between public attitudes and the intensity of antinuclear activity, and the latter was unaffected by the propaganda drive of 1983. Although disappointed on 10 February by the Church of England Synod's rejection of *The Church and the Bomb*'s unilateralist recommendation, activists were heartened early in March by the publication of *Medical Effects of Nuclear War,* a report by the British Medical Association's board of science, which preferred SANA's civil defense calculations to those of the government. They were further encouraged on 1 April by CND's successful fourteen-mile, 100,000-person chain connecting Greenham Common with the Royal Ordnance Factory at Burghfield, where research on the Trident warhead was being carried out. And even more cheering, when Thatcher called a snap general election for 9 June 1983, was the Labour party's unprecedented inclusion in its manifesto of a commitment to unilateralism that was (almost, as will be seen) unequivocal. It was not until the election campaign itself that CND and the unilateralist movement were to experience their first significant setback.

The two other main components of the nuclear-disarmament movement had run into difficulties sooner, although, because neither was a membership organization, support and impetus are rather harder to measure. Most obviously faltering was the WDC: concentrating as it had on collecting nearly 2.25 million signatures for its petition in support of the second United Nations special session on disarmament, it suffered an inevitable and major setback when that session, held from 7 June to 9 July 1982, coincided with the climax and immediate aftermath of the Falklands War and proved a disappointing flop. Four months later, on 9 October, Lord Noel-Baker died. By 1983 the WDC had been in effect replaced as the major multilateral-disarmament initiative by the "nuclear freeze" first proposed by American disarmers; after September 1982 this was being promoted by a Nuclear Weapons "Freeze" Advertising Campaign, organized by former anti-Concorde campaigner Richard Wiggs, [23] and by other groups. (After June 1983, as will be seen, a growing number of unilateralists came to give priority to the freeze campaign as an interim measure.)

Though continuing to expand its support in Britain, END's central policy assumptions were frustrated by international events, and the campaign also faced internal difficulties. Its main difference from CND was that it believed that cruise, Pershing II, and SS-20 missiles, though alarming in themselves and particularly convenient for dramatizing the issue to the mass public, were essentially symptoms of an underlying problem: the domination of Europe by the superpowers. END's whole credibility rested, therefore, on a loosening of NATO and Warsaw Pact ties, a political development with no necessary connection with nuclear disarmament, unilateral or otherwise: as de Gaulle had shown, it could in principle be promoted by European states developing their own independent deterrents.

If END was to pursue the simultaneous dissolution of the cold war alliances by means of a campaign against nuclear weapons, its strategy depended entirely upon reciprocation by Eastern Europe, whether by governmental action or the emergence of oppositional movements, an expectation that led it to be likened to "the appeasement of the 1930s" and dismissed as naive by a prominent Czech dissident in an open letter, under the pseudonym Vaclav Racek, to E.P. Thompson on 12 December 1980. [24] Nevertheless, the emergence of Solidarity in the Polish strikes of August 1980 and its steady assertion of power until its suppression in December 1981 seemed to offer a ray of hope. But, as Thompson later acknowledged, "in the aftermath of Polish martial law, transcontinental perspectives began to grow dim." The consequence, according to Thompson, was that the British peace movement as a whole became to its detriment "more nationally preoccupied" and "hence—by default rather than design—less clearly non-aligned and less aware of the reciprocal response from the Warsaw bloc."[25] As Thompson admitted: "Some ENDers suspected CND of being soft on the Soviet Union"; for its part END became extremely careful to emphasize that it was in no sense pro-Soviet.[26]

The initial END appeal of April 1980 had, however, failed properly to make this clear. Admittedly, it had insisted: "We do not wish to apportion guilt as between the political and military leaders of East and West. Guilt lies squarely upon both parties." But though it called for the United States not to deploy cruise or Pershing II missiles, it asked that the Soviet Union merely "halt production of the SS-20," despite the fact that 150 missiles were, on its own later admission,[27] already then deployed. And its demand "to free the entire territory of Europe, from Poland to Portugal, from nuclear weapons" could be construed as ignoring other missiles on Soviet territory. David Owen was quick to make this criticism; and as early as May 1980 Thompson was clarifying that END wanted "the withdrawal of *both* Cruise and Soviet SS-20 missiles: and for the creation of a zone free of all nuclear weapons in *all* Europe, and not only in western and central Europe."[28]

It was not unwelcome, therefore, when the official Soviet "peace movement" suddenly attacked END because of its continued efforts to encourage unofficial peace and other dissident groups in the East, including the Group to Establish Trust Between the USSR and the USA established in Moscow in June 1982 (the leader of which, Sergei Batrovin, was subsequently incarcerated for a time in a mental hospital), the Peace Group for Dialogue in Hungary, and Swords into Ploughshares in East Germany.[29] Although the first Convention for European Nuclear Disarmament, held in Brussels from 1 to 4 July 1982, included few delegates from Communist states other than Yugoslavia, it was announced that the second convention, to be held in May 1983, would invite both official and unofficial groups from the East and be held, moreover, in West Berlin. This provoked the president of the Soviet Peace Council, Zuri Zhukov, to send out in December 1982 to members of the British and West German peace movements fifteen hundred copies of a diatribe alleging that END was not only intensifying the cold war but even promoting German reunification.[30] END denied the charge but, when the second Convention for European Nuclear Disarmament met in West Berlin on 9 May 1983 and delegates from the West German Green party briefly got themselves arrested after staging a well-publicized demonstration in the eastern zone of the city, some members of the British peace movement did agree that such actions were exacerbating East-West tension for the sake of insignificant dissident peace groups in the Communist bloc. (Similar comments were expressed[31] when CND's two observers at the World Peace Council's World Congress For Peace And Life Against Nuclear War in Prague in June of 1983—which END had boycotted—had conspicuous contacts with the dissident Charter 77 group, to the annoyance of the Czech authorities.)

But although the Soviet Peace Council's criticisms were tributes to END's success in establishing that it was not pro-Soviet, the East European peace movements remained too weak for its strategy to be credible in the short term. In addition END faced, on top of mounting financial problems, disagreements both tactical and personal between Thompson and his associates on the one hand and Coates's Nottingham-based BRPF on the other. After December 1982 END's London office began to emphasize its independence by publishing the separate *END Journal* (instead of depending on the BRPF's *Bulletin*); the *Journal* established around itself a supporters' conference, which, meeting in Oxford on 2 and 3 July 1983, adopted a constitution and elected a new twelve-person coordinating committee, including Thompson, Dan Smith, and Mary Kaldor (editor of the *Journal*).[32] Yet despite these signs of vigor and the often high quality of its literature, it is clear that END faces a long uphill struggle, and lacks the broad appeal of CND.

Unlike WDC and END, the policies of which always required reciprocation by other states, CND and its associated local campaigns could preserve their momentum so long as they were perceived to have some chance of influencing British policy. The difficulties they face have been of two kinds.

The first has been the near impossibility, as CND had discovered during its first phase, of sustaining an ever fresh and ever more vigorous campaign that hits the headlines without, however, eventually being perceived as negative and irresponsible. In 1982 the Greenham camp was treated favorably by the media, its spirit in face of appalling living conditions being generally praised; by the late summer of 1983, however, it had become more newsworthy to mention its squalor and disorderliness. A turning point in this respect was 7 February 1983, when the defense secretary was reportedly jostled on his way into a Conservative party meeting in Newbury town hall. The peace movement was convinced that Heseltine fell because he was being rushed too fast through the crowd by police, but, whatever the real nature of the incident, it distracted attention from Heseltine's curt refusal of a public debate with Joan Ruddock. In August a case of dysentery at the peace camp was widely reported, even though it concerned a Dutch woman who had contracted it before arrival. By late September the view that "public sympathy with the Greenham ladies has rather evaporated" was voiced by Heseltine, who had wound up his "defence secretariat 19" and was being treated in the press as clear winner of the public relations battle. Following the arrests of over two hundred women, who, perhaps feeling that they had little to lose, had on 29 and 30 October assaulted the perimeter fence with wire-cutters (prompting Heseltine, in a rare lapse from subtlety, to warn that intruders could be shot), *The Times* could describe the Greenham women as the defense secretary's "most reliable allies in the battle for middle opinion." Equally valuable for Heseltine was the demonstrator at Manchester University on 15 November who sprayed him with paint in one of the nationwide protests that greeted the sudden arrival of the first cruise missiles and warheads on 14 and 15 November respectively. In another, three hundred demonstrators were arrested for illegally staging a peaceful protest in Parliament Square. By April 1984 a serious disagreement had manifested itself between CND and Action 84, a group reminiscent of the Committee of 100, over the scale of obstruction to be attempted at the time of the economic summit in London in June.[33] Yet, so far at least, aggressive incidents have been exceptional; and what has been most remarkable about the antinuclear movement of the 1980s has been its orderliness and nonviolence, even though the public seems decreasingly appreciative of this fact.

The second danger for unilateralists has been from political developments beyond their control. Even a purely cosmetic arms-control agreement would damage their ability to claim that they alone could check the arms race. In the event, however, the first political setback was domestic: the result of the 9 June 1983 general election. Having welcomed it initially as the "nuclear election" in the hope that the majority disapproval of cruise missiles and Trident consistently revealed by the opinion polls could help Labour to win, CND was disappointed by the ease of the Tory victory. Particularly galling was Labour's midcampaign row when deputy leader Denis Healey, backed by former Prime Minister James Callaghan, seized on the one ambiguous sentence in an otherwise clearly unilateralist manifesto to insist that Labour would renounce Polaris only as part of a multilateral agreement and not unconditionally. Thus, instead of attention being focused on cruise missiles and Trident, it was directed toward the more fundamental issue of complete unilateralism, for which support had already, according to at least one poll, fallen below 20 percent.

The election proved, superficially at least, a watershed in CND's fortunes: three days later, for instance, only a thousand people turned up at a CND rally at Wembley. From this time, moreover, the problems inherent in running a democratic mass movement, which had formerly been kept remarkably under control, began to surface: in August the national committee of Youth CND had to be suspended and the activities of CND's specialist groups reviewed, following a partial takeover by the Trotskyist Socialist League (involving members of an Oxford-based group that had shortly before been publicly accused of infiltrating British-Leyland's nearby Cowley automobile factory); and on 13 November Bruce Kent made a rare public relations blunder in delivering a speech of tribute for its peace efforts to a congress of the British Communist party. A growing awareness that the installation of cruise missiles could not be prevented from occurring (even if their subsequent practice dispersals along the country lanes of Berkshire might well be susceptible to disruption) further contributed to a sense that the antinuclear movement was at the crossroads.

The direction in which the leadership has tried to point the antinuclear movement has been toward a more gradualist policy. As early as April 1983 CND's national council had backed the nuclear-freeze proposal; and, during the "difficult summer" (as Joan Ruddock called it) that followed, most of its spokespersons came to insist that nuclear disarmers should cease to be "seen as all-or-nothing people," in Bruce Kent's words, but should instead "highlight disarmament mea-sures which are immediately possible and which, when carried out, will make further steps possible." In END, too, the freeze proposal was seen to be useful for its strategy of reaching "middle opinion in both West and East." In October its *Journal* noted: "Many European peace movements are discussing how to adapt the freeze idea to the European situation"; and, in urging support for CND's major rally on 22 October, E.P. Thompson insisted: "It is not a matter of whether people can cross every T or dot every I in the policies of CND."

Whether support from the leaders of CND and END was helpful to the freeze movement in its efforts to attract the moderate support it needed, however, was open to some doubt: the participation of fifty unilateralist groups among the nearly four hundred sponsors of the full-page advertisement placed in *The Times* on 28 September 1983 by the Nuclear Weapons "Freeze" Advertising Campaign merely enabled Lord Chalfont, a former minister for disarmament but a leading critic of the peace movement, to condemn the freeze as "creeping unilateralism." In cooperating with middle-of-the-road opinion, CND is handicapped also by its long–standing commitment (enshrined in its revised constitution of 1978) to "general and complete disarmament," which appears to rule out collaboration with the sizable force of moderates favoring increased conventional forces as the most practical way to reduce dependence on nuclear weapons, as well as by its opposition to NATO. The refusal of many of its activists to consider any "retreat from basic beliefs and principles of CND" led at the 1983 conference (held on 2-4 December) to a narrow defeat for the leadership's policy of supporting the nuclear freeze. [34]

But second-phase CND has proved more resilient than first-phase, and fully alive to the danger that prophesies of postelection decline would prove self-fulfilling unless challenged. Its successful London demonstration of 22 October 1983, at which even the police estimated an attendance of 200,000 (and the *Sunday Telegraph*, no friend of the peace movement, 250,000), marked a recovery of nerve, despite the attempt by the *Sunday Times* to write it off as "the last great gasp of a movement which has clearly failed"; national CND membership passed 82,000 by the end of 1983; and, despite the nuclear-freeze vote, the 1983 conference showed itself "realistic" enough to resist Trotskyist infiltration of its youth section. Also reassuring were: the refusal of Labour's 1983 conference and of the party's new leader, Neil Kinnock, to water down their unilateralism; the intensification of peace-camp activity to cover 102 bases simultaneously on 9 November; the U.S. invasion of Grenada (because it could be claimed to vindicate the peace movement's belief that Reagan was trigger-happy); the widespread and generally disciplined vigils and other demonstrations that greeted the arrival of cruise missiles; and a return in the autumn of 1983 to a more favorable treatment by the press of the Greenham women (perhaps in reaction against their being dubbed "the smellies" by the 3,000 troops and police guarding the base). Even the setbacks of 1984—the first token dispersals of cruise-missile vehicles (on the nights of 8/9 and 28/29 March), and the attempted eviction of the Greenham women (which began on 4 April, leaving them completely without shelter other than sleeping bags)—have been borne with fortitude. [35]

THE STATE OF THE MOVEMENT

A convenient way to sum up the second phase of Britain's nuclear-disarmament movement is to notice similarities with and differences from its first flowering.

As was true of all but the earliest stage of phase one, CND has lived up to its self-description as a *campaign*. It has not sought to lobby policymakers privately but has sought, by a mixture of traditional and innovative tactics, to mobilize mass support—at its peak on both occasions persuading almost one-third of the population to give unilateralist answers to public-opinion pollsters. It has been even more spontaneous, loosely organized, and democratic than formerly, with its officials and elected leadership (which contains fewer "stars") anxious not to be considerd "elitist." Once again the fact that the campaign coheres at all is more remarkable than the fact that it experiences rows and disputes, the latter being, moreover, less acute than in the past.

Its support encompasses the same elements as before, although the mixture is subtly different: Christians, Quakers, and nonconformists are now reinforced by increased numbers of Anglicans and Roman Catholics; and, among political groups, anarchists and Communists have become less important, and feminists, Labour left-wingers, and (as a disruptive minority) Trotskyists more so.

Once more, too, the movement's inspiration is eclectic, but held together by radicalism. E.P. Thompson, like A.J.P. Taylor a quarter of a century before, has been self-consciously renewing the radical tradition of which he is a distinguished historian. His initial response to cruise missiles was thus to condemn "the suppression of information, the manipulation of the media, and the exclusion of critical questions from the arena of national political life" implied by the NATO Council decision of 12 December 1979. In developing his doctrine of "exterminism," moreover, he finally broke with the Marxist emphasis on the primacy of the economic infrastructure and espoused the pure-radical view that defense bureaucracies, the distorted and self-interested perspectives of which fuel the arms race, do not differ significantly between capitalist and communist countries.[36] The radical strand in left-wing Labour thought has also been brought to the fore by the nuclear issue; in his speech on launching END on 28 April 1980, for instance, Tony Benn made the characteristic radical claim: "The real danger of nuclear weapons is that in the guise of defending people against a foreign threat, they place control of political action in the hands of the domestic military establishments."

Nor have CND's policies changed. Its fundamentalist opposition to all nuclear weapons and to NATO (the withdrawal from which was reaffirmed at the 1982 and 1983 conferences) has not been abandoned, though once again, after the early momentum has slackened a little, a gradualist interim policy has found support among the leadership. But the mix of policies is somewhat different this time. Because Reagan is a less reassuring president than Eisenhower or Kennedy, and also because British power has continued to decline, a combination of anti-Americanism (in the form of the allegation that a trigger-happy United States is planning for limited nuclear war in Europe) and escapism (in the form of the prudential argument that Britain would be too obscure to be a major military target were cruise missiles and similar weapons not based in Britain) has replaced the former preoccupation with the independent nuclear deterrent on moral grounds.

The change of emphasis within CND's overall aims introduces the first of three main differences from last time, which can be emphasized by way of a conclusion because of their significance for future developments. Whereas Britain dominated the politics of nuclear disarmament a quarter of a century ago, it is now but one actor in a worldwide campaign. Hostility to INF modernization has been more acute in Continental states, which, believing themselves at suddenly increased risk of having a limited nuclear war fought on their territory or very close to it, have been particularly responsive to the prudential antinuclear case. Because these states do not have their own independent deterrents, not only is the escapist case against having nuclear weapons on their soil reinforced by nationalism and anti-Americanism but the full force of principled antinuclearism is brought to bear, for want of an authentically national nuclear "distraction," on NATO's new missiles. And, because it can no longer be denied that the superpowers take all the crucial decisions concerning the arms race, it is obvious that the appearance in the United States of the nuclear-freeze movement is the most important antinuclear development of all. The British nuclear-disarmament movement is having to end its years of splendid isolation.

Nevertheless, NATO policy would be seriously challenged if any state went unilateralist, so domestic developments remain important, if only for their effort on superpower perceptions. In this respect a second difference can be stressed: the greater and more durable support given by the Labour party, which did much to make British unilateralism a real political possibility in the 1980s (although the party consistently refused to oppose NATO). Only if Labour both survives as a major political force and retains what seemed in June 1983 an electorally disastrous commitment to this policy will CND have any chance of achieving its primary goal. The first condition is more likely than the second to be fulfilled.

The third difference is that the second phase derives its mass appeal from concern with the arms race. For the first phase, the equivalent issue was atmospheric nuclear testing, a subject on which governments found it both possible and politic to make the concessions that satisfied middle-of-the-road opinion. If in the future lasting arms-control agreements can be secured, the nuclear issue will probably drop to a lowly place on the British political agenda, of the sort it occupied from 1945 to 1957 and 1965 to 1979. There is no significant neutralist or anti-NATO feeling to nourish opposition to nuclear weapons irrespective of the state of the arms race; and such anti-Americanism as exists is largely based on distrust of the Reagan administration. But in default of such agreements, and in the event of the West's being perceived as to a degree responsible for this state of affairs, the antinuclear movement will remain active and each new weapons–procurement decision by Britain or NATO will become ever more controversial. Certainly no such decision can ever again be explained to the British public as casually and incompetently as was that of 12 December 1979. This is not merely because of the revival of an organized protest movement; it is because of the growth of a politically moderate, attentive public for nuclear issues: as well as the peace societies, many groups are attempting radically to rethink European defense strategies (such as the Alternative Defence Commission), and there is a greatly increased academic and public interest in all aspects of the management of conflict in the international system.

Like most "cause" groups, the British nuclear-disarmament movement can do little to determine its own fate. Yet insofar as it can, this will depend on resolving the paradox inherent in CND. Its activist base, which is far stronger and more durable than that which any multilateralist body can expect to build, depends on the simple moral fervor that unilateralism alone inspires. But its main hope for political progress—barring a miraculous victory by a genuinely unilateralist Labour party—lies in mobilizing *all* those alarmed by the arms race, most of whom will regard one-sided disarmament as acceptable only if it elicits reciprocal concessions within a reasonable period. The future of the movement thus depends to some extent on how well CND makes what Dan Smith has called "the delicate choices which strike the right balance of radicalism and popular appeal, of short- and long-term goals, of British and international issues." [37]

NOTES

1. November 1983, with minor revisions in May 1984. This essay draws on research for my forthcoming history of Britain's twentieth-century peace movement. The major secondary sources so far for the antinuclear movement are (apart from those cited later): Christopher Driver, *The Disarmers: A Study in Protest* (London: Hodder & Stoughton, 1964); *From Protest to Resistance (Peace News* pamphlet no. 2; Nottingham: Mushroom, 1981); A.J.R. Groom, *British Thinking about Nuclear Weapons* (London: Francis Pinter, 1974); Vernon Richards, *Protest without Illusion* (London: Freedom Press, 1981); Nicolas Walter, "Damned Fools in Utopia," *New Left Review* (January 1962); and Peggy Duff, *Left, Left, Left* (London: Allison & Busby, 1971).
2. *Listener* (30 December 1954): 1135-36. For the evolution of Russell's views, see Ronald W. Clark, *The Life of Bertrand Russell* (London: Jonathan Cape and Weidenfeld & Nicolson, 1975).
3. The first CND minute book, in the Modern Records Centre of the University of Warwick, records the first meeting of the executive committee as occurring on 28 January 1958.
4. At Reading on 5 May 1957, cited in Michael Foot, *Aneurin Bevan: A Biography* (London: Davis Poynter, 1973), 2:554. The best account of Labour and unilateralism is in Philip M. Williams, *Hugh Gaitskell: A Political Biography* (London: Jonathan Cape, 1979).
5. *The Trouble Makers: Dissent over Foreign Policy, 1792-1939* (London: Hamish Hamilton, 1957).
6. Radicalism and the other popular ideas concerning the causes of war are discussed in my book on peace arguments to be published by Oxford University Press in its OPUS series.
7. "Accident Prone, or What Happened Next," *Journal of Modern History* 49 (March 1977):13.
8. For the controversy aroused by Hall's "Steps towards Peace" proposal, see CND's journal *Sanity* (June 1963).
9. See the account in Canon L. John Collins, *Faith Under Fire* (London: Leslie Frewin, 1966), pp. 315-40.
10. See Bruce Russett and Donald R. De Luca, "Theater Nuclear Forces and Public Opinion in Western Europe," *Political Science Quarterly* 98 (Summer 1983): 179-96.
11. *Sanity* (December 1978/January 1979).
12. See Raymond L. Garthoff, "The NATO Decision on Theater Nuclear Forces," *Political Science Quarterly* 98 (Summer 1983): 197-214.
13. *New Statesman* (21-28 December 1979):982.
14. Leonie Caldecott and Stephanie Leyland, eds., *Reclaim the Earth* (London: Women's Press, 1983), pp. 6-7.
15. See his September 1981 talk, "Why Is There a New Wave of Peace Activism in the UK?" printed in Barrie Newman and Malcolm Dando, eds., *Nuclear Deterrence: Implications and Policy Options for the 1980s* (Tonbridge Wells: Castle House Publications, 1982), p. 10.
16. The book was Richard Taylor and Colin Pritchard, *The Protest Makers: The British Nuclear Disarmament Movement of 1958-65, Twenty Years On* (Oxford: Pergamon Press, 1980); for Kent's member-

ship comment, at CND's 1980 conference, see *Sanity* (October/November 1980).

17. "The Politics of Nuclear Disarmament," *New Left Review* (November/December 1980):34.

18. In his contribution to John Minnion and Philip Bolsover, eds., *The CND Story* (London: Allison & Busby, 1983), p. 83.

19. A talk by Dr. Lynne Jones to the Oxford Women's Studies Committee, 25 October 1983; see also her book *Keeping the Peace* (London: Women's Press, 1983). I am grateful to Karmen Cutler for showing me her scrapbook of the first march to Greenham, and for talking to me about the early days of the peace camp.

20. *The Times*, 20 May 1983.

21. *The Times*, 29 April 1983.

22. For a useful survey of Marplan poll data, see the *Guardian*, 22 October 1983.

23. I am grateful to Mr. Wiggs for supplying me with information about his campaign, which issued its first public statement in the *Guardian*, 15 September 1982, and which published a full-page advertisement in *The Times*, 28 September 1983.

24. Printed in *New Statesman* (24 April 1981): 6-13.

25. *New Statesman* (24 June 1983):10.

26. In Minnion and Bolsover, *The CND Story*, p. 83.

27. Meg Beresford (secretary of END) in *New Statesman* (21 January 1983):14.

28. David Owen, *Negotiate and Survive* (London: Campaign for Labour Victory, 1980), p. 11; E.P. and Dorothy Thompson, letter, *The Times*, 21 May 1980. I am grateful to Ken Coates for helpfully answering my questions about END.

29. For these movements, see *END Journal* (June/July and October/November 1983), and END's special reports: *The New Hungarian Peace Movement, The Moscow Independent Peace Group, Voices from Prague.*

30. See *New Statesman* (14 January 1983):14.

31. For example, the letter from Douglas Peroni, *Sanity* (September 1983).

32. See the *New Statesman* articles by Sarah Benton and Duncan Campbell (14 January and 20 May 1983), and *END Journal* (December 1982/January 1983):23; (August/September 1983):28.

33. Interview with Michael Heseltine, *Guardian*, 24 September 1983; editorial, *The Times*, 3 November 1983. For Action 84, see Nicolas Walter, letter, *Guardian*, 3 May 1984.

34. Joan Ruddock, *Sanity* (October 1983); Bruce Kent, *Sanity* (September 1983); *END Journal* (August/September 1983) 2; E.P. Thompson, *Guardian*, 17 October 1983; Lord Chalfont, letter, *The Times*, 10 October 1983; Douglas Smith, *Sanity* (October 1983); Sarah Benton (on CND's 1983 conference), *New Statesman* (9 December 1983).

35. See *Observer*, 20 November 1983; *Daily Mirror*, 23 November 1983; *The Times*, 10 March 1984; *Guardian*, 5-7 April 1984.

36. *New Statesman* (21-28 December 1979): 982; "Notes on Exterminism," *New Left Review* (May/June 1980), reprinted in E.P. Thompson, *Zero Option* (London: Merline Press, 1982).

37. *Sanity* (November 1983).

11

ALL QUIET ON THE FRENCH FRONT?

Nicole Gnesotto

Though it may be stating the obvious, one cannot deny that during the three years of the Pershing missile issue, the French anachronism on the European pacifism scene has remained unchanged. An insignificant divided fringe movement, the antinuclear campaign has not succeeded in arousing the French, who remain reassured by their nation's deterrent force or merely indifferent to security issues. Defense policy, the responsibility of all the presidents of the Fifth Republic, has in fact enjoyed an apparently solid consensus for more than fifteen years. President François Mitterrand himself could become personally involved in the debate—before the Bundestag in January 1983, and on each of his European state visits—without provoking any real opposition. In the same way, the bill on military planning for 1984/88 legislating the modernization of strategic nuclear force, Force d'Action Rapide (FAR), drew criticism for virtually only financial, not political, reasons. Pershing or no Pershing missiles, the French public and all the French political parties—with the exception of the communist party—continue to lend their support to French defense policy, much to the detriment of the European antinuclear movements that are often irritated by the "splendid isolationism" of the French.

It would be inaccurate, or at least hasty, to say that French pacifism is nonexistent. Although it is a minor movement, the antinuclear campaign has in fact had at least two major political consequences:

- The first involves the French Communist party (PCF), main proponent of pacifism in France. A member of the government coalition, the PCF, for the first time since its decision to endorse a French deterrent policy, has in fact raised the question of the independence of French nuclear forces.

245

- The second involves the national consensus itself. Although the peace movement has failed to gain much public support, it has on the other hand forced the political parties and the French authorities to rethink their traditional positions taken on the security of the Federal Republic of Germany (FRG) and Europe in general.

One should not be deceived by the quiet on the French front. Though the pacifist debate does not attract much public attention, there is in fact a second debate taking place in political circles. Post-deployment events will undoubtedly establish the importance of this debate for the future of French defense policy.

REASONS FOR THE ANACHRONISM

The fundamental reason for the uniqueness of the French situation is of course its Gaullist heritage. Since the break with NATO in 1966 and the establishment of an independent deterrent force, the French seem to have resolved once and for all the need for national sovereignty and automony expressed today by other Europeans. The peace movement, particularly in the FRG, reflects a resurgence of nationalism that General de Gaulle's France experienced fifteen years ago. As fragile as it may be, the French national consensus on defense matters remains a current reality. Of course, this consensus is a more recent phenomenon than is sometimes thought: the Communist party did not back a national deterrent policy until 1977; the Socialist party endorsed it in 1978. Thus the consensus is only five years old, but in a democracy that is enough to constitute a tradition.

The Euromissile issue has undoubtedly left the French satisfied that they "made the right choice" at the time. This satisfaction springs from the fact that the national consensus is not concerned with the credibility of the French nuclear defense policy as much as it is with the myth of political independence accompanying that policy. In fact, most polls show that the French do not truly believe in the effectiveness of their defense system in the face of a real conflict.[1] All, on the other hand, continue to believe in the inviolable policy of national independence, often to the point of thinking France no longer has any connection to NATO. And this Gaullist heritage has triumphed today: no outside constraint forces France to accept U.S. missiles, while at the same time no restriction prevents her from officially intervening in the East–West strategic debate.

This comfortable situation is due to a second advantageous factor: the fundamental ambiguity of the French defense policy. Whether one considers the Three Circles Theory of General Poirier or the

1972 White Book on Defense, no government has ever decided on either the nationalist or European-Atlanticist interpretations of French strategic policy. Both the doctrine of the sanctity of national sovereignty and the doctrine of French responsibility to defend Europe have been maintained for at least two fundamental reasons: (1) to make an opponent unsure of French response in case of conflict, and (2) to ensure the cohesion and adhesion of all French political organizations to national deterrence. This ambiguity of the French strategy is indeed able to satisfy everyone: the "nationalists"—including the Communists, the RPR Gaullists, and CERES, the left wing of the Socialist party—as well as the "European-Atlanticists," who include the UDF and the Socialist party as a whole. Thus the national consensus on the issue of defense springs from a broad range of compromising factions. Under the Valery Giscard d'Estaing administration, France remained officially reticent on the Euromissile issue. Mitterrand, on the other hand, has chosen to support publicly NATO's double-track decision of 1979. Neither of these two approaches affected the national consensus.

This Gaullist legacy, essential to understanding France's unique position in the peace movement, introduces two additional points. The first revolves around the current political situation: because it is not part of NATO, France is not affected, at least not geographically, by the decision of 1979; no U.S. missile will ever "colonize" one square inch of French territory. Thus there is no fear. Moreover, opinion polls on this matter are very revealing on the difference in attitude felt by nuclear nations and nonnuclear nations: the possession of nuclear arms in fact lowers the fear that they inspire, and the French are, among all Western populations, the most placid with respect to the use of nuclear energy by the military. [2]

The second point revolves around ideology. Anti-Americanism is part of the Gaullist tradition, or at least the French themselves characterize it as such. Officially independent of military alliances for nearly fifteen years, France therefore has little need of pacifism to express its desires for autonomy, and the anti-Americanism found here in both the government and public opinion is often more virulent than in the rest of Europe. Socialist France has refined this tradition even further by referring to U.S. intentions to govern the world through MacDonald's, dollars, embargos, and even debarkations. It is a striking paradox to see a France so closely allied with Washington on all issues concerning European security and at the same time so sharply critical of the slightest U.S. economic or cultural encroachment on its territory. Seen in this context, French support for NATO's decisions can spring only from true solidarity, from responsibility, or from serious government intentions; at any rate, never from a sense of obligatory allegiance. Furthermore, anti-Americanism is usually found in protest or pacifist malaise. In France it is institutionalized in the political system itself. Thus pacifism loses much of its protest value, particularly in the eyes of the young.

In addition, the antinuclear movement also represents a more general protest against the values and options of a postindustrial society (the German contingent being here at the forefront of these alternative social movements) and as such is a reflection, albeit a few months later, of the same protest and desire on the part of the French: the election of a Socialist government in May 1981 demonstrated this desire for social and political change. Whether or not the new government has succeeded in satisfying the alternative utopic visions is of course another story. But the event had, on the other hand, two important political consequences for the fate of French pacifism.

Above all, the election of a Socialist government placed the Socialist party in a paradoxical situation. The European antinuclear movement was in fact largely based on leftist support: the British Labour party and the West German SPD strongly backed the peace movements. In France, on the other hand, these movements found the Socialist party to be one of their strongest opponents. Party unity meant that the Socialists stood behind the president's support of the deployment of the Pershing II. This endorsement was not always due to the members' own convictions but, rather, more often due to simple party discipline, yet that was effective enough to prevent certain antinuclear factions within the Socialist party from joining the peace movement. Furthermore, the personal involvement of Mitterrand in the French debate on the issue was also a major factor: another Socialist president might not have had the same ability to control and convince the French Socialist party.

The second consequence of the 1981 elections involved the Communist party. It was clearly the most effective driving force behind the French peace movement. In December 1979, during parliamentary debate on the double-track decision of NATO, the PCF immediately opposed deployment of the Pershing and cruise missiles, while the Socialist party refused to follow it in this unilateral opposition to U.S. missiles. In 1983 the PCF maintained its anti-Pershing policy and organized the only large street demonstrations that Socialist France has experienced thus far. However, the pacifist offensive was not a full-fledged attack. As a member of a government that supports the NATO decision, the PCF was obliged to avoid at all costs a casus belli and was thus obliged to never push its pacifist policy too hard; breaking with the Socialist party over a foreign policy issue would do irreparable political harm: it would give rise to accusations of favoring Moscow over Paris. The Communist party has thus continually and skillfully balanced its policies of pacifist opposition and coalition discipline. It is true that the Socialist leaders brought the Communists back into line as the deployment deadline approached. Then the PCF came up with a wondrous new feat of double-talk. After the Williamsburg summit the Politburo called for the French forces to be included in the Geneva talks, while the same time the four Communist ministers were faithfully backing Mitterrand's positions on the independence of French nuclear forces. Thus, while the PCF was the main supporter of French pacifism, it avoided going beyond the point of no return. [3]

To these historical and political reasons that explain, for the most part, the lack of support for the French peace movement must be added the cultural factors that also account for the uniqueness of France's position. On the ideological level, pacifism fits the pattern of failure of French alternative movements to gain popular support, whether they be ecology, terrorism, or various "purist" movements from elsewhere. They do not catch on. The French remain resistant to the half-romantic, half-moralistic, and always extremist movements that so often flourish in Italy, West Germany, or Great Britain. This is simply an observation; an explanation of the phenomenon is yet to be provided.

On the intellectual level, the activist tradition (anti-imperialist and anti-American) dissolved in the ruins of Vietnam, the tears of Cambodia, and the harsh realities of Gulag. Antitotalitarianism is now espoused by all French intellectuals, from Yves Montand to Andre Glucksmand; and the pacifism supported by eminent British and West German writers is viewed with suspicion by the French counterparts. Essentially mobilized by the Poles of Solidarity, the French intellectual milieu remains the president's strongest ally in matters concerning the balance of power in Europe and recognition of the Soviet threat.

In addition, French concepts of peace and freedom have historically followed for the most part the traditional political divisions between the Left and Right. In the immediate postwar period, after the Krouchenko affair and the creation of the organization Mouvement de la Paix under the aegis of the Communists, there was a complete break between the "Partisans of Peace" (the principal PCF slogan) and the "Defenders of Freedom" (the rallying cry of the others). Thirty years later, French pacifism continues to suffer from this ideological handicap. The PCF monopoly on the issues of peace and disarmament continue to cause most French citizens to greet these issues with skepticism. For this very reason, the Socialists themselves have certainly found additional reason for prudent silence.

The linking of "pacifism" with "communism" is thus a major reason for the French hesitancy in the peace movement. In Great Britain and West Germany it would be difficult, or at least hasty, to characterize the antinuclear movement as merely a communist movement. [4] In France, on the other hand, the relationship is both historic and natural. This is, then, the second distinguishing factor in the French peace movement: in addition to its low popularity, the movement is extremely politicized, following to a great extent the divisions found on the national political scene. In France, with peace as with all else, one is either Communist or one is not.

THE FRENCH PEACE MOVEMENTS

Since the beginning of the Pershing cruise missile affair, there has been division in the ranks of the French peace movement. The Mouvement de la Paix, an old organization connected with the PCF since the Stockholm Appeal of 1950, was the first organization to oppose the U.S. missiles. Reaction against the Communist influence in this organization led to the rise of a second, rival organization, CODENE, in November 1981. Since that time, the Mouvement de la Paix and CODENE have continued, at least apparently, to compete politically and ideologically for the leadership of the French peace movement.

THE MOUVEMENT DE LA PAIX AND THE FRENCH COMMUNIST PARTY

The Mouvement de la Paix, the oldest of the French pacifist organizations, established in Paris on 20 April 1949 and member of the World Peace Council, was most influential at the beginning of the fifties: fourteen million signatures were collected throughout the nation for the Stockholm Appeal against the atomic bomb. Based on the infrastructure and positions of the Communist party, the Mouvement de la Paix became involved in all the major problems of the postwar period, including the issue of German rearmament and the Algerian and Vietnam wars. Though its influence waned for a time, the Mouvement de la Paix nonetheless experienced a resurgence when the antinuclear protests gained momentum after NATO's double-track decision of 1979; it mobilized a half-million people in Paris on 25 October 1981 in the first major French demonstration against the installation of U.S. missiles on the Continent.

An analysis of the Mouvement de la Paix shows that it led an unrelenting condemnation of the Pershing II missiles, missiles in the vanguard of a strategy of a limited nuclear war fought on European territory. In the movement's eyes, the United States is the aggressor, not the Soviet Union, which is significantly weakened by its domestic economic and nationalist problems. On account of its inferior military position and domestic political instability, it is in the USSR's own interest to maintain peace and pursue detente. To the unequal balance of power in the world that favors the United States must be added a strategic analysis that, moreover, is shared by all the French pacifists: the Mouvement de la Paix decries the superiority of the Pershing II over the SS-20; the former can directly hit Soviet territory while Washington remains comfortably out of range of the latter. The European continent, of which the USSR is geographically a part, risks paying the price for U.S. isolationism. Therefore, Pershing and cruise missiles are not needed, because the SS-20 pose no additional threat to Europe; for that matter, even less, because NATO already has, with its submarines and U.S. Forward Based System (FBS), the clear capability of an adequate response.

As a result of this political-strategic analysis, the Mouvement de la Paix increased its disarmament initiatives during the Socialist government's first year. Two trends quickly developed within the organization: one involved the strategy of the movement itself, the other concerned the legislation on the French Nuclear Strategic Force.

For reasons of credibility in the eyes of the French public, the Mouvement de la Paix and the Communist party were so closely connected that the pacifism of the movement was thereby discredited; thus it was in its own best interest to disassociate itself as much as possible from the Communists. Therefore, in the spring of 1982, the pacifist strategy of the Mouvement de la Paix changed in tone, if not substance. Although the Pershing missiles had up to that point always been seen as the number-one enemy of world peace, the pacifist campaigns of the movement began to restrict themselves to the most benign and depoliticized abstract statements possible: No New Missiles in Europe, Long Live Peace, No War. The slogans were as mild as they could possibly get.

A second organization, seemingly encompassing several political trends and independent of the PCF, appeared in the spring of 1983 and called itself Cent (the Group of 100). Composed of well-known individuals from the entertainment industry, the universities, the media, and the scientific community, Cent picked up where the Mouvement de la Paix left off and successfully organized the huge Vincennes demonstration of 19 June 1983. Of course the goals were the same as those held by the PCF in 1981: halting any new U.S. missile installations on European territory. This depoliticization of the issue of peace (by the most politicized of all the organizatons) presented two advantages: it allowed the Communists to continue as an opposition party without risking a break with the Socialist party, and, above all, it also unloaded the problem of French nuclear forces.

In fact, it is on the issue of a national deterrent that the development of the first pacifist movement is the most remarkable. In 1981 there was no question of either the Mouvement de la Paix or the PCF's bringing up the issue of French missiles. Let the two superpowers negotiate first. France would await the "right moment" to participate in any arms-control negotiations. In 1983 both the Soviets and the situation had changed: President Yuri Andropov's proposal to limit his SS-20's pro rata with the French and British missiles dates from December 1982. This put the PCF in a delicate situation: how could it respect Mitterrand's government policy on the independence of a national deterrent without at the same time betraying its international Communist interests? For six months the PCF hesitated, and then after the Williamsburg summit its position became more cohesive. Now the PCF seems to be in solidarity with the Western heads of state on the issue of resolving the Pershing missile deployment through France. "The Geneva talks must be opened to all the European governments," declared the PCF Politburo following the Williamsburg summit.

This development in the Communist party stance is undoubtedly the greatest effect the antinuclear movement has had in France. The PCF endorsed a policy of a national deterrent in May 1977 in clearly nationalistic terms that left no room for any French participation in an integrated defense strategy for Europe. Five years later it is this very policy of national nuclear independence that the PCF calls into question. "No one can deny [that the French missiles] are basically aimed at Soviet territory," declared Georges Marchais, and "it is therefore to be expected that the USSR would want to count them."[5] Of course the PCF at the same time continues to maintain its support of the principle of the independence and modernization of French nuclear forces. It voted for allocations for the recent legislation on military planning for 1984-88 and abstained only on Article 1, which, for the first time ever in French legislative history, named the Soviet Union as the only plausible enemy of the nation. And only prodigious feats of verbal acrobatics later allowed the PCF to lobby simultaneously for "considering the inclusion" of French forces at Geneva. It is true that the pacifist organizations such as Cent or Mouvement de la Paix were quite helpful in this situation. Without repeating word for word the Politburo's arguments for the inclusion of France at the Geneva talks, these movements in fact adopted in July 1983 the rallying cry "A freeze on all nuclear weapons," a vague slogan but with the same objective. Whether it is a question of a freeze or participation in Geneva, the French nuclear forces would inevitably be halted at their 1983 level and from that point on be submitted to the Soviet right of verification.

CODENE

The Committee for the Denuclearization of Europe (CODENE) is undoubtedly the largest competitor of the Mouvement de la Paix in the French peace movement. It was in reaction against the pro-Soviet tendencies of the Mouvement de la Paix that a number of individuals and leftist organizations decided, in November 1981, to establish a nonaligned committee that would truly support the European antinuclear protest movement. Included in the group were ecologists, anarchists, Third Worldists, feminists, and nonviolent activists, as well as the Unified Socialist party (PSU), one of whose leaders, Mrs. Bouchardeau, is also a member of the Mauroy government.

CODENE can thus be described as a collection of all the non-Communist pacifists backing a simple platform: a halt to the arms race, recognition of the risk of war, mobilization against the deployment of the Pershing and cruise missiles, and for the reciprocal withdrawal of the SS-20. Since its inception, CODENE has differed from the Mouvement de la Paix in two essential ways:

One, its European ideology criticizes both the United States and the Soviet regime, thus assuring it a certain credibility in the eyes of the French public. CODENE does not hesitate to criticize sharply the totalitarianism that oppresses the Eastern Europeans. Actively supporting the Polish labor union Solidarity, the committee also maintains close ties with Hungarian and Czech dissidents as well as independent pacifists in Moscow and the German Democratic Republic. However, this impartiality with respect to the USSR does not imply particularly close ties with Washington. CODENE supports the idea of an independent Europe situated at arm's length from both of the equally dangerous and blameworthy superpowers. It considers the peace movements in Western Europe to be the equivalent of the dissident movements in Eastern Europe. In addition, it sees the arms race as merely a pretext for the two superpowers' desire to maintain political and economic control over the two Europes. Thus the military buildup is found to be fundamentally contrary to the European interest of returning to and strengthening detente. In CODENE's eyes, the Pershing IIs are doubly dangerous: politically, because they exacerbate Soviet fear of encirclement and prevent any internal liberation of the East European bloc; and militarily, because they allow a limited nuclear war to be conducted on European soil, although there is no imbalance in the forces in Europe. Thus, while calling for the withdrawal of the SS-20s, CODENE also attacks the U.S. missiles, thereby agreeing on this very point with the military-strategic analysis of the Mouvement de la Paix.

The second way in which CODENE differs from the Mouvement de la Paix is that CODENE calls into question the fundamental policy of the French defense strategy. Since 1981 it has decried both the uselessness and myth of the independence of the Strategic Nuclear Forces. In its opinion, the Socialist government has merely continued the masquerade that previous governments began concerning the autonomy of the French defense system with respect to NATO. Therefore the Soviets are correct in counting the Plateau d'Albion missiles among the missiles in the Atlantic alliance. However, where nuclear submarines are concerned, CODENE's position is less negative: because the missile-launching nuclear submarines (SSBNs) are still undetectable weapons, it is possible to keep them for their value as a true deterrent. Yet on the matter of land-based components of the French deterrent capability, CODENE does not hide its skepticism and strong opposition. CODENE remains convinced of the need for a "general denuclearization of the European continent, from Poland to Portugal," a slogan that gave rise to the organization's very name. And France must remain united with the rest of Europe in defending the Continent's interests against those of Washington: "War in Europe is in fact war in Russia, it is not war in America." [6]

In 1983 CODENE reaffirmed its anticommunist, antialliance, and anti-French nuclear policy positions. In contrast to the Atlanticist leanings of the Socialist government and the pro-Soviet tendencies of the pacifists, CODENE can be seen as the only peace movement in solidarity with the other European movements. During its large demonstration at the Plateau du Larzac in the summer of 1983, the committee declared itself in favor of a freeze of all nuclear arsenals, even if this meant the unilateral disarmament of France. It demanded that the Socialist government end all nuclear tests, halt the

HADES missile and neutron bomb programs, stop the development of the seventh SSBN, and abandon the use of plutonium for military purposes.

1981/1983: PACIFIST CONVERGENCES AND SOCIALIST DIVERGENCES

The evolution of French peace movements in the last three years has been quite remarkable. Differences of opinion found among them in 1981 concerning two major elements—analyses of the Soviet Union and attitudes toward the national deterrent force—have disappeared. The only remaining difference involves the ideological divergences with respect to totalitarianism. On the other hand, there is striking agreement on analysis of the balance of forces in Europe, opposition to the Pershing and cruise missiles, and, above all, challenging of the national nuclear force.

Essentially, whatever their political differences, the French peace movements have found themselves—at least tactically—in agreement on the basic issues: nondeployment of the Pershing II missiles and a freeze on the French arsenal. Does not the opening of Geneva talks to all European countries, including France, as called for by the Communists, mean a halt to the modernization of the French forces? It is hard to see the difference between the freeze called for by one group and the freeze called for by another.

In the beginning the French peace movement was clearly an imported movement for the most part; because French territory was not affected by the double-track decision of NATO, national pacifism seemed somewhat artificial. Today, on the other hand, pacifism has become a veritable national movement, still a minority one, of course, but one whose target now involves the French nuclear forces themselves.

As well as having partially agreed upon their stand concerning national deterrence, the pacifist movements have also expanded their support base. All the left-wing organizations, from leftist extremists to the Communist party have joined the antinuclear movement in 1983. The most significant occurrence in this evolution was when the CFDT (the second largest French labor union; closely associated with the Socialist party) supported CODENE in denouncing the deployment of Pershing II missiles. Of course, union leader Edmond Maire's central committee did not back CODENE on the issue of national defense, but its support for the peace movement demonstrations of 23 October surprised and somewhat troubled the Socialist party, the one major abstainer in the French pacifist debate.

Undoubtedly this abstention on the part of the Socialists has been a major factor in the failure of the peace movement, despite its growing numbers in the three years of the Pershing missile affair, to gain more popular support. This is not to say there is complete consensus within the Socialist party on the issue of the Pershing missiles or the fate of the French nuclear forces. On the contrary, there is debate among competing socialist factions, but it is a latent, underground, voluntarily restricted debate; the restraint reflects a desire to avoid strengthening the sustained pressure of the PCF pacifist stand, as well as a wish to maintain party discipline, but is above all a reflection of the pedagogical talent and personal investment of Mitterrand in the Euromissile issue. Nonetheless, the Socialist tendencies can be divided into two competing factions.

The first group consists of the traditional antinuclear advocates within the PS, though it is difficult to classify them as a true current within the party. However, in 1978, when the Socialists decided to support national deterrence, the antinuclear faction was in the majority at the grass-roots activist level. In 1983, though the faction remains officially silent, it has no less skepticism with regard to the credibility of the French nuclear force and the necessity of installing Pershing IIs. However, the faction's very real antitotalitarian attitude and its Atlanticist, or at least European, tendencies prevent it from joining an antinuclear movement that still seems, to it, quite legitimate.

The second group consists of CERES, the left wing of the Socialist party led by Mr. Chevenement. At the outset of the Euromissile affair in 1979, CERES publicly opposed the Pershing missiles and U.S. imperialist designs on Western Europe. In 1983 Chevenement continued to express the group's skepticism; he particularly criticized the illusion of connecting Europe to the United States via the Pershing II. But then, once again, party discipline prevailed and CERES, reliable even in a difficult situation, reluctantly supported the U.S. deployment as a last resort.

Thus the unanimity of the socialist party on the Euromissile issue can be categorized as actually quite fragile. The party's antinuclear faction and CERES were, for different reasons, opposed to the Pershing missiles: the former because it does not accept the logic of more nuclear arms and would rather see Europe look for conventional defense alternatives; the latter because, in its opinion, France did not need to get involved in NATO's problems and would do better to speed up efforts to modernize the French nuclear force. Herein lies the schism between these two Socialist factions: one skeptical of a national deterrent (because that deterrent is nuclear and anti-

European); the other favoring a stronger nuclear policy, clearly nationalistic. Perhaps this internal division in the party was also responsible for the absence of a true debate within the party. Rather than joining ranks in opposing the party line, the antinuclear faction and CERES were much more interested in neutralizing each other. In the end they both backed the government policy—the antinuclear proponents because of that policy's commitment to Europe, and CERES because of the policy's support of a national deterrent. Once again, the ambiguity of official French policy was due to diverging tendencies at the Socialist party level as well as at the more general level of the national consensus on defense.

PERSPECTIVES: THE OTHER DEBATE

As the internal disagreements within the Socialist party demonstrate, the national consensus on French defense policy does not appear to be stable. The French public has not been particularly interested in the Euromissile debate, which is not to say the debate's effect in political and defense circles has been any less. Parallel to the minor debate that has aroused the French pacifists, there is in fact a second, more basic debate being carried out in political circles, the effects of which may significantly change forever the national consensus on defense. Although the Pershing missiles have scarcely caused any ripples in France, the situation that follows their installation in Europe may, on the contrary, present new challenges because the very foundations of the national defense policy are now being questioned on two levels.

On one level there is the issue of arms control. The situation has been completely reversed; originally not affected by the double-track decision, France now finds itself at the center of the East-West strategic talks and in a very uncomfortable position: that of an irritating individualist whose stubbornness is the main obstacle to harmonious negotiations in Geneva. In December 1982 the Soviets let it be known that they were ready to reduce the number of SS-20s pro rata with the French and British forces. Certain conflicting opinions in the German cabinet have supported this as a solution to the Euromissile problem and, at any rate, the SPD has not hidden its preferences for such a scenario. U.S. Vice President George Bush's recent statements referring to the need to take the French forces into account should also be noted. Looking at these factors, we can see the extent of the evolution affecting the future of the independence of French defense. This is the truly unique situation France faces in 1983: the extraordinary gap between domestic tranquillity and foreign vulnerability. Moreover, the first deployment of the Pershing and cruise missiles has not resolved this problem. France must still face two fronts at once: at home, against the ever-possible pacifist leanings; abroad, against the crossfire of demands concerning national deterrence. Already, as we have seen, the PCF has undertaken to question national independence in nuclear weapons. And this first break in the consensus risks recurring at each stage of the Pershing deployments until 1989.

On the other level there is the issue of French responsibility to European security. The European antinuclear movement has in fact significantly affected the leaders of the four largest political parties, leaders who are aware of the dangers France must face when considering the resurgence of the German problem. The French strategic position assumes, in order to remain stable and credible, the continuation of at least two conditions: U.S. nuclear power continues to guarantee the safety of Western Europe and the FGR remains a trusted and faithful partner in the Atlantic alliance. The Euromissile issue has shaken these two assumptions and demonstrated the risks of an increasing loosening of European and U.S. ties on the one hand and ruptures in the German consensus on defense on the other. Thus it is the very definition of French strategy that is at issue, and each of the political parties has begun debating the role and responsibility of France vis-à-vis Germany and overall European security.

Perhaps even more important than the lack of a peace movement in France are the astonishing and contradictory developments to be found among the political elites on the issue of the defense of Europe. Undoubtedly the change in the Gaullists of the RPR is the most striking: Mr. Chirac was the first to surprise everyone by referring to the possible nuclear responsibility of the FRG. Though he was quickly forced to retreat from this position, the head of the RPR seems to have abandoned the nationalist tradition (still very much alive in his party) for one that calls for greater French participation in the defense of Europe. The same phenomenon occurred in the UDF, though Raymond Barre's position was the opposite of Chirac's: without denying his party's Atlanticist tradition, the former prime minister wants France to find "her own European policy, that is, appropriate to a German and Russian policy."[7] In the Socialist party Chevenement also indicates he is very concerned about the breach in the German consensus, but once again his solutions differ from those of his predecessors. In his opinion, France should rapidly modernize its nuclear deterrent force to broaden the guarantee; develop, with the FRG, cooperation in the realm of conventional defense; and support "raising the nuclear threshold" in Central Europe. Of course, the debate that forces the French leaders to rethink their positions vis-à-vis Europe as a whole and the FRG in particular so as to strengthen and consolidate the Atlantic alliance while palliating the uncertainties of the U.S. guarantee in Europe has only just begun. Whether it involves being on the front lines with a quick response (as implied by the Force d'Action Rapide), or involves nuclear armaments (which some say they are ready to share with the FRG), or involves increasing the umbrella of French (and British) missiles, these new questions have publicly appeared in France and shaken the comfortable ambiguity on defense that was previously held. Though pacifism has been above all a German affair, a reopening of the German problem risks becoming the major issue for the French in the years to come. Not having supported the peace movement up through December 1983, France may now find itself leading the way in considering the possibilities of an intra-European cooperation in defense and security.

NOTES

1. When asked about the usefulness of the French nuclear deterrent, 44 percent of those surveyed said that it served no purpose because "if we used it against a Superpower, we would be wiped off the map." *Ça m'intéresse*, no. 20 (October 1982).
2. Here are the results of a Louis Harris-Atlantic Institute for International Affairs poll, November 1983. Those who said they were very concerned about nuclear arms (in percentages): France, 26; FRG, 38; UK, 29; Italy, 35: Netherlands, 49; Norway, 38; Spain, 30; United States, 37; Japan, 34. However, it must be noted that the French are more worried now than in 1982 (18 percent) or in March 1983 (19 percent).
3. See N. Gnesotto, "Le Parti communiste français et les euromissiles," *Politiqe Etrangère*, no. 3 (1983).
4. For a comparative study of the antinuclear movements, see Pierre Lellouche, ed.,*Pacifisme et dissuasion* (IFRI/Economica, May 1983).
5. Interview with the French Communist party leader in *Témoignage Chrétien,* July 1983.
6. Alain Joxe, *Cahiers d'Etudes Strategiques du CIRPES*, no. 1, 1983.
7. Raymond Barre, interview, *Le débat*, no. 26 (September 1983).

12

THE CHURCHES AND THE PEACE MOVEMENT: THE BRITISH EXPERIENCE

Edward Norman

Both in Europe and in North America the churches have, in the last few years, demonstrated an extraordinary preparedness to represent fundamental Christian beliefs as inevitably on the side of general withdrawal from the defense of received values by military means. The change has been more dramatic in the case of the United States, where Christian pacifism has had, compared with Europe, a later growth. In both areas, however, it is the question of nuclear defense that has drawn the leaders of the churches into their present alignments with the "peace" movements. The change is to be seen as an aspect of the general secularization of the churches. With their supportive cosmology largely destroyed by nineteenth-century discoveries in the physical and social sciences, and their morality undermined by twentieth-century humanist ethicism, the churches have come to espouse the attitudes of their rivals and opponents to a degree that would astonish their own leaders—were they able to recognize that that is what has in fact occurred. But the change has taken place by stages and through stealth, and churchpeople are unaware of the extent of their own secularization, regarding their present positions on social, moral, and political questions as considered and necessary adaptations of their faith to contemporary circumstances.

At the heart of the matter is a view of humankind itself. In traditional Christianity men and women were regarded as being fallen and corrupted, the degree of their sin so great, and their capacity for error so wide and inclusive, that all their worldly actions were flawed and imperfect. There followed, from this, a view of society and its

260

organization: in classical Christian political thinking the powers of the state were limited because even authority given to human beings for the performance of good would inevitably also be productive of evil. The motives of human beings were a mixture of good intention, fallible delivery, and corrupt self-interest; the resulting actions were also seen to be morally ambiguous. Christ came into a fallen world not to make human beings better—that was outside the terms of reference of a corrupted human order—but to forgive, and to redeem human beings for eternity. The office of the church was to act as the mediator between the mysteries of the Kingdom of Heaven and humans' flawed perceptions—a specialized function, accommodated within a specialist literature, worship, and vocabulary of moral behavior.

At the center of Christianity was belief in God and the salvation offered through the extraordinary paradox of human participation: the treasure was in earthen vessels. The morality of Christianity was secondary. Not especially distinctive in content from preceding Judaic morality, and not widely different from the general moral sense of the ancient cultures of the Mediterranean and Middle East, Christian morality was centered in that cultivation of personal integrity and brotherly concern in which the flowers of spirituality were nurtured and flourished. The spiritual genius of Christ individualized morality: it was detached from its collective Judaic function and applied universally to each person. God was seen to be present no longer in the dealings of a single people and nation but with the whole of humanity.

How great is the contrast between this scheme of belief and contemporary Christian attitudes: now the churches appear to have adopted the secularized view of human beings characteristic of the humanism so widespread within the Western intelligentsia. Men and women are regarded as morally autonomous, as having "come of age"—to use an expression popular with theologians a decade ago—and as characterized by a great capacity for human goodness. It is no longer the individual person who is corrupt but social circumstances. Humankind can actually be made better, and more capable of reasoned choice, through environmental change and education. Christian writers and theologians have rushed to incorporate optimistic notions into their understanding of Christianity itself. At the center of their new version is no longer a fallen humanity but an ethicism that represents Christ as a sort of social reformer, more concerned with the material condition of men and women than with their "other-worldly" beliefs.

Contemporary Christians have become convinced supporters of

the concept of social pluralism, too—and go to great lengths to contend for variation of life-styles and the rights of minorities as essential expressions of "Christian" teaching about the "rights" of humans. The contemporary association of Christianity and human rights ideology—understood in its Western, liberal sense—is a further clear indication of the preparedness of church leaders to represent their faith in terms of basic human needs rather than as an intimation, amidst ambiguity, of a set of values other than worldly ones. The result is this: the churches have become preoccupied by human beings and their material needs (in the belief that this is "love of neighbor") and so have materialized the center of the churches' religion. The consequence is an obsession with human material progress and the conclusion that human life itself is more to be esteemed than the actual values an individual may espouse.

The obsession with human material progress and the conclusion concerning human life have two immediate outcomes. One is involvement with the politics of development: in global terms this means a general Christian support for the escalating expectations of the developing countries and an uncritical acceptance of hostile Third World attitudes toward the developed capitalist order. The other outcome concerns "peace." The churches have now reached the point at which they do not regard the received values of Western nations worth defending at high human cost. This is partly because they have, anyway, become skeptical of those values—because they now dislike capitalism and refer to their own societies as cultures of inequality and deprivation—and partly because they have adopted that reverence for human life itself that is characteristic of those secular thinkers who believe there is no other life. Contemporary Christianity no longer regards the world as a place of trial and suffering until the transformation of the Last Day; it now shares with secular humanism a belief that human material existence is the main area for the expression of essential values. Together, these attitudes have led the churches, for example, to lend their support to the destabilization of capitalist regimes in the developing world, even where this has meant assisting Marxist alternatives. They are repelled, that is to say, by the supposed injustices of capitalist inequality, and not offended by the materialism of Marxism because it is thought to be balanced by its human idealism.

In terms of global politics, the churches are shifting in our day from being guardians of the nonmaterial values incorporated within Western societies that have received Christianity into becoming a force for radicalization. The process is uneven and very incomplete, but it is clearly advancing. It is hardly surprising to find that some Christians have actually gone on to identify themselves and their faith with progressive politics, and that with their new allegiance come "progressive" views on defense and disarmament. Yet even among those Christians who have not gone on to the espousal of radicalized politics there has been an advance toward "soft" views on defense questions. There is a new reluctance to defend Western values by military means.

The reluctance is, to some extent, the fault of the values themselves. At the base of capitalism there is a calculated materialism—even though its central social consequence (quite apart from economic improvement generally) is the morality of choice. And the present acceptance of social and moral pluralism in Western societies, whatever its advantages, makes the defense of society (for any reason other than the preservation of the pluralism itself) morally ambiguous. Many, perhaps a large majority, of the people in Western nations are more grossly materialistic—and with more effective means of expressing it—than are the citizens in the socialist states. Perhaps the real defense of the West is that its people have freedom from the powers of the state—but even here the advance of collectivism in the middle years of the present century, and the effects of mass education in cultivating expectations that collective solutions will be found to social and moral evils are rapidly diminishing the area of individual expression. But in these complications the churches have not especially involved themselves. Their position is a simpler one. Despite their criticisms of evils in Western society, their general position is still to regard Western values as broadly desirable; their skepticism relates to the loss of life in the defense of those values. There is a growing feeling that the mass destruction of the lives of the citizens in an opposed country or alliance is not a Christian thing to contemplate in order to preserve one's own values or life-style.

It is at this juncture that the question of nuclear defense enters the development of opinion. There are, of course, Christian pacifists for whom all sorts of military defense are abhorrent. It is interesting to notice, in passing, that pacifism, too, has become secularized. In the medieval world it was a vocation undertaken by some religious people to express a specialized spiritual function—by people who still expected others to bear arms for the general protection. Contemporary Christian pacifism, however, derives from the moral rejection of all warfare made by small groups for religious reasons in the sixteenth and seventeenth centuries but now actually expressed within the sort of humanist ethicism characteristic of nineteenth-century freethinkers.

Whatever the pedigree of protest, the fact is that pacifism is clearly an established Christian basis for opposition to nuclear defense. Most Christian supporters of the "peace" movements, however, are not pacifists. Indeed, those who have also adopted radicalized political positions have been noticeable, in the last twenty years, for their support of violence in the movements for political change in the developing world. "Liberation theology" is essentially about the application in the modern world of the critiques and methods employed in the Old Testament to achieve social righteousness, and revolutionary violence is certainly among the methods endorsed, as is the notion of a war of liberation. There is often a curious identity of personnel, between those in international Christian agencies working for Third World armed struggles and those campaigning for nuclear disarmament. That they are able to do this with some appearance of consistency illustrates the concern of Christians, as of other "nuclear pacifists," to establish a moral isolation of nuclear weapons, and to show that they are completely unlike other weapons.

To do this, there has been a revival of what Christian writers have called "the just war theory"—but because the body of doctrines to which they refer was not theoretical but an actual series of concrete propositions, the word *theory* is not really appropriate. Nor was this collection of medieval conventions universally accepted. It is also somewhat inconsistent for modern churchmen to select these "just war" precepts—formulated originally for use in a society of feudal hosts—from medieval social culture without also considering other aspects of medieval political and moral practices. But they have, nevertheless, been suddenly accorded a new legitimacy and are now referred to by contemporary Christian thinkers as if they constituted an agreed, universal, and uncontroversial series of references for the conduct of warfare.

The "just war" precepts assume the legitimacy of conflict in some allowed situations, and are then concerned with the containment of the ensuing violence and the stipulation of moral conditions for its incidence. According to the "just war" rules, conflict must always be undertaken by governments, must be in support of a morally good cause, must always be a last resort, should follow a formal declaration, ought to have a reasonable hope of success, and should not result in destruction disproportionate to the object of the conflict. Once the violence has actually begun, it is to be conducted according to two criteria: the "principle of noncombatant immunity" and the "principle of proportion." According to the first of these, there are "innocent" parties involved in warfare within the civilian population whose persons and property should not be violated; and according to the second, no greater force should be used, and destruction procured, than are necessary for military success, and there should be no harm to third parties. Both Catholic and Protestant Christian leaders, in both Europe and North America, have in recent years referred to these ideas and conventions as an appropriate standard by which the issues of nuclear defense are to be judged. An increasing number have concluded that nuclear conflict can in no circumstances be morally justified—and this has applied even to the concept of nuclear deterrence because it is correctly recognized that for deterrence to be real, the parties employing it have actually to use nuclear weapons should occasion require it.

The churches, therefore, have faced the question of whether warfare conducted with nuclear weapons can ever be in pursuit of Christian aims. To those who now find the use of any force an anathema to the preservation or pursuit of Christian values, nuclear warfare is no different from any other; but for the majority of Christians it is not force as such but the inclusive destructive potential, coupled with the long-lasting environmental effects of nuclear weapons, that puts them in a class by themselves.

A recent development is to include chemical and biological agencies alongside nuclear ones in the list of morally unacceptable weapons, and for the same sorts of reasons. It is sometimes acknowledged that the death rates and destructive potential of modern conventional weapons, in a sustained conflict, are just as great as nuclear ones; but conventional arms are not held to have long-lasting effects upon the environment—to some a dubious conclusion in view of the effect upon civilian populations of the destruction, by conventional means, of water supplies, or of the economic means of sustaining life in highly urban societies.

A critique of the "nuclear pacifism" of so much contemporary Christian thinking should begin with its exceptionalizing of the consequences of nuclear warfare. It is obviously right to point to the wickedness of any need to destroy life, but it is also realistic to appreciate that it is a permanent characteristic of human society. This, furthermore, is because men and women are not merely material: they have a potential to perceive higher purposes for themselves and for human association than the provision of food for their bodies and shelter for their families. Humanity was endowed by God with reason, but its fallen and corrupted condition has meant that reason has been employed in the service of evil as well as of goodness. People differ among themselves about how to categorize the consequences, and about the appropriate forms in which life is most properly lived. The history of human organization for higher ends is therefore a history of conflict. It is a part of human life, inseparable from the pursuit suit of nonmaterial goals. Those who believe that peace is ever permanently attainable, or that violence or conflict are some sort of eradicable aberration, are, alas, at variance with the sad facts of human nature. That is why traditional Christianity, with its realism about human depravity, was so much more realistic than the contemporary *penchant* of Christians for adopting optimistic views about humanity borrowed from secular humanism.

Indeed, the "peace" brought by Christ that is at the center of the Christian message is not actually peace between nations—the Saviour himself predicted human conflict to the end of time—but inward peace, the peace of the heart, the paradoxical internal serenity attained by those who are nevertheless set within the violence of human conflict around them. In the Old Testament the righteousness of God's law for human beings was established by force; just as the chosen people of God occupied their land through the operations of a military host. In the warfare of the ancient world there was quite often both total destruction of whole populations, civilian as well as military, and environmental catastrophe—mysterious ravages and plagues procured by the divinities against those who opposed their sway, and the actual practice of laying waste the territories of defeated peoples. In scale and in effect upon the limited populations of the ancient world, the results of warfare were probably very comparable to a nuclear conflict today. Warfare, as a consequence, was greatly feared, yet familiarly recognized as a part of life.

During the last couple of centuries humankind has gone through an unusual and untypical period in which the growth of population outstripped the destructive capabilities of human conflict, and in which, in the transition from a limited view of government to modern collectivism, the constraints against military action have often held. The period has seen two world wars—for conflict is always a part of human life—but their destructive effects were very limited and human societies rapidly recovered from them. Now, suddenly, nuclear weapons have returned humankind to its normal condition: living a frail existence, in imminent expectation of the destruction of the familiar environment through its own action in pursuit of the preservation of its values. It is a situation full of traditional ingredients, and not at all the fearful novelty imagined by antinuclear activists. It stems from the human paradox: that people are gifted with reason and the divine potential to envisage perfection, yet are capable only of division and corruption. And now they have invented the means toward their own destruction in a way that is more efficient than anything known before; that, alone, is a novelty.

Because the general psychology of the nuclear world is a familiar one, it should have given Christianity the opportunity to point to the correctness of its own traditional diagnosis of human fallibility. Instead, however, it has been a measure of the secularization of the churches that they have joined in the shocked humanism of the Western intelligentsia—horrified at the revelation of the frailty of human life that nuclear weapons have disclosed to observers. The result has been a drift by the churches to support for the secular "peace" movements.

From a Christian point of view the "peace" movements ought to appear decidedly naive, for they assume two things that are contrary to Christian realism about human beings. In the first place they believe that mere survival at whatever ideological cost is preferable to defense of values at high human cost. Second, they believe that somehow "good" values will survive in an underground form in a society overrun by an ideological adversary—a situation thought morally preferable to nuclear defense—and will in due course resurface. The trouble with the first assumption is that it is, to use an old-fashioned word, ignoble. Human beings are dignified and find their own value through the defense of their inherited values; it is the very texture of human worth. The trouble with the second assumption is that it ignores the capacity of modern secular collectivist governments, with total materialist ideologies and the availability of mass communications and mass education, to remold the thoughts and beliefs of whole societies. Nothing stands still in human affairs, and the most total of total ideologies change and adapt with time, but there is no great possibility that submerged and conquered values will reappear in a recognizable form in a subject population. The survival of Christianity in the USSR is sometimes offered as a contrary example, but it is not a useful instance. Christianity in the Soviet Union shares the social and moral outlook of Soviet society in general—as witness the support of church leaders for the Soviet view of human rights in situations of present conflict in various parts of the world. And the Christianity that survives in the Soviet Union has become so socially marginated that it can scarcely be said to have resurfaced in a numerically significant form, despite optimistic expressions of opinion about it made periodically by Western observers.

Christians who believe, in the present debate about nuclear weapons, that their witness is to refuse to employ weapons of mass

destruction in defense of Christian values must face the prospect that
not to resort to armed conflict may result in the disappearance of
freedom from large parts of the world. Yet no one should be insensitive about his or her dilemma. However much conflict is a normal
part of human life, and however much it is recognized that one side
in a conflict is going to suffer anyway, it remains a terrifying choice
for Christians: to fight to preserve their values at the cost of millions
of lives. That is why the agreed first priority of all Christians should
be effective and controlled disarmament, in an attempt to lower the
threshold of terror; but it should not be one-sided disarmament, because that, in present circumstances, would produce only a dangerous imbalance and a general destabilization more, not less, likely to
lead to the breakdown of deterrence.

Of the main principle for the conduct of warfare in the "just war"
categories—the "principle of a noncombatant immunity"—there
should also be a good deal of reserve. In many recent church debates
the principle has been referred to as if it were conclusive against all
nuclear weapons, because of their inclusive effects upon civilian populations. But it is difficult to see why, in modern circumstances, civilians should be regarded as "innocent." The political relationships
between populations and their rulers in modern liberal democracies
is closer than it has been in any preceding arrangement of things, and
with modern collectivism providing a moral basis to mutual social
obligations, it can be argued that civilian populations are as legitimate a target in warfare as are those who are thought capable of
bearing arms. The whole of a people is responsible for the actions of
its government.

The "principle of noncombatant immunity," as implied in the
Hague Conventions of 1899 and 1907, and the Geneva Convention of
1949, doubtless applies to particular situations that may arise in a war
in which hostile action against a civilian group is unnecessary for the
efficient prosecution of military arms, but it is not a moral case
against the inclusive effects of nuclear weapons. Christians who speak
as if the principle operates in that way are simply being unrealistic.
They are the first to clamor for full democratic rights in the decisions
of governments, and must share in the consequences of the actions of
governments. The modern tendency to "politicize" Christianity—to
identify its essential content with action in the world to secure a
more just society—should actually give Christians an enhanced consciousness of the seriousness of political involvement.

Although the Christian churches have had, throughout their history, developed theological opinions and teachings about violence

and warfare, they do not seem to have any distinctively *religious* reasons for holding views about the nature of nuclear weapons. According to the sort of tests required in the "principle of noncombatant immunity," or the "principle of proportion" (in the "just war theory"), there has to be some way of knowing if nuclear weapons are really different in kind from other weapons. This involves exactly the sort of strategic and technical information that religious and spiritual knowledge is unable to supply. The noticeable result has been that, during the last forty years, the attitudes of the churches toward nuclear weapons has been determined by the same sorts of considerations that have informed secular moralists. Hence the easy integration with the "peace" movements made by those church leaders who have found nuclear defense unacceptable for moral reasons shared with the leaders of secular opinion.

Recent Christian debates on the nuclear issue in Europe and North America have been characterized by their involvement in political and strategic considerations rather than by any real theological content. The churches have actually found that their own spiritual insights have nothing uniquely religious to contribute. A survey of the attitudes of the churches toward the nuclear question during the last forty years illustrates this clearly. The observations that follow relate to the experience of the churches in England but they are not untypical of European and North American developments, and have the merit, for the present purpose, of standing institutionally somewhere midway between them.

The churches were actually quick to respond to nuclear power. Within a short time after the explosion of the first atomic bomb, the British Council of Churches and the Church of England (Anglican; Episcopalian) produced reports on nuclear warfare. Both, however, even at that early point, disclosed a division of opinion between those who believed that nuclear weapons should be absolutely outlawed and those who argued for their retention because of their utility as deterrents to conflict. It is a division that has continued to the present. The British Council of Churches report, *The Era of Atomic Power* (1946), was very candid about it: "We have no solution of the dilemma to offer . . . we do not believe that the Church is able with its present insight to pronounce between the two alternatives." The Anglican report (1948), *The Church and the Atom*, revealed as much division. The use of nuclear weapons was declared to be immoral, but some, a majority of the reporters, argued for the maintenance of nuclear arsenals as the lesser moral evil among alternatives. The Lambeth Conference of that year, and the Anglican Congress at Minneapolis, in 1954, called for international inspection and control of nuclear energy to prevent its development for military purposes.

The division of opinion within the churches became most clearly expressed in the later 1950s, in the gestation period of the Campaign for Nuclear Disarmament (CND). "The use of nuclear weapons is repugnant to the Christian conscience," and Anglican bishops at the Lambeth Conference of 1958 declared in their *Encyclical,* "Some of us would go further and regard such use in any circumstances as morally indefensible, while others of us, with equal conviction, would hold that so long as such weapons exist there are circumstances in which to use them might be preferable to political enslavement." The then archbishop of Canterbury, Dr. Geoffrey Fisher, disclosed a calm realism. Asked by a worried U.S. reporter about thermonuclear weapons, and the possibility that "the whole of humanity might be extinguished," the archbishop replied: "But they've all got to die sometime, and it shouldn't be all that dreadful if they all died at the same moment." It is not the sort of thing that is said today by church leaders.

But the essential divisions of view formulated in the late 1940s and early 1950s have remained. Church leaders have not found it easy to accommodate nuclear realities with their received notions of moral theology. In the Church of England's debate of the issue, in July 1979, the bishop of Truro, while declining to defend a rather moderate report before the synod, asked, rather in frustration, "What exactly those critics meant who had spoken in the debate of 'bringing the power of the cross to bear' on the problems before them." There is a sense that this is all new ground. The Catholics in England have found no surer footing. Opinion divided in just the same ways at the National Catholic Pastoral Congress, held in Liverpool in May 1979. All were agreed on the horrors and evil of nuclear weapons and, although some argued a case in support of a legitimate tactical use of such weapons, it was the majority opinion that both their possession and use must be condemned. The call, however, was for multilateral, not unilateral, disarmament—despite the agitation of such lobbies as Pax Christi. The hierarchies were urged to "oppose the introduction into this country of American nuclear cruise missiles."

Within the Catholic church, as in the others, the 1980s began with a drift of opinion toward unilateral nuclear disarmament. Indeed, the present chairman of CND is a Catholic priest. As yet still confined to pressure groups and individual, though influential, activists, the new campaign for unilateralism within the churches is much more respectable and quite different from the rather eccentric atmosphere that surrounded the clerical nuclear disarmers of the 1950s. The present shift of opinion has a number of causes. A primary incentive is the current revival of the CND; here, church leaders, as in so many other areas of social and moral concern, derive their inspiration from secular movements of opinion, and from the idealism of contemporary humanism. Another impulsion is the increasing costs of defense: money "wasted" on armaments, both nuclear and conventional, "diverts attention from the real needs of mankind," as the Lambeth Conference declared in 1978—"the eradication of poverty." The publicity given to ecological issues has provided a further dimension: there is a strong religious lobby against nuclear energy based upon fears about its real safety and its link with the provision of materials for nuclear weapons. But perhaps the most significant reason for the present adjustment of attitudes is the prevailing conviction, within influential Christian opinion, that the whole essence and purpose of religion is centered upon the eradication of human suffering and oppression—upon the satisfaction, in that context, of humanity's material needs. This is the idealism that regards the provision of material benefits, in the form of health care, education, housing, and so forth, especially in the developing world, as more important than the sort of ideology or political culture under which people live and from which, in the circumstances of the modern collectivist state, they derive so many of their values.

In February 1983, following an enormous amount of press and public interest, the General Synod of the Church of England once again debated the question of nuclear weapons and the moral propriety of deterrence. It had before it a report *(The Church and the Bomb)* drawn up by a committee it had appointed, under the chairmanship of the bishop of Salisbury, that had come out in favor of British unilateral nuclear disarmament. The report's moral basis claimed to derive from "just war" categories. Most of its pages were taken up with exactly the sort of political and strategic arguments as are found in the publications of the secular "peace" movements. The press, in fact, in commenting upon the synod's debate of the report, was almost unanimous in noting the political nature of the speeches—and how little real theological discussion took place. In the event, the synod rejected its own committee's recommendations by 338 votes to 100. But having defeated straightforward unilateral disarmament, the synod then proceeded at once, on a motion of the bishop of Birmingham, to pass a resolution "to forswear the first use of nuclear weapons in any form." The second resolution undermines the credibility of deterrence. The church had, in effect, faced both ways on the nuclear question.

It is impossible to escape the impression that the political and strategic emphasis in the attitudes of church leaders toward nuclear weapons is only because their own religious tradition fails to supply them with authentic religious data on the issues involved—there is also a strong suspicion that they experience a sense of revived public utility by involving themselves with the technical issues of defense. Now so often regarded as far removed from the centers of national and public life, the Christian clergy find in the discussion of such public issues as nuclear weapons a renewed sense of social relevance. A public opinion seemingly reluctant to listen to their views on sacramental grace, or the nature of the Trinity, is evidently concerned about a possible nuclear catastrophe. As in other dimensions of their present secularization and politicization, the churches seek to revive their social role through integration with the moral seriousness of contemporary opinion. That they actually have nothing distinctive to say, within the terms of reference they have set themselves, does not seem to be evident to those who speak for them. Their enthusiasm for the "peace" movements will rise and fall according to the independent fate of the movements themselves—not according to any external Christian judgment. The churches long ago lost control of public moral discourse to secular idealism. Now they follow the lines prescribed by their own replacements.

13

WAR AND PEACE AND THE GERMAN CHURCH

Siegfried Scharrer

The peace movement, the largest mass movement in Germany since World War II, arose or at least started to be publicly effective in the Federal Republic of Germany as a result of the NATO dual-track decision of 12 December 1979. A characteristic of the movement has been the involvement of Christians of both the Protestant and Catholic churches in a supportive role.

On 22 November 1983, a majority of the German parliament approved the stationing of U.S. medium-range missiles. This article will examine the arguments among Christians of the two churches and among the different denominations largely within this period. To present clearly the variety of positions, theological opinions, and arguments put forward by church groups and official church bodies, it is necessary for methodological reasons to consider three questions: (1) What are the aims behind the various positions? (2) Why are these aims pursued? (3) How is it proposed to achieve them? By distinguishing between these questions it will be easier to analyze at what points and for what reasons there is consensus of disagreement.

The subject is discussed by reference to attitudes toward three problems: war, deterrence, and disarmament. A further distinction needs to be made between nuclear and conventional armaments. A fourth point, the different interpretations of the word *peace*, will be clarified as well. I first set out the pattern of the present controversy; then inquire thoroughly into its theological background; then suggest a settlement and discuss its possible consequences; and, finally, briefly summarize the various aspects of the controversy.

NATURE OF THE DEBATE

The positions in the Protestant and Catholic churches have evolved in different ways, and thus it seems advisable to treat them separately.

THE ARGUMENT IN THE PROTESTANT CHURCH

Seen from abroad, it might appear that the discussion that is going on in the churches of the FRG is an entirely new phenomenon. At least as far as the Protestant churches are concerned, this would be a misconception. The discussion is fundamentally a repetition, although now on a much more publicly perceivable level, of old debating positions. To a certain extent even the same personalities are involved. To understand the present disagreements, a brief review of the decisive historical stages of the dispute will be helpful.

The Early History

Shortly after the end of the war, in October 1945, the Council of Evangelical Churches in Germany (EKD), the supreme body of all Protestant churches, issued a statement that later became referred to as the "Stuttgarter Schulldbekenntnis" (the Stuttgart confession of guilt). It stated, among other things: "Through us, infinite suffering has been brought upon many nations. . . . We did indeed fight for years in the name of Jesus Christ against the spirit which found its terrible expression in the National Socialist regime of violence; yet we still stand guilty of not having professed our faith more bravely, not having prayed more devoutly, not having believed more joyfully and not having loved more ardently." [1]

The statement, hesitant though it was, ignited an argument over the idea of collective guilt, about the relationship between guilt "in the eyes of God" and "in the eyes of mankind." The question people wondered about and were worried by was whether such ecclesiastical pronouncements might not be politically exploited against the German people, who after all had also had their share of suffering. Followers of the Swiss reform theologian Karl Barth argued with the Lutherans about the political relevance of ecclesiastical statements, one of the basic problems of the "two kingdoms doctrine" ("Zwei-Reich-Lehre"), as it is known.

The Second Phase: The Rearmament Debate

In May 1949, the FRG obtained its constitution; that of the GDR came into force in October. This "finalization" of separateness severely affected the Evangelical church—even until 1969 structurally an all-German organization. Again the Barthians, among them Pastor D. Niemoeller and the future Federal President Heinemann—at the time president of the synod of the EKD and a cosignatory of the "Stuttgarter Schuldbekenntnis"—were especially concerned that inclusion in the Western alliance might result in remilitarization and prevent the reunification of Germany. Discussion was made more difficult by nationalist overtones in Niemoeller's statements and his reservations about excessive Catholic influence. Typical was his description of the Adenauer government as "conceived in the Vatican and born in Washington." [2]

On the other hand, outspoken political statements against rearmament, particularly those of Niemoeller, an official church spokesman, provoked protests, particularly in Lutheran circles. Thus the regional council of the Evangelical-Lutheran church in Bavaria dissociated itself from Niemoeller's statements, and in the tradition of the Lutheran "Zwei-Reich" doctrine declared in October 1950: "The church cannot relieve Christians of the responsibility of political decision-making nor can it in the name of the Gospel impose particular political decisions upon them." [3]

The Third Phase: Controversy over Atomic Weapons

"The universal danger which threatens not only the present generation but our children and our children's children, demands of every individual a commitment to *outlaw and abolish* these means of mass destruction." [4] This was the response, issued in the form of a joint declaration of the deans of the theological faculties and the bishops of the GDR to the Göttingen declaration of 12 April 1957. In the manifesto, eighteen atomic scientists, among them C.F. von Weizsäcker, the future peace researcher, warned against the dangerous effects of nuclear weapons in light of plans to arm the Bundeswehr with such weapons: "In any case, none of the undersigned would be prepared to be involved in any way in the manufacture, testing or use of these atomic weapons." [5]

All major church bodies now also recognized and condemned the unspeakable threat. However, the new situation and the failure of traditional ethical criteria led to the drawing of contradictory conclusions. The theologian H. Vogel, a Lutheran connected with Barth, said in an address to the synod (July 1957): "There is in fact no objective which could justify or sanction the construction, testing or use of these weapons. Even if the entire Christian Occident were in the balance, or for that matter the Communist East, in other words everything that mankind considers of spiritual and material value, these things of value would not be defended by means of mass destruction but simply betrayed and obliterated. The dropping of an atomic bomb is an act of nihilism." [6]

Although the bishops of the United Evangelical-Lutheran churches of Germany (VELKD) issued similar stern warnings about the dangers, they saw the connection between theological and political statements differently: "We cannot put our trust solely in a security created by ourselves—neither in one based on the possession of nuclear weapons or on the renunciation of such weapons." [7]

On 30 April 1958, the EKD synod in Berlin passed a resolution that highlighted the tensions that had come to the surface. The synod rejected "total war waged with nuclear weapons as irreconcilable with man's conscience before God," but admitted that "the existing differences in our assessments of nuclear weapons run deep. They range from the conviction that the very construction and holding ready of means of mass destruction of any kind is sinful in the eyes of God, to the conviction that certain situations are conceivable where resistance with weapons matching those of the enemy may be acceptable in the eyes of God as being a duty to defend." [8] The EKD was close to breaking apart.

The "Heidelberg theses" of 28 April 1959 became especially important in terms of the historical effect they had on the subsequent debate. The theses were not a statement of a synod or bishops but of a commission of the "Evangelical study group" to which theologians of various opinions, such as Gollwitzer and Schlink, and scientists belonged. The theses were formulated by von Weizsäcker. Frequent reference will be made in this chapter to the theses—both pro and con. [9]

Thesis 1 reads: "World peace has become the condition of survival in the technological age." [10] It goes on to say that the doctrine of the "just war" is no longer of any assistance. The ethical dilemma of the present situation could be put as follows: Should we "defend bourgeois freedoms under the rule of law with atomic weapons or abandon them undefended to our enemies?" [11] The authors' answer to this question in Thesis 6 still has serious consequences today, at least in some respects: "We have to try to understand the various decisions of conscience taken in the dilemma of nuclear weapons as *complementary* actions." [12] In 1983, von Weizsaecker explained the formula of "ethical complementarity": "The two attitudes which are here at variance with each other are reconcilable, insofar as each can only be effective if the other also exists." [13] It follows from this that to renounce nuclear weapons is Christian (Thesis 7), and that (Thesis 8) "the church must recognize that participation in the attempt to secure peace in freedom by the presence of nuclear weapons still remains a possible mode of conduct for Christians." [14]

The important thing for the present controversy—apart from the fundamental theological question of the relationship between statements of belief and political statements—is the explosive potential contained in the expression "ethical complementarity." This, after all, is not to be understood as a static point of compromise but as a highly precarious period of reprieve, of which energetic use must be made.

At the political level, the idea of complementarity for a certain period of time found expression only twenty years later in the NATO dual-track decision—with the difference that there would be deployment if the negotiations failed. The implication of the "Heidelberg theses," on the other hand, is that the complementarity could be rescinded by the other side (in the form of conscientious objection) if the allotted time was not utilized. This point is important for the understanding of the present debate. [15]

The Present Debate: An Overview

Group: Live without Armaments: The Working Party for Ecumenicalism. In the period before the NATO dual-track decision, a Christian group with the name Live without Armaments: The Working Party for Ecumenicalism appeared, issuing a public appeal for the following personal pledge in its leaflet "To All Christians": [16] "I am prepared to live without the protection of military armaments. I intend to support the political development of the idea of peace without weapons in our country" (p.20).

The group explicitly referred to a demand of the fifth general assembly of the Ecumenical Council of Churches (late 1975) in Nairobi, Kenya, that was, however, addressed not only to the individual but to the church as such: "The Church should stress its willingness to live without the protection of weapons and should take important initiatives to press for effective disarmament. The churches, individual Christians and members of the public of all countries should urge their governments to see that national security is guaranteed without the use of massive weapons of annihilation" (p. 12).

Live without Armaments bases its call on the Christian creed in an almost trinitarian manner: "In the first article of faith all Christians proclaim God both as creator and sustainer of this world. As a God who wants life and not death. Can a Christian then even passively accept that preparations have already been made to destroy this entire creation several times over?" The reconciliation in Christ came about not through violence but in suffering. Christ's Easter victory was not a victory of power but of helpless suffering, which "does [not] bear the seed of the new war within itself" (p. 9). Can belief in Christ, who triumphed and brought reconciliation through helpless suffering, be perfected and simultaneously be based on "our Pyrrhic victories of violence"? (p. 9).

Decisive for this group is Christ's Sermon on the Mount, which for the group applies not only to the religious but also to the secular sphere. The sermon's validity is "unconditional and indivisible" (p.12). Although the state is justified in the last instance in enforcing the right, by force if necessary, in doing so it must not "overstep the limit which is the right to existence of the wicked" (p. 14).

In addition to rejecting nuclear deterrence and the arms race, and referring to the North-South problem ("Armaments spending in the midst of world famine," p.26), Live without Armaments demands steps toward unilateral disarmament. The risks involved are appreciated but obviously considered to be less than those of the present: "If we cling to the status quo, we will quite certainly be overtaken by destruction" (p. 29).

Group: Action Atonement/Peace Service. The group Action Atonement/Peace Service, which has existed since 1958, in 1980 called for the first time for a "peace week" throughout the FRG. Meetings took place in about 350 localities to discuss the theme "Create peace without weapons."

Returning quite consciously to the experiences of the "Bekennende Kirche" under Nazism and linking itself to the "Stuttgarter Schuldbekenntnis," Action Atonement/Peace Service bases its whole work theologically on the assumption that it is possible "to establish in this world provisional, fragmentary yet auspicious prefigurations of the peace of God that is to come." [17]

As far as its peace work is concerned, the group considers that the ruling principle hitherto has been "The fear I instill in my enemy secures my peace." In its opinion, however, there is a growing realization that "the fear I take away from my enemy guarantees my own security." The group thus supports calculated steps toward unilateral disarmament. [18] It appeals to all citizens personally to pledge: "I will do all that is in my power and ability to try to prevent the stationing of new U.S. medium-range missiles in our country," and to support "further controlled steps towards unilateral disarmament." [19] These first steps are to be taken in the expectation that the USSR will follow suit.

Group: Securing Peace. A contrary position is taken by the well-known theologians and scientists who form the group Securing Peace. In the summer of 1980, they spoke of the state's duty "to protect the lives of its citizens and their fundamental human rights" from both criminal internal enemies and external ones. [20]

Securing Peace stressed that in the nuclear age war could no longer be a legitimate instrument of policy; hence it is no longer possible to "wage just wars" (para. 2). In the spirit of the Sermon on the Mount, the group wrote, "If the community's giving way to foreign demands is the greater service to mankind and to peace, then Christians should . . . be prepared to be accommodating" (para. 2). This was true not only in the personal sphere but among nations as well. Yet this was not to give a "carte blanche to acts of violence" (para. 3). The commandment not to kill "is also an instruction to protect—if necessary with weapons—life, fundamental human rights and freedom" (para. 3). Thus "there is no contradiction between serving peace with or without weapons" (para. 6). The slogan "Live without armaments" might even help "increase the use of military practices in world politics" (para. 9). There exists, the group emphasizes, an obligation to provide the state with the means "to prevent acts of violence by individuals or entire states" (para. 4).

Group: Steps toward Disarmament. In May 1981, an Evangelical-Catholic working group, Steps toward Disarmament, put forward as a basis for discussion between a number of opposing views a gradualist concept of disarmament that was intended to provide security and reduce fear and mistrust. [21] The theological starting point here is the central message of the church itself, namely, "reconciliation with God and among men in justice and love." With the coming of Jesus Christ, the promised new world had "already begun in this world" (para. 19). The commandment to love one's enemy from Christ's Sermon on the Mount was not a demand for self-sacrifice but was intended to lead to reconciliation and was therefore "a reasonable commandment," the only chance to "halt the compulsion to retaliate" (para. 13).

Politically, the first steps of unilateral disarmament should be aimed at "anticipated reactions from the enemy." "*Without such reactions from the other side*, they would after a while come *to nothing*." The basis of such steps is "an adequate *deterrent capability*, for the moment still *nuclear*, which must be big enough to make an attack an incalculable risk for the enemy." The idea of a military "balance" should, however, be abandoned. Unilateral measures of disarmament should be pursued "over a considerable period" (para. 22).

Three concrete demands made by Steps toward Disarmament are "renunciation of new nuclear weapons" (para. 25), hence rejection of the NATO dual-track decision; and reduction of existing potential and "reequipment of the Bundeswehr" (para. 26) to provide effective defense while making the force "structurally incapable" of executing an attack beyond its own borders. Finally, the group calls for a "stop to arms exports" (para. 27) to areas outside NATO, in the interests of the nation's own security and on ethical grounds.

The Evangelical Church in Germany (EKD): Memorandum, "Preserve, Promote and Renew Peace." The EKD memorandum of 5 November 1981 entitled "Preserve, Promote and Renew Peace" brought new fuel to the argument. [22] Its nearly 100 pages are detailed, thorough, balanced, and historically oriented. Beginning with the acute dangers threatening peace, it gives a summary of the political efforts after 1945 and goes into the ecclesiastical controversies since 1959. There then follow a fundamental discussion of the theological mission of peace ("The aim of Christian ethics can only be peace not war," p. 45) and some concrete suggestions.

In its crucial section, the memorandum refers to the "Heidelberg theses": *"Even today, 22 years after* the Heidelberg theses, the church must accept that participation in the attempt to secure peace in freedom by nuclear weapons continues to be a possible mode of conduct for Christians" (p. 55; italics added). This statement is immediately qualified by something that in the subsequent debate has been mostly ignored (or at any rate not quoted): "But: this mode of conduct is only ethically defensible within a context in which every political effort is being made to reduce the causes of war, extend the possibilities of the nonviolent solving of conflicts and take effective steps toward lower armaments levels" (p. 55).

Concerning the slogan "Serve peace without weapons," the memorandum has this to say: "It must . . . be clear about the conditions that have to be achieved and preserved for a situation of peace without armaments to prevail. The slogan cannot be defended as an 'absolute' formula without this political context" (p. 57).

The memorandum continues to accept the phrase "serve peace with weapons," but stresses that this thesis is "only ethically justifiable in the context of a general peace policy" (p. 56).

The political/ethical content of the two positions—serve peace with/without weapons—has, the memorandum states, to be kept separate. Only thus could the discussion focus on the substantial problem areas of the mission for peace and avoid ending up as a "clash of political opinions" (p. 57).

The memorandum concerns itself directly with the NATO dualtrack decision. It shows understanding for the peace movement, because "many people can find in the actions of the politicians responsible for this decision no convinced or convincing perspective of how effectively to put an end to the nuclear arms race" (p. 54).

The Moderamen of the Reformed Federation: "The Confession of Jesus Christ and the Church's Responsibility toward Peace." On 12 June 1982, the most senior body of the Reformed Federation issued a statement. Its title, a significant one for the members of the Reformed church, is in the tradition of Karl Barth: "The Confession of Jesus Christ and the Church's Responsibility toward Peace." [23] Among other things, the statement renounces the "development, preparation and use of means of mass destruction" (p. 2).

The attitude of the EKD is explicitly mentioned as the cause of the statement: "It is the dubious 'balance,' the ambivalence and indecision in the EKD which have provoked this special vote" (p. 1). It continues: "We know that we are called to oppose the life-destroying *blasphemy* of nuclear weapons with the *confession of our faith*. The nuclear preparation of the universal holocaust is not an 'adiaphoron' (a thing indifferent, on which each may decide); it is in contradiction to the fundamental articles of the Christian faith....The peace question is a *question of faith*" (p. 1; first and third italics added).

The attitude the statement then adopts is derived directly from faith in Jesus Christ. The crucial initial thesis: "Jesus Christ is our peace. . . . All power in heaven and earth belongs to him who was crucified and resurrected" (p. 2). In obedience to his word we are to live at peace with all people. A little further on is the sentence so provocative to the Lutherans: "This confession of our faith is irreconcilable with the view that the question of peace on earth among men is a matter of political judgment and therefore to be decided independently of the gospel's message of peace." On the contrary, for the Reformed church the question is one having *"status confessionis,"* for what is at issue "in the question of attitudes to means of mass destruction" is "the profession or denial of the gospel" itself (p. 2).

In the appendix the issue is taken up again, where it is stated that while the Kingdom of God and the secular kingdom—God's peace and peace on earth—are not identical, they cannot be separated "because Jesus Christ is the Lord over all spheres of our life." Peace on earth is to be fashioned "in conformity with God's peace" (p. 11).

Similarly, another analogy leads us to the following argument: In Christ, God linked his peace with the promise and commandment of human justice. This faith is irreconcilable with approval or even toleration of a "security system" that is maintained "at the cost of the starving and the wretched of this earth and at the price of their death" (p. 2).

In the seven theses that follow, the theological arguments and their political consequences are discussed. The form of the theses is significant. First of all a confessional clause is formulated, which is followed in each case by: "This confession of our faith is irreconcilable with. . . . " The theses are consciously constructed to correspond to traditional confessional texts. For example, in the Lutheran Confessio Augustana, the positive confessional formulation is followed by a *"damnamus"* (there, however, it is other erroneous religious teachings and not other "political" opinions that are condemned).

The NATO dual-track agreement is not mentioned directly in the statement, but there is a clear demand for "renunciation of more and new weapons, an immediate end to the development and stationing of new means of mass destruction" (p. 2).

The Council of the EKD: Communiqué. A short while later, on 16-17 September 1982, the council of the EKD responded with a communiqué. In it the council stresses that both the EKD and the Reformed Federation agree on two goals: peace, and pursuing disarmament as a means toward peace. [24] Then we come to the point of disagreement: "No one at present is able to answer the question of *how* to reduce and put an end to the mutual nuclear threat in a way that satisfies all sides. None of us can know, when it comes to the problems which are the subject of negotiations, whether what he suggests or does might not bring about the opposite of what he intends" (p. 17). It was for this reason that the question of means could not have *"status confessionis."* The communiqué ends with the following—problematic—statement: "Questions of *survival* in this world, as important as they are, must not be confused with questions of faith and made into questions of confession" (p. 17 italics added). This argument still rages, threatening to split the EKD community.

THE CONTROVERSY IN THE CATHOLIC CHURCH

As with the various stages of development within Protestantism, we can here distinguish three phases.

The First Phase: After World War II

Along with thoughts of a "socialism based on Christian responsibility," it was pacifist ideas that predominated within the FRG's Catholic population—surveys show—as a reaction to World War II. As late as 1950, one could read in a commentary in a then-influential

Catholic paper: "The main body of German Catholic men rejects military service and war in principle. Hence all the discussion of re-militarization in Western Germany lacks any foundation in reality." [25]

The Second Phase: The Controversy over Rearmament

The predominantly pacifist mode began to change with time. Referring to the international political climate of the period, Cardinal Frings of Cologne, addressing the Catholic Conference in Cologne in July 1950, repeated the statements of Pius XII, and spoke of the duty to defend when the "deepest foundations of the divine order are under threat or attack." [26]

Adenauer's policy of rearmament was supported, or at least tolerated. No "theological objection of principle to either the permissibility or duty of military defense, that is to the core of the doctrine of the 'just war' " was raised. [27] The demands of the Sermon on the Mount were understood to refer not to the "what" but the "how." At the same time, despite the rejection of communism and the concern expressed about the Stalinist threat, this readiness to defend is not related directly to the Western world, for it "is decayed and rotten to its foundation." [28] A number of voices called for the defense of the Christian Occident, but others warned against Adenauer's restorationist policies.

The Catholic view of conscientious objection as expressed in the debate about rearmament also differs from the Protestant: "Absolute *conscientious objection,* which rejects every war, even the just defensive war, *is morally forbidden.*" [29] Papal pronouncements of the time also leave these decisions to the "erring conscience." "The doctrine of *bellum iustum* has validity for German Catholicism too." [30]

The Third Phase: The Argument over Nuclear Arms

On 5 May 1958, in the context of the situation at that time and of existing knowledge of nuclear weapons, a number of Catholic moral theologians judged, in conformity with the criterion of "controllability" (from the *bellum iustum* doctrine), "that it is, in the estimation of conscientious experts, erroneous to maintain that the effect of atomic weapons entirely evades this control. *Their use* is not therefore necessarily against the moral order or in every case a sin." [31] The Jesuit G. Gundlach, an adviser to Pius XII, put this very pointedly indeed: Not even defensive nuclear war that destroyed everything would necessarily be morally reprehensible, but might be permitted as a "manifestation of God's majesty and his order." "Yes, and even if the world were to be quite destroyed in the process this would still be no argument against our reasoning." [32]

Two people who strongly opposed this unchristian and inhuman distinction between values and the humans who embody them were the lawyer W. Boeckernfoerde and the philosopher R. Spaemann. The debate that ensued produced the realization that the *bellum iustum* doctrine ends in a dilemma: on the one hand, nuclear weapons stabilize peace; on the other, they are morally prohibited in terms of the criterion of controllability. [33] But if it might be morally prohibited to use nuclear weapons, would the threat of such use be morally prohibited as well? This question was hardly discussed, however, among Catholics.

Present Disagreements

Group: Christians against Nuclear Armaments. In March 1981, a number of Catholics, among them the well-known journalist W. Dirks, published a statement entitled "Christians against Nuclear Armaments." [34] The group arose as part of an initiative of the "Catholic grass-roots conference," a critical protest movement directed against the official organizers of the 86th German Catholic Conference in Berlin (June 1980). Its aim is to involve all Christians, but particularly Catholics, more strongly in peace work: "We unconditionally reject the use of nuclear weapons—regardless of whether they are to be used for defense or attack." Such use was "irreconcilable with the example and gospel of Jesus Christ and with the mission of the churches" (p. 156).

The group asks all Christians (p. 159): "Can we reconcile it with our faith in Jesus Christ to approve, or even remain silent before a possible use of nuclear weapons?" It asks what political significance the renunciation of force extolled in the Sermon on the Mount (Matt. 5-6)—"Blessed are they who use no force"—might have, or the commandment of love and our responsibility for the Creation that has been entrusted to us.

The group cites the Second Vatican Council and the Vatican's statement to the United Nations ("The Holy See and Disarmament," 1977), in which both the use of nuclear weapons and the arms race were "condemned in the sharpest manner" (p. 157). Using the precedent of the Protestant "Heidelberg theses," the group rejects any justification for the use of nuclear weapons by the traditional ethics of war. Christians should, rather, set about overhauling the "remnants of a theology of the Holy War, the misuse of the theory of the 'just war,' the retreat to mere personal responsibility in the private sphere (love of one's neighbor, obedience, sexual self-restraint, and so forth), as if politics had nothing to do with God or, therefore, with us Christians" (p. 159).

As far as military policy is concerned, the group demands gradual disarmament. The first step in this direction is seen to be "renunciation of the stationing of additional medium-range weapons (cruise, Pershing)" without any conditions (p. 157). Nuclear deterrence is rejected because it "necessarily" must reckon with the use of nuclear weapons.

The authors of the statement expressly refer to the Protestant groups Live without Arms and Action of Atonement, and the Catholic group Pax Christi.

"Platform of Pax Christi: Disarmament and Security." The work of the German section of the international Pax Christi movement was directed above all to reconciliation between the Germans and the French, later to that between the Germans and the Poles. It is a lay organization, with a bishop as its president (1967-72, Cardinal Doepfner, chairman of the German Bishops Conference; 1972-81, Bishop Moser; and since then, Bishop Kampe).

On 9 November 1980, a delegates' conference approved "Platform of Pax Christi: Disarmament and Security." [35] After a theological discussion, "The Church and Peace—the Church and War" (para. 3), the platform goes on to discuss the possibility of a concept of security going beyond military aspects, current disarmament models, and the tasks now facing the church.

The platform makes reference to Christ's Sermon on the Mount and the early Christian "ethos of love of one's neighbor and of non-violence" (para. 5). "The doctrine of just war," by contrast, "is less defensible than ever" (para. 9). There follows a quotation in support of this view: "John XXIII clarifies this with the words: 'It is therefore madness in this age of ours, this nuclear age as it calls itself, to consider war as still being a suitable means of restoring one's injured rights' " (para. 9).

The church's entanglement in the "present international state of non-peace" is to be blamed on the doctrine of just war, for this had provided the justification for it. In light of new understanding, however, peace is "a process of decreasing violence and increasing social justice at all levels of human activity" (para. 9). Christians have a duty to "suggest, demand and support steps directed toward a change in the international system, the gradual introduction of nonviolent methods of conflict-solving, and armaments reduction to the point of general and complete disarmament" (para. 10). "Every threat and use

of force in international affairs is prohibited under international law
(U.N. Charter, Art. 2, para. 4)" (para. 12).

In a historical passage, the document criticizes the doctrine of just
war for leading to

> the assumption in time of war that the legitimate state authority
> always has the right to wage war on its side. Hence at the beginning
> of World War I, the church supported, in some cases enthusiastically,
> the respective national war aims of the European countries. In World
> War II, the majority of the church in Germany, despite its philosophi-
> cal opposition to National Socialism and despite internal and exter-
> nal resistance within the ranks of the church, similarly upheld the
> soldier's obligation to do his loyal duty, even though Pope Pius XII
> had branded the invasion of Poland as unjust. After the Second
> World War (in different circumstances, to be sure, but following from
> the same tradition) the pacifism of the early postwar years was aban-
> doned within a short period in favor of an unquestioning and almost
> unanimous support for rearmament. Nor did the nuclear armaments
> debate of the late 50s meet with any great response within West Ger-
> man Catholicism [para. 47; italics added].

Many short-, medium-, and long-term perspectives and proposals
are mentioned. Among them is an appeal to the FRG "to influence
the USA in such a way that its negotiations with the Soviet Union
will be conducted with the aim of preventing the stationing of new
medium-range nuclear missiles in Europe" (para. 40).

*The Central Committee of German Catholics: "The Ethical Founda-
tions of Foreign and Defense Policy."* It is instructive, by way of complete contrast to the internal church peace initiatives, to look briefly
at the arguments about "the ethical foundations of foreign and defense policy" as they were put forward in a declaration of the Central
Committee of German Catholics (ZdDK) in February 1981. [36] At the
political level, the declaration states, what is required beside the supreme "commandment of love" is a "policy guided by common
sense" that is to be directed toward "universal well-being" (p. 11). In
this—and it is here that the chief difference to the previous approaches surely lies—"the first principle in all conflicts of power
must be that of reciprocity" (p. 13). "To protect and preserve the national interest against external threat is one of the rights of every
state and one of the obligations of its government toward the commonweal"; such national defense is "not immoral but an ethical imperative" (p. 14). Blind moral fervor is a danger to peace" (p. 17).

*The German Episcopal Conference: "Justice and Peace" and "Peace
and Security."* The German Episcopal Conference held its spring assembly 9-12 March 1981. Its statement, "Justice and Peace," in some

ways reflects official helplessness. [37] Without anything concrete being said, reference is made to the current "intense public controversy in our society" (p. 5), to unemployment, the armaments question, and the general crisis of meaning. "We German bishops share the bewilderment of so many people, particularly of the young." The statement then continues, after referring to the "complex technical issues," quoting a passage from the Bible (2 Tim. 1:7) to give encouragement against resignation, fear, and escalation, and to stress the responsibility of everyone: "Only justice creates true peace and only in peace can justice flourish" (p. 5).

"Peace and Security," the statement issued simultaneously to the press by the German Episcopal Conference, is more precise. [38] First, with "Gaudium et spes" (No. 81), the arms race is characterized as an "intolerable damaging of the poor." There follows—buttressed by further papal statements—a demand "for simultaneous, multilateral disarmament" (p. 6).

Having expressed their disappointment with the ineffectiveness of the church's appeals for peace in the past, the bishops speak of the tragic "tension between the demand for simultaneous, multilateral disarmament and the readiness to defend oneself" (p. 7). It is a tension that will have to be borne. The statement warns against "false pacifism" (p. 7). It concedes that the commandment against murder and the Sermon on the Mount's appeal not to practice violence are valid for every Christian. "Not a few understand this to mean radical rejection of any defense or self-defense" (p. 8). But Holy Scripture, the testimony of the early centuries of Christianity and of the constant doctrine of the church, of Vatican II, and the popes that came thereafter do not substantiate this interpretation: "There is no question of an absolute incompatibility between being a Christian and serving as a soldier" (p. 8). In the early church, only "some" and not all saints had refused military service.

While every individual has the right to forgo the defense of his freedom and subjugate himself to unjust force, "he is nonetheless duty bound" to protect "the freedom and integrity of his fellow men" (p. 8). And while the Sermon on the Mount's appeal for nonviolence applied to every individual believer, this could not "mean the state's ceasing completely to pursue justice or abandoning its self-defense or defense" (p. 9). Nonviolence was an aim, but this did not mean "abandoning defensive measures which are morally justified, i.e. which protect life *and freedom*," (p. 9; italics added). Governments, therefore, could not be denied the right to "morally permissible defense" (p. 10), just as conversely the individual must be given the right of conscientious objection. Both are services to peace. On particular issues, "such as the much-discussed questions of missile deployment and arms exports, it is possible for Christians 'of equal conscientiousness to come to different conclusions on the same question' " (p. 10).

The Federation of German Catholic Youth: "First Positions: Peace and Justice." In May 1981, the general assembly of the Federation of German Catholic Youth (BDKJ), the umbrella organization of Catholic youth organizations in the FRG (roughly 650,000 members), approved a working paper, "First Positions: Peace and Justice." [39] The paper is intended to give guidance to individual member organizations and groups over the next three years: "The number of young people who have made peace and justice a central preoccupation of their lives is already considerable and is growing steadily. This is also true of members and officials of the organizations of the BDKJ" (pp. 11-12).

The authors of the paper note with concern that for many of those involved in peace protests "the use of force has become subjectively permissible as means," in the sense of "counterviolence," against the threat to the foundations of life. These actions cannot simply be dismissed as the "actions of radical minorities" (p. 35). What is needed, rather, is a concept of how conflicts might be resolved without violence. The declaration criticizes the fact that today's pacifists are labeled naive. It further condemns the export of arms, particularly to Third World countries, as "morally scandalous" (p. 31).

The authors object to a policy of strength, which they claim increases the weaknesses of the deterrence system: "As part of such a policy we must consider the now official American strategy (Directive 59) that military installations (e.g. land-based nuclear missile sites) and centers of political decision making in the Soviet Union are targets for nuclear missiles. Such a strategy nurtures the dangerous illusion that nuclear wars can in the future be waged and won" (pp. 43-44). The FRG, however, the statement continues, cannot be defended. Thus the BDJK demands a reorientation of peace and defense policy and a search for alternative concepts.

One of the preconditions of disarmament would be for the negative stereotype of the enemy to be dismantled and "the security needs of the other side to be taken into consideration." [40] Defense readiness would have to be subordinated to the primacy of peace policy.

Characteristic of the present controversies is the explosive potential of the old "complementarity formula." This is evident in the attitude taken toward conscientious objection: in 1969 the BDJK regarded "peace service without weapons" (civilian service) and "peace service with weapons (Bunderswehr) as "equal" decisions. [41] Service with arms was described as the precondition of service without arms because it "secures the state of nonwar," thereby making the other peace services possible. However, changes in "the conditions of military technology and military strategy" meant that this conclusion was now "only conditionally" true. "The likelihood of weapons being able to safeguard the state of nonwar is getting smaller!"

The Chairman of the German Episcopal Conference: "The Peace Problem in the Light of Christian Belief." In an address at the opening of the general assembly of the German Bishops Conference (September 1981, in Fulda), the chairman of the conference, Cardinal Höffner, discussed "the peace problem in the light of Christian belief." [42] He made no mention of the BDKJ declaration *expressis verbis*. To begin with, he considered the eschatalogical "Eternal Peace" (p. 4). Then he turned to peace "in this eon," which is realized as peace with God, in one's own heart, in society and state, and, last, among nations (p. 8). In connection with this last point, he analyzed in detail the doctrine of the just war. He then depicted the unimagineable and dreadful potential of present arms technology—including nuclear weapons.

Finally, the cardinal mentioned three paths that have recently been followed but that "have not led to the goal" (p. 16). This is important to note, for he here discussed the three central problems of the present controversy from his position as the most senior Catholic dignitary in the FRG: pacifism, the Sermon on the Mount, and revolutionary violence. He began by saying that the mouthing of "slogans that whip up emotion," such as "Peace at any price!" "Better red than dead!" "Destroy what destroys you!" (Gollwitzer), "Make peace without weapons!" and "Unilateral disarmament!" does no service to the cause of peace (p. 16). In so saying, the cardinal was also delivering a reprimand to well-known Protestant theologians and large Protestant groups. Emotions, he continued, get in the way of the real issues. He quoted Pope Paul VI, who warned against the "insidiousness of purely tactical pacifism, . . . which anaesthetizes the opponent one wishes to conquer and kills the sense of justice, duty and sacrifice in men's spirits" (p. 17).

While the nonviolence and renunciation of retaliation found in the Sermon on the Mount should be the "disposition" (p. 17) of every Christian and of states, too, these exhortations of Christ's do not mean "that law and order are suspended." A government is in fact "obliged to defend the life and freedom of its citizens against unjust aggressors" (p. 18).

Taking issue with the theologians of "revolution" (Giulio Girardi, J. B. Metz, Ernesto Cardenal), the cardinal argued that here "the demand of traditional doctrine, made in the interests of peace, that forces and movements within the state . . . are not permitted to wage war" is being undermined (p. 18). Violence is to be rejected. "It is unchristian to say that shooting people is a good thing when done by the Left, bad when done by the Right—or vice versa" (p. 19).

A certain tension exists, however, not noted by the cardinal, between this and the right to defense that he then adduced, quoting from the Christmas message of Pope Pius XII in 1948: there are values "the violation of which by an aggressor state is an attack on God's majesty" (pp. 21-22). Values " 'of such importance to human coexistence that to defend them against unjust aggression is without doubt entirely justified' " (p. 22). The cardinal went on to name these "supreme existential values of a nation: the right to life, justice, freedom of conscience, of religion and *such things*" (p. 22; italics added). In his view, attitudes toward deployment and arms exports are questions of how to secure peace "on which Christians 'of equal conscientiousness' can come to different conclusions" (p. 24).

The German Episcopal Conference: "Justice Creates Peace." The ninety-one-page 'Word of the German Episcopal Conference on Peace," entitled "Justice Creates Peace" (April 1983),[43] begins with a veiled reference to the peace movement: "Large sections of the young and members of other age groups are giving expression to their longing for peace" (p. 5). A broad outline of the biblical (Old and New Testaments) understanding of peace ("man's peace with God, man's peace with himself, in his own heart, men's peace amongst themselves all belong together," p. 11) is followed by a survey of the doctrine of just war through the ages. This in turn is followed by a number of statements concerning the all-embracing tasks of peace of Christians and by exhortations to work for peace.

Within the biblical section, the most important theological passages are concerned with the Sermon on the Mount, the contents of which apply "not only to the disciples . . . but to the church as a whole" (p. 17). At the same time, Jesus' message of peace cannot be directly translated into political action. The instructions of the Sermon on the Mount cannot be declared ethical norms for political action "to be binding of themselves alone, without evaluation of given circumstances and values." Yet the sermon should not be thought to be about "unreal, ideal conditions" but ought, despite eschatalogical reservations, to be effective "in the here and now." It is out of this tension that the conference's conception of the relation between the sermon and politics emerges: The Sermon on the Mount was aimed at "fundamental attitudes," which could not be applied schematically as if they were laws. Thus a renunciation of violence "at the cost of others' well-being, especially third parties' . . . [could be] contrary to Jesus' intention" (p. 18).

As for the theory of the just war, although the bishops do not condemn it as obsolete in principle, they do considerably restrict and alter it; it had above all been Pius XII who had "taken up the theory in an official capacity" and elaborated it "in its theological-ecclesiastical manifestation." "The 'just cause' of war is concentrated in the defense of fundamental legal values, insofar as they are under direct violent threat." It would therefore be more proper to speak of the " 'just defense.' " This is particularly necessary in view of the effects of the secular theory of the "just war" (p. 33). (Earlier the bishops had attacked Lenin's theory.)

It is also important to distinguish between the military and the political dimensions of deterrence: "In this intra-Catholic discussion" in the FRG, unlike in the statements of the pope or from within Protestantism, "the political dimension of the threat of nuclear weapons" had tended to take second place (p. 34). Though not suspended, the doctrine of the just defense is incorporated into a comprehensive peace-promoting concept "based on the recognition of the well-being of mankind in freedom and justice" (p. 37).

Because the effectiveness of nuclear deterrence is disputable, criteria have to be named that deterrence must satisfy if it is to *continue* to be ethically acceptable: "Those military measures which have either already been taken or which are planned must neither make war more wageable nor more probable" (p. 53). The measures must be reduced to the minimum level required and not "suggest any striving for superiority." This, however, was no excuse for standing still; "alternatives to the threat of mass destruction" should be sought (p. 54).

The stress here is also obviously on the criterion of controllability, for a little later it is stated unequivocally that "the use of nuclear weapons or other means of mass destruction to annihilate *population* centers or other *predominantly civilian* targets is in no way justifiable. War of annihilation can never be an alternative, is never permitted" (p. 55; italics added).

THEOLOGICAL BACKGROUND

As our description of the various positions and controversies has shown, sociopsychological, military-strategic, and theological arguments all play an important role in the discussion. It is not always clear, however, what is the general major premise and what the contingent condition in the arguments supporting a given view. Common to all the positions, though in varying intensity, are:

- The experience of World War II, or youth's reflection upon it:
- The awareness of the failure of Christians at that time; and
- The emotional conviction that similar events must never be allowed to happen again.

These viewpoints and experiences were much more thoroughly debated by Protestants after the war than by the Catholic church. In addition, there is in both ecclesiastical currents—generally speaking —an awareness of the North-South problem, which exposes the East-West category as a dangerous shorthand.

These four elements of a sociopsychological approach derive, to an extent anyway, from a "Christian sense of existence," which does not always use the usual theological categories or, if it does, then quite often in rather unusual ways.

MILITARY-STRATEGIC THEMES

As far as military strategy is concerned, the new quality of the weapons of mass destruction was quickly recognized by the Protestants as part of the ethical problem, however varied opinions might have been on the matter. Among Catholics, the problem tended to be hidden by the category of the just war, especially as rejection of communist ideology was given priority. Later there was an increasing awareness of the ethical problems posed by the new weapons. For all the differences of opinion among Protestants, they were always clear that there could be no "religious war" against the East. Official Catholic opinion—with a few exceptions—tends not to speak explicitly about this, but such a view would tend to be subsumed under the expression "just defense."

A pacifist tendency does exist (except of course in the official postures of the Catholic church), but not for the most part in the sense of total pacifism, which appears as more of a long-term objective. The tendency is probably a reaction to the failure of all disarmament attempts so far—and therefore is to be understood as a sign of increasing mistrust of present conflict-solving strategies or those persons politically responsible for them. Seen from this angle, genuinely Christian possibilities are again taken seriously—in contrast to the toning down that has taken place in the existing ecclesiastical tradition. And they are understood by many who have not been able to "relate" to traditional dogma.

POINTS OF THEOLOGICAL CONTENTION

All the opinions, positions, and proposals we have discussed are justified theologically by their proponents. How far this applies to the "grass roots" in each case is difficult to determine, for no empirical studies are available. What are the central points of theological contention?

The first decisive theological question: What is to be understood by the word *God?* Remarkably enough, this question is never dealt with explicitly in the controversies, although one would think it needs to be settled before the second question could be answered, namely, What is the relationship between "'God" and "the world," "the Kingdom of God" and "the empirical world and states as they exist," between "the peace of God" and "peace in the world"? How are worldly political questions connected to questions of faith? How is a realistic assessment of political conditions related to trust in God? How is trust in law and power related to trust in God?

The classic answer to the second question is sought (predominantly among Catholics) with the aid of the concept of the just war and (mainly, but not exclusively, in the Protestant sphere) with the help of various interpretations of Christ's Sermon on the Mount. Behind both these attempted answers lie pointed problems: How do humans relate to certain values? And what, exactly, is sin?

Finally—considered from the viewpoint of epistemology—there is the question: Exactly what type of statements are theological statements? How do they relate to empirical statements?

In what follows I shall look more closely at the theory of the just war as it was used, rejected, or modified in the various approaches to which we have so far referred. I shall then discuss the various interpretations—important above all for the Protestant debate—of the Sermon on the Mount. This will lead back to the theories of the "doctrine of the two kingdoms" and of "the reign of Christ."

THE THEORY OF THE JUST WAR

The theory of the just war is not really a theory but, rather, a number of different arguments strung together, attempting to answer the question of whether "waging war is always a sin." [44] The relationship of particular arguments to one another is often not very clear.

The history of the doctrine sheds some light on its problematical character. I will briefly describe some of the decisive stages of its development, in order to show the doctrine's inappropriateness to the present day and the reinterpretation it has occasionally undergone, and to explain the protest against it.

In view of the dilemma posed by the doctrine of the just war as this has appeared in the controversy so far, it is astonishing that none of the opponents of this idea has made reference, to my knowledge, to the fact that the doctrine is known to be heathen in origin, being traced back to the Roman Cicero. Cicero distinguished between *bellum iustum* and *bellum iniustum: iniusta bella* are those that are ventured upon *sine causa.* [45] The cause can be retaliation or defense against enemies. In Cicero's view, only wars that are proclaimed, declared, and waged for reasons of reparation are just. Ideally, a state would wage no wars except *"pro fide auto pro salute."* [46] It is interesting to note what Augustine says apropos of *"salus"*: what Cicero wants is "for the state to wage war for the good of its everlasting existence, while the individual citizens may die and be born, as the olive, the laurel and similar trees always stay green despite the fall and new growth of their individual leaves." [47] The words *retaliation, defense,* and *salus*—and the relationship this touches on between the state and the individual citizen—epitomize the most important elements that then continue to recur, in modified form, in the subsequent tradition. Augustine cites Cicero; Thomas Aquinas refers back to Augustine.

For Augustine, war is permissible only as a means to achieve peace, never as an end in itself. It must be directed against an injustice that has been committed, must be declared by the legitimate authority, and must be waged in a "humane" manner, i.e. the waging of war should be free from passions, "such as delight in causing damage, cruel lust for revenge, unforgivingness, retaliatory fury, mania for conquest. . . . " [48]

Thomas Aquinas, basing himself on Augustine, incorporates his thoughts on war into the comprehensive doctrine and aim of the "common good" as a partial aspect of moral human behavior seen from the viewpoint of the virtue of love. He, too, names three conditions:

• The just war must be ordered by the "auctoritas principii." [49] Then there must be
• a *"causa iusta"* [50] (viz., punishment of injustice) and
• an *"intentio . . . recta"* (i.e. the intention "of multiplying the good and avoiding evil"). [51]

These very vague conditions leave room for much subsequent discussion and elaboration.

In 1924 the Catholic theologian F. Stratmann brought the traditional arguments together in ten conditions to show that no actual war would again fall under them:

1. *serious injustice* on the side of one and *only* one of the conflicting parties;
2. serious *formal moral guilt* on one of the two sides (material injustice done is not sufficient);
3. undoubted *proof* of this guilt;
4. the *inevitability* of military conflict, after all attempts at reconciliation, undertaken with the utmost seriousness and effort, have failed;
5. a *proportion* between guilt and means of punishment. A punitive measure *exceeding* the measure of guilt is unjust and not permissible;
6. moral *certainty* that victory will be *on the side of right;*
7. the *right intention,* of *furthering good* by waging war and of *avoiding evil.* The benefit to the state to be expected from the war must exceed the expected evil;
8. the war to be *conducted in a proper manner:* to be kept within the boundaries of justice and humanity; . . .
9. *avoidance of any severe harm to other states, or to Christianity as a whole,* not directly involved in the war action;
10. a *declaration of war* by the *legally empowered authority,* in the name of God to execute His justice. [52]

Pius XII adopted the three conditions laid down by Thomas Aquinas and two further conditions from sixteenth-century theology (all peaceful attempts at reaching an understanding must have proved ineffective; "moral certainty of success" [53]). He restricted the meaning of *causa iusta* and *intentio recta* as well. The "just cause" is, he said, provided by those values of humankind, of which some are "of such importance to human coexistence that to defend them against unjust attack is without question entirely justified." [54] The "proper intention" is qualified as follows: "If . . . the use of this means leads to such an extension of the harm that it passes completely beyond man's control, then its use must be rejected as totally immoral." [55] These imprecise formulations triggered a debate about whether "controllability" was to be applied to the new weapons themselves and their effects, or to the human "act of fusing them." [56]

The formulation of Vatican II in the form "Gaudium et spes" (No. 80) stands in the same tradition: "Any act of war which *aims indiscriminately* at the destruction of *entire* cities or *wide* areas and their populations, [57] is a crime against God and against man, and is to be firmly and resolutely rejected."

Despite these restrictions, therefore, the doctrine of the just war survives as a doctrine of the just defense. [58] The just cause is "limited to the defense of fundamental legal values, where they are under direct, violent threat." [59]

THE IRRITATION OF THE THEORY OF THE JUST WAR

The doctrine of the just war, persisting in this official reinterpretation but emptied of meaning by its evolution and the present situation, is under fire on two counts. First, in its *premise:* that its justification by natural law is undermined by the dynamics of reflection upon biblical texts. This is reinforced by lay interpretations of the Bible. The increasing use in twentieth-century Catholicism of vernacular biblical texts, the greater emphasis on biblical tradition in the Catholic church since Vatican II, and the increased self-reliance of the laity have all contributed to this development. Second, the doctrine is questioned because of its *intent:* the new qualities of weapons have made the category of a just war untenable. It has become inappropriate, for, even according to Pope John XXIII, it goes against reason "still to consider war a suitable means of restoring injured rights." [60] Nuclear war cannot be fought in a humane manner. The values that are to be defended, or their upholders, are destroyed by their very act of defense. Similarly, the self-defense category no longer appplies; it is senseless, if the life of the person under attack is more endangered by the defense than by the attack itself.

This is the opening for the peace movements. The category of the just war appears untenable beside the churches' anathematization of war in principle. It hangs in midair: its premise cannot be biblically substantiated and is being questioned; in its intent, it has been shown to be inappropriate.

The official Catholic church has tried to save itself with a reinterpretation—that of "justified defense" (at the cost of considerable vagueness in its statements). But precisely because of these characteristics the statements might produce unwanted side effects. [61] The careful formulations of Vatican II could, in view of the simultaneous (and recently renewed [62]) stress on the duty to defend and such vague generalizations as the "commonwealth" or "universal justice," lead to greater precision in nuclear technology (and thereby to the possibility of controllability). This has not actually been said as of yet—but is probably perceived as a hidden danger by the peace movement. For instance, the theory of the just war is considered by German Catholic bishops as needing improvement not because it could be exposed as a means toward fulfilling the common good but because the common good could also be taken over by Marxism-Leninism. Unfortunately, we have here a structural element common to both ideologies.

The Catholic church's interpretation ultimately leaves the question of means unclear. Even where there is a morally justified duty to defend, is such a defense with nuclear weapons morally justifiable? The —initially sensible—distinction between political and military deterrence conceals the fact that political deterrence is psychologically effective only when there is a willingness to use the weapons in a military way. Therein lies the paradox of deterrence. It is possible that, as a result of ecumenical ideas, a new, sharper conception of sin and guilt is gaining ground in Catholic circles: in Reformed eyes, even the best intentions are signs of humankind's fallen existence. In this view, there is never any such thing as a just war or a just defense. On the contrary, it should rather be said—in the negative mode, so as to express the mark of fallen humanity: decision A is *less bad* than decision B. The criterion here is (should be) the protection of the life of each actual human being. If the categories of natural law and common sense ultimately fail, then, in view of the increasing sensitivity to the traditional biblical texts, it must be asked how the demands of the Sermon on the Mount can be made fruitful in the context of this discussion. But for the moment let us look at a fundamental objection that is continually brought up at this stage of the present debate.

To assess nuclear dangers and all the related questions requires an enormous amount of expert knowledge of the subject. Has the church any right to interfere at all? And, in addition, can it justifiably refer to the Sermon on the Mount? These questions were discussed in a much-quoted speech given by (Protestant) State President Carstens at the reopening of the St. Petrius Cathedral in Bremen in April 1981.

I respect . . . the utterances [of the church] even when I am of a different opinion, and even when I consider them dubious. An example would be when demands are made by the church for one-sided measures in the area of disarmament, or when the principle of political and military balance is rejected, which I am convinced and which historical experience shows is a guarantee of security and peace. I consider these arguments to be mistaken and I think it is particularly disquieting if references are made to the Sermon on the Mount to justify them. [63]

In such ways doubts about the Sermon on the Mount are indirectly expressed, or particular interpretations of it put forward from political quarters.

THE CENTRAL PROBLEM: CHRIST'S SERMON ON THE MOUNT

The Sermon on the Mount is the name given to a collection of sayings of Jesus in Matthew 5-7. They contain radical demands, such
as—as far as our subject is concerned—loving one's enemy and renouncing the desire for retaliation. Jesus' demands are preceded by
words of comfort known as the beatitudes: precisely those are blessed
and praised whom one would least expect to be: the weak, the poor,
the underprivileged, the peacemakers. The radical demands and
words of encouragement lead to a reformulation of values. What is
being talked about is the sacrifice of right and might, but in politics
everything revolves around right and might. It is understandable why
it has often been said by Helmut Schmidt among others, [64] that one
cannot govern the world with the Sermon on the Mount. But how is
the Sermon on the Mount to be interpreted or its overall meaning to
be characterized?

Briefly, there are two problems to be distinguished in regard to the
Sermon on the Mount:

1. To whom is the Sermon on the Mount addressed? Only the individual Christian? Or the whole congregation, the church, or humankind pure and simple?
2. Can the radical demands of the Sermon on the Mount be fulfilled
   in the real world?

*MAJOR POSITIONS ON THE INTERPRETATION OF THE SERMON ON
THE MOUNT*

The "Classic" Catholic Position

The demands of the Sermon on the Mount are not intended for all
Christians in the classic Catholic interpretation. From as far back as
the doctrine of the two paths of the Didache (c. 90-100 A.D.), we are
told, according to the outline of ethics to which the radical injunctions of the Sermon on the Mount also belong, and which should be
impressed upon the baptized: "If you are able to bear the whole yoke
of God, then you will be perfect [teleios]. But if you are not able to
bear it, then keep to what you can." [65] This distinction between perfect and ordinary Christians leads to the classic differentiation between *consilia* and *praecepta*.

The ten commandments of the Decalog apply to all Christians; the
consilia evangelica, to ascetics and monks. The *consilia* comprised not
only the three classic monastic vows but up to twelve injunctions,
most of them based on those of the Sermon on the Mount. This leads

to a dangerous set of two-tiered ethics. No doubt for this reason the distinction has come under strong criticism in present-day Catholic theology, which has effectively gone over to the evangelical (Lutheran) view. Remnants are still to be found in pronouncements such as that of the German Bishops Conference, wherein with regard to conscientious objection by Christians in the Old Church, it is argued that not all but only "some" saints were objectors.

The "Two Kingdoms Doctrine": Luther's Position

Luther himself protested against the division of Christian into two groups. The injunctions of the Sermon on the Mount apply equally to all Christians. But the Christian is seen in two functions, leading to the "two kingdoms doctrine," as it is known. Luther makes a distinction within the person of the Christian: Mr. X as a Christian in his private life, when just he himself is involved, and Mr. X as a Christian in his official capacity (as a judge, for example, or as a soldier). If—as in the first case—the issue is personal interests, then right and might and resistance are to be renounced and (unconditional) love is to be shown. In his official capacity—as in the second case—when Mr. X, in his social responsibility, is acting for others, he must use might and enforce the right. At this point we find the seeds of a new argument.

To avoid misunderstandings and misinterpretations of Luther's position, certain points should be noted: even in the Christian's official capacity, the Christian is characterized by love, which expresses itself in a manner not its own (in the form of power and right). Thus, the love of parents can take, for example, the form of punishment. Here, too, it is important to note that, motivated by love, right and might must be applied for the protection of others.

The dangers of Luther's solution are threefold, and these dangers have, in fact, been realized in history. One, the danger of privatizing the Sermon on the Mount. Two, the separation into personal and official spheres, and the idea (possibly) linked to it, of the later sphere's having "a law of its own." The third danger is Luther's theological inconsistency in not having recognized, as a result of this process of justification, the ranks of classes (*Stände*) of society as sufficiently "fallen." In an analogous way, little is asked about the structural consequences of the rule of God that is already dawning here and now.

The Doctrine of the "Kingship of Christ"

The doctrine of the "Kingship of Christ" was developed by Karl Barth, not directly as an interpretation of the Sermon on the Mount but as a reaction to the Lutheran "two kingdoms doctrine" (or rather its abuse, particularly during the Third Reich). The problem, however, is the same as that posed by the confrontation between the Sermon on the Mount and any political situation. How do faith and political action, the church and the political order relate to each other?

As a whole, Karl Barth's theology could be described as a Christ-centered concentration of theology. Thus, all aspects of the world are under Christ's rule. The consequence of this for the relationship between church and state is the following: they behave like two concentric circles, with Jesus Christ as their center. The smaller circle, the church (Barth: the Christian community), sets the authoritative example for the wider circle, the state (Barth: the civil community). [66]

What now is the task of the church toward the state? First, as its "archetype and ideal" (p. 41), it is simply to exist in an exemplary way. How, then, can concrete ethical guidance be given on political issues? Here, as a bridging principle, the *"analogia fidei"* (or *"analogia relationis,"* as they are known) are brought in to help. Relations at the human level correspond to "inner godly" relations (cf., for example, the analogous derivation of marriage: "As the invoking I in God's being is to the thou which invokes . . . , so in human existence itself is the I to the thou, the man to the woman." [67]

In the same way, God's action in Jesus Christ becomes the criterion for the forming of political life, in its structural relationship, by the community of Christians: in its relationship to the Kingdom of God, the state exists in the tension between "equivalence" and "inequivalence" as an "allegory, a correspondence, an analogy to the Kingdom of God believed in within the Church and proclaimed by the Church" (p. 23).

The "analogy" idea appeared explicitly in the argument of the Moderamen or council of the Reformed Federation: the Kingdom of God and the kingdom on earth are "not identical," but neither can they "be divided"; they are to be seen as "corresponding" to each other. Karl Barth himself gives this example: "The Christian community is founded on the knowledge of the one eternal god, who as such became man and thus man's closest neighbour." For the Christian community it follows from this that in "the political sphere and in all circumstances it will put mankind first and not any one cause or other" (p. 25). Another example: According to Barth, the Christian community lives "in the dawn of the day of the Lord, and its duty to the world is to awaken it and tell it that this day has dawned." In short, through Christ, God's light entered the world. "The necessary political equivalent of this state of affairs is that the Christian community is the sworn enemy of all secret diplomacy" (p. 30).

In a sharp, methodologically consistent critique, Helmut Thielicke reduces this interpretative scheme *ad absurdum* by actually deriving secret diplomacy, with the help of the same "method," from theological precepts of the "messianic secret." [68] One can understand Thielicke's fundamental objections to Barth at that time, as one can those of the EKD and even of some Reformed voices to the Moderamen today, [69] given the methodological arbitrariness of this reasoning—despite its meaningful motives and aims. The arguments simply lack a rational, verifiable methodological foundation.

The consequence—even in the case of committed Christian politicians, such as Helmut Schmidt and Hans Apel [70]—can then only be (hopefully) to distrust this theological arbitrariness and effectively (unfortunately) to propound a misunderstood "two kingdoms doctrine" as a counter to those positions. This is why we must now ask: How can the Sermon on the Mount be taken seriously and its sociopolitical consequences assessed without our succumbing to theological capriciousness?

SUGGESTIONS FOR A SETTLEMENT

In the following reflections, some hidden and unrealized tendencies in the present discussion, as well as some clear positions and some thoughts of my own, will be construed and examined, for the purpose of finding a proposal for settling the present debate. This can also help to clarify, classify, and evaluate the many positions better. Settlement of the debate will require the following:

• a search for a new ethical measure of judgment;
• clarification of the relationship between human beings and values;
• examining the meaning of "sin"; and
• understanding the relationship between theological statements and empirical statements.

THE SEARCH FOR A NEW MEASURE OF JUDGMENT

The motif of the "two kingdoms doctrine" advanced by the Lutherans can be helpful: the rule of God is to be proclaimed over the worldly domain. His love holds good here, even if in a modified form. At the same time, from the methodological-rational point of view, the doctrine allows the derivation of a fundamental distinction between

ethical-theological statements and descriptive empirical statements.
This Lutheran motif ought to be combined with concentration on
Jesus of Nazareth. Not, however, with an abstract, ahistorical Chris-
tology—the preexistence of Jesus [71]—but with the actual Jesus of Nazareth.

In Jesus' actions and words (the Sermon on the Mount) God's original will is made clear: "Jesus lives God." Thus, at the same time he is
considered the "true human." According to God's original will, man
was to be the "image of God" (Gen. 1:26). If the Old Testament prohi-
bition of images, intended to preserve his intangibility, holds in relation to God, so here, by analogy, it is claimed for the human being
that the human being has an intangible value. Through the life and
sayings of Jesus of Nazareth this claim is made even more extreme. It
applies to every single individual, even the enemy, the outcast, and
the weak. This process should not be limited to human motives but,
rather, should be formulated as a basic ethical norm. The empirical
phenomena and their consequences could then be evaluated in light
of this norm. The danger of Protestant theology is that it might not
put forward any such norm. The danger of Catholicism is that it will
formulate general values that, because of their vagueness, deteriorate
into mere empty phrases.

I propose as the basic norm that every human being has an intangible value, and one should act accordingly. Only from this basis are
human rights then to be derived and differentiated. This fundamental norm applies to everyone. In actual fact, however, we restrict, we
touch upon, we deter—in many different ways. That is why it is simultaneously a norm of protest: our talk of the intangible value of a
human being is a continual protest against the domination of human
beings by human beings. The most extreme form of this domination
is the killing of another human being. This is why this fundamental
norm is simultaneously a minimal criterion of ethical behavior. It
demands the protection of each human being's unconditional right to
life—worldwide. This requirement implies a host of consequences.

The Sermon on the Mount is the "law" of life of the congregation,
the church. Its injunctions are directed at everyone, without exception. Because biblical thought, in contrast to platonic thought—still
widespread today—does not recognize any split between the body
and the soul, the difference between "inner" and "outer" does not
apply either. It is the whole human being that is meant. No one can
escape this. The injunctions of the Sermon on the Mount expose the
most secret of thoughts. At the same time the sermon expresses
promise and encouragement: "blessed are . . . " and "ye shall. . . . "

These statements refer to the beginning of the "new" human being. Hence a dialectic arises: If the injunctions of the Sermon on the Mount expose each one of us, the beatitudes invoke a "new state of being" (grace). The person who lives life as a disciple of Christ will love his or her enemies. According to the latest research, this corresponds to the fundamental structure of the Decalog. The fifth commandment ("Thou shall not kill"), which is expressed even more radically in the Sermon on the Mount, is theologically comprehensible only on the basis of the first commandment ("I am the Lord, thy God").

According to Luther, "God" is what I put my heart into. Following this, the (Old Testament) promise could be correctly expressed as: If your life has no other ground and no other goal than "the Lord thy God," then you will not kill. In New Testament terms, this reads: If you follow Jesus with your whole heart and self, you will be able to love your enemy. When human beings live in this way "out of God," their existence is characterized as one due to itself alone—as opposed to an existence formed by mechanisms of self-assertion. This basic norm applies to all human beings. The Sermon on the Mount puts the norm in extreme terms and speaks of the power of Jesus to make things possible.

In addition, we ought to discuss—and this is touched upon in the controversial theses of the Catholic journalist Franz Alt [72] —the rationality of the Sermon on the Mount in its empirical sociopsychological aspect: Our existence can be understood—seen from the point of view of the Sermon on the Mount—as a life ruled by the "echo law," a life in the deterrence spiral or within a well-rehearsed "circle of rules" that obeys its own laws.

The acts and words of Jesus, on the other hand, point to a way of breaking out of the circle of rules. Methodologically speaking, this is clear from his dialogues and his reaction to catch questions. For instance, in the story of Caesar's tax (Mark 12:13-17), in which Jesus breaks the double bind of whether or not to pay taxes: "Render to Caesar the things that are Caesar's and to God the things that are God's" (Mark 12:17). By this answer he draws the questioners into the far larger question of to whom they themselves belong. In other words, the radical demands of the Sermon on the Mount are not aimed at "passive acceptance" [73] but at "nonsensical action." "'Turn the other cheek!' 'Give him your shirt!'; 'Give him your cloak as well!'; 'Go with him for two miles!'" [74] These demands are not for literal ways of behavior but for something of greater psychological depth: with his "new" rule, Jesus distances himself from the "old" rule—"an eye for an eye," "as you do to me, so I will do to you"—so as to reduce accepted "behavior by the rules ad absurdum." [75] In this way he makes a change of attitude possible. We are given the chance "of recognizing our neighbor in our enemy." [76] Here, then, is the hidden rationality in Jesus' behavior. Beyond the "echo law," he opens up a freedom of alternatives, a space for alternative interpretations and actions.

Today, this rationality could be the only sensible way of reacting to the threatened failure of deterrence. As with most decisions, there is a risk here, too: to behave according to Christ's example does not necessarily lead to success. For the Christian, this is the burden of the discipleship of Jesus: suffering.

Even Luther said that the individual Christian should be prepared to suffer. And for Luther, suffering is a sign of the church of Christ. *Suffering* in the New Testament sense means renouncing right and might and expecting everything "from God." A church that bears the sign of the cross stands on the side of the weak, the outcast, and the poor. In this way, it could radiate love through powerlessness and then gain the power of the promise of resurrection of Jesus: "In powerlessness lies strength." Or as St. Paul put it: "My grace is sufficient for thee: for my strength is made perfect in weakness" (2 Cor. 12:9).

This is not a recommendation for politicians but a paving of the way that could become contagious. And to an extent it is an invitation to the politicians. "The church can make a moral demand its own, even if it knows that it may take a long time for it to be fulfilled." [77] The basic norm we have established should, however, enter into the considerations of every politician as a normative criterion regardless of whether or not the politician intends to follow the Sermon on the Mount.

THE RELATIONSHIP BETWEEN THE HUMAN BEING AND VALUES

Even the basic norm implies a radical rethinking in light of the Sermon on the Mount. True, it is a fundamental value that is expressed there, but in such a way that its content is meant to be each actual human being. The human being, in his or her existence, stands above all other values. Hence, there can be no fatal separation in a (usually platonic) realm of values between the actual human being in whom values are embodied and the values themselves. As a result, even meaningful values such as justice, freedom, peace, and the common good take on secondary significance. They describe the task of a harmonizing function in light of the high valuation, conceived as applicable throughout the world, of every individual human being and his or her right to life.

It follows from this that the individual must never become a function of "the universal" or "the whole"—regardless of their conceptual content. Herein lies the root of the contradiction, concealed within a number of the positions adopted in the present debate, between pacifist demands, in relation to Central Europe, and the demands for revolutionary justice in the countries of the Third World. And the placing of values above actual human beings permeates opposing views, as a common structure.

It is therefore not surprising that Cardinal Höffner does not criticize, in the reasoning of his theological antipodes, J.B. Metz and his positive assessment of revolutionary overthrow as such, insofar as its aim is the improvement of the "commonweal"—even though in the process human life might be sacrificed. Rather, he sees the problem as being that the revolution might come about illegally, "as a result of private arrogance." [78] Here, moreover, lies the root of the argument about the connections—conjunctions in the logical sense—between the (possibly empty) terms peace and freedom on the one hand, and *peace* and justice on the other. But from the point of view of the fundamental norm, the issue is whether the life of an individual human being may be sacrificed at all in the name of any value whatsoever.

The divorcing of values and human beings also leads to internal contradictions. Thus, the Catholic church, in particular, is criticized for the contradictions and, as it were, logical inconsistency of its position on abortion on the one hand, and the question of armaments on the other—one of the critics being Heinrich Albertz. [79] The Catholic journalist Alt is one of the few—logically consistent on this point, at least—to stress his unified view of both problems. [80] Affirmation of the life of an actual human being is a necessary precondition for improving the quality of his or her own life. To this extent the basic norm provides a minimal criterion for the evaluation of alternative possibilities of action. How and by what means can it be achieved, throughout the world, that as few people as possible are killed, or rather that their deaths (as far as it is not their own choice) are not permitted?

THE UNDERSTANDING OF SIN

The formulation of the basic norm and the statements derived from it contain, through their negative context, the theological awareness of the radical nature of sin. To this extent, the norm expresses skepticism both about "good," "just" solutions and about definitive solutions.

It appears that the standpoint embodied in Catholic pronouncements is close to the radicalism of the Reformed conception of sin. At the same time, it is true that theological discourse about sin runs the fundamental risk of sin's becoming "ontologized." This would also mean—applied to all human beings—that a universal statement is formulated: All human beings are sinners. Like all universal statements, this statement cannot be tested. If it is nevertheless maintained as dogma—in the sense of renunciation of its ability to be tested—then it may possibly prevent ideas of peace from being developed. In addition, if sin is ontologized, there would be no room for the entrance of "God's Kingdom"; it would be, to all intents and purposes, ineffective. It would be scientifically legitimate, on the other hand, to interpret the theological conviction of sin as a relatively well-confirmed hypothesis intended to serve as a reminder of the need for both skepticism and caution.

At the level of the empirical manifestations of sin, it follows from these differentiations that often in the debate, a false inference is drawn, namely, that from the universal statement of the sinfulness of human beings it must follow that war and killing cannot be abolished. But, even if sinfulness were understood ontologically, the only thesis that could be maintained would be: The forces that underlie war—aggression, for instance, as a potentiality that could be actualized in various ways—cannot be abolished. Both in the closed ontological view and in the open worldview, the following demands must be made: War as an institution must be done away with; aggressions must be institutionally restrained and other ways of channeling them evolved.

THE RELATIONSHIP BETWEEN IDEOLOGICAL STATEMENTS AND EMPIRICAL STATEMENTS

Finally, it would be of help for the entire discussion if the question of how theological statements relate to nontheological empirical statements could be clarified. Without being able to go into this ultimately decisive question in any depth, we may nevertheless suggest the following: From the theologian's (or Christian's) fundamental convictions—such as the fundamental norm—he or she formulates prescriptive statements. For a concrete political decision to be reached, however, additional, empirically descriptive statements concerning the actions and their alternatives, the conditions of the situations, and the means and measures are necessary. Further, descriptive statements need to be made about the possible consequences of the various alternative actions. And last, statements are needed that express evaluations of the probability of the consequences' occurring.

All the empirical-descriptive statements we have mentioned have a hypothetical status. These empirically desirable consequences should now be evaluated in light of our proposed basic norm. In this way one would arrive, under the ethical premise of our established basic norm, at a rational theory of decision taking in situations of risk. Only if this methodological differentiation is observed is it possible to establish where exactly there is dissension or consensus—at the level of values, at the descriptive level, or in the evaluation of probability. To give just one example: C.F. von Weizsaecker maintains that there will "probably"[81] be a third world war. The supporters of the group Live without Armaments, on the other hand, say there will "definitely"[82] be a third world war. Here dissension may exist not at the level of values but at the level of empirical information and (concealed) sociopsychological assumptions, which led to differing assessments of probability.

CONSEQUENCES OF THE PROPOSED SETTLEMENT

Again taking up some arguments from the current discussion, we will now briefly consider the consequences of our reflections in light of the proposed basic norm. First, it will be asked how political the church is allowed to be. Then consequences are inferred relating to the arms problem, which the church communities might introduce into the political discussion as suggestions. Finally, there is a discussion of the church's own general responsibilities toward the problem.

How Political May the Church Be?

The question How political may the church be? is wrongly put. The church is in actual fact (by what it does or does not do) always politically active, whether it knows it or not, whether it wants to be or not. By apparently declining to make political statements, it sanctions, intentionally or unintentionally, prevailing political opinion. This is particularly the case when the criteria of church opinions are formulated in such a way that, in terms of values, political positions of very differing kinds can be derived from them (cf. the just war). The question must therefore be phrased thusly: What should the criterion be for political statements by the church?

My suggestion is the above-mentioned basic norm. The church should apply this to various possible decisions and recommend to the politicians and decision makers: In a situation where decisions have to be made involving risks, that course of action is to be preferred whose consequences least contradict the basic norm.

In view of the considerations outlined above, the churches should in principle reject the instrument of nuclear deterrence. Moral obloquy does not solve anything, but it does give expression to a fundamental conception of values, the "negative framework" of all further considerations. Otherwise there would be a danger, that of the "just war" of deterrence being understood as an expression of good, just action. Within these positions of principle, responsible and rational ideas must be thought out step by step. At the same time, these would need to be permanently reexamined, criticized, and reformulated.

According to the following assessments of the situation, the decision to deploy missiles is to be rejected (or reversed):

- In the opinion of many experts it is superfluous because of the "military balance."
- If the "balance" is understood not only militarily but in a more general sense (economic strength; political stability), then deployment becomes even less necessary.
- Quite apart from deployment, the situation of deterrence is already an extremely risky one in view of the manifold potential for destruction and the possible sources of technical and other error.
- When set against the starvation throughout the world, missile deployment and the costs involved cannot be defended.

Regarding the next demand, that for gradual unilateral disarmament, even without deployment the present situation is extremely ominous. Moreover, in the face of the ethical problem of the North and South, it is ethically indefensible to maintain the status quo.

Valentin Falin of the Soviet Union has said: "Together, we and the Americans already have enough nuclear weapons to obliterate all life on earth fifteen times over. Why fifteen times? Is not twice enough?" [83] For this reason, unilateral disarmament to the necessary level of deterrence is the first requirement. At the same time, it must be admitted that "naturally, a policy of security through disarmament is not free of either. On the other hand, military security policy is attended with immeasurably greater risks." [84]

Reequipping with Structural Defensive Weapons

According to Article 2b of the Basic Law of the FRG, wars of aggression are unconstitutional even in the potential state of preparation. In the meantime, concepts have been developed for the FRG that require further critical examination. [85]

The Immediate Development and Long-Term Planning of Social Defense

It is true that in terms of the basic norm, defense of "freedom" is better than a life of "nonfreedom." But it is also true that if the defense of freedom involves killing people, the value of freedom does not justify the killing. This idea necessarily leads to measures of social defense. Social defense is to be understood as a nonmilitary form of defense, primarily of "social institutions and only indirectly . . . of the state's territory," [86] acting to deter possible aggressors. At the moment the existing projects still seem utopian, but there is an urgent need for them to be developed further and critically examined.

Normatively speaking, priorities of values must be worked out within the framework of the basic norm, and must be capable of attracting the sympathies of broad sections of the population. From the empirical methodological point of view, what is important is—in contrast to the working methods of the main protagonist of this concept in the FRG, Theodore Ebert, a member of the EKD synod—to apply some of the critical methods of the empirical social sciences. Until now the only approaches taken have been either that of Marxist "conflict theory" [87] or the extremely problematical [88] "functionalist" approach. [89]

There is a long-term aim that should not be lost sight of in all this discussion, namely, to make possible an *internal world policy* (C.F. von Weizsäcker), [90] with a kind of world police to control conflicts. This concept might least infringe upon the basic norm, that of the intangible value of every individual.

I would like to propose the following general aims as the special tasks of Christian congregations:

1. Christians should constantly remind themselves that all stated opinions—even theological ones—are no more than provisional. One thing is particularly true of disarmament issues: timid adherence to certain theories (for or against) can under certain circumstances be fatal. This requirement of provisionality is to be applied to the dogmatic question and answer of theology as well.
2. Christians should live in appreciation of the individual human being. Every one should be or become sensitive to whatever group pressure under which he or she or others live. Even in church circles there is an increasingly "fascistoid" emotional group pressure manipulating the behavior of individuals.
3. The liberating possibilities that the Gospel opens up for life should be lived to the fullest extent. The theological "process of

justification" means the human being's unconditional acceptance by God. As a result, weakness can be admitted and perhaps overcome. But there are barriers to this happening that must be dismantled. In this way, the congregation will acquire a radiating function.

4. Christians have to learn to admit their prejudices. Only by doing so can they work together to overcome them.
5. Church congregations should extend invitations to politicians and develop permanent contacts with them. Test questions could be posed in the context of the basic norm.
6. Christian congregations should invite political and church groups from the Warsaw Pact countries, thereby nurturing international contacts aimed at reconciliation.
7. The words and concepts *people, nation,* and *fatherland* should be demythologized. Today these have ceased to be meaningful political categories. They should be used only in a cultural context. Paul indicated that faith calls for the overcoming of such relative differences: "You are all one in Jesus Christ" (Gal. 3:28).
8. Christians and their congregations must see to it that concrete measures are introduced to overcome hostility toward foreigners. They should be particularly directed at the prejudice shown toward Turks in the FRG.

SUMMARY

It would be not only fascinating but also relevant to our subject to examine and differentiate between the controversies in the churches of the GDR. In the context of this paper, however, there is space for only a few brief notes against the background of what has been written so far.[91]

THE VARIOUS CONTINGENT CONDITIONS

First, one must consider the different sociopolitical conditions: the churches exist in a socialist state that is also a most loyal Warsaw Pact member. Their existence is that of a minority, especially that of the Catholic church. Nevertheless, they are the only tolerated non-state organizations and as such offer a niche for a number of nonconformists.

The central organization of the (numerically larger) Protestant churches is the Federation of Churches in the GDR. After a long and difficult history, they have become—since top-level discussions between the then-chairman of the federation, Bishop Schönherr, and the chairman of the state council of the GDR, Honecker—socially "accepted." The church now officially understands itself as a "church within socialism." Despite this restriction, it still has an opportunity to make a fruitfully and critically clear peace offer of its own—in particular contrast to the official state thesis of "socialism equals peace."

There seems to have been no direct mutual influence of the peace movements in the two German states upon each other. Initially, the Protestant churches of the GDR took part in the general discussion in Germany as a whole. Later—after their organizational separation —they tended increasingly to seek contact with the ecumenical debate. The Catholic church, because of its conception of the church and its organization, has from time immemorial been much more tied into an international frame of reference.

PROBLEMS AND UNDERCURRENTS

The problems and undercurrents in the GDR have an accent different from those in the FRG, and this is in large part due to the different sociopolitical conditions. The encroaching international situation has brought out a tendency different from that in the FRG, one that is visible in the consequences drawn from the Heidelberg "thesis of complementariness." Because the official state position recognizes only service in the National People's Army as "peace service," the tendency of the church attitude has been to lean toward pacifism.

In the GDR young Christians are currently faced with three alternatives: to do their service as soldiers in the National People's Army; to do an alternative service with (military) construction units (as "construction soldiers"); or to choose total conscientious objection (the usual consequence of which is imprisonment).

While the West German churches tend to see civilian service and military service as being equivalent, for the churches of the GDR there is a definite gradient within the three possibilities:

> It will not be able to be said that the peace witness of the churches has taken form with the same clarity in each of the three decisions taken by young Christians in the GDR today. The *conscientious objectors,* who pay for their obedience by suffering personal loss of freedom in penal camps, and the construction soldiers, who have taken on the burden of questions of conscience and situational decisions, give *clearer witness* of today's peace commandment of our Lord. [92]

It is in such ways that the authors of the working paper "Pacifism in the Current Peace Discussion" (November 1981) have tried to win some sympathy for pacifism in the Protestant congregations of the GDR. In the paper, which, it should be noted, was published by the

GDR Federation of Churches, impulses for a future (political) concept of pacifism are derived from a historical overview of pacifism—pacifism as a commandment of political reason. [93]

Even for the Catholic bishops of the GDR, the talk of nonviolence in the Sermon on the Mount has a rational expressiveness unsuspected hitherto. [94] Thus, the official bodies of both churches have come out emphatically against state-ordered military science lessons in the schools.

The Protestant Federation of Churches has even developed its own concept of peace education. And the Catholic church stresses in traditional manner the "inalienable right of parents to educate." [95] Both churches have warned against the general militarization of society seen in the glorification of violence on television and in war toys, for example. It is understandable, from this, how the "social peace service" initiative that developed at the grass-roots level was then given official church support.

As one further example of action from below we should mention the movement Schwerter zu Pflugscharen (swords into plowshares). The way in which the state has dealt with it, and for that matter is still dealing with it, has its tragicomic sides. The picture printed on cloth stickers (with a biblical slogan) is at the same time a Soviet symbol (cf. the statue in New York donated by the USSR to the UN). Although the churches have in principle supported this spontaneous movement, they had to say, due to the risks involved in wearing the sticker, "We cannot protect you." [96]

The Protestant churches have advised against supporting the Berlin appeal "Peace without weapons" [97] because it contains clear political demands (including a nuclear-free zone). But the churches are standing up for the signatories of the appeal who have gotten into trouble. This attitude on the part of the churches can certainly be understood in terms of the Lutheran "two kingdoms doctrine," but, in view of the continued conditions, it can also be interpreted differently. On the other hand, church leaders, on the occasion of the Luther anniversary, have been tending to interpret the "two kingdoms doctrine" more along the lines of our proposed settlement. W. Krusche, the former regional bishop of Magdeburg, is opposed to any abridged interpretation of Luther's position; citing Luther's warnings to the rulers of that time, he has said: "To act according to the commandment of love of the Sermon on the Mount is therefore eminently sensible." [98]

The Catholic church more or less propounds the contradictory papal position: on the one hand, there is no disputing the right to morally permissible defense; on the other, war is "madness" (John XXIII). "A war waged with modern weapons of mass destruction is in every case immoral in itself . . . but even conventional weapons are reaching an increasingly deadly perfection." [99]

The path of the "church within socialism" shows us that within restrictive social structures, the churches put the accent on nonviolence and a greater willingness to sacrifice in the face of the North-South conflict—in an economic situation certainly more difficult than that in the FRG. Both are genuinely Christian options.

NOTES

1. In M. Greschat, ed., *Die Schuld der Kirche* (Munich, 1982), p. 102.
2. Quoted in W.W. Rausch and Chr. Walther, eds., *Evangelische Kirche in Deutschland und die Wiederaufruestungsdiskussion in der Bundesrepublik 1950-1955* (Guetersloh 1978), p. 47, n. 10.
3. Quoted in Rausch and Walther, *Evangelische Kirche in Deutschland*, p. 68.
4. Quoted in Chr. Walther, ed., *Atomwaffen und Ethik. Der deutsche Protestantismus und die atomare Aufruestung 1954-1961. Dokumente und Kommentare* (Munich, 1981), p. 69, n. 11 (italics added).
5. In C.F. von Weizsäcker, *Der bedrohte Frieden* (Munich, 1982), p. 29f.
6. Quoted in Walther, *Atomwaffen*, p. 28.
7. Ibid., p. 75.
8. Ibid., p. 139.
9. von Weizsäcker, *Der bedrohte Frieden*, p. 95ff.
10. Ibid., p. 95.
11. Ibid., p. 99.
12. Ibid., p. 100 (italics added).
13. C.F. von Weizsäcker, "Geistiger und politischer Hintergrund der Entwicklung seit dem Kirchentag 1967: Wie hat die geltende Sicherheitspolitik die Gnadenfrist des atomaren Gleichgewichts genutzt und wie wird es weitergehen?" in *epd-Dokumentation* (Frankfurt), no. 6/83, p. 5f.
14. Von Weizsäcker, *Der bedrohte Frieden*, p. 102.
15. To keep the number of notes to a minimum in what follows, I give the relevant source in the notes. In the text, the page number is given in parentheses, and always refers, unless otherwise stated, to the particular source in question.
16. In "Ohne Ruestung Leben," in *Ohne Ruestung leben*, ed. Arbeitskreis von Pro Oekumene (Guetersloh, 1981), p. 20ff.
17. In H. Anslem and W. Schindelin, eds., *Umkaempfter Frieden* (Munich, n.d. Arbeitshilfe für den Evangelischen Religionsunterricht an Gymnasien. Themenfolge 49b), p. 110.
18. The appeal, "Create Peace without Weapons," of the group In the Name of Atonement/Peace Services (ASF), delivered at the second national peace week, 15-21 November 1981, in In the Name of Atonement

Aktion Suehnezeichen/Friedensdienste, ed., *Aktionshandbuch 2, Frieden schaffen ohne Waffen* (Bornheim-Merten, 1981), p. 14f.

19. Cf. partial reproduction in Pax Christi, ed., *Frieden und Sicherheit. Eine ausgewaehlte Dokumentation von Friedensdenkschriften (1) and (2)*, in *Probleme des Friedens,* info no. 5-12/1982 (quotation, 9-12/1982, p. 31f.).

20. *Sicherung des Friedens* (Bad Boll, n.d.), p. 2. In the following text the numbers in parentheses refer to paragraphs in source.

21. In *epd-Dokumentation* (Frankfurt), No. 21a/81. The numbers in parentheses refer to paragraphs in source.

22. Ibid., no. 48/81 (italics added).

23. Ibid., no. 38a/82.

24. Ibid., no. 45/82, p. 17f.

25. Quoted in Herder—Korrespondenz, vol. 5, 1950/51, p. 154.

26. Quoted in P. Engelhardt, "Die Lehre vom 'gerechte Krieg' in der vorreformatischen und katholischen Tradition. Herkunft—Wandlung-Krise," in *Der gerechte Krieg: Christentum, Islam, Marxismus,* R. Steinweg ed. (Frankfurt, 1980), p. 107.

27. E.J. Nagel and H. Oberhem, *Dem Frieden verpflichtet. Konzeption und Entwickungen der katholischen Friedensethik seit dem Zweiten Weltkrieg* (Munich/Mainz, 1982), p. 29.

28. Quoted in A. Doering-Manteuffel, *Katholizismus und Wiederbewaffinung* (Mainz, 1981), p. 101.

29. J. Mausbach and G. Ermecke, *Katholische Moraltheologie,* 9th ed. (Muenster, 1953), 3:95.

30. Nagel and Oberhem, *Dem Frieden verpflichtet,* p. 32.

31. Quoted in Herder—Korrespondenz, vol. 13, 1958/59, p. 396 (italics added).

32. F. Fundlach, "Die Lehre Pius XII. vom modernen Krieg" (lecture delivered in 1959); Fundlach, *Die Ordnung der menschlichen Gesellschaft* (Koeln, 1964), 1:650.

33. Nagel and Oberhem, *Dem Frieden verpflichtet,* p. 33.

34. In At. Batke, ed., *Atomruestung-christlich zu verantworten?* (Duesseldorf, 1982), p. 156ff.

35. In Pax Christi, ed., *Dokumentation,* no. 4, 5th ed. (Frankfurt, 1982). The numbers in parentheses refer to paragraphs in source.

36. In Sekretariat der Deutschen Bischofskonferenz, ed., *Frieden und Sicherheit,* Arbeitshilfen, no. 21 (Bonn, 1981), p. 11ff.

37. Ibid., p. 5.

38. Ibid., p. 6ff.

39. The page numbers in parentheses in the following text refer to *Frieden und Sicherheit. Eine ausgewaehlte Dokumentation von Friedensdenkschriften* (1), ed. Pax Christi, in *Probleme des Friedens,* info. no. 5-8/1982, p. 11ff.

40. Ibid. (2), in *Probleme des Friedens,* info. no. 9-12/1982, p. 9.

41. All the following quotations, ibid., p. 40.

42. Sekretariat der Deutschen Bischofskonferenz, ed., Joseph Kardinal Höffner, *Das Friedensproblem im Licht des christlichen Glaubens* (Bonn, 1981).

43. Sekretariat der Deutschen Bischofskonferenz, ed., *Gerechtigkeit schafft*

Frieden. Wort der Deutschen Bischofskonferenz zum Frieden, Die Deutschen Bischoefe, no. 34 (Bonn, 1983).

44. Thomas von Aquin, *Summa theologica,* II-II, 40, 1. (German Thomas edition, ed. Albertus-Magnus-Akademie Walberberg bei Koeln, vol. 17B [Heidelberg/Graz-Wien-Koeln, 1966], p. 82.)

45. Cicero, *De republica,* 3, 23. (Latin-German edition, ed. K. Buechner [Stuttgart, 1979], p. 282.)

46. Ibid., p. 280.

47. Augustinus, *De civitate dei,* 22, 6. (*Vom Gottesstaat,* trans. W. Thimme [Munich, 1978], p. 758f.)

48. Augustin, *Contra Faustum,* XXII, 74, CSEL 25/1, p. 672. (*Voelkerrecht,* I, trans. E. Reibstein [Freiburg/Munich, 1958], p. 135.)

49. *Summa theologica,* II-IIq, 40, a, 1. (German Thomas edition, ed. Albertus-Magnus-Akademie Walberberg bei Koeln, p. 83.)

50. Ibid., p. 84.

51. Ibid., p. 85.

52. *Weltkirche und Weltfriede* (Augsburg, 1824), p. 103f.

53. J. Endres, in German Thomas edition, ed. Albertus-Magnus-Akademie Walberberg bei Koeln, p. 452.

54. In A.F. Utz and J.F. Groner, eds., *Aufbau und Entfaltung des gesellschaftlichen Lebens. Soziale Summe Pius XII* (cited herafter as U-G), 2 vols. (Freiburg/Schweiz, 1962², no. 4133ff. (=Acta Apostolica Sedis 41 [1949] p. 5ff.), quotation, no. 4154.

55. U-G. III (Freiburg/Schweiz, 1961), no. 5364 (=AAS 46(1954) 590).

56. Fundlach, *Die Ordnung der menschlichen Gesellschaft,* p. 640.

57. For texts of Second Vatican Council see K. Rahner and H. Vorgrimler, *Kleines Konzilkompendium,* 15th ed. (Freiburg/Basel/Wien, 1981), p. 540 *"abgestellt."* At this point the teaching of "dual-effect-action" was inserted; in the original council proposal it said: *"secumfert";* it now reads *"tendit."* Cf. N. Glatzel, "Neueste kirchliche Lehrverkuendigung zur Sicherheits-und Ruestungsdebatte ab 1945," in *Frieden in Sicherheit,* ed. N. Glatzel and E.J. Nagel (Freiburg/Basel/Wien, 1982²), p. 127 (italics added).

58. German Thomas edition, ed. Albertus-Magnus-Akademie Walberberg bei Koeln, vol. 17B, p. 33.

59. Ibid.

60. *Pacem in Terris,* no. 127, Quoted, ibid., p. 34.

61. German Thomas edition, ed. Albertus-Magnus-Akademie Walberberg bei Koeln, vol. 17B, p. 33.

62. Cf. Pope John Paul II., message delivered at the World Peace Day Celebration 1 January 1984 (Pressedienst der Deutschen Bischofskonferenz 22 December 83).

63. In *epd-Dokumentation* (Frankfurt), no. 25/81, p. 2 (italics added).

64. Cf. the interview in *Evangelische Kommentare,* April 1981. Cf also, *epd-Dokumentation* (Frankfurt), no. 18a/81, p. 1ff.

65. *Didache* VI/2 (my translation of K. Bihlmeyer and W. Schneemelcher, eds., *Die Apostolischen Vaeter* [Tuebingen, 1956], p. 5).

66. The page numbers in parentheses in the following text refer to K. Barth, *Christengemeinde und Buergergemeinde,* Theologische Studien (Zurich, 1946).

67. K. Barth, *Die Kirchliche Dogmatik*, III/1, 4th ed. (Zurich, 1970), p. 220. The page numbers in parentheses in the following text refer to this book.
68. H. Thielicke, *Theologische Ethik*, II/2, (Tuebingen, 1966²), p. 717.
69. Cf., for example, for Reformed view, Th. Lorenzmeier, in *Abschaffung des Krieges*, ed. G. Brakelmann and E. Mueller (Guetersloh, 1983), p. 52ff.
70. Cf. *epd-Dokumentation* (Frankfurt), no. 18a/81, p. 6, and no. 30/81, p. 7.
71. Cf. this critique of K. Barth: H.Thielicke, *Theologische Ethik*, I (Tuebingen, 1965³), p. 230ff.; Thielicke, *Glauben und Denken in der Neuzeit* (Tuebingen, 1983), p. 431ff.
72. F. Alt, *Frieden ist moeglich. Die Politik der Bergpredigt* (Munich, 1983).
73. P. Hoffmann, "Evangelium und Friedenshandeln," in *Revolution der Gewaltlosigkeit*, ed. H. Pfister (Waldkirch, 1981), p. 14.
74. Ibid.
75. Ibid.
76. Ibid.
77. *Moeglichkeiten und Probleme auf dem Weg zu einer vernuenftigen Weltfriedensordnung* (Munich, 1982²), p. 22.
78. Cf. Sekretariat der Deutschen Bischofskonferenz, *Gerechtigkeit schafft Frieden*, p. 19.
79. Cf. H.J. Luhmann and G. Nevling, eds., *Deutscher Evangelischer Kirchentag* (Hamburg, 1981). *Dokumente* (Stuttgart/Berlin, 1981), p. 683.
80. Cf Hoffmann, "Evangelium und Friedenshandeln," p. 102.
81. Cf. Sekretariat der Deutschen Bischofskonferenz, *Gerechtigkeit schafft Frieden*, p. 10.
82. Cf. Arbeitskreis von Pro Oekumene, "Ohne Ruestung leben," p. 29.
83. *Der Spiegel*, no. 51 (1980), p. 102.
84. *Denkschrift*: Deutsche Gesellschaft fuer Friedens-und Konfliktforschung, e.V.-DGFK-PP, No. 26, p. 6 (quoted in E. Eppler, *Wege aus der Gefahr* [Reinbek, 1981], p. 95).
85. H. Afheldt, *Verteidigung und Frieden. Politik mit militaerischen Mitteln* (Munich/Wien, 1976); Afheldt, *Defensive Verteidigung* (Reinbek, 1983).
86. Th. Ebert, "Das Konzept der sozialen Verteidigung," in Pfister, *Revolution der Gewaltlosigkeit*. p. 29.
87. Th. Ebert, *Soziale Verteidigung. Formen und Bedingungen des zivilen Widerstandes* (Waldkirch, 1981) 2:37.
88. Cf. K.K. Opp, *Methodologie der Sozialwissenschaften* (Reinbek, 1970), p. 208; W. Stegmueller, *Probleme und Resultate der Wissenschaftstheorie und Anlytischen Philosophie*, vol. 1, *Wissenschaftliche Erklaerung und Begruendung* (Berlin/Heidelberg/New York, 1969), p. 558ff.
89. Ebert, *Soziale Verteidigung*, p. 37.
90. C.F. von Weizsäcker, "Bedingungen des Friedens," in von Weizsäcker, *Der bedrohte Frieden*, p. 131ff.
91. I refer in the following, if not otherwise stated, to the presentation by R. Henkys, "Die Friedensfrage in der Diskussion der evangelischen Kirchen in der DDR," in *Christliche Ethik und Sicherheitspolitik,* ed. E. Wilkens (Frankfurt, 1982), p. 181 ff; Henkys, "Zwischen Militarismus und Pazifismus. Friedensarbeit der evangelischen Kirchen," in *Friedensbewegung in der DDR; Texte 1978-1982,* ed. Buescher et al.

(Hattingen, 1982), p. 14ff. The major sources quoted are Buescher et al., *Friedensbewegung in der DDR*; K. Ehring and M. Dallwitz, eds., *Schwerter zu Pflugscharen. Friedensbewegung in der DDR* (Reinbek, 1982). Further sources are named with the relevant quotations.

92. *Handreichung zur Seelsorge an Wehrpflichtige*, partially reproduced in Buescher et al., *Friedensbewegung in der DDR*, p. 54 (italics added).
93. Ibid., p. 245ff.
94. "Gemeinsamer Hirtenbrief der katholischen Bischoefe in der DDR zum Welfriedenstage 1983," in *Bischoefe zum Frieden*, ed. Sekretariat der Deutschen Bischofskonferenz, Stimmen der Weltkirche, no 19 (Bonn, 1983), p. 177ff. (quotation, p. 180).
95. Ibid., p. 181.
96. Letter of the synod to the youth of the Saxony regional church (24 April 1982), in Buescher et al., *Friedensbewegung in der DDR*, p. 290 ff. "Wir muessen Euch aber sagen, dass wir nicht mehr in der Lage sind, Euch vor Konsequenzen, die das Tragen des Aufnaehers jetzt mit sich bringen kann, zu schuetzen" (p. 291).
97. In Buescher et al., *Friedensbewegung in der DDR*, p. 242ff.
98. Quoted from Herder-Korrespondenz, Freiburg No. 12/1983, p. 544.
99. Both quotations cf. note 94 above, p. 179.

14

THE ORIGINS AND AIMS OF THE GERMAN PEACE MOVEMENT

Peter Graf von Kielmansegg

Movements of fierce, indeed passionate protest against the defense policies of the North Atlantic alliance, or peace movements, as they called themselves, emerged in a number of countries of the Western alliance at the beginning of the eighties. The Federal Republic is only one of these countries, but it is a special case. In no other country did the political configurations change so rapidly or so dramatically. After more than two decades of what had seemed unshakable stability, the consensus of politicians and defense experts over the strategy of deterrence collapsed almost overnight. After years of indifference and disinterest toward the problems of defense policy in the nuclear age, a public debate suddenly erupted, to be conducted almost immediately with something approaching monomania and, as it progressed, to divide the country more and more sharply into two camps. A movement formed that in a short time proved capable of bringing hundreds of thousands of people into the streets in repeated demonstrations and that then—armed with this capability—proceeded to lead a more dramatic fight against the NATO dual-track decision than did any other peace movement. In a word, the sudden violence with which the German peace movement erupted into the republic's political life and the support it garnered both there and beyond its borders are without parallel.

But there is a second reason that the Federal Republic is a special case. If the West German peace movement eventually achieves its aims, if it succeeds in gaining even a measurable amount of influence on German policy, the consequences would be extremely far-reaching, for the Federal Republic is not just one member of the alliance among others: it is the strongest of the nonnuclear powers within the alliance; its position in Central Europe gives it a key importance; politically and territorially it is on the Federal Republic that the U.S. presence in Europe is essentially based. In other words, the German peace movement is operating in an area from which the severest shocks could be delivered to the Western alliance. It therefore merits our careful attention.

The questions an attentive observer would like answered fall into three groups. First, What were the roots and origins of this peace movement? What is the explanation for its abrupt entrance onto the political scene? Then, Who does the peace movement actually consist of? What groups and what currents have merged to form it? What is its program, and what are the strategies it employs to achieve its political ends? And finally, What kind of support has the peace movement found in the Federal Republic? What is its real strength, and how much stronger might it become? What effect has it had so far, and what further effects might it have? These are the questions to which we shall endeavor to find an answer.

I

In its short history, the Federal Republic has seen few dramatic debates about defense policy that have lasted any length of time or excited great public interest. In the early fifties, there were conflicting views over the issue of rearmament—but then it would have been surprising if the idea of creating a new army so soon after the catastrophe of 1945 had been accepted with complete unanimity or equanimity. Then in 1957, when it was learned that allied forces stationed in the Federal Republic—including the Bundeswehr—were to be armed with tactical nuclear weapons, a new argument broke out. While it became very heated, by the second half of 1958 it was dying out almost as abruptly as it had arisen. For the two decades since then defense has not been a cause of public excitement. What controversies there have been were argued out among those with official responsibility. It was the peace movement, coming together at the beginning of the eighties, that brought defense back into the arena of public debate.

The peace movement does not, then, have a strong and living tradition behind it. Nevertheless, it will be worth taking a short look at the Kampf dem Atomtod (Fight Nuclear Death) movement of the years 1957-58. Our assessment of the peace movement will be more reliable and closer to the mark if we consider it against this background;

if we ask ourselves why the peace movement of the eighties, beginning as it did in much the same way as the Fight Nuclear Death movement, has not already vanished without trace after the fashion of its predecessor.

The very name of the campaign that erupted in the spring of 1957 clearly indicates what its cause was: nuclear weapons. More precisely, what provided the impulse that brought the movement into being and continued to give it momentum was the sudden transformation of the abstract knowledge of the existence of nuclear weapons into a concrete yet incredible vision of the horror of a nuclear war in Germany, sparked by the debate about the stationing of tactical nuclear weapons in the Federal Republic. The starting point was the famous March 1957 Göttingen declaration signed by eighteen physicists. The cause was then quickly espoused by the SPD, some of the trades unions, and the DGB. Voices of protest were raised in local councils and in the universities. In early 1958, the Fight Nuclear Death movement was formally called into being by a declaration in the Frankfurt Paulskirche, supported by the SPD, the DGB, professors, artists, and representatives of the Evangelical church. There were demands for a national referendum, and this very soon became a central element in the campaign. Two-thirds of the population, according to opinion polls, were against arming the Bundeswehr with nuclear weapons; 52 percent of those questioned even supported a strike to prevent the Bundeswehr from being so armed (Brand et al., p. 54). It was questioned whether parliament had the right to take decisions that were "against the people's will." Several big demonstrations, spontaneous labor stoppages, a resolution at the SPD party congress, and a vote in the synod of the Evangelical church, together with a decision by some SPD-controlled regional parliaments and local councils to hold a referendum, marked, from April to early summer 1958, the real climax of the campaign.

There is no doubt that much in this narrative recalls the events of the early eighties. But with even greater speed than it had arisen, the movement fell away. By the end of the year it had lost all its strength and importance. A faint echo lived on in the Easter Marches, organized along the lines of the British Campaign for Nuclear Disarmament of 1960, but they met with little public support. It is the suddenness of the protest's demise, the sharp contrast between the powerful, very spectacular way it erupted and the speed with which it died away, that raises questions. A number of explanations have been offered: the judgment of the Federal Constitutional Court declaring regional and local referenda on defense policy unconstitutional; the state elections in Northrhine-Westphalia of July 1958, which resulted in a remarkable victory for the CDU: Khrushchev's Berlin ultimatum of November 1958, which gave the Germans a harsh reminder of how threatened the divided city was; and above all, the SPD's political shift to the center, which was to lead in 1959 to the Godesberg program. It is useful to bear in mind these explanations of the campaign's failure as we try to explain the success of the peace movement of the eighties and assess its prospects. We shall therefore occasionally have to return to them.

Between the late fifties and the early eighties lie the sixties and the seventies. This is not just a statement of the obvious. It is an allusion to the profound change of consciousness that took place in that interval: Western industrial society began to question itself, became alienated from itself. The tangible expression of this change was the wave of protest movements that, kindled by a variety of causes, burst upon the political life of many Western countries, the Federal Republic in particular, toward the end of the sixties. The student revolt in Germany was a kind of prelude, a rehearsal, changing the atmosphere and testing out new forms of provocation and insubordination. What it lacked was a cause to bring it wide support. Neo-Marxist critiques of capitalism might fascinate a few intellectuals for a while but did not have any really impelling force. It was not until the rapid emergence of the ecological movement in the seventies that industrial society's protest against itself found an authentic form. A new existential sense arose, a sense of living in the shadow of impending catastrophe, on the edge of the abyss; a fear of the self-destructive power of a civilization created by human beings but no longer controlled by them; a vague yet definite feeling that things could not continue as they were, that the established order and existing institutions had nothing more to offer, that new forms of existence would have to be found.

This new existential feeling that affected many people in the seventies was, of course, not due only to the abrupt impact of the ecological crisis on the consciousness of industrialized societies, frighteningly sharp though this was. A number of processes of social change seem to combine to produce the same effect: people experiencing the world in which they live as alien, hostile; people no longer feeling at home in society as it is currently ordered. The decline of the family as a powerfully integrating institution and the early separation of the generations may have played a key role in this; or the steadily increasing concern of many over the last few years whether they will find their place in this society's world of work—to name but two recent critical developments. However we may try to explain them, the findings themselves are clear: we are faced with a process of mass emigration from the existing social order, emigration not to another country but—experimentally so to speak—to another world; or at least with a mass disposition to such emigration.

It manifests itself in various attempts to "live differently"; but even more in a constant readiness to protest against, reject, say no to the demands of the old world. This readiness can be actualized by different causes. The first great constituent cause was the ecological crisis. For the time being, in the Federal Republic anyway, this has now been replaced (for reasons we shall soon discuss) by the cause of peace. This is in no way to suggest that what we have is a sort of diffuse potential for protest that allows itself to be driven blindly onto the barricades by any odd cause it comes across. The threat to the basis of natural life and the threat to peace—these are certainly not "any odd cause." What is meant is, rather, that the disposition we have mentioned, the disposition to protest, to reject, to say no to a world to which one no longer feels one belongs, is not as characterized by specific causes as it seems in its manifestations. New causes can provide new points of crystallization for the movement.

Most observers hold the view that the younger generation has played a key role in the developments we have outlined. This is indeed the case. There is no overlooking the fact that it is largely the young who, in loud protest or silent retreat, are dropping out of the ranks of Western industrial civilization, of the collectivity in which they live, into political homelessness. It can be seen on the streets and it can be seen in the attitude profiles revealed by the opinion polls. The younger generation has an unmistakable profile of its own, a profile of sharper detachment from the society in which it lives, of greater inclination to reject it, of greater concern about the threats of the future. Nevertheless, it would be an oversimplification to talk only of youth movements and youth protests. The disposition we have described permeates the whole of society; not even the ecological movement was a pure youth movement, and the peace movement, as we shall see, is even less so.

We have sketched out a landscape, a landscape of disquiet, of fear of the future, of revolt. This landscape is the background out of which, at the beginning of the eighties, the peace movement made its astonishingly rapid, almost explosive appearance. The extraordinary support that it has found cannot be understood without an appreciation of how far the ground and the atmosphere had been prepared in advance. In other words, it is impossible to understand the rise of the peace movement without also seeing it as a new manifestation of the self-doubt, the self-disgust by which Western industrial society has been gripped for a decade and a half. As far as the Federal Republic is concerned, the peace movement could never have become what it has if from the late sixties a politically active subculture of protest had not developed that was receptive to any cause able to spark resistance against existing reality. This thesis, however, offers no explanation of why it was at the beginning of the eighties that peace became the cause of a new protest movement in the Federal Republic, more vehement and forceful than its predecessors. Although the ground had been prepared, a catalyst was still needed. It is to this that we must now turn.

Peace in Europe, the strategy of deterrence, and the Federal Republic's membership within the Western defense alliance—none of these things had occupied the restless and protest-hungry spirits of the early and mid-seventies, neither the student rebels nor the militant environmentalists. At most, the rapid increase in conscientious objectors from the early seventies onward was a forewarning of the new cause. It was not until the NATO deployment decision of December 1979 that the new pattern emerged.

It appears that at least in open societies the strategy of nuclear deterrence is felt to be bearable only for as long as the possibility of its failure is not seriously considered. Once the possibility of nuclear war is perceived behind the strategy of nuclear deterrence, not as an abstract thing but in the form of a threat to one's own world, the consensus, being much more a consensus of passive acceptance than of positive approval, collapses. It would be surprising if this were not the case. It seems that, as far as the West German public is concerned, the horror of nuclear war shows itself behind the strategy of nuclear deterrence only when a decision is to be made about the stationing of nuclear weapons in the Federal Republic. This was the issue in 1957/58 and it has again been the issue since 1979. It is nuclear weapons on one's own soil—weapons not under one's own control, in a country that would inevitably be the battlefield in any European war—that conjure the unbearable vision of nuclear war. It is possible to get used to nuclear weapons in one's own country, or to forget them, as they were forgotten after 1958, but whenever a fresh decision has to be made, the vision rises up again. With some certainty we can state that whatever else NATO might have decided, if part of its decision had not been the plan to station nuclear weapons in the Federal Republic, there would have been no West German peace movement of the kind that has actually emerged. The key significance of the deployment decision is clear from all the testimonies the peace movement has given of itself; as we shall soon go on to show, that decision and in some sense it alone is the target of its political struggle.

Naturally, the deployment decision could precipitate the reaction it did only in combination with other factors. Foremost among these was the political rhetoric of President Reagan and his administration, which had the direst effect. This rhetoric allowed the president's new course to be misinterpreted—and misinterpreted it eagerly was —as meaning that the United States was conducting an offensive against the Soviet Union with the aim of achieving strategic superiority; and to this end was employing means involving the risk of a nuclear war in Europe; and further, that Washington was actually planning a limited nuclear war in Europe. Considerations of how to respond to a Soviet attack in Europe had the most dangerous intentions read into them. And the end result, achieved not without demagogy, was the arousal of a widespread suspicion that the United States was quite consciously and as a matter of cold calculation running the risk of involving Europe in nuclear war.

The peace movement regards this suspicion as certain fact. It is omnipresent in its political argumentation and its rhetoric. It is not the Soviet Union's threat to its freedom that Europe has to be frightened of; Europe and Germany must, rather, be on their guard against the threat to peace presented by the United States, which, in its struggle for hegemony with the Soviet Union, is playing, light-headedly and cold-bloodedly at the same time, with the risk of nuclear war. Without this interpretation of U.S. policy, the deployment decision would have been much less provocative. To put this another way, it is no accident that the West German peace movement was not formed until 1981, over a year after the deployment decision had been taken, and during the Reagan administration's first year.

The NATO twin-track decision, Reagan's new course, and the rhetoric that so irritated the Europeans can also be seen together in another context. In 1980 the East-West conflict entered a new phase. It was becoming increasingly clear that as a political program, detente, on which for a whole decade so many hopes had been pinned, had not really succeeded in altering the character of the East-West conflict. The Soviet arms program, the invasion of Afghanistan, and the strangulation of Poland on the one hand, and NATO's and Reagan's responses on the other—the events that put such an abrupt end to the dream of detente's irreversible progress—are familiar enough. There is no doubt that the Federal Republic's awakening from this dream was especially rude. Nowhere else had the policy of detente been extolled, if not pursued, with such ardor and emphasis by those responsible for it. Peace had been made more secure, we were assured again and again. Indeed, was it not true that since the end of the sixties we had had a stable and peaceful *modus vivendi* with the Soviet Union, which was now jeopardized by the sudden decision to station a new type of nuclear weapon in the Federal Republic? Thus intense irritation, disappointment, and disorientation at a moment of climactic change in world affairs were also part of the circumstances attending the peace movement's birth.

II

The peace movement is a loose alliance of numerous groups and organizations, and many of those who consider themselves its members do not belong to any of these groups or organizations. Nevertheless, it would not be oversimplifying greatly to say that there are three main sources from which the peace movement has drawn its members, three currents that have merged to form it. First, there is the ecological movement, in the broadest sense. Second, there is pacifism, or, more frequently, nuclear pacifism, based to a greater or lesser extent on Christianity. And third, there is the traditional Left, with its socialist faith. By taking a closer look at these three sources of origin, we should at least be able to draw a first sketch of the peace movement's profile.

Reference has already been made to a kind of rudimentary affinity between the ecological movement and the peace movement. In both movements, it was argued, the same predisposition can be seen. Both had their roots in the same soil. The older movement had, so to speak, prepared the ground for the more recent one. Nevertheless, it was some time before the ecological movement made peace a cause of its own. The reason that it never questioned the defense consensus until the end of the seventies was quite simply that defense policy and the whole issue of war and peace lay outside its field of vision. In the occasional contacts it had with pacifist organizations, its attitude tended to be one of distrust because these organizations were under communist influence—the ecologists were reluctant to be pushed into a left-wing corner. On the other hand, peace was a cause the ecological movement had long been on the way toward. From the middle seventies at the latest, it had committed itself entirely to opposing nuclear power stations. And if one wages an unconditional campaign against nuclear power stations, there is no way to avoid the subject of nuclear weapons and with them the strategy of nuclear deterrence in the long run. All that was needed was a catalyst, which was provided in 1980. Another link between ecology and the peace cause was of some significance. Toward the end of the seventies more and more complaints were heard from the ecological movement that even in peacetime military activity was responsible for natural destruction (on training grounds, for example); and arms spending, it was argued, represented an unacceptable squandering of scarce resources. Here again, it was its own deepest concerns that brought the ecological movement closer to peace as an issue.

Once the cause of peace had been adopted, there was no difficulty in formulating a sort of unifying philosophy for the ecological and peace movements; it was undertaken very forthrightly and with little ado. "Live and Survive" (leben and überleben) is the slogan—the struggle for life has grown into a struggle for survival. To quote Petra Kelly, who led the way for many others from the ecological movement to the peace movement, "The common ground between ecology and the peace movement is the threat to existence, which emanates equally from modern weapons and from large-scale industrial technology. Thus both movements have become movements of survival, with the aim of averting a global catastrophe for mankind" (Kelly and Leinen, p. 11).

Christian-inspired involvement in the peace issue, of no less significance for the peace movement than that of the ecological movement, is primarily a Protestant involvement. Not that the Protestant church has officially affiliated itself with the peace movement or even given it its unreserved approval; on the contrary, the church, at the moment, maintains the view, against the strongest opposition, that as a church it cannot take sides in the argument. In the end, no more than one of the seventeen regions of the West German Protestant church came out formally against NATO deployment. But this is only one side of the coin. The other is that the peace movement has met with an extraordinary response among West German Protestants. In one sense, the Evangelical synod of 1981 was the first great peace demonstration. Since then, large numbers of Protestant pastors have identified themselves with the peace movement, which, in view of the influence they exert on their congregations, gives the peace movement some key forward positions. Pacifist church groups such as the Aktion Sühnenzeichen and the Live without Armaments group founded in 1978, earlier very much fringe groups, have suddenly begun to exercise a strong appeal, their slogan "Make peace without weapons" (*Frieden schaffen ohne Waffen*) finding a wide response. And even in circles where the peace movement tends to meet with disapproval rather than sympathy, it is still true that over the past few years peace has become the central issue of German Protestantism.

West German Catholicism presents a somewhat different picture. The episcopacy has been neither as critical in its statements on nuclear deterrence as the U.S. bishops nor as affirmative as the French. Speaking in somewhat muted tones, it has pursued a middle course. In the Catholic clergy, the peace movement has found nothing like the active backing it received from Protestant pastors. The Central Committee of German Catholics, which represents the Catholic laity, has come down firmly against the peace movement. The only two groups within organized Catholicism that are close to the peace movement are Pax Christi and Catholic Youth. None of this of course means that there are no Catholics to be found in the peace movement. What it does mean is that West German Catholicism has contributed nothing crucial to the peace movement.

Here we have a further illustration that since 1945 it is Protestantism that, politically speaking, has been the more restless of the two great faiths, the more critical, the cooler in its attitude to the state. It is tempting to see this as the result of a—largely unconscious—effort by Protestantism to dissociate itself from its past, from the alliance of "throne and altar" of bygone centuries, and from accusations of failure under National Socialism. There is no doubt that the past causes more pain to Protestantism than to Catholicism. The fact that Christian pacifism since 1945 has generally felt more at home within Protestantism than Catholicism may not be entirely unconnected with this. The organizational structure of the two churches may also play a part. Protestantism, being less hierarchical and centralized, is more exposed to the currents of the time, more receptive, to put it more pejoratively, to passing fashions.

Whether Protestant or Catholic, Christian involvement in the peace movement is primarily a Christian revolt against nuclear weapons. There is, of course, a committed, total pacifism—the slogan "Make peace without weapons" has already been mentioned. But, primarily, what won the peace movement support in the Christian congregations and elsewhere was the fear of nuclear war suddenly aroused by the debate over deployment. Nor was the heated theological dispute that began in the shadow of the public debate so much a discussion of war and peace in general as of nuclear weapons. At least one official organization of West German Protestantism, the Reformierte Bund (Federation of the Reformed Churches), has taken the argument to its ultimate logical conclusion. Through its leadership it has raised the unconditional rejection of nuclear weapons, and thus also the policy of deterrence based on nuclear weapons, to an article of faith, in other words to a question that decides who is a Christian and who not. This position has not met with general acceptance, but it underlines what might be said to be the prevailing mood and frame of mind of Christians involved in the peace movement: a Christian must give an unqualified no to nuclear weapons. So here again, nuclear weapons are the decisive issue. As soon as the possibility of a nuclear catastrophe, emerging out of the shadow of the strategy of nuclear deterrence, dawned again on the public awareness, it became—as in the 1950s—a challenge to Christians and theologians, and as such acted as the chief force behind a strong Christian involvement in the peace movement.

This involvement has taken its characteristic tone from appeals to the Sermon on the Mount, which had suddenly and surprisingly assumed a central importance to the Christian case. More exactly, it is not appeals to the Sermon on the Mount as such that have met with an extraordinary response but, rather, the idea that, in the situation created by a nuclear arms race, the radical ethical requirements of the Sermon on the Mount and the promptings of political common sense coincide. *Frieden ist möglich,* the peace movement's most successful book (by Franz Alt, a Catholic journalist; München 1983), which has sold over 700,000 copies, is entirely based on the idea that loving our enemies as the Sermon on the Mount commands us to do and doing to them as we would be done by them is the only way out of the arms race, with all its dangers to mankind. At the same time, Alt's book makes quite clear what is the ultimate basis of this equivalent of the Sermon on the Mount and political good sense: it does not for one moment consider the possibility of the Soviet Union's not reacting differently from the way the author hopes.

Had the ecological movement not made the cause of peace its own and had this same cause not met with such a response among Christians, albeit mainly among Protestants, the peace movement would never have become a mass movement. True though this is, the movement's third source of origin is still important. Groups and individuals from the socialist camp, of both orthodox and unorthodox persuasion, have from the very beginning played an important part in the peace movement. The pacifist and conscientious objectors' organizations had already gone over to this camp a while earlier. Here, too, are to be found many intellectuals whose view of the defense policies of the Western alliance had always been ultracritical. The Moscow-inspired Communists are here as well, of course, alongside some of their strongest opponents in the peace movement, however, such as

Rudolf Bahro. In a word, this camp is the meeting ground of the "old warriors" of the fifties and the lean sixties and seventies and the "new" peace movement. The socialist wing is probably also the most political element of the peace movement. It has more political experience behind it, and tactical and strategic political thinking comes more naturally to it, all of which contributes to its influence on the peace movement. Incidentally, one must bear in mind that it is almost impossible to draw a sharp dividing line between the ecological movement and the nondogmatic socialist opposition, for in the last few years the Green movement has—in round terms—grown "redder and redder."

To identify three fields of origin in this way, three different tides that have run together in the peace movement, is of course somewhat crude. A closer look would reveal a multiplicity of organizations and groups held together in a loose alliance. Loose though it is, however, this does not mean that the groups do not have a very strong awareness of the common goal. On the contrary. The word *loose* here means that the peace movement as such is barely institutionalized. The alliance is geared to action. The groups get together, forming a joint committee when there is something to be done, which means more often than not when there is to be a demonstration. The peace movement has no body that could be described as its presidium; and there is no center from which the movement could be reliably directed. Nor are there any outstanding or charismatic figures within the peace movement capable of carrying the masses with them, of pointing the masses in a given direction, or acting as spokespersons. The way the movement sees itself discourages the emergence of such people.

It would be just as hard for one of the peace movement's member organizations to run the movement as it is for anyone to try to direct it from the center. This applies as much to the Green party, which sees itself as a part of the peace movement, as to the DKP, whose influence on the movement is the subject of constant speculation. There can be no denying that, both as a party and through its various auxiliary organizations, the DKP is active in the peace movement. It is also known that the party's financial clout (a large portion of its funds originate in East Berlin) and its organizational talents secure it a certain influence. But it has to guard against making itself too prominent. For although there is only faint objection in the peace movement to cooperation with the Communists, it would become very much louder if Communist influence were to become overriding. It is not in the DKP's interests to provoke such objections, for as long as the peace movement continues to fight deployment, in other words, tries to force the West to disarm unilaterally, it is to all intents and purposes a confederate of the DKP, however great or small the party's influence on the movement might be.

The peace movement has no real political program to speak of. It was brought together and continues to be held together by rejection of the NATO dual-track agreement. At best, one might consider the call for a nuclear-free zone, first in Central Europe then in Europe as a whole, as one item in a common platform. There is a suggestion here that Europe can sidestep the East-West conflict, which is seen essentially as a conflict between the two world powers, the USSR and the United States. But at present, it would even be difficult to get the peace movement to agree on a demand for the Federal Republic to withdraw from NATO.

Thus, the consensus on rejection of the dual-track decision does not, then, cover very much more. The spectrum of attitudes ranges from complete pacifism to nuclear pacifism, to those in favor of "social defence," to those who have not completely discarded the idea of deterrence by military means but who just consider Pershing and cruise deployment as superfluous and dangerous. Hitherto, however, this variety of attitude has far from weakened the peace movement. Precisely because rejection of deployment was the only link that bound them all together, the movement has fought for it with uncompromising firmness of purpose.

In the unifying force and passionate intensity of this rejection one can sense a missionary zeal, the mission being to avert the threat of nuclear death at the eleventh hour. It is the movement's conviction that it is struggling against a threat surpassing the human imagination that enables it to claim a unique moral legitimacy. Again we find that it is the struggle against nuclear weapons that is the peace movement's constituent cause. And here one may make another observation: the peace movement's unshakable conviction that it is in possession of the truth also has something to do with its having its own technical expertise, its own "counterexperts" to call on. Rarely have a few specialists found so many credulous followers as the retired officers who have entered the ranks of the peace movement. It is to these specialists that the peace movement owes, among other things, its precise "knowledge" that while the Pershing II is a first-strike weapon, the SS-20 is not. The contribution of such "knowledge" to the movement's self-confidence can hardly be exaggerated.

Those who believe they are fighting to prevent universal catastrophe inevitably find themselves considering whether the end does not justify the means. The question must pose itself, if no shadow of doubt in one's own judgment is left. This doubt, which is the lifeblood of democracy's conflicts of opinion, is obviously something of which the peace movement is ignorant. As a result, it is convinced that the government and parliamentary majority's decisions on deployment are illegitimate; that, in other words, the issue gives opponents a right of civil disobedience (which the movement itself misleadingly refers to as a "right of resistance," *Widerstandsrecht*). True, the overwhelming majority of the peace movement is committed to "nonviolent" disobedience. And, contrary to the fears of some, particularly before the "hot autumn" of 1983, its large demonstrations have in fact actually gone off peacefully. But its concept of violence is a narrow one: causing harm to persons and destroying things. Blockades, on the other hand, preferably of military installations, are in the peace movement's view nonviolent, even when in legal terms they amount to duress and illegal detention.

There can be no question that what we have here are the beginnings of an insidious undermining of the principle of democratic legality. Where it will lead is uncertain. What is particularly uncertain is whether the peace movement will allow itself to be driven across the line it itself has drawn between nonviolent and violent disobedience, should it seriously begin to practice the resistance it has hitherto only preached. At this crossroads, the important question will be whether there will be agreement within the peace movement that civil disobedience has only a symbolic function or whether it views civil disobedience as a means to achieve its ends in defiance of the constitutional authorities. The question has still not really been decided, because up to this point the peace movement has not been a mass movement of civil disobedience. From staging spectacular demonstrations to going before the constitutional court, it has squeezed the democratic right of opposition to the very last drop without, however, by and large overstepping the mark. Now that missiles are being stationed in the Federal Republic, the peace movement will be faced with new decisions.

It follows from everything that has been said about the internal structure of the peace movement that it is far from being an entirely harmonious coalition. Until now, what has caused controversy has tended to be matters of tactics and style. The one unifying aim, to prevent deployment, had unanimous support. Issues that went beyond this immediate objective were prudently kept in the background. Now that deployment has begun, this will no longer be so easy. In the future we can expect more evidence of the variety of opinion within the peace movement. The next question is, then, how will more serious and more frequent internal conflict be dealt with? Hitherto, the conviction that the preservation of the movement's unity comes before everything else has always triumphed (a tendency the Communists, eager to throw a cloak of silence over the Soviet arms buildup, were not the least to benefit from). But it remains to be seen whether this conviction can withstand any great pressure. Its hold might well weaken when the common objectives are less concrete and tangible than they were.

III

In the short history of the Federal Republic there has been no political campaign to compare with that of the peace movement against deployment. The support the campaign attracted has been quite extraordinary. The peace movement has proved capable of winning over millions of people, of bringing hundreds and thousands out into the streets in one huge demonstration after another, and of making its cause the main, indeed the dominant theme of public debate over a number of years. But what does this mean? What is the movement's real strength? What has it actually achieved?

Data obtained from surveys can take us some of the way toward answering these questions. In the summer of 1983, 2 percent of those questioned described themselves as active members and about the same proportion stated they "would definitely get actively involved." Nine percent stated they "might get actively involved." A further 31 percent declared themselves in sympathy with the movement but were not intending to take any active part in it. (From unpublished results of surveys undertaken by the Konrad-Adenauer-Stiftung.) Surveys undertaken as far back as 1981 produced very similar results (*Der Spiegel*, nos. 48, 49, 50, 1981). So the quantities we are dealing with are relatively stable ones: 10-15 percent firm supporters, of which, however, only a small minority have actually committed themselves; and about 30 percent (or more, depending on how the question is phrased) of sympathizers in a broader, vaguer sense. The younger generation is disproportionately represented in both groups, particularly the first. About 30 percent of those under thirty are to be found in this first group. Further, of those actively involved, a disproportionate number have had a higher education.

The really difficult question is, clearly, What does sympathizing "in a broader, vaguer sense" mean? Is sympathy for the peace movement basically sympathy for the appeal for peace? Or also for the path the peace movement has taken? Do those who express sympathy for the peace movement agree with its concrete demands? The data give us no clear picture. Particularly as far as deployment is concerned, it is clear that the answers are largely determined by the questions, and, further, that there is much uncertainty. The more unambiguously the question is directed toward the stationing of missiles in the Federal Republic, the clearer the preponderance of nos. If the question is about the twin-track decision in general or if it emphasizes the principle of military balance between East and West, then different answers are received. And things are even more complicated: a survey in January 1983 inquiring whether in the event of the Geneva negotiations' failing, NATO should station missiles in Western Europe, the replies were 37 percent yes, 35 percent no, and 28 percent undecided (*Newsweek*, 31 January 1983). A few months later—the questions were almost identically phrased except "Western Europe" was replaced by "The Federal Republic"—two-thirds of those questioned said no (*Die Zeit*, 7 October 1983). There are many more examples of such contradictory figures. In the end, we can draw only one main conclusion: there is a majority against the emplacement of medium-range missiles in the Federal Republic, and it is this majority that the peace movement's referendum idea is aimed at. But many, far from sure of their own views, continue to vacillate and are easily swayed.

The picture is no clearer when the questions go beyond deployment. The opinion and attitude profiles remain strikingly inconsistent, even when the controversies of day-to-day politics are left behind. Thus one in three sympathizes with pacifism, but only one in four of these is ready to accept an East-bloc military superiority. Or again, one in three favors neutrality along Austrian lines, but only one in four of those replying in this way is also in favor of U.S. withdrawal from Europe (*Der Spiegel*, nos. 48, 49, 50, 1981). All that can be read with any certainty into these figures is that there is still a clear majority—two-thirds to three-quarters of those questioned—in favor of the Federal Republic's membership in NATO, while 20-30 percent of the FRG's population is prepared to entertain the idea of neutrality and thus, presumably, unilateral disarmament. But these are figures that, with some oscillation, have been valid for quite a while. In other words, the peace movement has been unable to bring about any significant change of opinion on this key issue. The most that could be said is that three years of heated public debate have resulted in greater uncertainty among the uncommitted.

One further word needs to be said about the relative significance of all the data we have been considering. They tell us nothing of what general importance the issue may have for those questioned. There are many indications that even in years of intense discussion the subjects of peace, defense, and arms do not occupy an especially important place in most people's minds. It is only a minority that are convinced that the Federal Republic is on the threshold of a nuclear war, and that deployment represents an immeasurable catastrophe for the country. Certainly, this minority, readily assisted by the media, succeeded in stirring up a controversy that created the impression that the entire Federal Republic had been gripped by a kind of deployment mania. But for the majority, concern about their jobs still, in reality, looms largest. Thus it was that in March 1983, the federal elections were won, despite the polls showing a clear mood against deployment, by the parties that—as everyone knew—supported the dual-track decision.

The election returns obviously mean that one cannot reach an opinion on the success of the peace movement or the effect it has had solely on the basis of opinion surveys. The peace movement has not achieved the aim that it set itself, which was to prevent deployment. It will probably now never achieve it. Has it then failed? One reason that it cannot be said to have failed is its success in attracting one of the FRG's two great parties, the SPD, to its banner. Not wholly, of course, but at least insofar as the SPD, executing a change of course probably without parallel in the history of democratic parties, renounced the NATO twin-track agreement in an almost unanimous vote of the party conference. It is not our task here to explain how this reversal came about. Relevant to our present purpose is, rather, that it would have been unimaginable without the pull, the pressure exerted by the peace movement. This is undoubtedly the greatest success the peace movement has yet achieved, and there is little question that the way to it was effectively paved by the long-standing cross-connections between the SPD left wing and the peace movement, personified in the two SPD politicians Eppler and Lafontaine.

Unlike 1958, when the SPD was moving unstoppably toward the center, the peace movement's influence on the SPD could increase. This is true not only because under the leadership of Brandt and Vogel the SPD intends to try to win over voters who sympathize with the peace movement but also because the SPD is moving closer to the Green party, which sees itself as part of the peace movement and which is in fact an important bastion of the movement in the Bundestag and the state parliaments. If the SPD is looking for ways of cooperating with the Greens—and it seems that both sides have made up their minds to experiment with some sort of alliance—this will be certain to have its effect on the party's defense policy.

The peace movement has also gained ground within the trade unions. Some unions, including that of the metalworkers (IG Metall), one of the largest, have more or less aligned themselves with the peace movement—in opposition to deployment anyway—or at the least made no secret of their sympathies. None, however, has entered a formal alliance. Others such as the chemical and mining unions (IG Chemie and IG Bergbau) have remained aloof, one of their main reproaches being that the peace movement is deaf and blind to the dangers of the Soviet arms buildup. Yet others have tried to steer a middle course. The trade-union umbrella organization, the DGB, had little freedom of action in this situation. It had to tack carefully for fear of colliding with someone. It had also to take account of the fact that it was more often the officials, and the far left ones at that, than the rank and file who sympathized with the peace movement. Many members tend to be conservative when it comes to external security. This was why there was never any chance of the idea of a general strike against deployment, calls for which were heard here and there, getting off the ground. No union seriously backed the idea.

The churches and the extraordinary response the peace movement has met with among Protestants have already been mentioned. It is hardly necessary to add that there has been no lack of involvement by artists, writers, and professors. Scientists and doctors, making much of their special competence, have also spoken out in public, forgetting that their protest against deployment was based in the last analysis on political and strategic assumptions that they had no scientific authority to make. The peace movement attracted a high level of attention from the mass media right from the beginning, attention that in the case of the public television and radio companies often enough was synonymous with sympathy. In a nutshell, then: while the peace movement may have failed to halt deployment, it can set against that its enormous success in mobilizing masses of people. The peace movement has altered the consciousness of society. Doubts have been sown about the policy of nuclear deterrence; the seeds have taken root, have flourished, and will remain fertile in the future.

IV

The preceding remarks bring us to our final question: What of the future? First of all, of course, the deployment controversy will be carried on: the peace movement still has its case before the constitutional court, it is planning to carry out a referendum, and calls are going out for mass conscientious objection to military service. But as the stationing of the missiles proceeds, so the peace movement loses its key cause and its impetus. This is significant because the movement is by nature action oriented. It is, so to speak, only in and through action that it comes into being. But action presumes concrete targets for protest and resistance to ignite against. Disagreement on principles alone is not enough. Moreover, sooner or later it will become increasingly apparent that the peace movement has no real joint program of defense policy to fight for.

Are its future prospects then, despite its extraordinary ability to mobilize large numbers of people, not very good? Or could one argue that even if it does lack a program, it represents a mood that is important for the future? This question is customarily followed, especially outside Germany, by another: Might the peace movement not be evidence of a new awakening of German nationalism?

To begin with, it is true that the peace movement is in a number of respects quite specifically German. Not in the sense that what we have here is an expression of a supposedly innate German mentality —presumptions of this kind are mere arbitrary speculation—but, rather, that the Federal Republic's special position and Germany's special history are not without importance for the peace movement. The country would inevitably be a battlefield if there were to be a catastrophe in Europe; the country would not be master of its own fate because others would be deciding about the use of nuclear weapons on its territory; and as to their history, the Germans have lost two world wars this century and, incidentally, did not have the opportunity to learn the lesson Britain and France have learned from the pacifism of the thirties. But there is a great difference between discussing such peculiarities in the peace movement's origins and seeing in it the embryo of a new German nationalism. Certainly, the German question is one of the peace movement's themes, though not a prominent one. But this is so because the whole subject of Germany is unavoidable in any attempt to question the confrontation of the two blocs in Europe or to break out of this confrontation in Central Europe. Among the opponents of Adenauer's foreign policy in the fifties, it was the other way around: their aim was reunification and they accepted neutrality as the precondition of achieving it, whereas for the peace movement unification is far from being an important or prominent objective in itself. If anything is to be seen as nationalist about the movement, it is at most its aversion for the alliance and the alliance's predominance, its attempt to sidestep the competition between the superpowers and seek shelter from the storm. But this is more like an egocentricity of survival than nationalism in the traditional sense. It could even be argued that what sometimes appears to be a lack of self-assertiveness in many Germans has something to do with a lack of national self-confidence.

Be that as it may, if the peace movement is to have a future, it will not be on the basis of a program recommending the Federal Republic's withdrawal from the Western alliance. The overwhelming majority of the Federal Republic's citizens remain convinced that for their country to abandon the alliance of West Europeans and North Americans would be a fatal step. The peace movement's future, if it has one, is bound up with the question of nuclear weapons. In the controversies of the last few years, the Germans have been made so aware of the permanent, terrifying ambivalence of the strategy of nuclear deterrence that they will not easily forget it. The peace movement will do everything to prevent the consensus it has destroyed from reforming. In this it will be aided not only by the fact that the subject of nuclear weapons excludes consensus by its very nature but also by its ability—unlike the movement of the late fifties—to rely on that widespread negative, predisposition that we mentioned at the beginning. On the other hand, there will be a process of habituation to the new status quo, if peace in Europe proves not to have become less secure than it was in the fifties, sixties, and seventies. Defense policy, caught between these two tendencies, will for the time being remain the tempestuous seas into which it sailed at the beginning of the decade, even if the tempest should slowly begin to subside.

SELECT BIBLIOGRAPHY

GENERAL STUDIES

Günther Schmidt, *Sicherheitspolitik und Friedensbewegung. Der Konflikt um die "Nachrüstung"* (Munich, 1982).
Karl-Werner Brand, Detlef Büsser, and Dieter Rucht, *Aufbruch in eine andere Gesellschaft. Neue soziale Bewegungen in der Bundesrepublik* (Frankfurt/New York, 1983).

THE PEACE MOVEMENT ABOUT ITSELF

Petra K. Kelly, Jo Leinen, eds., *Prinzip Leben. Ökopax—die neue Kraft* (Berlin, 1982).
Hans A. Pestalozzi, Ralf Schlegel, and Adolf Bachmann, eds., *Frieden in Deutschland. Die Friedensbewegung: wie sie wurde, was sie ist, was sie werden kann* (Munich, 1982).

Reiner Steinweg, ed., *Die neue Friedensbewegung. Analysen aus der Friedensforschung* (Frankfurt, 1982).

THE PROTEST MOVEMENTS OF THE FIFTIES AND SIXTIES

Hans-Karl Rupp, *Ausserparlamentarische Opposition in der Ära Adenauer, Der Kampf gegen die Atombewaffnung in den fünfziger Jahren* (Köln, 1970).
Karl A. Otto, *Vom Ostermarsch zur APO. Geschichte der ausserparlamentarischen Opposition in der Bundesrepublik, 1960-1970* (Frankfurt/New York, 1977).

The analyses of results of surveys referred to in the text can be found in *Der Spiegel*, nos. 48, 49, 50/1981; *Frankfurter Allgemeine Zeitung*, 30 October 1981 and 16 September 1983; *Die Zeit*, 7 October 1983. The unpublished survey results were made available by the Konrad Adenauer Foundation.

15

THE ARGUMENTS OF THE GERMAN PEACE MOVEMENT

Ulrich de Maiziere

The Federal Republic of Germany has never experienced such a passionate and searching debate about the way to achieve peace among nations, or about the political and ethical justification of military means for securing peace. Groups involved in the debate range from those acting out of purely political motives to others moved by moral and Christian considerations. The result has been a network of social movements inspired for the most part by humanitarian and idealistic aims and feelings but forming as yet no coherent political movement. This is not, however, to deny that Communist elements are trying to make use of the movement and to infiltrate it.

The peace debate is not confined to the German Federal Republic. It is taking place in other democracies in the Western hemisphere, if with varying degrees of intensity. It has even found an echo inside the German Democratic Republic, primarily within the Evangelical church. Despite the differences from one country to another, the debate has crossed national and international frontiers and for this reason alone deserves to be taken seriously by responsible policymakers. It is in the Federal Republic, however, that the peace debate has had its most visible consequences.

It would be a mistake to think of the peace movement as being solely concerned with problems of war and peace. The subject of peace is only one of a large bundle of worries besetting people for which solutions have not yet been found. Among these are environmental destruction, the North-South problem, and technological development, as well as what are believed to be limited training and job opportunities. A mood of pessimism about the present and the future has spread among the younger generation, a mood summed up in the slogan "No future." The result is either resignation, to the point of wanting to "drop out" of society entirely, or an attitude of protest, anger, and resistance, to the point of being prepared to use force to bring about change.

In this context, the NATO double-track decision of December 1979 acted as a catalyst. It brought the question of how best to preserve peace into the center of the debate while simultaneously concentrating attention on nuclear weapons, which are regarded as the real threat to peace. After two decades during which defense policy and nuclear weapons were discussed by only very few, with the whole subject more or less repressed—consciously or unconsciously—in the public mind, political events in the years just before and after 1980 brought the seriousness, complexity, and dangers of nuclear policy back into public awareness. The effect was one of shock. Repression has turned into heated obsession. The new nuclear debate is the moving expression of a deeply felt longing for peace.

The critical arguments presented by the German peace movement originate in some very diverse sets of attitudes. There are the pacifists, who on political or ethical grounds consistently reject the possession or use of all weapons. They want peace at any price, declining to discuss the political content of a state of peace or the consequences arising from their position. Others accept that military power is necessary to safeguard peace in honorable conditions but call for strategies and structures different from those on which the NATO strategy of balance of power and flexible response, agreed on by all member states since 1967, is based.

In analyzing the peace movement's arguments in what follows, I have chosen to ignore the ideas that have quite clearly been brought in by Communists for their own political purposes. I shall be concerned only with those sections of the peace movement whose bona fides cannot be questioned.

I

Many groups within the peace movement start from the belief that it is primarily arms and soldiers that create tension and endanger peace. Their argument runs as follows: If armies and weapons were done away with or at least reduced, then political tensions could be surmounted. All arms have a tendency to increase, resulting in a spiraling arms race. Once arms have reached a certain level, they demand to be used. War, then, is in the end inevitable, unless one can halt it in time. In view of the defense spending by both blocs over the last ten to fifteen years and with the West proceeding to introduce medium-range missiles in Western Europe, the danger of war in Europe has increased dramatically.

Disillusion over the tangible results of a decade of detente increases the fear of war; the fear in turn fuels itself on nuclear weapons. With nuclear weapons, the argument continues, humankind for the first time in its history possesses the means to destroy itself and the world completely. As a result, war has lost its meaning, for warfare would destroy the very thing military defense is supposed to protect. In the nuclear age war can no longer be an instrument of policy. Moreover, as long as states continue to possess nuclear weapons, there is a danger of the weapons' slipping out of political control or of a nuclear war's being unleashed by a technical or human error. The supposed guarantee of peace would then have been the cause of a world catastrophe.

There are doubts, too, about the effectiveness of nuclear deterrence as a means of maintaining peace. Deterrence, it is argued, can be effective only if one is actually prepared to use the weapons if deterrence fails. But this would lead inevitably to all-out nuclear war, which would in turn mean suicide and is therefore not credible. Even if one admits that deterrence has contributed to the maintenance of peace in Europe hitherto, there are no grounds for assuming that the "balance of terror" can fulfill the same function for another thirty or fifty years. The idea, it is claimed, is outmoded. The nations of the world are now in the position of a climber stuck on a rock face, with no way forward and only a terrible drop below. The time has come to turn back. Someone has to make the first move and set an example, for instance, by renouncing the stationing of U.S. medium-range missiles in Europe. Wholesale rejection of "deployment" was the lowest common denominator on which all groups within the peace movement were able to agree.

Because the medium-range missiles do not cease to be U.S. missiles after they have been stationed, rejection has extended to U.S. policy and U.S. forces. Anti-Americanism is steadily becoming a second common cause of the peace movement. Occasional, not wholly unjustified criticisms of the U.S. government since the election of President Reagan have been generalized and taken to extremes. Forgetting what the United States has done and still does for the freedom of Europe, including West Berlin, people concentrate their worries and objections on what they claim are the dangerous consequences of a supposed U.S. "policy of strength," whose aims are reputed to be military superiority over the Soviet Union and U.S. world domination.

Some of those who reject nuclear weapons outright do so on theological grounds. God, it is argued, entrusted the earth and all its riches to humankind to keep and multiply, but with modern means of mass destruction, humankind is in a position to destroy them. The production, possession, and use of nuclear weapons are therefore against the commandment of God; they are a *sin* and irreconcilable with the Christian conscience.

Other Christians, invoking the Old and New Testaments, go further and question whether the use of any kind of weapon can be morally justified. Taking the fifth commandment, "Thou shalt not kill," quite literally and concretely, they even deny the right of self-defense, with weapons at least. The Sermon on the Mount's exhortation to love one's enemy and not to resist evil are understood not just as requirements of the Christian as an individual but in all spheres of life including politics. Many are prepared to accept any unpleasant consequences this may lead to, including physical suffering, without asking themselves whether they are entitled to expect, let alone demand, the same of their neighbor.

One very common conviction among many young people today is that a person has no higher duty than to *preserve life.* No value, they say, is worth the sacrifice of a human life. Military defense, because it necessarily involves loss of life, is thus unacceptable in principle, even if the alternative is subjection. For those who have grown up in security, freedom, and relative affluence, who have no personal experience of life under a totalitarian dictatorship, this may be a view honorably held and based on honest conviction, but a glance at history shows that human beings have always been, as they still are, prepared to risk life and limb in the cause of greater freedom and self-determination for themselves and their children.

In an attempt to demonstrate the earnestness of their convictions and, as their immediate aim, to prevent deployment of new missiles, many in the peace movement have believed it right to employ methods of "nonviolent resistance," as they call it. They stretch the right of public assembly and demonstration to include the blockading of roads, military bases, and other installations, even if this involves intimidation or a breach of the peace. They train themselves in "civil disobedience," knowing in advance that their actions will result in infractions of regulations or of the law itself. While they accept the risk of breaking the law and of the punishment that might ensue, they try to avoid violence to others, however fluid the line between the two may be. In defense of such methods, they try to argue that the decision to deploy the new missiles is so serious and such a danger to peace and life that morality is no longer in line with the law. Hence, the decision is a "nonvotable matter," on a par with basic civil rights, the constitutional prohibitions of the death penalty, and preparation for a war of aggression—questions that have been removed from the normal democratic majority-vote principle. Their interpretation of resistance is, therefore, a very broad one. It is not the legality of the manner in which the decision was reached by the various constitutional organs that is disputed—the Basic Law would provide no defense for such dispute—but the *legitimacy of the moral substance of the decisions*. These, it is argued, conflict with the spirit of the constitution and the values embodied in it. Resistance is therefore justified, a course further vindicated by Article 20 of the Basic Law.

II

Up to this point we have concentrated on those who for political and moral reasons criticize or reject the war-prevention and defense measures adopted by the Atlantic alliance but who have failed to come forward with any counterproposals. Let us now turn to some of the concrete alternatives advanced by some of the groups within the peace movement.

One alternative is the concept of "social defense" developed by Theodor Ebert, a peace researcher from West Berlin. In his view, the Federal Republic's dangerous position between two blocs, its density of population, and its economic structure do not allow any possibility of meaningful military defense. Any use of modern weapons systems would mean, in practice, total destruction. The only possible alternative is nonviolent defense, i.e. passive resistance. The solution Ebert offers is thus a deterrence based on the preparation of nonviolent, civil resistance by the whole population. It should be made clear to the enemy that an invasion would be met not by military resistance but by a resolute withdrawal by the authorities and general population of all cooperation. The "entry price"—the concept behind Austria and Switzerland's strategic thinking—would not be high but the "staying price" in the occupied country would have to be kept so high that in the long run the costs of aggression and occupation would outweigh their presumed value—with the result that the aggressor would finally give up and leave.

Ebert admits that the historical precedents for nonviolent defense have been only partially successful, but he argues that it can be built up and developed further. He cites as examples the resistance in the Ruhr in 1923, the nonviolence of Mahatma Gandhi, and the civil resistance to the Soviet occupation of Czechoslovakia in 1968. Ebert concedes that attainable and effective social defense demands political and psychological requirements currently unfulfilled. West German citizens do not yet have the sense of self-sacrifice, or the readiness to suffer the hardships to be expected, particularly under a harsh and determined occupying power. The conditions Ebert describes as being necessary for the realization of social defense ultimately require even of peacetime society a level of cohesion that could be achieved only at the risk of "militarization." Political scientist Kurt Sontheimer has made a pertinent criticism of social defense: "For all its pseudo scientific trimmings, the idea of social defense is wishful thinking. It rests on pure hope, not on any assessment of conflict situations even remotely connected with reality."

A second alternative proposes unilateral disarmament as a declaration of goodwill. The underlying assumption is that the real cause of East-West conflict lies in mistrust, in sterotyped images of the enemy, and fears of being threatened. But if one side was to declare its defensive intentions by a series of concrete measures, making its desire for understanding and detente credible by deliberately forgoing parity, unilaterally reducing its arms, and revealing its military plans, this would not, it is argued, be without its effect on the other side. An atmosphere of trust would arise, causing the Soviets to undertake comparable measures. These declarations of intent could be initiated gradually, starting with unilateral measures of a more symbolic character, scarcely affecting security. A case in point would be to extend the confidence-building measures defined for the first time in the final accords of the Helsinki Agreement. With this as a basis, one could move on to more far-reaching measures of unilateral disarmament, even if in opening up—as they would—gaps in security these would be more of a risk. Some even more radical proposals go as far as total unilateral disarmament in the nuclear sphere.

What those in favor of such gradualism or unilateralism, as it is known, overlook is that the United States undertook unilateral steps of arms reduction and de-escalation in the 1970s. These included reductions in the size of the armed forces, the ending of compulsory military service, cuts in real defense expenditure, and the decision not to produce either the B-1 bomber or the neutron bomb. To this should be added the unilateral withdrawal of a thousand nuclear warheads from Central Europe in 1981. The Soviet Union offered no response, except to draw back, with much hue and cry, twenty thousand soldiers and a thousand tanks from the GDR and install them a few hundred kilometers further east. On the contrary, the 1970s were a period of intense Soviet arms buildup.

The only area to offer any hopeful signs has been that of the *confidence-building measures.* The announcement of troop movements and maneuvers and the exchange of observers have been steps in the right direction. Here there is room for progress, and it is to some degree a road that can be traveled unilaterally if the Soviet Union refuses to reciprocate. A further reduction in European stockpiles of warheads for short-range nuclear missiles could also be aceptable. To this extent gradualism has provided some positive impulses.

A third proposal, with the same objective, is the suggestion that our own forces should be armed exclusively with weapons of defense. The armed forces would thus take on a *defensive structure,* making clear to everyone that although they are able to repel an attack they are not capable of launching one. Such a step would, it is hoped, lessen the other side's sense of threat and fear of attack. At the same time it has to be made clear that the nation would not bow to blackmail and that a potential aggressor would always be met by an opponent prepared to defend itself. Finally, this option is considered to offer a chance of halting the ams race, insofar as it abandons what is seen as the fateful idea of strategic balance and restricts itself to a different, more simplified arms policy and structure, tailored to defensive political aims.

The man who has thought through most of the logical implications of this idea is Horst Afheldt, the originator of the concept of defense-in-depth. Afheldt dispenses with tanks, artillery, a tactical air force, U.S. troops, forward defense, and mobile operations. He rejects all weapons systems and military installations that might offer enemy weapons a worthwhile target in the hope that an aggressor would then be either unwilling or unable to use destructive heavy weapons, including nuclear ones. Instead, he puts faith in a tight network of independent "techno-commandos" spread across the whole of the Federal Republic, armed with antitank weapons and light ground-to-air missiles. Such defense-in-depth would, it is supposed, whittle down the numerical superiority of the Soviet tanks and frustrate the attack. Heated criticism later led Afheldt to refine and modify his thinking. His basic idea has remained the same, however, and has been taken up by many others, who approve Afheldt's clear restriction of weapons to those they consider purely defensive, namely, antitank weapons and ground-to-air missiles. They have also called for a thorough restructuring of the forces stationed in Central Europe. They accept that these ideas would mean the denuclearization of Central Europe and the extension of hostilities to the whole of West German territory.

The objections to this idea are largely political; they will be discussed later in a different connection. But the military expert has criticisms, too. Defense-in-depth throws the whole burden of the fight against the Soviet tank onto the antitank weapon. This goes against long-standing and recently reconfirmed experience, which shows that it is a grave mistake to rely on *one* weapons system alone or to gear the structure of the armed forces to only *one* anticipated manifestation of war. If conditions change or the aggressor switches to a different kind of operation, we would be unprepared. Changing the structure of the armed forces is no short-term undertaking. Only a mixed weapons system can meet all the requirements of a defensive war. Mixed weapons systems do have their particular emphases, though, and in point of fact these are actually the repulsion of the aggressor's tanks and tactical air force. The idea is basically sound, therefore, but is made more dangerous than helpful by being so one-sided.

A fourth suggestion, a *nuclear-free zone* in Central Europe, is not new. It has been put forward in many guises, with slight differences in detail each time, since the mid-fifties. The basic idea has remained the same, however, namely, that no nuclear weapons should be stationed within a given zone, yet to be precisely defined. As far as possible, this zone should cover territories to the same depth each side of the border between the two blocs. The Soviet Union has never given any indication that it would be seriously prepared to allow parts of any territory it controls, of whatever nationality, to be included in a nuclear-free zone only on the Western side. Others have suggested that nuclear weapons systems should be withdrawn from all states that, not having nuclear weapons under national ownership, are unable themselves to make the decision as to their use. Such proposals need not, it is argued, lead to the dissolution of the alliance. Nor would the principle of the balance of power be threatened. A nuclear disengagement of the blocs would, it is said, lead to a lowering of tension: it would scale down direct confrontation and banish the danger of an early nuclear escalation. Some have pointed out that the Warsaw Pact's conventional superiority would then become effective and would have to be countered. But even this necessity could be avoided, it is claimed, if the suggestion were carried further and Central Europe were completely demilitarized and *neutralized*. For the Germans, this might even be a first step toward reunification.

The risks of adopting such proposals are easily overlooked. Not even a nuclear-free zone will solve the East-West conflict. And if it did come to a military contest between the superpowers, Central Europe's geographical position alone would prevent its being spared. It remains a battlefield and a potential nuclear target area. It is not so much the siting as the range of nuclear weapons that is important. The crucial point is still to prevent nuclear weapons from being used at all. It is not resiting but reduction and control that reduce the nuclear threat.

III

The peace movement has proved most attractive to educated young people and young adults; it is they who form the active and dynamic part of the movement. It should not be overlooked, however, that recently much broader sections of the population, of all ages, have been caught up in the movement or at least have begun to sympathize with its ideas. Much goodwill is evident. With some exceptions, there is no doubting the honesty of motive. On the other hand, there have been signs of hysteria, sometimes assuming a neurotic form.

We have already mentioned the phenomenon of fear. Fear is freely admitted, is indeed considered a matter of pride, a sign of special sensitivity to the problems of our times. Anyone claiming to have no such fear is thought of as blind to the dangers of the future or, even worse, unwilling even to acknowledge them. But, as has been mentioned, the fear goes much further than the threat of war. It is fed by concern about the preservation of a healthy environment, about clean air, about limited resources of water and raw materials, about the unforeseeble consequences of modern technology, and about hunger and overpopulation in the Third World. In Germany these fears are compounded by shortages of training and job opportunities.

Ecology, rejection of technological progress, Third World policy, and the peace movement are all closely connected. People have doubts whether the established structures are capable of solving these manifold and pressing problems. Many have lost faith in the prevailing order. They no longer believe official statements or the declarations of responsible politicians, claiming they cannot see either the ethical legitimacy of those in power or the moral basis of the decisions they make. They therefore want a new and different political order, although they cannot say how it would look in detail. They are united on only one thing: the grass roots should be more closely involved in political decisions. There is no mistaking the tendency toward plebiscitary ideas in their criticisms of representative parliamentary democracy. There is therefore a danger that out of the peace movement may grow a real crisis of confidence in the state, far exceeding the movement's original aims. The desire for "alternative" policies may easily develop into fundamental opposition. This would be an expression of the despair of social groups who, out of fear of the future and their sense of political impotence, have fled into negativity and violence.

Fear is a feeling. It is thus not surprising that emotion should, whether unconsciously or as a consciously employed tool, play a large part in the debate. Emotion offers a way of standing up to the rationality and logic of the apparently so self-assured experts—the politicans and soldiers—and the inescapable realities they like to invoke. It is cold rationality, so the argument goes, that is on its way to destroying the whole world. Irrational enthusiasm can awaken new forces. A sense of moral superiority increases the reluctance to take part in sober discussion.

This attitude produces an impressive spontaneity. The emotional involvement of the young gives them energy and dynamism. True, they lack organizational experience and suitable structures. Enthusiasm and commitment by themselves do not add up to political muscle. A political movement must have more than merely short-term objectives. A loose coalition of different groups is not yet a political movement with a future. And yet the peace movement is more than a passing fad; it is capable of both mobilizing masses of people and giving them an inspiring sense of community, a quickening sense of belonging together in an endangered environment. And within the media it has not been slow to find support.

IV

The movement's strength is also a source of weakness. To be successful, a peace policy has to be based on sober evaluation and assessment of the facts, and it must also be politically achievable. Unthinking fear and anxiety distort one's view of reality. The peace movement's chief characteristics, and its chief failing, thus seem to me to be its lack of realism. If one closes one's eyes to the harsh realities, it is all too easy to clutch at hopes and illusions. At that point one is no longer accessible to rational argument and perceives only those things that seem to confirm one's own view of the world.

One sobering thought that has been subject to this kind of suppression is that there will never again be life without nuclear weapons. Weapons of mass destruction can of course be forbidden, or abolished, or scrapped, but the knowledge of how such weapons are manufactured can never be extinguished. The same is true, incidentally, of chemical weapons, which are equally terrible. As Karl Jaspers said long ago, we must learn to "live with the bomb." What we need is not so much the abolition of nuclear weapons—which does not mean we should not try to reduce them to the lowest possible level—as the abolition of war pure and simple. And those who consider such an idea wishful thinking should at least try to help prevent war between the nuclear powers.

Another victim of the peace movement's lack of a sense of reality has been awareness of the political, military, and ideological threat posed by Soviet Communism. The free press of the Western democracies is able to publish and speculate more about the West's defense than the East's. In the West information is plentiful; in the East detailed facts about defense and the armed forces are kept a close secret. As a result, little or no notice has been taken of the Soviet arms buildup of the last twelve years. Many consider the Soviet Union to have reached a saturation point and to be concerned only with preserving what it already has. Its policy objectives and armaments are seen as defensive. That the aim of Soviet foreign policy is hegemony is no longer recognized, nor that its ideology is one of revolution, pursued with revolutionary zeal. People no longer feel threatened. It is not difficult to see how people who think in this way can measure the United States and the Soviet Union by the same yardstick. They distance themselves equally from both. They forget the fundamental differences between the two world powers' systems of government and their moral foundations.

The Soviet Union is a totalitarian dictatorship. It claims for itself a "world-historical mission." As recently as 1982, after his appointment as general secretary, Andropov said: "Revolution is destructive, but without destruction it is impossible to create a new socialist world." Human rights are respected only on paper. The Soviet Union uses its military strength as a means of cowing others, of exerting pressure to the point of blackmail, of altering the political situation to the advantage of the Communist camp. But it does not shy away from armed conflict when this involves no risk to itself.

The United States, by contrast, is a parliamentary democracy. Freedom and human rights are not only theoretical constitutional principles but daily political realities safeguarded by a parliament and a free press. The United States is our ally. It protects us. Its policy is defensive. Its military strength serves to preserve peace in freedom. NATO and with it the United States will never fire the first shot. They have renounced the first use of any and all weapons. If the United States had ever entertained ideas of conquest, it could easily have realized them in the years after 1945, when it had a monopoly on nuclear weapons. What the United States actually did, however, was propose that all nuclear weapons be brought once and for all under the control of the United Nations (the Baruch Plan). The plan was defeated by the opposition of the Soviet Union.

The Soviet Union's aim is the victory of socialism, if possible without war. The aim of the United States and its allies is securing liberty without war. To remain equally detached from the two superpowers is not only to do a grave injustice to the Americans, to whom Western Europe owes its freedom, but to ignore basic political realities. On political grounds as much as on those of shared ideals, the Federal Republic of Germany must align itself with the United States.

There is further lack of realism in wanting to make the fifth commandment and the Sermon on the Mount the basis of all political decision making, as many Christians with a new moral rigor now want to do. Martin Luther himself grappled with the conflict between love of one's enemy and love of one's neighbor. He distinguished between a Christian's duties to self and to neighbor. Although Christians should suffer injustice themselves, they are obliged to avert violence and injustice from their neighbors. And to this end they may also use violence.

It is to the Christian as an individual that the Sermon on the Mount is addressed; it is a challenge to be lived up to. But the Sermon on the Mount is certainly not a political program. No state can be governed in accordance with the Gospel. So there can be no "politics of the Sermon on the Mount." Governments have responsibility for those they govern and for the common good. In their plans and actions, they must be guided by what the likely consequences will be, for which they have to bear responsibility. Part of their responsibility is to take precautions against violent attack. This follows from the right to self-defense. For a community to renounce its right to self-defense would be tantamount to giving itself up to the enemy;

politically speaking, it would mean subjugation—and could a peace in subjugation, involving as it would the renunciation of freedom and justice, still be described as peace? Large sections of the peace movement are in danger of believing that the purity of their own motives will elicit a pacifist response from the other side. There are no historical precedents for this, however, especially where dictatorships are concerned.

The recent reinvolvement of religion, or more accurately, the churches, in politics is an interesting new development. The churches are actively concerned about the ethical aspects of nuclear policy. They have not been content merely to sketch out the framework of the kind of action that would be ethically acceptable; some church leaders have felt entitled to go much further, proposing or warning against concrete political measures when they themselves do not have to bear the political consequences. In so doing they restrict the freely elected politicians' freedom of decision, as well as their responsibility. While political action cannot remove itself from moral judgment, it must at the same time do justice to the conflicts of human existence. Ethics have to stand the test of the practical world in which men and women must live. Christians know that they incur guilt in every action they take, but to take no action can incur just as much guilt. Let us remember Martin Luther's saying: *"Pecca fortiter, sed crede fortius,"* which I would translate today as: Act boldly in the faith, even when you know you will be guilty if you do.

The great emphasis on nuclear weapons has made the peace debate too narrowly concerned with military equipment and technical details, at the expense of the wider political background. East-West tension ultimately originates in all irreconcilable antagonism between the two political, economic, and ideological systems, in the contradiction between freedom and dictatorship. The threat is a political one. If there is a threat to the Soviet Union, it comes not from Western arms but from the existence and appeal of the free democratic states on its borders and elsewhere in the world. The threat to the West is that of a totalitarian hegemonial regime buttressed by superior military strength.

An example of the poor political judgment found within the peace movement has been its overestimation of Germany's freedom of action and the extent of its possible influence. The German peace movement is demanding the abolition or reduction of weapons owned not by the Germans but by someone else. It forgets that while the Federal Republic of Germany may be strong economically, politically it is a nonnuclear, middle-ranking power without a permanent seat in the Security Council. As long ago as 1955, the Federal Republic set an outstanding example by renouncing the production of nuclear weapons and having a national finger on the button. But it must also accept the conseqences of this: The Federal Republic is a "security importer" and thus cannot make nuclear decisions alone; only within the North Atlantic alliance does Germany have a voice in nuclear policy. Only in this forum can its national interests be represented. If the Federal Republic were to leave the alliance, it would no longer even be able to exert influence, let alone pressure. In nuclear matters the FRG would fade from being a country with an active voice in decision making to one passively tolerating decisions made for it.

A similar tendency to overestimate Germany's freedom of action is revealed in some of the proposals made for changes in the structure of the armed forces or for a new type of operations. For many years now, six allied nations have had forces permanently stationed alongside the Bundeswehr on German soil, their numbers roughly equaling the number of Bundeswehr units under NATO's operational command. Only half of the Central European area is secured by German troops. Changes in structure or weapons or a new plan of operations in Central Europe are thus possible only if they include all the forces involved in deterrence and defense in that area. These are not national but alliance decisions. Alliance decisions are the only politically feasible ones. A withdrawal of our allies from Central Europe would, however, make an attack more of a calculable risk for the Soviet Union, thereby making military conflict more likely.

This brings us to the fundamental criticism we have of the strategic and operational alternatives set out in part III. The keystone of NATO's strategy is deterrence, deterrence of both military aggression and political pressure. All measures that assist deterrence have priority over the consideration of various "war-fighting options." Each alternative must first be assessed in light of what it can contribute to the prevention of war, to making certain that member states of the alliance will never be faced with a choice between the surrender of their freedom and involvement in war. Deterrence, which presupposes the right combination of means, cannot of course guarantee peace beyond all doubt—no system can—but there is a very high probability of its doing so. No NATO government, of whatever political complexion, has so far managed to decide to abandon the alliance's strategy while there is as yet no other security system available offering as high a probability of peace.

V

The peace movement is still a minority, albeit a vociferous one, which in a brief time has attracted much sympathy and approval. No one could or would want to dismiss lightly the peace movement's fears and concerns, least of all those whose duty is to the common good and who are responsible for defense. Nor can there be any doubt that the peace movement has made some positive contributions to the political debate about the best method of securing peace.

The public had been too little informed about defense matters for too long. Some politicians may well have been quite pleased not to have to talk about such unpopular subjects in public or be made to argue their case. The suddenness with which the discussion of the urgent question of nuclear weapons revived, and its vehemence, surprised and frightened politicians. They have given voters the mistaken impression that the problems are quite new, at least in their seriousness, whereas in fact they have been in existence since the early sixties.

The peace movement has therefore become a necessary, if uncomfortable, critic of traditional defense policy. In view of the gravity of the decisions involved, politics needs such criticism. It obliges policymakers constantly to review their own position in an unbiased manner, making it easier for them to adapt to changing circumstances and—what has been omitted hitherto—requiring them to expound their chosen policy convincingly and comprehensibly to the public, not just once but repeatedly at all levels.

The peace movement has initiated a debate about the ethical justification of using arms to secure peace and about the legal and ethical limitations on measures of self-protection taken on the basis of the state's right to defend itself. Until a few years ago, these limitations were not as obvious to some of those in power.

The peace movement has raised the question not just of security—which, because of what the older generation had experienced, was its main consideration—but of the meaning of life itself. This generation, which has had the good fortune to have lived its life in great freedom and relative prosperity, needs a convincing answer to this question.

It will be helpful to recognize that there is some common ground between the two sides in the peace debate, which is a hopeful sign. Everyone wants peace, everyone wants an end to the tension between East and West, wants talks, negotiation, and economic cooperation. Everyone is looking for a way to make the use of weapons of mass destruction unnecessary, and everyone insists that there should be a limitation and reduction of arms in East and West. If it were clear to all that these are common aims, it ought to be possible for each side to listen to the other and to take it seriously. This would encourage moderation of thought and action, reduce polarization, and make it easier to seek a common path.

The most important impulse, however, has come from the peace movement's doubts about the credibility and effectiveness of deterrence. It is asked, understandably, if we can assume that the deterrence that has hitherto been so successful will continue to be effective for another thirty or fifty years. How much longer can we count on the Americans linking their fate with ours? How much longer will we be prepared to live with the paradox that peace must be defended by weapons whose actual use can destroy the whole of mankind? Must not one's long-term aim be to replace deterrence by a better system? Are there not other possibilities that might lift the pressure of nuclear weapons from us without jeopardizing peace in freedom? No future political leadership will be able to sidestep these questions, even if it must, and wishes to, maintain the present strategy until a convincing better alternative that meets with the approval of the majority has been found.

VI

What can be done to parry the dangers sparked by the peace movement while at the same time utilizing the impulses it has provided?

1. The peace debate should be repoliticized. It is all too easy for the larger political issues to be lost behind the comparisons for military strength or, even more, the counting of missiles. The differences in the political aims and values of East and West must be brought more prominently before the public. The part played by the Federal Republic in world events should be soberly spelled out. It is not just peace as a general aim we are concerned with but the form of peace, the *content of peace.*

2. Attempts must of course continue to be made to diminish political tension. This implies talks with the Soviets. Without cooperation with the Soviet Union, nothing can be done to alleviate the situation of the Germans in the other part of Germany. But such talks will have a chance of success only if the West has taken sufficient defensive measures to be able to withstand political and military pressure.

3. In the long term, ways should be sought to reduce dependency on nuclear weapons. While there can be no argument about the political aim of "peace and freedom," there might be changes in methods, means, and structures.

- Efforts should be pursued to reach a signed agreement on balanced and verifiable reductions of nuclear weapons to lower levels in both East and West. This is the most hopeful path. Its achievement will require cooperation on both sides.
- Strengthening conventional defenses could raise the nuclear threshold appreciably; the costs, however, would be considerable.
- Might not a technological breakthrough entirely alter the role of nuclear weapons? If new nonnuclear defensive weapons that could be guaranteed to neutralize aggressive nuclear missiles are discovered, nuclear weapons would then lose their terror. In the final analysis they could be scrapped completely. This may be only a vision today but it may also be a hope based not entirely on illusion.

4. Last but not least, we should make efforts to overcome the paralyzing pessimism that feeds on fear. It makes it difficult if not impossible to arrive at meaningful and promising solutions. Dietrich Bonhoeffer, the theologian who gave his life in the resistance against Adolf Hitler, wrote during World War II: "No one should decry optimism, the will for a better future." And he went on: "Tomorrow may be the Last Judgement and if it is, we will gladly lay aside our work for a better future, but not before."

16

NEUTRALISM AND THE MORAL ORDER IN WEST GERMANY

Jeffrey Herf

The four years from 1979 to 1983 were tumultuous ones in West Germany. Now that the first of the scheduled deployments of NATO's intermediate-range missiles have taken place, some observers have already accorded the largest peace movement in the Federal Republic's history the status of a flash in the pan. The solid pro-Western majority has elected a conservative government while Social Democratic politicians insist that their rejection of the NATO missiles is a disagreement over policy within the context of the Atlantic alliance. In light of this exhausted calm after the storm, we will examine the temporary and permanent features of the peace movement and the SPD Left. What were the causes of the peace movement? Why did the SPD move away from missile deployment? What lessons can we draw from the events of the past four years for Western foreign and defense policy? What was and what will be the connection between the German question and European security?

The vote of the Social Democratic party in the Bundestag in November 1983 against the NATO dual-track decision was the most dramatic manifestation of the erosion of the security consensus in West Germany. It also indicated that the West German peace movement, although a minority of the electorate, achieved considerable success in a relatively short time in pushing an albeit not unwilling SPD to positions considerably to the left of its last chancellor, Helmut Schmidt. The immediate controversy over the 1979 NATO dual-track decision, the heightened superpower tensions following the Soviet invasion of Afghanistan, the Polish crisis, and the increased fears of nuclear war that existed in Western Europe and the United States in general in the early 1980s were the international context for the emergence of pacifist and neutralist sentiment in the Federal Republic. To understand why these tensions had a particularly acute impact on West German domestic politics, it is important to keep in mind the impact of the intellectual Left in the universities and the media, as well as to recall some of the unintended consequences of *Ostpolitik* and detente as articulated by the Brandt wing of the SPD since the 1960s. The virulence of the missile debate in West Germany was due to the deep fears aroused by nuclear weapons as well as to the fact that an articulate minority among the young and highly educated challenged some of the fundamental aspects of the legitimacy of West Germany's political institutions.

The debate over the future of the Western alliance is essentially a struggle over recreating the validity of a set of ideas that went into NATO's formation: there is an insurmountable distinction between Western liberty and freedom and Communist dictatorships; the Western alliance is a defensive voluntary association of democracies that sustains both peace and freedom in Western Europe by nuclear and conventional deterrence; and the presence of U.S. power in Europe preserves a balance of power that, upset by a U.S. withdrawal or a West German move out of the alliance, would soon lead to the erosion of political freedom in Western Europe due to the expansion of Soviet power.

The peace movement challenged these foreign policy assumptions as well as ideas central to the political and moral consensus of the Federal Republic articulated in its early years. We would do well to recall its fundamental elements. First, the Center-Left and Center-Right rejected totalitarianism—Nazism in the past, communism in the present. The Federal Republic was to be a pluralist democracy in the Western sense. This shared antitotalitarianism made Bonn a "militant democracy," ready to do battle with antidemocratic ideas of the Right—now utterly discredited—and the Left.

Second, and related to this view, the Federal Republic would be integrated into the West, both militarily and politically. Gone would be the days when the Germans rejected "Western civilization" for the charms of German *Kultur.* Political freedom demanded that German politics be freed from anti-Western resentments. Moreover the power of the Red Army in Eastern Europe sent the same message: only a semblance of a balance of military power in Europe could preserve free political institutions.

Third, restoration of a United Germany was subordinated to the preservation of free institutions in its Western half. It was hoped that integration into the Western alliance would offer a promise in the very long run—depending on the policies of the Soviet Union—for eventual reunification. Integration into the Western alliance would offer the basis on which to carry on the possible reunification of Germany. It is because all of these assumptions have been severely challenged, above all by the political and intellectual Left, that the security consensus cracked. [1]

While all of the capitalist democracies in the 1960s experienced cultural revolution of the young, the West German New Left promised to fill a void left by a perceived absence of romantic politics in the postwar period. Its links to earlier manifestations of romantic anticapitalism, generous support in the rapidly expanding universities and in the welfare state, an SPD government whose reform efforts could always be criticized as insufficient, and sympathy in the press and media all contributed to a remarkable persistence of the influence of the intellectual Left in West Germany.

Indeed, there is hardly a single theme in today's peace and ecology movements that was not articulated then. Consider just a few of the following standard criticisms of West German society: It is authoritarian. Its parliamentary institutions do as much, indeed more, to stifle democratic will as they do to allow its articulation. The schools and family are factories of authoritarian socialization serving an overarching system of domination. The logic of instrumental reason has displaced politics based on moral criteria. An amoral expertise obscures political controversies in the guise of technical language. Capitalism and the modern technology it develops are dehumanizing, fostering false needs while exhausting the earth's limited resources for the benefit of a wealthy minority of the globe's population. [2]

These general assaults on capitalism were complemented by an attack on the claim of the Federal Republic to be a fundmental break with the Nazi regime. According to Marxist analysts, because the Federal Republic was not born out of socialist revolution, it amounted to a restoration of the same capitalist system from which National Socialism had emerged. This "continuity" of the Third Reich and the Federal Republic suggested that a relapse into a "neo-" or "proto-" fascism could not be excluded. Moreover, the radical Left denounced the antitotalitarian consensus that had been the source of pride to the militant democrats of the early 1950s as little more than ideological cover for capitalist restoration and avoiding "coming to terms with the Nazi past."

The result, in the words of the political theorist Kurt Sontheimer, has been *Verunsicherung* or "loss of certainty," which placed the political consensus of the Federal Republic on the defensive and made the political elites of a very young republic less sure of the moral order that supported its political institutions.[3] Where the founding generation focused on the shift from dictatorship to democracy, the New Left saw in the first decade of the new republic economic growth and an orgy of forgetting, instead of a coming to terms with the Nazi past. For the New Left, the "continuity" of capitalism from the Third Reich to the Federal Republic was a more important fact than the consolidation of parliamentary institutions. For the Left, NATO was merely the foreign policy accoutrement of capitalist restoration, and U.S. hegemony. Hence the Federal Republic is not, in fact, a genuine democracy. Its parliamentary institutions are rituals that serve only to obscure the real locus of power in the economic and political elites. A lack of internal democracy went hand in hand with a loss of sovereignty to the United States.[4]

The antiauthoritarianism of the New Left meant that it would not be comfortable with existing Communist societies, especially the Soviet Union and Eastern Europe. But it also rejected the label of totalitarian as appropriate for them. To the extent to which the New Left thought about existing Communist regimes, it argued that they were not really socialist, that a host of historical contingencies had diverted the revolution in question from its proper goal, that their goals were preferable to those of capitalist societies, that their faults were due to the aggressive capitalist states that encircled them, or finally and most importantly, that they were merely another variant of a universal system of domination. The Soviet Union, in particular, no longer served as the beacon of revolutionary hopes. The radical Left's criticisms of the Soviet bloc did not require a moral or political choice in favor of Western societies. If the East is bad, the West is not appreciably better. Herbert Marcuse's "Great Refusal" of the 1960s has become the "Great Equation" of East and West in the 1980s. It, and the fear of nuclear war, are the core idea of the recent peace movements in Western Europe. The juxtaposition of free and totalitarian regimes was discarded as a "relic of the Cold War" hence bad, obsolete, wrong, and reactionary.

The theory of the New Left exerted an influence in the universities in the SPD's *Jusos,* in the high schools through political propaganda called "emancipatory pedagogy," in the social science and humanities faculties in the universities, and in the print and visual media. All of these general notions concerning the repressive nature of Western society tended to dampen enthusiasm for thinking about what would be needed to defend it. Indeed, they raise the issue of whether such a system of domination is worth defending at all.

Of most direct relevance to the emergence of the peace movement of the early 1980s was *kritische Friedensforschung* or critical peace research. Its growth is a remarkable story: a government financially subsidizes a whole new, and rather dubious, academic "discipline" whose every practical proposal is aimed at criticizing or dismantling the structure of defense laboriously constructed since West Germany's integration into NATO.[5] One of the paradoxes of an antimodernist peace movement is the importance of *Gegenexperten* or critical peace researchers who have learned the language of deterrence to attack it. Developed since the late 1960s, critical peace research in West Germany was well established at peace research institutes with considerable government funding. The analyses move on a continuum from charlatanry to sincere efforts to raise the nuclear threshold with criticisms of NATO policy that have existed in official circles as well. Their political importance for the peace movement lies in lending an angst-ridden, apocalyptic, utopian ideology a certain intellectual aura of science and rationality, and in "democratizing" the debate over Western security beyond the previously small circle of strategic and defense experts.[6]

The peace movement of the early 1980s was a breakthrough into public consciousness of a decade of intellectual criticism of the basic assumptions of Western deterrence. In the late 1960s, the Norwegian peace researcher Johan Galtung distinguished between personal violence and structural violence, negative peace and positive peace. Structural violence is contained in all relationships of exploitation and inequality, be they between social groups within a society or between richer and poorer societies. Hence the "mere" absence of active war is a "negative peace" that contains within it unresolved conflicts. "Positive peace" demands the end of all of the social inequalities that "deny human potential," hence it may require the use of "counter-violence," that is, revolutionary violence. Galtung's arguments served primarily as a justification of violence by Third World "liberation" movements, but they also had the effect of dismissing the accomplishments of the Atlantic alliance in the postwar period. After all, preserving "negative peace" was hardly an impressive accomplishment.[7]

In West Germany, Dieter Senghaas's critique of deterrence theory, *Abschreckung und Frieden,* a "critique of organized peacelessness" (*organisierter Friedlosigkeit*) first published in 1969 and reissued several times since, has been the central theoretical attack on deterrence.[8] Critical peace research, an outgrowth of the student New Left of the 1960s, echoes some of the Marxist and Marcusian themes of the period. First, it is not the fundamental conflict of values and political institutions between free and totalitarian societies that lies at the root of the U.S.-Soviet conflict but primarily the internally generated sources of expansion that life in Western capitalism promotes. It is deterrence, what Senghaas called "the threat system," that itself is the cause of the problem. Given that they argue that it is the weapons themselves that generate a mutually reinforcing arms spiral, the work of the critical peace researchers manifests a peculiarly technocratic, rather morbid fascination with particular dimensions of the East-West conflict.

Second, the U.S.-Soviet conflict serves to contain social conflicts within each of the blocs. In the literature, lip service is given to the benefits the Soviets may derive from their rhetoric about fears of capitalist encirclement. The focus lies on the "function" anticommunism serves in the West in stifling reform and radicalism by focusing on the external enemy. The aggression that has accumulated in Western capitalist societies finds an outlet in the Soviet scapegoat. This is primarily a social psychological theory of the causes of the arms race. Deterrence is not then a response to real Soviet threats but an ideological rationale that undergirds the status quo in the West.

The third notion developed by the critical peace research is that because the arms race gets its primary political and social momentum from the internal dynamics of Western, viz., U.S. society, it is the perceptions of a—nonexistent—Soviet threat that must be changed. The dynamic of the arms race begins in the West but continues due to a "symmetry of behavior" between the superpowers as this psychopathology develops into mutual projection and hostility, combined with technology out of control. The political differences between West and East pale beside their similarities insofar as the arms race is concerned. This analysis combines the tones of evenhandedness—between the United States and the Soviet Union—with proposals for Western unilateral disarmament. If it is U.S. and Western *Feindbilder*—images of the enemy that have set the arms race in motion—then *Entfeindung*, or a psychological change in perceptions of the Soviets, is necessary to reverse the arms race.[9] Such an intellectual edifice largely precludes grappling with the purposes of Soviet political and military power as anything more than responses to U.S. initiatives. It not only offers arguments against any proposals for Western defense beyond the most minimal notions of "social defense" but also criticizes any juxtaposition of democratic and total-itarian political values as contributing to tensions that only lead to acceleration of the arms race.

The underlying assumption of critical peace research is that the past history of conflicts among nations has all been a terrible mis-take that can be corrected with sufficient radical enlightenment. Power politics, international relations, the balance of power are all to be rejected—along with capitalism. It is a program that argues that "social change" in Western societies is the prerequisite for ending the specter of nuclear war. Once the roots of structural violence and the limits of "negative peace" are overcome, the lamb will lie down with the lion. This was not a worldview brought into existence by the Reagan administration of the 1979 dual-track decision, but it was one that played an important role in the attack on this decision. [10]

As important as the theoretical legacy of the New Left has been in the formation of the new social movements of the 1970s and today's peace movement, it is important to note that the romantic, utopian dimensions of the radicalism of the 1960s have been deepened and extended over the last decade. The contrast to Weimar is striking. Then, the Right was the romantic exponent of cultural revolution, while, with the exception of a few romantic Marxists such as Ernst Bloch, the Left stood for "progress." Today, there is no significant antidemocratic Right, while the anticivilizational, cultural revolu-tionary themes are articulated by the Left. The effort to blend the anticivilizational mood with the more traditional left-wing analysis of capitalism, the so-called red-green synthesis, has not been a uniquely German enterprise. But the romantic legacy within Marx-ism in the Frankfurt school and especially in the work of Bloch give the West German Left a philosphical basis for ecological leftism that is far more elaborate than that of the new social movements else-where. [11] While the New Left's cultural revolution petered out in the United States, in West Germany the appeals for reconciliation with nature, gloom over the dialectic of enlightenment, and visions of a new and alternative technology were, if anything, more pervasive in the 1970s Left than in the 1960s.

The red-green synthesis has been forcefully articulated by Rudolf Bahro, the former East German dissident Communist and author of *The Alternative in Eastern Europe,* a critique of "real existing social-ism" that led to his imprisonment in East Germany before a cam-paign on his behalf in the West won his release and emigration to the Federal Republic in 1977. [12] Because Bahro expresses in pristine form the blend of romanticism and ecology that animates the peace movement, there is a tendency to dismiss him. Yet his is one of the most articulate and forceful vioices in favor of neutralism, dissolution of the blocs, and a link between the peace issue and the German question. Bahro gives clearest expression to what others express with reservations and qualifications. [13]

Bahro, like the former leader of the West German New Left, Rudi Dutschke, believed that the West German Left must be at once romantic, national, and ecological, a view that led both men to the Green party and to conflict with more conventional leftists. Bahro's hopes that conservatives would also join in the new ecological politics have met with only modest success. The main impact of the new romanticism has been on the Left. He has urged a deemphasis on traditional socialist anticapitalism in favor of a more apocalyptic vision of impending ecological catastrophe: unless the West's way of life is completely transformed and its consumption drastically reduced, the unjustified appetites of Western societies will mean that "between now and the end of the century at least 200 million people will die of hunger." What is needed in this context is not another left-wing sect but a party that touches "existential interests" and "forms an autonomous yet integrated component of the wider constructive forces that stand against the decomposition and self-destruction of our civilization." In place of Left and Right, Bahro stressed the crisis of civilization that would draw adherents from across the political spectrum. While the Green party in fact remains primarily a left-wing party, the romantic component so powerful in Bahro's thought suggests the possibility of speaking in the name of civilization, or more modestly, only of the whole nation rather than the proletariat. [14]

To prevent imminent catastrophe, Bahro argues that German anticapitalism must be a cultural as well as socioeconomic revolution. His vision also has a pronounced religious dimension. He seeks support from "committed Christians" who agree that "capitalism is the epoch furthest from God." "Religious transcendence" and a "real cultural transformation" demand a "mobilization" that has stretched right into this most intimate sphere of human motivation. Central and Northern Europe are witnessing "a movement for conversion in the metropolises" that regards arguments, facts, evidence, negotiations, diplomacy, and "policies" as hopelessly beside the point. In view of the coming apocalypse, it is nonpolitical or extrapolitical forces leading to "an overwhelming moment of conversion" that are crucial. Only the peace movement—not the governments—can save civilization by bringing about a fundamental break in cultural continuity, destroying the traditional consensus that supports the state, and above all constructing a new consensus by bringing about changes within individuals. [15]

What conclusions does Bahro draw from these views for the more prosaic question of East-West politics and Euromissiles? First, security and peace are not the same thing. "If you seek security, you practice distrust and take precautions which in turn feed the mistrust of the other side." Security has led to the current nuclear powder keg. Anyone who claims to pursue peace and security together is deceiving their listeners. What has up to now been called security really means suicide." Second, "the apocalyptic situation gives me courage" because it impels so many to take risks to prevent the worst from happening. The moral lesson of Hitlerism for the antinuclear movement is to prevent catastrophe, to stop the "Great Machine." [16]

Bahro is an advocate of neutralism, that is, freedom and independence from both blocs for Central Europe. Only by breaking out of the blocs can the West and East Germans regain their sovereignty, and help to disband the confrontation of the blocs. "Power elites" in East and West agree on continuing to play foreign policy games over the heads of the population. Each thrives on the existence of the other as an enemy for "they use these images to legitimate their internal monopoly of force" and the continuation of the arms race. A new internationalism of the peoples against the governments is necessary.

While Bahro's romanticism led to differences with more orthodox Marxists, his views of the Soviet Union were quite conventional. They amounted to asserting that it will no longer threaten Western Europe if it is no longer threatened. It needs its troops to patrol the satellites. Thus a conventional offense against Western Europe is "unthinkable." It is "absurd" to count Soviet tanks and soldiers. A new Rapallo? "Then, why not? . . . Today all of Western Europe finds itself in the middle position in which earlier Germany always found itself alone." A new Rapallo would break Europe from the the United States, and Eastern Europe perhaps from the Soviet Union. Western Europe alone would be both economically and culturally stronger than each of the superpowers. It might indeed have a Gaullist component, but with a *force de frappe.* [17]

Like E.P. Thompson, one of the leading representatives of the British peace movement, Bahro stresses the similarity of East and West: both contribute to the exterminist dynamic. Fundamental opposition against both blocs is the answer, though in his view Soviet foreign policy has always been a defensive reaction to Western capitalism. His plea for a third way is that of a new internationalism, with its own set of illusions about Soviet power. It is humanity, not Germany, that he seeks to renew. He combines the enlightenment universalism of East German Marxism-Leninism with the apocalyptic message of a new North European Protestant Reformation. It is possible to puncture his illusions—a neutral and disarmed Europe would be tempting to the Soviets indeed—but the arguments that would be necessary would pass him by just as they pass by much of the peace movement. "A movement for conversion in the metropolises" is not much impressed by the difference between early, delayed, or no-first-use of nuclear weapons. In fact, it is impervious to improvements and/or modifications in the remote world of policy and strategy. What it succeeds in doing is discrediting any talk of such nature. In terms of the balance of political-psychological forces, Bahro's views rule out rational discourse concerning deterrence. The very language is part of the exterminist logic he seeks to destroy. "Policy" has no answer to this essentially conspiratorial view of elites plotting the end of humanity. [18]

Bahro's apocalyptic rhetoric often obscures his shrewdness as a tactician. His aim is to use the Greens to move the SPD away from its position under Schmidt as the "party of moderate exterminism" to an ally of the peace movement. Bahro argues that the SPD's adherence to "NATO's insane armaments policy is riddled with fallacies from start to finish." These fallacies are that an unprovoked attack from the East is plausible, that security can be purchased by arms, that sustaining the military equilibrium will lead to anything but more arms race, that governments rather than peoples can insure peace, that the Atlantic alliance offers Europe and the Federal Republic more security independence from the opposing blocs, or that with the SS-20s the Soviets have upset the military balance, something that "has by no means been sufficiently exposed as a calculated lie in the media by such magazines as *Der Spiegel* and *Der Stern*."

Bahro practically accuses the SPD of treason to the nation. The peace movement exerts pressure on the SPD by accusing it of being a lackey of Washington's policies of making preparations for a "war on German soil." The SPD, Bahro insists, cannot be a peace party and a party of moderate exterminism at the same time. The Brandt wing of the leadership must be encouraged to support detente over and against the policy of East-West tension. "The immediate task is to bring about an open breach with the CDU/CSU on all the basic questions of foreign policy." But the SPD must be pushed. In short, there is both a need and an opportunity for alliances between the SPD and the Greens. When Bahro hopes that the new peace movement "gives Germans the right to emancipate themselves from the political tutelage of the victors," is this not similar to the SPD's subsequent *linke Patriotismus*? Bahro's romantic leftism first found organizational expression in the Greens, but by 1982 paler versions of his views could be heard within the SPD. [19]

Although it is unlikely that the Greens will move much beyond their current parliamentary representation and may even expire under the tensions of being both a party and a movement, while the SPD takes away its monopoly of the peace issue, they did exert a continuous pressure on the SPD Left. For the SPD to gain, in Brandt's words, a majority left of the CDU, it had to seek the votes of those drawn to the Greens as well. The Greens advocated neutralism, and did so in language that combined neo-Marxism, anti-imperialism, anarchism, feminism, and ecology. They supported a "European peace policy" that they defined in the following manner: unilateral disarmament leading to a nuclear-free zone in Europe; West German withdrawal from NATO; an end to the arms race and to deterrence, which they viewed as a euphemism for preparation for mass murder and collective suicide; dismantling the Bundeswehr, with "social defense" based on a decentralized, lightly armed civilian militia; the immediate dissolution of the military blocs, above all NATO and the Warsaw Pact, as a result of which the division of Europe and thus the division of Germany will be overcome; and rejection of the NATO dual-track decision combined with verbal pleas for dismantling of the Soviet's SS-20s. [20]

The Greens' view of the East-West conflict assumed that there are not, in fact, fundamental political differences between NATO and the Warsaw Pact. The West was not defending democracy, while the Soviet Union, as unattractive as it may be, pursued a defensive foreign policy. The main, indeed the only, danger was the self-perpetuating exterminist logic of the arms race, in the middle of which the peoples of Europe are caught. The aggressive foreign policy of the United States places the Soviets on the defensive and therefore increases the Soviet threat to Western Europe. Only U.S. and Western withdrawal and the dismantling of anticommunist *Feindbilder*—ideological distortions of the East bloc as a dangerous totalitarian dictatorship—can diminish the prospect of war. Peace will result from *Entfeindung* or dissolution of these images of the enemy, not strong defenses.

Hence the Europeans, especially the Germans, are victims of the East-West conflict, not parties to it. Germany is particularly victimized because inclusion in the blocs and the presence of foreign occupiers in both Germanys deprive them of their sovereignty. Bloc confrontation both prevents eventual reunification and serves to stifle social and political reform within East and West. The Greens suggest that the CDU/CSU and the SPD, by pursuing a policy of Western integration, cement the country's division and make Germany the future battleground of a war between the superpowers. While the Greens have not stressed the German question as much as the ecological message, they agree that membership in NATO is a betrayal of German national interests. To the extent that the Greens have developed a concrete utopia of a future Germany, it would be demilitarized, neutralist, pacifist, and deindustrialized. Petra Kelly summarized the Greens' Weltanschauung succinctly: "the [present] system is bankrupt." [21]

Although the Greens called themselves neutralists, the burden of their anger was directed against the United States. At a "Nuremberg trial" held in the spring of 1983, the Greens convicted the United States of waging atomic war in 1945, initiating each step in the arms race, and thus providing the Soviet Union with a rationale for its arms buildup. On the one hand, they argued that the military balance makes no difference; on the other hand, they rejected Western information about Soviet military power as propaganda.

The Greens denounced both tactical nuclear weapons already in the Federal Republic as well as the new intermediate-range weapons able to reach the Soviet Union, because both weapons systems threatened a nuclear war limited to Europe. In rejecting the NATO LRTNF deployments, Gert Bastian, a former general who belonged to the Greens until he left the parliamentary group in early 1984, argued that SS-20s did not open new possibilities for nuclear war-fighting in the way that the NATO deployments did. The accuracy and speed of the new missiles made them first-strike weapons that would invite Soviet preemptive strikes. Thus while the intentions behind the dual-track decision were to offer tangible evidence of coupling the U.S. deterrent to the defense of Europe and thus convince the Soviets of the unlikelihood of limiting nuclear war to Central Europe, the Greens saw the deployments as part of a new phase in U.S. nuclear strategy: a shift from mutually assured destruction to nuclear war-fighting, with Germany as the prime victim. Deployment of the missiles would be further confirmation of Germany's loss of any right to self-determination.

The "European peace policy" of the Greens linked the missile issue to national sovereignty. The way for Germany to regain sovereignty is to dissolve the blocs, and create a nuclear-free zone in

Central Europe. This process would be initiated by unilateral disarmament, which would create a cycle of disarmament by removing the threats that now hold the East bloc together. Once the pressure on Moscow is alleviated, it will reciprocate with disarmament measures of its own, leading in turn to U.S. reciprocity and worldwide disarmament. The first step toward a "bloc-free Europe" must be taken in Germany by dissolving West German ties with NATO. Then West Germany will no longer be a territory serving the aggressive striving of the United States for hegemony, "thus delivering itself up to atomic destruction." West Germany would then propose freedom from the blocs to East Germany and the rest of the East bloc. With the *Feinbild* of revanchist reactionary Germany a thing of the past, both Germanys would move toward complete demilitarization. Bloc-free status would reopen the question of Berlin as well.

A demilitarized, nonaligned Germany including Berlin would undermine the bloc system entirely, thereby removing what the Greens see as the central cause of conflict in Europe—U.S. and Soviet forces standing face-to-face at the Continent's center. A nonviolent Germany would be welcomed by other Europeans and would induce the Soviets to loosen their grip on Eastern Europe, allowing future movements for reform to take place without military interventions. At last, the wounds of the cold war would be healed and the division of Europe ended. Further, it would be a fundamental step toward worldwide peace because both superpowers would be weakened. [22]

The Soviet Union has on several occasions proposed exactly such a resolution of the German question: reunification in exchange for withdrawal from NATO. [23] This is a formula for extending Soviet influence over all of Western Europe. The striking thing about the peace movement is that its illusions about the Soviet Union serve to mesh with Moscow's foreign policy without, as in the period of the Comintern, requiring the active intervention of Communists. The spontaneity of the Greens includes spontaneously advocating policies that amount to capitulation in the face of the military power they dismiss as meaningless. Whatever their subjective intentions may be, the neutralism of the Greens "objectively" serves the foreign policy goals of the Soviet Union, above all to split Western Europe and the United States and prevent the emergence of a politically united Western Europe that could mount a credible defense.

Despite the obviousness with which such proposals serve the Soviet Union's goals, the new peace movement is animated more by the "Geist der Blockfreiheit" rather than explicit sympathy for the Russians. The Russians are not coming. Bahro, for example, rejects both anti-Sovietism and anti-Americanism. Neutralism suggests merely a negation, while dissolution of the blocs is a positive utopia, a vision of both a "third way" and a world turned upside down. A revolution in consciousness will displace the balance of power, dissolve the irrational fears that hold the blocs together. Bahro is for a third way between East and West, for both East and West are "two sides of one and the same coin." The security policy of the Greens, if one can call it that, means a leap from *Abschreckung* (deterrence) to *Entfeindung* (undoing the image of the enemy).

The Greens thus offer both a vision of total catastrophe as well as the image of complete salvation. In place of alienated, divided Europe and Germany there would emerge a new, nonalienated, autonomous Continent finally able to realize the goals of European civilization without interference from the Americans and Soviets. *Neutralism* is far too pallid a term to capture the vision of a world made right and turned upside down that these modern radical utopians promise.

The peace movement provided an outlet for expression of an inchoate yearning, principally but not exclusively on the Left, for a new West German national identity. It was not primarily the result of a new nationalist upsurge, but nationalist themes werre inseparable from its diagnoses of nuclear weapons. Both sympathetic and critical observers have noted that the new social movements and now the peace movement celebrate the virtues of *Gemeinschaft*, emotions, and immediacy in ways strikingly reminiscent of earlier antimodernist and nationalist youthmovements. [24]

One young left-wing journalist, Wolfgang Pohrt, described the peace movement as potentially movement of national awakening, whose main slogan could be *"Ein Volk, ein Reich, ein Frieden."* [25] In fact, the specter of nuclear war limited to East and West Germany by the machinations of both superpowers was the theme most frequently repeated in the peace movement literature. West Germany, the argument went, like East Germany, has lost its political sovereignty to its superpower. The new nationalists complained that West Germany has been victimized by cultural Americanization as much as by direct political interference with the sovereignty of the Federal Republic.

In the early and mid 1970s, Rudi Dutschke, one of the leaders of the extraparliamentary opposition of the 1960s, was urging the West German Left to reject both "Americanization and Russification" and to take up the national question. More recently, Willy Brandt's son Peter has urged the Left to give up its reservations concerning the national question and not to make the same mistake of the Weimar

Left, namely, leaving the national question to the political Right. [26] In terms of the experience of the West German Left since the 1960s, interest in national identity was, as Pohrt put it, a kind of *Endstation* —last stop—on a journey in search of political identification that experienced repeated disappointments with the international proletariat, and with the Third World in assorted national guises. This return home was not a return to soulless, bureaucratic Bonn but to the still unfocused antimodernist *Heimat. Die Linke fuhlt sich Deutsch* (the Left feels itself German) but no less estranged and alienated from capitalist, industrial society, and no less inclined than earlier political pilgrims to deny the harsher realities of communist power. [27]

Intellectuals within the SPD, such as Horst Ehmke, Peter Glotz, and Günter Gaus, also wrote books and articles on the Left and the national question. In 1979, the sociologist Jürgen Habermas, edited a widely read essay collection, *Stichworte zur 'Geistigen' Situation der Zeit* that devoted considerable space to the issue. [28] The essays made clear as well that the yearning for a new national identity was part of the larger anticivilizational mood that affected the new social movements generally in West Germany. As I said above, it represented a willingness of the intellectual and political Left, by no means restricted to the Greens, to blend romantic themes of cultural revolution beginning in the 1960s into its more conventional analysis of capitalism.

The revival of left-wing interest in the national question included the following common denominators. The Federal Republic, as Habermas put it, was witnessing a "colonization of the life world" by capitalist technocracy. [29] The postwar era was above all an era of economic growth and forgetting and repressing the past. But growth alone would not provide a collective identity. Today, Glotz and others argue for a "new patriotism" that can envisage a Germany that is something other than the soulless technocracy of Bonn. As the author Martin Walser puts it, both German states "lack depth"; neither arouses deep conviction. [30] Another contributor to the Habermas collection, Dietrich Wellershof, bemoaned the lost opportunities of the immediate postwar years. Instead of coming to terms with the past there was a "deficit of meaning," NATO instead of reunification, cold war instead of neutralist, democratic socialism. [31] "Growth" and anticommunism were opiates of reconstruction that the political sociologist Wolfgang Mommsen worries created *Modell Deutschland*—an economic giant without adequate legitimations for its political institutions. In Mommsen's words, "We are still very far from a real, democratic consensus which does not rest only on material values (which change with time and are abandoned) but rather on secure foundations of ideas."[32] In Fassbinder's films, and in Hans-Jürgen Syberburg's epic about Hitler, the scorn for the 1950s among the younger leftists but by no means Marxist intellectuals is apparent. As Syberburg puts it, it is "in its volunatry relinquishing of its creative irrationality and perhaps in this alone, that Germany really lost the Second World War."[33] The political theorist Iring Fetscher drew the logical conclusion from this lament: West Germany can no longer recover its national identity in the arid realms of socialist internationalism but must opt out of the global industrial, capitalist, consumerist race toward ecological balance.[34] The talk of national identity, like the new social movements generally, was, as Richard Lowenthal put it, a return of the repressed romantic impulse in German society.

In the same collection, Horst Ehmke linked the national question to detente and *Ostpolitik*.[35] Continuation of *Ostpolitik* rather than rigid adherence to Adenauer's policy of strength offers some hope of bringing the two Germanys closer together, increasing human contacts between them, and reopening the German question. The longer detente continues, the more East and West Germans understand themselves still as belonging to one nation. But further progress in the German question can take place only in the context of development of "peace and detente policies," policies that cannot get anywhere against the will of the Soviet Union and thus require good relations with the Soviets. For Ehmke it is the great task of Social Democracy today to take up the national question in a way that the bourgeoisie and the political Right could not, namely, by fusing the call for national unity with that of political freedom through democratic, true socialism, in both East and West Germany.

One of the most notorious documents of the early 1980s dealing with the national question was *Die deutsche Einheit kommt bestimmt* (1982), an essay collection that includes the radical right-wing historian, Helmut Diwald, as well as the far Left, represented by Peter Brandt and Herman Ammon.[36] The main interest of the collection lay in the way in which the nuclear issue brings the political extremes together. Its principal theme was that Germany had been victimized for thirty years by the superpowers and must now become a subject, not an object, of history and its own destiny.

All of the authors agreed that German reunification was the only guarantee for peace in Europe. Since 1949, the German people had been denied their right of "self-determination" due to the division of the nation. The postwar status quo amounted to the hegemony of the

United States and the Soviet Union over Europe, a strategy of "bipolar imperialism." While the Germans accepted "subjugation" and division in exchange for material progress and peace, the economic, ecological, and international crises of the 1980s reminded the Germans of the emptiness of material progress and of the threat of limited nuclear war. Rather than engage in the East-West conflict, Germans must work for a Germany for Germans. "No German blood for Moscow or Washington" must be the new essence of politics in Bonn and East Berlin. In the face of possible nuclear catastrophe, "peace" and the "nation" are categories that transcend the traditional cleavages of Right and Left. The contributors to the collection were adamant in their conviction that only a neutral Germany can recapture the national identity and preserve peace in Europe. They understood that this solution would mean closer ties to the Soviet Union, loosening of the blocs, and the end of West German participation in NATO. For these new nationalists, the issue was either a new national identity and peace, or continued integration into the Western alliance and war. Neither survival nor a new identity were compatible with continued integration in the Western alliance.

The peace movement, then, is not only the result of the debate over deployment of the missiles. Its significance also lies in its character as a *Bewegung,* a movement, one that promises realization of utopia.[37] While it and the other new social movements cannot be equated with the romantic nationalism of the nineteenth century, the youth movements, Völkish ideologues, or National Socialism, they have revived some of their basic features. Both the old and the new *Bewegungen* made the same claim and effort, namely, to offer a life-affirming alternative to a world that had become hopelessly lifeless and degraded, to extend this alternative to the whole of society, and through the power of the movement to replace the mechanisms of established politics.

The new social movements of the last decade have been on the Left rather than the Right—through a very unconventional notion of the Left—and heatedly rejected the notion that they represented a return of the repressed romantic, irrationalist, and antidemocratic traditions that helped to destroy the Weimar Republic. However, even sympathetic analysts of the new social movements saw these continuities: "In the new social movements, very different motifs of the critique of Western civilization are combined into a heterogeneous movement whose common self-understanding is drawn from the experience of the dehumanizing and life-destructive consequences of industrial growth, and of the industrial model of civilization generally. The

Angst in the face of the future, feelings of alienation and psychic burdens grounded in this experience are synthesized into a movement of resistance and protest which gains its driving force and perspective from the antimodernist myth of the 'natural,' of the simple, transparent, spontaneous life oriented to needs." [38]

As Sontheimer has emphasized, a new myth, a new *Lebensgefühl,* a new form of life, a new longing for meaning, a perception of the existing world and its developmental tendencies as disastrous and self-destructive and that will be replaced by the mirror image of a healed and natural world are all themes common to the past *Bewegungen* of modern German history. Despite the existence of hundreds of organizations and an equally impressive number of theoretical disputes, at bottom, the different movements of the past decade and a half and their organizations are the diffusion of one great social and cultural movement that seeks to replace the old politics with an alternative politics guided by the belief that we are living in the midst of an epochal break, as the result of which the old must give way to the new if there is to be a chance for human existence in the future. It is the coalescence of different protests into one oppositional movement, and the connection of this political romanticism to a revival of the issue of national identity that distinguishes the West German antinuclear movement from the peace movements in the other NATO countries in Western Europe.

The recent peace movements draw on the ideas and in some cases the leadership of the Kampf dem Atomtod movement of the 1950s against stationing tactical nuclear weapons in West Germany. While many of the themes of both movements are similar, the differences are important. First, the recent movements are much bigger. Given the preponderance of the young and educated, it is reasonable to assume that the recent peace movements are one of the unintended consequences of the rapid and considerable growth of the German university system since the 1960s. Second, the new social movements are supported by a considerable network of alternative newspapers and magazines. This expansion of the alternative scene also entailed a growth of "counterexperts." Where the debates of the fifties juxtaposed strategists and the people, by the 1980s the people could mobilize the resources of at least the language, if not always the substance, of strategic insight. Third, the Social Democrats present a more ambiguous picture in the 1980s. Unlike the SPD before Bad Godesberg, the party is unambiguously in favor of the Atlantic alliance. However, the militant anticommunism of Schumacher would now be out of favor as a relic of the cold war. Fourth, the romantic dimension in politics was studiously avoided by the Left in the 1950s; after the 1960s, it again became part of the left-wing repertoire. Fifth, where the peace movements of the 1950s were attacking the cold war with reference to their own views of European security, the peace movements of the 1980s often attacked the "new cold war" in the name of principles of *Ostpolitik* and detente articulated by the SPD from 1969 to 1982 while it was the governing party.

It was in the SPD that the peace movement had its most important political impact. Willy Brandt, Egon Bahr, Erhard Eppler, Gunter Gaus, and Oskar Lafontaine to different degrees have adopted the positions of the peace movement. From 1979 on, a considerable body of opinion in the SPD qualified its support for the 1979 decision, accentuating the negotiating track of the dual-track over the possible need actually to deploy the missiles. Helmut Schmidt found himself increasingly isolated within his own party, leading the CDU to charge correctly that he no longer was representative of the views of his party. A reading of the proceedings of the SPD party congresses from 1979 to 1983, when it voted against deployments, demonstrates that views changed relatively little over those four years. Schmidt and the minority that agreed with him supported both a strong defense as well as negotiation with the Soviets, while Brandt and Bahr talked of a European peace order and disarmament, and the dangers of the arms race without offering the ritual defense of a strong security policy.

The divisions over foreign policy added to already existing differences over fiscal and social policy within the SPD. The split between the Schmidt and Brandt wings of the party eventually became so severe that the Free Democrats left the social-liberal coalition in 1982 and formed a new government with the CDU/CSU in the fall of 1982. Both Brandt and Bahr were receptive to Soviet proposals to include British and French missiles in the Geneva negotiations over the NATO intermediate-range missiles, and raised doubts about the seriousness of the U.S. negotiating position in Geneva. Eppler juxtaposed the wisdom of the people and the madness of the experts, while Lafontaine and Bahr stressed the dependent position of the Federal Republic in matters concerning nuclear strategy and decision making. By late winter of 1983, Hans Joachim Vogel, once considered in the right wing of the party, ran as the party's candidate for chancellor with the slogan "in German interests." The SPD was now the advocate of a "patriotism of the Left"—because it was willing to reject the NATO decision. By the fall of 1983, a majority at a special party congress and again in the Bundestag voted against the deployments. In so doing, the victorious faction in the party claimed that the vote was not a repudiation of NATO or even the double decision but a statement that the negotiating track of the decision had not been pursued in good faith and that the deployments would bring less, not more, security to the Federal Republic. Schmidt's impassioned plea for the party to demonstrate its reliability and commitment to defense and detente largely fell on deaf ears. Without the penetration of the ideas of the peace movement, the peace movement would not have received public attention inside and outside West Germany. Of course, while rejecting the missiles the SPD affirmed its support for NATO, but it was undeniable that many of the arguments made by the peace movement had found a sympathetic hearing in the party.

Moreover, fear of nuclear war in the early 1980s was not restricted to new social movements. The foreign policy elites of the United States and Western Europe were also divided. In 1982, George Kennan, speaking at the German book fair after receiving its peace prize, rejected the NATO double-track decision as an answer to the Soviet intermediate-range missiles. The "whole complicated science" of strategic thinking about nuclear weapons was "morbid, nightmarish, and hopeless;" and the idea that nuclear war could be limited, was untenable. Kennan also bemoaned the militarization of U.S. foreign policy, and called for complete dismantling of the nuclear arsenals of all nations. [39]

Carl Friedrich von Weiszäcker repeatedly argued that more nuclear weapons were bringing less, not more, security and were increasing the danger of nuclear war, and that such a war was "probable" in the 1980s unless the arms race was stopped and reversed. Within U.S. politics, Paul Warnke, Robert McNamara, and McGeorge Bundy all expressed deep reservations about NATO nuclear policies. Although the no-first-use proposal was intended to foster increased conventional defense and hence deterrence, its public effect was to add to the antinuclear—and antidefense—chorus directed against NATO. [40]

The press, in particular *Der Spiegel* and *Der Stern*, has skillfully interpreted U.S. dissent to legitimate opposition to the 1979 decision, while placing official statements of the U.S. administration in the worst possible light. The role of the West German press as a filter of U.S. policy to its public was one of the residual effects of the radicalization of the intellectuals in the 1960s and played a crucial role in the growth of the peace movement. *Der Spiegel* devoted considerable attention to the theme of limited war, first-strike weapons, the loss of

West German sovereignty in nuclear matters, the peace movement in East Germany, and to Americans who were critical both of the NATO deployments and of the Reagan administration's foreign and military policies.

If *Der Spiegel* and *Der Stern* were ardent partisans against deployment, the Center as represented by *Die Zeit* was uncertain and on the defensive. Firmly rooted in th West, *Die Zeit* has given the dual-track decision lukewarm, almost resigned support, while often granting to left-wing critics fundamental points: Yes, deterrence causes insecurity but what else is there? No, the NATO weapons serve no military purpose and they probably do as much to couple as decouple Western Europe from the United States. Yes, the Americans have not been forthcoming enough in Geneva, but the Russians have been even worse. No, the real threat does not come from the NATO deployment but from a revival of a new cold war. When the dangers of nuclear war are vivid and the benefits of Western deterrence seem obscure, passion and conviction belong to the disarmers. The Center became insecure. The political-psychological balance of West German politics did indeed shift.

Especially during the first two years of the Reagan administration, the hard line and harsh words in Washington gave fuel to the peace movement in Western Europe. If the rhetoric of detente had led to U.S. wishful thinking about the Soviet Union, in Germany, detente's benefits were more tangible for the Germans. The U.S. strategic statements seeking to articulate a policy that would make changes in the technology of the arms race and in the size and quality of the Soviet arsenal reinforced the sense of dependence and limited sovereignty in West Germany. In the last year of the Carter administration and first year and a half of the Reagan administration, statements by the president and other leading officials about limited nuclear war offered the peace movement new debating points: The Americans want to displace the locus of nuclear conflict from the United States to Europe, especially Germany; Presidential Directive 59 (PD 59) issued in August of 1980, meant that the United States had now moved away from mutually assured destruction to a new nuclear war-fighting doctrine that assumed nuclear war could be won; the U.S. buildup was in preparation for a first strike against the Soviet Union using Western Europe as a convenient launching pad. The most-right-wing strategists who spoke the most casually about nuclear weapons were repeatedly quoted by the European peace movement and by the liberal and left-leaning press. Although the strategic insight of the peace movement is not, in fact, deep, it had learned to speak the language of nuclear jargon with a certainty that furthered the sense of fear and uncertainty, as if the *Friedensbewegung* were really the only group in society that cared about the preservation of peace.

Several themes were especially important in the expansion of the peace movement. First was the idea that the nuclear arms race is an irrational self-generating dynamic independent of the political motivations of the United States and Soviet Union. Because of the "overkill" capacities contained in the size of the existing nuclear arsenals, the peace movement attacked new weapons systems as superfluous and dangerous, and of such nature as to add to the likelihood of nuclear war. It argued that deterrence itself was the cause of this growing imminence of war. Second, the peace movement disputed the factual material presented by Western governments concerning the conventional and nuclear military balance in Europe and worldwide, as well as the very category of balance of military power as important in sustaining peace. On the one hand the peace movement presented figures to suggest that the military balance was not in favor of the Soviet Union in Europe but on the other hand, when faced with the issue of Soviet preponderance in intermediate-range land-based missiles, discounted the military and political significance of the SS-20s.

In view of the hostility to strategic argument in the peace movement, its fascination with particular weapons systems and the relative neglect of political issues that distinguished its public statements is interesting. Ultimately, opposition to the new missiles rested on three main assumptions. First, they were first-strike weapons turning West Germany into target and launching pad for an aggressive United States. Second, the NATO deployments, not the Soviet buildup, had upset the military balance (this even though at other times it was argued that the military balance no longer mattered). Third, the NATO deployments were a U.S. effort to limit nuclear war to Europe. [41]

The peace movement would have done better in the public debate if the Soviets had been less heavy-handed. Without any SS-20s at all, the Soviet Union's SS-4s and SS-5s outnumbered the British and French strategic weapons. In 1979, when the Soviets had deployed only thirty SS-20s with ninety warheads, Brezhnev claimed a balance of forces to exist in Europe. As the numbers grew over the four-year period to over 350 SS-20s with over 1,000 warheads without any NATO deployments, the Soviets continued to insist a balance existed. The peace movements in the West were placed on the defensive by such doublethink and by their own refusal to organize protest demonstrations at the Soviet embassies in the West. Who could really claim to speak for "German interests" and ignore the Soviets' attempt to redefine the meaning of nuclear parity to mean equality with all of their potential enemies combined?

The issue of the first-strike capabilities of the Pershing II was more telling, but the peace movement could not successfully explain how 108 single-warhead missiles could threaten 300 launch-control centers and 2,350 Soviet ICBMs and submarine-launched missiles. Even if the Pershing II had a range capable of reaching Moscow, which it is said not to have, it falls well short of the ICBM bases further to the east. A first-strike weapon leaving most of the Soviet arsenal intact would be pointless. In view of developments in U.S. submarine technology, the cruise and Pershing II do not offer the United States significant strategic advantages in terms of capacity to strike the Soviet Union.

The peace movement made a great deal of the fact that the Pershing II would take less than ten minutes to reach the Soviet Union, thus reducing warning time and forcing the Soviets to a launch-on-warning strategy that in a period of tension could increase the possibility of nuclear war. But it had little or nothing to say about the fact that the SS-20s would take no less time to reach Western Europe, or that the British and French missiles and the United States submarine missiles assigned to NATO since the 1960s have equally short warning times. Soviet submarines capable of launching missiles close to the United States coasts have not forced the United States into a launch-on-warning policy. What the Scowcroft Commission report said about the vulnerability of land-based U.S. missiles applies to the controversy over the Pershing II. If the Pershing IIs were launched at the Soviet Union, any element of surprise from missiles fired from the United States would be gone, for the Soviets would then be launching under attack, not launching on warning. Missiles fired from "close in"—for example, from West Germany to the Soviet Union—act as irrefutable proof that an attack has begun, thus making a "successful" first strike impossible. [42]

The argument that the United States wanted to limit nuclear war to Europe and therefore went ahead with the dual-track decision is the crux of the connection between the nuclear debate and the new national consciousness. This accusation was made despite the following facts: First, it was the West German chancellor, Helmut Schmidt, who first warned that the Soviet intermediate-range weapons should not be neglected in arms control agreements dealing with strategic weapons of the superpowers. Second, the purpose of the deployments was to reassure Western Europeans that the United States would not decouple from its commitments to Western Europe in face of the Soviet buildup. Third, it made no sense to leave 300,000 American troops and their dependents in Europe if the United States was planning a nuclear war that would destroy them as well. Fourth, U.S. missiles capable of reaching the Soviet Union mean that war is no longer limited to Central Europe, something that the shorter-range tactical nuclear weapons in Germany could not do. Hence they reinforce in the minds of the Soviet leadership the belief that an attack on Europe would lead to attacks on Soviet territory. Fifth, if the main goal of the United States were to limit a nuclear war to Europe, there were two more dependable methods. The first would be to do nothing and instead rely on tactical nuclear weapons and conventional forces now in existence. The second would be to withdraw from the Atlantic alliance. The 1979 dual-track decision was an effort to sustain both treaty commitments and peace.

The upshot of the peace movement's case was to reverse the rationale of the 1979 dual-track decision—from coupling to decoupling, from extended deterrence to limiting war, from renewing a U.S. commitment to run risks for the defense of Europe to indicating a U.S. willingness to defend Europe down to the last smoldering European—and to forestall reflection on the political purposes of the SS-20s as an ideal weapon to limit a nuclear war to *Western* Europe and exert political pressure. [43]

The successes the peace movement did have must be attributed in part to the vividness and clarity of the public's fear of nuclear war. Next to "Euroshima" in ruins, the arguments in favor of deterrence sound cold and heartless, for the arguments in favor of deterrence presuppose that if the West does not defend itself adequately, Western Europe would suffer the loss of its political freedom. But the image in the public mind of what that would mean is far less vivid or clear. Would the Soviets invade? If not, what would Soviet influence mean? However bad it might be, one could live to fight another day. Hence, the peace movement succeeded in convincing large numbers of people, especially the educated young, that the only clear and present danger about which Western Europe must think is nuclear war, rather than nuclear war and the specter of the Soviet Union and its growing military power. In so doing, the peace movement claimed moral superiority while at the same time suggesting that the moral values of the West are of little consequence compared to the prospect of nuclear holocaust.

Four groups have been at the forefront of the peace movement: the

Protestant churches, the alternative and ecological movements, communist-oriented groups, and independent socialists.

First, the Protestant churches were in the forefront of those stressing angst and fear of war. Pacifist ministers urged that the ethic of the Sermon on the Mount replace the cold calculations of power politics in the nuclear era. They called for one-sided disarmament and sought to ground particular political proposals such as rejection of the NATO dual-track decision with religious reasons. They contributed little to the discussion of security policy other than to argue that security lies in Western steps to disarmament, which will then lead to Soviet reciprocity. In place of supposedly threatening NATO policies, the Protestant ministers favored "social defense," a nonviolent form of "defense without weapons" that is claimed will deter aggression by signaling the potential aggressor that the country at risk would be ungovernable if conquered because of the resistance of the civilian population. This ooze of good intentions has been politically consequential above all in the annual *Kirchentag*, which in 1981 and 1982 brought together up to 150,000 young people to reinforce one another's angst concerning nuclear weapons and to denounce the NATO double-track decision. The Protestant churches must be given considerable credit for extending the peace movement beyond the left-wing ghetto. The highly emotional mixture of religion and politics characteristic of this aspect of the peace movement makes it an apocalyptic movement. [44]

The religious dimensions of the peace movement in West Germany recall the issues raised by Max Weber in "Politics as a Vocation" (1920), namely, the conflict between the ethics of absolute conviction *(Gesinnungsethik)* and the ethics of responsibility *(Verantwortungsethik)*. Then Weber was addressing his criticisms to young left-wing communists and anarchists who believed that the ethic of the Sermon on the Mount could replace the realities of force and violence in relations between states. Certainly if Weber had read works such as *Frieden ist Moglich: Die Politik der Bergpredigt,* a book by one of West Germany's most well known televison news personalities, Franz Alt, he would have noticed the ethics of absolute conviction live on. [45] Alt's book is of interest both for its intrinsic contents—visions of imminent catastrophe, emotionalism, politicized religion, and a moralistic contempt for politics as usual, combined with utopian visions of the world turned upside down—and because it is a genuine best-seller that reaches beyond the Left and the universities to a broader, television-watching public.

The message is simple: We are militarily preparing for "the end of creation." It is "an illusion" to believe that diplomacy and common sense can prevent the worst from happening. However, the means to prevent nuclear holocaust is at hand, namely, the politics of the Sermon on the Mount. "If you want peace, prepare for peace." To begin with, we need a transformation of our hearts, for we are all already "psychologically contaminated" by nuclear weapons. Then the West should reject the NATO deployments, which are the quintessential product of political expertise; they will make the Federal Republic a launching pad for U.S. missiles and a target for the Soviets' SS-20s. The laity must take matters into its own hands to "save the world" from the politicians and military experts who are leading us down the road to "the end of humanity and the planet."

The goal is great but the path is clear. "Make peace without weapons" or, more realistically, "with ever fewer weapons." This, in Alt's view, is simply practical reason, not the irrationality of the "pure reason" that fills the heads of nuclear strategists. The nuclear cul-de-sac is the result of our "split" and excessive rationality. Peace demands that the schools once again encourage us to return to our emotions and intuitions, our "fantasies of survival." In view of the prospect of nuclear holocaust, the old questions of "capitalism and socialism" are of minor importance compared to the primacy of life and peace. In their nuclear policies, both superpowers do what they accuse the other of doing.

The nuclear abyss reopens the German question. For the first time since 1945, there is "a really all-German idea," the idea of peace that binds both East and West Germans together. The conflict of "systems" has become unimportant, for the main enemy, nuclear weapons, is "beyond the ideologies of the blocs." Alt urges that both Germanys be part of a demilitarized, nuclear-free zone that, along the lines Bahro has discussed, leads to a new national identity. The peace movement is a "liberation movement" seeking to free Germans from the inability to feel sorrow and sadness, from the obsession with power and wealth, "not from insecurity but from our security complex. . . . Only he who frees himself is free. . . . Salvation is not for the next world. This world is not beyond salvation." [46]

The emergence of Protestant moralism on the Left is one of the most significant changes in the political and moral landscape of the Federal Republic and has done much to spread the peace movement beyond the confines of left-wing intellectuals, the alternative scene, and the SPD Left—although some of these groups, especially the SPD Left, overlap with the new Protestant moralism and pacifism.

Ökopax is the acronym that suggests the synthesis of the ecology and peace movements.[47] The ecology movement sees in nuclear weapons and defense policy generally a waste of resources that could be used for social purposes at home and for the Third World. More important it sees in nuclear weapons the horrific end point of *"Grosstechnologie"*—large-scale technology—and the domination of nature. The extension of an airport runway in Frankfurt aroused large and continuing protest—far more than did the Polish coup and the suppression of Solidarity—that focused on the destruction of forest needed to complete the project as well as on what were alleged to be the military uses of the runway. The ecologists argued that the way to avoid war is not through military preparation but through an ecological program of soft-energy and conservation that will make possible energy autarky. There is much talk of "alternative security policy" from the Ökopax current in the peace movement, most of which refers to the proposals by peace researcher Horst Afheldt for a national network of decentralized, locally based "techno-guerrillas" armed with modern antitank weapons.[48] The Afheldt proposals address the dilemma of defense versus deterrence in West Germany, but do so without serious consideration for the scope of the power of the Warsaw Pact's military buildup. They combine hopes in decentralized technology with the mistrust of the centalized state and forms of organization that is common in the ecology movement. Their appeal lies in the image of a citizens' militia carrying out guerrilla operations against the invader. It is that rather than any serious contribution to raising the nuclear threshold which accounts for whatever appeal the proposals may have received.[49]

The third group active in the peace movement is independent socialists who seek a "third way" between capitalist, industrial societies and the bureaucratic state socialism of the Communist countries. They view the peace movement as an attempt to break the logic of "bipolarity" that the superpowers impose on Europe. They argue that the sovereignty and independence of German politics require that the Federal Republic decouple from the United States as a precondition for peace in Germany. The corollary to these views is interest in neutralism, an illusory hope for the cooperation of both German states in the securing of peace that could lead to the process of national reunification. By the late 1970s, independent socialists had incorporated many of the themes of the ecologists, and the overlap in outlook and persons was considerable.[50]

The fourth main group in the peace movement, aside from a large, nonorganized group of nuclear pacifists who are suspicious of any kind of nuclear deterrence, is the groups and organizations organized and directed by Communist groups loyal to and dependent on East Germany and the Soviet Union. They played a not unimportant role in the first large public letter of the peace movement, the Krefeld appeal, were active in the organization of the mass demonstrations in Bonn protesting NATO deployments, and assumed a role far out of proportion to their numbers in peace movement organizations. The Communist groups did not dominate the peace movement. A movement as heterogenous as the peace movement is not directed from the outside; however, the very heterogeneity of the new social movements did allow the Communist groups to exploit their own organizational coherence and play a role more important than their numbers would suggest. Despite the declared "plague-on-both-your-houses" outlook of most of the peace movement, the least common denominator in the movement remains opposition to the NATO deployments, and this goal does, of course, suit the interest of the Soviets.

For Communist groups such as the German Communist party (DKP) the peace movement was a classic example of a popular front. German youth, the ecology movements, churches, trade unions, feminists, and peace groups mobilized around the least common denominator: in this case, no new nuclear weapons in Europe (thus excluding the Soviets' SS-20s), unilateral disarmament in the West, which will supposedly lead to Soviet reciprocity, and a nuclear-free zone in Europe. The Communist groups in the peace movement were not interested in the great utopian visions of the Greens, nor did they make their mass appeal on the basis of class struggle or nationalization of the means of production. Rather, they presented themselves as the true representatives of peace and national independence, and sought support on that basis. While Communist-oriented groups remained a very small minority of the movement, the fact remains that no large-scale demonstrations were ever organized against missiles already deployed against Western Europe by the Soviet Union. [51]

At the end of four years of controversy over the NATO dual-track decision, the political balance sheet read as follows. The Greens were in parliament but internally torn by conflicts between fundamentalists and pragmatists. The coalition of the FDP and CDU/CSU had weathered the missile deployments and was hoping for economic recovery to sustain its electoral majority. The SPD was in a state of exhausted ambiguity. Its yes to NATO and no to the missiles in the fall of 1983 provoked conflicting interpretations—a party of neutralism or nuclear sanity, depending on one's point of view.

In thinking about where the Social Democrats will be headed for the remainder of the 1980s, it is useful to remember that they were not dragged against their will to sympathize with the peace movement and reject the NATO deployments. The peace movement pushed the SPD to the left but the interpretation of detente and *Ostpolitik* articulated by Brandt and Bahr also lent encouragement and conceptual weight to the movements from below. Both the break in the consensus over Western security and the emergence of the peace movement in the early 1980s are inexplicable without taking into account the hopes—and illusions—raised during the preceding decade of detente. East-West detente continued the delegitimation of anti-communism begun during the war in Vietnam among large segments of public opinion while fostering the view that the East-West conflict itself was either over or in a state of permanent latency. Hence the need for a strong Western military defense appeared anachronistic if the Soviet Union was, in Egon Bahr's term, in a relationship of *Sicherheitspartnerschaft* with Western Europe.

In West Germany, detente brought additional benefits: better relations with the GDR, more access for families in both countries, and the hope that the U.S.-Soviet thaw would loosen up the blocs and perhaps leave room for resolving the German question. As Pierre Hassner has noted, to be told that the party was over, that the old bad news about the Soviets must be taken seriously, and that more money was needed for the military during a period of economic difficulty produced bitterness and denial of unpleasant facts. The reversal of a positive development was hard to bear, entailing as it did a return to values and priorities of the older generation that had been under severe attack for a decade and that were based on completely different postwar experience. To add insult to injury, the main purveyor of the bad news—other than the left–wing Guallists with their own independent nuclear deterrent—was the most conservative U.S. president in half a century. [52]

Detente, in Bahr's view, also expanded West German room for maneuver in foreign policy. Superpower bipolarity and tension "leads without doubt to an expansion of military thinking and to its predominance over political thinking. It leads to a weakening of Europe, to easier domination of Western Europe by the United States." Security thus means reducing tensions between the superpowers. This will allow for increased room for maneuver to reopen the German question. Certainly war would mean the end of the German nation. Peace is thus the basic presupposition for dealing with the German question. In Bahr's view, threats to peace in Europe in the late 1970s and early 1980s came as much from the United States as from the Soviet Union. While claiming to support a strong defense policy, Bahr also attacked the CDU/CSU for slavish obedience to U.S. policy and suggested that U.S. and West German interests in matters of war and peace were not always convergent. [53]

The dialectic between *Ostpolitik,* the emergence of the peace movements, and West German neutralism was most fully articulated by one of detente's earliest and most articulate advocates, Peter Bender, in *Das Ende des Ideologischen Zeitalters* (1981). [54] Bender puts forth the following theses:

First, the time has arrived for Europe, meaning Eastern as well as Western Europe, to assert its own identity in the face of growing superpower tensions. This form of European self-assertion and independence calls for efforts to reduce the dangerous tensions between the United States and the Soviets, to remove Europe gradually from their conflict, and to move toward a settlement of the postwar division of the Continent. What unites Europe above all is a defense of detente against the efforts of both superpowers to undermine it.

Second, detente and *Ostpolitik* mark the end of the age of ideological struggle between East and West. The "real existing socialist states" have become normal states with whom a normal diplomatic relationship is possible and desirable based on mutual self-interest independent of ideology. The age of totalitarianism is over. The totalitarian enemy of yesterday has become today's security and trade partner. Interdependence has replaced bitter rivalry. The Communists no longer define themselves as involved in a historically necessary conflict with the noncommunist world, while in the West noncommunists have abandoned anticommunism as a primitive relic of a simpler age. "With emancipation from the communities of faith, the old world began a new chapter."

Third, the nature of European security has changed. It now amounts to expanding East-West economic and cultural contacts rather than sustaining a military balance that is impossible to define anyway. Furthermore, Europe and especially divided Germany must pursue a security policy different from that of the United States, one more suited to West Germany's geographical proximity to the East. The real threat to Europe's security is not the Soviet Union but the Soviet-U.S. relationship. Resistance to U.S. bellicosity and fixation on the communist menace is crucial for European security. The Europeans must leave the arms race or "become satellites in a conflict that is no longer their own."

Fourth, the Soviet Union does not present a serious security threat to Western Europe. The internal economic difficulties of the USSR, the centrifugal pulls of empire in Eastern Europe, and the growing power of China all suggest that the Soviets are more interested in co-operation than conflict with Western Europe. To assume that the Soviets would use their nuclear arsenal to blackmail Western Europe is simplistic militaristic thinking that mistakenly assumes that rockets and soldiers can provide security. For Bender, the balance or imbalance of military power becomes a decidedly secondary issue to that of war and peace.

Fifth, the solution of the German question must be part of a gradual reduction of tensions and loosening of the alliances in Eastern and Western Europe. So long as Western Europe holds onto Atlanticism, reform in Eastern Europe will be impossible. Only when Western Europe ceases to be a platform for U.S. rockets and radio stations will the Soviets allow the spread of democracy in Eastern Europe. Bender repeats the lament of "national denial" in both East and West Germany in the postwar years. The false identifications of the fifties must give way to greater consideration of West Germany's geographical, cultural, military, and emotional proximity to the East.

Sixth, while Bender denies that he is advocating neutralism or leaving the Atlantic alliance, his view of the role of alliance membership focuses on making it an instrument for detente and for exerting a moderating influence over the Americans. He argues that West German foreign policy can do more to moderate U.S. foreign policy toward the Soviets by remaining formally in the alliance than by leaving it. But what would remain of NATO as a military alliance remains unclear.

In light of such views, it is not surprising that Bender rejects the NATO dual-track decision with arguments that are identical to those of the peace movement. The weapons were part of a U.S. first-strike strategy. They were an attempt to see that nuclear war would not touch the United States. Western Europe was for the Americans what Cuba was for the Soviets in 1962: a highly vulnerable launching pad. He accepts the Soviets' view that their SS-20s should be counted against British and French missiles in the INF talks. Real European security for Bender lies in making Europe a nuclear-free zone and restricting nuclear deterrence to the United States and the Soviet Union.

The strategic objections to Bender's analysis of the dual-track decision are obvious and have been repeated often. The purpose and effect of the NATO deployments are to couple the United States even more firmly to the defense of Europe and to balance a growing threat from the Soviet Union's military buildup. The decision was originally a West European initiative. Limiting war to Europe is not done by deploying missiles that reach the territory of one's main opponent. But strategic debates are beside the point in the absence of a political and moral consensus as to the meaning of the Atlantic alliance. It is this consensus that Bender's interpretation of detente undermines.

There was nothing left here of the antitotalitarian consensus of the postwar years. Anticommunism was simply an embarrassment. The hopes for European unity founded on a shared commitment to the West and a self-reliant common defense are now based on a desire to be left out of a conflict that, for Bender, was and is not really Europe's business. What is manifest is a wholly one-sided interpretation of the meaning of detente. The Soviet Union has not ceased its ideological assault on Western capitalist democracies. The ideological age that Bender believes has ended applies only to the willingness of the West to continue the intellectual and moral struggle with the Soviet Union. In this sense, *Das Ende des Ideologischen Zeitalter* is a plea for a unilateral, moral, and political cease-fire that precedes and rationalizes unilateral military restraint.

Bender's views on the Soviet Union were disproven by events. As its military power grew he argued that military power no longer guarantees security. As it deployed ever more missiles aimed at Western Europe, he denied that they could be used for purposes of blackmail or political pressure. While the Soviets crush free trade unions in Poland for reasons having absolutely nothing to do with the Atlantic alliance, Bender suggested that a U.S. withdrawal from Western Europe would serve the cause of reform in the East. While he spoke of a Europeanized Europe, his views of the Soviet Union and the needs of Western security would leave Western Europe open to the very blackmail and pressures he assured his readers are part of a bygone era. In the last analysis, Bender is telling us that the conflict between "both superpowers" does not involve a fundamental clash of political and moral values, and that to suggest that it does is to consign oneself to the primitive certainties of a simpler and bygone age.

The Polish crisis of the early 1980s also points to problems in Bender's assumptions concerning the degree of commonality between the governments of Western and Eastern Europe and their respective publics, as well as the degree of autonomy the governments of Eastern Europe possess in relation to Moscow. *Ostpolitik* has important accomplishments to its credit, but as the events in Czechoslovakia and Poland have shown, the optimistic view that Western detente diplomacy and economic assistance would lead to political reform and economic revival in Eastern Europe that the Soviet Union would or could tolerate has proven to be excessive. The idea that

Western detente could lead to liberalization in Eastern Europe was one grounded more in a mixture of Western goodwill and economic self-interest than in real developments within the Soviet bloc. It has been the fear of contagion of solidarity within the Warsaw Pact, not the threat of NATO, that led to martial law in Poland. The arguments of the peace movements of Western Europe in the last five years concerning the commonality of themes in the peace movements of East and West suggest that the wish was father to the thought. Even if, which is doubtful, the old "ideological" contrast between freedom and dictatorship were not important to the dissidents in East Germany because of the primacy of the national issue, this would be the exception in Eastern Europe. In Poland and Czechoslovakia, the basic themes of protest have been civil and political freedom, free trade unions, pluralism, and renewal of civil society, not peace and ecology.

It is not surprising that after nearly fifteen years in which ideas such as Bender's about East-West relations, the nature of the Soviet Union, and purposes of the Atlantic alliance have been expressed by a significant segment, indeed now a majority, of the Social Democratic party both in and out of power, the young generation in West Germany should have taken some of these ideas to heart. The peace movement—and ultimately neutralism—are the last stop of detente according to Bender, Brandt, and Bahr. When Brandt repeatedly says that in the nuclear era there is no alternative to a policy of negotiation with the Soviet Union, he is certainly right. But what he neglects to add is that negotiations can be successful only if conducted from a position of strength. The leitmotif of Helmut Schmidt's views on German foreign policy was precisely the need for such a balance between cooperation and strategic balance, political competence and moral leadership. It was the inability to sustain this complexity, that is, to defend both negotiation and deterrence, to defend liberty while maintaining peace within the Social Democratic party in the 1970s that furthered the development of the peace movement from below in the early 1980s.

For Brandt and Bahr, *Wandel durch Annäherung* (change through rapprochement) meant that communism would moderate the rigidity of its ideology if the West moderated its rejection of that ideology. What the Brandt school of detente has refused to face is that this was always a one-sided game. The integrity of communist ideology is more important for communist politics than detente implied. Even in Poland, where communist ideology collapsed in a spectacular fashion, the concept of the leading role of the Communist party—even if carried out by the army—remained an unshakable article of faith. *Wandel durch Annäherung* transformed the doctrine of detente as a doctrine of coexistence demanded by foreign policy in the nuclear age, that is, a pragmatic adjustment in the face of the power of the atom, into what it was not intended to be, namely, a doctrine of ideological coexistence. As Hermann Lubbe has rightly pointed out, a policy of successful coexistence requires more, not less, ideological defense and confrontation; more, not less, clarification of the issues at stake precisely because one must coexist with an ideological opponent. If the West refuses to continue the conflict on an intellectual, moral, and ideological level, detente becomes *Wandel durch Annäherung*, but it is the West, not the Soviet Union, that faces the loss of its identity. Anticommunism is not an alternative but must remain a constitutive element of the blend of the West's detente and deterrence. The point is not only that to drop ideological conflict is tantamount to unilateral disarmament on the moral and intellectual level, or only that the Soviet Union has never stopped its ideological assault on the West and its values. The most corrosive consequence of detente defined as "change through rapprochement" is the debilitating but logical conclusion drawn by Peter Bender: Why bother? The differences between East and West are too minimal to justify running such high risks. [55]

CONCLUSION

First, when political complexity is not sustained by political leaders, it will not survive at the grass roots either. The advocates of *Ostpolitik* turned detente from a means in an ongoing conflict with the Soviet Union into an end in itself. In so doing, they suggested that the balance of power had ceased to matter in the preservation of peace and freedom in Europe.

U.S. foreign policy has often been justly criticized for lack of complexity, for reducing political issues to an exclusively military dimension. The emergence of the peace movements and the turn away from the NATO deployments by the SPD represented an erosion of complexity of an opposite sort, namely, neglecting the military dimensions of diplomacy as well as the political aspects of the strategic balance of power.

Second, neutralism has a constituency in West German intellectual and political life. Neo-Marxism, left-wing Protestant moralism, the romanticism of the Greens, the counterexpertise among the peace researchers, new patriotism in the media, and the SPD Left all contributed to a search for a third way. Any U.S. president who was determined to proceed with the NATO dual-track decision would have incurred the wrath of these currents. Given that these trends have been rather long in developing, it would be unreasonable to assume that they will soon cease to have an impact on West German politics and public opinion. But they are far from soon representing a majority viewpoint.

Third, the peace movement was an explosion of utopian hope and apocalyptic fear whose main vision was of a neutralist, nuclear-free, bloc-free Germany at last out from under the historical burdens of the war and postwar settlement. In the late 1970s, the West German Left returned home. Utopia was no longer sought in Vietnam or Cuba but in Frankfurt and Berlin. The peace movements have not emerged in Eastern Europe nor have the "first-strike weapons" been launched. "Antiauthoritarianism" has bumped up against Soviet negotiating tactics. But there are many missiles yet to be deployed. In short, the peace movement may subside, but the issues it has raised will continue on in West German politics.

Fourth, the SPD will remain a fog of political ambiguity, softly claiming adherence to Atlanticism while loudly warning of the dangers of the arms race and the need for arms control for the sake of the interests of the Germans. To claim that the SPD turned against missile deployment because it enjoyed the luxury of being in the opposition is to forget that it fell into the opposition in considerable degree because large parts of the party had never really accepted the need for the missiles to begin with. If the SPD should return to power in the next several years, its verbal Atlanticism will be put to the test, perhaps in the context of economic difficulties. At present, the meaning of its commitment to Western defense is unclear.

The contrast between the German Social Democrats and the French Socialists in their view of the Soviet Union and European security is striking in every regard. In the 1970s, the left-wing intellectuals in France turned to anti-Sovietism, while the West German Left rediscovered the nation and defended detente. The defense of nation in Mitterand's France has incorporated the left into the Gaullist consensus—independence and autonomy over nuclear weapons while remaining outside NATO—and has fostered French desires for more European defense efforts. In the same period, defense of the nation for the Left in West Germany meant defense of detente and rejection of the revised version of Soviet capabilities and intentions that had come to predominate in Paris. Finally, where the French spoke of the need for greater European defense efforts to balance the power of the

Soviet Union, to create a basis for autonomy from U.S. policy, and to ward off the specter of West German neutralism, the West German Left believed the path to national autonomy for nonnuclear Germany lay in a gradual movement toward overcoming the division of the country through more detente, and distancing from U.S. policy.

Fifth, what of the Soviet Union? It failed to prevent deployment of the missiles or to split Western Europe off from the United States. True, North European Social Democracy turned against the missile deployments, but the French and Italian Socialists did not. The Soviets failed to make the missile issue a simple battle between the forces of imperialism and war and those of class struggle and peace. European socialism is too complex for that. European political unity remains a distant goal but so does the Soviet hope of splitting the Western alliance. If the two Germanys want to talk to each other, it may be that the Federal Republic will be able to play the game well enough to separate its policy toward the GDR from its policy toward the Soviet Union. Detente can be divisible in both directions. The Soviets have already deployed their missiles, have no demonstrations to worry about, and can patiently wait for more West European annoyance with the stubborn Americans. One hopeful sign may be that Soviet diplomacy proved itself too heavy-handed to play on the anxieties of the Western publics. A cause for concern is that the military "balance" remains unbalanced and a considerable West European effort will be required in the years to come to correct it. [56]

Sixth, one lesson of the Euromissile episode is that it is important to recognize the basically asymmetrical relations between the two Germanys and between West Germany and the Soviet Union. If West German-Soviet detente is made irreversible for the sake of continued good relations between East and West Germany regardless of the actions of the Soviet Union in Eastern Europe and the Third World, or in terms of its military buildup directed at Western Europe itself, the Soviets gain leverage in undermining Western unity and in potentially isolating the Federal Republic from the West. Lack of symmetry is also inherent in East-West arms-control negotiations in which public pressure is applied to only one side for agreements. Contrary to what became the conventional wisdom concerning the end of the era of bipolarity, detente has not diminished East German integration into the Warsaw Pact, while it has encouraged West German visions of an emancipation from Atlanticism. The triangular relationship between the Soviet Union, the GDR, and the Federal Republic exposes the West Germans to a strategy of manipulation that can be effectively countered only by Western correction of the strategic imbalance, and not by negotiations alone. Only a West Germany firmly rooted in the Western alliance can aim at "Finlandization" of East Germany and avoid being "Finlandized" itself.

Seventh, a stable parliamentary democracy exists on German soil, a fact that deserves more mention in discussions about the absence of an adequate national identity in the Federal Republic. The differences between the political systems of the two Germanys have not precluded and ought not to preclude many contacts, but these many contacts have not diminished the dictatorial essence of the German Democratic Republic. At some point in the (probably distant) future, the Soviet Union may conclude that it must put its own house in order and release its East European satellites. In the meantime, hopes for German cultural and political unity should be combined with the hope for freedom in Eastern Europe as well. "German interests" will be best served by stressing the indivisibility of peace and freedom. [57] Germany does not need yet another national identity grounded in romanticism and anti-Western sentiments. The Federal Republic is a welcome break with German illiberalism. Only a search for national identity firmly rooted in the liberal traditions of democracy and individual liberty can avoid the errors and illusions that caused so much grief in the last century. [58]

Finally, it is tempting to focus on the gap between the experts and the people as a contributing factor to West Germany's political uncertainties. But the erosion of the security consensus in the Federal Republic was not primarily the result of the challenge of democracy to technocracy. Rather, the moral order of liberal democracy was fractured under the combined impact of a return of political romanticism and the national question, the legacies of the radical Left from the 1960s, and the erosion of complexity in foreign policy in the era of detente. Neutralist sentiment and the illusions of a third way grew on confusion over the moral foundations of the Western alliance. Relegitimation of the alliance, of West Germany's role in it, and of deterrence as a strategy calls for political leadership willing and able to draw upon and articulate the meaning of the West's often unappreciated traditions of political freedom and liberty.

NOTES

1. On the political consensus of the Federal Republic, see: Karl Dietrich Bracher, *Geschichte und Gewalt* (Berlin: Severin & Siedler, 1981); Richard Lowenthal, "Why German Stability Is So Insecure," *Encounter* (January 1982): 31-37; *Kulturkrise und Gesellschaftswandel* (1976); and Kurt Sontheimer, *Die verunsicherte Republik* (Hamburg: Hoffman & Campe, 1979).

For poll data on the extent of neutralist or pacifist sentiments, see Elisabeth Noelle-Neumann, ed., *The Germans: Public Opinion Polls, 1967–1980* (London: Greenwood Press, 1981); and the polls of the Emnid Institut on West German attitudes toward the United States, Russia, neutralism, and NATO. On the political views of university students, see Christian Krause, *Zwischen Revolution und Resignation. Alternativkultur, politische Grundströmungen und Hochschulaktivitäten in der Studentenschaft* (Bonn: Friedrich Ebert Stiftung, 1980). On the prevalence of neutralism, see Dieter Just and Peter Caspar Mulhens, "Zur Wechselbeziehung von Politik und Demoskopie—Das Beispiel der aktuellen Sicherheitspolitik," *Das Parlament* (8 August 1981): 23-27. On the radicalization of the young, see Stephen F. Szabo, *The Successor Generation: International Perspectives of Postwar Europeans* (London: Butterworth, 1983). For a report from *Der Spiegel* on angst that is an excellent example of the use of public opinion data to try to bring about the attitudes being examined, see Joe Leinemann, *Die Angst der Deutschen* (Hamburg: Rowohlt Verlag, 1982). For a general view of changes in West Germany's political culture, see Kenneth Baker, Russell J. Dalton, and Kai Hildebrand, *Germany Transformed* (Cambridge: Harvard University Press, 1981). The major conclusions of the public opinion polls are the following: First, there is a strikingly persistent and firm majority of the electorate that for over three decades favors integration into the Western alliance, and an equally persistent minority—between 25 and 40 percent—that favors equally good relations with the United States and the Soviet Union. Second, those in favor of leaving NATO are a small minority, but those who support "equally good relations with both superpowers" are considerably larger in number, especially among the young, where over 40 percent have advocated such views in recent years. Third, support for the NATO dual-track decision varies widely depending on how questions are asked; consistently about 30 to 40 percent are in favor, about an equal number opposed, and the rest undecided. Claims that a majority of the population are opposed to the dual-track decision are not borne out by polls that include questions about the Soviet's SS-20s and the importance of arms control. In short, while nationalism, nuclear pacifism, and neutralism have won the day for the time being in the SPD, they have not won the hearts of the electorate. An honest reader of the poll data would conclude that neutralism is not the path to take for politicians eager for electoral triumphs. However, the support for the peace movement and the Greens is higher among the young and educated, the "successor generation," those born since 1950. A 1981 survey conducted by German Shell found that of those between 15 and 24 years of age, 32 percent had no party affiliation; 20 percent supported the Greens; 24 percent the SPD; 18 percent, the CDU; and 6 percent, the Liberals. A number of polls have indicated that 41 percent of the 36-year-olds with higher education constitute the activist base of the peace movement; that 43 percent of self-described pacifists are under 29 years of age; that the young and better educated are the most likely to support the goals of the peace movement, to oppose INF deployment, nuclear deterrence, and defense spending, to be sanguine about the military balance, and less likely to be disturbed by the prospect that the Soviet Union would use military force for political ends in Europe. In the famous "red or dead" choice offered by pollsters, in the early 1980s 56 percent of postwar German respondents chose the "red" compared to 44 percent of the prewar generation. There has also been a dramatic rise in the number of conscientious objector applications, from 3,000 per year in the 1960s to 50,000-60,000 in the early 1980s.

2. See Kurt Sontheimer, *Das Elend unserer Intellektuellen* (Hamburg: Hoffman & Campe, 1976).

3. Kurt Sontheimer, *Die Verunsicherte Republik* (Munich: Piper Verlag, 1979). In his speech to the SPD Parteitag in November 1983 in defense of the NATO dual-track decision, Helmut Schmidt, in addition to offering reasons concerning deterrence, the military balance, and the Western alliance, stressed the importance of constitutionalism, parliamentary majorities, and democracy. In reference to the peace movement, he said, "Whoever disregards these rules can endanger freedom!" Helmut Schmidt, "Die Deutschen müssen berechenbar bleiben," *Frankfurter Allgemeine Zeitung*, 21 November 1983, p. 2.

4. For a representative expression of the antiparliamentary stance of the radical Left, see Roland Roth, ed., *Parlamentarisches Ritual und politische Alternativen* (Frankfurt/Main: Campus Verlag, 1980), in particular essays by Claus Offe, Wolf-Dieter Narr, Joachim Hirsch, and Herbert Kitschelt, all of which seek to demonstrate that the claim of parliamentary democracy to express rule by the people is a fiction. In proposals declaring a specific city a "nuclear-free zone" or calls for referenda on the NATO deployments, the peace movement has expressed impatience with parliamentary democracy. On the antiparliamentary aspects of the peace movement, see George Paul Hefty's critical commentary on the movement's proposals for a national referendum on the NATO deployments, "Angriff auf die Demokratie," *Frankfurter Allgemeine Zeitung,* 6 July 1983, p. 1.

5. See *Friedensforschung—Entscheidungshilfe Gegen Gewalt*, ed. Manfred Funke (Munich: Paul List Verlag, 1975) for a representative collection of critical peace research. For an incisive critical commentary, see Frederick Tenbruck's essay "Frieden durch Friedensforschung? Ein Heilsglaube unserer Zeit," pp. 425-39.

6. Typical of the criticisms of (Western policies and strategies) deterrence are Carola Bielfeldt and Peter Schlotter, *Die militärische Sicherheitspolitik der Bundesrepublik* (Frankfurt/Main: Campus Verlag, 1980); *Das kontrollierte Chaos: Die Krise der Abrüstung*, ed. Reiner Steinweg (Frankfurt/Main: Suhrkamp Verlag, 1980); *Alternativen zur Abschreckungs Politik*, ed. Jürgen Tatz (Freiburg, Br.: Dreisam-Berlag, 1983). For a representative example of "peace pedagogy," much criticized as unvarnished propaganda, see *Friedenspädagogik Heute: Theorie und Praxis*, ed. Hermann Pfister (Waldkirch: Waldkircher Verlag, 1980). *Der Stern* and *Der Spiegel* reproduce the arguments of the critical peace researchers. See, for example, a book by two editors of *Der Stern*: Wolf Perdelwitz and Heiner Bremer, *Geisel Europa* (Berlin: Olle & Wolter, 1981).

7. On Galtung, see Pierre Hassner, "On Ne Badine Pas Avec La Paix,"

Revue français de science politique 23 (December 1973): 1268-1303; Tenbruck, "Frieden durch Friedensforschung?"; Helmut Schelsky, *Die Arbeit tun die Anderen* (Opladen: Westdeutscher Verlagn, 1975), pp. 290-97; Sontheimer, *Das Elend unserer Intellektuellen.*

8. Dieter Senghaas, *Abschreckung und Frieden: Studien zur Kritik organi-sierter Friedlosigkeit* (Frankfurt/Main: Europäische Verlagsanstalt, 1969, 1981).

9. See *Feindbilder*, ed. Reiner Steinweg (Frankfurt/Main: Suhrkamp Ver-lag, 1975). Other topics covered in the series published by Suhrkamp, one of West Germany's largest publishers of trade books, include: un-derdevelopment, aggression and socialization, wars in the Third World, and anticommunism (but nothing on the armaments of the So-viet Union).

10. Some examples of the mobilization of critical peace research against the NATO dual-track decision are Dieter Lutz, ed., *Weltkrieg wider Willen? Die Nuklearwaffen in und für Europa* (Hamburg: Rowohlt Ver-lag, 1981)—Lutz is the director of the institute for peace research and security policy at the University of Hamburg; Alfred Mechtersheimer, ed., *Nachrüsten? Dokumente und Positionen zum NATO-Doppelbesch-luss* (Hamburg: Rowohlt Verlag, 1981)—Rowohlt has played an impor-tant role in publishing material attacking the NATO deployments. *Weltkrieg wider Willen*, bursting with charts and numbers of weapon systems, is a good example of the strangely apolitical and quite tech-nocratic fascination for the details of weapons systems found in the generally antimodernist and apocalyptic peace movement.

11. For Bloch's analysis of the Left's excessive rationalism in the years be-fore 1933, see *Erbschaft dieser Zeit* (Frankfurt/Main: Suhrkamp Verlag, 1962). For a recent combination of socialist and ecological themes, see the report of a 1978 conference held at the University of Tübingen, *Marxismus und Naturbeherrschung* (Offenbach: Verlag 2000, 1978).

12. Rudolf Bahro, *Die Alternative* (Frankfurt/Main: Europäische Verlags-anstalt, 1979).

13. In *Elemente einer neuen Politik* (1980); translation, *Socialism and Sur-vival* (London: Heretic Books, 1982).

14. Ibid., p. 16.

15. Ibid., pp. 138-39.

16. Rudolf Bahro and Michael Vester, "Seven Taboos and a Perspective," *Telos* 51 (Spring 1982): 45-52.

17. Bahro, *Socialism and Survival*, p. 143.

18. Ibid., "Who Can Stop the Apocalypse? Or the Task, Substance and Strategy of Social Movements," pp. 143-57.

19. Rudolf Bahro, "The SPD and the Peace Movement," *New Left Review.*

20. For a very helpful report on the Greens, see Robert Pfaltzgraff, Jr., et al, *The Greens of West Germany: Origins, Strategies and Transatlantic Implications* (Cambridge, Mass.: Institute for Foreign Policy Analysis, 1983). The Greens' general program and "analyses on the atomic threat and on paths to peace," respectively, are to be found in *Die Grünen: Das Bundesprogramm* (Munich, n.d.) and *Entrüstet Euch* (Munich, n.d.). *Entrüstet Euch* is a collection of essays on disarmament including

contributions by peace researchers Horst Afheldt and Alfred Mechtersheimer, the Protestant theologian Helmut Gollwitzer, Petra Kelly, E.P. Thompson, and Rudolf Bahro.

21. See Petra Kelly and Jo Leinen, eds., *Prinzip Leben: Okopax—die neue Kraft* (Berlin: Olle & Welter, 1982). The title of one of Kelly's essays, "The System Is Bankrupt: New Forces Must Emerge," reflects the totality of the rejection of Western society and the hope for a wholly new order that permeates this collection. Peter von Oertzen, a member of the SPD Bundesvorstand since 1973, reflects on "Reality and Utopia—On the Political Possibilities (and Dangers) of a New Way," pp. 140-59. Von Oertzen's realism begins with rejection of the NATO deployment, includes more talk of SPD-Green coalitions, and "more discussion" of nuclear-free zones, alternative conventional defense, "greater political independence from the United States—without leaning to the Soviet Union," though how these circles are to be squared remains a mystery. To dramatize their accusations against both superpowers, the Greens staged "Tribunal Against First-Strike and Mass Destruction Weapons" in Nuremberg in February 1983. Not surprisingly, the bulk of the testimony was directed against NATO and the United States; both were found guilty of preparing for nuclear holocaust. See "Heftige Angriffe gegen Politik der Atomächte," *Frankfurter Rundschau*, 20 February 1983, p. 1.

22. *Die Grünen: Das Bundesprogramm*, p. 19.

23. Soviet foreign policy has long aimed at splitting the Atlantic alliance and keeping Western Europe from transforming its economic power into a potent united political-military unit. On this, see Adam Ulam, *Dangerous Relations* (New York: Oxford University Press, 1983); Pierre Hassner, "Moscow and the Western Alliance," *Problems of Communism* (May-June 1981): 37-54; John van Oudenaren, *The 'Leninist Peace Policy' and Western Europe* (Cambridge: Center for International Studies, MIT, 1980); *Soviet Strategy in Europe*, ed. Richard Pipes (New York: Crane & Russak, 1976), esp. the essays by Pipes and by Lothar Ruehl. And on Soviet relations with Germany, see Angela Stent, "The USSR and Germany," *Problems of Communism* (September-October 1981); Elizabeth Pond, "Andropov, Kohl and East-West Issues," *Problems of Communism* (July-August 1983).

24. See, for example, Kurt Sontheimer, *Zeitenwende? Die Bundesrepublik Deutschland zwischen alter und alternativer Politik* (Hamburg: Hoffmann & Campe, 1983); Josef Joffe, "The Greening of Germany," *New Republic* (14 February 1983); 18-23; Walter Laqueur, "Germany's Fall," *New Republic* (17 October 1983): 19-23.

25. Wolfgang Pohrt, *Endstation: Uber die Wiedergeburt der Nation* (Berlin: Rotbuch Verlag, 1982). This report on the Left and alternative scene in West Germany contains valuable insights as well as a refreshing manifestation of independent thought. Peace movement representatives have not infrequently referred to Germany and/or Central Europe as the new Auschwitz and to Europeans as inmates of a nuclear concentration camp. See, for example, the writer Günther Anders's speech upon receiving the Theodor Adorno prize from the City of Frankfurt in fall 1983, reprinted in *Pflasterstrand* (Frankfurt) 168 (8-21 October, 1983): 40-42.

26. Peter Brandt and Herbert Ammon, "Patriotismus von Links," in *Die Deutsche Einheit kommt bestimmt*, ed. Wolfgang Venohr (Bergisch Gladbach: Gustav Lübbe Verlag, 1982), pp. 119-59.

27. Also see Henryk Broder, "Die Linke fühlt deutsch," *Der Spiegel* (21 Feb., 1983): 190-93; Rudi Dutschke, "Die Deutschen und der Sozialismus," ibid., pp. 334-35, and "Zur nationalen Frage," ibid., pp. 350-51; Hennig Eichberg, "National ist revolutionär," in *Die Linke und die nationale Frage: Dokumente zur deutschen Einheit seit 1945*, ed. Peter Brandt and Herbert Ammon (Hamburg: Rowohlt, 1981), pp. 351-52; other contributors include Günter Grass, Egon Bahr, Robert Havemann, Rudolf Augstein, and Hans Magnus Enzensberger. Also see Hennig Eichberg, *Nationale Identität: Entfremdung und nationale Frage in der Industriegesellschaft* (Munich: Langen-Müller, 1978). Eichberg urges a recovery of genuine, regional, national cultures from the homogenization brought about by the multinationals and the "ITT speech." For a very lucid analysis of the peace movement and nationalism, see Sigrid Mueschel, "Neo-nationalism and the Peace Movement," *Telos* 56 (Summer 1983): 119-30. For a general analysis of estrangement and utopian politics of left-wing intellectuals with important implications for the peace movement intellectuals, see Paul Hollander, *Political Pilgrims* (New York: Oxford University Press, 1981).

28. *Stichworte zur 'Geistigen Situation der Zeit': I. Band: Nation und Republik*, ed. Jürgen Habermas (Frankfurt/Main: Suhrkamp Verlag, 1979).

29. Jürgen Habermas, "Einleitung," in Habermas, *Stichworte*, p. 18.

30. Martin Walser, "Händedruck mit Gespenstern," in Habermas, *Stichworte*, pp. 39-50.

31. Dieter Wellershoff, "Deutschland—ein Schwebezustand," in Habermas, *Stichworte*, pp. 77-114.

32. Wolfgang Mommsen, "'Wir sind wieder wer.' Wandlungen im politischen Selbstverständnis der Deutschen," in Habermas, *Stichworte*, p. 209.

33. Hans Jürgen Syberberg, *Hitler, ein Film aus Deutschland* (Reinbek: Rowohlt Verlag, 1978), p. 9, cited by Iring Fetscher in "Die Suche nach der nationalen Identität," in Habermas, *Stichworte*, pp. 115-131.

34. Iring Fetscher, "Die Suche nach der nationalen Identität," in Habermas, *Stichworte*, pp. 115-31. Fetscher's essay documents a renewed interest in the sixties Left in returning to German profundity after a decade of seeking identification in foreign revolutions. Fetscher, a political theorist who has written sympathetically on English liberalism, favorably refers to Italian critic Pier Passolini's warnings of the totalitarian nature of Western consumerism.

35. Horst Ehmke, "Was ist das deutsche Vaterland?" in Habermas, *Stichworte*, pp. 39-50. Günter Gaus, the first representative of the Federal Republic in East Germany, is another member of the SPD who has raised the German question.

36. Venohr, *Die Deutsche Einheit kommt bestimmt*. In addition to the essay by Brandt and Ammon see Helmut Diwald, "Deutschland—was ist es?" pp. 17-35.

37. Sontheimer, *Zeitenwende*; Joseph Rovan, *L'Allemagne du Changement* (Paris, 1983); "La République Fédérale et la Tentation Neutralisté," *Esprit* (January 1982): 26-41.

38. Karl-Werner Brand, *Neue Soziale Bewegungen* (Opladen: Westdeutscher Verlag, 1982), p. 7. Also see Karl Werner Brand, Detlef Busser, and Dieter Rucht, *Aufbruch in eine neue Gessellschaft; Neue soziale Bewegungen in der Bundesrepublik* (Frankfurt: Campus Verlag, 1983);

39. George F. Kennan, *Die Zeit*, 28 August 1981. The *Frankfurter Rundschau* presented Kennan's speech as a "radical renunciation of nuclear deterrence," 10 October, 1981.

40. Carl Friedrich von Weizsäcker, *Wege in der Gefahr* (Munich: Carl Hanser Verlag, 1976). Von Weizsäcker urges adoption of the "Afheldt proposals" for "techno-guerrillas," a kind of high-tech, antitank civilian militia. Aside from the military drawbacks to this scheme—the Warsaw Pact's using planes, artillery, and tanks would wipe out such a defense with no trouble, and, second, such a defense would exact massive destruction within West Germany and abandon any effort to carry the battle into East Germany—von Weizsäcker's efforts to devote some thought to raising the nuclear threshold through conventional defense have not received much attention in the peace movement. His emphasis on conventional defense may be good policy, but it will not draw much support from those who are now demonstrating against the NATO nuclear deterrent. Generally, proposals for "alternative" security policies do not advocate spending more for conventional defense and advocate "political rather than military" avenues toward sustaining peace. See, for example, the proposals by the Hessische Stiftung Friedensforschung, "NATO-Strategie in der Kontroverse," *Frankfurter Rundschau*, 21 Jan. 1983, pp. 10-11. For U.S. discussions of conventional defense, see *Strengthening Conventional Deterrence in Europe*, Report of the European Security Study (New York: St. Martin's Press, 1983); Samuel P. Huntington, ed. *The Strategic Imperative* (Cambridge, Mass.: Ballinger Publishing Co., 1982); and John Steinbrunner and Leon V. Sigal, eds. *Alliance Security: NATO and the No-First-Use Question* (Washington, D.C.: Brookings Institution, 1983).

41. For some representative samples of the peace movement's claim that Germany will be the "shooting gallery" of the superpowers, see Perdelwitz and Bremer, *Geisel Europa*; and Hans A. Pestalozzi, ed., *Frieden in Deutschland* (Munich: Wilhelm Goldmann Verlag, 1982). *Der Spiegel* has been very important in the antimissile campaign, running numerous articles suggesting that the NATO deployments are a U.S. effort to regain nuclear superiority, to limit war to Europe, to use the Euromissiles to pressure the Soviets if tension arises outside Europe (especially in the Middle East), or to facilitate a first strike against the Soviet Union. See, for example, Wilhelm Bittorf, "Raketen töten nicht-Menschen töten," *Der Spiegel*, nos. 9, 10 (February 1983). For critical responses see Jeffrey Herf, "Western Strategy and Public Discussion: The Double Decision Makes Sense," *Telos* 52 (Fall 1982): 114-28; Mark Helprin, "Drawing the Line in Europe: The Case for Missile Deployment," *New York Times Magazine*, 4 December, 1983.

42. *Report of the President's Commission on Strategic Forces* (Washington, D.C., April 1983), pp. 7-8.

43. Stanley Kober, "Can NATO Survive?" *International Affairs* (Summer 1983); Raymond Aron, "Hope and Despair in the Western Camp," *Encounter* (June-July 1982): 121-29; Michael Howard, "Surviving a Protest," in *The Causes of War* (Cambridge: Harvard University Press, 1983), pp. 116-33.

44. See Kurt Sontheimer, *Zeitenwende*, pp. 229-40; Peter Hertel and Alfred Paffenholz, *Fur eine politische Kirche: Schwerter zu Pflugscharen* (Hannover: Fackelträger Verlag, 1982); *Christen im Streit um den Frieden* (Freiburg, Br.: Dreisam Verlag, 1982); and the best-selling application of the Sermon on the Mount to the purposes of nuclear pacifism by Franz Alt, one of West Germany's best-known television personalities, *Frieden ist Möglich: Die Politik der Bergpredigt* (Munich: R. Piper Verlag, 1983). Also see "Das Bekenntnis zu Jesus Christus und die Friedensverantwortung" of the Moderamens des Reformierten Bundes of the Evangelical Church, *Frankfurter Rundschau,* 4 September 1982, p. 14; Trutz Rendtorff "Der Friedensstreit bedeutet Gefahr für die Kirche," *Frankfurter Allgemeine Zeitung,* 25 October, 1982, p. 8, for a critique of efforts to give the status of religious commands to political judgments concerning security policy.

45. Alt, *Frieden ist Möglich*, pp. 98-99.

46. Ibid., p. 101. On the conflict between the ethics of responsibility and absolute convictions, see Helmut Schmidt, "Bemerkungen zu Moral, Pflicht und Verantwortung des Politikers," *Merkur* 35 (May 1981): 449-65.

47. Kelly and Leinen, *Prinzip Leben.*

48. Von Weizsäcker, *Wege in die Gefahr,* "Europäische Verteidigung," pp. 215-35.

49. See Johanno Strasser and Klaus Trauber, *Die Zukunft des Fortschritts: Der Sozialismus und die Krise des Industrialismus* (Bonn: Verlag Neue Gesellschaft, 1981).

50. See the publications of the Sozialistische Büro, *Sozialistische Friedenspolitik: Thesen des Sozialistischen Büro* (Offenbach: Verlag 2000, 1982); Andreas Büro, *Zwischen sozial-liberalem Zerfall und konservativer Herrschaft* (Offenbach: Verlag 2000, 1982); and the monthly journal of political commentary *Links.* The socialist intellectuals are sometimes made uncomfortable by the religious, nationalist, romantic aspects of the new social movements and tend to stress the economic motivations of U.S. hegemony in Europe.

51. Der Bundesminister des Innern, *Linksextremistische Einflüsse auf die Kampagne gegen die NATO-Nachrüstung* (Bonn, June 1983). The report of the Ministry of the Interior estimated that of the 1.5 to 3 million participants in the peace movement, no more than 3 to 5 percent are "left-wing extremists," i.e. members of Marxist-Leninist and/or Maoist organizations. But they were believed to constitute 20 percent of the demonstrators and 40 percent of the speakers at rallies, while the DKP alone accounted for over 50 percent of those active in the most important organizations. It described the DKP as "the largest and most active group" in the peace movement, with a membership of 100,000 and

an annual budget of 60 million marks. The focus of its efforts has been in Protestant peace groups, the trade unions, the Greens, and the SPD Left. For the views of the German Communist party on the peace movement, see *Grundsätze kommunistischer Bündnispolitik in der Friedensbewegung* (DKP Anschriften, 1983). There has been considerable press coverage of Communist involvement in the peace movement. See R.v. Woitowsky, "Taktik und Kreis des Krefelder Appells," *Die Welt*, 4 December, 1981; "Friedensdemonstration: Das Stichwort kam aus Moskau," *Die Welt*, 6 October, 1981; "Kommunisten in der Friedensbewegung," *Süddeutsche Zeitung*, 9 December, 1982; "Ostermärsche scheinen von DKP gesteuert," *Frankfurter Allgemeine Zeitung*, 24 March 1982. On the conflict within the Greens over working with Communists, see Rudolf Bahro, "Die DKP ist ein Fremdkörper," *Der Spiegel* (12 April, 1982): 30; "Streit in der Friedensbewegung über Friedensgruppen in der DDR, *Frankfurter Allgemeine Zeitung*, 6 April, 1982, p. 2; "Ideologischer Ballast der DKP," *Frankfurter Rundschau* 20, April 1982, p. 4.

52. Pierre Hassner, "Zwei deutsche Staaten in Europa: Gibt es gemeinsame Interessen in der internationalen Politik?" in Werner Weidenfeld, ed., *Die Identität der Deutschen* (Munich: Hanser Verlag, 1983), pp. 294-323.

53. Egon Bahr, *Was wird aus den Deutschen?* (Hamburg: Rowohlt Verlag, 1982); Egon Bahr, "Die Priorität bleibt fur den Frieden," *Vorwärts* (20 October, 1983). Also see Günter Gaus, *Wo Deutschland liegt. Ein Ortsbestimmung* (Hamburg: Hoffmann & Campe Verlag, 1983). See Karl Kaiser's criticisms of Bahr for separating the issues of peace and freedom, and obscuring the causes of the conflict between the Soviet Union and the West in "Prioritäten sozialdemokratischer Aussen-und Sicherheitspolitik," *Vorwärts* (6, 13 October, 1983).

54. Peter Bender, *Das Ende des Ideologischen Zeitalters* (Berlin: Severin & Siedler, 1981). For some brief critical comments on the effects of detente, see Hermann Lübbe, *Endstation Terror* (Stuttgart: Seewald Verlag, 1978), pp. 115-22. Willy Brandt summarized his rather similar views in his speech to the SPD Parteitag urging rejection of the NATO deployments. Both superpowers are stronger than they need to be. Detente must continue. *Sicherheitspartnerschaft* remains the key concept. A European peace policy must replace the spiraling arms race, beginning with a nuclear freeze and a nuclear-free zone along the German border. See Willy Brandt, "Die Beiden Supermächte sind stärker als es gut ist, der Begriff der Zukunft heisst Sicherheitspartnerschaft," *Frankfurter Allgemeine Zeitung*, 21 November 1983, p. 2.

55. Lübbe, *Endstation Terror*, esp. "Wandel durch Annäherung—auch ideologisch?" pp. 115-18.

56. On the past disappointments and future prospects for a strong West European defense, see Stanley Hoffmann, *Dead Ends: American Foreign Policy in the New Cold War* (Cambridge, Mass.: Ballinger Publishing Co., 1983), esp. "Drift or Harmony" and "Security in an Age of Turbulence"; Theodore Draper, *Present History: On Nuclear War, Detente, and Other Controversies* (New York: Random House, 1983); Raymond Aron, *In Defense of Decadent Europe* (South Bend: Regency/Gateway, 1977); Walter Laqueur, *A Continent Astray: Europe, 1970-78*

(New York: Oxford University Press, 1979). While these observers differ in their assessments of U.S. foreign policy, all agree that Western Europe must get its own house in order, beginning with defense at home, to overcome or at least minimize dependence on the United States.

57. Hassner, "Zwei deutsche Staaten in Europa," p. 320.
58. Kurt Sontheimer, "Ein deutscher Sonderweg?" in *Die Identität der Deutschen*, ed. Werner Weidenfeld (Munich: Hanser Verlag, 1983), pp. 324-35.

17

APOCALYPSE NOW: THE AMERICAN PEACE MOVEMENT IN THE 1980s

David Thomas

INTRODUCTION

Freud in his *Civilization and Its Discontents* observed that the primary cause of humankind's present psychological discomfort and mood of anxiety was the realization that the forces of nature have been mastered to such an extent that, with their help, the human race could readily exterminate itself. [1] In a general, psychological sense, Freud's observation could be adduced to explain the establishment of a new U.S. peace movement preoccupied with arms control, disarmament, and the danger of nuclear war, for this peace movement could be diagnosed as merely a periodic manifestation of the inchoate perennial fear of nuclear war residing within the general public.

In truth, neither a preexisting apprehension about nuclear weapons nor the rediscovery of the nuclear arms race adequately explains the dramatic florescence of a peace movement in the United States in 1980. The Atomic Age and the Bomb have been with Americans since 1945. The general public from time to time has experienced war scares in connection with international crises. Yet, in no instance in the past, either before or after any crisis, did a peace and disarmament movement arise that could be compared in respect to size and emotional intensity with the "peace crusade" that is presently perturbing the United States with books, demonstrations, symposia, political petitions, theological incantations of a nuclear apocalypse, and scientific admonitions about impending doom. Thus, the question may be asked: Whence the new fear of the arms race and nuclear war?

In this interpretive essay on the U.S. peace and disarmament movement in 1984, an attempt is made to address this question by discussing the recent history of the movement, its composition, the main views and activities of the most important peace organizations, the strengths and weaknesses of the central views of the movement, and the issue of Soviet manipulation and Communist participation. Of necessity, the discussion assumes the form of a *tour d'horizon* that focuses restrictively upon the peace organizations exclusively concerned with arms control and disarmament issues. Thus, only passing attention is paid to the amorphous, amoeba-like conglomeration of left-wing political groups that nominally associate themselves with the activities and views of the peace movement but are otherwise engaged with causes and issues that have nothing to do with arms control, disarmament, and peace. [2]

RECENT HISTORY OF THE PEACE MOVEMENT

The peace movement of 1984 is the lineal descendant of the anti-Vietnam war movement (1965-1975), and of the succession of ad hoc coalitions that constituted the so-named antidefense lobby between 1975 and 1980. Until 1975, the peace movement was more or less synonymous with the antiwar movement. That movement consisted of a progression of national coalitions that incorporated new peace groups formed in direct response to the Vietnam war and peace organizations of long standing, for example, the American Friends Service Committee (AFSC), SANE, the War Resisters League (WRL), and Women's International League for Peace and Freedom (WILPF). Upon the collapse of South Vietnam in 1975, the antiwar movement formally dissolved. The various peace groups that belonged to it either lapsed into political ennui and became progressively moribund or assumed a series of new organizational forms in the search for a new cause around which to coagulate. [3]

The immediate successor of the last antiwar coalition was the Coalition to Stop Funding the War (CSF). In 1975, the CSF was succeeded by the Ad Hoc Coalition for New Foreign Policy (CNFP), an omnibus organization of notable ideological versatility, whose formal program included opposition to the defense budget. The CNFP in 1976 evolved into the Campaign for a Democratic Foreign Policy (CDFP). The CDFP included nearly every peace group that had belonged to the anti-Vietnam war movement and that would later join the peace movement of the 1980s. The broad purpose of the CDFP was to establish a movement strong enough to restrict U.S. "imperialism" by compelling Congress to reduce the defense budget. In 1976, the CDFP undertook a program of educational and legislative activity designed to confute the gathering public discussion about the Soviet military buildup initiated by the Committee for the Present Danger, and to obtain congressional support for reducing the defense budget and transferring funds from military to domestic programs. The best-known lobbying effort of the CDFP in this connection was the successful campaign against the B-1 bomber in 1976. [4]

The CDFP transmuted itself into another antidefense coalition, the Coalition for a New Foreign and Military Policy (CNFMP). In 1977, the Disarmament Working Group of the CNFMP published a document entitled "Disarmament Appeal to President Carter." In hindsight, this document looks like the spiritual ancestor of the nuclear-freeze proposal circulated for the first time in 1980. The 1977 appeal proposed major arms reductions, leading in stages to general and complete disarmament. It also implored the U.S. government to undertake a continuing series of highly publicized acts of restraint and to invite the Soviet Union to reciprocate them. [5] Against the background of the SALT II negotatiations that were in progress at the time, the CNFMP did not attract national attention.

During 1978 and 1979, the CNFMP carried out a vigorous program of organizational and educational activity and lobbying on behalf of the Comprehensive Test Ban Treaty with the Soviet Union and the second Strategic Arms Limitation Treaty (SALT II). The CNFMP position on SALT qualified its endorsement of the limitations on the number of strategic nuclear-delivery vehicles and the number of warheads with an objection to the treaty's failure to require "early, significant mutual reductions of strategic weapons." The CNFMP insisted upon the need for the United States to take independent steps to limit U.S. weapons programs, under the argument that this would be an important complementary approach to controlling the strategic arms race. [6]

The CNFMP never obtained broad popular support for any of its public positions on the defense budget and arms control. However, by the end of the Carter administration, the CNFMP had positioned itself at the center of the antidefense lobby and had acquired useful experience in legislative lobbying, the utilization of the media, and the coordination of its forty-three member organizations and numerous working groups. Every one of the peace groups associated with the

CNFMP emerges as part of the peace movement after 1980 in connection with the campaign for a nuclear freeze. [7]

The educational and lobbying activity of the CNFMP in 1979 and 1980 foundered on events. The Soviet invasion of Afghanistan derailed the SALT II treaty and deprived the arguments of the proponents of reduced military spending, peaceful coexistence, and strategic arms control of their urgency. The Iranian hostage crisis not only preoccupied the government and the public but also provided voters in the 1980 presidential election with unequivocal evidence that the United States was not surrounded by friends and well-wishers.

In early 1980, the director of an obscure arms control group in Cambridge, Massachusetts, the Institute for Defense and Disarmament Studies, came out with a proposal entitled "Call to Halt the Nuclear Arms Race." The document appealed for the adoption of a "mutual freeze on the testing, production, and deployment of nuclear weapons" as an essential, verifiable first step toward lessening the risk of nuclear war and reducing the nuclear arsenals of the United States and the USSR. [8] The genesis of the idea of the nuclear freeze proposed in the appeal can be traced to the "Disarmament Appeal to President Carter" (1977) and to a provision in the Hatfield Amendment to the SALT II treaty (1979), which appended a "freeze" on the research, testing, development, manufacture, and deployment of new nuclear weapons and strategic delivery systems. It is not clear whether the publication of the freeze proposal was the result of consultation among the peace groups that endorsed the original appeal of Randall Forsberg. In the event, after the 1980 presidential election, the idea of a nuclear freeze became the basis of a revivified peace movement. [9]

The 1980 election and the avowed defense and arms-control policies of the new president galvanized the existing collection of peace groups associated with the CNFMP and the Mobilization for Survival (MFS), another coalition of peace organizations that had first appeared in 1977 at a conference sponsored by the World Peace Council (WPC), the AFSC, the WRL, WILPF, and Clergy and Laity Concerned (CALC). The activity of the disarmament movement in Western Europe and Britain provided a working example of a successful peace movement. But the freeze proposal furnished the essential ingredient for the organization of a new coalition of peace groups: an issue with political and emotional appeal.

In March 1981, the National Strategy Conference for a Nuclear Freeze was convened in Washington, D.C., by representatives of all major peace groups, with members of various European peace organizations also in attendance. [10] The conference established the Nuclear Weapons Freeze Campaign, Inc. (NWFC), and the NWFC immediately became the organization nominally responsible for the national coordination of the activities of all major peace groups.

With amazing speed, the existing group of peace organizations that had been associated recently with the CNFMP and the MFS, a number of left-wing groups concerned with Central America and the Middle East, and a new peace organization, the United States Peace Council (USPC) recast their agenda, refurbished their depleted memberships, and swiftly coalesced into a national peace movement under the ostensible banner of the nuclear freeze campaign. In addition, there sprang up a plethora of new peace organizations, study groups, committees, and "institutes" for research on defense policy—from the Children's Campaign for Nuclear Disarmament in Plainfield, Vermont, to the Esalen Institute Soviet-American Exchange Program in San Francisco, California. [11]

In 1981 and 1982, the original freeze proposal was translated into a joint resolution of Congress, and numerous petitions, referenda, and resolutions calling for a freeze were endorsed by town meetings, state legislatures, church bodies, and so forth. [12] On 12 June, 1982, and 27 August 1983, the new movement staged its first large peace demonstrations. Since 1981, the peace movement has become more or less synonymous with the nuclear freeze campaign in the public mind. Under the aegis of the NWFC, the various peace groups have initiated educational activities in support of the freeze on the local, state, and national levels to mobilize public anxiety about nuclear weapons and the arms-control policy of the Reagan administration.

COMPOSITION

Every movement inherits the offspring of others; the new peace movement is no exception. In its present incarnation as the nuclear freeze campaign it did not spring *de novo* or *ex nihilo*. Nor should the peace movement be seen as an eruption from below. The roots of the movement are in the various national coalitions that once made up the anti-Vietnam war movement and later the antidefense lobby of the late 1970s. The membership of the peace groups that belonged to the antiwar movement was predominantly of left-wing origin. [13] Since many of the same groups now are marching under the banner of the nuclear freeze, it would be fair to say that the new peace movement retains a sizeable element of the now old New Left of the 1960s and 1970s. However, it has been leavened by an influx of environmentalists and apolitical, affluent suburban dwellers, and by a large number of like-minded idealists, pacifists, clergy, scientists, and retired public officials who are in general liberal and left of center in political orientation and are not ideologues.

The organizational composition of the peace movement on the national level can be delineated according to six general categories: [14] (1) religious peace organizations; (2) pacifist organizations; (3) environmental groups; (4) medical and scientific associations; (5) public interest organizations; (6) left-wing political organizations. Because there are now some 1,250 registered peace groups in the United States, including numerous local and regional affiliates of the prominent national peace organizations, the conspectus of groups belonging to each of these categories is necessarily brief and selective. It should be noted that the number of groups is deceiving. The full-time staffs are small (five to fifteen persons on average), most employees are not paid, and the typical annual budget is $250,000 or less (1982-83 figures). Most of the national and local groups thus depend upon a cadre system to carry on their activities: a small permanent staff directs the work of volunteers, and mobilizes on the occasion of large events such as demonstrations a diverse body of unaffiliated but sympathetic supporters.

In respect to social origin, the peace movement has been predominantly middle and upper-middle class in background, and it remains so as of this writing. In this respect, the supporters and sympathizers of the peace movement conform to George Orwell's characterization of pacifists: they are commonly individuals who have led sheltered lives and have grown up in exceptional or comfortable circumstances. The supporters of the peace movement drawn from this stratum include members of the liberal and progressive professoriate, especially from the faculties of the social sciences and the humanities; clergy; educated professionals, in particular, from nonprofit organizations, the public sector, and occupations associated with the creation and dissemination of knowledge; metropolitan intellectuals; and students.

CONSPECTUS

1. Religious organizations. The Protestant groups include: (a) The Friends Committee on National Legislation (1943); (b) United Church of Christ, Office of Church in Society (1976); (c) Riverside Church Disarmament Progam (1978); (d) Unitarian Universalist Association (1979); (e) United Methodist Church, Department of Peace and World Order (1940); (f) Clergy and Laity Concerned (1965). For

the Catholic church: (g) Pax Christi USA (1973); (h) Catholic Peace Fellowship (1964). Three Jewish groups are on register; (i) New Jewish Agenda (1980); (j) Rainbow Sign (1981); (k) Union of American Hebrew Congregations (1961).

2. Pacifist organizations. The best-known include: (a) War Resisters League (1923); (b) Fellowship of Reconciliation (1915); (c) American Friends Service Committee.

3. Environmental groups. (a) Common Cause (1970); (b) Council for a Livable World (1962); (c) Environmental Policy Institute (1974); (d) Friends of the Earth (1969); (e) Greenpeace USA/Disarmament Project (1971); (f) National Resources Defense Council, Nuclear Nonproliferation Project (1970).

4. Medical and scientific associations. (a) Federation of American Scientists (1946); International Physicians for the Prevention of Nuclear War (1980); (c) Union of Concerned Scientists, Nuclear Arms Program (1969); (d) Physicians for Social Responsibility (1979).

5. Public interest organizations. (a) American Committee on East-West Accord (1977); (b) Arms Control Association (1971); (c) Center for Defense Information (1972); (d) Ground Zero (1981); (e) Fund for Peace (1967); (f) Institute for Defense and Disarmament Studies (1980); (g) International Student Pugwash (1979); (h) National Peace Academy Campaign (1976); (i) Nuclear Freeze Foundation (1982); (j) SANE, Inc. (1957); (k) The Stanley Foundation (1956); (l) Nukewatch, Inc. (1979).

6. Left-wing political organizations. (a) Center for International Policy (1975); (b) Center for War/Peace Studies (1977); (c) Coalition for a New Foreign and Military Policy (1976); (d) Council on Economic Priorities (1969); (e) Institute for Policy Studies (1963); (f) Jobs with Peace (1981); (g) Mobilization for Survival (1977); (h) National Campaign to Stop the MX (1981); (i) Lawyers Committee on Nuclear Policy (1981); (j) National Council of Soviet-American Friendship; (k) U.S. Peace Council (1979); Women for Racial and Economic Equality; (m) Women's International League for Peace and Freedom (1915); (n) Women Strike for Peace (1961).

ACTIVITIES AND MAIN VIEWS

On a broad view, the principal peace organizations are shown by their public statements and official literature to agree on three basic points: (1) a nuclear freeze is the best, practical first step that the United States could take toward genuine arms reduction and disarmament; (2) the nuclear arms race must be opposed because it has become uncontrollable and endangers the survival of the planet; (3) the Reagan administration is making nuclear war inevitable by its arms-control and defense policies. Most of the activity of the major national peace groups is dedicated to implementing a nuclear freeze at least in the United States. This activity includes community education and organizing; fund-raising and administration; production of materials; issue research; media activities; political action; national and international policy development.

It would be impossible in this space to discuss the principal views of every important peace organization. For this reason, the analysis presented here restricts itself to the following points: first, a summation of the general viewpoint of the peace movement; second, a recapitulation of the key assumptions about the nuclear freeze proposal itself because the freeze is the *raison d'être* of the peace movement; third, a review of the views of the nonreligious peace groups; fourth, an extended discussion of positions adopted by the religious peace organizations and the churches, owing to their importance in conferring moral legitimacy on the peace movement as a whole. Let it be admitted in advance that the admixture of generalization and specificity provided is unavoidably uneven.

The general view of the peace movement can be summarized as follows. There are two paths to disarmament. The first involves international agreements, such as the SALT treaties, which control but do not reduce nuclear weapons. The second consists of independent initiatives by the United States, accompanied by invitations to the Soviet Union (and other nations) to reciprocate. [15] The new generation of U.S. strategic weapons under development is inherently destabilizing. The deployment of these weapons in response to a Soviet military buildup and a Soviet threat, both of which have been grossly exaggerated by the military-industrial complex and the Reagan administration, will ignite an uncontrollable arms race. The present size of the nuclear arsenals of the United States and the Soviet Union already exceed the requirements of deterrence. These arsenals cannot provide genuine security, and they have become instruments of coercion, intimidation, and an aggresive foreign policy—especially in the case of the United States. [16] The traditional strategy of deterrence, indeed, the concepts of a balance of terror and mutual assured destruction that undergird it, are immoral and repugnant to U.S. values. [17] The arms race itself imposes an intolerable burden upon the United States. Unconscionable sums are being wasted on defense, while Americans are suffering because there is not enough money for senior citizens, education, the handicapped, racial minorities, medical care, and even basic scientific research. [18] The freeze offers the best means of ending the arms race. The opponents of the freeze are in the minority, and they have a vested interest in perpetuating the arms race. [19] They do not understand the extent of nuclear "overkill," and they are ignorant of the extent to which the military forces and production systems of the superpowers are known and are capable of verification. [20]

Five popular assumptions about the nuclear freeze attach to the aforementioned general view: (1) The use of nuclear weapons and the threat of such use are immoral; therefore, disarmament is the only answer to the moral dilemma posed by nuclear weapons. (2) The nuclear arms race endangers the survival of the planet. (3) The existence of a condition of overkill. (4) A freeze could be verified by "national technical means." (5) A mutual freeze would lead to the negotiation of a comprehensive arms-reduction agreement with the Soviet Union.

The first assumption embodies the theological argument advanced by the National Council of Catholic Bishops in the controversial "Pastoral Letter on War and Peace" published in 1983. Briefly, the historic argument of *ius ad bellum* (just war), which subsumes the right of legitimate self-defense, is limited in the case of nuclear weapons, and does not constitute a moral justification for the use of these weapons against innocent noncombatants. Therefore, nuclear deterrence based on the threat of inflicting inescapable retaliation upon defenseless civilian populations is immoral.

The theological argument is examined in more detail below. [21] Here, suffice to state that it has three weaknesses. First, nuclear deterrence has been the principal factor in preventing a war between the United States and the Soviet Union, and this is a moral achievement. Second, the U.S. doctrine of deterrence, which embodies the assumption of mutual assured destruction as the basis of deterrence itself, has always provided for the use of nuclear weapons against military targets to deter a Soviet attack; retaliation against civilian targets has not been an essential element of the strategy of deterrence. Third, the bishops who drew up the original version of the argument did not base their explication of the technical military problems and the political dimension of deterrence on divine authority or historical church doctrine; rather, they imbibed it from a gamut of secular strategists and academic authorities associated for the most part with the traditional strategy of deterrence based on retaliation against nonmilitary targets. [22]

The second assumption is metaphysical. The metaphor of an arms race has been used by peace movements in the United States since the late nineteenth century. For instance, the metaphor was applied to the dreadnought competition between Imperial Germany and

Great Britain, and later, to the U.S. naval construction program under President Theodore Roosevelt. [23] The premise behind the assumption of an arms race is that U.S. strategic weapon programs ineluctably compel the Soviet Union to build comparable systems, either to catch up or to maintain parity. It does not consider the possibility or the fact of an independent, unilateral Soviet motivation for developing and deploying strategic weapons systems. Nonetheless, the cycle of action-reaction is presumed to be the fault of the United States. The military establishment or the intelligence community invariably analyze the worst-case implications of any Soviet reaction to U.S. programs. The threat of new Soviet systems is always exaggerated to obtain unjustifiable increases in defense spending to build more weapons. [24]

The main weakness of this assumption is the actual history of the U.S.-USSR military competition since 1950. The Soviet Union began to develop ICBMs on its own initiative. The buildup of Soviet strategic nuclear forces in the early 1960s was not prompted in the first instance by the Cuban missile crisis, or by the expansion of U.S. strategic forces undertaken by the Kennedy and Johnson administrations. On the contrary, as should be self-evident from Soviet military thinking, the buildup was initiated unilaterally to satisfy the new requirements of Soviet military strategy and doctrine, in accordance with a conception of security quite different from its U.S. counterpart. [25] Until the true dimension of the enormous Soviet strategic military buildup became apparent, it was commonly believed by many well-meaning people that the United States was racing with itself because the Soviet Union either could not challenge U.S. nuclear superiority, or would accept a position of strategic inferiority. When the Soviet Union began to catch up, it was presumed that it intended merely to achieve parity. When it achieved parity in respect to strategic nuclear weapons but went on to increase the size of its strategic forces and began to deploy large ICBMs manifestly capable of destroying U.S. ICBM silos (thereby weakening the credibility of U.S. deterrence by imperiling the U.S. retaliatory capability), [26] the peace movement of the day was preoccupied with the Vietnam war. The Soviet buildup that continued during the decade of SALT occasioned no peace demonstrations nor any audible protest from U.S. peace groups.

The third assumption—the existence of overkill—leads immediately to the conclusion that the procurement of new strategic weapons systems by the United States is unnecessary because the possession of more weapons (delivery systems or warheads) by one side or the other is irrelevant, and the idea of nuclear superiority is meaningless, by definition. The presumption that the United States possesses an excessive number of strategic nuclear delivery systems or warheads rests upon a misunderstanding of the fundamental requirements of the strategy of deterrence. U.S. forces must be sufficient in numbers, destructive power, and accuracy to deter a Soviet attack. In the event that deterrence should fail, the U.S. retaliatory force must be large enough to sustain the unavoidable losses that a Soviet first strike would inflict, and still be capable of inflicting, in turn, an unacceptable level of damage on the Soviet Union with a second strike. Soviet nuclear targeting strategy is a counterforce strategy, that is, it is directed against U.S. military targets and national command centers in the first instance, not against cities and industrial areas. To guarantee the ability of the U.S. retaliatory force to absorb a Soviet first strike, and then deliver upon the Soviet Union an attack capable of inflicting a (predetermined) level of catastrophic destruction, it is necessary to maintain more than the minimum number of strategic nuclear delivery systems that supporters of the freeze imagine would suffice to deter the Soviet Union. [27]

Thus, the notion of overkill and of an arms race associated with it for which the United States alone is responsible cannot be reconciled with reality. In 1967, the United States unilaterally established force levels of approximately 1,054 ICBMs and 656 SLBMs, which it has maintained ever since. Only the number of warheads that these missiles are capable of delivering has been increased (through technical improvements). In comparison, the Soviet Union doubled the size of its ICBM force between 1967 and 1980, from a base figure of roughly 460 ICBMs and 130 SLBMs in 1967 to the present estimated total of 1,398 ICBMs and 950 SLBMs. [28] Furthermore, technical improvements have increased the accuracy of Soviet ICBMs to a level that approaches U.S. standards. As a result, there is general agreement that the Soviet Union is within reach of a capacity to destroy a large portion of the U.S. ICBMs in a surprise attack, using a relatively small proportion of its own ICBM force.

The fourth assumption, that a freeze could be verified, is the most important, because the credibility of the freeze proposal itself turns on it. Nowhere in the literature of the freeze campaign is the definition of verification clearly expounded. *Prima facie*, freeze proponents have to mind the same forms and methods of verification as are currently used to monitor compliance with existing arms-control agreements. Accordingly, verification would encompass the process of monitoring Soviet adherence to the provisions of a freeze agreement, to the extent necessary to safeguard adequately national security. This process would use primarily national technical means (sensor and reconnaissance satellites, ground radars, etc.), which could not be interfered with, or impeded by, deliberate measures of concealment, for example, encryption of missile telemetry, ground camouflage, and antisatellite weapons. [29]

The ability of U.S. intelligence to verify Soviet compliance with any arms control agreement is debatable. The ratification of SALT II foundered on uncertainty about verification, and this uncertainty has not been resolved since 1979. It is still disputed whether watertight procedures of verification can be devised in respect to all phases of the development, testing, production, and deployment of the Soviet strategic weapons systems regulated under the present arms control agreements.

SALT I and SALT II restricted the objective of arms control to what could be verified adequately by U.S. technical means. However, there is still no firm consensus about what constitutes adequate verification. [30] Supporters of SALT II, for example, supposed that the treaty was adequately verifiable because the Soviets could not violate the treaty to an extent that would enable them to alter the strategic military balance without provoking timely and adequate U.S. compensatory action. This assertion is impossible to prove, *a posteriori*: no agreed standard exists by which to measure the stability of, or alterations to, the strategic balance. Nor it is possible to evaluate the potential for compensatory U.S. action under various circumstances. Moreover, the term *violation* has several meanings. It is also argued that adequate verification is a function of U.S. assumptions about the U.S.-USSR strategic balance. The more stable this balance is assumed to be, the less the need for verification. [31]

The opponents of SALT II observed that the verification process constituted a paradox: the inconsistency between criteria of significance and verifiability. Any characteristic of Soviet strategic forces or the Soviet military-industrial establishment pertinent to the agreement, but which U.S. intelligence was incapable of verifying, could not be incorporated in the SALT II treaty. On the other hand, any element that was significant could not be excluded. Therefore, these two criteria as applied to an arms-control agreement meant that what was significant would have to be verifiable, but that what was insignificant would be unverifiable, by definition. Because it was admitted that the absolute number, and the location and identification of Soviet warheads and missiles could not be verified, only that of fixed launchers and silos, in practice "significance" reduced to the capacity to count all agreed categories and numbers of strategic offensive systems, specifically launchers (including missile tubes in submarines), and to collect technical data about the testing, performance characteristics, and operational capabilities of Soviet strategic weapons. [32]

The supporters of the freeze overlook the troubled history of verification. [33] Either they assume that the imposition of comprehensive ceilings on nuclear weapons can be verified, or they believe that the stabilization of the strategic nuclear balance would reduce the need for precise verification. The implicit assumption is that any arms-control or arms-reduction agreement makes the process of verification easier. A freeze [34] that simply stops deployment, production, and testing would be less difficult to monitor than a complex arms-control treaty such as SALT II, for it would be necessary to verify only activity in violation of the freeze. It is left unsaid how the subsequent, comprehensive arms-reduction treaty envisioned by supporters of the freeze would be verified. The gathering evidence of Soviet violations of the SALT II treaty should give pause. Soviet honesty in compliance appears to be like the Loch Ness monster: one cannot say that it exists.

The last assumption is that a mutual nuclear freeze would greatly increase the chance of negotiating an arms-reduction agreement that would vouchsafe substantial cuts in the size of the U.S. and Soviet arsenals. This belief does not appear to be grounded in a coherent understanding of Soviet military doctrine, the history of SALT negotiations, and the actual strategic nuclear balance.

No publication of any major peace group, nor any public statement by a leading proponent of the freeze, can be said to explain the purpose of the Soviet buildup in the 1970s, or to furnish any credible evidence for the belief that the Soviet Union is prepared to negotiate an arms-reduction treaty of serious proportions upon the implementation of a mutual nuclear freeze. The present Soviet strategic force structure has been acquired at enormous expense and great economic cost to the Soviet state. [35] This force structure fulfills the requirements of Soviet military doctrine, in particular, Soviet nuclear targeting strategy. [36] The statements of high-ranking Soviet military leaders, including Marshal Nikolai Ogarkov, former chief of the Soviet General Staff, about the Soviet view of detente, the correlation of forces, the character of nuclear war, and so on contain no explicit evidence that the Soviet Union is prepared to reduce drastically its strategic nuclear forces. Such a step would be tantamount to forfeiting the instrument that Soviet official writing explicitly states has been responsible for the advantageous shift in the correlation of forces in favor of socialism. To quote Marshal Ogarkov (1979): "The Soviet Union has military superiority over the United States. Henceforth, the United States will be threatened. It had better get used to it." In this light, the last assumption seems to be the weakest of all. For it cannot be reconciled with Soviet reality. [37]

Turning to the main categories of nonreligious peace groups, the broad view of the left-wing and pacifist organizations, for example, the USPC, WRL, FOR, IPS, WSP, and WILPF, is antidefense, without qualification. These groups oppose any increase in military spending, even for conventional forces. In the main, they blame the United States for the arms race and the existence of international tension, or they argue that one side is more or less as bad as the other. Thus, Afghanistan equals Grenada; El Salvador equals Poland; the Pershing II equals the SS-20; and so forth. On the other hand, these groups do not impartially condemn the United States and the USSR. For instance, they did not protest the Soviet military buildup in the 1970s, nor did they condemn the Soviet Union for defending socialism in Afghanistan, or for compelling the Polish army to save Poland from the horrors of self-government. As Michael Myerson, chairman of the USPC, put it: "It may not be kosher to say so in this political climate, but we do say that the United States is terribly irresponsible and the Soviet Union is responsible." [38]

Indeed, for the supporters of these peace groups, the real, though unadmitted, motive for supporting the nuclear freeze campaign and the peace movement, is hatred of U.S. democracy per se and admiration for the Soviet form of "progressive socialism." The United States is held to be the greatest threat to peace, as shown by the Vietnam war, the machinations of the CIA in the Third World, and the official support for dictatorships. Accordingly, any form of arms control or disarmament that would weaken U.S. military and political power is believed to further the cause of peace and reduce the risk of war. [39]

The pacifism espoused by some of these groups has undergone a certain corruption. In traditional form, U.S. pacifism has opposed any resort to violence in any form for any cause. It is therefore surprising to find the pacifist groups associated with the U.S. peace movement espousing the cause of Marxist "liberation struggles" in the Third World, [40] and supporting such "liberation movements" as the Palestine Liberation Organization. [41] The identification of revolutionary Marxist socialism with justice, liberation, and the forces of peace is not uncommon in the publications representing the pacifist viewpoint. Nor is it a rarity to read in this literature how the United States is the chief source of racism, militarism, imperialism, and economic exploitation in the world.

The general views about arms control, U.S.-USSR relations, and disarmament associated with the main public interest research organizations are factual, articulate, and generally sincere.[42] *Grosso modo*, organizations under this heading such as the American Committee on East-West Accord, Ground Zero, and so on exemplify in their advocacy of the freeze the conventional wisdom of the liberal and left-of-center portion of the official arms-control establishment. Many of the organizations in this category are directed by, or include as prominent members, high-ranking, former officials of the diplomatic service, the intelligence community, and the Arms Control and Disarmament Agency. Their support for the freeze is sometimes subject to the influence of an unduly benign view of Soviet intentions and military thinking, but it is sincere, and it does not reflect knowingly an ulterior ideological agenda or foreign influence. Support for the freeze issues from a view that the United States can achieve the objective of preserving the strategy of deterrence at lower levels of armament while reducing the danger of war through arms control. On the other hand, there are former officials associated with the general viewpoint of these organizations who themselves have expressed reservations about SALT-type negotiations, and favor instead a series of prearranged bold initiatives coupled with reciprocal measures of restraint.

George Kennan is perhaps the best known of the advocates of unilateral U.S. disarmament on a limited scale as the first step to stopping the unrestrained competition in the development of nuclear weaponry.[43] The above viewpoint includes advocacy of a U.S. renunciation of the principle of first use of nuclear weapons in Western Europe. But this position is complemented by a recognition of the need to restore strategic parity in conventional weapons and forces. It is understood that reducing dependence upon nuclear weapons will require the expansion of conventional forces in order to guarantee the ability of the United States to defend Western Europe.

The scientific organizations and medical groups in the peace movement are concerned primarily with educational programs designed to acquaint the public with the substantive issues that shape arms-control policy, and with the scientific effects of nuclear war itself. The literature, the public testimony, and the statements of representatives of groups such as the Federation of American Scientists

(FAS) and the Union of Concerned Scientists (UCS) are factual and informed in some cases by experience in the development of nuclear weapons.

The FAS is the oldest group in the United States concerned with controlling the arms race and preventing the use of nuclear weapons. Many of its original members had worked on the Manhattan Project. The FAS in the postwar period played a major role in establishing civilian control of nuclear weapons through the creation of the Atomic Energy Commission. The expert testimony before governmental bodies of FAS members was of great importance in the public debates about the Nuclear Test Ban Treaty of 1963, the Anti-Ballistic Missile Treaty, and the SALT agreements.

The Union of Concerned Scientists is committed to reducing the risk of nuclear war. The group has devised a four-point program, the individual tenets of which have been adopted selectively or *in toto* by the nuclear freeze campaign and some religious peace organizations. The program advocates a freeze on strategic weapons and delivery systems; a comprehensive test ban; a policy of no first use of nuclear weapons in Western Europe; and deep cuts in the nuclear arsenals of the United States and the Soviet Union. [44]

The strength of the position adopted in general by the scientific groups associated with the peace movement is exemplified by the testimony of Sidney Drell before the Subcommittee on Investigations and Oversight of the House Committee on Science and Technology, and the informative exchange of views between Drell and Soviet nuclear physicist Andrei Sakharov that this testimony prompted. [45]

The growing involvement of environmental organizations in the peace movement is the logical result of the opposition to commercial nuclear power, which these groups set afoot in the 1970s. The same transition to opposition to nuclear weapons was made by the Green party in West Germany, and by environmental groups in Denmark and Holland. To date, the entry into the freeze campaign of groups such as the Sierra Club has been cautious. The various temporary, *ad hoc* alliances and coalitions that sprang up in the 1970s after the Vietnam war to oppose the expansion of nuclear power, for example, the Clamshell Alliance, have been less reluctant. The issue of commercial nuclear power has peaked in respect to public attention, leaving those environmentalists who had invested in the movement against nuclear reactors, without a cause in the 1980s. [46]

The Catholic church and the liberal Protestant churches now provide powerful institutional and moral support to the nuclear freeze campaign and the peace movement. The participation of religious peace groups confers upon the peace movement an aura of divine legitimacy that the political peace organizations cannot furnish. The third draft of a pastoral letter published in 1983 by the National Conference of Catholic Bishops, "Pastoral Letter on War and Peace," presents the most acceptable formulation of a moral justification for renouncing the use of nuclear weapons conceived by any peace group. The arguments advanced in the letter have been variously praised and criticized. In any event, they have placed a theological imprimatur upon the mundane ideological and pacifist arguments against nuclear weapons and deterrence. [47] If the Catholic debate on nuclear war is characterized by carefully reasoned argument and appreciation of the moral and political complexity of the issues, it cannot be said that depth of thought or breadth of argument are distinctive features of the pronouncements on disarmament served up by some of the liberal Protestant churches since 1981. These statements adopt an apocalyptic tone and simply cobble together the most fashionable pieties about nuclear war and U.S. arms–control policy. Other Protestant church publications and official statements adopt an apologetic tone toward the Soviet Union and advocate what can be described as nuclear pacifism. In the Protestant view of the nuclear freeze and disarmament, there is an unmistakable unilateralist strain.

The Catholic "Pastoral Letter on War and Peace" argues that nuclear war is immoral because no nuclear war can be just. Nuclear weapons by their nature are indiscriminate because innocent civilians inevitably would be slaughtered as the result of the weapons' use. The letter condemns the use of nuclear weapons in the abstract and issues three prohibitions.

First, under no circumstances may nuclear weapons or other instruments of mass slaughter be used for the purpose of destroying civilian population centers. Second, no situation can be conceived in which the deliberate initiation of nuclear warfare, on however restricted a scale, can be morally justified. Third, there is no moral justification for submitting the human community to the risk of limited nuclear war. The bishops enjoin that it is necessary, for the sake of prevention, to build a barrier against the concept of nuclear war as a viable strategy of defense, and they admonish that there should be a clear public resistance to the rhetoric of winnable nuclear wars, surviving nuclear exchanges and strategies of protracted nuclear war. [48]

Thus, the pastoral letter argues that the strategy of deterrence is morally flawed, and that it is equally immoral to threaten to use nuclear weapons. Under the bishops' argument, the very possession of nuclear weapons constitutes a threat to peace. However, instead of endorsing a policy of immediate unilateral disarmament to resolve this dilemma, the logical conclusion of the argument is evaded through the equivocation that deterrence may still be judged morally acceptable, provided that it is used as a step toward progressive disarmament. Accordingly, the bishops served up a recommendation for arms control that is more or less identical with the central proposal of the nuclear freeze campaign: arms reductions should be effected forthwith by immediate, bilateral verifiable agreements to halt the testing, production, and deployment of new strategic weapons. However, in the bishops' view, the situation requires that the United States should be prepared to undertake independent initiatives in the absence of such agreements, "to reduce some of the gravest dangers and to encourage a constructive Soviet response." [49] Thus, in the last analysis, the pastoral letter moves very close to a unilateralist position.

The Protestant churches are divided in their response to the freeze campaign and the peace movement. The fundamentalist denominations and the more conservative established churches either have not endorsed the freeze proposal or have done so only in a tentative way. On the other hand, the liberal churches that were previously involved in the anti-Vietnam war movement or the antidefense lobby of the late 1970s have transferred their activity to the peace movement. The United Methodist Church, the United Church of Christ, the United Presbyterian Church, the Unitarian Universalist Church, the American Quakers, and the Episcopal Church have formally endorsed the nuclear freeze either individually or in an ecumenical manner through the National Council of Churches. It is not clear that the views advocated by elected church officials and the national governing bodies of these liberal denominations always replicate the beliefs and positions of the rank-and-file membership. In the event, these views as reflected in the publications, pronouncements, and pastoral letters prepared at the national level and submitted to the laity for endorsement, or retailed in religious magazines such as *Christianity and Crisis, Christianity Today,* and *Christian Century,* have infused the freeze campaign with an element of religious pacifism and eschatology. There is no space for a systematic rehearsal of these views. But the rapid survey attempted here may provide some idea of the main tenets.

The liberal Protestant churches have endorsed the freeze as the first step toward what is envisioned as total nuclear disarmament. During the 1970s, the national governing bodies of the liberal denominations endorsed ratification of the SALT I and SALT II agreements. Thus, the support for the nuclear freeze is a natural extension of this earlier support for arms control. However, since 1980, some of the same bodies have manifested in their statements an impatience with the conventional policy of negotiating arms-control agreements from a position of strength and with formal arms-control agreements per se. The standard objection to formal arms-control negotiation on the pattern of SALT or START (Strategic Arms Reduction Talks) is now that they are ineffectual and inadequate because they preserve the existing strategic nuclear balance, do not compel drastic reductions in nuclear arsenals, and do not ameliorate the danger of nuclear war. The position tacitly or formally endorsed in the statements of a number of national bodies can be described as unilateral disarmament. [50]

For example, two resolutions adopted by the Governing Board of the National Council of Churches (NCC) "Resolution on a Nuclear Weapons Freeze" (1981) and "Swords and Ploughshares" (1982), both advocate unilateral initiatives by the United States as the means of halting the nuclear arms race. The 1981 statement urged the United States and the Soviet Union to adopt a mutual freeze, but it simultaneously pledged support for unilateral arms reduction initiatives to demonstrate good faith and induce the other side to adopt similar measures. [51] The 1982 resolution endorsed the freeze but called for unilateral U.S. initiatives at the Second Special Session on Disarmament in the United Nations—including a declaration of no first use of nuclear weapons, and a willingness to implement a freeze on the production and deployment of U.S. strategic weapons. The same resolution enjoined the member communions of the NCC to commit themselves to change the institutions in U.S. society that are an obstacle to peace, and to urge the American people to turn away from an attitude of reliance upon nuclear weapons as the source of national security. The communions were also admonished to assume the task of developing more effective political means to resolve international conflicts without the threat or use of armed force. This resolution communicated to churches in Eastern Europe and in other parts of the Soviet bloc the readiness of the NCC to join with them in common pursuit of the goal of disarmament. [52]

Two recent pastoral letters bring the advocacy of unilateral disarmament into clearer focus. The first, "Identity, Pilgrimage, and Peace," published in 1982 by the Episcopal House of Bishops, provides a composite jeremiad against nuclear weapons and deterrence compiled from fashionable secular arguments. The strategy of deterrence is condemned, *ex cathedra*, as intrinsically evil because it cannot be reconciled with a free nation's commitment to justice. The expenditure of economic and natural resources on nuclear weapons is immoral and unjust, for it constitutes an act of aggression against the starving children in the world. What the bishops describe as the "American fever to match the Soviet Union weapon for weapon" is blamed directly for damaging the personality structure of a whole generation. According to the letter, a belligerent nuclear arms policy not only distorts the spiritual and moral formation of children but also defeats free nations from within. The conclusion of the letter is that it is the responsibility of the United States to take the bold initiative in nuclear disarmament, and to keep on taking it. [53]

The second letter, "Pastoral Letter to a People Called Methodist," was approved by the United Methodist Council of Bishops in 1982. This document endorses the freeze and disarmament under the shadow of impending nuclear catastrophe. It is stated that even the arguments concerning parity have become irrelevant because of the frightening capacity of overkill possessed by the United States and the Soviet Union. The Methodist letter therefore advocates the immediate dismantlement of nuclear stockpiles and the reallocation of military resources for civilian purposes. [54]

In addition to the views set forth in official statements and pastoral letters, many of the same Protestant churches in their publications on arms control and international relations embrace views about disarmament and the Soviet Union that are not dissimilar to the double standard of selective morality and conditional pacifism practised by the left-wing and pacifist peace organizations discussed earlier.

Protestant literature on international relations is often chary of explicit discussions of Soviet nuclear strategy, Soviet military power, and Soviet actions that might be thought to have endangered world peace, ignored human rights, or contributed to international tension. For instance, a prominent publication such as *Christianity and Crisis* rarely notices the situation of the Catholic church in Poland or events in Afghanistan. A recent report on the occasion of a visit of an NCC delegation to Russian Orthodox churches and church officials in the Soviet Union neglected to mention the official campaign of anti-Semitism, the persecution of Soviet Christians, and the situation regarding human rights for dissidents. Yet, this report did applaud the vigor and the dedication of the Soviet religious community, and it urged the expansion of an exchange program between U.S. and Soviet church groups concerned with peace so as to improve efforts of both on behalf of arms control. [55] A tract published by the press of the NCC and used in the international affairs programs of several liberal denominations furnishes a number of startling apologies for the

Soviet Union. The book, *Must Walls Divide?,* states that the Soviet bloc is more or less the equal of the Western democracies in vouchsafing basic human rights and in spiritual dedication to the cause of peace. A basic tenet of *Must Walls Divide?* is that U.S. Christians must find their way into the dialogue between Christianity and Marxism, and the United States and the USSR, so that Americans might remove the "ideological constraints" now limiting the mission of peace and justice. The mission is described elsewhere as ensuring progress toward reconciliation with the Communist countries. [56]

In summary, the views of the Catholic church and of certain Protestant churches on disarmament and arms control are distinguished either by a thoughtful attempt to grapple with the moral dilemma of nuclear weapons and the danger of nuclear war, or by the less compelling idea that the arms race and the danger of nuclear war finally represent a human problem as opposed to a political problem that in the first instance concerns the United States *and* the Soviet Union. The implicit premise of Catholic and Protestant views about disarmament and arms control is that there is no temporal, scientific, or political solution to the nuclear threat. The solution must involve a moral judgment to abolish these weapons, and the essence of the morality that informs this judgment is, in the final analysis, pacifism. [57] The universal validity of this belief even in a religious context is not clear. It is said that to abjure violence, it is necessary to have no experience of it. The providential view that evil will eventually defeat itself, and, therefore, that it need not be resisted in the present, is the foundation of pacifism. Perhaps for these reasons, Jewish peace organizations with a national standing are noticeable by their absence. The religious experience of Jews in the twentieth century has been tempered by profane events that do not affirm the validity of the belief that evil will somehow destroy itself if it is not resisted.

SOVIET MANIPULATION AND COMMUNIST PARTICIPATION

It is an article of faith among right-wing extremists that foreign agents enkindled the nuclear freeze campaign and that the peace movement is procommunist. [58] No probative evidence is on hand to substantiate this fancy. On the other hand, there is no doubt that the Soviet Union and the Communist party in the United States (CPUSA) regard the peace movement as a natural target of opportunity. After all, it is no secret that peace campaigns have served as standard instruments of Soviet propaganda and Soviet political and psychological warfare since the Bolshevik Revolution. Nor is it a revelation that foreign communist parties maintain a tradition of using front organizations both to recruit innocents for purposes beyond their comprehension and to manipulate noncommunist popular movements for the benefit of Soviet foreign policy.[59] The issue is whether or no the Soviet Union or the CPUSA is attempting to penetrate, influence, and mobilize the nuclear freeze campaign and the peace movement. An assessment of the available evidence is contained in a recent report of the FBI, "Soviet Active Measures Relating to the U.S. Peace Movement."[60]

According to the FBI report, the Soviet organizations principally involved in the Soviet peace campaign in the United States are the First Chief Directorate of the KGB, the International Department of the Central Committee, the Communist party of the Soviet Union, and the Institute for the U.S.A. and Canada. The CPSU International Department orchestrates the activities of Soviet-controlled international front organizations, e.g. the National Council of American-Soviet Friendship (NCASF), the U.S. Peace Council (USPC), and the Lawyers Committee on Nuclear Policy (LCNP). The KGB carries out a wide range of overt and covert activities, including the dissemination of officially sponsored propaganda, attendance at disarmament conferences, friendship and cultural events, and speaking engagements in the guise of accredited Soviet diplomatic and official representatives and journalists, providing interviews for U.S. media, the planting of oral and written disinformation, the cultivation of official and informal contacts with peace groups and their principal members, and the collection of information about the views of peace organizations and their membership. The Institute for the U.S.A. and Canada conducts sophisticated propaganda and disinformation activity designed to influence prominent opinion makers, professors, foreign policy experts, journalists, and leaders of the peace movement. It supervises closely official and nongovernmental exchanges in the Soviet Union between U.S. and Soviet delegations. Delegations and individual spokesmen from the institute often represent the Soviet Union at academic conferences and public speaking engagements on the subject of arms control convened in the United States. Georgi Arbatov, the director of the institute, provides interviews to the U.S. media.[61]

Under instruction from the CPSU International Department, the CPUSA has placed high priority on the issues of arms control and disarmament, and the peace movement. In 1979, the CPUSA founded the USPC as the U.S. affiliate of the World Peace Council (WPC). Since 1979, the USPC has assumed the sponsorship of WPC activities in the United States, and it has utilized conferences, demonstrations, and publications to promote Soviet views on arms control and disarmament.[62] The USPC has also joined various peace coalitions, including the MFS and the national nuclear freeze campaign. Another CPUSA front organization, the NCASF, has arranged meetings, press conferences, radio and television interviews, and lecture or speaking engagements for Soviet officials assigned to the United States and for visiting Soviet delegations. The USPC, the NCASF, and several other CPUSA front organizations were among the sponsors of the large 12 June, 1982 peace and disarmament demonstration in New York City. The organizations played a decisive role in the planning and organization of the demonstration, and in the selection of the themes and slogans adopted by the peace movement for the occasion.[63]

Nonetheless, despite these attested instances of Soviet or CPUSA involvement, the FBI assessment affirmed that it was difficult to determine the extent to which various peace organizations and coalitions were being influenced or manipulated by the Soviet Union. The report concluded that the Soviets do not play a dominant role in the U.S. peace and nuclear freeze movements, and that they do not directly control or manipulate the movements. It is argued that the Soviets do not regard direct control or manipulation as an essential condition for a successful active-measures campaign. The Soviet peace campaign in the United States is designed to direct public attention to new U.S. strategic nuclear weapons (e.g. the MX and Trident II), and to nurture the spurious impression that the Soviet Union alone is interested in serious disarmament and arms-control negotiations. Therefore, the Soviet campaign does not require direct control or manipulation to be effective. Under the FBI analysis, these objectives can be achieved through a well-contrived series of arms-control proposals that are embroidered to suit the preconceptions, emotions, and sentiments of the peace movement.[64]

The peace movement is heterogeneous. A substantial portion of its supporters appear to be politically naive, untutored in the history and the nuances of progressive popular fronts or front organizations, and predisposed for a variety of reasons to oppose either Republican or Democratic arms-control and defense policies. There appears to be a consensus among the major peace groups that any public discussion of Communist participation abets criticism and red-baiting of the peace movement, or is tantamount to left-wing McCarthyism.[65] For these reasons, it is clear that both the nuclear freeze campaign and the whole peace movement are susceptible to the influence of domestic Communists and fellow travelers. Nevertheless, at present, any putative Communist influence must be described as minimal.

The peace movement of 1984 is simply not the same as the League for Peace and Democracy of the 1930s or the Stockholm Peace campaign of the early 1950s. The main effect of Soviet contact with peace groups in the United States and the participation in the movement of the USPC is the frequent discovery in U.S. peace literature of bowdlerized or congenial versions and fragments of Soviet official statements and propaganda about arms control, disarmament, and U.S. foreign policy. The presence of this material is not proof of covert manipulation or direct influence as much as it is of successful impregnational propaganda techniques. Through constant repetition of the Soviet viewpoint before an American audience predisposed to self-doubt or credulity, and the regurgitation before sophisticated audiences of U.S. views disguised as Soviet opinion, the Soviet officials in touch with the peace movement and the USPC have achieved some success in defining the views of U.S. peace groups about certain issues. [66]

CONCLUSION

In 1984, the peace movement is more a feeling than it is a political program. The beliefs of many supporters are rooted in emotion: they are felt to be true. No peace organization has assembled a feasible political strategy with which to secure the implementation of a nuclear freeze or a unilateral U.S. initiative for disarmament. The strengths of the movement remain its weakness. An endless arms race and the absence of a coherent government policy concerning arms control helped to kindle the peace movement. Neither is difficult to oppose, and the solutions envisioned by the peace movement have the advantage of aiming at the impossible. Thus, they demand very little in reality, and this situation makes it difficult to translate emotion and belief into a concrete political program, for a large movement has no critical faculty, and it has a tendency to think in images and make predictions that are amplified by appeals to the emotions.

The nuclear freeze could still develop into an effective political force. The fourth annual National Freeze Conference of the National Weapons Freeze Campaign in December 1983 adopted a strategy for 1984 the essence of which is a coordinated lobbying effort, "Freeze Voter '84." The purpose is to press Congress to enact parts of a comprehensive freeze, including the suspension of funding for the testing of nuclear warheads and the testing and deployment of ballistic missiles. The 1984 strategy seeks to obtain congressional restrictions on funds for the verifiable aspects of nuclear weapons testing and deployment. The Soviet Union would be challenged to cease its own activities of this kind. It would be insisted that such a halt must be followed quickly by negotiations between the United States and the Soviet Union. The negotiations would result in a full freeze, and this freeze would be followed by reductions in each country's nuclear arsenals. The conference also adopted a resolution urging Congress to oppose funding for testing, production, and deployment of specific weapons systems, including the MX, Trident II, cruise and Pershing II missiles, and ABM and antisatellite systems. [67]

The 1984 program is essentially a recycled version of the original freeze proposal of 1981. But it is a concrete program, and in an election year a change in public opinion about the size of the defense budget might infuse it with political utility. On the other hand, the new freeze proposal ignores the other factor that would be decisive in the implementation of a freeze, the Soviet Union. [68]

It is fitting in 1984 to recall what Orwell—who knew something about peace movements—said about the sincerity of pacifists and peace movements: it can be judged by the subjects they avoid. The alternatives to the arms race, or deterrence, or the nuclear balance, and so forth that are offered by the peace groups or the nuclear freeze campaign provide a useful test, for they seem to avoid many things that have to do with the world as it is. Closer relations with the Soviet Union are recommended by the public interest peace groups such as the Committee on East-West Accord. But would these improved relations affect the internal dynamism of Soviet military doctrine, which has driven Soviet weapons systems development and deployment for twenty years?

To advocate bold unilateral initiatives, or no resistance, or a moral solution to the dilemma of nuclear weapons would be the same as ignoring the historical record and Soviet thinking on the subject of pacifism. The record can be made to disclose that governments that refuse to use armed force in their own defense usually cease to exist very quickly. The Soviet leadership presumably would not be affected by unilateral gestures of goodwill and moral sincerity, for it is on record as regarding pacifists in the West either as "useful idiots" (Lenin's phrase) or as simple-minded people of goodwill who adhere to illusory perceptions of war and peace because they seek to solve problems of war and peace outside the class struggle, by means of abstract morality. [69] To rebel against extinction is one thing, but to claim that continued existence cannot be achieved unless those who believe in peace reinvent politics and the world itself, is to avoid the subject of human aggression and the admittedly unsavory history of many modern nation-states. These are the basic prescriptions of the peace movement. They are not particularly realistic, despite the abstract terms and the imagery with which they are often clothed. And they ignore a great deal, for which reason they need not be judged as sincere. *"Fere libenter homines id quod volunt credunt."*

NOTES

1. Sigmund Freud, *Das Unbehagen in der Kultur* (Frankfurt am Main, 1976), pp. 128-29. See Bruno Bettelheim, "Obsolete Youth," in *Surviving and Other Essays* (New York, 1980), esp. pp. 354ff.
2. For more detail, see Leon Wieseltier, "Nuclear War, Nuclear Peace," *New Republic* (17 January 1983): 9-15; Rael and Jean Isaac, "The Counterfeit Peacemakers: Atomic Freeze," *American Spectator* 15 (June 1982): 3-11; Fox Butterfield, "Anatomy of the Nuclear Protest," *New York Times Magazine*, 11 July 1982, pp. 14, 17, 32, 34, 38-39; William Greider, "The New Abolitionists," *Rolling Stone* (17 March 1983): 9-11; Pamela Haines, "'No Nukes' Is Not Enough," *Progressive* 45 (March 1981): 34-42; Leon Sigal, "Warming to the Freeze," *Foreign Policy* (Fall 1982): 54-65.
3. See Charles DeBenedetti, "The American Peace Movement, 1941-1971," *World Affairs* 141 (January 1978): 123ff.; Irving Louis Horowitz, *Ideology and Utopia in the United States, 1956-1976* (New York, 1977), ch. 19. See, on the antidefense lobby, "The Anti-Defense Lobby: Part III. Coalition for a New Foreign and Military Policy," *Institution Analysis*, no. 12 (Washington, D.C.: Heritage Foundation, 1979).
4. See "The Anti-Defense Lobby," pp. 33-36.
5. Ibid., pp. 55-56. A letter drafted and circulated by the Disarmament Working Groups of the CNFMP, dated 23 March 1979, urging President Carter to conclude the Comprehensive Test Ban Treaty, was signed by the Institute for Policy Studies, Council on Economic Priorities, Clergy and Laity Concerned, SANE, U.S. Peace Council, Women Strike for Peace, Fellowship of Reconciliation, National Council of Churches, and Women's International League for Peace and Freedom, among other organizations.
6. See *Coalition Close-up* (Summer 1979), as reproduced in "The Anti-Defense Lobby," pp. 57-58.
7. The membership of the CNFMP in 1976 included the following organizations: American Friends Service Committee; Business Executives Move for New National Priorities; Campaign for a Democratic Foreign Policy; Church of the Brethren; Clergy and Laity Concerned; Coalition on National Priorities and Military Policy; Common Cause; Episcopal Peace Fellowship; Environmental Action; Fellowship of Reconciliation: Friends Committee on National Legislation; Jesuit Conference; Movement for Economic Justice; SANE; United Church of Christ-U.S. Power

and Priorities Team; United Methodist Board of Global Ministries; Women's International League for Peace and Freedom; and Women Strike for Peace.

8. See Barbara Welling, "Nuclear Freeze Debate," *Quarterly Report* (The Mershon Center) 7 (Winter 1982-83): 1-2; *The Nuclear Freeze. A Study Guide for Churches Prepared by the Institute for Religion and Democracy* (Washington, D.C., 1982), pp. 7-8. See also Christopher Kojm, ed., *The Nuclear Freeze Debate* (New York, 1983).

9. See Sidney Lens, "Revive the Ban-the-Bomb Movement," *Progressive* (1982) in *The Apocalyptic Premise*, ed. Ernest Lefever and E. Stephen Hunt (Washington, D.C., 1982), p. 96; Ron Freund, "It Wasn't a Quick Freeze," *Christianity and Crisis* 42 (July 1982): 204, 222-23.

10. See John Barron, "The KGB's Magical War for 'Peace,'" in *The Apocalyptic Premise*, ed. Ernest Lefever and E. Stephen Hunt (Washington, D.C., 1982), p. 128, for a list of groups.

11. See *1983 Handbook. Arms Control and Peace Organizations/Activities* (Washington, D.C.: Forum Institute, 1983), for a selection. See also *The Peace Catalogue* (New York, 1982); Peter DeLeon, "Freeze: The Literature of the Nuclear Weapons Debate," *Journal of Conflict Resolution* 27 (March 1983): 181-89.

12. See "The Nuclear Freeze Proposal," *Congressional Digest* 61 (August-September 1982); Senate Committee on Foreign Relations, *Nuclear Freeze Proposal: Report to Accompany S.J. Resolution 2* (Washington, D.C.: Government Printing Office, 1983).

13. See Horowitz, *Ideology and Utopia*, pp. 348-50; Stanley Rothmann and S. Robert Lichter, *Roots of Radicalism: Jews, Christians, and the New Left* (New York, 1982), pp. 25-40; 387-94. For an official view, CIA, Office of Current Intelligence, "International Connections of the U.S. Peace Movement," *Study* (15 November 1967): 1-28 (Lyndon Johnson Library, released 24 September 1981).

14. See *1983 Handbook*, with "U.S. Disarmament Organizations," *Congressional Record—Senate*, 97th Cong., 2d sess., 29 September 1982, 128: 12522-31.

15. See, in general, E. Raymond Wilson, "The Pillars of Peace," *World Affairs* 148 (Fall 1978): 169-70.

16. See, for example, "Prepared Statement of Terry Herndon, President, Citizens Against Nuclear War, Washington, D.C.," in Senate Committee on Foreign Relations, 98th Cong., 1st sess., *Hearings, United States-Soviet Relations*, p. 247; "Statement of Randall Kehler, National Coordinator, Nuclear Weapons Freeze Campaign," ibid., p. 259.

17. See Sidney Lens, "The Deterrence Myth," *Progressive* 48 (February 1984): 16-17; Sidney Bailey, "Deterrence: Wrong in Law and Morals," *Christianity and Crisis* 41 (January 1982): 377; Roger Shinn, "A Dilemma Seen from Several Sides," ibid., 372-76.

18. See, e.g., "Statement of Susan Kemetty Catania, Illinois State Representative, 1973-1983," in Senate Committee on Foreign Relations, *Hearings, United States-Soviet Relations*, p. 245.

19. See Francesco Calogero, "Why Arms Control Empowers the Hawks," *Christianity and Crisis* (January 1982): 381-83.

20. Thus Randall Forsberg, "If We Share a Single Goal, We Can Stop the

Arms Race," ibid., p. 384. See also *Hope: Facing the Music on Nuclear War in the 1984 Elections* (New York: Ground Zero, 1984), p. 77.

21. See Philip Munion, ed., *Catholics and Nuclear War. A Commentary on the Challenge to Peace. The U.S. Catholic Bishops' Pastoral Letter on War and Peace* (New York, 1983), esp. pp. 276-85, 290-95, and 295-305 for key passages. See also Bishop John O'Connor, "The Church's Views on Nuclear Arms," in *The Apocalyptic Premise*, ed. Ernest Lefever and E. Stephen Hunt (Washington, D.C. 1982), pp. 295-308.

22. See Albert Wohlstetter, "Bishops, Statesmen, and Other Strategists on the Bombing of Innocents," *Commentary* (June 1982): 15-35, for a critique. See Munion, *Catholics and Nuclear War*, pp. 291-92, nn. 61, 62, for reference to secular authorities cited by the bishops. On U.S. targeting strategy, Desmond Ball, *Targeting for Strategic Deterrence*, Adelphi Papers No. 185 (London: International Institute for Strategic Studies, 1983), pp. 17-25.

23. See William Isaac Hull, *The New Peace Movement* (Boston, 1912), p.v; Charles Chatfield, *For Peace and Justice* (Knoxville, 1971), pp. 239ff.; *The Peace Movement in America* (Boston, 1908), pp. 99-109, esp. p. 101: "Each nation, for example, argues that it can protect its own peace only or best by increasing its armaments." See also Florence Boeckel, *Between War and Peace. A Handbook for Peace Workers* (New York, 1928), 25.

24. See Randall Forsberg, "A Bilateral Nuclear-Weapon Freeze," *Scientific American* (November 1982): 52-61. See also Andrew Cockburn, *The Threat* (New York, 1983).

25. See Robert Berman and John Baker, *Soviet Strategic Forces* (Washington, D.C.: Brookings Institution, 1982), pp. 41-69, for a good summary. Also William Lee, "Soviet Perceptions of the Threat and Soviet Military Capabilities," in *Soviet Perceptions of War and Peace*, ed. Graham Vernon (Washington, D.C.: National Defense University, 1981), esp. 77ff.

26. See *Report of the President's Commission on Strategic Forces* (Washington, D.C., 1983), esp. pp. 3-6, on the current nuclear balance. Also Benjamin Lambeth, *Arms Control and Defense Planning in Soviet Strategic Policy*, RAND P-6644 (Santa Monica, 1981), esp. pp. 4-9; Lambeth, *Soviet Strategic Conduct and the Prospects for Stability*, RAND R-2579-AF (Santa Monica, 1980), pp, 6-7. On the buildup, Albert Wohlstetter, *Legends of the Strategic Arms Race*, USSI Report 75-1 (Cambridge, Mass.: United States Strategic Institute, 1975).

27. See Patrick Glynn, "Why an American Arms Buildup Is Morally Necessary," *Commentary* (February 1984): esp. 22-26.

28. *Soviet Military Power* (Washington, D.C.: U.S. Department of Defense, 1983), p. 19.

29. See U.S. Department of State, "SALT II Agreement," Selected Documents No. 12B, pp. 60-63 (glossary); William Potter, ed., *Verification and SALT* (Boulder, 1980); William Kincade, "Verification and SALT II," in *SALT II and American Security* (Cambridge, Mass.: Institute for Foreign Policy Analysis, 1980), pp. 28-52; Stuart Cohen, "SALT Verfication: The Evolution of Soviet Views and Their Meaning for the Future," *Orbis* (Fall 1980): 657-83.

30. See Geoffery Levitt, "Problems in the Verification and Enforcement of

SALT Agreements in Light of the Record of Soviet Compliance with SALT I," *Harvard International Law Journal* 22 (Spring 1981): 391-94, 396-403. Add Senate Committee on Armed Services, 96th Cong., 2d sess., *Report of Hearings, Military Implications of the Proposed SALT II Treaty Relating to the National Defense*, pp. 13-15; 88-89.

31. Senate Select Committee on Intelligence, 96th Cong., 1st sess., *Report, Principal Findings on the Capabilities of the United States to Monitor the SALT II Treaty*, p. 5; Department of State, "SALT I: Compliance and SALT II: Verification," Selected Documents No. 7 (Washington, D.C., 1978).

32. See Amron Katz, *Verification and SALT* (Washington, D.C.: Heritage Foundation, 1979), pp. 3ff.; Jacquelyn Davis, Patrick Friel, and Robert Pfaltzgraff, eds., *SALT II and U.S.-Soviet Strategic Forces* (Cambridge, Mass.: Institute for Foreign Policy Analysis, 1979), 39-41. See also Richard Perle, "What Is Adequate Verification?" in *SALT II and American Security*, pp. 53-65.

33. See David Sullivan, *Soviet SALT Deception* (Boston, Va.: Coalition of Peace Through Strength, 1979), for examples of violations.

34. For example, the testimony of William Colby on behalf of the Committee for National Security in Senate Committee on Foreign Relations, *Hearings, United States-Soviet Relations*, pp. 274-75.

35. See William Lee, *Soviet Defense Expenditures in an Era of SALT*, USSI Report 79-1 (Washington, D.C., 1980); Abraham Becker, *The Burden of Soviet Defense*, RAND R-2752-AF (Santa Monica, 1981), esp. pp. 20-21. Also House Permanent Select Commitee on Intelligence, 96th Cong., 2d sess., *Hearings, CIA Estimates of Soviet Defense Spending*.

36. William Lee, "Soviet Nuclear Targeting Strategy and SALT," in *World Communism at the Crossroads*, ed. Steven Rosefielde (Boston, 1980), pp. 55-88.

37. Albert Weeks and William Bodie, eds., *War and Peace: Soviet Russia Speaks* (New York: National Strategy Information Center, 1983), p. 19. See also Lee, "Soviet Perceptions of the Threat and Soviet Military Capabilities," pp. 88-89. See *Hope: Facing the Music on Nuclear War*, p. 57: "The ongoing hostility between the United States and the Soviet Union is a little like the legendary feud between the Hatfields and the McCoys."

38. See David Corn, "Peace Council Raises Questions," *Nuclear Times* (May 1983): 8. Compare the explanation of the Korean Airlines incident in "The Soviet Crime, The Reagan Response," *Christianity and Crisis* 43 (October 1983): 348: "The more evidence we have that the Soviets are fearful to the point of paranoia, the more urgent is our need to avoid emplacement of redundant nuclear weaponry that could lend itself to use in a first-strike attack." Cf., *Hope: Facing the Music on Nuclear War*, p. 62.

39. See Paul Hollander, "Intellectuals, Estrangement and Wish Fulfillment," *Society* (July-August 1983): esp. pp. 18-24.

40. For examples, "Why Does Elliot Abrams Weep for the Churches of Nicaragua?" (editorial); *Christianity and Crisis* 42 (September 1982): 250-51; R. Scott Kennedy, "Northern Ireland's 'Guerrillas of Peace,'" *Christian Century* (7 September-31 August 1977): 746-51; Anne Nelson,

"El Salvador's Struggle. The Revolution Has a History," *Christianity and Crisis* 43 (June 1983): 231-38; "Words, Too, Are Weapons" (editorial), *Christianity and Crisis* 42 (July 1982): 202-3.

41. See Marvin Maurer, "Quakers and Communists—Vietnam and Israel," *Midstream* 25 (November 1979): 30-35. Cf., Scott Kearney and Diana Hurwitz, "Sartawi and the Palestinians," *Christianity and Crisis* 43 (May 1983): 181-82.

42. See, e.g., the excellent background book by Ground Zero, *What about the Russians and Nuclear War?* (New York, 1983).

43. See George Kennan, *The Nuclear Delusion: Soviet-American Relations in the Atomic Age* (Boston, 1982), esp. pp. 179-81.

44. See *1983 Handbook*, p. 253.

45. Sidney Drell, *Facing the Threat of Nuclear Weapons* (Seattle, 1983).

46. See Anna Gyorgy and John Clewett, "Ties that Bind Arms & Energy," *Nuclear Times* (March 1983): 22-23; John Surrey, "Opposition to Nuclear Power. A Review of International Experience," *Energy Policy* 4 (December 1976): 286-307; Harvey Wasserman, "The Clamshell Alliance: Getting It Together," *Progressive* 41 (September 1977): 14-18; Deborah McKenzie, "Seduced and Abandoned," *Environmental Action* 13 (April 1982): 28-30.

47. See Thomas Fox, "The Next Step: Acting on Faith," *Nuclear Times* (February 1983): 9-11; John Deedy, "The 'Peace Catholics' Speak Out," *Nation* (March 1982): 321, 338-40; William O'Brien, "The Peace Debate and American Catholics," *Washington Quarterly* 5 (Spring 1982): 219-22; William Greider, "The Power of the Cross," *Rolling Stone* (April 1983): 11-12, 17, 74, 76-77; L. Bruce Van Voorst, "The Churches and Nuclear Deterrence," *Foreign Affairs* 61 (Spring 1983): 827-52; James Wood, "The Nuclear Arms Race and the Churches," *Journal of Church and State* 25 (Spring 1983): 219-29.

48. See "The Challenge to Peace," in Munion, *Catholics and Nuclear War*, p. 302 (no. 188): "If nuclear deterrence exists only to prevent the *use* of nuclear weapons by others, then proposals to go beyond this to planning for prolonged periods of repeated nuclear strikes and counterstrikes, or 'prevailing' in nuclear war, are not acceptable." And, "Nuclear deterrence should be used as a step on the way toward progressive disarmament."

49. See ibid., pp. 307-8 (nos. 203-208), with Bruce Russet, "The Doctrine of Deterrence," ibid., 149-67.

50. See J. Ronald Newlin, "The Protestant Churches and the Nuclear Freeze," *Fletcher Forum* (Summer 1983): 355-64; John Stott, "Calling for Peacemakers in a Nuclear Age," *Christianity Today* (March 1980): 7ff. For a listing, see Federation of American Scientists, *American Religious Organizations and the Nuclear Weapons Debate* (Washington, D.C., 1983).

51. See "Resolution on a Nuclear Weapons Freeze," in *The Apocalyptic Premise*, ed. Ernest Lefever and E. Stephen Hunt (Washington, D.C. 1982), pp. 347-48.

52. "Swords into Ploughshares," in *The Apocalyptic Premise*, ed. Ernest Lefever and E. Stephen Hunt (Washington, D.C., 1982), p. 349.

53. "Identity, Pilgrimage and Peace," in *The Apocalyptic Premise*, ed.

Ernest Lefever and E. Stephen Hunt (Washington, D.C., 1982), pp. 343-45, Cf., Robert Lifton and Richard Falk, *Indefensible Weapons* (New York, 1982), chs. 8, 16.

54. "Pastoral Letter to a People Called Methodist," in *The Apocalyptic Premise,* ed. Ernest Lefever and E. Stephen Hunt (Washington, D.C., 1982), pp. 345-46.

55. See Arch Puddington, "The New Soviet Apologists," *Commentary* (November 1983): 26-28. Compare Billy Graham, "Graham's Mission to Moscow," *Christianity Today* (18 June, 1982): 20-23; Tom Minnery, "Graham and the Soviet Union," *Christianity Today* (18 June 1982): 42-44, 48-49, 51-52, 54-55, 59.

56. See James Will. *Must Walls Divide?* (New York, 1983), esp. pp. 26, 41-43, 46-50, 106-108. See also John McDougall, "An American among the Soviets," *America* 149 (December 1983): 351-52.

57. See, for example, Gordon Zahn, "Pacifism and Just War," in Munion, *Catholics and Nuclear War,* pp. 119-31, and esp. p. 19, on the scriptural promises that God's power will me made perfect in man's infirmity, and that no matter how hopeless and threatening the situation may appear, "the gates of hell will not prevail." See also Bishop Mahoney, "The Case for Nuclear Pacifism," in *The Apocalyptic Premise,* ed. Ernest Lefever and E. Stephen Hunt (Washington, D.C., 1982), pp. 279-93.

58. See, for example, John Rees, "Reds and the Peace Movement," *Review of the news* 18 (8 December, 1982): 39-41, 43, 45, 47, 49, 51-52.

59. For historical precedents, see Eugene Lyons, *The Red Decade* (New York, 1941), pp. 195-203, 382-92; William McNeill, *A better World* (New York, 1982), ch. 1; Louis Budenz, *Men without Faces* (New York, 1950), pp. 208-46.

60. See "Soviet Active Measures Relating to the U.S. Peace Movement, March, 1983," 24 March 1983, *Congressional Record—Senate,* 129, n. 39-2: 4-10. For a definition of *active measures,* see House Select Committee on Inteligence. 97th Cong., 2d ses., *Hearings, Soviet Active Measures,* pp. 31-50. See also John Barron, *The KGB Today* (New York, 1983).

61. "Soviet Active Measures," p. 4.

62. See Ronald Radosh. "The 'Peace Council' and Peace," *New Republic* (31 January 1983): 14-17.

63. "Soviet Active Measure," pp. 7-8.

64. Ibid., p. 10.

65. See *Nuclear Times* (May 1983): 7.

66. See Baruch Hazan, *Soviet Impregnational Propaganda* (Ann Arbor, 1982). An example is the regurgitation by Soviet scientists and physicians of U.S. nuclear war studies and scenarios. See *The Danger of Nuclear War Soviet Physicians' Viewpoint* (Moscow, 1982). See also Joseph Douglass. "The Growing Disinformation Problem," *International Security Review* (Fall 1981): 333-53.

67. See Robert Meriwether, "Renewed Plans for a Freeze," *Washington Peace Center Newsletter* (January 1984): 1, 6.

68. Compare Neal Pierce, "Nuclear Freeze Proponents Mobilize on Local Referenda, House Elections," *National Journal* (18 September, 1982): 1602-5.

69. See, for example, M.V. Petrov, "Problems of War and Peace and the World Revolutionary Process," in *Selected Readings from Military Thought, 1963-1973*, Studies in Communist Affairs, vol. 5, part II (Washington, D.C.: GPO, n.d.), pp. 114, 118.

ABOUT THE CONTRIBUTORS

Martin Ceadel has since 1979 been a fellow of New College, Oxford, and a lecturer in politics in the University of Oxford. He did his undergraduate work and his doctorate at Oxford, and held lectureships at first Sussex University then Imperial College (University of London). In addition to various articles, he is author of *Pacifism in Britain, 1914-1945: The Defining of a Faith* (London and New York: Oxford University Press, 1980), and is currently completing two further books for the same publisher: an analysis of "peace arguments," and a history of Britain's twentieth-century peace movement.

Theodore Draper is a member of the Council on Foreign Relations and the American Academy of Arts and Sciences. He has written ten books and has contributed to the *New York Review of Books, Encounter, Dissent, Commentary,* and other publications. His most recent publication is *Personal History,* a collection of his most important essays and articles of the past ten years.

Nicole Gnesotto is director of research at the Institut Français des Relations Internationales in Paris, and has published various studies on French defense policy, including "La France fille aînée de l'Alliance," in *Pacifisme et dissuasion* (IFRI/Economica, 1983), and "Defense européenne, histoire d'une passion française," in *l'Express,* July 1984.

Niels Jorgen Haagerup served for many years as an editorial writer on foreign and defense affairs for the *Berlingske Tidende* of Copenhagen. Since 1978 he has headed the Danish Institute of International Studies, and he has been a Liberal member of the European Parliament since 1979. He is the author of a number of books and pamphlets on foreign policy and international security.

Pierre Hassner is a senior research associate at the Centre d'Etudes et des Recherches Internationales, Fondation Nationale des Sciences Politiques, in Paris. His most recent publications include "Pacifism and Terror," *Atlantic Quarterly* (Spring 1984) and "France, Deterrence and Europe," *International Defense Review* (February 1984).

Jeffery Herf is a research associate at the Center for European Studies, Harvard University, and he also teaches for the Committee on Degrees in Social Studies. He was a postdoctoral fellow at the Center for International Affairs at Harvard during 1983-84. Herf is the author of *Reactionary Modernism: Technology, Culture and Politics in Weimar and the Third Reich* (Cambridge University Press, 1984) as well as another book on Western strategy and public discussion during the controversy over the NATO dual-track decision, to be published at a future date.

Robert Hunter, coeditor of this volume, is director of European studies and senior fellow in Middle Eastern studies at the Georgetown University Center for Strategic and International Studies. He is also contributing editor of the *Washington Quarterly.* During the Carter administration, he served on the National Security Council staff as director of West European affairs (1977-79) and then as director of Middle East affairs (1979-81). He has also been foreign policy advisor to Senator Edward M. Kennedy, and was a speechwriter for Vice-President Hubert Humphrey. He recently served as special advisor on Lebanon to the speaker of the House of Representatives and lead consultant to the National Bipartisan Commission on Central America (the Kissinger Commision). Dr. Hunter is the author of *The Soviet Dilemma in the Middle East, Security in Europe,* and *Presidential Control of Foreign Policy,* and writes regularly for the *Los Angeles Times.*

William G. Hyland is the editor of *Foreign Affairs,* the journal published by the Council on Foreign Relations in New York. He served in the CIA, the National Security Council, and the White House before joining the Georgetown Center for Strategic Studies, and subsequently becoming a senior associate at the Carnegie Endowment for International Peace.

Henry Kissinger was the fifty-sixth U.S. secretary of state. He also served as assistant to the president for national security affairs and, more recently, as the chairman of the National Bipartisan Commission on Central America. He taught at Harvard University prior to entering government service, and at Georgetown University after leaving the Department of State. Dr. Kissinger has written extensively on NATO and the future of the Western alliance as well as on U.S. foreign policy, international affairs, and diplomatic history.

Irving Kristol is the John M. Olin professor of social thought at the NYU Graduate School of Business Administration. He is a senior fellow of the American Enterprise Institute, a member of the President's Commission on White House Fellowships, and a member of the Council on Foreign Relations. He is the author of *On the Democratic Idea in America* (1972), *Two Cheers for Capitalism* (1978), and *Reflections of a Neoconservative* (1983).

Walter Laqueur, coeditor of this volume, serves as chairman of the International Research Council of the Georgetown Center for Strategic and International Studies (CSIS), and as editor of two of the center's publications series, *The Washington Papers* and *The Washington Quarterly.* He is also director of the Institute of Contemporary History and Wiener Library in London, and the founder and coeditor of the *Journal of Contemporary History.* Laqueur is University Professor in the Department of Government at Georgetown University, professor of history at the University of Tel Aviv, Israel, and has been visiting professor of history at various other U.S. universities. He is the author of numerous books on contemporary history and current affairs, including *The Struggle for the Middle East: The Soviet Union in the Mediterranean, 1958-1968, Young Germany* (1961), *The Fate of the Revolution* (1967), *Europe Since Hitler* (1970), *Guerrilla: A Historical and Critical Study* (1976), *Terrorism* (1977), *A Continent Astray* (1979), and others.

Ulrich de Maiziere is a retired general of the Bundeswehr and former chief of the Armed Forces Staff, which comprises the eight ranking officers of the Bundeswehr. He is the recipient of many prestigious international awards, among them the Legion d'Honour of France and the Legion of Merit from the United States. General de Maiziere is the author of *Bekenntnis zum Soldaten* (1971), *Führen im Frieden* (1974), and *Verteidigung in Mitteleuropa* (1975).

Edward Norman, dean of Peterhouse College at Cambridge University, is also a lecturer in history at Cambridge. He is the author of *The Catholic and Ireland* (1965), *The Early Development of Irish Society* (1969), *Christianity and the World Order* (1979), and several other books.

Uwe Nerlich is director of research at Stiftung Wissenschaft und Politik, vice-president of the European-American Institute for Security Research in Los Angeles, and a council member of the International Institute for Strategic Studies. He has been a fellow at the Center for Advanced Study in the Behavioral Sciences at Stanford University and visiting distinguished professor at the Naval Post-graduate School in Monterey, California. He has published widely on international relations, strategy, and arms control, including *Beyond Nuclear Deterrence* (coedited with Johan J. Holst).

Siegfried Scharrer is professor of theology at the University of Hamburg specializing in systematic theology and social ethics. He is the author of *Theologische Kritik der Vernunft* (1977), *Theologische Kritik der Moral* (1979), and *Grundfragen christlichen Glaubens* (1984). He has also written about scientific-theoretical questions, medical ethics, and problems of foreign policy.

David Thomas is a research assistant to the Honorable Helmut Sonnenfeldt, and a free-lance defense analyst in Washington, D.C. He has also worked as a defense consultant with Canby and Luttwak Associates.

Frans A.M. Alting von Geusau is the chairman of the Advisory Commission on Disarmament and International Security to the Government of the Netherlands, as well as a member of the International Institute for Strategic Studies, London, and vice-chairman of the Executive Board of the European Cultural Foundation. He is the author and editor of many books and articles on European integration, East-West relations, and problems of peace, security, and arms control. *Beyond the European Community* (1969), *NATO and Security in the Seventies* (1971), *Uncertain Detente* (1979), and *Allies in a Turbulent World: Challenges to U.S. and Western European Cooperation* (1982) are among his many publications.

Peter Graf von Kielmansegg has been professor of political science at the University of Cologne since 1971. He also served as the Konrad Adenauer professor at Georgetown University's School of Foreign Service in 1976-77. He is the author of *Deutschland und der Erste Weltkrieg* (1968), *Volkssouveränität* (1977), and *Nachdenken über Demokratie* (1980).

INDEX